Writing from Sources

Writing from Sources

SEVENTH EDITION

Brenda Spatt

The City University of New York

BEDFORD/ST. MARTIN'S   Boston ◆ New York

For Bedford/St. Martin's

Developmental Editor: John Elliott
Production Editor: Ryan Sullivan
Production Supervisor: Jennifer Wetzel
Marketing Manager: Karita dos Santos
Project Management: Books By Design, Inc.
Photo Research: Naomi Kornhauser
Cover Design: Sarah Beth Wiley
Cover Art: *Falling Cubes*, Hiroshi Yagi. © Hiroshi Yagi/Getty Images.
Composition: Books By Design, Inc.
Printing and Binding: R. R. Donnelley & Sons Company

President: Joan E. Feinberg
Editorial Director: Denise B. Wydra
Editor in Chief: Erica Appel
Director of Marketing: Karen Melton Soeltz
Director of Editing, Design, and Production: Marcia Cohen
Manager, Publishing Services: Emily Berleth

Library of Congress Control Number: 2006920123

Manufactured in the United States of America.

5 4 3 2 1 0
f e d c b a

For information, write: Bedford/St. Martin's, 75 Arlington Street, Boston, MA 02116 (617-399-4000)

ISBN-10: 0-312-54386-7
ISBN-13: 978-0-312-54386-0

Acknowledgments

To the Instructor

For twenty-five years, *Writing from Sources* has been the book instructors have used when they wanted to give their students a thorough grounding in the skills and techniques needed to write a freshman research essay. It remains unique as a focused, step-by-step guide, with the research and writing processes broken down into manageable segments of progressive difficulty. *Writing from Sources* builds up to the research essay organically, concentrating on providing instruction and practice in each skill, with minimal repetition or digression, so that the student is prepared to undertake the final assignment with confidence.

With each new edition, I have adjusted both the content and the method to make *Writing from Sources* more effective in an era of new technology and changing student interests. In the sixth edition, for example, I placed a new emphasis on Internet research, with extensive sections on finding and evaluating sources on the Web. For the seventh edition, it seemed to me time to review the book's basic structure, not with the intention of changing an approach that has worked well for so many instructors, but in an attempt to provide a better balance among topics and a richer, more complete experience for students. In doing so, I've taken the opportunity to respond to suggestions made by instructors over the past few years. What have your counterparts all over the country asked for?

You've asked for *Writing from Sources* to provide your students with a stronger sense of their academic environment. The seventh edition features a broad range of readings to suit all levels of student achievement, from newspaper articles to scholarly works. The latter are all presented with their original documentation so that, from the beginning of the course, students become aware of the need to cite sources appropriately. Each essay and excerpt longer than a paragraph is preceded by a brief biography of the author so that students can start to judge for themselves the credibility of the source. And at a pivotal stage in the process—learning how to write a multiple-source essay using two or three readings—I've introduced new models and exercises using academic sources. As some of you have pointed out, it's never too soon to introduce students to basic principles of documentation. Finally, I have added a brief, but explicit discussion of the dangers of plagiarizing Web material.

You've asked for more practice in the basic skills that students need. The best way for students to learn how to write research essays is to concentrate fully on each specific stage of the process, not to be confused by exposure to more topics than they can handle. To add more depth at crucial points in the sequence, I've added new exercises that fit into a three-stage learning model: (1) Students observe the way a skill—quotation, for example—is handled by a source in a model reading. (2) Students read a second source and consider how they would apply that skill if they were writing about that source—what phrases or sentences would they choose to quote? (3) Finally, students are provided with a third source and asked to incorporate it into a paragraph of their own, focusing on quoting, or paraphrasing, or documentation. In this way, students experience sources both as readers, learning to analyze a text as they'll need to do in most of their college courses, and as writers, learning how to incorporate the mixture of voices in their own essays. With a broad range of exercises to choose from, as well as several on the *Writing from Sources* Web site, you will find it easier to tailor your exercise assignments to your students' level of competence. (You'll find the Web site at bedfordstmartins.com/writingfromsources.) Most of the new exercises can be used as classroom activities, individually or in small groups.

You've asked for more examples and illustrations. Throughout the book, I've included many more short readings to illustrate complex points, to provide models, and to serve as exercise materials. An expanded Chapter 1 contains new material on analyzing the author's intention, thesis, and use of evidence and logic, all of which provides copious illustrative examples of good practice and bad. For the first time, *Writing from Sources* includes some of the pictures that originally accompanied certain readings; these pictures serve as examples for analysis in a new section showing students how to use visuals in their research essays.

You've asked for *Writing from Sources* to be easier to use. In the seventh edition, I've tried to provide greater clarity of structure and design. Each of the three basic skills—summary, quotation, paraphrase—now has its own chapter. Similarly, I've integrated some of the appendixes into the main text so that important topics will no longer seem like afterthoughts. Within the text itself, I've made the sequence of topics clearer and the information more accessible by using space, headings, bullets, and other signals to break up blocks of text that might otherwise seem too dense and forbidding. In presenting some model sources, I've replaced textual commentary with a marginal gloss that's easier to follow and requires less page-turning. In addition, certain perennial topics that used to be discussed at only one stage of the book, where they ran the risk of being overlooked, now appear—usually briefly—both early and late. "Bias" and "tone," for example, are introduced in the first chapter as well as in their usual place in the chapter on evaluating sources.

The readings in this edition of *Writing from Sources* cover a broad range of topics that I think you and your students will find interesting to work with. A couple of these topics become running themes. Several essays deal with educational issues, such as whether schools are really necessary, or whether a liberal education has any value, or whether students should be assigned more homework! The casebook focuses on patriotism and military ethics, and, in a similar vein, essays by authors such as Martha Nussbaum and Jeffrey Rosen touch on 9/11. Other authors and topics include Anne Hollander on fashion, Neal Gabler on celebrity, Leon Kass on courtship, Ruben Martinez on tolerance, and Anthony Swofford on a soldier's experiences.

Here is a summary of the changes in and additions to the seventh edition of *Writing from Sources*:

- A stronger focus on academic writing throughout the book, with examples of documentation presented throughout and more frequent practice in working with academic sources

- Nine new exercises to provide practice on topics such as selecting quotable material, identifying plagiarism, and documenting sources

- Expanded sections in Chapter 1 on analyzing sources to determine the author's thesis, method, intention, use of evidence, and possible logical fallacies

- A new section on incorporating visual materials, ranging from charts to pictures to film clips, into the research essay

- A new chapter sequence that makes *Writing from Sources* easier for you and your students to use

- A new, easier-to-follow layout that includes more headings, lists, and marginal annotations

- A new section on writing introductions and conclusions

- A new model research essay—"Looking at Horror Films"—using MLA documentation and including an opinion survey.

ACKNOWLEDGMENTS

I am particularly grateful to the instructors whose reviews provided the basis for many of the changes and additions in this edition and whose comments were notably thoughtful and sensitive to the special qualities of *Writing from Sources*: Chandra Speight Cerutti, East Carolina University; Kelly Erickson, Washington State University; Judith Gardner, University of Texas at San Antonio; Anne Gossage, Eastern Kentucky University; Kathryn Henkins, Mt. San Antonio College; Terri R. Hilgendorf, Lewis and Clark Community College; Mary L. Otto Lang, Wharton County Junior College; Vincent Marianiello, Bemidji State University; David G. Miller, Mississippi College; Lyle W. Morgan, Pittsburg State University; James Murphy, Southern Illinois University–Edwardsville; and Margaret Rozga, University of Wisconsin–Waukesha. My editors, Nancy Perry and John Elliott, have done their best to help me make this new edition responsive to your needs and those of your students. I remain obliged to Eve Zarin, who prepared the original draft for the section on "Interviewing and Field Research" for the fourth edition. As always, this edition is dedicated to all the students—mine and yours—who are at the heart of *Writing from Sources*.

Brenda Spatt

To the Student

Every day, as you talk, write, and work, you use sources. Most of the knowledge and many of the ideas that you express to others originate outside yourself. You have learned from your formal schooling and from observing the world around you, from reading, from watching television and movies, from the Internet, and from a multitude of other experiences. Most of the time, you do not consciously think about where you got the information; you simply go about your activities, communicating with others and making decisions based on your acquired knowledge.

In college, however, using sources becomes more concentrated and deliberate. Each course bombards you with new facts and ideas. Your academic success depends on how well you can understand what you read and hear in your courses, distinguish the more important from the less important, relate new facts or ideas to what you already have learned, and, especially, communicate your findings to others.

Most college writing is both informative and interpretive; that is, it contains material that you take from sources and ideas that are your own. Depending on the individual course and assignment, a college paper may emphasize your own conclusions supported by knowledge you have gathered, or it may emphasize that knowledge, showing that you have mastered a certain body of information. In any case it will contain something of others and something of you. If twenty students in your class are all assigned the same topic, the other nineteen papers will all be somewhat different from yours.

The main purpose of college writing assignments is to help you consolidate what you have learned and to expand your capacity for constructive thinking and clear communication. These are not merely academic skills; in most careers, success depends on these abilities. You will listen to the opinions of your boss, your colleagues, and your customers; or read the case histories of your clients or patients; or study the marketing reports of your salespeople or the product specifications of your suppliers; or perhaps even analyze the papers of your students! Whatever your job, the decisions that you make and the actions that you take will depend on your ability to understand and evaluate what your sources are saying (whether orally or in writing), to recognize any important pattern or theme, and to form conclusions. As you build on other people's ideas, you certainly will be expected to remember which facts and opinions came from which source and to give appropriate credit. Chances are that you will also be expected to draft a memo, a letter, a report, or a case history that will summarize your information and present and support your conclusions.

To help you see the connection between college and professional writing, here are some typical essay topics for various college courses, each followed by a parallel writing assignment that you might have to do on the job. Notice that all of the pairs of assignments call for much the same skills: The writer must consult a variety of sources, present what he or she has learned from those sources, and interpret that knowledge in the light of experience.

ACADEMIC ASSIGNMENT	PROFESSIONAL ASSIGNMENT	SOURCES
For a *political science* course, you choose a law now being debated in Congress or the state legislature and argue for its passage.	As a *lobbyist, consumer advocate,* or *public relations expert,* you prepare a pamphlet to arouse public interest in your agency's program.	debates Congressional Record editorials periodical articles your opinions
For a *health sciences* course, you summarize present knowledge about the appropriate circumstances for prescribing tranquilizers and suggest some safeguards for their use.	As a *member of a medical research team,* you draft a report summarizing present knowledge about a specific medication and suggesting likely directions for your team's research.	books journals government and pharmaceutical industry reports online abstracts
For a *psychology* course, you analyze the positive and negative effects of peer-group pressure.	As a *social worker* attached to a halfway house for adolescents, you write a case history of three boys, determining whether they are to be sent to separate homes or kept in the same facility.	textbooks journals case studies interviews Web sites personal experience
For a *business management* course, you decide which department or service of your college should be eliminated if the budget were cut by 3 percent next year; you defend your choice.	As an *assistant to a management consultant,* you draft a memo recommending measures to save a manufacturing company that is in severe financial trouble.	ledgers interviews newspapers journals financial reports Dow Jones news
For a *sociology* or *history* course, you compare reactions to unemployment in the 1990s with reactions in the 1930s.	As a *staff member in the social services agency* of a small city, you prepare a report on the social consequences that would result from closing a major factory.	newspapers magazines books interviews statistics Web sites

ACADEMIC ASSIGNMENT	PROFESSIONAL ASSIGNMENT	SOURCES
For a *physical education* course, you classify the ways in which a team can react to a losing streak and recommend some ways in which coaches can maintain team morale.	As a *member of a special committee of physical-education teachers,* you help plan an action paper that will improve your district's performance in interscholastic sports.	textbooks articles observation and personal experience Web sites
For an *anthropology* course, you contrast the system of punishment used by a tribe that you have studied with the penal code used in your home or college town.	As *assistant to the head of the local correction agency,* you prepare a report comparing the success of eight minimum-security prisons around the country.	textbooks lectures articles observation and personal experience
For a *physics* course, you write a definition of "black holes" and explain why theories about them were fully developed in the second half of the twentieth century—not earlier, not later.	As a *physicist* working for a university research team, you write a grant application based on an imminent breakthrough in your field.	books journals online abstracts e-mail Web sites
For a *nutrition* course, you explain why adolescents prefer junk food.	As a *dietician* at the cafeteria of a local high school, you write a memo that accounts for the increasing waste of food and recommends changes in the lunch menu.	textbooks articles interviews observation Web sites e-mail
For an *engineering* course, you describe changes and improvements in techniques of American coal mining over the last hundred years.	As a *mining engineer,* you write a report determining whether it is cost-effective for your company to take over the derelict mine that you were sent to survey.	books articles observation and experience e-mail Web sites

Writing from Sources will help you learn the basic procedures that are common to all kinds of academic and professional writing and will provide enough practice in these skills to enable you to write from sources confidently and successfully. Here are the basic skills.

1. *Choosing a topic:* deciding what you are actually writing about; interpreting the requests of your instructor, boss, or client, and determining the scope and limits of the assignment; making the project manageable.

2. *Finding sources and acquiring information:* deciding how much supporting information you are going to need (if any) and locating it; evaluating

sources and determining which are most suitable and trustworthy for your purpose; taking notes on your sources and on your own reactions; judging when you have sufficient information.

3. *Determining your main idea:* determining your intention in writing this assignment and your probable conclusions; redefining the scope and objective in the light of what you have learned from your sources; establishing a thesis.

4. *Presenting your sources:* using summary, paraphrase, and quotation; deciding when each skill is most appropriate.

5. *Organizing your material:* determining what must be included and what may be eliminated; arranging your evidence in the most efficient and convincing way, so that your reader will reach the same conclusions as you; calling attention to common patterns and ideas that will reinforce your thesis; making sure that your presentation has a beginning, middle, and end, and that the stages are in logical order.

6. *Writing your assignment:* breaking down the mass of information into easily understood units or paragraphs; constructing each paragraph so that the reader will receive a general idea that will advance your main idea, as well as providing supporting examples and details that will make it convincing; writing an introduction, and, as needed, a conclusion; if appropriate, choosing visuals to supplement your essay.

7. *Giving credit to your sources:* ensuring that your reader knows who is responsible for which idea; distinguishing between the evidence of your sources and your own interpretation and evaluation; assessing the relative reliability and usefulness of each source so that the reader can appreciate your basis for judgment.

This list of skills may seem overwhelming right now. But remember: You will be learning these procedures *gradually.* In Part I, you will learn how to get the most out of what you read and how to use the skills of summary, quotation, and paraphrase to provide accurate accounts of your sources. In Part II, you will begin to apply these skills as you prepare an essay based on a single reading and then a synthesis essay drawing on a group of sources. Finally, in Part III, you will begin the complex process of research. The gradual increase in the number of sources will make each stage of the process more complex and demanding, but not essentially different.

The best way to gain confidence and facility in writing from sources is to master each skill so thoroughly that it becomes automatic, like riding a bicycle or driving a car. To help you break the task down into workable units, each procedure will first be illustrated with a variety of models and then followed by exercises to give you as much practice as you need before going on to the next step. As you go on to write essays for other courses, you can concentrate more and more on *what* you are writing and forget about *how* to write from sources, for these methods will have become natural and automatic.

A NOTE ABOUT DOCUMENTATION
AND ACADEMIC WRITING

Colleges are academic institutions that expect you to understand and adhere to generally accepted standards of scholarship. At the simplest level, this means that you don't cheat when you take examinations, and you don't plagiarize when you prepare your written assignments. If you present the words or ideas of someone else as your own, you are guilty of plagiarism. By academic standards, plagiarism violates the very principles and the body of knowledge that you've come to college to learn.

To make sure that you don't inadvertently abuse the rules that define academic integrity, *Writing from Sources* asks you to devote a great deal of time and attention to learning how to document your sources: giving appropriate credit to each of the authors whose ideas or words you use when you write your essay. As indicated above, you'll learn how to use summary, quotation, and paraphrase to present your sources, and you'll learn how to ensure that your reader knows who these sources are and where and when they were published, as well as which material in your essay is theirs and which material is yours.

There are complex systems of documentation that make the attribution of sources absolutely clear, and you will probably be asked to use at least three of them during your time at college. The MLA (Modern Language Association) and APA (American Psychological Association) systems both use names and page numbers in parentheses at the end of material obtained from sources; the footnote/endnote system places information about sources at the bottom of the page or the end of the essay, keyed by a set of numbers. In Chapter 11, you can see three research papers, each using one of these three common systems. Every system of documentation requires the inclusion of a bibliography, which usually comprises all the works mentioned (or "cited") in the essay, article, or book. Different disciplines require different forms of documentation, and your instructor will generally tell you which one to use.

As you look through the readings in *Writing from Sources*, you will notice that some of them use documentation—most often endnotes—to cite their sources, and some do not. That's because some of the authors were writing for an academic audience, and some were not. Most nonfiction books, as well as articles in newspapers and popular magazines, are intended to provide information and commentary for a general audience. The authors are expected to include the names of their sources (and, as appropriate, the name of the specific book or article being cited), but the need for formal documentation does not apply. Not so for the authors you'll find in this book whose work was published in scholarly journals or by academic presses. And so you will see endnotes or parenthetical citations included in some readings. When you prepare research papers for your courses, you may use mostly popular sources, or mostly academic sources, or a combination of both; that will depend on your assignment. But, as a student in an academic institution, you'll always be expected to provide full documentation for all your sources.

Finally, rather than risk distracting you with my own parenthetical citations or endnotes, I've left the discussions of the readings in *Writing from Sources* undocumented. But if you're curious about where and when the readings originally appeared, you can find a list of acknowledgments at the end of the book, just before the index.

Contents

PART II
PRESENTING SOURCES TO OTHERS 57

2 *Summarizing Sources* 59

PART IV
WRITING THE RESEARCH ESSAY   301

7   *Finding Sources*   305

9 *Writing the Research Essay* 411

Writing
from Sources

Part I

MAKING SOURCES
YOUR OWN

Academic writers continually study and use the ideas of others. However good and original their own ideas may be, they must explore the work of authorities in their field, determine its value and relevance to their own work, and then integrate the ideas and words of others with their own. We call this process *research*.

To make use of another person's ideas in developing your own work, you first need to appreciate (and even temporarily share) that person's point of view. In this chapter, you will learn to better understand what you read by asking basic questions about the author's words and meaning, and by writing down (or typing out) what interests and puzzles you alongside the text. This skill is called *annotation*. Then, as your questions become more complex, you start to focus on identifying the text's main idea or *thesis* and the strategies the author uses to present and support that thesis. By asking these questions, you can eventually understand *what* the author wants to say, and *how* and *why* he or she is trying to say it. This chapter ends by examining some *argumentation* techniques, including an analysis of *inference* as a logical tool and a review of some methods of presenting *evidence*. Throughout, as you work with texts by a range of authors, you will learn how these concepts apply to your own writing.

▪1▪

Reading for Understanding

Before class began, I happened to walk around the room and I glanced at some of the books lying open on the desks. Not one book had a mark in it! Not one underlining! Every page was absolutely clean! These twenty-five students all owned the book, and they'd all read it. They all knew that there'd be an exam at the end of the week; and yet not one of them had had the sense to make a marginal note!

Teacher of an English honors class

Why was this teacher so horrified? The students had fulfilled their part of the college contract by reading the book and coming to class. Why write anything down, they might argue, when the ideas are already printed on the page. All you have to do is read the assignment and, later on, review by skimming it again. Sometimes it pays to underline an important point, but only in very long chapters, so that you don't have to read every word all over again. Taking notes wastes a lot of time, and anyway, there's never enough space in the margins.

Reading is hard work. Responding to what you are reading and participating in a mental dialogue between yourself and an author requires concentration. But only such involvement can prevent your eyes from glazing over and your thoughts from wandering off to next weekend or next summer.

As with any job, active reading becomes more rewarding if you have a product to show for your labors. In active reading, this product is *notes*: the result of contact (even friction) between your mind and the author's.

UNDERLINING

Underlining is used for selection and emphasis. When you underline, you are distinguishing between what is important (and worth rereading) and what you can skip on later readings. Underlining text on a first reading is usually

3

> ### *Guidelines for Effective Reading*
>
> - As you read and reread, note which ideas make you react.
> - Pause frequently—not to take a break but to think about and respond to what you have read. If the reading has been difficult, these pauses will provide time for you to ask questions.
> - Have a pen or pencil in your hand so that you can make lines, checks, and comments in and around what you are reading. You may even want to use several colors to help you distinguish between different ideas or themes as they recur. Of course, if you don't own the book or periodical, make a copy of key pages or take notes on separate paper. If you underline or write in a library copy, you are committing an act of vandalism, like writing graffiti on a wall. If the material comes from a computer screen, print out key pages and work with a "hard" copy. Or if the material is downloaded into a file, type comments and questions into the text [using brackets to indicate your own work].

hard, since you don't yet know which material is crucial to the work's main ideas.

Underlining can be a sophisticated analytical skill, the active sign of passive reading. But, too often, underlining merely indicates that the eyes have run over the lines. Many pages are underlined or "highlighted" so completely that there is hardly anything left over. Everything has been chosen for emphasis.

Underlining means selection. Some points are worth reviewing, and some are not. You probably would want to underline:

- important generalizations and topic sentences
- examples that have helped you understand a difficult idea
- transitional points, where the argument changes

Try *circling* and *bracketing* words and phrases that seem worth rereading and remembering. Or try using *checks in the margin*. However you choose to mark the text, deciding what to mark is an important step.

ANNOTATING

Annotation refers to the comments you write in the margins when you interpret, evaluate, or question the author's meaning, define a word or phrase, or clarify a point.

You are annotating when you jot down short explanations, summaries, or definitions in the margin. You are also annotating when you note down an idea of your own: a question or counterargument, perhaps, or a point for comparison. Not every reading deserves to be annotated. Since the process takes time and concentration, save your marginal notes for material that is especially difficult or stimulating.

Here is an example of a passage that has been annotated on the second reading. Difficult words have been defined; a few ideas have been summarized; and some problems and questions have been raised. (As you can see, the author uses footnotes to document his sources. Later, you will learn how to use several systems of documentation. At this stage, it's not necessary to annotate the notes.)

A finalist in 1993 for the National Book Award for nonfiction, *Land of Desire* is concerned with America's development as a consumer culture. In this part of the book, William Leach, a professor of history at Columbia University, is demonstrating some of the ways in which stores and restaurants encouraged people to patronize them.

from LAND OF DESIRE: MERCHANTS, POWER, AND THE RISE OF A NEW AMERICAN CULTURE
William Leach

[margin notes left: why quotes? / entrust: customers are precious possessions / all European / True of all service workers? / depends on luck, not good service / tastes and manners of the upper classes / meals at any time; more choice in return for higher prices / why extremely?]

[margin notes right: service grew faster than industry (same in recent years) / Did they speak English? Who trained them? / sweatshops = long hours/ low wages / barely endure / "American Plan"- based on middle-class culture / luxurious? expensive? / middle class attracted by upper class style / Hours were longer because of tipping or because of greater service?]

To make customers feel welcome, merchants trained workers to treat them as "special people" and as "guests." The numbers of service workers, including those entrusted with the care of customers, rose fivefold between 1870 and 1910, at two and a half times the rate of increase of industrial workers. Among them were the restaurant and hotel employees hired to wait on tables in exchange for wages and "tips," nearly all recent immigrants, mostly poor Germans and Austrians, but also Italians, Greeks, and Swiss, who suffered nerve-wracking seven-day weeks, eleven-hour days, low wages, and the sometimes terrible heat of the kitchens. Neglected by major unions until just before World War I, they endured sweated conditions equal in their misery only to those of the garment and textile workers of the day.[83]

Tipping was supposed to encourage waiters and waitresses to tolerate these conditions in exchange for possible windfalls from customers. Tipping was an unusual practice in the United States before 1890 (although common in the luxurious and aristocratic European hotels), when the prevailing "American Plan" entailed serving meals at fixed times, no frills, no tipping, and little or no follow-up service. After 1900 the European system of culinary service expanded very quickly in the United States, introduced first to the fancy establishments and then, year by year, to the more popularly priced places. By 1913 some European tourists were even expressing "outrage" at the extent of tipping in the United States.[84] Its effect on workers was extremely mixed. On the one hand, it helped keep wages low, increased the frenzy and tension of waiting, and lengthened the hours. "The tipping business is a great evil," wrote an old, retired waiter in the 1940s. "It gives the waiter portrayed as victim

waiter <u>an inferiority complex</u>—makes him feel he is <u>at the mercy of the customers</u> all the time."[85] On the other hand, some waiters were stirred by the "speculative excitement" of tipping, the risk and (chance). *chance = luck, not opportunity*

cliché

statement of theme expressed in parag. 2

all these quotation marks are distracting

all an illusion

For customers, however, tipping was intended to have only one effect—to make them feel at home and in the (lap of luxury.) On the backs of an ever-growing sweated workforce, it aristocratized consumption, <u>integrating upper-class patterns of comfort into the middle-class lifestyle.</u> Tips rewarded waiters and waitresses for making the customer "feel like 'somebody,'" as one restaurant owner put it. Such a "feeling," he wrote, "depends" on the "service of the waiter," who ushers us to "our table" and "anticipates our every want or whim." "Courteous service is a valuable asset to the restaurateur. There is a curious little twist to most of us: We enjoy the luxurious feeling of affluence, of being 'somebody,' of having our wishes catered to."[86]

3

tipping as a marketing device

it's the customer who has the inferiority complex

[83] Matthew Josephson, *The History of the Hotel and Restaurant Employees and Bartenders International Union, AFL-CIO* (New York, 1955), pp. 4–5, 84–95.

[84] Barger, *Distribution's Place*, pp. 4, 92–93. Also, on the earlier "American plan," see Josephson, pp. 4–5.

[85] Quoted in Josephson, p. 90.

[86] W. L. Dodd, "Service, Sanitation, and Quality," *The American Restaurant* (August 1920): 37.

As this passage demonstrates, annotation works by reminding you of ideas that you have thought about and understood. Some marginal notes provide no more than a shorter version of the major ideas of the passage. Others remind you of places where you disagreed with the author, looked at the ideas in a new way, or thought of fresh evidence. Your marginal notes can even suggest the topic for an essay of your own.

You can also make marginal comments about pictures or other graphics that accompany a text. In "The Weight of the World," published in the *Atlantic Monthly* in 2003, Don Peck uses maps to support his analysis of the increase in obesity worldwide. In fact, the maps are more thought-provoking—and therefore worth annotating—than is Peck's text. Here's what an annotated excerpt from the text and some of the maps might look like:

The United States contains more fat people—by a large margin—than any other nation. Sixty-four percent of American adults are overweight, versus 47 percent in 1980. Some nine million Americans are now "morbidly obese," meaning roughly a hundred pounds or more overweight, and weight-related conditions cause about 300,000 premature deaths a year in this country—more than anything else except smoking.

17% rise in 23 years

What determines ideal weight? Does it vary according to environment or only by sex and age?

Why Michigan?

Mississippi and Louisiana are poor states

West remains thin; so does New England

No pattern here—why is Oregon worse than surrounding states?

Finally, when you write marginal notes, *try always to use your own words* instead of copying or abbreviating a phrase from the text. Expressing it yourself will help you to understand and remember the point.

EXERCISE 1: ANNOTATING A PASSAGE

Read the following passage from *Sex and Suits* by Anne Hollander. Then reread it carefully, underlining and circling key ideas and inserting annotations in the margins. Remember to include the photograph and its caption in your marginal comments.

Anne Hollander is an art historian who specializes in the history of fashion and fashion trends. *Sex and Suits* focuses on male clothing as an expression of sexuality.

from SEX AND SUITS
Anne Hollander

Costume = male undershirts

Tee-shirts began as male undershirts; but so in fact did all shirts in the dim past. The shirtsleeves costume for men still retains a socially forbidden quality in some   1

worn under

contexts, held over from the shirt's ancient days as underwear. But tee-shirts have a stronger one, since they were originally meant to be worn *under* tailored shirts, an even more intimate protective layer.

erotic? vs elegant

teeshirts as underwear

Men's fashion has never used provocative exposure as part of a formal scheme; and shirts, once invisible under medieval doublets, became elegant status symbols when they began to emerge, not erotic elements. The important parts that showed, the collar, cuffs and some of the bosom, were incorporated into the imposing and skin-concealing surface composition, but the rest remained hidden—still underwear, still humiliating as public costume. Traditionally, a man in nothing but underwear is undignified and ridiculous, or vulnerable and perhaps even sacrificial, but symbolically stripped naked, not enticingly semi-nude.

second skin?

artless / point - clear

decolletage = low neckline

tee shirt = artless naked

Nevertheless, half undressed with his pants on and his coat off, he's an attractive image of unselfconscious readiness for work or play, stripped for action to his second skin, which is there to soak up the honorable sweat of his sport or labor. With the shirt collar open and the sleeves rolled up, he may indeed be very erotically exposed; but that effect, unlike deliberate feminine décolletage, only succeeds by looking artless. A man can thus be attractively undressed in ordinary shirtsleeves and trousers; but he can obviously look even more so in a tee-shirt, the under-undergarment. An extreme naked vulnerability is still there, lurking behind the zeal. The combination is very appealing.

emblem?

It's therefore not surprising that tee-shirts were the other phenomenon besides jeans that swept the world in the last third of [the twentieth] century, encompassing all sexes and classes and nations in a universal common nakedness. On top of this artless skin now goes a favored emblem, lexical or not, something that dresses the

Publicity photograph, Marlon Brando in *A Streetcar Named Desire*, 1951.

Subversive masculine modes in the second half of this century began with the tee-shirts and bluejeans of rural laborers, later adopted by rebellious urban youth. Brando shows an awareness that a tee-shirt is male underwear, and that its display is as sexy as his expression or his muscles.

[margin annotation: ambling?]
[margin annotation: law(lessness) rebellious]

person in a provisional tattoo, transcending mere clothing. Tee-shirts began skin-tight; but it's clear that they really make the wearer <u>even more</u> naked if they're loose and keep all specific bumps and hollows from intruding on the eye. Such freedom from fit only adds to the idea that the wearer is really not dressed at all; just an ⊙ambling bare body, casually flashing the message on its chest.

[margin annotation: white shirts identity of freedom]

[margin annotation: sex not the issue. based on naked]

Because poor adolescents in cities also wore the original jeans-and-tee-shirt costume, it had the repeatedly modish look of youthful ⊙lawlessness along with its older flavor of honest work. In the 1960's, it became the new *sans-culotte* costume, the scary dress of the restive ⊙urban masses. Like the original one, it came to stay and develop great variety in all social groups. Tee-shirts and jeans keep their fashionable subversive authority, their ability to weigh heavily among any proposed set of modes and to keep looking new, chiefly because their form is old and familiar, but also because they always suggest the naked man. When women wear them they still suggest Naked Man, the universal human being, dressed in <u>neutral bareness</u> to show that sex is not the issue for the moment.

[margin annotation: 5 urban = costume of jeans + tee shirt]

Annotating: "A Question of Degree"

The next step is to apply these skills to a full-length essay. Written by Blanche Blank, who was a professor of education at Hunter College of the City University of New York, "A Question of Degree" is 17 paragraphs long. Here is what the first two paragraphs look like with basic annotations about the meaning of words and phrases:

[margin annotation: everyone believes it]

Perhaps we should rethink an idea fast becoming an <u>undisputed premise</u> of American life: that a college degree is a ⊙necessary (and perhaps even a ⊙sufficient) precondition for success. I do not wish to quarrel with the assumptions made about the benefits of orthodox education. I want only to expose its ⊙false god the four-year, all-purpose, degree-granting college, aimed at the so-called college-age population and by now almost universally accepted as the stepping-stone to "<u>meaningful</u>" and "<u>better</u>" jobs.

[margin annotation: 1 necessary vs. sufficient? = false idol quotes mean B.B. doesn't agree]

[margin annotation: inconsistencies]
[margin annotation: high salary + expensive possessions]

What is wrong with the current ⊙college/work cycle can be seen in the following ⊙anomalies we are selling college to the youth of America as a take-off pad for the ⊙material good life. College is literally ⊙advertised and packaged as a means for getting more money through "better" jobs at the same time that Harvard graduates are taking jobs as taxi drivers. This situation is a ⊙perversion of the true spirit of a university, a perversion of a humane social ethic and, at bottom, a ⊙patent fraud. To take the last point first, the economy simply is not geared to guaranteeing these presumptive "better" jobs; the colleges are not geared to training for such jobs; and the ⊙ethical propriety of the entire enterprise is very questionable. We are by ⊙definition (rather than by ⊙analysis) establishing two kinds of work: work labeled "better" because it has a degree requirement tagged to it and nondegree work, which, through this logic, becomes automatically "low level."

[margin annotation: college leads to work]
[margin annotation: 2 presented to the public = corruption = obvious colleges can't deliver what they promise]

[margin annotation: morality definition = by saying so]
[margin annotation: analysis = by observing what's right and real]

ASKING QUESTIONS

As you read actively and try to understand what you read, you will start asking questions about the text. Sometimes you will want to write your answers down; sometimes answering your questions in your head is enough.

As the questions in the box below suggest, to understand what you read, your mind has to sweep back and forth between each sentence on the page and the larger context of the whole paragraph or essay. You can misunderstand the author's meaning if you interpret ideas out of context, ignoring the way in which they fit into the work as a whole.

Understanding takes time and careful reading. Being a fast reader is not necessarily an advantage. In fact, it is usually on the second reading, when you begin to grasp the overall meaning and structure of the work, that questions begin to pop into your head and you begin to read more carefully.

Questions to Aid Understanding

- What is the meaning of this word?
- How should I understand that phrase?
- Where do I have difficulty understanding the text? Why? Which passages are easy for me? Why?
- What does this passage remind me of?
- What is the topic sentence of the paragraph?
- What is the connection between these two points?
- What is the transitional word telling me?
- This concept is difficult: how would I express it in my own words?
- Is this point a digression from the main idea, or does it fit in with what I've already read?
- Can the whole page be summarized briefly?
- What point is the writer trying to make?

Asking Questions: "A Question of Degree"

Now, read the entire essay, and answer the questions asked in the margins. These questions go beyond the simple definitions of the previous annotation, asking *why* and *how*. Your answers can be brief, but *use your own words*.

Some of the sample questions may seem very subtle to you, and you may wonder whether you would have thought of all of them yourself. But they are model questions, to show you what you *could* ask if you wanted to gain an especially thorough understanding of the essay.

When you're sure of the answers to these questions, you're sure of the author's meaning. Then, compare your answers with those on pages 15–19.

A QUESTION OF DEGREE
Blanche D. Blank

A. In what context can a college degree be a false god?

B. Why does Blank put "meaningful" and "better" in quotation marks?

C. What conclusion can be drawn from the "Harvard graduates" sentence?

D. How many perversions does Blank mention? Can you distinguish between them?

E. In the last two sentences, what are the two types of "fraud" that are described?

F. What is the "practical curriculum"?

G. What is the danger to the universities?

H. What groups have suffered as a result of "compulsory" college?

Perhaps we should rethink an idea fast becoming an undisputed premise of American life: that a college degree is a necessary (and perhaps even a sufficient) precondition for success. I do not wish to quarrel with the assumptions made about the benefits of orthodox education. I want only to expose its false god: the four-year, all-purpose, degree-granting college, aimed at the so-called college-age population and by now almost universally accepted as the stepping-stone to "meaningful" and "better" jobs. 1

What is wrong with the current college/work cycle can be seen in the following anomalies: we are selling college to the youth of America as a take-off pad for the material good life. College is literally advertised and packaged as a means for getting more money through "better" jobs at the same time that Harvard graduates are taking jobs as taxi drivers. This situation is a perversion of the true spirit of a university, a perversion of a humane social ethic and, at bottom, a patent fraud. To take the last point first, the economy simply is not geared to guaranteeing these presumptive "better" jobs; the colleges are not geared to training for such jobs; and the ethical propriety of the entire enterprise is very questionable. We are by definition (rather than by analysis) establishing two kinds of work: work labeled "better" because it has a degree requirement tagged to it and nondegree work, which, through this logic, becomes automatically "low level." 2

This process is also destroying our universities. The "practical curriculum" must become paramount; the students must become prisoners; the colleges must become servants of big business and big government. Under these conditions the university can no longer be an independent source of scientific and philosophic truth-seeking and moral criticism. 3

Finally, and most important, we are destroying the spirit of youth by making college compulsory at adolescence, when it may be least congruent with emotional and physical needs; and we are denying college as an optional and continuing experience later in life, when it might be most congruent with intellectual and recreational needs. 4

Let me propose an important step to reverse these trends and thus help restore freedom and dignity to both our colleges and our workplaces. We should outlaw employment discrimination based on college degrees. This would simply be another facet of our "equal opportunity" policy and would add college degrees to 5

I. What is Blank's
contribution to "our
'equal opportunity'
policy"?

J. What does "legitimacy"
mean in this context?

K. What point(s) does
the example of Joe
help to prove?

sex, age, race, religion and ethnic group as inherently unfair bases for employment selection.

People would, wherever possible, demonstrate their capacities on the job. Where that proved impractical, outside tests could still serve. The medical boards, bar exams, mechanical, mathematical and verbal aptitude tests might still be used by various enterprises. The burden of proof of their legitimacy, however, would remain with the using agencies. So too would the costs. Where the colleges were best equipped to impart a necessary skill they would do so, but only where it would be natural to the main thrust of a university endeavor.   6

The need for this rethinking and for this type of legislation may best be illustrated by a case study. Joe V. is a typical liberal-arts graduate, fired by imaginative art and literature. He took a job with a large New York City bank, where he had the opportunity to enter the "assistant manager training program." The trainees rotated among different bank departments to gain technical know-how and experience and also received classroom instruction, including some sessions on "how to write a business letter." The program was virtually restricted to college graduates. At the end of the line, the trainees became assistant bank managers: a position consisting largely of giving simple advice to bank customers and a modest amount of supervision of employees. Joe searched for some connection between his job and the training program, on the one hand, and his college-whetted appetites and skills on the other. He found none.   7

In giving Joe preference for the training program, the bank had bypassed a few enthusiastic aspirants already dedicated to a banking career and daily demonstrating their competence in closely related jobs. After questioning his superiors about the system, Joe could only conclude that the "top brass" had some very diffuse and not-too-well-researched or even well-thought-out conceptions about college men. The executives admitted that a college degree did not of itself ensure the motivation or the verbal or social skills needed. Nor were they clear about what skills were most desirable for their increasingly diverse branches. Yet, they clung to the college prerequisite.   8

Business allows the colleges to act as recruiting, screening and training agencies for them because it saves money and time. Why colleges allow themselves to act as servicing agents may not be as apparent. One reason may be that colleges are increasingly becoming conventional bureaucracies. It is inevitable, therefore, that they   9 should respond to the first and unchallenged law of bureaucracy: Expand! The more that colleges can persuade outside institutions to restrict employment in favor of their clientele, the stronger is the college's hold and attraction. This rationale becomes even clearer when we understand that the budgets of public universities hang on the number of students "serviced." Seen from this perspective, then, it is perhaps easier to understand why such matters as "university independence," or "the propriety" of using the public bankroll to support enterprises that are expected to make private profits, can be dismissed. Conflict of interest is difficult to discern when the interests involved are your own. . . .

L. What are the colleges' reasons for cooperating with business?

M. What is the conflict of interest?

What is equally questionable is whether a college degree, as such, is proper evidence that those new skills that are truly needed will be delivered. A friend who works for the Manpower Training Program feels that there is a clear divide between actual job needs and college-degree requirements. One of her chief frustrations is the knowledge that many persons with the ability to do paraprofessional mental-health work are lost to jobs they could hold with pleasure and profit because the training program also requires a two-year associate arts degree. 10

Obviously, society can and does manipulate job status. I hope that we can manipulate it in favor of the greatest number of people. More energy should be spent in trying to upgrade the dignity of all socially useful work and to eliminate the use of human beings for any work that proves to be truly destructive of the human spirit. Outlawing the use of degrees as prerequisites for virtually every job that our media portray as "better" should carry us a long step toward a healthier society. Among other things, there is far more evidence that work can make college meaningful than that college can make work meaningful. 11

N. What does this sentence mean?

O. Is Blank recommending that everyone go to work before attending college?

My concern about this degree/work cycle might be far less acute, however, if everyone caught up in the system were having a good time. But we seem to be generating a college population that oscillates between apathy and hostility. One of the major reasons for this joylessness in our university life is that the students see themselves as prisoners of economic necessity. They have bought the media messages about better jobs, and so they do their time. But the promised land of "better" jobs is, on the one hand, not materializing; and on the other hand the student is by now socialized to find such "better" jobs distasteful even if they were to materialize. 12

P. What does "prisoners of economic necessity" mean?

One of the major improvements that could result from the proposed legislation against degree requirements for employment 13

Q. What are the "compulsory schools" and how would their role change if Blank's proposal were adopted?

would be a new stocktaking on the part of all our educational agencies. Compulsory schools, for example, would understand that the basic skills for work and family life in our society would have to be compressed into those years of schooling.

Colleges and universities, on the other hand, might be encouraged to be as unrestricted, as continuous and as open as possible. They would be released from the pressures of ensuring economic survival through a practical curriculum. They might best be modeled after museums. Hours would be extensive, fees minimal, and services available to anyone ready to comply with course-by-course demands. Colleges under these circumstances would have a clearly understood focus, which might well be the traditional one of serving as a gathering place for those persons who want to search for philosophic and scientific "truths."

R. What role does Blank envisage for the university in a healthier society?

This proposal should help our universities rid themselves of some strange and gratuitous practices. For example, the university would no longer have to organize itself into hierarchical levels: B.A., M.A., Ph.D. There would simply be courses of greater and lesser complexity in each of the disciplines. In this way graduate education might be more rationally understood and accepted for what it is— more education.

S. What are the "strange and gratuitous practices" of the universities? What purpose do they serve?

The new freedom might also relieve colleges of the growing practice of instituting extensive "work programs," "internships" and "independent study" programs. The very names of these enterprises are tacit admissions that the campus itself is not necessary for many genuinely educational experiences. But, along with "external degree" programs, they seem to pronounce that whatever one has learned in life by whatever diverse and interesting routes cannot be recognized as increasing one's dignity, worth, usefulness or self-enjoyment until it is converted into degree credits.

T. What, according to Blank, would be a "rational order of priorities"?

The legislation I propose would offer a more rational order of priorities. It would help recapture the genuine and variegated dignity of the workplace along with the genuine and more specialized dignity of the university. It should help restore to people of all ages and inclinations a sense of their own basic worth and offer them as many roads as possible to reach Rome.

14

15

16

17

Answering Questions: "A Question of Degree"

Paragraph One

A. In what context can a college degree be a false god?

A. Colleges are worshiped by students who believe that the degree will magically ensure a good career and a better life. Blank suggests that college degrees no longer have magic powers.

B. Why does Blank put "meaningful" and "better" in quotation marks?

B. Blank doesn't believe the adjectives are applicable; she is using quotation marks to show her disagreement with the idea that some jobs should be seen as better or more meaningful than others.

Paragraph Two

C. What conclusion can be drawn from the "Harvard graduates" sentence?

C. If Harvard graduates are driving taxis, a degree does not ensure a high-level job.

D. How many perversions does Blank mention? Can you distinguish between them?

D. When degrees are regarded as vocational qualifications, the university's proper purpose is perverted; society's conception of proper qualifications for employment and advancement is perverted; and, by implication, young people's belief in the reliability of rewards promised by society is perverted.

E. In the last two sentences, what are the two types of "fraud" that are described?

E. One kind of fraud is the deception practiced on young college students who won't get the good jobs they expect. A second type of fraud is practiced on workers without degrees whose efforts and successes are undervalued because of the division into "better" and "worse" jobs.

Paragraph Three

F. What is the "practical curriculum"?

F. "Practical curriculum" refers to courses that will train college students for specific jobs; the term is probably being contrasted with "liberal arts."

G. What is the danger to the universities?

G. The emphasis on vocational training perverts the universities' traditional pursuit of knowledge for its own sake, as it makes financing and curriculum very closely connected with the economic needs of the businesses and professions for which students will be trained.

Paragraph Four

H. What groups have suffered as a result of "compulsory" college?

H. Blank has so far referred to four groups: students in college; workers who have never been to college; members of universities, both staff and students, interested in a liberal-arts curriculum; and older people who might want to return to college after a working career.

Paragraph Five

I. What is Blank's contribution to "our 'equal opportunity' policy"?

I. Blank suggests that a college degree does not indicate suitability for employment and therefore that requiring it should be classed as discriminatory, along with sex, age, etc.

Paragraph Six

J. What does "legitimacy" mean in this context?

J. If certain professions choose to test the qualifications of aspirants, professional organizations should prove that examinations are necessary and that the results will measure the applicant's suitability for the job. These organizations should be responsible for the arrangements and the financing; at present, colleges serve as a "free" testing service.

Paragraphs Seven and Eight

K. What point(s) does the example of Joe help to prove?

K. Joe's experience supports Blank's argument that college training is not often needed in order to perform most kinds of work. Joe's expectations that his college education would prepare him for work were also pitched too high, as Blank has suggested, while the experience of other bank employees who were passed over in favor of Joe exemplifies the plight of those workers without college degrees whose experience is not sufficiently valued.

Paragraph Nine

L. What are the colleges' reasons for cooperating with business?

L. Colleges are competing for students in order to increase their enrollment; they therefore want to be able to assure applicants that many companies prefer to hire their graduates. Having become overorganized, with many levels of authority, the bureaucratic universities regard enrollment as an end in itself.

M. What is the conflict of interest?

M. The interests of an institution funded by the public might be said to be in conflict with the interests of a private, profit-making company.

Paragraph Eleven

N. What does this sentence mean?

N. Instead of discriminating between kinds of workers and kinds of work, we should distinguish between work that benefits everyone and should therefore be considered admirable, and work that is degrading and should, if possible, not be performed by people.

O. Is Blank recommending that everyone go to work before attending college?

O. Although Blank is not insisting that working is preferable to or should have priority over a college education, she implies that most people gain more significant knowledge from the work experience than from college.

Paragraph Twelve

P. What does "prisoners of economic necessity" mean?

P. Young people who believe that a degree will get them better jobs have no choice but to spend a four-year term in college, whether or not they are intellectually and temperamentally suited to the experience.

Paragraph Thirteen

Q. What are the "compulsory schools" and how would their role change if Blank's proposal were adopted?

Q. Compulsory schools are grade and high schools, which students must attend up to a set age. If students were not automatically expected to go on to college, the lower schools would have to offer a more comprehensive and complete education than they do now.

Paragraph Fourteen

R. What role does Blank envisage for the university in a healthier society?

R. Blank sees the colleges in a role quite apart from the mainstream of life. Colleges would be easily accessible centers of learning, to which people could go for intellectual inquiry and stimulation in their spare time.

Paragraph Fifteen

S. What are the "strange and gratuitous" practices of the universities? What purpose do they serve?

S. The universities divide the process of education into a series of clearly defined levels of attainment. Blank finds these divisions "gratuitous" or unnecessary, perhaps because they are "hierarchical" and distinguish between those of greater or lesser achievement and status.

Paragraph Seventeen

T. What, according to Blank, would be a "rational order of priorities"?

T. Blank's first priority is the self-respect of the average member of society who currently may be disappointed and frustrated at not being valued for his or her work. Another priority is restoration of the university to its purely intellectual role.

EXERCISE 2: UNDERSTANDING WHAT YOU READ

Read "Victim of Circumstance" twice. On the second reading, answer the comprehension questions in the margins. You will notice that some of the "questions" resemble instructions, very much like examination questions, directing you to explain, define, or in other ways analyze the reading. *Answer in complete sentences*, and use your own words as much as you can.

Jane Bernstein teaches creative writing at Carnegie Mellon University and has published both fiction and nonfiction. This essay appeared in the *New York Times Magazine* prior to its publication as part of Bernstein's memoir, *Bereft: A Sister's Story*.

VICTIM OF CIRCUMSTANCE
Jane Bernstein

A. All the details of Laura's murder are stated in a single sentence. Why?

B. What information are we initially given about the killer? Why is that information important?

C. Bernstein uses three negatives in the space of two sentences: "did not discuss"; "never asked"; "weren't informed." What's the effect of doing so?

D. How can a Victims' Bill of Rights apply to someone who has been murdered?

In September 1966, my sister, Laura, a 20-year-old college student in Tempe, Arizona, was chaining her bike to a window grate when she was stabbed six times and left to die on the pavement. My parents did not discuss the murder, so for years, all I knew was that the killer, David Mumbaugh, was a teenager, like me, and a stranger to my sister, that he had confessed to the crime and that he had been sent to prison. 1

We never asked what became of Mumbaugh, and maybe it was just as well, because in 1966 criminal files were sealed and murder victims' families weren't informed of parole hearings, which inmates' families were encouraged to attend. It took 24 years before Arizona passed a Victims' Bill of Rights. 2

That was why in 1990 I was informed that Mumbaugh was petitioning for his release from prison and invited to write an "impact 3

E. Why is "impact statement" in quotation marks?

statement." I asked a lot of questions about this hearing—my first and Mumbaugh's 10th. The advocate assigned to my case tried to re-assure me that the procedural details were unimportant. Just tell the board your feelings, she said. Your statement will be the single most important thing it will hear. Only you can say if Mumbaugh's debt has been paid.

F. "Can a debt be paid for murder?" What does the question mean at this point in the essay?

G. What do the contrasting attitudes in paragraph 4 tell us about the possibility of paying this debt?

Can a debt be paid for murder? The wardens, cops and prosecu-tors I asked all said, "An eye for an eye." One official said, "Your sis-ter didn't get a chance, why should he?" Those in the "forgiveness community" talked about forgiveness's healing qualities. Anger and hate are corrosive, they said. Use mercy to turn tragedy into "a growth experience."   4

H. Bernstein is once again contrasting her life with Mumbaugh's. Why?

Neither of these positions addressed Mumbaugh or his 24 years   5
behind bars—years in which I had gone from being a teenager to being the mother of a teenager. What if Mumbaugh had been psy-chotic when he murdered my sister and had been languishing in prison for decades, no longer sick? What if he had worked hard in prison and shown genuine remorse? I had read about such a man—

I. Why is Hamm introduced?

James Hamm—who had served part of his sentence in the same fa-cility as Mumbaugh. Hamm had enrolled in every work program, in stress-reduction and self-improvement classes, had earned a B.A. with honors, had his sentence for first-degree murder commuted and was paroled after 17 years. Could I approve Mumbaugh's release if he had served his time this productively?

I obtained Mumbaugh's file and learned that he had served his time   6
well, if quietly. But his record was marred by certain "self-injurious incidents"; in 1984 he swallowed insecticide and in 1989 stabbed

J. What changes in Bernstein do the active verbs—"I *obtained*"; "I *spoke*"—and the shorter sentences convey?

himself in the thigh. So I spoke against Mumbaugh's release, citing these bizarre acts to suggest that rage still percolated beneath his placid exterior. No debate or discussion followed. Mumbaugh was simply sent back to prison.

I attended a second hearing in 1993. This time two of the board   7
members seemed eager to give Mumbaugh a chance. Again I voiced

K. "The gate crashed down" is a rare instance of figurative language in this essay. What does its use signify?

my opposition. The gate crashed down. Mumbaugh's petition was immediately and unanimously denied.

I was chilled by my power. Regardless of my reasons, or Mum-   8
baugh's behavior over the last 27 years, my "no" was all the board

L. By committing suicide, has Mumbaugh paid his debt?

had to hear. Two months later he was found dead, more than likely a suicide.

Had the system swung too far on the side of victims? I had been   9
mulling this question when I saw a newspaper article about Hamm. Upon his release, he had enrolled in tax-supported public law school

M. Why does Bernstein want to meet Hamm?

N. What's the significance of Hamm's T-shirt?

(at the same university my sister had attended at the time of her murder) and had thereby started a bitter controversy. I phoned him in 1994 to ask if we could talk. When we met, at a crowded restaurant, he was wearing a T-shirt with "Law" emblazoned across his powerful chest.

Hamm would not speak about his past, only of the moment in prison when he acknowledged the "absolute irrevocability" of his actions and decided that serving his time well was a way of paying in the only coin he had.

10

O. What is Hamm's "only coin"? Does he believe that he has paid his debt? Has he forgiven himself?

Was he the same person who had committed the murder? I asked. He couldn't relate to that other self. What did he say to death-penalty proponents? It was their perspective. And victims—now that we had so much power, what responsibility did he feel we had?

11

His expression clouded, as if my question was distasteful. "You have no responsibility," he said.

12

P. In what sense is Hamm a "free man"?

For a moment I believed him. But when I stepped away, years away, I was struck by the carelessness of his words; for only a free man can wear his guilt as openly as a law-school T-shirt.

13

Q. Can a debt be paid for murder? How has Bernstein's view changed?

R. At the end of the essay, in what way does Bernstein identify with Mumbaugh?

Murder is irrevocable. When Mumbaugh killed my sister, he put a knife into my family's heart. There is no full payment for all that we lost. And yet, I am part of a society that stopped throwing prisoners into dungeons to rot, part of a culture that claims to be humane. Allowing victims a role in the decision about a prisoner's release is just and humane. Giving us the power to dictate someone's fate is not.

14

QUESTIONING THE AUTHOR

Asking questions about a text helps you to understand the meaning of words, sentences, and paragraphs. Still, having done so, you may not yet fully understand the meaning of the text itself: the author's *reason* for writing it, the *validity* and *persuasiveness* of the ideas. Has the author's point been made? Was it worth making?

To analyze these issues of *intention*, you need to use some standard vocabulary: thesis, bias, and tone.

Thesis

A thesis is a statement of intention and purpose, expressing the central idea of an essay. Once committed to a thesis, the author undertakes to support and validate this central idea thoroughly and convincingly.

The thesis should be a substantial generalization that can stand by itself. It should not be confused with a *topic*.

- The thesis should be a *statement*, not a question. The author is not raising a question for exploration, but attempting to *answer a question*.

These are topics, not theses.

Unacceptable: Who should go to college?

Unacceptable: How can students succeed in college?

Acceptable: Only students who will make the fullest use of their education should go to college.

- The thesis should be *broad* enough and *arguable* enough to be worth defending. It should not be an obvious truth.

Who would disagree? It's hardly worth arguing.

Unacceptable: Poorly prepared students can find college work difficult.

Too narrow a thesis to sustain an essay.

Unacceptable: Some of the students in my history course found the second assignment too difficult.

Solves the problem— how can students succeed in college?

Acceptable: To help unprepared students succeed, colleges should provide a full range of support services.

Answers the question—who should go to college?—by *defining* that group.

Acceptable: Since college can be difficult for poorly prepared students, admission should depend on the applicant's meeting certain standards of achievement.

- The thesis should define the *scope* and *limits* of the essay. The author should stay within the boundaries of the thesis and not digress into other topics. Which of the following theses correctly corresponds to the scope of "A Question of Degree"?

Too narrow.

Unacceptable: Employment discrimination arises from an overemphasis on college degrees.

Too broad.

Unacceptable: College is wasted on the young.

A good thesis, which is often complex, cannot always be expressed in a short sentence.

Acceptable: Regarding the college degree as a prerequisite for a good job and a better life can only discourage a fair and efficient system of employment and subvert the true purpose of higher education.

Intention

The author's general purpose in writing is to present a thesis clearly and support it convincingly. The thesis will vary according to the nature of the topic and what the author intends to do with it.

If thesis denotes *what* the essay is about, intention suggests *how* it will be developed. Take, for example, the topic of *college drinking*. In this group of four theses, notice how the author's intention changes with each one.

What Is a Thesis?

The thesis will be a broad statement, worth defending, that defines the scope and limits of the essay.

1. The thesis will be a substantial generalization that can stand by itself. It should not be confused with a *topic*.
2. The thesis will be *broad* enough and *arguable* enough to be worth defending. It will not be an obvious truth.
3. The thesis will define the *scope* and *limits* of the essay. The author should stay within the boundaries of the thesis and not digress into other topics.

---

1. Students have ample opportunity to drink to excess on our campus.

The author's intention is to *explain* why it's easy to get drunk at her college—probably by citing *facts* and *statistics* such as the number of bars near campus and the rules on liquor in dormitories, as well as *anecdotes* and *examples*. With a thesis like this one, the reader can't easily tell whether the author approves of, disapproves of, or is indifferent toward the drinking.

2. The behavior of students who drink to excess can represent a cry for help.

Here, the author has made an interesting observation and undertakes to *analyze* or *interpret* it. Developing a theory about the habits of college drinkers and what they signify requires a more complex level of inquiry and speculation than does exploring how easy it is to get access to alcoholic beverages. Such a theory might also be supported by anecdotes and examples, as well as the "hard" evidence of facts and statistics, but that evidence will have to be correctly interpreted if the reader is to be convinced. While the thesis might be controversial—you can disagree with it—the author intends to do something other than merely defend one side of the issue.

3. Students who drink to excess should be expelled.

No question here that the author will be engaged in *persuasion*, defending a thesis that represents a particular point of view. Doing so may or may not include the explanation and analysis mentioned above, but it will certainly require presenting a *line of reasoning* for the reader to follow.

4. Because the deficiencies of their colleges cause many students to drink to excess, colleges ought to provide a better environment for learning.

This thesis combines elements from all three of the previous examples. Do many students drink to excess? **Explain and demonstrate.** Why do they drink to excess? **Analyze and interpret.** What should be done about this problem?

("Deficiencies" indicates that this writer isn't going to be neutral about this is-sue.) **Argue and persuade.**

Developing a Thesis

Authors can develop a thesis in several ways, depending on their inten-tion. Most complex theses involve several methods of approach, usually including:

- explanation,
- analysis and interpretation,
- argument and persuasion.

Recognizing Intention

You can often determine an author's intention just by reading the first few paragraphs of an essay and asking some questions. Look at the following examples:

Botstein's *thesis* is clear and upfront: his *intention* is to *persuade* his readers that high schools should be abolished. He starts by alluding to the worthless values prevalent in schools.

A. *The national outpouring after the Littleton shootings has forced us to confront something we have suspected for a long time: the Ameri-can high school is obsolete and should be abolished. In the last month, high school students present and past have come forward with sto-ries about cliques and the artificial intensity of a world defined by in-siders and outsiders, in which the insiders hold sway because of superficial definitions of good looks and attractiveness, popularity and sports prowess.*

LEON BOTSTEIN, from "Let Teenagers Try Adulthood"

Jekanowski is citing statistics to *explain* and *demonstrate* one aspect of his *thesis* about the need for time-saving products.

B. *With today's hectic lifestyles, time-saving products are increasingly in demand. Perhaps one of the most obvious examples is fast food. The rate of growth in consumer expenditures on fast food has led most other segments of the food-away-from-home market for much of the last two decades. Since 1982, the amount consumers spent at fast food outlets grew at an annual rate of 6.8 percent (through 1997) compared with a 4.7 percent growth in table service restaurant ex-penditures. The proportion of away-from-home food expenditures on fast food increased from 29.3 to 34.2 percent between 1982 and 1997, while the restaurant proportion decreased from 41 to 35.7 percent.*

MARK D. JEKANOWSKI, from "Causes and Consequences of Fast Food Sales Growth"

Bok's likely
intention is to
analyze and
interpret this
aspect of Roman
behavior. We
can't tell yet what
her *thesis* will be.

C. *No people before or since have so revelled in displays of mortal com-*
bat as did the Romans during the last two centuries BC and the first
three centuries thereafter, nor derived such pleasure from spectacles
in which slaves and convicts were exposed to wild beasts and killed
in front of cheering spectators. According to Nicolaus of Damascus,
writing in the first decade AD, Romans even regaled themselves with
lethal violence at private banquets; he describes dinner guests relish-
ing the spectacles of gladiators fighting to the death:

> *Hosts would invite their friends to dinner not merely for other*
> *entertainment, but that they might witness two or three pairs of*
> *contestants in a gladiatorial combat; on these occasions, when*
> *sated with dining and drink, they called in the gladiators. No*
> *sooner did one have his throat cut than the masters applauded*
> *with delight at this feat.*

SISSELA BOK, from *Mayhem: Violence as Public Entertainment*

Bias

Because authors often have strong feelings about and even a personal stake
in proving their point, they may, knowingly or unintentionally, be less than
objective in their choice of methods, evidence, and words. For example, a work
can lose credibility if the author's bias leads him or her to omit or distort
evidence.

If you think you detect bias at a specific point in a text, consider the entire
presentation. Determine whether the presentation is *balanced* and all relevant
points are given a fair hearing, or whether the author consistently gives unrea-
sonable weight to one side of the issue.

Knowing something about the author's background may help you to determine whether he or she has an ax to grind. In a previous example, we can't be
sure whether Mark D. Jekanowski is extolling fast food or merely recording its
growth in popularity. Knowing that, at the time of writing, he was an agricultural economist with the U.S. Department of Agriculture might reassure you
about his objectivity. Does that impression change when you learn from a
Google search that he subsequently became a senior consultant, with responsibilities including research on consumer demand, for a consulting firm specializing in agribusiness? (See pp. 362–363 and 368–369 for more information about
detecting bias in sources.)

Tone

Most academic authors write in a measured, straightforward style; serious
subjects call for a serious tone. But, outside of academia, there are many exceptions. Some writers use *humor* to win over their readers. Others will try *irony* to

make a point, so that readers, unsure whether the author means what she says, have to question apparently obvious assumptions. In describing how snobbery works, Joseph Epstein establishes a light, almost flippant tone, poking fun at himself as well as others:

> Nearly every human being deserves respect, but the question is, how much? And who does the calculations? By one's own reckoning, it is safe to say that a great deal of respect is owed. By the world's reckoning, the estimate is, somehow, almost inevitably likely to be lower. Journals kept by the young tend to give off a strong whiff of depression, chiefly because the world doesn't yet recognize the youthful journal keeper's genius, however unproven it may be. Sometimes one feels one isn't getting the consideration (another euphemism for deference) one deserves as a veteran, senior man or woman, someone whose mettle has been established. Awaiting a decision from an editor that takes longer than I think it ought, I find myself mumbling about the ignorance of people who don't understand that I am much too important to be kept waiting so long.
>
> JOSEPH EPSTEIN, from *Snobbery: The American Version*

Sometimes the tone of a work is *strident and overbearing*, which can be a clue to the possibility of bias: the author is so eager to make his case that he may be willing to cut corners to do so. Such a work may be a *polemic*—an argument that aggressively courts controversy. Here, for example, is a passage filled with sweeping generalizations in which the author is rejecting what he says is a common form of American patriotism:

> Many of our superpatriots love this country because it is considered a land of opportunity, a place where people can succeed if they have the right stuff. But individual success usually comes by prevailing over others. And when it comes to the really big prizes in a competitive, money-driven society, almost all of us are losers or simply noncontestants. Room at the top is limited to a select few, mostly those who have been supremely advantaged in family income and social standing from early in life. Even if the U.S. economy does reward the go-getters who sally forth with exceptional capacity and energy, is the quality of life to be measured by the ability of tireless careerists to excel over others? Even if it were easy to become a multimillionaire in America, what is so great about that? Why should one's ability to make large sums of money be reason to love one's country? What is admirable about a patriotism based on the cash nexus?
>
> MICHAEL PARENTI, from *Superpatriotism*

In another example of immoderate tone, Waller Newell's anger at the misappropriation of the song "Imagine" spills over into his prose:

> I am rarely at a loss for words, and like most political junkies I enjoy a good rant, especially after a dose of the television and newspaper opinion makers who can

be counted on to make my blood boil—and stir my appetite for more reasoned polemics. But I must confess my stupefaction at how, in the painful months after 9/11, in schools, church basements, and community centers across the land, children's sweet voices swelled in repeated performances of John Lennon's 1970s ballad. That decent people truly believe this song is an appropriate tribute to the victims, that it contains some profound lesson for these trying times, sums up more completely than any other single example how much we desperately need some better guides for manly reflection.

WALLER NEWELL, from *The Code of Man*

The author's perception of the likely *audience* for the work may affect the tone. Writing for a general audience reading a popular magazine will be different from writing for an audience of specialists reading a scholarly journal, and writing for an audience inclined to agree with a thesis will probably be less challenging than writing for its opponents. The author has to make assumptions about the readers, and the style of the essay changes accordingly. (For more information on audience, see pp. 363–365.) Identifying an essay's characteristic tone and probable audience can help you to understand how well the author succeeds in supporting the thesis.

Questioning the Author: "The Kindness of Strangers"

Read through "The Kindness of Strangers" by Rubén Martínez, looking at the marginal comments as you read. Some of the annotations are concerned with basic points about the author's meaning; others are more general comments about thesis, method, intention, and tone. Notice how some of them try to sum up what the author has said so far. Others point to a transitional place where the author is turning from one idea to another. Familiarize yourself with this advanced process of annotation, which resembles carrying on a dialogue with the author. What other questions could you ask?

Rubén Martínez teaches creative writing at the University of Houston and has written essays and opinion pieces on political issues for a range of newspapers and magazines. His books include *Crossing Over: A Mexican Family on the Migrant Trail* (2002) and *The New Americans* (2004), the text that accompanied a PBS series. "The Kindness of Strangers" appeared as an op-ed article in the *New York Times*.

THE KINDNESS OF STRANGERS
Rubén Martínez

anecdote   The young couple knocks on the heavy wooden door. They are weary and the hour is late; it is bitterly cold.   1

The husband says: "En nombre del cielo, os pido posada," in the name of heaven, I ask thee for lodging.   2

simple style,
like a
fairy tale

From behind the door comes the answer: "Este no es mesón, sigan adelante, yo   3
no debo abrir, sea algún tunante," this is not an inn, move along, I shouldn't open
up, it may be a thief.

story has
universal
relevance—
part of the
Mexican-
American
experience

The centuries-old tradition of las posadas is celebrated throughout Mexico and in   4
practically every Mexican neighborhood in America in the days before Christmas.
José and María trudge from door to door, turned away again and again until they
are finally allowed to bed down in the humble manger where the Christ child is
born. Everyone in the neighborhood gets a part in the play.

RM turns to
interpretation
of the story

parable = story
with a moral

to grasp the
moral, we should
play both roles:
identify with
innkeepers
(native-born)
and immigrants

Like many traditions, this one can resonate with different tones according to the   5
political tenor of the times. And with the immigration debate on the national
agenda—President Bush is once again promoting "guest worker" legislation—this
Christmas parable asks us to step inside the shoes of both the protagonists and
antagonists, the migrant couple seeking shelter and the innkeepers who, momen-
tarily, hold such power over the couple's fate.

Las posadas is a story about hospitality, certainly a "moral value," but not one poll-   6
sters ask about. Based on the notion of pilgrimage, a spiritual journey undertaken
through the flesh, it is present in practically all the world's religions. Without the
hospitality of those who live along the roads of one's pilgrimage—be it the hajj of
Islam or a Catholic penitent's journey to a shrine—one would never arrive at one's
destination. Hospitality implies reciprocity: the pilgrim received with generosity
will one day have the occasion to return the favor. To shut the door on the wayfaring
stranger would be to negate the possibility of one's own journey.

moral = we are
interdependent

hospitality
= kindness
to guests
(do guests
= strangers?)

giving and
receiving
hospitality
are
essential
to achieving
a state of
grace

Of course, we shut the door all the time. We conclude, as the innkeepers do in
the posada play, that José and María aren't pilgrims at all; they are "thieves" intent
on taking from us and giving nothing in return. That is precisely what a strong majority of voters in Arizona apparently believed in November when they passed
Proposition 200, which denies most public benefits to illegal migrants; on Wednesday, a federal judge cleared the way for the proposition to become law. "They"
have come here merely to feed off America's welfare state—to take something for
nothing. We do not extend hospitality to thieves.

we misinterpret
the migrants'
motives; we
can't imagine
ourselves in
their situation

political
parallel

Philosophers have long debated the ethics of hospitality, which raises a series of
existential, legal and moral questions. Is pure hospitality practicable in a world of human unpredictability? Or is hospitality an indispensable practice precisely because of
human unpredictability? In the post-9/11 world, we ponder the question more in
terms of national security. How does one discern between the stranger to whom
hospitality should be extended, and the stranger who poses a threat? Does war
automatically exempt us from showing hospitality? Does a "war without end" permanently suspend such values?

more abstract
tone

RM moves
beyond simple
parable

"thief" becomes
"terrorist"

8
asking
questions =
a way of
raising issues
without
committing to
answers

RM moves
from the
spiritual
("pilgrimage")
to the
political
(protecting
borders)

Americans have long had a troubled, contradictory relationship with immigrants.
We famously say that we are immigrants, indeed a "land of immigrants," and just
as famously render them "them." While Liberty opens her arms to the tired, poor
and huddled masses, we also greet the immigrant with ethnic slurs and sweatshop

parallels the
double role of
innkeeper and
migrant

RM is repeating the parable in terms of the nation

Why should one open the door to a stranger? act of faith?

"thieves"

Here, RM is completely identifying with the migrants. Does his sympathy become bias?

shift in point of view from nativist to migrant

like a spiritual pilgrimage

RM's identification with migrants deepens

We're asked to take this view of migrants on faith—RM's language has become spiritual, not analytical as before

i.e., both sides ignore the urgent need for hospitality

borders are artificial and porous

summarizing sentence

returns to the theme of reciprocity

laws are good (realistic) and bad (disguise reality)

Biblical image

wages, with savage and simplistic representations on our movie and TV screens. We are immigrants who despise immigrants. To enact hospitality in this context is a radical act: it automatically erases the border between us and them. To open one's door to the stranger is to recognize that he no longer is one.

10   The nativist reacts against the immigrant with prosaic notions of "law and order." José has broken the law by crossing the river without the proper documents. María breaks the law by baby-sitting for money under the table. (The nativist has little to say about the natives who also break the law by hiring illegal aliens; he gains nothing politically by implicating himself in the crime.) But immigration codes are very human laws, born of economic and political realities—laws that blind us from perceiving the migrants for who they really are.

11   This notion of the foreigner as an economic mercenary has no relation whatsoever to the way migrants regard themselves. Ask Mexicans why they cross the Rio Grande and they will invariably say, "to seek a better life." They do not mean only material gain. Migrants travel through space and time, and are transformed by their encounter with the newness of the landscape, beginning with language. They are changed by their encounter with their other, with us.

12   Anyone who has grown up with more than one culture knows that to switch between languages is more than a matter of grammar and accent; meaning itself shifts, sometimes subtly, sometimes profoundly. To travel from one country to another, one language to another, is a journey of both spirit and flesh. The migrants sense this. In America, they are among our most fervently religious communities. In the barrio storefront church, they meditate on and give meaning to their passage—their sacrifice, their yearning for the transcendent, their crossing of the river.

13   And so now it is time again to face our contradictions head-on. The Bush administration is pushing an immigration agenda that is questioned from both the right and the left. The proposal offers documentation to immigrants who can prove gainful employment in the form of "contracts" of up to three years. President Bush on Monday repeated that the program would not be an amnesty (like that granted several million illegal immigrants in 1986). Nevertheless, conservatives argue that the program would reward criminals and pose a threat to national security. Liberals complain about institutionalizing the exploitation of foreign labor and the impact on native workers. Both sides reduce the immigrant to caricature. And both still imagine—in their rhetoric, at least—that the broken border between the United States and Mexico can be fixed.

14   But there was never enough of a border between us for it to have come undone. Immigration laws have always been enforced selectively, largely according to the needs of the labor economy. To a great extent, there is no functioning border, but we insist on believing there is one: imagining a borderless world is a leap into unfamiliar territory, a place where, in a sense, we would all be strangers.

15   Yet perhaps it is only in such a place where we might begin to offer genuine hospitality. At the very moment one opens the door to the stranger, one also crosses

a border and sees not an immigrant, not an illegal alien, not a Mexican, but a face—a human face.

return to "story"

Tonight, in the final representation of the posada, José and María will wearily   16
walk from door to door seeking shelter in the barrios, even as thousands of Josés
and Marías arrive at the shore of the Rio Grande, the river they dream of as Jor-
dan. They look to the other side, imagining la vida mejor. The Border Patrol stops
some of them. Other migrants, in distress, find doors shut to them when they seek
help. But most find a bed to sleep in. With family, with friends, even with strangers—

RM switches point of view again

that is the story of immigration in America these days. Perhaps we are a hospitable
land, after all. How else could we have become this "land of immigrants"?

In New Mexico, one of the most lyrical metaphors in the posada tradition is that   17
of the farolitos, votive candles that glow inside paper sacks weighed down by sand.

We are all pilgrims, but nativists deny the pilgrimage

These light the path toward that place where José and María will finally be recognized for who they are: pilgrims seeking shelter on the road, faces that serve as
mirrors to our own.

Thesis: For Rubén Martínez, the problem of immigration would be solved by each
of us finding enough faith to extend hospitality to strangers.

Method: Broadly interpreting a parable to support the thesis.

Questioning the Author: Points to Consider

- What is the thesis?
- What method is the author using to support this thesis?
- For which audience is the author writing? the general public? peers?
- Is the presentation serious or flippant or ironic?
- Does the author have any special interest in the topic that might amount to bias?
- Does the author try to manipulate the reader in any way?
- Are you inclined to believe everything that you read?
- How well does the author support the thesis? Is the reader convinced?

EXERCISE 3: EXAMINING INTENTION

Read "Cosmopolitan Emotions?" by Martha C. Nussbaum, using the margins
to ask questions and make comments about the meaning of the author's words
and phrases and her thesis and intention.

Martha Nussbaum, a Distinguished Professor of Law and Ethics at the University of Chicago, is a leading figure in the American Philosophical Association and the author of numerous books. This essay is the introduction to *For
Love of Country?*—a volume of essays about the limits of patriotism.

COSMOPOLITAN EMOTIONS?
Martha C. Nussbaum

In the aftermath of September 11, we have all experienced strong emotions for our country: fear, outrage, grief, astonishment. Our media portray the disaster as a tragedy that has happened to our nation, and that is how we very naturally see it. So too the ensuing war: it is called "America's New War," and most news reports focus on the meaning of events for us and our nation. We think these events are important because they concern *us*. Not just human lives, but American lives. In one way, the crisis has expanded our imaginations. We find ourselves feeling sympathy for many people who did not even cross our minds before: New York firefighters, that gay rugby player who helped bring down the fourth plane, bereaved families of so many national and ethnic origins. We even sometimes notice with a new attention the lives of Arab-Americans among us, or feel a sympathy with a Sikh taxi driver who complains about customers who tell him to go home to "his country," even though he came to the United States as a political refugee from persecution in the Punjab. Sometimes our compassion even crosses that biggest line of all, the national boundary. Events have led many Americans to sympathize with the women and girls of Afghanistan, for example, in a way that many feminists had been trying to get people to do for a long time, without success.

All too often, however, our imaginations remain oriented to the local; indeed, this orientation is implicit in the unusual level of our alarm. The world has come to a stop—in a way that it never has for Americans, when disaster befalls human beings in other places. Floods, earthquakes, cyclones—and the daily deaths of thousands from preventable malnutrition and disease—none of these typically makes the American world come to a standstill, none elicits a tremendous outpouring of grief and compassion. The plight of innocent civilians in the current war evokes a similarly uneven and flickering response.

And worse: our sense that the "us" is all that matters can easily flip over into a demonizing of an imagined "them," a group of outsiders who are imagined as enemies of the invulnerability and the pride of the all-important "us." Compassion for our fellow Americans can all too easily slide over into an attitude that wants America to come out on top, defeating or subordinating other peoples or nations. Anger at the terrorists themselves is perfectly appropriate; so is the attempt to bring them to justice. But "us-them" thinking doesn't always stay focused on the original issue; it too easily becomes a general call for American supremacy, the humiliation of "the other."

One vivid example of this slide took place at a baseball game I went to at Chicago's Comiskey Park, the first game played there after September 11—and a game against the Yankees, so there was a heightened awareness of the situation of New York and its people. Things began well, with a moving ceremony commemorating the firefighters who had lost their lives, and honoring local firefighters who had gone to New York afterward to help out. There was even a lot of cheering

when the Yankees took the field, a highly unusual transcendence of local attachments. But as the game went on and the beer flowed, one heard, increasingly, the
chant "U-S-A, U-S-A," a chant left over from the Olympic hockey match in which the
United States defeated Russia. This chant seemed to express a wish for America
to defeat, abase, humiliate its enemies. Indeed, it soon became a general way of expressing the desire to crush one's enemies, whoever they were. When the umpire
made a bad call that went against the White Sox, the same group in the stands
turned to him, chanting "U-S-A." In other words, anyone who crosses us is evil and
should be crushed. It's not surprising that Stoic philosopher and Roman emperor
Marcus Aurelius, trying to educate himself to have an equal respect for all human beings, reports that his first lesson was "not to be a fan of the Greens or Blues at
the races, or the light-armed or heavy-armed gladiators at the Circus."

Compassion is an emotion rooted, probably, in our biological heritage. (Although   5
biologists once portrayed animal behavior as egoistic, primatologists by now recognize the existence of altruistic emotion in apes, and it may well exist in other
species as well.) But this history does not mean that compassion is devoid of
thought. In fact, as Aristotle argued long ago, human compassion standardly requires
three thoughts: that a serious bad thing has happened to someone else; that this
bad event was not (or not entirely) the person's own fault; and that we ourselves are
vulnerable in similar ways. Thus compassion forms a psychological link between
our own self-interest and the reality of another person's good or ill. For that reason it is a morally valuable emotion—when it gets things right. Often, however,
the thoughts involved in the emotion, and therefore the emotion itself, go astray, failing to link people at a distance to one's own current possibilities and vulnerabili-
ties. (Rousseau said that kings don't feel compassion for their subjects because
they count on never being human, subject to the vicissitudes of life.) Sometimes, too,
compassion goes wrong by getting the seriousness of the bad event wrong: sometimes, for example, we just don't take very seriously the hunger and illness of people who are distant from us. These errors are likely to be built into the nature of
compassion as it develops in childhood and then adulthood: we form intense attachments to the local first, and only gradually learn to have compassion for people who are outside our own immediate circle. For many Americans, that expansion
of moral concern stops at the national boundary.

Most of us are brought up to believe that all human beings have equal worth.   6
At least the world's major religions and most secular philosophies tell us so. But our
emotions don't believe it. We mourn for those we know, not for those we don't
know. And most of us feel deep emotions about America, emotions we don't feel
about India, or Russia, or Rwanda. In and of itself, this narrowness of our emotional lives is probably acceptable and maybe even good. We need to build outward from meanings we understand, or else our moral life would be empty of
urgency. Aristotle long ago said, plausibly, that the citizens in Plato's ideal city, asked
to care for all citizens equally, would actually care for none, since care is learned in

small groups with their more intense attachments. If we want our life with others to contain strong passions—for justice in a world of injustice, for aid in a world where many go without what they need—we would do well to begin, at least, with our familiar strong emotions toward family, city, and country.

But concern should not stop with these local attachments. Americans are unfortunately prone to such emotional narrowness. So are all people, but the power and geographical size of America have long contributed to its particularly strong isolationist roots. When at least some others were finding ways to rescue the Jews during the Holocaust, America's inactivity and (general) lack of concern was culpable, especially in proportion to American power. It took Pearl Harbor to get us even to come to the aid of our allies. When genocide was afoot in Rwanda, our own sense of self-sufficiency and invulnerability stopped us from imagining the Rwandans as people who might be us; we were therefore culpably inactive toward them. So too in the present situation. Sometimes we see a very laudable recognition of the interconnectedness of all peoples, and of the fact that we must join forces with people in all nations to defeat terrorists and bring them to justice. At other times, however, we see simplifying slogans ("America Fights Back") that portray the situation in terms of a good "us" crusading against an evil "them"—failing to acknowledge, for example, that people in all nations have strong reasons to oppose terrorism, and that the fight has many active allies.

Such simplistic thinking is morally wrong, because it encourages us to ignore the impact of our actions on innocent civilians, and to focus too little on the all-important project of humanitarian relief. It is also counterproductive. We now understand, or ought to, that if we had thought more about support for the educational and humanitarian infrastructure of Pakistan, for example, funding good local nongovernmental organizations there the way several European nations typically do in India, young people of that nation might possibly have been educated in a climate of respect for religious pluralism, the equality of women, and other values that we rightly prize, instead of having fundamentalist *madrasas* as their only educational alternative. Our policy in South Asia has showed for many years a gross failure of imagination and sympathy; we basically thought in terms of cold war values, ignoring the real lives of people to whose prospects our actions could make a great difference. Such crude thinking is morally obtuse; it is also badly calculated to advance any good cause we wish to advance, in a world where all human lives are increasingly interdependent.

Compassion begins with the local. But if our moral natures and our emotional natures are to live in any sort of harmony we must find devices through which to extend our strong emotions and our ability to imagine the situation of others to the world of human life as a whole. Since compassion contains thought, it can be educated. We can take this disaster as occasion for narrowing our focus, distrusting the rest of the world, and feeling solidarity with Americans alone. Or we can take it as an occasion for expansion of our ethical horizons. Seeing how vulnerable our

7

8

9

great country is, we can learn something about the vulnerability all human beings share, about what it is like for distant others to lose those they love to a disaster not of their own making, whether it is hunger or flood or ethnic cleansing.

There are hopeful signs in the present situation, particularly in attempts to edu-   10
cate the American public about Islam, about the histories of Afghanistan and Pakistan, and about the situation and attitudes of Arab-Americans in this country. But
we need to make these educational efforts consistent and systematic, not just fear-
motivated responses to an immediate crisis.

Our media and our systems of education have long given us far too little infor-   11
mation about lives outside our borders, stunting our moral imaginations. The situation of America's women and its racial, ethnic, and sexual minorities has to some
extent worked its way into curricula, at various levels, and into our popular media.
We have done less well with parts of the world that are unfamiliar. This is not surprising, because such teaching requires a lot of investment in new curricular initiatives, and such television programming requires a certain temporary inattention to
the competition for ratings. But we now know that we live in a complex, intercon-
nected world, and we know our own ignorance. As Socrates said, this is at least
the beginning of progress. At this time of national crisis we can renew our commitment to the equal worth of humanity, demanding media, and schools, that nour-
ish and expand our imaginations by presenting non-American lives as deep, rich,
and emotion-worthy. "Thus from our weakness," said Rousseau of such an education, "our fragile happiness is born." Or, at least, it might be born.

ANALYZING THE USE OF EVIDENCE
AND REASONING

The author asserts a thesis and attempts to prove it; the reader decides whether the thesis is convincing. Whether the author is writing an explanatory, analytical, or persuasive essay, the credibility of the thesis depends upon the strength of the evidence and reasoning. If intention is the "how" of an essay, evidence and reasoning are the "why." Why should you believe this thesis? Because the author offers solid evidence as *proof* and uses a process of *logical reasoning* to persuade you.

Evidence

Evidence refers to any kind of *concrete information* that can support a thesis. Just as evidence is necessary for a criminal to be convicted in court—there, the thesis to be proved is that John Doe robbed Richard Roe—so authors are expected to cite evidence in supporting a thesis.

Evidence can take several forms. Most authors use more than one.

Facts and Statistics

Authors usually offer *facts* and *statistics* to back up their thesis, especially when they are working in the social sciences. When Mark D. Jekanowski (see p. 24) assures the reader that "the proportion of away-from-home food expenditures on fast food increased from 29.3 to 34.2 percent between 1982 and 1997 . . ." he is using statistics to support his thesis about the growing popularity of fast food.

To prove a thesis about excessive drinking on a college campus, an author might cite the college's policy governing drinking in the dormitories (facts), the number of bars near the campus (statistics), the number of students who frequent those bars (statistics), the number of students who have sought help from college counselors for drinking problems (statistics), and so on. Some of this evidence might be obtained from surveys that the author personally has carried out. Or to provide a broader context for the argument, the author might consult government Web sites or publications such as the *Chronicle of Higher Education* to find additional data about practices on campuses nationwide.

Whatever the source, the data must be reliable. Surveys and polls, for example, depend upon *generalizing from a representative sample*, based on an appropriate "population." In other words, they use limited evidence (the opinions of, say, 1,000 respondents) to predict the opinions of a much larger group—possibly the entire nation—by assuming that the opinions of the smaller group reflect proportionately the opinions of the larger. So, a 1989 poll surveying almost 4,000 people from three countries about the state of their national health care was able to conclude that 89 percent of all Americans regarded their health-care system as "fundamentally flawed." The author is using the responses of the 4,000 people surveyed to make larger claims about whole national groups.

The same rules of samples and populations would apply to a survey cited as evidence in an essay on college drinking. How many people took part in the survey? If percentages are cited, what was the base population? If an author says that 60 percent of those students surveyed drank excessively, does that mean five, or fifteen, or fifty people? How many drinks were defined as "excessive," and was drinking measured by the day, by the week, or by the month?

Examples

An example is a *single representative instance* that serves to support a thesis. Blanche Blank uses the example of Joe V. to show her readers that college graduates are overqualified for many kinds of work. In the following passage from *Mapping Human History*, Steve Olson provides a series of examples to demonstrate the absurdity of ethnic enmities:

> Many of the harshest conflicts in the world today are between people who are indistinguishable. If someone took a roomful of Palestinians and Israelis from the Middle East, or of Serbs and Albanians from the Balkans, or of Catholics and Protestants from Ireland, or of Muslims and Hindus from northern India, or of Dayaks and Madurese from Indonesia, gave them all identical outfits and haircuts, and

forbade them to speak or gesture, no one could distinguish the members of the other group—at least not to the point of being willing to shoot them. The antagonists in these conflicts have different ethnicities, but they have been so closely linked biologically throughout history that they have not developed marked physical differences.

Yet one of the most perverse dimensions of ethnic thinking is the "racialization" of culture—the tendency to think of another people as not just culturally but genetically distinct. In the Yugoslavian war, the Croats caricatured their Serbian opponents as tall and blond, while the Serbs disparaged the darker hair and skin of the Croats—even though these traits are thoroughly intermixed between the two groups. During World War II the countries of Europe fiercely stereotyped the physical attributes of their enemies, despite a history of intermarriage and migration that has scrambled physical characteristics throughout the continent. In Africa, the warring Tutsis and Hutus often call attention to the physical differences of their antagonists, but most observers have trouble distinguishing individual members of the two groups solely on the basis of appearance.

Keep in mind, though, that because examples are only single instances of a broad and complex situation, they may provide only limited support for the thesis. Specific examples of students whose drinking resulted in academic, social, or emotional difficulties may catch your attention, but shouldn't by themselves persuade you that the problem is widespread or serious enough to require action. Rather, they should serve as supplements to more broad-based evidence.

Anecdotes

Anecdotes are stories—extended examples with a beginning, middle, and end—that illustrate the point an author wants to make. Here's the way Stephen L. Carter starts an essay on civility:

> Let us begin with a common and irritating occurrence. As you sit down to dinner with your family, the telephone rings. When you answer, you find that you are being offered a subscription to the local paper or invited to donate to the volunteer fire department. And although you may enjoy reading your local paper and admire the volunteers who keep the city from burning to the ground, if you are like me, a wave of frustration passes through you, and you face the serious temptation to say something rude. . . .

And Carter continues to describe how his family deals with this dinnertime interruption. He has used an anecdote as a vivid way of introducing his point about the disappearance of common courtesy in daily life.

Like examples, anecdotes attract and interest the reader (and, for that reason, they are often placed at the beginning of essays). But they can take up a great deal of space. "Anecdotal evidence" is never enough to prove a thesis.

Appeal to Authority

Authors often support their theses by citing their own research or the work of acknowledged authorities. Data and examples have considerably more credibility when they are endorsed by sources with a reputation as *experts in the field*. An author needs to cite the evidence of such sources in reasonable detail and, if possible, convey the strength of their credentials. A thesis should not depend on nameless sources such as "1,000 doctors" or "authorities in the field." (Chapter 8 discusses how you can determine which sources are authoritative and which are not.) In an essay exploring the effects of cloning on human rights, John Harris quotes Dr. Hiroshi Nakajima, specifically identifying him as the Director General of the World Health Organization: "WHO considers the use of cloning for the replication of human individuals to be ethically unacceptable as it would violate some of the basic principles that govern medically assisted procreation.[41]"

An author writing about college drinking is likely to find evidence in *published sources*: books, magazines, scholarly journals, and *reliable* Web sites. The source of that evidence must be acknowledged in the text, with documentation containing the author's name, the work, and the place and date of its publication. In this way, when you read the essay, you can determine whether the author is citing a reputable and appropriate source and, if you wish, locate that source and find out more about the topic. In John Harris's essay, the citation of Dr. Nakajima's statement about cloning is documented by a footnote that refers the reader to a WHO press release, specifying the date.

Looking for Evidence

- Does the author use facts and/or statistics to support the thesis? If so, do they seem reliable?

- Does the author use examples and anecdotes? If so, are they the main or only evidence for the thesis?

- Are the sources for the evidence acknowledged?

- Do these sources seem credible?

- Are there some points that are not supported by evidence?

- Does the author seem biased?

- Based on the evidence provided, do you accept the author's thesis?

INTERPRETING EVIDENCE: INFERENCE

When you actively read and ask questions about a text, you may sometimes find yourself projecting your own thoughts and assumptions into what you are reading. You may even find it difficult to differentiate between your own ideas, inspired by what you have read, and the factual evidence found in the source. Should such confusion occur, you can easily attribute to your source ideas that are not there at all. When you generalize from specific facts—statistics, for example—you have to be especially careful to make sure that your statement is based on a correct interpretation of the evidence.

There are several different ways to describe how an author uses evidence and how you form conclusions from that evidence: *stating, proving, implying,* and *inferring*. These terms will be explained and illustrated with excerpts from an article about patterns of marriage in America during the early 1980s.

Quoting a Census Bureau report, this 1984 *New York Times* article begins by *stating* that:

> More and more young Americans are putting off marriage, possibly to begin careers. . . .

At this point in the article, the *Times* is offering no specific evidence to support this statement. You probably accept it as true because you know that the *Times* is a newspaper of record, and you assume that the Census Bureau provided statistics that justify the claim. And, in fact, several paragraphs later, we find evidence to *prove* the statement:

> The trend toward postponed marriage has been growing steadily in recent years. The study found that 74.8 percent of men aged 20 to 24 had never married, compared with 68.8 percent in 1980 and 54.7 percent in 1970. Among women aged 20 to 24, 56.9 percent were single in this year's survey, as against 50.2 percent in 1980 and 35.8 percent in 1970.

Here is an example of a statement (in italics) that is immediately followed by proof:

> *Traditional married couples continue to make up the majority of family households in the United States, but the report documents the steady erosion of this group's dominance.* The 50.1 million traditional families constitute 58.6 percent of American households, compared with 60.8 percent in 1980 and 70.5 percent in 1970.

So far, we have been examining only what the article *explicitly states* or what it *proves*. But, in addition, most sources inform you indirectly, by *implying* obvious conclusions that are not stated in so many words. The implications of a statement can be easily found within the statement itself; they just are not directly expressed. For example, according to the Census Bureau report, in 1980:

> Three-quarters of American men and more than half of American women under 25 are still single.

Although it does not say so, the report *implies*—and it would be perfectly safe to conclude—that *more men than women have been waiting until they are over 25 to marry.* The following paragraph also contains implication as well as statement:

Many of these young adults may have postponed their entry into marriage in order to further their formal education, establish careers or pursue other goals that
might conflict with assuming family responsibilities," said the bureau's study of
households, families, marital status and living arrangements. The report also found
that Americans are once again forming new households at high rates after a decline, apparently recession-induced, last year.

In addition to several *statements* about likely reasons for postponing marriage, the paragraph also provides you with an important *implication: economic
conditions seem to be a factor in predicting how many new households are formed in the
United States.*

Finally, it is perfectly acceptable to draw a conclusion that is not implicit in
the source, as long as you reach that conclusion through reasoning based on
sound evidence. Unlike implication, *inference* requires the analysis of information—putting 2 and 2 together—for the hidden idea to be observed. The text
implies; the reader infers.

In the following brief and factual statement from the article, little of interest is
implied, but important conclusions can be *inferred*:

A slight increase was noted in the number of unmarried couples living together;
they totaled almost two million as of March and represent about 4 percent of the
couples.

From this information, as well as previous evidence provided about postpone-
ment of marriage, it would be safe to *infer* that *one reason why people were marrying later may have been that they were living together as unmarried couples first.*

Since the article is about postponing marriage and also refers to the increasing number of unmarried couples living together, you might jump to the
conclusion that, in 1984, most households in the United States consisted of unmarried couples or single-parent families. As the statistics cited in the excerpts
above clearly indicate, that would be a *false conclusion.*

What inferences can you draw from the following paragraph, when you put
this information together with everything else that you have read in the article?

Though the report said that most young people are expected to marry eventually,
it noted that the longer marriage was delayed the greater the chance that it would
not occur. "Consequently, the percentage of today's young adults that do not ever
marry may turn out to be higher than the corresponding percentage of their predecessors," the report speculated.

First, notice that the connection between delaying marriage and never marrying at all is *stated*, not *proved*. Assuming that the statement is correct, and realizing that the years of fertility are limited, it would be reasonable to *infer* that
*the trend to marry later in life may have been a factor in the declining birth rate in the
early 1980s.*

Because inferences are not totally rooted in the information provided by your source, they tend to be expressed in tentative terms. Both inferences cited above, for example, use "may have been" to convey an appropriate degree of uncertainty. The following inference hedges in a different way: *if the trend toward later marriages continues at a steady rate, eventually there will be no more married couples in this country.* Here, the sweeping and improbable generalization—no more married couples—is put into some perspective through the conditional: "*if* this trend continues at a steady rate. . . ." However, given the variety of unpredictable influences affecting the decision to marry, the negative trend is unlikely to continue at a steady rate. In fact, this inference is absurd.

EXERCISE 4: DRAWING INFERENCES

Read "The Other Gender Gap." Then decide which of the sentences that follow are *stated*, which are *implied*, which can be *inferred*, and which are *unsupported*, according to the information in the article.

Marshall Poe is a historian who is on the staff of the *Atlantic Monthly*, where this article appeared in 2004.

THE OTHER GENDER GAP
Marshall Poe

The women's movement has taught us many things, one of the more surprising being that boys are not performing in school as well as they might.   1

Three decades ago reformers' attention was focused on the "higher-education gap"—the fact that not as many girls went on to college, graduate school, and professional school as boys. Advocates of equality between the sexes fought hard to create gender-specific education programs, fair admissions policies, and professional societies for women. Their efforts were rewarded: from 1970 to 2000 the number of women attending college rose by 136 percent, graduate school by 168 percent, and professional school by 853 percent.   2

Yet soon the higher-education gap opened again—but this time girls were on the other side of it. In the late 1970s more girls than boys began to enroll in college, and the disparity has since increased. Today women make up approximately 56 percent of all undergraduates, outnumbering men by about 1.7 million. In addition, about 300,000 more women than men enter graduate school each year. (The gap does not particularly affect professional school; almost as many women as men attend.) In short, equal opportunity brought an unequal result.   3

The advance of girls relative to boys might well have been predicted from patterns in K–12 schooling, where girls have long been outperforming boys on several measures. In both primary and secondary school girls tend to receive higher marks than   4 boys. Since the inception, in 1969, of the National Assessment of Educational Progress (a standardized exam given to nine-, thirteen-, and seventeen-year-olds), girls at all grade levels have scored much higher, on average, than boys in language skills, and about the same in math. (True, college-bound boys have long outperformed girls overall on the SAT, but it is likely that boys' average scores are statistically elevated by the fact that roughly 10 percent fewer of them take the exam—and those who opt out tend to be lower achievers.) It is hardly surprising, then, that once various cultural barriers were removed, girls began entering college at a greater rate.

The continuing advance among girls has thrown a spotlight on the stagnation of boys. During the past decade the percentage of boys who complete high school (about 70), enter college (about 40), and go on to graduate school (about eight) has risen only slightly or not at all. And this despite the fact that the economic payoff of higher education has never been greater. Whereas girls continue to demonstrate that society has not yet reached any "natural" limit on college-attendance rates, boys have somehow gotten stuck. If boys and girls have roughly equal abilities, then why aren't they doing equally well? 5

From kindergarten on, the education system rewards self-control, obedience, and concentration—qualities that, any teacher can tell you, are much more common among girls than boys, particularly at young ages. Boys fidget, fool around, fight, and worse. Thirty years ago teachers may have accommodated and managed this behavior, in part by devoting more attention to boys than to girls. But as girls have come to attract equal attention, as an inability to sit still has been medicalized, and as the options for curbing student misbehavior have been ever more curtailed, boys may have suffered. Boys make up three quarters of all children categorized as learning disabled today, and they are put in special education at a much higher rate (special education is often misused as a place to stick "problem kids," and children seldom switch from there to the college track). Shorter recess times, less physical education, and more time spent on rote learning (in order to meet testing standards) may have exacerbated the problems that boys tend to experience in the classroom. It is no wonder, then, that many boys disengage academically. Boys are also subject to a range of extrinsic factors that hinder their academic performance and pull them out of school at greater rates than girls. First among these is the labor market. Young men, with or without high school diplomas, earn more than young women, so they are more likely to see work as an *alternative* to school. Employment gives many men immediate monetary gratification along with relief from the drudgery of the classroom. 6

But boys' educational stagnation has long-term economic implications. Not even half the boys in the country are taking advantage of the opportunity to go to college, which has become almost a prerequisite for a middle-class lifestyle. And languishing academic attainment among a large portion of our population spells trouble 7 for the prospects of continued economic growth. Unless more boys begin attending college, the nation may face a shortage of highly skilled workers in the coming decades.

The trouble with boys is not confined to the United States; boys are being out-performed by girls throughout the developed world. The United Kingdom and Australia are currently testing programs aimed at making education more boy-friendly. Single-sex schools, single-sex classes, and gender-specific curricula are all be-ing tried. Here the United States lags: there are several local initiatives aimed at boys, but nothing on the national level—perhaps owing to a residual anxiety over the idea of helping boys in a society where men for so long enjoyed special advantages. 8

1. On the whole, girls get better grades than boys.
2. Boisterous and inattentive behavior was considered natural for boys 30 years ago.
3. Women are likely to earn less than men, so they have to perform better in school to get ahead.
4. Most boys don't like school.
5. Girls' ability to focus on a task allows them to do well in school.
6. Performance in primary and secondary school is a good predictor of ad-mission to college.
7. Our culture rewards those who conform to standards of good behavior.
8. It is very difficult to engineer educational opportunities so that both sexes benefit equally.
9. The increased number of women with college degrees may not be able to compensate for the diminished number of men without advanced skills entering the labor market.
10. Three times as many boys as girls are considered learning disabled.
11. Boys' poor educational performance might be improved if they had more outlets for their energy during the school day.
12. Western culture has at last begun to compensate women for previous in-justices.

LOGICAL REASONING

The structure of most texts used in research consists of a *logical progression of general points that lead to an overall thesis or conclusion*; each point is followed by more concrete statements of supporting evidence. The sequence of generaliza-tions is determined by logical reasoning. For instance, if you look out a window and observe that the street and sidewalk are wet and the sky is overcast, you would most likely conclude that it had rained recently. You didn't directly ob-serve the rain, but you can generalize from past experiences with the same evidence and apply this generalization to a specific experience in the present. Although this may seem like a simpleminded illustration, it is typical of the reasoning we all engage in every day.

There are two types of reasoning in formal logic—*deductive* reasoning and *inductive* reasoning, each a distinct process for arriving at defensible conclusions based on available evidence.

Deductive Reasoning

The classic format for deductive reasoning is the *syllogism*, which consists of a series of carefully limited statements, or premises, pursued to a circumscribed conclusion:

All reptiles are cold-blooded.	[premise]
Iguanas are reptiles.	[premise]
Therefore, iguanas are cold-blooded.	[conclusion]

This is a line of reasoning based on classification, that is, the creation of a generalized category based on shared traits. Members of the group we call "reptiles" have cold-bloodedness in common—in fact, cold-bloodedness is a defining trait of reptiles. Iguanas are members of the group reptiles, which means that they must also have that shared trait.

Notice that the opening premise of a syllogism is a statement that the reader will be willing to grant as true without explicit proof. For example, in her essay "Danger to Human Dignity: The Revival of Disgust and Shame in the Law," Martha C. Nussbaum begins with a (presumably) shared premise:

The law, most of us would agree, should be society's protection against prejudice.

Deductive reasoning always begins with beliefs or knowledge that the author and reader have in common, and the syllogism builds from that undisputed statement.

Deductive reasoning follows an almost mathematical rigor; provided the premises are true and the line of reasoning valid, the conclusion must necessarily be true.

Inductive Reasoning

In inductive reasoning, a conclusion or common principle is reached by generalizing from a body of evidence. The conclusions reached through inductive reasoning are always conditional to some extent—that is, there's always the possibility that some additional evidence may be introduced to suggest a different conclusion. Given the available evidence, you are perfectly justified in concluding that a wet street and overcast sky always mean that it has rained; but suppose one day, observing these conditions, you turn on the radio and learn that a water main in the area has broken overnight. That overcast sky may be coincidental, and you should be prepared to revise your original conclusion based on the new information.

Inductive reasoning uses the available evidence to construct the most likely conclusion.

Using Logic to Establish Common Ground with the Reader

Whether source materials are explanatory, interpretive, or argumentative, most of them contain elements of both inductive and deductive reasoning. The author attempts to prove a claim by presenting evidence and reasoning so that the reader will recreate the author's logic and view an issue as the author does. The core of the reasoning is usually *deductive*, but rarely based on a classical syllogism; rather, it consists of a series of *premises* or *assumptions* that the reader shares—or can be persuaded to share—with the author. These premises often depend on *common cultural values*. That is why a thesis can lose its force over time as values change. One hundred years ago, authors could safely reason from the premise that heroism is defined by slaying the enemy in battle, or that engaging in sex before marriage warrants a girl's expulsion from polite society, or that whipping young children is an effective and acceptable punishment. Today, those statements would not have such wide credibility.

To establish common ground with the reader, the author usually needs to spell out these assumptions and define them so precisely that they seem not only true but inevitable. For instance, few people would challenge a claim that cruelty to animals is wrong, but there is a wide range of opinion regarding exactly what constitutes cruelty, or whether certain specific activities (the use of animals in scientific research, for instance) are or are not cruel. If inflicting pain serves some larger purpose, is it still cruel, or does "cruelty" refer only to *unnecessary* or *unjustifiable* pain? Before contesting the ethics of medical research practices, the author would have to begin by establishing a premise—in this case, a definition of "cruelty"—that the reader will also find acceptable.

Using Logic for Persuasion

To be fully convincing, the reasoning that emerges from your premises must be inductive as well as deductive. It must be supported by a range of evidence, which you present, analyze, and interpret for your reader.

Logical Flaws

Not every explanation, interpretation, or argument convinces us to accept the author's conclusion. What undermines the credibility or persuasiveness of an author's logic?

- The reasoning may be based on an initial premise that is unconvincing.
- The line of reasoning that connects premise to premise may be flawed.
- The evidence itself may be misrepresented in some way.

It's easy to accept *initial premises* uncritically because they're generally expressed with confidence in the reader's agreement—remember, the author assumes that the reader will accept the opening premises without explicit proof. As you read, you should be careful to identify the assumptions an author uses in constructing a line of reasoning. For example, look at the following opening premise, from the second paragraph of an unsigned editorial attacking the logic of a proposed ban on tobacco products. The editorial appeared in the magazine *National Review* in 1994.

> Even though nine-tenths of smokers don't die of lung cancer, there are clearly health dangers in cigarettes, dangers so constantly warned about that smokers are clearly aware that these dangers are the price they pay for the enjoyment and relaxation they get from smoking.

The author claims here that because the health risks connected with smoking have been widely publicized, the decision to smoke is rational—that is, based on smokers' weighing their desire for "enjoyment and relaxation" against the potential health risks. You might grant that the dangers of smoking have been well documented and publicized, but does it necessarily follow that knowing the risks involved ensures a rational decision? If, as has also been widely demonstrated, cigarettes are addictive, then the decision to keep smoking may *not* be entirely rational.

The author here is committing a common logical lapse known as **begging the question**. The assumption here is false; it assumes that a crucial point is self-evident and requires no further support. The key word here is "clearly"—"smokers are clearly aware"—which may persuade the careless reader that the point has already been proven. When an author is begging the question, you often find language that preempts the issue and discourages scrutiny: "obviously," "everyone knows," or "it goes without saying."

Sometimes, the process of begging the question is more subtle. Here, an author arguing against euthanasia begins with a strong statement:

> Every human being has a natural inclination to continue living. Our reflexes and responses fit us to fight attackers, flee wild animals, and dodge out of the way of trucks. In our daily lives we exercise the caution and care necessary to protect

ourselves. Our bodies are similarly structured for survival right down to the molecular level. . . . Euthanasia does violence to this natural goal of survival. It is literally acting against nature because all the processes of nature are bent towards the end of bodily survival.

By limiting his view of existence to purely bodily functions, J. Gay-Williams simplifies the complex issue of euthanasia. What he omits are the key functions of the mind, will, and emotions, which, some would say, can override the force of the instinct toward "bodily survival" and make the choice to die. The key here is the first sentence: "Every human being has a natural inclination to continue living." This broad assumption allows for no exceptions. *It begs the question by telling only part of the story.*

Logical Fallacies

Even if the author's premises are valid, there may be *fallacies* in the reasoning that holds the premises together. Logical fallacies are breakdowns in reasoning; they occur when the author makes *unjustifiable* generalizations like the one above or draws *unjustifiable* conclusions from the available evidence.

Post hoc ergo propter hoc

Cause-and-effect reasoning can slide into before-and-after fallacies (known as post hoc ergo propter hoc—after this, therefore because of this). This fallacy assumes that an event that precedes another must somehow cause the second event. It is often true that one event causes a second, later event, as in the case of rain causing the wet street you observe the next morning. But if you make that reasoning a universal rule, you might, for instance, conclude that because swimsuits habitually appear in your local clothing stores in May, and summer follows in June, swimsuits somehow cause summer. It may be perfectly true that swimsuits appear in stores in May and that summer usually begins in June, but this argument fails to consider alternative explanations—in this case, that the approach of summer actually causes manufacturers to ship and retailers to display swimsuits in May, rather than the other way around; the swimsuits *anticipate,* rather than cause, summer.

False Dilemma

Most fallacies result from a tendency to oversimplify issues, to take shortcuts in dealing with complex and diverse ideas. With the false dilemma, an author limits the ground for disagreement by proceeding as if there are only two alternatives; everything else is ignored. Here is part of the argument presented by an author who supports euthanasia:

Reality dictates the necessity of such laws because, for some dying patients experiencing extreme suffering, a lethal prescription is the only way to end an extended and agonizing death. Consider the terrible dilemma created when so-called passive measures fail to bring about the hoped-for death. Are we to stand helplessly by while a patient whose suicide we legally agreed to assist continues to suffer and deteriorate—perhaps even more so than before? Or do we have a moral imperative, perhaps even a legal responsibility, to not only alleviate the further suffering we have brought about but to take action to fulfill our original agreement [to withdraw life support]?

Barbara Dority has reduced the situation to a simple choice: passive doctor and patient in agony versus active doctor who brings an end to suffering, abides by morality, and keeps her promise. There are many possibilities for intervention between these two extremes, but at least at this point in her argument, the author does not acknowledge them. Through her language, she also loads the dice: does one identify with the doctor "stand[ing] helplessly" by or with the doctor with a "moral imperative" who knows how to "take action" to "alleviate . . . suffering"?

Hasty Generalization

The tendency to oversimplify, to base claims on insufficient evidence, can result in the hasty generalization. A convincing generalization will be supported by strong evidence. Beware of generalizations made on the basis of one or two examples. And when an author does cite examples, consider whether they clearly support the claim. Gertrude Himmelfarb, for example, builds her argument about the decline of morality in our society by criticizing what she claims is an increasing tendency to be nonjudgmental. She offers the following generalization:

> Most of us are uncomfortable with the idea of making moral judgments even in our private lives, let alone with the "intrusion," as we say, of moral judgments into public affairs.

To support her generalization, she observes that public officials, such as the president's cabinet and the Surgeon General, tend to avoid using the word "immoral." In one of her two examples, the Secretary of Health and Human Services is quoted as saying:

> I don't like to put this in moral terms, but I do believe that having children out of wedlock is just wrong.

This last quotation, in itself, hardly strengthens Himmelfarb's initial point since many would consider "wrong" a judgment equivalent to "immoral." Then, on the basis of these limited examples, she reiterates her original claim:

> It is not only our political and cultural leaders who are prone to this failure of moral nerve. Everyone has been infected by it, to one degree or another.

The argument has moved around in a circle, from one hasty generalization to another.

Ad Hominem

An especially unpleasant kind of logical fallacy is the *ad hominem* [about the man] argument, a personal attack in which an author criticizes a prominent person who holds opposing views without considering whether the criticism is relevant to the issue. As you have doubtless realized, the ad hominem argument is often used in political campaigns and other well-publicized controversies.

Paul McHugh, for example, spends the first half of an argument against euthanasia demonstrating why he regards Dr. Jack Kevorkian, who facilitated a number of mercy killings, as "'certifiably' insane." McHugh compares him with other zealots who would do anything to advance their cause and finally cites "the potential for horror in an overvalued idea held by a person in high authority" such as Adolf Hitler. Certainly, the comparison is strained—Dr. Kevorkian is not "in high authority." Yet, even though McHugh now moves to a completely different basis for argument, the opprobrium generated by the association between Kevorkian and Hitler reverberates throughout the rest of the essay.

False Analogy

Authors often support their points by *reasoning through analogies*. They may compare a disputed idea or situation to some other, less controversial idea in order to reveal an inconsistency or to advocate a particular course of action. For instance, some might claim that the wide availability of foreign-made consumer products is analogous to an infection that threatens to destroy the health of the nation's economy. What similarities in the two situations are being exploited? What parallels can be drawn between them? In both cases, some entity (in the first case a nation, and in the second a human being) is "invaded" by something potentially harmful (such as a Japanese-made VCR or German-built car in the case of the nation, and a virus or bacterial infection in the case of the person). Analogies can provide vivid and persuasive images, but they are easily distorted when pushed too far.

In a false analogy, *the two ideas or circumstances being compared are not actually comparable*. To illustrate the pitfalls of false analogy, let's return to the editorial on the proposed tobacco ban from the *National Review*. Here's the entire paragraph:

> Even though nine-tenths of smokers don't die of lung cancer, there are clearly health dangers in cigarettes, dangers so constantly warned about that smokers are clearly aware that these dangers are the price they pay for the enjoyment and relaxation they get from smoking. As mortals we make all kinds of trade-offs between health and living. We drive automobiles knowing that forty thousand people die in them in the U.S. each year; we cross busy streets, tolerate potentially explosive gas in our homes, swim in fast-moving rivers, use electricity though it kills thousands, and eat meat and other foods that may clog our arteries and give us heart attacks and strokes. All the . . . demagoguery about the tobacco industry killing people could

be applied with similar validity to the automobile industry, the electric utilities, aircraft manufacturers, the meat business, and more.

Here, the reader is asked to compare the health risks associated with smoking with those of parallel but comparatively uncontroversial activities, such as crossing a busy street. According to the author, the situations are comparable because both involve voluntarily engaging in activities known to be health risks, and that similarity is used to suggest that laws *prohibiting* smoking would be logically inconsistent because we don't prohibit other risky activities. If potential health risks justify regulation or even prohibition, then any number of modern activities should, by analogy, be regulated. Yet, in spite of the risks in crossing busy streets, no one ever suggests preventing people from doing so for their own good; smoking, however, is singled out for regulation and possible prohibition. The reader can further *infer* from this line of reasoning that, since we daily engage in all kinds of risky activities, individuals in all cases should be allowed to decide without government interference which risks to take.

In writing based on false analogies, the reasoning can be attacked merely by demonstrating that the differences in the two situations are more significant than the similarities. In this case, we need to consider:

- if the decision to smoke and the decision to cross a busy street are *genuinely* comparable; and
- if there may be sound reasons for regulating smoking, and equally sound reasons for *not* regulating crossing the street.

Most people could not live a normal life without crossing a busy street, but the same cannot be said of smoking. In addition, if a minimal amount of caution is exercised in crossing busy streets, most people will not be injured; when injuries do occur, they're the result of accidents or some other unexpected or unusual set of events. The same is true of the other "hazards" described in the editorial (driving automobiles, using gas appliances, and so on): injuries result from their *misuse*. By contrast, cigarettes pose a serious health threat when used exactly as intended by their manufacturers; no amount of caution will protect you from the risks associated with cigarettes.

You might also object to this argument on grounds that go beyond the logic of the reasoning to the ways the evidence is presented. The author mentions, for instance, only that 9 in 10 smokers don't die of lung cancer, implying not only that a 10 percent death rate is insignificant but that death or lung cancer is the only potential health risk connected to smoking worth mentioning. The author also states that "forty thousand people die" in automobiles each year in the United States, but because that number isn't presented as a percentage of all drivers on the road over the course of the year, it doesn't really address the *comparable* level of risk—those 40,000 may represent fewer than 1 percent of all drivers, which would make driving considerably less risky than smoking. Misrepresenting the evidence in this way prods the careful reader to question the author's trustworthiness and credibility.

> ## *Analyzing an Author's Logic*
>
> 1. What assumptions is the author making as the basis for the thesis? Is it reasonable to assume that the reader shares these assumptions?
> 2. Does the text provide a logical sequence of assertions that can be easily followed and that lead to a persuasive conclusion? Are there any convincing alternatives to the conclusion that the author has drawn?
> 3. Is the reasoning primarily inductive (deriving generalizations from probabilities established by the author) or is it deductive (deriving specific conclusions from broad assertions that are tested and proved)?
> 4. Are there appropriate and sufficient data and examples provided?
> 5. Are the sources of the evidence clearly indicated?
> 6. Has the author lapsed into any fallacies that distort the logic and support a false conclusion?
> 7. What inferences does the author make from the evidence provided? Are they reasonable, or does the author attempt to manipulate the reader's perception of the evidence to suit the purposes of the thesis?

EXERCISE 5: ANALYZING AN AUTHOR'S LOGIC

Read this excerpt from "Courage," a chapter from *The Code of Man*, by Waller R. Newell, and make marginal comments about the logical processes used by the author (including deduction and induction), the presence of logical fallacies (if any), and the appropriateness and sufficiency of the evidence provided. Note: *The Code of Man* contains an index but no bibliography or notes.

Waller R. Newell teaches political science at Carleton University in Ottawa, Canada. The author of two other books, he also writes for the *Weekly Standard* and other publications. In *The Code of Man*, Newell is arguing in favor of a return to traditional ideals of masculinity.

Here are some questions to start you off:

Which sentences support the author's thesis?

Which sentences introduce a new premise or a turn in the argument?

Which sentences contain evidence that supports the thesis? What kind of evidence?

Are there any flaws in the reasoning?

How would you sum up the thesis in your own words?

Are you convinced?

from THE CODE OF MAN
Waller R. Newell

Have you ever met a boyosaurus? That is the term coined by the Canadian journalist Joseph Brean to describe something that everyone has observed about boys:

> Film makers and paleontologists have long known this simple fact to be true:
> Boys love dinosaurs. Boys are suckers for loud roars and inaccurate computer-
> generated terror. They shudder in their seats. They have the nightmares. They
> buy the toys.

The love of young boys for maximum dinosaur violence is recognized by the film
industry. According to the anthropologist Douglass Drozdow–St. Christian, "The
first *Jurassic Park* was a girl's movie, because it had a strong environmentalist theme."
The third installment of the series, by contrast, was marketed exclusively to boys,
because "this one is about fear and conquering monsters."

Girls and boys relate to their dinosaurs in very different ways. Girls want to
nurture them. Boys want to become their comrades. According to Joseph Brean,
when boys visit museums, "they expect the dinosaurs to be large and vicious. . . .
Girls, on the other hand, like to imagine taking the vegetarian hadrosaur home as
a pet." Gayle Gibson, who spent eleven years leading the dinosaur tours at the Royal
Ontario Museum in Toronto, sums up her experience of thousands of kids' visits:
"For the girls, a dinosaur is kind of a secret friend, but for the boys it's a secret
protector."

I can confirm these stories with my own tour of that same dinosaur skeleton
collection with my ten-year-old nephew. Nothing in the museum interested him
more than the dinosaurs, and he asked the guide dozens of questions. By contrast,
when it came time to look at the rock collections, he literally fell prone to the
floor with boredom. Only the Egyptian mummies interested him half as much, and
then it was mainly the mummy of a small boy that caught his eye. He asked me if
we could do that to his younger brother. (I said no.)

As I read these reports about boys and dinosaurs, one phrase jumped out at
me: that boys liked *Jurassic Park III* because it was about "fear and conquering monsters." As we'll see in this chapter, that in a nutshell sums up many discussions of
courage in the Western tradition. Courage is a virtue we summon out of ourselves when confronted with someone or something terrifying.

But is courage a trait we should really be encouraging in boys? Is it, in fact, a virtue,
as the traditional view from Homer, Aristotle, and the Bible to Theodore Roosevelt and JFK has consistently maintained? Or does any praise for the use of force
merely serve to exacerbate what is already a strong built-in tendency in boys to
be violent? Instead of praising some kinds of aggression as virtuous, should we perhaps be working harder to get rid of it altogether?

As numerous studies demonstrate, boys are certainly more prone than girls to   7
spontaneous aggressiveness and combativeness. This trait can have its lighter side,
as seen in the boyosaurus. But it's not always a laughing matter. Sometimes little
boys who are fascinated with the power of a *Tyrannosaurus rex* grow into older
boys who actually want to destroy people they perceive to be their foes. Many times
throughout the 1990s, the same ghastly scenario unfolded—an underfathered young
man suddenly and without any previous signs of violence sprays his classmates and
teachers with bullets.

The most notorious case involved Timothy McVeigh, the product of a broken   8
home, who looked for something to blame for his terminal drift and rootlessness,
and decided his own government was the oppressor. The result was a libertarian
Jihad fed by the fantasies of the lunatic Right that the American government is in fact
the "Zionist occupying authority," suppressing individual liberties on behalf of the
world Jewish conspiracy. But often there's no ideological or political motivation. The
killers at Columbine and other high schools were usually just kids who felt
excluded from the In Crowd of the beautiful and the athletic—Tom Sawyer in
fatigues, hefting an assault rifle in place of the more innocent slingshot.

Parents, educators, and political leaders have all agonized over these developments   9
as signs that the culture is in crisis. Some have made the case that virtual violence
in video games and action movies has become a model for real life. Young men
who, in a previous era, would have picked a fistfight, or confined their anger to their
private feelings, now find it all too easy to make a direct transition from the violence
that washes over them from TV, movies, and video games into their own situations,
and to apply the methods of a Rambo in their own suburban enclaves.

To me, there is little doubt that this entertainment culture of virtual violence con-   10
tributes to an atmosphere that prompts real-life rampage killings. There may not
be a direct cause-and-effect relationship: It may not be possible to demonstrate,
with complete empirical rigor, that Person A killed Person B because Person A
watched Movie C. But the virtual violence does have an indirect and corrosive effect
on morality. Its endless stream of fantasies of solitary omnipotence and open-ended
violence cannot help but undermine those ethical and psychological mechanisms
of self-restraint which a civilized society must ingrain in all its members.

According to Charles Mandel, a journalist specializing in the entertainment cul-   11
ture, a recent study shows that "roughly one in four children is addicted to [video]
gaming (specifically, 24 percent play between seven and thirty hours a week)." And
what games they are. How many parents, Mr. Mandel asks, know what their kids
are playing on the computer? Here's an example:

> Duke Nukem runs forward, grabs the shotgun and pumps a round into the cham-
> ber. "Groovy," intones the video-game hero in his gravelly voice, just before he
> starts blasting alien scum into a gory pulp.

Sound violent? Mandel continues: 12

Not to some video-game developers, apparently. Major U.S. software companies are about to make such infamous "splatter" games as Duke Nukem and Doom seem like child's play as they prepare to release a new wave of titles this fall that enable players to manipulate photorealistic images of humans into acts of torture, mutilation and even—if you can believe it—prostitution.

One of the innovators in digitalized carnage is Interplay Productions, whose sales   13
for the previous six months had been $81 million. Now you don't have to proceed directly to massacring your enemies. You can have some extra fun by torturing them first! Mandel goes on:

> Interplay Productions proudly promotes its Wild 9 as the first-ever action game that encourages players to torture enemies. Shiny Entertainment, a subsidiary of Interplay, is completing work on Messiah, a game in which a cherub tries to cleanse the world of corruption. "Ever seen a body with 10,000 volts run through it?" the game's advertising slogan teases. "Want to?" Not to be outdone, Virgin Interactive is set to release Thrill Kill, a series of gladiator-style battles between demented characters that bite and tear at each other in a torture-chamber setting.

Lieutenant Colonel Dave Grossman, a retired infantry officer and an expert on   14
the psychology of violence, has labored tirelessly to alert parents to the corrosive effects of what he calls "television's virus of violence." He believes there is a direct link between television's glamorization of violence and the search for recognition by alienated boys through rampage killings of the kind that took place at Columbine High.

What disturbs him the most is the resemblance he sees between television vio-   15
lence and techniques used by the Marines and other military organizations to desensitize soldiers to the moral impact of inflicting death in combat. Killing loses its horror when it becomes a repetitive act carried out against enemies whom you are conditioned to regard as completely alien to yourself. However, while the military uses these techniques only in the dire situation of war, the last resort of national self-defense, television and other electronic media desensitize young men to the existence of their own fellow citizens, schoolmates, and parents. And, of course, while professional soldiers are taught to direct their ability to kill beyond U.S. borders, restricted to those comparatively rare episodes when foreign combatants imperil Americans, the climate of violence fed by the entertainment culture spreads indiscriminately to target one's own fellow citizens.

By a strange coincidence, Jonesboro, Arkansas, where one of the school shootings   16
took place, is Colonel Grossman's hometown. It is a cruel irony that his worst fears about the "virus of violence" spread among young men by the entertainment culture were played out in the ghastliest way in the small town to which he returned after retiring from the Marines. He writes:

Before retiring here, I spent almost a quarter of a century as an army infantry officer and a psychologist, learning how to enable people to kill. Believe me, we are very good at it. And just as the army enables killing, we are doing the same thing to our kids—but without the military's safeguards.

He believes that violence has been trivialized by its prevalence on television, to   17
the point where the young people watching it cannot distinguish between the fantasy version and the real thing:

The TV networks are responsible for traumatizing and brutalizing our children as they watch violent acts—a thousand a month, according to the latest research financed by the cable industry itself—at a young, vulnerable age when they cannot tell the difference between reality and fantasy. Children really only know what they have been taught, and we have taught them, ever so cleverly, to laugh and cheer at violence. In Jonesboro we saw an indication of just how good a job we have done.

Even when they confront it directly, children can confuse real-life violence with   18
something they've seen on a screen and react as if they were detached spectators enjoying a completely fictitious act of carnage. Grossman witnessed this creepy spectacle firsthand in the aftermath of the Jonesboro incident:

I spent the first three days after the shooting at Westside Middle School, counseling teachers, students, and parents. One high school teacher told me about the reaction she got when she informed her students that someone was shooting at their little brothers, sisters, and cousins in the middle school. "They laughed," she told me in amazement. "They laughed." We have raised a generation of barbarians who have learned to associate violence with pleasure, like the Romans who cheered and snacked as the Christians were slaughtered in the Colosseum.

As accounts like this one make disturbingly clear, before we can think about how   19
best to prevent young men from committing acts of pointless violence, we have to think about why they may be psychologically prone to them. We must pose the disturbing but crucial question: Is warlike aggression natural to man? Only if we know why men are warlike will we know how to direct their courage toward good aims and away from bad ones.

Even posing this question goes against a powerful grain in our academic culture   20
and the opinion elites influenced by it. Some believe that the use of force is always regrettable—that there is no ethical distinction between using force for just and unjust purposes. People holding this view are often drawn to the idea that warlike behavior can be explained only by an involuntary biological drive in males, since it falls beyond the pale of rational discussion or moral justification under any circumstances. Typical of this reductionist approach is a recent study by the psychologists Neil Wiener and Christian Mesquida. "How do you explain the universality of war?" Dr. Wiener asks. "It's ubiquitous." Using demographic data provided by the

United Nations to compare war zones in El Salvador, Northern Ireland, Croatia, Kosovo, Albania, and Chechnya, he and his colleague came up with a single answer: "Wars are not triggered by ideology or religion, but by a society that has too many young, unmarried men."

This kind of broad empirical generalization has the seductive appeal of providing a single answer for the occurrence of violence everywhere in the world. Unfortunately, upon reflection, I believe it obscures rather than clarifies the nature of war and courage. Drs. Wiener and Mesquida begin by setting aside the complex conditions that make each war zone they analyzed unique. They take what is in fact the least interesting and informative characteristic in every one of these cases— the predominance of unmarried males under thirty years old—and elevate it to the most interesting and informative characteristic. But in each case studied, what is primarily motivating the belligerents is their conviction that they are fighting for honor, justice, and the dignity of their people or faith. These views are in turn rooted in complicated competing views of the histories of the opposing sides—how each side interprets the cultural, religious, and ethnic experiences of its people, perceptions of oppression, insult, and grievance, culminating in a feeling on both sides of justified zealotry and the need to reestablish dignity and freedom. In short, contrary to what the researchers maintain, wars *are* "triggered by ideology and religion." Any psychology of male aggression must be able to comprehend those deeper motives. 21

In order to arrive at the simplistic and reductionist conclusion that all wars are "caused" by young males, we have to set aside our entire accumulated knowledge of history, politics, and civilizational clashes. We have to ignore the reasoned opinions that belligerents advance to justify their cause in favor of the view that wars are driven by a dumb subrational compulsion akin to the need to eat. Above all, the empirical approach prevents us from arriving at a substantive conception of male psychology that includes an understanding of courage as a virtue connected to the aspiration for honor and the service of justice. When we look at war and violence from that perspective, we find that the predominance of young males is not the *cause* of war but its *effect*. Men don't fight wars because they're young. Men fight wars because a desire for justice, honor, and human dignity is intrinsic to human nature, and that desire is often threatened, challenged, or derided by other people or by external events. Fighting wars for those reasons requires young men. Wars are caused by the need to fight for justice. 22

Part II

PRESENTING SOURCES TO OTHERS

Now, you are making the transition from reader to writer. To use what you have learned from your reading and to write about your sources in an essay, you must next learn about basic methods of *presenting sources* fairly and accurately.

- Chapter 2 shows you how to present a source through *summary*: the technique of expressing a group of related ideas briefly yet completely.
- Chapter 3 describes the rules to follow when you use *quotation*: the acknowledgment that a source, not yourself, is responsible for the precise language, as well as the ideas, contained in quoted text.
- Chapter 4 gives you practice in *paraphrase*: the method of expressing the ideas of others in your own words.

Summary, quotation, and paraphrase are the building blocks of writing from sources. They enable you to demonstrate your understanding of the source while integrating these ideas into your own work. They also help you to avoid the dishonest "borrowings," called *plagiarism*, that occur when the reader cannot tell who wrote what and so gives you credit for work that you did not do.

When you write, you must make it clear to your reader whether a specific idea, phrase, sentence, or group of sentences is the product of your own work or that of another. For example, whether you summarize, quote, or paraphrase, you must always *acknowledge* your source with a clear *citation* of the author's name. That process is called *documentation*.

▪2▪

Summarizing
Sources

When you annotate a text, when you ask yourself questions about its contents, you are helping yourself to understand what you are reading. When you write a summary, you are *recording* your understanding for your own information. When you include the summary in an essay of your own, you are *reporting* your understanding to your reader. In fact, you have already been using summary in your marginal notes when you express an author's idea in a phrase or sentence.

Summarizing a source usually means *condensing ideas or information*. It is neither necessary nor desirable to include every repetition and detail. Rather, you extract only those points that seem important—the main ideas, which in the original passage may have been interwoven with less important material. A summary of several pages can sometimes be as brief as one sentence.

When writing a brief summary, you should add nothing new to the material in the source, nor should you change the emphasis or provide any new interpretation or evaluation. For the sake of clarity and coherence, you may rearrange the order of the ideas; however, as summarizer, you should strive to remain in the background.

The writer of a research essay is especially dependent on the brief summary as a means of referring to source materials. When you discuss another piece of writing, you generally have to summarize the contents briefly to establish for your reader the ideas that you intend to analyze. Through summary, you can condense a broad range of information, and you can present and explain the relevance of a number of sources all dealing with the same subject.

SUMMARIZING A PARAGRAPH

Before you can begin to summarize a short text—a paragraph, for example— you must read the passage carefully and understand the significance of each idea and how it is linked to the other ideas. Sometimes, the paragraph will contain a series of examples that can be summarized inductively.

The following paragraph can be summarized adequately by one of its own sentences. Which one?

> It is often remarked that science has increasingly removed man from a position at the center of the universe. Once upon a time the earth was thought to be the center and the gods were thought to be in close touch with the daily actions of humans. It was not stupid to imagine the earth was at the center, because, one might think, if the earth were moving around the sun, and if you threw a ball vertically upward, it would seem the ball should come down a few feet away from you. Nevertheless, slowly, over many centuries, through the work of Copernicus, Galileo, and many others, we have mostly come to believe that we live on a typical planet orbiting a typical star in a typical galaxy, and indeed that no place in the universe is special.
>
> GORDON KANE, from "Are We the Center of the Universe?"

Both the first and last sentences are possibilities, but the first is a broader generalization and a more comprehensive summary. Usually, even when you find a strong sentence that suggests the main idea of the paragraph, you will still need to tinker with that sentence, expanding its meaning by giving the language a more general focus.

Here is a paragraph in which no one sentence is broad enough to sum up the main idea, but which contains a scattering of useful phrases:

> In a discussion [with] a class of teachers, I once said that I liked some of the kids in my class much more than others and that, without saying which ones I liked best, I had told them so. After all, this is something that children know, whatever we tell them; it is futile to lie about it. Naturally, these teachers were horrified. "What a terrible thing to say!" one said. "I love all the children in my class exactly the same." Nonsense; a teacher who says this is lying, to herself or to others, and probably doesn't like any of the children very much. Not that there is anything wrong with that; plenty of adults don't like children, and there is no reason why they should.

But the trouble is that they feel they should, which makes them feel guilty, which makes them feel resentful, which in turn makes them try to work off their guilt with indulgence and their resentment with subtle cruelties—cruelties of a kind that can be seen in many classrooms. Above all, it makes them put on the phony, syrupy, sickening voice and manner, and the fake smiles and forced, bright laughter that children see so much of in school, and rightly resent and hate.

JOHN HOLT, from *How Children Fail*

Here, you might begin by combining key phrases: "a teacher who says" that she "loves all the children" "is lying to herself, or to others," and makes herself and the children "feel resentful." However, this kind of summarizing sentence resembles a patchwork, with the words and phrasing pulled straight out of the original. Even if you acknowledged the borrowings, by using quotation marks, as above, you would still be left with a weak sentence that is neither yours nor the author's. It is far better to construct an entirely new sentence of your own, such as this one:

In John Holt's view, although it is only natural for teachers to prefer some students to others, many teachers cannot accept their failure to like all equally well and express their inadequacy and dissatisfaction in ways that are harmful to the children.

Finally, some paragraphs give you no starting point at all for the summary and force you to write an entirely new generalization. How would you summarize this paragraph?

To parents who wish to lead a quiet life, I would say: Tell your children that they are very naughty—much naughtier than most children. Point to the young people of some acquaintances as models of perfection and impress your own children with a deep sense of their own inferiority. You carry so many more guns than they do that they cannot fight you. This is called moral influence, and it will enable you to bounce them as much as you please. They think you know and they will not have yet caught you lying often enough to suspect that you are not the unworldly and scrupulously truthful person which you represent yourself to be; nor yet will they know how great a coward you are, nor how soon you will run away, if they fight you with persistency and judgment. You keep the dice and throw them both for your children and yourself. Load them then, for you can easily manage to stop your children from examining them. Tell them how singularly indulgent you are; insist on the incalculable benefit you conferred on them, firstly in bringing them into the world at all, but more particularly in bringing them into it as your children rather than anyone else's. Say that you have their highest interests at stake whenever you are out of temper and wish to make yourself unpleasant by way of balm to your soul.

Harp much upon these highest interests. Feed them spiritually upon such brimstone and treacle as the late Bishop of Winchester's Sunday stories. You hold all the trump cards, or if you do not you can filch them; if you play them with anything like judgment you will find yourselves heads of happy, united God-fearing families, even as did my old friend Mr. Pontifex. True, your children will probably find out all about it some day, but not until too late to be of much service to them or inconvenience to yourself.

SAMUEL BUTLER, from *The Way of All Flesh*

A summary of this paragraph could recommend that parents intimidate their children and thus put them in their place. However, although such a generalization sums up the series of examples contained in the paragraph, it does not convey the fact that, in his caricature of family life, Butler is exaggerating outrageously. A comprehensive summary, then, would have to include not only the essence of Butler's recommendations, but also his implied point: that he does not expect anyone to follow his advice. *Irony* is the term used to describe the conflict between Butler's real meaning—parents should not be monsters, but sometimes are—and the meaning apparently expressed by his words as he urges them to treat their children tyrannically. Here is one way to summarize the paragraph:

> When he ironically suggests that parents can gain domestic tranquillity by tyrannizing over their children and making them feel morally inferior, Samuel Butler seems to be urging parents to treat their children with respect and justice.

Notice that this summarizing sentence includes Butler's name. Mentioning the author's name emphasizes that what you are summarizing is not your own work. By making it clear who is responsible for what, you are avoiding any possibility of *plagiarizing*—borrowing from your source without acknowledgment.

Summarizing a Brief Passage

1. Find a summarizing sentence within the passage (and, if you are using it in your own essay, put it in quotation marks); *or*
2. Combine elements within the passage into a new summarizing sentence; *or*
3. Write your own summarizing sentence.
4. Cite the author's name somewhere in the summary, and use quotation marks around any borrowed phrases.

EXERCISE 6: SUMMARIZING A PARAGRAPH

Summarize each of the following paragraphs by doing *one* of three things:

1. Underline a sentence that will serve as a comprehensive summary; or
2. Combine existing phrases; then rewrite the sentence, based on these phrases, to create a comprehensive summary; or
3. Invent a new generalization to provide a comprehensive summary.

Be prepared to explain your summary in class discussion.

A. The neurotic individual may have had some special vulnerability as an infant. Perhaps he was ill a great deal and was given care that singled him out from other children. Perhaps he walked or talked much later—or earlier—than children were expected to, and this evoked unusual treatment. The child whose misshapen feet must be put in casts or the sickly little boy who never can play ball may get out of step with his age mates and with the expectations parents and other adults have about children. Or a child may be very unusually placed in his family. He may be the only boy with six sisters, or a tiny child born between two lusty sets of twins. Or the source of the child's difficulties may be a series of events that deeply affected his relations to people—the death of his mother at the birth of the next child or the prolonged illness or absence of his father. Or a series of coincidences—an accident to a parent, moving to a new town and a severe fright—taken together may alter the child's relationship to the world.

MARGARET MEAD, from *Some Personal Views*

B. Ever wonder why divorce rates are so high? The real culprit isn't some kind of moral collapse. It's excessive expectations, driven and fueled by the civic religion of romance. For a lucky few, infatuation sometimes does lead to lasting love, and love to family, and family to all the other virtues our preachers and politicians regularly celebrate. For the other 99 percent of us, relationships are, at best, useful economic bargains and, if we're lucky, successful sexual transactions—better than the alternative, which has long been close to social death. But thanks to the civic religion of romance, we constantly expect more and quit what we have in search of more. For the essence of romantic love is not the company of a lover but the pursuit. It's all promise with the delivery of the postal service.

ANDREW SULLIVAN, from "The Love Bloat,"
New York Times Magazine

C. The biggest problem [affecting the comic book industry] is the transformation of American culture itself. The last decade of the twentieth century saw a phenomenal expansion in the entertainment choices available to young people and a glutted market for adolescent obsessions. Widely accessible cable television stations constantly air films, programs, and music videos directed at youth sensibilities. At least one station, the Sci-Fi Channel, is devoted exclusively to the kind of programming that overlaps with the fantasy appeal of comic books. Video and computer games have become one of the largest growth sectors of the entertainment industry by offering the kind of hands-on fantasy experience that comic books simply cannot match. And the Internet holds a potential for fantasy entertainment that is only beginning to be realized. Rather than simply reading about superheroes, interactive technology now makes it possible for young people to become virtual superheroes themselves. While comic book characters have successfully crossed over into all of these media, the consequences for the comic books themselves are less clear. Recognizing the significance of the new technology, Stan Lee, in his late seventies and serving as an honorary chairman of Marvel, launched a venture in 1999 to publish comic books exclusively over the Internet. With so many appealing avenues for young people to indulge their angst and fantasies, the comic book industry has never faced more formidable competition.

BRADFORD W. WRIGHT, from *Comic Book Nation:*
The Transformation of Youth Culture in America

D. On large plantations, only a small percentage of slaves worked as house servants. Although those jobs seemed on the surface to be more pleasant and higher in prestige, many women tried to avoid them, and some deliberately failed at their house chores in order to get back into the fields. Their impulses were similar to the ones that made young white women prefer even the more unpleasant types of factory work to domestic service. Housework meant being under the close watch of a mistress who had high expectations when it came to her family's comfort, and who might not know how to give clear directions. House slaves had no downtime—even their meals had to be grabbed on the run. When white people were in the room, they had to remain standing. (A spiritual from the era says, "I want to be in heaven sitting down.") Residents of the Big House even expected slaves to sleep at the foot of their beds, in case they wanted something during the night. Angelina Grimke said she knew of a black woman who had been married eleven years "and yet has never been allowed to sleep out of her mistress's chamber." The image of the slave lying at the foot of the bed like a dog sometimes was extended further. Some slaves reported that, as children, they were encouraged to sit under the table during dinner and beg scraps from their mistress.

GAIL COLLINS, from *America's Women*

E. When we pick up our newspaper at breakfast, we expect—we even demand—that it bring us momentous events since the night before. We turn on the car radio as we drive to work and expect "news" to have occurred since the morning newspaper went to press. Returning in the evening, we expect our house not only to shelter us, to keep us warm in winter and cool in summer, but to relax us, to dignify us, to encompass us with soft music and interesting hobbies, to be a playground, a theater, and a bar. We expect our two-week vacation to be romantic, exotic, cheap, and effortless. We expect a faraway atmosphere if we go to a nearby place; and we expect everything to be relaxing, sanitary, and Americanized if we go to a faraway place. We expect new heroes every season, a literary masterpiece every month, a dramatic spectacular every week, a rare sensation every night. We expect everybody to feel free to disagree, yet we expect everybody to be loyal, not to rock the boat or to take the Fifth Amendment. We expect everybody to believe deeply in his religion, yet not to think less of others for not believing. We expect our nation to be strong and great and vast and varied and prepared for every challenge; yet we expect our "national purpose" to be clear and simple, something to give direction to the lives of nearly two hundred million people and yet can be bought in a paperback at the corner drugstore for a dollar.

DANIEL BOORSTIN, from *The Americans:*
The National Experience

F. Family love indeed subverts the ideal of what we should feel for every soul in the world. Moral philosophers play with a hypothetical dilemma in which people can run through the left door of a burning building to save some number of children or through the right door to save their own child. If you are a parent, ponder this question: is there *any* number of children that would lead you to pick the left door? Indeed, all of us reveal our preference with our pocketbooks when we spend money on trifles for our own children (a bicycle, orthodontics, an education at a private school or university) instead of saving the lives of unrelated children in the developing world by donating the money to charity. Similarly, the practice of parents bequeathing their wealth to their children is one of the steepest impediments to an economically egalitarian society. Yet few people would allow the government to confiscate 100 percent of their estate, because most people see their children as an extension of themselves and thus as the proper beneficiaries of their lifelong striving.

STEVEN PINKER, from *The Blank Slate:*
The Modern Denial of Human Nature

SUMMARIZING AN ARTICLE

When you want to summarize a longer text in a few sentences, how do you judge which points are important and which are not? Some texts, especially newspaper articles, have rambling structures and short paragraphs, so you don't even have fully developed paragraphs in which to search for summarizing topic sentences. Are there any standard procedures to help you decide which points to summarize?

Summarizing an Article

1. Read the entire article more than once and note down key points.
2. Ask yourself why the article was written and published.
3. Look for repetitions of and variations on the same idea.

Read "Holdup Man Tells Detectives How to Do It" by Selwyn Raab, a former crime reporter for the *New York Times,* where this article appeared. Some of the main points are indicated in the margins. Would you add any? How would you turn these notes into a summary?

HOLDUP MAN TELLS DETECTIVES HOW TO DO IT
Selwyn Raab

conceals face
peers out

1 His face hidden by a shabby tan coat, the career holdup man peeked out at his audience of detectives and then proceeded to lecture them on how easy it was to succeed at his trade in New York.

nothing the cops can do

2 "I don't think there's much any individual police officer can do," the guest lecturer told 50 detectives yesterday at an unusual crime seminar sponsored by the Police Department. "Once I knew what the police officer on the beat was up to I wasn't much concerned about the cops."

won't give full name
police couldn't catch him

3 The holdup man, who identified himself only as "Nick," is serving a prison term of 6 to 13 years. He said his most serious arrest occurred after he was shot three times by a supermarket manager—not in any encounter with the police.

strengthen deterrent

4 When asked by a detective taking a course in robbery investigations what the best deterrent would be against gunmen like himself, Nick replied crisply: "Stiffer sentences."

5 After being seriously wounded in his last robbery attempt, Nick said he decided it was time to retire.

6 "I'm close to 40 and not getting any younger," he explained. "I just don't want to spend any more time in jail."

7 Nick also offered the detectives some tips on how robbers pick their targets and make their getaways in the city.

no disguise
tries to be anonymous

8 Except for wearing a hat, Nick said he affected no disguise. "I usually picked a store in a different neighborhood or in another borough where I was unknown."

casual preparation

9 Leads on places to hold up usually came from other criminals or from employees. There were no elaborate plannings or "casings," he said, adding:

fear of getting shot

10 "I liked supermarkets because there's always a lot of cash around. Uniformed guards didn't deter me because they're not armed, they usually just have sticks. It's

don't stand out

better to pick a busy area rather than the suburbs. The chances of someone notic- ing you are greater in residential or suburban areas."

11 The detectives, sitting at desks with notepaper in front of them, were rookies as well as veterans. Besides city detectives, the audience included policemen from the Transit Authority, the Housing Authority, the Yonkers Police Department and from Seattle.

avoid the cops

12 They listened carefully as Nick outlined how he or a confederate would inspect the area for signs of uniformed or plainclothes police officers.

stay concealed

13 The retired robber said he had preferred supermarkets or stores with large win- dow advertisements or displays because these materials prevented him from being seen by passers-by on the street.

14 "I was always a little nervous or apprehensive before a job," he continued. "But once you're inside and aware of the reaction of the people and you know the pos- sibilities then your confidence comes back."

disappear into the crowd

15 Nick said he always made his escape in a car and he preferred heavily trafficked roads because it made the getaway vehicle less conspicuous than on little used side streets.

guns easy to get

16 In New York, cheap handguns were selling from $15 to $70, he told the detec- tives. Such weapons as shotguns or automatic rifles, Nick said, could be rented for about $100 an hour.

17 Nick said he had been a holdup man since the age of 20 and had committed about 30 "jobs," but was uncertain of the exact number. The biggest robbery he had par- ticipated in netted a total of $8,000, and overall he got about $30,000 in his crimi- nal activities.

motive = self- aggrandizement

18 Asked why he went back to robbing after his first arrest, Nick said: "I wanted whisky, women and big autos. Like most who rob I was not socially accepted. Big money elevates you above the people you think are looking down on you."

short sentence = poor deterrent

19 Short prison sentences, for first arrests, Nick asserted, probably do little to dis- courage holdup men. "I see them laying up in jail and it doesn't make any difference," he said. "They just go ahead planning the next one in a different way."

not violent

20 During his "on-and-off" criminal career, Nick said he had never fired any of the guns he carried.

stays concealed

21 After his one-hour appearance as guest lecturer, Nick, his face still covered by his coat, was escorted out of the classroom back to his cell at an undisclosed prison.

1. *Read the entire article more than once and note down key points.*

Pay attention to *minor facts and interesting details.* Notice that most of the marginal notes in this article support and illuminate the central ideas. For ex- ample, the fact that Nick chose to hide his face during and after his "lecture" hardly seems worth considering and would never by itself be regarded as cru- cial. But taken together with some of Nick's remarks, that minor fact helps you to recognize a key point of the article: The robber's reliance on *anonymity* enables him to commit a successful crime; Nick may at some point wish to resume his profession despite his "retirement." Although you should always identify your key points, remember to reread and consider every part of the article as you prepare your summary.

2. *Ask yourself why the article was written and published.*

What does the newspaper want its readers to learn? A news article's purpose is frequently twofold—to describe an event and to suggest the event's significance—and so it is easy to confuse the *facts* being recorded with the underlying *reasons* for recording them. Here are two one-sentence summaries of the article that are both off the mark because they concentrate too heavily on the event:

> Nick, a convicted retired criminal, was guest speaker at a police seminar and
> told detectives how robbers pick their targets and make their getaways in
> New York.

> Nick, after committing thirty robberies, suggested to detectives some possible
> methods of thwarting future robberies.

Both writers seem too concerned with Nick's colorful history and the peculiarity of his helping the police at all. They ignore the significance of what Nick was actually saying. The second summary—by emphasizing the phrase "thwarting future robberies"—is misleading and almost contradicts the point of the article; in fact, Nick is really suggesting that the police will continue to be ineffectual.

A news article can also mislead you into thinking that a headline is a summary: the headline "Holdup Man Tells Detectives How to Do It" does not summarize the material in the article, but, because it is broad and vague, it "sounds" good. What, for example, is meant by the "it" of the headline—robbery or detection?

3. *Look for repetitions of and variations on the same idea.*

There is one concrete point that Selwyn Raab and his readers and the police and Nick himself are all interested in: *ways of preventing criminals from committing crimes.* Not only are we told again and again about Nick's contempt for the police, but we are also given his flat statement that only fear of imprisonment ("stiffer sentences") will deter a hardened criminal.

A brief summary of this article, then, would mention *tougher sentencing as a way of preventing crime.* But, in addition, the theme of *the criminal's need for anonymity* ought, if possible, to be incorporated into a complete summary. In Nick's opinion, his career has been relatively successful because he has managed to appear normal and blend into the crowd. The primary and secondary ideas can be joined in a summary like this one:

> An article in the *New York Times* describes Nick, the successful robber, who observes with contempt that the police have rarely been able to penetrate his "anonymous" disguise. Nick argues that the presence of police will not deter most experienced criminals and that only "stiffer sentences" will prevent crime.

EXERCISE 7: SUMMARIZING AN ARTICLE

Carefully read "Crying Foul over Fans' Boorish Behavior" by Eric Hoover, a reporter for the "Students" section of the *Chronicle of Higher Education*, where this article appeared. Determine the article's purpose and make notes of the points that the author emphasizes. Then write a comprehensive summary in two or three sentences.

CRYING FOUL OVER FANS' BOORISH BEHAVIOR
Eric Hoover

The final buzzer sounded at the National Collegiate Athletic Association men's basketball championship this week, ending a season in which student spectators cheered, jeered, and hurled four-letter words. 1

In sports arenas throughout the nation, boos have become passé, and fans are getting personal. 2

During a basketball game at the University of Kentucky last month, for instance, students both chanted "Matt is gay" at Matt Walsh, a forward on the visiting University of Florida team, and then hoisted signs that insulted his girlfriend, a *Playboy* magazine Playmate. 3

In January students at Iowa State University yelled "rapist!" at Pierre Pierce, a guard for the University of Iowa who pleaded guilty to an assault-causing-injury charge in 2002. 4

Last December students at Florida taunted D. J. Strawberry, a guard for the University of Maryland at College Park, by referring to the drug problems of his father, Darryl Strawberry, a former professional baseball player. 5

Incivility at sporting events is as old as blood-boiling collegiate rivalries, and perhaps, just as inevitable. Still, some administrators, tired of plugging their ears, are trying to promote more tasteful cheering—a delicate task in an era when students believe they have a right to say what they please while supporting the home team. 6

Although some institutions, including St. Joseph's University, boot students out of arenas for bad language, many colleges tolerate isolated showers of expletives in deference to fans' free-speech rights. But some legal experts say both public 7

Travis Garrison, a sophomore forward for the Maryland Terrapins, is taunted by Duke fans at Cameron Indoor Stadium.

and private colleges can prohibit indecent language at athletics events without stomping on the First Amendment.

Last month an assistant attorney general of Maryland advised the state's flagship   8
institution that it could constitutionally restrict vulgar chants and signs at games with a "carefully drafted policy."

Even if the law supports them, college officials who have confronted the issue   9
say efforts to clean up speech must include—if not begin with—students themselves. Lectures or warnings from administrators alone might not inspire anyone to put soap in his own mouth.

"It has to sink in with students at some kind of a voluntary level that they are foul-   10
ing their own nest," says Gary M. Pavela, director of judicial programs at Maryland. "If your dominant image of a particular university is that of a howling, obscene mob, then you are not going to be favorably disposed."

Maryland's administrators had red faces after a nationally televised home bas-   11
ketball game against Duke University on January 21. Dozens of students at the game sported T-shirts that applied the F-word to the visiting team. They also chanted an expletive at J. J. Redick, a Duke guard who scored a game-high 26 points.

National sports commentators lampooned the Terrapins' fans. Maryland alumni,   12
some of whom had taken their children to the game, complained about the coarse language, a recurring problem at basketball games. (Students have long chanted, "Hey, you suck!" at visiting players before tipoff.)

After the Duke game, Maryland's president, C. D. Mote Jr., asked the state at-   13
torney general's office if the university had any latitude to adopt a speech policy prohibiting offensive language at athletics events.

In a March 17 letter to Mr. Mote obtained by *The Chronicle*, John K. Anderson,   14
the state's chief counsel for educational affairs, advised the university that such a policy was feasible. "While First Amendment law is complex, it does not seem reasonable for the university to be utterly without any means to address a
phenomenon that has proved to be upsetting to large numbers of fans," Mr. Anderson wrote. "The applicable case law does not, in my view, leave the university
powerless."

In his analysis, Mr. Anderson noted that the speech policy could not include   15
criminal punishments, citing *Cohen v. California*, a 1971 case in which the U.S. Supreme
Court held that states could not remove a particular word, however offensive,
from the public's vocabulary: "One man's vulgarity," Justice John Marshall Harlan
wrote in the majority opinion, "is another's lyric."

The speech in question at Maryland is constitutionally protected because it is nei-   16
ther defamatory nor obscene under the Supreme Court's definition. Nonetheless,
Mr. Anderson wrote that the Court's reasoning, in *Cohen* and in other cases, suggested that states could regulate "lewd or profane words" in specific locations,
particularly those where "captive auditors," including children, are present.

At Maryland's arena, he wrote, "offensive language comes without warning . . .   17
people attending the game cannot avoid it by averting their eyes. They are captives whose only recourse is to leave the stadium or stop attending games."

The university would have to word such a policy carefully, ensuring it was nei-   18
ther too broad nor too vague. Maryland would also have to publicize the restrictions, train its arena personnel to enforce it, and perhaps provide a means of
contesting sanctions, which could include ejection from the arena and campus-
judiciary punishments for students.

Such "practical problems" might persuade the university to regulate speech only   19
if all other means were ineffective, Mr. Anderson concluded.

Officials at the university say they will consider a speech policy, among other   20
strategies, over the summer.

Maryland's Mr. Pavela concedes that enforcing a speech restriction may be im-   21
practical: Sending a battalion of security officers after swearing students could spawn
"First Amendment martyrs" who might cause a greater stir than foul-mouthed
fans.

But he says the university can refer to the nuances of the law to inform discus-   22
sions of sportsmanship among students, who tend to believe the First Amendment
protects them against any restraint of expression.

"If we frame it at the outset as a punishment issue, then we will probably lose—   23
then it's not about the sportsmanship standards involved," Mr. Pavela says. "We've
got to get students to think. . . . We're not just dealing with the First Amendment
rights of speakers, but also with the rights of people in the audience."

Some athletics conferences have confronted the issue with policy changes. Last   24
summer the Big Ten passed new crowd-control measures, stating that it would
hold colleges "responsible" for student sections that singled out athletes for verbal abuse. But those measures do not include procedures for disciplining or ejecting
students during games.

One complication for colleges is that students know that administrators welcome   25
most of the noise they make. Coaches encourage students to make their home
courts "hostile" environments, places their opponents fear. Some arenas were designed to intimidate: At Maryland's new Comcast Center, the stands behind the
visitor's basket during the second half rise at a steep angle, thrusting a "wall of
fans" into the action.

So how do administrators ask students to go crazy, but not too crazy?   26

"It's very difficult in a college setting because you're trying to market to differ-   27
ent groups," says Bob D'Amelio, an assistant athletics director at Western Michigan University. "You want students there, you want families there, you want them to
coexist peacefully."

Athletics officials say students tend to listen to appeals from coaches and play-   28
ers. After Western Michigan students rained the F-word on a referee during an
ice-hockey game a few years ago, the university's hockey coach took the ice before the following game and urged students to refrain from swearing.

Mr. D'Amelio says that fans' behavior improved, though some problems endure.   29
When a player on the visiting team goes to the penalty box, some students continue to yell, "See ya, bitch!"

Security officers occasionally remove fans for shouting the F-word. (Mr. D'Ame-   30
lio could only remember one such instance this season.) Students who get booted
must report to the campus judiciary office, where they receive "verbal reprimands,"
Mr. D'Amelio says.

Some colleges recommend that coaches talk to students at the beginning of the   31
season, before problems arise. Broadcasting reminders about sportsmanship from
coaches or players just before big games may help, too. Western Michigan's code
of conduct for sporting events, which includes warnings about using abusive language, is read over the public-address system before each game and posted in the
arena.

Daniel L. Wann, a professor of social psychology at Murray State University and   32
the editor of *Sports Fans: The Psychology and Social Impact of Spectators* (Routledge,
2001), says students are more likely to engage in verbal abuse when facing a bitter
rival whom "they perceive as a threat."

Persuading fans to root a certain way is not easy, though, given that many of them   33
believe they can influence the outcome of a game.

"When fans yell at officials, there's no belief in their mind that it will help the   34
team—it's just aggression," Mr. Wann says. "But when they yell at opposing players, they feel like they're helping the team win, doing their part."

Students are matter of fact about why they give visiting teams hell. 35

"We get into their heads," says Donald Wine, a senior at Duke and a member 36
of the university's infamous "Cameron Crazies," who see themselves less as spectators than as participants in basketball games.

Mr. Wine gets so worked up in the stands that he spends hours afterwards just 37
sitting around, chugging orange juice and vitamins. He is certain, though, that he
and his fellow Crazies helped limit Julius Hodge, North Carolina State University's
star forward, to just seven points on January 15 by chanting "anything and everything" at him all night.

Duke students pride themselves on creative cheers and publicly eschew the use 38
of expletives. Their philosophy stems from a 1984 letter Terry Sanford, then the
president of Duke, sent to students, criticizing them for their "crudeness, profanity, and cheapness" during games. The missive, which Mr. Sanford titled "An Avun-
cular Letter," urged students to clean up their language and to "taunt with style."

But Duke fans have their four-letter lapses, as some Crazies admit. When play- 39
ing host to its hated rival, the University of North Carolina at Chapel Hill, Mr. Wine
says, the "line" distinguishing appropriate from inappropriate fan behavior shifts,
allowing for more vicious and personal jibes.

Among student fans, politeness is a relative term. Before the game against Mary- 40
land this season, some Duke students debated whether they should taunt Mr. Strawberry about his father's drug abuse (one idea was to fill sandwich bags with sugar
and shake the "cocaine" at him). The Crazies decided against the tactic, though
decency was not necessarily the deciding factor.

"Strawberry was not a big threat," explains Matt Kawecki, a senior at Duke. "It 41
wouldn't have been worth any sort of fallout."

The Crazies usually enjoy a good relationship with Duke's athletics department 42
and Mike Krzyzewski, the men's basketball coach, who also tells fans when their
chants cross the line.

Other colleges cite communication between students and administrators as a key 43
to improving fan behavior.

After students at Stanford University hoisted fake joints to taunt a visiting player 44
with a drug history in the late 1990s, administrators told them the stunt was too
personal. Now the athletics department regularly discusses its expectations with
leaders of the student fan group.

At the University of Missouri, a notorious student group known as the Antlers 45
lost its priority seating at basketball games because the athletics department became
frustrated with the students' "questionable" chants and signage, says Chad Moller,
the university's director of sports information.

Now Missouri reserves prime seats for two university-approved groups, the 46
Student Athletic Board and the Zoo Crew, which both emphasize sportsmanship.
Each group has a faculty sponsor, "which lends them a little more credibility," Mr.
Moller says.

Following the game against Duke in College Park, Coach Gary Williams talked   47
to students about the importance of appropriate behavior. Fans did not reprise their
profane January performance for the rest of the season.

Administrators at the university are working with student leaders to develop a   48
game plan for better sportsmanship.

In February Ben Maggin, a senior at Maryland who was frustrated by the four-   49
letter jeers, created "the Sixth Man," a student group that plans to organize more
creative—and decent—cheers in the next season. Within weeks of its founding,
more than a hundred students had signed up to help.

Mr. Maggin, who has attended Terrapins games since he was a child, attributes stu-   50
dents' bad behavior to "a combination of frustration and not having anything else
to say."

He encountered some resistance from students who worried that he was try-   51
ing to stifle their passion, but Mr. Maggin says the group will not dictate how fans behave—just provide a presence that might help prevent "a lapse back into profanity."

And there are indications that wit may replace invective in the stands. Recently   52
some Maryland students appeared at games holding signs that read "Expletive" and
"I dislike the other team."

SUMMARIZING A COMPLEX ESSAY

Sometimes, you need to summarize a reading containing a number of complex and abstract ideas, a reading that may be disorganized and therefore difficult to understand and condense. The best way to prepare for such a summary
is to make marginal notes and then write a list with each key point expressed in
a sentence.

Here is an essay by Bertrand Russell, a distinguished British mathematician
and philosopher of the early twentieth century. The essay is annotated with
marginal notes and followed by a preliminary list of key ideas, a statement of
Russell's thesis, and the final summary.

Russell's essay is difficult, so be sure to read it slowly, and more than once. If
you get confused at any point, try referring to the list of notes that follows; but
be sure to *go back to the essay* after you have identified and understood each
numbered point.

First Stage: Marginal Notes

THE SOCIAL RESPONSIBILITY OF SCIENTISTS
Bertrand Russell

responsibility   Science, ever since it first existed, has had important effects in matters that lie   1
for how
discoveries   outside the purview of pure science. Men of science have differed as to their re-
are used?   sponsibility for such effects. Some have said that the function of the scientist in   2
society is to supply knowledge, and that he need not concern himself with the use

some
scientists:
no

scientists
as public-
spirited
citizens

to which this knowledge is put. I do not think that this view is tenable, especially in our age. The scientist is also a citizen; and citizens who have any special skill have a public duty to see, as far as they can, that their skill is utilized in accordance with the public interest. Historically, the functions of the scientist in public life have generally been recognized. The Royal Society was founded by Charles II as an antidote to "fanaticism" which had plunged England into a long period of civil strife.

3

some
scientists
work in the
public
interest;
others work
for the
government

The scientists of that time did not hesitate to speak out on public issues, such as religious toleration and the folly of prosecutions for witchcraft. But although science has, in various ways at various times, favored what may be called a humanitarian outlook, it has from the first had an intimate and sinister connection with war. Archimedes sold his skill to the Tyrant of Syracuse for use against the Romans; Leonardo secured a salary from the Duke of Milan for his skill in the art of fortification; and Galileo got employment under the Grand Duke of Tuscany because he could calculate the trajectories of projectiles. In the French Revolution the scientists who were not guillotined were set to making new explosives, but Lavoisier was not spared, because he was only discovering hydrogen which, in those days, was not a weapon of war. There have been some honorable exceptions to the subservience of scientists to warmongers. During the Crimean War the British government consulted Faraday as to the feasibility of attack by poisonous gases. Faraday replied that it was entirely feasible, but that it was inhuman and he would have nothing to do with it.

4

influence
of the
media

Modern democracy and modern methods of publicity have made the problem of affecting public opinion quite different from what it used to be. The knowledge that the public possesses on any important issue is derived from vast and powerful organizations: the press, radio, and, above all, television. The knowledge that governments possess is more limited. They are too busy to search out the facts

5

6

governments
lack
information

for themselves, and consequently they know only what their underlings think good for them unless there is such a powerful movement in a different sense that politicians cannot ignore it. Facts which ought to guide the decisions of statesmen— for instance, as to the possible lethal qualities of fallout—do not acquire their due importance if they remain buried in scientific journals. They acquire their due importance only when they become known to so many voters that they affect the course of the elections. In general, there is an opposition to widespread publicity for

7

special
interests
suppress
information

such facts. This opposition springs from various sources, some sinister, some comparatively respectable. At the bottom of the moral scale there is the financial interest of the various industries connected with armaments. Then there are various effects of a somewhat thoughtless patriotism, which believes in secrecy and in what

public is
squeamish

is called "toughness." But perhaps more important than either of these is the unpleasantness of the facts, which makes the general public turn aside to pleasanter topics such as divorces and murders. The consequence is that what ought to be known widely throughout the general public will not be known unless great efforts are made by disinterested persons to see that the information reaches the minds and hearts of vast numbers of people. I do not think this work can be

8

*scientists
have a
public duty
to speak*

successfully accomplished except by the help of men of science. They, alone, can   9
speak with the authority that is necessary to combat the misleading statements of
those scientists who have permitted themselves to become merchants of death. If
disinterested scientists do not speak out, the others will succeed in conveying a
distorted impression, not only to the public but also to the politicians.

*scientific
research
depends on
funding*

   It must be admitted that there are obstacles to individual action in our age which   10
did not exist at earlier times. Galileo could make his own telescope. But once
when I was talking with a very famous astronomer he explained that the telescope
upon which his work depended owed its existence to the benefaction of enormously rich men, and, if he had not stood well with them, his astronomical discoveries would have been impossible. More frequently, a scientist only acquires access
to enormously expensive equipment if he stands well with the government of his
country. He knows that if he adopts a rebellious attitude he and his family are likely
to perish along with the rest of civilized mankind. It is a tragic dilemma, and I do
not think that one should censure a man whatever his decision; but I do think—
and I think men of science should realize—that unless something rather drastic is
done under the leadership or through the inspiration of some part of the scientific world, the human race, like the Gadarene swine, will rush down a steep place
to destruction in blind ignorance of the fate that scientific skill has prepared for it.

   It is impossible in the modern world for a man of science to say with any honesty, "My business is to provide knowledge, and what use is made of the knowledge is not my responsibility." The knowledge that a man of science provides may fall
into the hands of men or institutions devoted to utterly unworthy objects. I do
not suggest that a man of science, or even a large body of men of science, can altogether prevent this, but they can diminish the magnitude of the evil.

*support more
benign
research*

   There is another direction in which men of science can attempt to provide lead-   11
ership. They can suggest and urge in many ways the value of those branches of science of which the important and practical uses are beneficial and not harmful.
Consider what might be done if the money at present spent on armaments were
spent on increasing and distributing the food supply of the world and diminishing the
population pressure. In a few decades, poverty and malnutrition, which now afflict
more than half the population of the globe, could be ended. But at present almost all
the governments of great states consider that it is better to spend money on killing
foreigners than on keeping their own subjects alive. Possibilities of a hopeful sort
in whatever field can best be worked out and stated authoritatively by men of science; and, since they can do this work better than others, it is part of their duty
to do it.

   As the world becomes more technically unified, life in an ivory tower becomes increasingly impossible. Not only so; the man who stands out against the powerful organizations which control most of human activity is apt to find himself no longer
in the ivory tower, with a wide outlook over a sunny landscape, but in the dark and
subterranean dungeon upon which the ivory tower was erected. To risk such a habi-
tation demands courage. It will not be necessary to inhabit the dungeon if there   12

Speaking out together lessens the risk

are many who are willing to risk it, for everybody knows that the modern world depends upon scientists, and, if they are insistent, they must be listened to. We have it in our power to make a good world; and, therefore, with whatever labor and risk, we must make it.

Second Stage: List of Notes

1. Should scientists try to influence the way their discoveries are used?

2. One point of view: the scientist's role is to make the discovery; what happens afterward is not his concern.

3. Russell's point of view: scientists are like any other knowledgeable and public-spirited people; they must make sure that the products of their knowledge work for, not against, society.

4. In the past, some scientists have made public their views on controversial issues like freedom of religion; others have been servants of the war machine.

5. The power to inform and influence the public is now controlled by the news media.

6. Government officials are too busy to be well informed; subordinates feed them only enough information to get them reelected.

7. It is in the interests of various groups, ranging from weapons makers to patriots, to limit the amount of scientific information that the public receives.

8. The public is reluctant to listen to distasteful news.

9. Since the public deserves to hear the truth, scientists, who are respected for their knowledge and who belong to no party or faction, ought to do more to provide the public with information about the potentially lethal consequences of their discoveries. By doing so, they will correct the distortions of those scientists who have allied themselves with warmongers.

10. It is very difficult for scientists to speak out since they depend on government and business interests to finance their work.

11. While scientists cannot entirely stop others from using some of their discoveries for antisocial purposes, they can support other, more constructive kinds of research.

12. Speaking out is worth the risk of incurring the displeasure of powerful people; since the work of scientists is so vital, the risk isn't too great, especially
if they act together.

Third Stage: Establish a Thesis

Russell's thesis: Contrary to the self-interested arguments of many scientists
and other groups, scientists have a social responsibility to make sure that their
work is used for, not against, the benefit of humanity.

Fourth Stage: Summary

two views of the scientists' responsibility   Some scientists, as well as other groups, consider that they need not influence
the way in which their discoveries are used. However, Bertrand Russell, in "The
Social Responsibility of Scientists," believes that scientists have a responsibility
to make sure that their work is used for, not against, the benefit of humanity. In
modern times, he argues, it has been especially difficult for concerned scientists
obstacles to scientific freedom of speech   to speak out because many powerful groups prefer to limit and distort what the
public is told, because government officials are too busy to be thoroughly
informed, because scientists depend on the financial support of business and
government, and because the public itself is reluctant to hear distasteful news.
Nevertheless, Russell maintains that scientists have the knowledge and the prestige to command public attention, and their work is too vital for their voices to be
suppressed. If they act together, they can warn us if their work is likely to be
the need to act despite obstacles   used for an antisocial purpose and, at least, they can propose less destructive
alternatives.

This summary of Russell's essay is not a simple compilation of phrases taken
from the text, nor a collection of topic sentences, one from each paragraph.
Rather, it is a clear, coherent, and unified summary of Russell's ideas, expressed
in the writer's own voice and words.

A *framework* is immediately established in the first two sentences of the summary, which contrast the two alternative views of the scientist's responsibility.
The next sentence, which describes the four obstacles to scientific freedom of
speech, illustrates the rearrangement of ideas that is characteristic of summary.
While reviewing the list of notes, the summarizer has noticed that points 6, 7, 8,
and 10 each refer to a different way in which scientific truth is often suppressed;
she has therefore brought them together and lined them up in a parallel construction based on the repeated word "because." Finally, the last two sentences
contain a restatement of Russell's thesis and point out that the obstacles to action are not as formidable as they seem.

Notice that the Russell summary excludes points 1, 4, and 5 on the list of notes: point 1 is included in the presentation of points 2 and 3; point 4 is an example, one that is not essential to an understanding of the essay; and point 5 is not directly related to Russell's argument. In summarizing Russell's essay, you should not include extraneous points, such as the dangers of making scientific secrets public, for that would be arguing with Russell. Such ideas should be reserved for a full-length essay in which you develop an argument of your own.

Summarizing a Complex Essay

1. *The summary must be comprehensive.* You should review all your notes, and include in your summary all those ideas that are essential to the author's development of the thesis.

2. *The summary must be concise.* Eliminate repetitions in your list, even if the author restates the same points. Your summary should be considerably shorter than the source.

3. *The summary must be coherent.* It should make sense as a paragraph in its own right; it should not be taken directly from your list of notes and sound like a list of sentences that happen to be strung together in a paragraph format.

4. *The summary must be independent.* You are not being asked to imitate or identify yourself with the author whose work you are summarizing. On the contrary, you are expected to maintain your own voice throughout the summary. Even as you are jotting down your list of notes, you should try to use your own words. Nevertheless, while you want to make it clear that *you* are writing the summary, avoid introducing comments or criticisms of your own. (That is most likely to occur if you strongly disagree with the material that you are summarizing.) Make it clear to your reader when you are summarizing directly from the text and when you are inferring from or explaining what is being summarized. Cite the author's name somewhere in the summary, and use quotation marks around any borrowed phrases.

ASSIGNMENT 1: SUMMARIZING AN ESSAY

Summarize one of the following three essays. Before you begin your summary (on your second reading), underline and annotate key ideas and arguments, make a preliminary list of points, and identify the thesis. Use your own words as much as possible.

Shannon E. French has published *The Code of the Warrior: Explaining Warrior Values Past and Present*, an exploration of military ethics across the centuries. The essay that appears here was published in the *Chronicle of Higher Education*.

Neal Gabler has published several books on Hollywood and popular entertainment, and has made numerous appearances on TV, commenting on contemporary culture. This essay appeared in the *Chronicle of Higher Education*.

John Taylor Gatto was named New York City Teacher of the Year three times before he left the teaching profession in 1991. His campaign for school reform has included giving speeches all over the United States and publishing three books. This article (which is shortened here) appeared in *Harper's*.

WHEN TEACHING THE ETHICS OF WAR IS NOT ACADEMIC
Shannon E. French

I remember watching the 1991 gulf war on television while I was working toward my Ph.D. in philosophy at Brown University. On philosophical grounds, I concluded that the war was justified. My study of history and the just-war tradition persuaded me that Saddam's aggression had to be checked. I was furious when the coalition forces stopped short of removing Saddam from power. I knew in my gut that he would pop up again like one of those gophers in a carnival mallet game. I did not want our troops to have to return to the desert. What I did not know then was just how directly I would know and care about those troops by the time that call came.   1

In 1997, I accepted a tenure-track position in the ethics section of the department of leadership, ethics, and law at the U.S. Naval Academy. My students are intelligent, well-rounded, surprisingly earnest, and extremely likable young people. My six years of teaching philosophy to these future Navy and Marine Corps officers have made it impossible for me to see discussion about the ethics of war as a mere academic exercise. The men and women in my classes have volunteered to be America's warriors. It is important for all of us to understand what that means.   2

With that in mind, in the spring of 1998 I developed a new elective course, "The Code of the Warrior," which in turn inspired my book, *The Code of the Warrior: Exploring Warrior Values Past and Present*. The aim of both the course and the book is to examine the values that are explicit and implicit within the "warrior ethos" and to try to make sense of those values in a modern American context. My students and I study the warrior's codes associated (in fiction or in fact) with the ancient Greeks, the Romans, the Vikings, the Celts, medieval knights, Zulus, Native Americans, Chinese monks, and Japanese samurai. We talk about how the purpose of a code is to restrain warriors, for their own good as much as for the good of others. The essential element of a warrior's code is that it must set definite limits on what warriors can and cannot do if they want to continue to be regarded as warriors, not murderers or cowards. For the warrior who has such a code, certain actions remain unthinkable, even in the most dire or extreme circumstances.   3

Some people might fear that encouraging young warriors to study the warrior traditions of the past will lead them to become Rambo-like or to embrace outrageous bigotries and out-of-date ideals. Granted, some of the qualities that ancient warriors or warrior archetypes possess do not play well in the twenty-first cen-   4 tury. The key is to select for preservation only what is consistent with the values cherished by contemporary warrior cultures. For example, modern American warriors should resurrect only those traditions that cohere with the letter and spirit of the Constitution they have sworn to uphold and defend. They can emulate the humility, integrity, commitment to "might for right," courtesy, and courage of a Round Table knight without taking on board his acceptance of an undemocratic, stratified society (in which most of the population is disenfranchised and women and serfs are treated as property) or his determination to "pursue infidels."

Although warrior traditions may seem outmoded, the genuine emotional connection of today's warriors to an intentionally idealized warrior tradition and their sense that they must not betray that legacy is more important than ever. That connection and devotion may help them summon the will to show restraint in situations that will sorely tempt them to throw self-control out the window, for the world is no longer arranged in such a way that conflicts are likely to arise among great powers that are evenly matched.   5

The privileged warriors of today increasingly will find themselves pitted against adversaries who fight without any rules or restraints because they see no other way to advance their objectives. These desperate adversaries are likely to employ methods that are rightfully viewed as horrific and appalling by the rest of the civilized world, such as terror attacks on civilian populations and the use of chemical and biological weapons. Since these adversaries already are willing to die, they will not be deterred by any threat of punishment for continuing to disregard the laws of war.   6

In the spring semester following the attacks of September 11, 2001, and the start of President Bush's "war on terror," I gave an unusual assignment to my students. I asked them to write essays detailing exactly why they are different from terrorists. The midshipmen were to spell out as clearly as possible how the roles they intended to fill as future Navy and Marine Corps officers are distinct in morally relevant ways from that of, say, an Al Qaeda operative. They dubbed the assignment "creepy," but gamely agreed to do it. After they had read their efforts aloud, I gave the project a twist. I had them exchange papers, and told them each to write a critical response to their classmate's paper, from the point of view of a terrorist. Then I had them read those responses aloud.   7

The midshipmen found the entire exercise very disturbing because it forced them to reflect on that thin but critical line that separates warriors from murderers. In their initial essays, several of them stressed the facts that as members of the U.S. military they will not target innocent people, and that there is a moral difference between intentionally causing civilian deaths and doing so unintentionally as the result of attacks on legitimate military targets, or what is known as "collateral damage."   8

Here is a segment of an argument from a student in that class: "It is wrong to kill innocent people even if it does further the cause of the United States. There are rules to war. . . . We learned in 'Naval Law' [class] about the Law of Armed Conflict and the Rules of Engagement. There are targets that are acceptable and have   9 'military value' and there are targets that are simply killing for the sake of killing. Terrorists see targets of military value as too difficult to strike. They do not have the means to strike these targets. They instead will take out the easy targets for shock value, just to disrupt the lives of those they hate."

The second part of the "Why are you different from a terrorist?" assignment required my students to try to get inside the heads of those who commit terrorist acts. It forced them to consider how easy it might be for someone to rationalize crossing the line between "warrior" and "murderer" in the interest of what he believes to be a noble cause. As most of the students recognized, terrorists do not see themselves as murderers. They believe that they are warriors—"freedom fighters" struggling against those they have dubbed their "oppressors." But no matter how they may justify their actions, if they refuse to accept any rules of war, they forfeit the right to be regarded as warriors. 10

While there are many differences among them, warrior codes tend to share one point of agreement: the insistence that what distinguishes warriors from murderers is that warriors accept a set of rules governing when and how they kill. When they are trained for war, warriors are given a mandate by their society to take lives. But they must learn to take only certain lives in certain ways, at certain times, and for certain reasons. Otherwise, they become indistinguishable from murderers and will find themselves condemned by the very societies they were trained to serve. Individuals can fight for an objectively bad cause or a corrupt regime and still be warriors, as long as they have a warrior's code that requires them to observe the rules of war. There can be no honor in any conflict for those who believe that they have no moral obligation to restrain their behavior in any way. 11

Some of my students reported having trouble understanding how anyone, no matter what his convictions, could agree to take part in terrorist operations that are not limited by moral constraints and that involve intentionally targeting innocent civilians. They wondered: Are the people who can do these things inhuman monsters? How can they create meticulous plans to slaughter unsuspecting civilians without being stopped in their tracks by impossible-to-ignore pangs of conscience? 12

We discussed the fact that it is unlikely that those who have been bewitched by the rhetoric of Osama bin Laden and others like him feel no revulsion at the thought (or in the act) of killing unarmed, helpless civilians. Rather, it is more probable that they are persuaded that any apparent pricks of conscience they may feel are not the screams of their precious humanity hoping to be heard but rather their human weakness battling against their will to perform their sacred duty. They would therefore consider it a triumph of will to carry out the charge to kill without mercy or discrimination. 13

I gave my students this assignment because they need to understand how the line between warrior and murderer can be crossed, so they can avoid crossing it themselves. Unfortunately, it is most difficult for warriors to keep from slipping over that line when they are fighting against those who have already crossed it. In his 14 modern classic on the experience of war, *The Warriors: Reflections on Men in Battle*, J. Glenn Gray, a U.S. veteran of World War II, brings home the agony of the warrior who has become incapable of honoring his enemies and thus is unable to find redemption.

Gray describes how the atrocities committed by Japanese soldiers (including the 15 torture and murder of prisoners of war and wounded GIs) in the Pacific theater during World War II led Allied soldiers to view their enemies as unworthy of any respect or humane treatment. Otherwise unthinkable actions, such as collecting enemy body parts as "trophies" (a practice that also occurred in the Vietnam War) and refusing to accept surrenders, became acceptable within some circles of Allied fighters. As Gray notes, "The ugliness of war against an enemy conceived to be subhuman can hardly be exaggerated."

Gray's conclusions match those of psychologists Jonathan Shay, author of *Achilles* 16 *in Vietnam: Combat Trauma and the Undoing of Character*, and Lt. Col. Dave Grossman, author of *On Killing: The Psychological Cost of Learning to Kill in War and Society*. Both Shay and Grossman have worked extensively with American combat veterans. Their research reveals that the lasting psychological damage suffered by some veterans (such as debilitating post-traumatic stress) is most often the result of experiences that are not simply violent, but which involve what Shay calls the "betrayal of 'what's right.'" Veterans who believe that they were directly or indirectly party to immoral or dishonorable behavior (perpetrated by themselves, their comrades, or their commanders) have the hardest time reclaiming their lives after the war is over.

It is easier to remain a warrior when fighting other warriors. When warriors fight 17 murderers, they may be tempted to become like the evil they hope to destroy. Their only protection is their code of honor. The professional military ethics that restrain warriors—that keep them from targeting those who cannot fight back, from taking pleasure in killing, from striking harder than is necessary, and that encourage them to offer mercy to their defeated enemies and even to help rebuild their countries and communities—are also their own protection against becoming what they abhor.

It is not just "see the whites of their eyes" frontline ground and Special Forces 18 troops who need this protection. Men and women who fight from a distance— who drop bombs from planes and shoot missiles from ships or submarines—are also at risk of losing their humanity. What threatens them is the very ease with which they can take lives. As technology separates individuals from the results of their actions, it cheats them of the chance to absorb and reckon with the enormity of what they have done. Killing fellow human beings, even for the noblest cause, should never feel like nothing more than a game played using the latest advances in virtual reality. Modern warriors who dehumanize their enemies by equating them with blips on a computer screen may find the sense that they are part of an honorable undertaking far too fragile to sustain. It is important for warriors to show respect for the inherent worth and dignity of their opponents. Even long-distance warriors can achieve that by acknowledging that some of the "targets" they destroy are in fact human beings, not demons or vermin or empty statistics.

In class, I try to stress the point that once that thin line between warrior and murderer has been crossed, the harm to the individual who crossed it may be severe. In response to this, a student in my 2002 "Knowing Your Enemy" seminar raised the issue of whether a warrior who had crossed the line and allowed himself to become a murderer could ever find redemption and, in a sense, regain his warrior status. 19

My response was that I believe it depends a great deal on the individual's own reaction to having crossed that line. If he refuses to examine the immorality of his actions, he may do further damage to his character. He may tell himself that it was naive ever to have clung to a code—that there is no real difference between, for example, killing an enemy combatant in the thick of a firefight and killing an unarmed civilian in cold blood. On the other hand, if he rejects his ignoble behavior rather than excusing it, he may be able to restore his sense of honor and renew his commitment to the path of restraint. 20

In 1989, my father had a conversation with a World War II fighter pilot who knew firsthand what it feels like both to see an enemy cross the line from warrior to murderer and, in response, to cross the line himself. The veteran described an experience that had haunted him for more than 40 years. He and his friend Jimmy had been in a dogfight with three German ME-109s. Jimmy was hit and bailed out. One of the German pilots shot him while he was drifting down in his parachute. The veteran was horrified and went after the German pilot, forced him to bail out, and killed him in *his* parachute. My father asked the veteran how it had felt to take that revenge. At first, the man claimed that it had felt good. A moment later, however, he admitted, "No. . . . OK, . . . I cried." 21

Legend has it that when a Spartan mother sent her son off to war, she would say to him, "Come back with your shield, or on it." If a warrior came back without his shield, it meant that he had laid it down in order to break ranks and run from battle. He was supposed to use his shield to protect the man next to him in formation, so to abandon his shield was not only to be a coward but also to break faith with his comrades. To come back on his shield was to be carried back either wounded or dead. Thus the adage meant that the young warrior should fight bravely, maintain his martial discipline, and return with both his body and his honor intact. 22

The warriors' mothers who spoke this line were not heartless—far from it. It was spoken from great love. They wanted their children to return with their sense of self-respect intact, feeling justifiably proud of how they had performed under pressure, not tortured and destroyed by guilt and shame. To come back with their shields was to come back still feeling like warriors, not like cowards or murderers. The Spartan mothers' message is timeless. Everyone who cares about the welfare of 23 warriors wants them not only to live through whatever fighting they must face, but also to have lives worth living after the fighting is done.

The warrior's code is the shield that guards our warriors' humanity. Without it, they are no good to themselves or to those with whom and for whom they fight. Without it, they will find no way back from war. I have dear friends—many of them former students and Naval Academy colleagues—who are currently in harm's way. They are our pilots, surface-warfare officers, submariners, Navy SEALs, and Marines. Come May, more of my current students will join them. When and if they go into combat, I want them to be able to return from war intact in body and soul. I want all of them, every last one, to come back with their shields. 24

OUR CELEBRITIES, OURSELVES
Neal Gabler

It has been more than 40 years since the historian Daniel Boorstin, in a now famously clever turn of phrase, defined a celebrity as someone who is known for being well known. If he were writing about celebrity today, Boorstin might describe it less flippantly as one of America's most prominent cottage industries and one of television's fastest-growing genres—one in which spent entertainers can find an afterlife by turning their daily existence into real-life situation comedy or tragedy. Anyone caring to stargaze can see *The Osbournes*, *The Anna Nicole Smith Show*, *Star Dates*, *The Surreal Life*, and the network prime-time celebrity interviews conducted by Barbara Walters, Diane Sawyer, Jane Pauley, and others. A reality series for VH1 capturing the life of the former star Liza Minnelli was derailed by a spat between the network and the principals. Meanwhile, cable networks continue to troll for celebrities eager to expose their lives to the public. Programs on the drawing boards include one in which over-the-hill stars spend the weekend with typical families, and another in which stars return to their hometowns and revisit their roots. 1

When Boorstin was writing in the early '60s, celebrity was one of those absurdities of contemporary culture—a large and ever-growing class of public figures for which there had been no precedent. Celebrities existed not to entertain, though they usually were entertainers, but rather to be publicized. Their talent, as Boorstin put it, was to grab the spotlight, whether or not they had done anything to deserve it. Now they have not only become an entertainment themselves, a kind of ambulatory show, but are also a cultural force with tremendous appeal, though exactly what that appeal is has been hard to determine. Most conventional analysts, from the popular historian Barbara Goldsmith to the pundit Andrew Sullivan, find celebrity a form of transport—a vicarious fantasy that lifts audiences out of the daily grind. Others, like Joshua Gamson in *Claims to Fame: Celebrity in Contemporary America*, see celebrity-watching as a ritual of empowerment through deconstruction. The audience doesn't seek to be elevated; it seeks to bring the celebrities back to earth. Still others, notably the rulers of the media, attribute the rapid rise of 2 celebrity to mundane financial considerations, like the cheapness of programming real-life celebrities as opposed to fictional stories, and to the power of celebrities to sell magazines and tabloids by appearing on the cover.

There is no doubt some truth to each of those explanations—particularly the last one—but none of them fully expresses the range and power of celebrity in contemporary America, or its rampant march through the culture. None really gets to the root of the matter. To do that, one may have to think of celebrity in an entirely new way—not as a status that is conferred by publicity, but as a narrative form, written in the medium of life, that is similar to narratives in movies, novels, and television.

The only difference, really, is that since it is written in the medium of life, it requires another medium, be it television or print, to bridge the gap between the narrative lived and the narrative watched. In fact, celebrity narratives are so pervasive, with so many being generated, that they have subordinated other narratives and commandeered other media, until one could argue that life itself has become the dominant medium of the new century, and celebrity its most compelling product. Though purists will blanch at the thought, celebrity may even be the art of the age.

When you think of celebrity as a form of narrative art—the romances and divorces, the binges, the dysfunctions, the triumphs, the transgressions—you can immediately appreciate one of its primary appeals, which is the appeal of any good story. Boorstin was wrong: Celebrities aren't known for being well known. They are known for living out real-life melodramas, which is why anyone from Elizabeth Taylor to Joey Buttafuoco can be a celebrity. All one needs is a good story and a medium in which to retail it, and the media, always in desperate need of a story, are only too happy to oblige. And so we get the saga of Ozzy Osbourne, one-time Goth-rock star now stumbling through life as an addled dad to his own teenagers, or Whitney Houston insisting that she isn't addicted to drugs even as she crumbles before our eyes, or Mariah Carey telling us how she has rebounded from a nervous breakdown (she was really just exhausted) and a series of career disasters.

Of course, conventional narratives can provide equally riveting tales, but celebrity has advantages over fiction, not the least of which is novelty. Traditional narrative forms are so familiar to us now, especially with the proliferation of television programs and the staggering number of books published—well over 100,000 each year—that they have become exhausted, attenuated, predictable. We feel as if we've seen it all before. Celebrity is an antidote to that sense of exhaustion. Though celebrity narratives themselves have certain conventions—already, the idea of a famous eccentric displaced into normal life, which *The Osbournes* introduced a year ago, has been stolen by Anna Nicole Smith—they also have a *frisson* that so-called imaginative narratives lack.

3

4

5

6

Part of that *frisson* is the intensification of one of the staples of any form of story-   7
telling: suspense. Readers or viewers always want to know what's going to happen
next, and there are some readers for whom that tension is so excruciating that
they race to the end of the book for the outcome so that they can then read comfortably and without anxiety. Celebrity, playing out in real time, obviously has suspense, since there is no author to imagine the finish, only life itself to devise the next
scene. One never knows what will happen. Who knew that Sharon Osbourne
would be diagnosed with cancer? Who knew that Michael Jackson would dangle
his infant son from a hotel balcony, or that his nose would erode into a nub after
multiple plastic surgeries? Who knew whether Winona Ryder would be convicted
or acquitted of her shoplifting charges, or what the sentence would be? Who knows
whether Jennifer Lopez and Ben Affleck will be wed or whether something will
happen to spoil their idyll? No one knows. The scenes just keep unspooling, and
we wait, like Dickens's nineteenth-century readers eagerly snatching the next installment of his new novel, or like the moviegoers in the '30s watching the weekly
chapters of a serial—only it is not just the *what* that we anticipate, it is the *when*
or even the *if*. Fictional narratives have closure. They end, and the characters are
frozen in time. Celebrity narratives resist closure. They go on and on and on.

Celebrity has another advantage over conventional narratives. All narratives de-   8
pend on our emotional connection to the material—not only on our anticipation
of what will happen, but also on our caring about what happens. In the case of fictional tales, we must, in the timeworn phrase, suspend our disbelief, because we
know that what we are watching or reading is not real, although to be conscious
of the unreality would seriously undermine, if not destroy, our sense of engagement. We must believe that these are not fictional creations but people, and that
there is something at stake in the outcome of their story. That is one reason Henry
James insisted on "felt life" as his aesthetic standard.

Great works still compel us to suspend our disbelief and convince us that we   9
are watching life itself, but that is a harder and harder sell at a time when many
Americans, particularly younger ones, are aware of narrative manipulations and regard all imaginative fiction as counterfeit. Celebrity, on the other hand, doesn't require one to suspend disbelief, because it is real, or at least purports to be. The
stakes are real, too. Sharon Osbourne may eventually die of her cancer. Kelly Clark-
son would get a record contract if she won *American Idol*. The various celebrities
who beam at us from the cover of *People* each week will find romance or will re-
cover or will succeed—or they won't. Either way, something is at stake. There are
consequences that we will be able to see down the road. It matters.

Finally, there is the appeal of voyeurism that is heightened precisely because   10
celebrity is unavoidably contrasted with the fictional narratives in which most
celebrities find themselves. For many fans today, the roles that celebrities play, both
on television and in movies, and the roles they assume as they project themselves
in the media, operate as a kind of disguise. They obscure the real person. Celebrity

purportedly allows us to peek behind the disguise and see the real person in real joy or torment. This has resulted in an odd reversal that further underscores the power of celebrity. There was a time when celebrities, with a few exceptions, interested us only because of the work they did; their movies, books, albums, TV shows piqued our curiosity. We wanted to know more. But the ratio of interest in the work to interest in the personalities within the work has changed. Now the work they do serves as a curtain that celebrity draws, but since celebrities almost always have a larger appeal than that work—more people certainly know about the Osbournes than buy Ozzy's albums, just as more people are following the exploits of J. Lo and Ben Affleck than watch their movies—the work is almost an excuse for the celebrity. In effect, you need a curtain so that you can reveal what is behind it. Celebrity, then, is the real narrative—the real achievement.

After the terrible events of 9/11, some predicted that the days of celebrity ob-   11
session were over, and that Americans would prefer the comforts of closure to the roilings of reality. It hasn't turned out that way. If anything, 9/11 itself delivered a narrative of such extraordinary impact that it was impossible for fictional narratives to equal or approximate it, and it may even have created a new aesthetic divide—not between good stories and formulaic ones, but between real stories and imagined ones. In that context, celebrity, for all its seeming triviality and irrelevance, survives and thrives because it still has the mark of authenticity.

That element of authenticity is critical in understanding the public's attraction not   12
only to the text of celebrity, but also to its subtext, without which celebrity would just be a bundle of melodramatic, albeit real, stories. The deeper appeal of these narratives is that they address one of the central tensions in contemporary America: the tension between artifice and authenticity, between the image and the reality.

The celebrity narrative is especially well suited to reify that issue. One is likely   13
to think of celebrities as creatures of artifice. They wear makeup and costumes (even when they are not before the cameras, the hottest ones are dressed by designers), they rely on public-relations stunts and gossip to promote themselves, and they play roles and affect attitudes. That isn't just the public's view. Celebrities often think of themselves in the same way. Cary Grant was once quoted, perhaps apocryphally, as having said that it wasn't easy being Cary Grant. Presumably he meant that the persona was vastly different from the person who inhabited it, and that the latter was always having to work to become the former.

That idea—of a distance between the celebrity as public figure and the person   14
within the celebrity narrative—is, indeed, the basis for almost every celebrity narrative that features an entertainer, as opposed to narratives, like those of Joey Buttafuoco or John Wayne Bobbitt or Kato Kaelin, that create the celebrity in the first place, out of notoriety. As I wrote in *Life the Movie*, virtually every celebrity profile, be it in *People*, *Vanity Fair*, *The New Yorker*, or on *Entertainment Tonight* or *Access Hollywood*, focuses on the celebrity's battle to find himself or herself, to achieve some

genuineness, to understand what really constitutes happiness instead of settling for the Hollywood conception of happiness.

These stories are all chronicles of self-discovery. Now that she is rid of Tom Cruise, Nicole Kidman can find herself. Having broken up with her boyfriend, Justin Timberlake, Britney Spears is flailing about trying to find herself. Winona Ryder's shoplifting was a cry for help to enable her to find herself. Whitney Houston is now in a state of denial, but she will eventually have to find herself or perish. Lost in romance, drugs, abuse, failure, breakdowns—you name it—celebrities must fight through the layers of image to discover who they really are. Whether that is just more public-relations blather or not, those are the stories we read and see every day.

It is the same process that is charted on the new celebrity television shows. Ozzy Osbourne may be brain-fried and distracted, but his life, for all its oddities and even freakishness, is touchingly ordinary in its emotional groundedness. Ozzy has found himself in his family, which makes the program remarkably old-fashioned and life-affirming. Next to the F-word, the word most often used on the program is "love." Similarly, Anna Nicole Smith, the former *Playboy* centerfold now overweight and bovine and searching for love, may be a moron, but there is something attractive in her almost pathetic ordinariness beneath all her attempts at grandeur. Watching her and Ozzy and the minor stars from old sitcoms now looking for love on *Star Dates*, one is reminded not how different these celebrities are from us but how similar they are once they have recognized the supposed falsity of the celebrity way of life.

All of that may seem a very long way from the lives of those who read and watch the celebrity narrative—us. Not many Americans, after all, have had to struggle with the sorts of things, like romantic whirligigs, drug detoxification, and sudden career spirals, that beset celebrities. And yet in many respects, celebrity is just ordinary American life writ large and more intense. In an image-conscious society, where nearly everyone has access to the tools of self-invention and self-promotion—makeup, designer clothes, status symbols, and quirks of behavior, language, and attitude—people are forced to opt for a persona or else to find out who they really are. That is the modern condition. Each of us, to a greater or lesser degree, is fighting the same battle as the celebrities, which is why celebrity, for all its obvious entertainment value, resonates psychically in a way that few modern fictional narratives do. Celebrity doesn't transport us from the niggling problems of daily life. It amplifies and refines them in an exciting narrative context.

And so we keep watching as we might watch any soap opera, engaged by the melodrama, or any sitcom, amused by the comedy. We watch not because, as Boorstin wrote, we are too benumbed by artifice to recognize the difference between celebrities and people of real accomplishment who are more deserving of our attention. Rather we watch because we understand, intuitively or not, that these celebrities are enacting a kind of modern parable of identity, with all its ridiculousness and all its tragedy. We watch because in their celebrity—Ozzy's and Anna Nicole's and Whitney's and Winona's and J. Lo's and Mariah's and even Jacko's—we somehow manage to find ourselves.

AGAINST SCHOOL
John Taylor Gatto

I taught for thirty years in some of the worst schools in Manhattan, and in some   1
of the best, and during that time I became an expert in boredom. Boredom was
everywhere in my world, and if you asked the kids, as I often did, *why* they felt so
bored, they always gave the same answers: they said the work was stupid, that it
made no sense, that they already knew it. They said they wanted to be doing something real, not just sitting around. They said teachers didn't seem to know much
about their subjects and clearly weren't interested in learning more. And the kids
were right: their teachers were every bit as bored as they were.

Boredom is the common condition of schoolteachers, and anyone who has spent   2
time in a teachers' lounge can vouch for the low energy, the whining, the dispirited
attitudes, to be found there. When asked why *they* feel bored, the teachers tend to
blame the kids, as you might expect. Who wouldn't get bored teaching students who
are rude and interested only in grades? If even that. Of course, teachers are themselves products of the same twelve-year compulsory school programs that so thoroughly bore their students, and as school personnel they are trapped inside structures
even more rigid than those imposed upon the children. Who, then, is to blame?

We all are. My grandfather taught me that. One afternoon when I was seven I com-   3
plained to him of boredom, and he batted me hard on the head. He told me that I was
never to use that term in his presence again, that if I was bored it was my fault and
no one else's. The obligation to amuse and instruct myself was entirely my own,
and people who didn't know that were childish people, to be avoided if possible. Certainly not to be trusted. That episode cured me of boredom forever, and here and
there over the years I was able to pass on the lesson to some remarkable student.
For the most part, however, I found it futile to challenge the official notion that boredom and childishness were the natural state of affairs in the classroom. Often I had
to defy custom, and even bend the law, to help kids break out of this trap.

. . . By the time I finally retired in 1991, I had more than enough reason to think   4
of our schools—with their long-term, cell-block–style, forced confinement of both
students and teachers—as virtual factories of childishness. Yet I honestly could
not see *why* they had to be that way. My own experience had revealed to me what
many other teachers must learn along the way, too, yet keep to themselves for fear
of reprisal: if we wanted to we could easily and inexpensively jettison the old, stupid structures and help kids *take* an education rather than merely *receive* a schooling. We could encourage the best qualities of youthfulness—curiosity, adventure,
resilience, the capacity for surprising insight—simply by being more flexible about
time, texts, and tests, by introducing kids to truly competent adults, and by giving
each student what autonomy he or she needs in order to take a risk every now
and then.

But we don't do that. And the more I asked why not, and persisted in thinking   5
about the "problem" of schooling as an engineer might, the more I missed the point:

What if there is no "problem" with our schools? What if they are the way they are, so expensively flying in the face of common sense and long experience in how children learn things, not because they are doing something wrong but because they are doing something right? Is it possible that George W. Bush accidentally spoke the truth when he said we would "leave no child behind"? Could it be that our schools are designed to make sure not one of them ever really grows up?

Do we really need school? I don't mean education, just forced schooling: six classes a day, five days a week, nine months a year, for twelve years. Is this deadly routine really necessary? And if so, for what? Don't hide behind reading, writing, and arithmetic as a rationale, because 2 million happy homeschoolers have surely put that banal justification to rest. Even if they hadn't, a considerable number of well-known Americans never went through the twelve-year wringer our kids currently go through, and they turned out all right. George Washington, Benjamin Franklin, Thomas Jefferson, Abraham Lincoln? Someone taught them, to be sure, but they were not products of a school *system*, and not one of them was ever "graduated" from a secondary school. Throughout most of American history, kids generally didn't go to high school, yet the unschooled rose to be admirals, like Farragut; inventors, like Edison; captains of industry, like Carnegie and Rockefeller; writers, like Melville and Twain and Conrad; and even scholars, like Margaret Mead. In fact, until pretty recently people who reached the age of thirteen weren't looked upon as children at all. Ariel Durant, who co-wrote an enormous, and very good, multi-volume history of the world with her husband, Will, was happily married at fifteen, and who could reasonably claim that Ariel Durant was an uneducated person? Un-schooled, perhaps, but not uneducated.

We have been taught (that is, schooled) in this country to think of "success" as synonymous with, or at least dependent upon, "schooling," but historically that isn't true in either an intellectual or a financial sense. And plenty of people throughout the world today find a way to educate themselves without resorting to a system of compulsory secondary schools that all too often resemble prisons. Why, then, do Americans confuse education with just such a system? What exactly is the purpose of our public schools?

Mass schooling of a compulsory nature really got its teeth into the United States between 1905 and 1915, though it was conceived of much earlier and pushed for throughout most of the nineteenth century. The reason given for this enormous upheaval of family life and cultural traditions was, roughly speaking, threefold:

1. To make good people.
2. To make good citizens.
3. To make each person his or her personal best.

These goals are still trotted out today on a regular basis, and most of us accept them in one form or another as a decent definition of public education's mission, however short schools actually fall in achieving them. But we are dead wrong. Compounding our error is the fact that the national literature holds numerous and surprisingly consistent statements of compulsory schooling's true purpose. We have, for example, the great H. L. Mencken, who wrote in *The American Mercury* for April 1924 that the aim of public education is not

> to fill the young of the species with knowledge and awaken their intelligence. . . . Nothing could be further from the truth. The aim . . . is simply to reduce as many individuals as possible to the same safe level, to breed and train a standardized citizenry, to put down dissent and originality. That is its aim in the United States . . . and that is its aim everywhere else.

. . . It was from James Bryant Conant—president of Harvard for twenty years, WWI poison-gas specialist, WWII executive on the atomic-bomb project, high commissioner of the American zone in Germany after WWII, and truly one of the most influential figures of the twentieth century—that I first got wind of the real purposes of American schooling. Without Conant, we would probably not have the same style and degree of standardized testing that we enjoy today, nor would we be blessed with gargantuan high schools that warehouse 2,000 to 4,000 students at a time, like the famous Columbine High in Littleton, Colorado. Shortly after I retired from teaching I picked up Conant's 1959 book-length essay, *The Child, the Parent and the State*, and was more than a little intrigued to see him mention in passing that the modern schools we attend were the result of a "revolution" engineered between 1905 and 1930. A revolution? He declines to elaborate, but he does direct the curious and the uninformed to Alexander Inglis's 1918 book, *Principles of Secondary Education*, in which "one saw this revolution through the eyes of a revolutionary." 10

Inglis, for whom a lecture in education at Harvard is named, makes it perfectly clear that compulsory schooling on this continent was intended to be just what it had been for Prussia in the 1820s: a fifth column into the burgeoning democratic movement that threatened to give the peasants and the proletarians a voice at the bargaining table. Modern, industrialized, compulsory schooling was to make a sort of surgical incision into the prospective unity of these underclasses. Divide children by subject, by age-grading, by constant rankings on tests, and by many other more subtle means, and it was unlikely that the ignorant mass of mankind, separated in childhood, would ever re-integrate into a dangerous whole. 11

Inglis breaks down the purpose—the *actual* purpose—of modern schooling into six basic functions, any one of which is enough to curl the hair of those innocent enough to believe the three traditional goals listed earlier: 12

1. The *adjustive* or *adaptive* function. Schools are to establish fixed habits of re-action to authority. This, of course, precludes critical judgment completely. It also pretty much destroys the idea that useful or interesting material should be taught, because you can't test for *reflexive* obedience until you know whether you can make kids learn, and do, foolish and boring things. 13

2. The *integrating* function. This might well be called "the conformity function," because its intention is to make children as alike as possible. People who conform 14

are predictable, and this is of great use to those who wish to harness and manipulate a large labor force.

3. The *diagnostic* and *directive* function. School is meant to determine each student's proper social role. This is done by logging evidence mathematically and anecdotally on cumulative records. As in "your permanent record." Yes, you do have one. 15

4. The *differentiating* function. Once their social role has been "diagnosed," children are to be sorted by role and trained only so far as their destination in the social machine merits—and not one step further. So much for making kids their personal best. 16

5. The *selective* function. This refers not to human choice at all but to Darwin's theory of natural selection as applied to what he called "the favored races." In short, the idea is to help things along by consciously attempting to improve the breeding stock. Schools are meant to tag the unfit—with poor grades, remedial placement, and other punishments—clearly enough that their peers will accept them as inferior and effectively bar them from the reproductive sweepstakes. That's what all those little humiliations from first grade onward were intended to do: wash the dirt down the drain. 17

6. The *propaedeutic* function. The societal system implied by these rules will require an elite group of caretakers. To that end, a small fraction of the kids will quietly be taught how to manage this continuing project, how to watch over and control a population deliberately dumbed down and de-clawed in order that government might proceed unchallenged and corporations might never want for obedient labor. . . . 18

There you have it. Now you know. We don't need Karl Marx's conception of a grand warfare between the classes to see that it is in the interest of complex management, economic or political, to dumb people down, to demoralize them, to divide them from one another, and to discard them if they don't conform. Class may frame the proposition, as when Woodrow Wilson, then president of Princeton University, said the following to the New York City School Teachers Association in 1909: "We want one class of persons to have a liberal education, and we want another class of persons, a very much larger class, of necessity, in every society, to forgo the privileges of a liberal education and fit themselves to perform specific difficult manual tasks." But the motives behind the disgusting decisions that bring about these ends need not be class-based at all. They can stem purely from fear, or from the by now familiar belief that "efficiency" is the paramount virtue, rather than love, liberty, laughter, or hope. Above all, they can stem from simple greed. 19

There were vast fortunes to be made, after all, in an economy based on mass production and organized to favor the large corporation rather than the small business or the family farm. But mass production required mass consumption, and at the turn of the twentieth century most Americans considered it both unnatural and unwise to buy things they didn't actually need. Mandatory schooling was a godsend on that count. School didn't have to train kids in any direct sense to think 20 they should consume nonstop, because it did something even better: it encouraged them not to think at all. And that left them sitting ducks for another great invention of the modern era—marketing.

Now, you needn't have studied marketing to know that there are two groups of people who can always be convinced to consume more than they need to: addicts and children. School has done a pretty good job of turning our children into addicts, but it has done a spectacular job of turning our children into children. Again, this is no accident. Theorists from Plato to Rousseau to our own Dr. Inglis knew that if children could be cloistered with other children, stripped of responsibility and independence, encouraged to develop only the trivializing emotions of greed, envy, jealousy, and fear, they would grow older but never truly grow up. In the 1934 edition of his once well-known book *Public Education in the United States*, Ellwood P. Cubberley detailed and praised the way the strategy of successive school enlargements had extended childhood by two to six years, and forced schooling was at that point still quite new. This same Cubberley—who was dean of Stanford's School of Education, a textbook editor at Houghton Mifflin, and Conant's friend and correspondent at Harvard—had written the following in the 1922 edition of his book *Public School Administration*: "Our schools are . . . factories in which the raw products (children) are to be shaped and fashioned. . . . And it is the business of the school to build its pupils according to the specifications laid down."   21

It's perfectly obvious from our society today what those specifications were. Maturity has by now been banished from nearly every aspect of our lives. Easy divorce laws have removed the need to work at relationships; easy credit has removed the need for fiscal self-control; easy entertainment has removed the need to learn to entertain oneself; easy answers have removed the need to ask questions. We have become a nation of children, happy to surrender our judgments and our wills to political exhortations and commercial blandishments that would insult actual adults. We buy televisions, and then we buy the things we see on the television. We buy computers, and then we buy the things we see on the computer. We buy $150 sneakers whether we need them or not, and when they fall apart too soon we buy another pair. We drive SUVs and believe the lie that they constitute a kind of life insurance, even when we're upside-down in them. And, worst of all, we don't bat an eye when Ari Fleischer tells us to "be careful what you say," even if we remember having been told somewhere back in school that America is the land of the free. We simply buy that one too. Our schooling, as intended, has seen to it.   22

Now for the good news. Once you understand the logic behind modern schooling, its tricks and traps are fairly easy to avoid. School trains children to be employees and consumers; teach your own to be leaders and adventurers. School trains children to obey reflexively; teach your own to think critically and independently. Well-schooled kids have a low threshold for boredom; help your own to develop an inner life so that they'll never be bored. Urge them to take on the   23 serious material, the *grown-up* material, in history, literature, philosophy, music, art, economics, theology—all the stuff schoolteachers know well enough to avoid. Challenge your kids with plenty of solitude so that they can learn to enjoy their own company, to conduct inner dialogues. Well-schooled people are conditioned to dread being alone, and they seek constant companionship through the TV, the computer, the cell phone, and through shallow friendships quickly acquired and quickly abandoned. Your children should have a more meaningful life, and they can.

First, though, we must wake up to what our schools really are: laboratories of   24
experimentation on young minds, drill centers for the habits and attitudes that corporate society demands. Mandatory education serves children only incidentally; its real purpose is to turn them into servants. Don't let your own have their childhoods extended, not even for a day. If David Farragut could take command of a captured British warship as a preteen, if Thomas Edison could publish a broadsheet at the age of twelve, if Ben Franklin could apprentice himself to a printer at the same age (then put himself through a course of study that would choke a Yale senior today), there's no telling what your own kids could do. After a long life, and thirty years in the public school trenches, I've concluded that genius is as common as dirt. We suppress our genius only because we haven't yet figured out how to manage a population of educated men and women. The solution, I think, is simple and glorious. Let them manage themselves.

▪ 3 ▪
Quoting Sources

I hate quotations. Tell me what you know.

Ralph Waldo Emerson (1849)

By necessity, by proclivity, and by delight, we all quote.

Ralph Waldo Emerson (1876)

Like Emerson in 1849, most writers hope to rely entirely on what they know and to express their knowledge in their own words. But, as Emerson realized later, we rarely write about ideas that no one has ever explored. Someone has usually gone part of the way before, so why not build on that person's discoveries?

To do so, you will need a working knowledge of another method of presenting a source's ideas to your readers: *quotation.*

REASONS FOR QUOTING

In academic writing, presenting the words of another writer through quotation is the most basic way to support your own ideas. Quotation enables you to give credit to your sources for both borrowed ideas and borrowed words.

- *Correct quotation* tells your reader that you respect your sources, that you know how to distinguish between your own work and theirs, and that you will not *plagiarize*—make unacknowledged use of another writer's words and ideas.

- *Appropriate quotation* tells your reader that you know when to quote and that you are not allowing your sources' words to dominate your writing.

Experienced writers use quotation marks only when they think it essential to present the source's exact words.

Reasons to Use Quotation

1. To support a point
2. To preserve vivid or technical language
3. To comment on the quotation
4. To distance yourself from the quotation

---

1. Quoting for Support

You will most often refer to another writer's work as evidence to support one of your own points. To ensure that the evidence retains its full meaning and impact, you may retain the author's original language, instead of putting the sentences in your own words. Very often, quoted material appears in an essay as an *appeal to authority*; the source being quoted is important enough or familiar enough with the subject (as in an eyewitness account) to make the original words worth quoting. For example, the only quotation in a *New York Times* article describing political and economic chaos in Bolivia presents the opinion of a government official:

> Even the Government acknowledges its shaky position. "The polity is unstable, capricious and chaotic," Adolfo Linares Arraya, Minister of Planning and Coordination, said. "The predominance of crisis situations has made the future unforeseeable."

The minister's words in themselves seem vague and glib, and therefore not especially quotable. But his position as representative of the government makes the minister's exact words necessary evidence for the reporter's presentation of the Bolivian crisis.

2. Quoting Vivid or Technical Language

The wording of the source material may be so ingenious that the point will be lost if you express it in your own words. *You will want to quote a sentence that is very compact or that relies on a striking image to make its point.* For example, here is a paragraph from a review of a book about Vietnamese history:

> Not many nations have had such a history of scrapping: against Mongols and Chinese seeking to dominate them from the north, and to the south against weaker and more innocent peoples who stood in the way of the Vietnamese march to the rich Mekong Delta and the underpopulated land of Cambodia. Mr. Hodgkin [the

author] quotes from a poem by a medieval Vietnamese hero: "By its tradition of defending the country / the army is so powerful it can swallow the evening star."

The quotation adds authentic evidence to the reviewer's discussion and provides a memorable image for the reader.

It is also important to retain the precise terminology of a *technical or legal document*. Changing one word of the text can significantly change its meaning. Here is a sentence from the final paragraph of a Supreme Court decision upholding the civil rights of three tenth-graders who had been suspended by school officials for "spiking" the punch at a meeting of an extracurricular club:

> We hold that a school board member is not immune from liability for damages if he knew or reasonably should have known that the action he took within his sphere of official responsibility would violate the constitutional rights of the student affected, or if he took the action with the malicious intention to cause a deprivation of constitutional rights or other injury to the student.

Virtually every word of the sentence has potential impact on the way this decision will be interpreted in subsequent legal suits. Note, for example, the distinction between "knew" and "reasonably should have known" and the way in which "intention" is qualified by "malicious."

3. Quoting Another Writer to Comment on the Quotation

In your essay, you may want to analyze or comment on a statement made by another writer. Your readers should have that writer's exact words in front of them if they are to get the full benefit of your commentary; *you have to quote it in order to talk about it*. Thus, when a writer reviewing Philip Norman's biography of the Beatles wants to criticize the biographer's style, he must supply a sample quotation so that his readers can make up their own minds.

> Worst of all is the overwritten prologue, about John Lennon's death and its impact in Liverpool: "The ruined imperial city, its abandoned river, its tormented suburban plain, knew an anguish greater than the recession and unemployment which have laid Merseyside waste under bombardments more deadly than Hitler's blitz." A moment's thought should have made Norman and his publishers realize that this sort of thing, dashed off in the heat of the moment, would quickly come to seem very embarrassing indeed.

4. Quoting to Gain Distance

Authors generally use quotation to distinguish between themselves and other authors they are citing. Sometimes, however, you want to distance yourself from your own choice of language. For example, you may use quotation marks to indicate that a word or phrase is not in common or standard use. A phrase may be *obsolete*, no longer in current usage:

> Many "flower children" gathered at the rock festivals of the late 1960s.

Or a phrase may be *slang*, not yet having been absorbed into standard English:

> She tried to "cop out" of doing her share of the work.

In effect, you want to use the phrase and at the same time "cover" yourself by signaling your awareness that the phrase is not quite right: you are distancing yourself from your own vocabulary. On the whole, it is better to take full responsibility for your choice of words and to avoid using slang or obsolete vocabulary, with or without quotation marks.

You can achieve a different kind of distance when you use quotation marks to suggest *irony*:

> The actor was joined by his "constant companion."

The quoted phrase is a familiar *euphemism*, a bland expression substituted for a more blunt term. Again, by placing it in quotation marks, the author is both calling attention to and distancing him- or herself from the euphemism.

Quotation marks also serve as a means of *disassociation* for journalists who wish to avoid taking sides on an issue or making editorial comments.

> A fire that roared through a 120-year-old hotel and took at least 11 lives was the work of a "sick arsonist," the county coroner said today. Robert Jennings, the Wayne County coroner, said that he had told county officials that the building was a "fire trap."

The author of this article did not want the responsibility of attributing the fire to a "sick arsonist" or labeling the building a "fire trap"—at any rate, not until the findings of an investigation or a trial make the terminology unquestionably true. Thus, he is careful not only to use quotation marks around certain phrases, but also to cite the precise source of the statement.

USING QUOTATIONS

Quoting requires two actions:

1. By *inserting quotation marks*, you indicate that you are borrowing certain words, as well as certain ideas, that appear in your writing.
2. By *inserting a citation* containing the source's name, you give credit for both ideas and words to the author.

Citation	Quotation
Theodore Roosevelt said,	"Speak softly and carry a big stick; you will go far."

Direct Quotation: Separating Quotations from Your Own Writing

The simplest way to quote is to combine the citation (written by you) with the words you are quoting (exactly as they were said or written by your source). This method of quotation joins together two separate statements, with punctuation—comma or colon—bridging the gap and a capital letter beginning the quoted sentence.

St. Paul declared, "It is better to marry than to burn."

In his first epistle to the Corinthians, St. Paul commented on lust: "It is better to marry than to burn."

In both these forms of direct quotation, the quoted words are not fully integrated into the grammatical structure of your sentence. In addition to the quotation marks, the *comma or colon* and the *capital letter* at the beginning of the quoted sentence separate the two parts, making it clear that two voices appear in the sentence: yours and your source's. In general, you should choose this kind of direct quotation when you want to differentiate between yourself and the quoted words, perhaps because you disagree with them.

The *colon* is used less frequently than the comma. It usually follows a clause that can stand alone as a complete sentence. As such, the colon separates a complete idea of your own from a complementary or supporting idea taken from your source.

Direct Quotation: Integrating Quotations into Your Sentences

In an alternative kind of direct quotation, *only the quotation marks indicate that you are using someone else's words.*

St. Paul declared that "it is better to marry than to burn."

Alvin Toffler defined future shock as "the shattering stress and disorientation that we induce in individuals by subjecting them to too much change in too short a time."

There is no other signal for the reader that separates citation from quotation—no comma or colon, no capital letter. The first word of the quoted material, in this second type of direct quotation, is *not* capitalized, even if it was capitalized in the source.

Original

Beware of all enterprises that require new clothes.

HENRY DAVID THOREAU

Quotation

Thoreau warned his readers to "beware of all enterprises that require new clothes."

The effect is very smooth, and the reader's attention is not distracted from the flow of words.

The Two Kinds of Direct Quotation

Separated

- Comma or colon and quotation marks separate citation and quotation.
- The first letter of the quotation is capitalized.
- You are distinguishing between your ideas and those of your source.

Integrated

- No punctuation but quotation marks separates citation and quotation.
- The first letter of the quotation is not capitalized.
- You are integrating your ideas with those of your source.

Because integrating the quotation tends to blur the distinction between writer and source, you must be careful to avoid confusion. Look, for example, at the various ways of quoting this first-person sentence, which was originally spoken by a motorist: "I hate all pedestrians."

Separated Quotation

The motorist said, "I hate all pedestrians."

Integrated Quotation

The motorist said that "I hate all pedestrians."

The first method, quoting with separation by punctuation, requires no alteration in the original sentence. But in the second version, quoting with integration, the original wording does not quite fit.

- The first-person "I" conflicts with the third-person "motorist" (the reader may wonder who "I" is—the motorist or the writer!).
- The present-tense "hate" conflicts with the past-tense "said," so "hate" must be turned into "hated."

But once the person [I] and the tense [hate] of the original statement have been altered for clarity and consistency, only two words—"all pedestrians"—are actually being quoted:

Direct Quotation

The motorist said that she hated "all pedestrians."

You may even prefer not to put quotation marks around the remaining two words taken from the original source. If so, you are not quoting anything directly; you are using *indirect quotation*. In indirect quotation, you report rather than quote what has been said.

Indirect Quotation

The motorist said that she hated all pedestrians.

However, the absence of quotation marks in the indirect quotation could be confusing. If you were collecting evidence for a legal suit, quotation marks would indicate that the motorist was responsible for the precise wording. Therefore, direct quotation, separated from the citation by punctuation, is probably the most appropriate method of presenting the motorist's opinion of pedestrians.

> **As a rule, the writer has the obligation to insert quotation marks when using a source's exact words, whether written or oral.**

Direct Quotation

Robert Ingersoll condemned those who deny others their civil liberties: "I am the inferior of any man whose rights I trample underfoot."

Indirect Quotation

Robert Ingersoll proclaimed that he was the inferior of any man whose rights he trampled underfoot.

The indirect quotation does not indicate exactly who wrote this sentence. Even if you change "I" to "he" and the present to the past tense, you are still not using your own words; the basic phrasing of the sentence remains Ingersoll's. *To imply, as this indirect quotation could, that the wording is yours, not Ingersoll's, would be plagiarism.*

For this reason, writers should use indirect quotation with great care. If one of the two forms of direct quotation does not seem appropriate, you should invent your own wording—called *paraphrase*—to express the source's original statement.

The Historical Present Tense

Certain ideas and statements remain true long after their creators have died. By convention, or general agreement, writers often refer to these statements in the present tense.

> Shakespeare <u>states</u>, "This above all: to thine own self be true."

When you are devoting part of your own essay to a "discussion" with another writer, you may prefer to conduct the discussion on a common ground of time and use the present tense, called the *historical present*. The historical present is also useful to place a variety of different sources on equal terms, especially when they are from different eras. In the following example, the introductory verbs, all in the present tense, are underlined:

> While Shelley <u>acknowledges</u> that poets are creators of language and music and art, he also <u>asserts</u> that they have a civic role: "They are the institutors of laws, and the founders of civil society, and the inventors of the arts of life." Writing one hundred years later, Benedetto Croce <u>affirms</u> Shelley's insistence upon the social and spiritual responsibilities of the poet. According to Croce, Shelley <u>sees</u> poetry "as the eternal source of all intellectual, moral, and civil vitality."

Finally, the historical present is almost always used when you refer to important documents (often written by a group of people, rather than a single author) that remain in force long after they were created. Obvious examples include the Constitution, the Declaration of Independence, the laws of Congress, Supreme Court decisions, the charter of your state government, and the bylaws governing your college or university.

> The Constitution <u>guarantees</u> that women—and, indeed, all citizens—shall have the vote in elections; Amendment XIX <u>states</u> that the right to vote "shall not be denied or abridged by the United States or by any State on account of sex."

Punctuating Direct Quotations

You have already learned about punctuating *the beginning of the quotation*:

1. In a separated direct quotation, the citation is followed by a comma or a colon.
2. In an integrated direct quotation, the citation is followed by no punctuation at all.

Some writers tend to forget this second point and include an unnecessary comma:

Incorrect Quotation

Ernest Hemingway believed that, "what is moral is what you feel good after and what is immoral is what you feel bad after."

Remember that *an integrated quotation should have no barriers between citation and quotation*:

Correct Quotation

Ernest Hemingway believed that "what is moral is what you feel good after and what is immoral is what you feel bad after."

In the integrated direct quotation, note that the first letter of the quotation is not capitalized.

There is no easy way of remembering the proper sequence of punctuation for *closing a quotation*. The procedure has been determined by conventional and arbitrary agreement, originally for the convenience of printers. Although other countries abide by different conventions, in the United States the following rules apply—and *there are no exceptions.*

1. All periods and commas are placed inside the terminal quotation marks.

It does not matter whether the period belongs to your sentence or to the quoted sentence: it goes *inside* the marks. This is the most important rule and the one most often ignored. Don't resort to ambiguous devices such as placing the marks directly over the period (".").

P. T. Barnum is reputed to have said that "there's a sucker born every minute."

P. T. Barnum is reputed to have said that "there's a sucker born every minute," and Barnum's circuses undertook to entertain each and every one.

Notice that, in the second example, the comma at the end of the quotation belongs to the framework sentence, not to the quotation itself; nevertheless, it goes *inside* the marks.

2. Semicolons, colons, and dashes are generally placed outside the terminal quotation marks.

They should be regarded as the punctuation for *your* sentence, and not for the quotation.

George Santayana wrote that "those who cannot remember the past are condemned to repeat it"; today, we are in danger of forgetting the lessons of history.

Occasionally, when a semicolon, colon, or (most likely) a dash appears at the end of the material to be quoted, you will decide to include the punctuation in the quotation; in that case, the punctuation should be placed inside the marks. In the following example, the dash appears in Lucretia Mott's original statement, so it is placed inside the quotation marks.

> Lucretia Mott argued urgently for women's rights: "Let woman then go on—not asking favors, but claiming as a right the removal of all hindrances to her elevation in the scale of being—" so that, as a result, she might "enter profitably into the active business of man."

3. Question marks and exclamation points are sometimes placed inside the quotation marks and sometimes placed outside.

- If the quotation is itself a question or an exclamation, the mark or point goes *inside* the quotation marks.
- If your own sentence is a question or an exclamation, the mark or point goes *outside* a quotation placed at the very end of your sentence.

> In 1864, General Sherman signaled the arrival of his reinforcements: "Hold the fort! I am coming!"

The exclamation is General Sherman's; the exclamation point goes inside the quotation.

> Can anyone in the 1980s agree with Dumas that "woman inspires us to great things and prevents us from achieving them"?

Dumas was *not* asking a question; the question mark goes at the very end of the sentence, after the quotation marks.

> Sigmund Freud's writings occasionally reveal a remarkable lack of insight: "The great question that has never been answered, and which I have not yet been able to answer despite my thirty years of research into the feminine soul, is: What does a woman want?"

Freud himself asked this famous question; the question mark goes inside the quotation.

> Freud was demonstrating remarkably little insight when he wrote, "What does a woman want?" citing his "thirty years of research into the feminine soul"!

The exclamation is the writer's, not Freud's; the exclamation point goes outside the quotation marks.

It is possible to construct a sentence that ends logically in two question marks (or exclamation points): one for the quotation and one for your own sentence. In such cases, you need include only one—and, by convention, it should be placed *inside* the quotation marks:

What did Freud mean when he asked, "What does a woman want?"

These rules about punctuation apply only to the quotation of complete sentences or reasonably long phrases. Whether it is a quotation or an obsolete, slang, or ironic reference, a single word or a brief phrase should be fully integrated into your sentence, without being preceded or followed by commas.

Winston Churchill's reference to "blood, sweat and tears" rallied the English to prepare for war.

Be careful not to quote words or phrases excessively. Using more than one quotation, however brief, in a sentence or quoting phrase after phrase suggests that you cannot express your thoughts in your own words.

Interrupting Quotations

Sometimes you want to break up a long quotation or to vary the way you quote your sources by interrupting a quotation and placing the citation in the middle.

"I do not mind lying," wrote Samuel Butler, "but I hate inaccuracy."

Butler's statement is divided into two separate parts, and therefore you need to use *four* sets of quotation marks: two introductory and two terminal. The citation is joined to the quotation by a comma on either side. There are two danger points:

- If you forget to use the marks at the beginning of the second half of the quotation, you are failing to distinguish your words from Butler's.

- You must also put the first comma *inside* the terminal quotation marks (because commas *always* go inside the terminal quotation marks) and put the comma that concludes the citation *before* the quotation marks (because it is *your* comma, not Butler's).

Quoting inside a Quotation

Sometimes a statement that you want to quote already contains a quotation. In that case, you must use two sets of quotation marks, double and single, to help your reader to distinguish between the two separate sources.

- *Single quotation marks* are used for the words already quoted by your source (and this is the *only* time when it is appropriate to use single quotation marks).

- *Double quotation marks* are used around the words that you are quoting.

  Goethe at times expressed a notable lack of self-confidence: "'Know thyself?' If I knew myself, I'd run away."

  At the beginning of World War I, Winston Churchill observed that "the maxim of the British people is 'Business as usual.'"

The same single/double procedure is used even when there is no author's name to be cited.

  A Yiddish proverb states that "'for example' is not proof."

EXERCISE 8: QUOTING CORRECTLY

A. Correct the errors in the following sentences:

1. "The man who views the world at fifty the same as he did at twenty," remarked the boxer Mahommad Ali, has wasted thirty years of his life

2. Do you agree with Jerry Seinfeld that: "A bookstore is one of the only pieces of evidence we have that people are still thinking?"

3. Three may keep a secret" Benjamin Franklin cynically remarked, "if two of them are dead".

4. "A fool learns from his experience, said Otto von Bismarck". The German Chancellor tells us "A wise person learns from the experience of others."

5. The American historian Barbara Tuchman wrote about the ineptitude of generals, arguing that: "The power to command frequently causes failure to think".

6. Ralph Waldo Emerson warned his readers that, "Life is not so short but that there is always time enough for courtesy.

7. Donald Trump offered this advice—"there's the old story about the boxer after a fight who said: 'that wasn't so tough." What was really tough was my father hitting me on the head with a hammer."

8. Before the Revolutionary War, Patrick Henry made a passionate speech, "is life so dear or peace so sweet, as to be purchased at the price of chains and slavery"? "Forbid it, Almighty God"! I know not what course others may take, but as for me, give me liberty or give me death."!

B. Use quotations from the following group as directed:

- Choose one quotation and write a sentence that introduces a direct quotation with separation.

- Choose a second quotation and write a sentence that introduces a direct quotation with integration.
- Choose a third quotation and write a sentence that interrupts a quotation with a citation in the middle.
  1. I've seen my own men commit atrocities, and should expect to see it again. You can't stimulate and let loose the animal in man and then expect to be able to cage it up again at a moment's notice. (A British colonel during World War I)
  2. I'm basically an optimist in life but this doesn't prevent me from deducing as a scientist that we are probably doomed. (Vladimir Chaloupka, physicist, University of Washington, regarding mankind's potential misuse of technology)
  3. Like dear St. Francis of Assisi I am wedded to poverty, but in my case the marriage is not a success. (Oscar Wilde)
  4. The reason so many people showed up at his funeral was because they wanted to make sure he was dead. (Samuel Goldwyn on L. B. Mayer)
  5. I feel sorry for people who don't drink. When they wake up in the morning, that's as good as they're going to feel all day. (Frank Sinatra)
  6. Money, it turned out, was exactly like sex, you thought of nothing else if you didn't have it and thought of other things if you did. (James Baldwin)
  7. There is no use whatever trying to help people who do not help themselves. You cannot push anyone up a ladder unless he be willing to climb himself. (Andrew Carnegie)
  8. You can't say civilization don't advance, however, for in every war they kill you in a new way. (Will Rogers)

QUOTING ACCURATELY

Quoting is not a collaboration in which you try to improve on your source's words. Don't make minor changes or carelessly leave words out, but faithfully transcribe the exact words, the exact spelling, and the exact punctuation that you find in the original.

Original

Those who corrupt the public mind are just as evil as those who steal from the public purse.

ADLAI STEVENSON

Inexact Quotation

Adlai Stevenson believed that "those who act against the public interest are just as evil as those who steal from the public purse."

Exact Quotation

Adlai Stevenson believed that "those who corrupt the public mind are just as evil as those who steal from the public purse."

Even if you notice an error (or what seems to be an error), you still must copy the original wording. For example, old-fashioned spelling should be retained, as well as regional or national dialect and spelling conventions:

One of Heywood's *Proverbes* tells us that "a new brome swepeth clean."

In one of his humorous stories, Colonel Davy Crockett predicted the reactions to his own death: "It war a great loss to the country and the world, and to ole Kaintuck in particklar. Thar were never known such a member of Congress as Crockett, and never will be agin. The painters and bears will miss him, for he never missed them."

If the material that you are quoting contains errors of syntax, punctuation, or spelling, you can use a conventional way to point out such errors and inform the reader that the mistake was made not by you, but by the source. The Latin word *sic* (meaning "thus") is placed in square brackets and inserted immediately after the error. The [*sic*] signals that the quotation was "thus" and that you, the writer, were aware of the error, which was not the result of your own carelessness in transcribing the quotation.

In the following example, [*sic*] calls attention to an error in subject-verb agreement:

Richard Farson points out that "increased understanding and concern has [*sic*] not been coupled with increased rights."

You may also want to use [*sic*] to indicate that the source used archaic spelling:

In describing Elizabeth Billington, an early nineteenth-century singer, W. Clark Russell observed that "her voice was powerful, and resembled the tone of a clarionet [*sic*]."

It would be tedious, however, to use [*sic*] to indicate each misspelling in the Davy Crockett quotation; in your essay about Crockett, you could, instead, explain his use of dialect as you discuss his life and writing.

TAILORING QUOTATIONS TO FIT YOUR WRITING

There are several ways to change quotations to fit the quoted material naturally into your own sentences. Like [*sic*], these devices are conventions, established by generally accepted agreement: *you cannot improvise; you must follow these rules.* Usually, the conventional rules require you to inform your reader that a change is being made. In other words, they make clear the distinction between your wording and the author's.

Changing Capital and Small Letters

The first way of altering quotations depends entirely on how and where the quotation fits into your sentence.

- When a quotation is *integrated* completely into your sentence (usually when your citation ends in "that"), the first letter of the quotation will be small, whether or not it is a capital in the original. (Two exceptions are the pronoun "I" and proper nouns, which are always capitalized.)
- When a quotation is *separated* from your sentence, and your citation ends in a comma or a colon, the first letter of the quotation will be a capital, whether or not it is a capital in the original.

Integrated Quotation

The poet Frost wrote that "good fences make good neighbors."

Separated Quotation

The poet Frost wrote, "Good fences make good neighbors."

As a rule, it is not necessary to indicate to your readers that you have altered the first letter of your quotation from small to capital or from capital to small.

Using Ellipses to Delete Words

It is permissible to delete words from a quotation, provided that you indicate to the reader that something has been omitted. Your condensed version is as accurate as the original; it is just shorter. But you must remember to insert the conventional symbol for deletion, *three spaced dots*, called an *ellipsis*. Once made aware by the three dots that your version omits part of the original, any reader who wants to see the omitted portion can consult the original source.

Original

It is not true that suffering ennobles the character; happiness does that sometimes, but suffering, for the most part, makes men petty and vindictive.

W. SOMERSET MAUGHAM

Quotation with Ellipsis

Maugham does not believe that "suffering ennobles the character; . . . suffering, for the most part, makes men petty and vindictive."

Notice that:

- The three dots are spaced equally, with one space between each dot and the next, and before the first and after the last.
- The dots *must* be three—not two or a dozen.
- The semicolon is retained, to provide terminal punctuation for the first part of the quotation.

If you wish to delete the end of a quotation, and the ellipsis coincides with the end of your sentence, you must use the three dots, plus a fourth to signify the sentence's end.

Quotation with Terminal Ellipsis

Maugham does not believe that "suffering ennobles the character; happiness does that sometimes. . . ."

Here, you'll note:

- There are four dots, three to indicate a deletion and a fourth to indicate the period at the end of the sentence.
- The first dot is placed immediately after the last letter.
- The sentence ends with quotation marks, as usual, with the marks placed *after* the dots, not before.

Three dots can also link two separate quotations from the same paragraph in your source; the ellipsis will indicate the deletion of one or more sentences. You may do this only if the two sentences that you are quoting are fairly near each other in the original. *An ellipsis cannot cover a gap of more than a few sentences.* When you use an ellipsis to bridge one or more sentences, use only *one* set of quotation marks. Your full quotation, with an ellipsis in the middle, is still continuous—a single quotation—even though there is a gap.

When an ellipsis is used following a quoted complete sentence, the period of the quoted sentence is retained so that a total of four dots is used, as in the following example.

Original

In one sense there is no death. The life of a soul on earth lasts beyond his departure. You will always feel that life touching yours, that voice speaking to you, that spirit looking out of other eyes, talking to you in the familiar things he touched, worked with, loved as familiar friends. He lives on in your life and in the lives of all others that knew him.

ANGELO PATRI

Quotation with Ellipsis

Patri states that "in one sense there is no death. The life of a soul on earth lasts beyond his departure. . . . He lives on in your life and in the lives of all others that knew him."

An ellipsis should be used to make a quotation fit more smoothly into your own sentence. It is especially convenient when you are working with a long passage that contains several separate points that you wish to quote. But ellipses should *not* be used to condense long, tedious quotations or to replace summary and paraphrase. If you want to quote only a brief extract from a lengthy passage, then simply quote that portion and ignore the surrounding material.

The meaning of the original quotation must always be exactly preserved, despite the deletion represented by the ellipsis.

Original

As long as there are sovereign nations possessing great power, war is inevitable.

ALBERT EINSTEIN

Inexact Quotation

Einstein believes that "as long as there are sovereign nations . . . war is inevitable."

It would not be accurate to suggest that Einstein believed in the inevitability of war merely because sovereign nations exist. To extract only a portion of this statement with ellipsis is to oversimplify and thus to falsify the evidence.

Using Brackets to Insert Words

Brackets have an opposite function: ellipsis signifies deletion; *brackets signify addition or alteration.* Brackets are not the same as parentheses. Parentheses would be confusing for this purpose, for the quotation might itself include a parenthetical statement, and the reader could not be sure whether the parentheses contained the author's insertion or yours. Instead, brackets, a relatively unusual form of punctuation, are used as a conventional way of informing the reader that material has been inserted. (You have already seen how to use brackets with [sic], which enables you to comment on the material that you are quoting.) You simply insert the information *inside* the quotation, placing it in square brackets.

The most common reason for using brackets is to clarify a vague word. You may, for example, choose to quote only the last portion of a passage, omitting an important antecedent:

Original

Man lives *by* habits, indeed, but what he lives *for* is thrills and excitement.

WILLIAM JAMES

Quotation with Brackets

William James argues that "what he [man] lives *for* is thrills and excitement."

William James argues that "what [man] lives *for* is thrills and excitement."

In the second example, the vague word "he" has been deleted entirely; the brackets themselves indicate that there has been a substitution, but the reader doesn't know what was originally there. For that reason, unless the presentation of both wordings seems very awkward, *it is better to follow the first example: quote the original and also provide the clarification in brackets.* This way, you will leave your reader in no doubt about your source's words.

Brackets can also be used to complete a thought that depends on an earlier sentence which you have left out of the quotation.

Original

A well-trained sensible family doctor is one of the most valuable assets in a community. . . . Few men live lives of more devoted self-sacrifice.

SIR WILLIAM OSLER

Quotation with Brackets

The great surgeon Sir William Osler had enormous respect for his less famous colleagues: "Few men live lives of more devoted self-sacrifice [than good family doctors]."

Here, the quotation marks are placed *after* the brackets, even though the quoted material ends after the word "self-sacrifice." The explanatory material inside the brackets is considered part of the quotation, even though it is not in the source's own words.

Reasons to Use Brackets

- To explain a vague word
- To replace a confusing phrase
- To suggest an antecedent
- To correct an error in a quotation
- To adjust a quotation to fit your own writing

You may put your own explanatory comments in brackets if they are brief. You might, for example, want to include an important *date* or *name* as essential background information. But whatever is inside the brackets should fit smoothly into the syntax of the quotation and should not distract the reader. For example, do not use brackets to argue with the author you are quoting. The following running dialogue with the entertainer Sophie Tucker is poorly conveyed through the use of brackets.

Confusing Use of Brackets

Sophie Tucker suggests that up to the age of eighteen "a girl needs good parents. [This is true for men, too.] From eighteen to thirty-five, she needs good looks. [Good looks aren't that essential anymore.] From thirty-five to fifty-five, she needs a good personality. [I disagree because personality is important at any age.] From fifty-five on, she needs good cash."

EXERCISE 9: USING ELLIPSES AND BRACKETS IN QUOTATIONS

  A. Choose one of the following quotations. By using *ellipses*, incorporate a portion of the quotation into a sentence of your own; remember to include the author's name in the citation.

  B. Choose a second quotation. Incorporate a portion of the quotation into another sentence of your own; insert words in *brackets* to clarify one or more of the quoted words.

    1. Politicians are the same all over: they promise to build a bridge even where there is no river. (Nikita Khrushchev)

    2. I have never taken any exercise, except sleeping and resting, and I never intend to take any. Exercise is loathsome. And it cannot be any benefit when you are tired, and I am always tired. (Mark Twain)

    3. Naturally the common people don't want war. But after all, it is the leaders of the country who determine policy, and it is always a simple matter to drag the people along, whether it is a democracy, or a fascist dictatorship, or a parliament or a communist dictatorship. All you have to do is to tell them that they are being attacked, and denounce the pacifists for lack of patriotism and exposing the country to danger. It works the same in any country. (Hermann Goering)

    4. An engaged woman is always more agreeable than a disengaged. She is satisfied with herself. Her cares are over, and she feels that she may exert all her powers of pleasing without suspicion. (Jane Austen)

    5. The whole aim of practical politics is to keep the populace alarmed (and hence clamorous to be led to safety) by menacing it with an endless series of hobgoblins, all of them imaginary. (H. L. Mencken)

6. Anyone who knows anything of history knows that great social changes are impossible without feminine upheaval. Social progress can be measured exactly by the social position of the fair sex, the ugly ones included. (Karl Marx)

WRITING CITATIONS

Citing the Author's Name

The first time that you refer to a source, use the author's full name—without Mr. or Miss, Mrs., or Ms.

First Reference

John Stuart Mill writes, "The opinion which it is attempted to suppress by authority may possibly be true."

After that, should you need to cite the author again, use the *last name only*. Conventional usage discourages casual and distracting references such as "John thinks," "JSM thinks," or "Mr. Mill thinks."

Second Reference

Mill continues to point out that "all silencing of discussion is an assumption of infallibility."

When you cite the author's name:

- At first reference, you may (and usually should) include the *title* of the work from which the quotation is taken:

  In *On Liberty*, John Stuart Mill writes . . .

- Avoid referring to the author twice in the same citation, once by name and once by pronoun.

  In John Stuart Mill's *On Liberty*, he writes . . .

- If there is a long break between references to the same author, or if the names of several other authors intervene, you may wish to repeat the full name and remind your reader of the earlier citation.

  In addition to his warnings about the dangers of majority rule, which were cited earlier in the discussion of public opinion, John Stuart Mill also expresses concern about "the functions of police; how far liberty may legitimately be invaded for the prevention of crime, or of accident."

- Finally, unless you genuinely do not know the author's name, use it! There is no point in being coy, even for the sake of variety:

> A famous man once made an ironic observation about child-rearing: "If you strike a child, take care that you strike it in anger. . . . A blow in cold blood neither can nor should be forgiven."

Your guessing game will only irritate readers who are not aware that this famous man was George Bernard Shaw.

Choosing the Introductory Verb

The introductory verb in the citation can tell your reader something about your reasons for presenting the quotation and its context in the work that you are quoting. Will you choose "J. S. Mill says," or "J. S. Mill writes," or "J. S. Mill thinks," or "J. S. Mill feels"? Those are the most common introductory verbs— so common that they have become boring! Whenever appropriate, select less stereotyped verbs. As the senses are not directly involved in writing, avoid "feels" entirely. And, unless you are quoting someone's spoken words, substitute a more accurate verb for "says."

Here are some introductory verbs:

argues	adds	concludes
establishes	explains	agrees
emphasizes	believes	insists
finds	continues	maintains
points out	declares	disagrees
notes	observes	states
suggests	proposes	compares

Of course, once you stop using the all-purpose "says" or "writes," you have to remember that verbs are not interchangeable and that you should choose the verb that best suits your purpose.

The citation should suggest the relationship between your own ideas (in your previous sentence) and the statement that you are about to quote.

You should examine the quotation before writing the citation to define the way in which the author makes a point:

- Is it being asserted forcefully?
  Use "argues" or "declares" or "insists."

- Is the statement being offered only as a possibility?
  Use "suggests" or "proposes" or "finds."

- Does the statement immediately follow a previous reference?
  Use "continues" or "adds."

For clarity, the introductory verb may be expanded:

X is aware that . . .
X stresses the opposite view
X provides one answer to the question
X makes the same point as Y
X erroneously assumes . . .

But make sure that the antecedent for the "view" or the "question" or the "point" can be found in the previous sentences of your essay.

Note that all the examples of introductory verbs are given in the *present tense*, which is the conventional way of introducing most quotations.

Varying Your Sentence Patterns

Even if you choose a different verb for each quotation, the combination of the author's name, introductory verb, and quotation can become repetitive and tiresome. One way to vary the citations is occasionally to place the name of the source in a less prominent position, tucked into the quotation instead of calling attention to it at the beginning.

1. You can interrupt the quotation by placing the citation in the middle.

"I made my mistakes," acknowledged Richard Nixon, "but in all my years of

public service, I have never profited from public service. I have earned

every cent."

The verb and the name may be placed in reverse order (instead of "Richard Nixon acknowledged") when the citation appears in the middle of the quotation. Remember to include two commas: one at the end of the first portion of the quotation (*inside* the quotation marks), one at the end of the citation.

One citation is quite enough. There is no need to inform your reader back to back, as in this repetitive example:

"The only prize much cared for by the powerful is power," states Oliver Wendell

Holmes. He concludes, "The prize of the general . . . is command."

2. You can avoid the monotonous "X says that . . ." pattern by phrasing the citation as a subordinate clause or phrase.

In Henry Kissinger's opinion, "Power is 'the great aphrodisiac.'"

As John F. Kennedy declares, "Mankind must put an end to war or war will put

an end to mankind."

3. You should avoid placing the citation after the quotation.

The author's name at the end may weaken the statement, especially if the citation is pretentiously or awkwardly phrased:

Awkward Citation

"I am the inferior of any man whose rights I trample underfoot," as quoted from the writings of Robert Ingersoll.

Clear Citation

A champion of civil liberties, Robert Ingersoll insisted, "I am the inferior of any man whose rights I trample underfoot."

Two rules should govern your choice of citation:

1. Don't be too fancy.
2. Be both precise and varied in your phrasing.

Presenting an Extended Quotation

Occasionally, you may have reason to present an extended quotation, a single extract from the same source that runs *more than four printed or typewritten lines.* For extended quotations, you must, by conventional rule, set off the quoted passage by *indenting the entire quotation on the left.*

- Introduce an extended quotation with a colon.
- Start each line of the quotation 10 spaces from the left-hand margin; stop each line at your normal right-hand margin.
- Some instructors prefer single-spacing within extended quotations; some prefer double-spacing. If possible, consult your instructor about the style appropriate for your course or discipline. If you are given no guidelines, use double-spacing.
- Omit quotation marks at the beginning and end of the quoted passage; the indented margin (and the introductory citation) will tell your readers that you are quoting.

Here is an example of an extended quotation:

Although he worked "hard as hell" all winter, Fitzgerald had difficulty finishing *The Great Gatsby.* On April 10, 1924, he wrote to Maxwell Perkins, his editor at Scribner's:

While I have every hope & plan of finishing my novel in June . . . even [if] it takes me 10 times that long I cannot let it go unless it has the very best I'm capable of in it or even as I feel sometimes better than I'm capable of. It is only in the last four months that I've realized how much I've—well, almost *deteriorated*. . . . What I'm trying to say is just that . . . at last, or at least for the first time in years, I'm doing the best I can.

DECIDING WHAT TO QUOTE

Use quotation sparingly! If quoting seems to be your primary purpose in writing, your reader will assume that you have nothing of your own to say. *Quote only when you have a clear reason for doing so*: when you are intending to analyze a quotation, when you are sure that its wording is essential to your argument, or when you simply cannot rephrase it in your own words.

Descriptions can be more difficult to rephrase than ideas. If your source states that the walls of Charles Dickens's parlor were painted sea-green and the furniture was made out of mahogany and covered with light-brown velvet, you may find it next to impossible to find an appropriate way of presenting these descriptive terms. Dark brown wood covered with fuzzy beige fabric? Is aquamarine the same as sea-green? Better to retain the source's original words, and without quotation marks if the words are common, everyday ones and used sparingly in a sentence that is clearly yours—not the source's—in structure and phrasing. If a man's eyes are described as dark blue, don't alter the phrasing to "piercing blue" or "ocean pools." If you place "dark blue" in a sentence that is otherwise your own writing, you may omit the quotation marks.

You will probably want to quote authorities in the field, especially *primary sources*: original works—often by historical figures—that other authors have commented on. (For an explanation of primary and secondary sources, see pp. 365–366.) Here, for example, Lewis Lapham, the editor of *Harper's*, is writing about America as a nation of immigrants, citing first an American president and then a notable explorer:

> We are a nation of parvenus, all bound to the hopes of tomorrow, ^(full citation of the source) or next week, or next year. John Quincy Adams put it plainly in a ^(context for the quotation) letter to a German correspondent in the 1820s who had written on behalf of several prospective émigrés to ask about the requirements for their success in the New World. "They must cast off the ^(citation in the middle) European skin, never to resume it," Adams said. "They must look forward to their posterity rather than backwards to their ancestors."
>
> We were always a mixed and piebald company, even on the seventeenth century colonial seaboard, and we accepted our racial or cultural differences as the odds that we were obliged to overcome

citation   or correct. When John Charles Fremont (a.k.a. The Pathfinder) first
descended into California from the East in 1843, he remarked on the
context   polyglot character of the expedition accompanying him south into
the San Joaquin Valley:

long extract/
no quotation
marks

ellipsis

> Our cavalcade made a strange and grotesque appearance, and it
> was impossible to avoid reflecting upon our position and com-
> position in this remote solitude . . . still forced on south by a
> desert on one hand and a mountain range on the other; guided
> by a civilized Indian, attended by two wild ones from the Sierra;
> a Chinook from the Columbia; and our own mixture of Ameri-
> can, French, German—all armed; four or five languages heard at
> once; above a hundred horses and mules, half-wild; American,
> Spanish and Indian dresses and equipments intermingled—such
> was our composition.

John Quincy Adams's statement is tightly phrased, with the first half of each
sentence balancing the second; Lapham would have found it difficult to express
it half as well in his own words. Fremont's description has the authenticity of
experience that is hard to capture using secondhand words.

Historical celebrities aren't the only ones who merit quotation. In this extract
from *A Consumer's Republic*, Lizabeth Cohen, who teaches American Studies at
Harvard University, describes the rise of the shopping center or, as she puts it,
the "feminization of public space." The marginal notes suggest why Cohen's
sources—many of them ordinary people from the 1950s and 1960s—are worth
quoting. Unlike Lapham's article, this is an academic work, based on extensive
research, and so the sources are documented with footnotes. The need for documentation is explained in greater detail at the end of this chapter and in Chapter 10.

The first shopping centers were planned with the female consumer in mind. As women patrons increasingly drove their own cars,
they found parking spaces at the shopping center designed wider
than usual for the express purpose of making it easier for them—
many of whom were new drivers—to park.[48] Women then entered

quotes suggest   a well-controlled "public" space that made them feel comfortable
unusual use of the   and safe, with activities planned to appeal especially to them and
word "public"   their children. From the color schemes, stroller ramps, baby-sitting

"wraps" = archaic   services, and special lockers for "ladies' wraps" to the reassuring
term   security guards and special events such as fashion shows, shopping

quotation from a   centers were created as female worlds. "I wouldn't know how to de-
key primary source   sign a center for a man," admitted Jack Follet of John Graham, Inc.,
a firm responsible for many shopping centers. And if New Jersey res-
ident Mrs. Bonnie Porrazzo was any indication, designers like Follet
knew what they were doing. Four or five times a week, she visited

Large, open, well-lighted departments with year-round air conditioning permit Bambergers to handle large crowds easily.

Do-it-yourself delivery is popular with suburban customers—and so is the "togetherness" of family shopping.

This page from Macy's annual report to shareholders the year its Garden State Plaza opened conveyed the prevalence of women shoppers but also hinted at the growing importance of the "togetherness of family shopping," referred to in the bottom caption. Reproduced from R. H. Macy & Co., Inc., *1957 Annual Report*. (Courtesy of Robert F. Wagner Labor Archives, New York University, from its Department Store Workers, Local 1-S Collection)

a shopping center three minutes from her suburban home because "it's great for women. What else is there to do?" The reported shopping priorities of women like Bonnie Porrazzo—convenience to home, one-stop shopping, big stores, self-service, and evening hours—fit well with what shopping centers had to offer.[49]

authentic colloquial speech

But for all the attention that early shopping centers lavished on women, their growing presence in the suburban landscape did not increase women's social and economic power in postwar society. Consumers' growing interest in shopping as families even when orchestrated by women, the increasing use of credit in purchasing, and the kind of jobs that women secured at shopping centers all conspired to limit the gains in domestic and public authority that a feminized suburban space might otherwise have encouraged.

summary

no sources; therefore, no quotes

2

Whenever suburban and downtown shopping were compared in the 1950s and 1960s, shopping centers were singled out for their greater family appeal. In typical fashion, *Redbook*'s 1957 film *In the Suburbs* depicted the "happy-go-spending," "buy-it-now" generation passing great amounts of time together as a family in the local shopping center: "Like the rest of life in suburbia, shopping has a family flavor," the narrator observed while footage showed couples buying while their children trailed along or played nearby. These young adults, he went on, "have a 'let's-go-see quality' that brings crowds to community events and promotions" sponsored by the centers. A study comparing family shopping in downtown Cincinnati with its suburban shopping centers found that while 85 percent of downtown patrons shopped alone, only 43 percent of shopping center patrons did; most of them were accompanied by family members. Other surveys showed as many as two-thirds of female suburban customers shopping with someone else. Women shoppers in Bergen County surveyed by the Pratts conformed to these patterns. In the first few years after the centers opened, four in ten families were spending more time shopping, three in ten were making more shopping trips, two in ten were taking the children more often, and two in ten were including husbands more often than before the malls were built.[50]

interrupted quotation— slogan provides flavor of the period

3

When "the whole family [was] shopping together," as marketer Pierre Martineau put it in 1958, men played a greater role in household purchasing. Survey after survey documented husbands' increasing presence alongside their wives at shopping centers, which made evenings and weekends by far the busiest time there, creating peaks and valleys in shopping that had not affected downtown stores nearly as much. In many suburban centers more than half the volume was done at night. At Bergen Mall the peak traffic count was at

This was a new phrase in 1958.

4

8 p.m., and shopping was very heavy on Saturdays as well. A May Company executive described how this imbalance created special problems in branch-store operation: "The biggest day in the suburban store will be ten times the poorest day, instead of five as it usually is downtown." The manager of the Tots'n Teens toy store in Shoppers World in Framingham, Massachusetts, tried to explain to less experienced mall sellers how the new-style suburban shopping actually worked: "It's a curious thing about a shopping center. Most of our daytime shoppers are women who are just looking around. It's hard to sell them during the day but if they're at all interested, they'll be back at night—with their husbands. That's when we do the real business."[51]

quotation— succinct, but is the quotation needed?

authentic voice

Shopping centers responded to suburban couples' growing tendency to shop together with stores and programming specifically designed to further encourage families to turn shopping chores into leisure time spent at the mall. William M. Batten, board chair of JCPenney, for example, recalled "the broadening of our lines of merchandise and our services to encompass a fuller spectrum of family activity" as the company began building stores in shopping centers rather than on Main Street in the late 1950s and 1960s. Only then did Penney's start selling appliances, hardware, and sporting goods, and offering portrait studios, restaurants, auto service, and Singer sewing instruction. *Business Week* reported that department stores were scurrying to respond as well: Federated Department Stores started a new Fedway chain to attract the whole family and in its F. & R. Lazarus store in Columbus was "making a real effort to take the curse of femininity off the big store" by selling more male-oriented merchandise. Atlanta-based Rich's Department Store added a "Store for Men" adjoining its main store. Automobile shows, Saturday "kids' movies," student art exhibits, and circus clowns were only a few of the many events designed to attract men and children. In time, shopping centers themselves would be constructed as less feminized space, with all family members, not just women, in mind. As families strolled and shopped together at the mall, more and more they engaged in a form of activity that may have been female-directed, but reflected greater sharing of responsibility for household purchasing between husbands and wives.[52]

Quote sounds like a board chair! Is it needed?

striking phrase— integrated quotation

5

Notes

[48]On women driving, and specifically using a car for shopping, see Rich, *Shopping Behavior of Department Store Customers*, pp. 84–85, 137–38; L. Pratt, "Impact of Regional Shopping Centers in Bergen County"; Voorhees, *Shopping Habits and Travel Patterns*, p. 17.

[49]Herzog, "Shops, Culture, Centers—and More," *NYT Magazine*, p. 35; "Busy Day in Busy Willowbrook Mall," *NYT*, Apr. 2, 1972; Harris, *Cultural Excursions*, p. 281; Wolff, *What Makes Women Buy*, pp. 220–25.

[50]On Film, Inc., for *Redbook* magazine, *In the Suburbs*, 1957, 19:30 minutes, 35 mm, from Rick Prelinger, ed., *Our Secret Century: Archival Films from the Darker Side of the American Dream*, vol. 6, *The Unchartered Landscape*, Voyager CD, 1996; Rich, *Shopping Behavior of Department Store Customers*, pp. 64, 71–74; Sternlieb, *Future of the Downtown Department Store*, pp. 27–28, 184; Wolff, *What Makes Women Buy*, p. 226; L. Pratt, "Impact of Regional Shopping Centers in Bergen County."

[51]Martineau, "Customers' Shopping Center Habits Change Retailing," p. 16; Feinberg, *What Makes Shopping Centers Tick*, p. 97; Oaks, *Managing Suburban Branches of Department Stores*, p. 72; Irving Roberts, "Toy Selling Techniques in a Shopping Center," *Playthings*, July 1953, p. 112; also see "Lenox Toy & Hobby Selects Good Location in Atlanta Shopping Center—1,200 Sales a Week," *Playthings*, May 1961, p. 99.

[52]JCPenney, "An American Legacy, A 90th Anniversary History," brochure (1992), pp. 22, 25, JCPenney Archives, Plano, TX; Mary Elizabeth Curry, *Creating an American Institution: The Merchandising Genius of J.C. Penney* (New York: Garland, 1993), pp. 311–13; William M. Batten, *The Penney Idea: Foundation for the Continuing Growth of the J.C. Penney Company* (New York: Newcomen Society in North America, 1967), p. 17. The opening of the JCPenney store in Garden State Plaza in 1958 is featured in a film, *The Past Is a Prologue* (1961), which is one of several fascinating movies made by the company that has been collected on a video, *Penney Premieres*, available through the JCPenney Archives. Also see *Penney News* 24 (November–December 1958): 1, 7 on the new Paramus store; JCPenney Archives. On activities for family members, see R. H. Macy & Company, *Annual Report for 1957*, p. 26; "Bait for the Male Shopper," *BW*, Apr. 5, 1952, p. 40; "300,000 Prospects Ten Minutes Away," *Playthings*, February 1955, p. 308; Samuel Feinberg, "The Spirit of Garden State Plaza," *Women's Wear Daily*, Feb. 29, 1960.

EXERCISE 10: WHY QUOTE?

Read this passage from *America's Women* by Gail Collins, make marginal notes, and be prepared to comment on Collins's use of quotation. Gail Collins edits the editorial page of the *New York Times* and is a former columnist for that newspaper. *America's Women* was intended for a popular, not an academic market, and so Collins provides a bibliography (so that readers can locate her sources) but no formal documentation.

Selecting Quotations

1. *Never quote something just because it sounds impressive.* The style of the quotation—the level of difficulty, the choice of vocabulary, and the degree of abstraction—should be compatible with your own style. Don't force your reader to make a mental jump from your own characteristic voice and wording to a far more abstract, flowery, or colloquial style.

2. *Never quote something that you find difficult to understand.* When the time comes to decide whether to quote, rapidly read the quotation and observe your own reactions. If you become distracted or confused, your reader will be, too.

3. *Quote primary sources—if they are clear and understandable.* A person who witnessed the Chicago Fire has a better claim to have his original account presented verbatim than does a historian, decades later.

from AMERICA'S WOMEN
Gail Collins

One of the things that separated nineteenth-century women from their colonial forebears was their belief that bathing is a good idea. Middle-class Americans became attached to the idea of personal hygiene even before they acquired running water or central heating. Lucy Larcom, the mill girl turned author, remembered watching her sister in 1835 taking a full bath before going to work, "even though the water was chiefly broken ice. . . . It required both nerve and will to do this at five o'clock on a zero morning in a room without a fire."

Cleanliness, like most of the transformations of the pre–Civil War period, was mainly a phenomenon of the larger towns and cities. William Alcott, the health reformer, estimated in 1850 that a quarter of New England's population bathed their whole bodies less than once a year, and the numbers of unwashed Americans in the South and western states must have been staggering. (The girls at the Euphradian Academy in Rockingham, North Carolina, had to get special permission from their parents to take a full bath.) But the people setting the pace—the prosperous urban families—had decided that cleanliness was, if not next to godliness, at least a sign of gentility. By midcentury, every middle-class bedroom had a water pitcher and washbasin.

Still the concept of real head-to-toe bathing was slow to catch on. By 1860 there were only about 4,000 bathtubs in Boston, which had a population of 178,000. Washing generally didn't include soap; people stood in tubs and rubbed themselves with a wet sponge, followed by a brisk toweling. Some women boasted that they could take a complete bath in a carpeted room without spilling a drop. "Females, with all their scrupulous attention to cleanliness, are . . . too sparing in their use of water," advised *The American Lady's Medical Pocket-Book.* "Many ridiculously suppose that its free and repeated application to the skin gives it a disagreeable roughness, and otherwise injures its beauty." The idea of washing one's body was still so novel that people believed in waiting two hours after eating for even a sponge bath.

Women were also being counseled to keep their hair clean, but shampoo was still in the future. Health and beauty books were full of recommendations about what to use when washing your hair: a beaten egg yolk, cold tea, castor oil mixed with brandy and bay rum, or olive oil in which flowers had been allowed to stand. Although magazines urged readers to brush their teeth, visitors from abroad still commented on the poor quality of American dental care and many women became toothless very young. "The loss of my teeth has been the severest mortification to which my vanity has ever been subjected," wrote Sarah Gayle, the wife of the future governor of Alabama. Gayle was one of the rare Americans who consulted a dentist, but her efforts weren't rewarded. The dentist not only subjected her to "unspeakable" pain, he eventually gave her a fatal case of tetanus.

4

EXERCISE 11: WHAT TO QUOTE

Read each of the two passages below and decide which phrases or sentences, if any, would be worth quoting in a research essay. In real life, your choice would depend on your essay topic and proposed thesis. For this exercise, it may be helpful to imagine some topics that would lead you to consult sources dealing with the history of running or with Arab countries' rejection of Western modernity.

Edward Tenner, former science editor at Princeton University Press, has a special interest in technology—its history and its practical uses and consequences—and has written widely on the way everyday things work.

Fareed Zakaria has been the editor of the journal *Foreign Affairs* and is currently the editor of *Newsweek International.* In addition to publishing books and newspaper columns, Zakaria has regularly appeared on television as an analyst of American foreign policy and the war on terrorism.

A. Running may be the oldest sport of the West. It played an important part in ancient Egyptian festivals. Egyptians recorded times for distance running that compare with those of the best nineteenth-century European athletes, and the Egyptians were almost certainly barefoot. In Greece, at the first Olympics in 776 BC, races of from about 192 meters to 5,000 meters were run without shoes. Although Greek message carriers ran in soft leather boots called *endromides*, and although the Greeks were aware of spiked shoes used in the icy Caucasus, they had no interest in footwear for athletics. The original Olympic starting line had grooves for runners' toes, and in the absence of cleats even sprinters are pictured standing upright at the start rather than leaning forward on their hands. Bare feet were, of course, part of male athletic nudity, a custom that scandalized foreigners but served the Greeks themselves as proof of their superiority to barbarians. Even "hoplite" foot races based on warfare, run with shields and at first with helmets, omitted sandals. (Women, who ran wearing light clothing at special events for them, at least sometimes wore sandals.) The Greeks applied their ingenuity to running terrain rather than foot coverings. They went to some expense to prepare the track for bare feet. The soil was weeded and dug up before the events, and covered with fine sand. At Delphi the cost of the sand alone was considerable: over 83 staters, the equivalent of more than ten months' wages for a laborer. Runners trained for this surface, practicing on deeper sand. Today's experts recommend grass as the best running surface and warn that running on beaches endangers the Achilles tendon, but in antiquity, a carefully prepared layer of sand over dirt may have been the state of the art. Late in the Olympics, during Roman rule, Greek athletes did begin to wear a type of sandal called the *krepis*, probably owing either to the influence of Roman customs or to changing standards of track maintenance. By the time of Diocletian (AD 245–313) there is a reference to shoes called *gallica* used for running. But, having been born with the Romans, the athletic shoe appears to have vanished in the West with the end of the Olympics and the disappearance of Greco-Roman physical culture under Christianity.[8]

> EDWARD TENNER, from *Our Own Devices:*
> *The Past and Future of Body Technology*

[8]Wolfgang Decker, "Die Lauf-Stele des Königs Taharka," *Kölner Beiträge zur Sportwissenschaft*, vol. 13 (1984), 7–37; E. Norman Gardiner, *Athletics of the Ancient World* (Oxford: Clarendon Press, 1930), 128–33, fig. 87; E. Norman Gardiner, *Greek Athletic Sports and Festivals* (London: Macmillan, 1910), 271–73; H. A. Harris, *Greek Athletes and Athletics* (London: Hutchinson, 1964), 66–77; Marc Bloom, "Judging a Path by Its Cover," *Runner's World*, vol. 32, no. 3 (March 1997), 54–62; Melvin P. Cheskin, *The Complete Handbook of Athletic Footwear* (New York: Fairchild Publications, 1987), 2–3.

B. About a decade ago, in a casual conversation with an elderly Arab intellectual, I expressed my frustration that governments in the Middle East had been unable to liberalize their economies and societies in the way that the East Asians had. "Look at Singapore, Hong Kong, and Seoul," I said, pointing to their extraordinary economic achievements. The man, a gentle, charming, erudite, and pro-Western journalist, straightened up and replied sharply, "Look at them. They have simply aped the West. Their cities are cheap copies of Houston and Dallas. That may be all right for fishing villages, but we are heirs to one of the great civilizations of the world. We cannot become slums of the West."

This sense of pride and fall is at the heart of the Arab problem. It makes economic advance impossible and political progress fraught with difficulty. America thinks of modernity as all good—and it has been almost all good for America. But for the Arab world, modernity has been one failure after another. Each path followed—socialism, secularism, nationalism—has turned into a dead end. People often wonder why the Arab countries will not try secularism. In fact, for most of the last century, most of them did. Now people associate the failure of their governments with the failure of secularism and of the Western path. The Arab world is disillusioned with the West when it should be disillusioned with its own leaders.

The new, accelerated globalization that flourished in the 1990s has hit the Arab world in a strange way. Its societies are open enough to be disrupted by modernity, but not so open that they can ride the wave. Arabs see the television shows, eat the fast foods, and drink the sodas, but they don't see genuine liberalization in their societies, with increased opportunities and greater openness. They don't see economic opportunities and dynamism, just the same elites controlling things. Globalization in the Arab world is the critic's caricature of globalization, a slew of Western products and billboards with little else. For the elites in Arab societies it means more things to buy. But for some of them it is also an unsettling phenomenon that threatens their comfortable base of power.

This mixture of fascination and repulsion with the West—with modernity— has utterly disoriented the Arab world. Young men, often better educated than their parents, leave their traditional villages to find work. They arrive in the noisy, crowded cities of Cairo, Beirut, Damascus or go to work in the oil states. (Almost 10 percent of Egypt's working population worked in the Gulf states at one point.) In their new world they see great disparities of wealth and the disorienting effects of modernity; most unsettlingly, they see women, unveiled and in public places, taking buses, eating in cafes, and working alongside them. They come face to face with the contradictions of modern life, seeking the wealth of the new world but the tradition and certainty of the old.

Globalization has caught the Arab world at a bad demographic moment. Its societies are going through a massive youth bulge; more than half of the Arab world is under the age of twenty-five. Fully 75 percent of Saudi Arabia is under the age of thirty. A bulge of restless young men in any country is bad news. Almost all crime in every society is committed by men between the ages of fifteen and twenty-five. Lock all young men up, one social scientist pointed out, and violent crime will drop by more than 95 percent. (That is why the socialization of young men—in schools, colleges, and camps—has been one of the chief challenges for civilized societies.) When accompanied by even small economic and social change, a youth bulge produces a new politics of protest. In the past, societies in these circumstances have fallen prey to a search for revolutionary so-lutions. France went through a youth bulge just before the French Revolution in 1789, as did Iran before its revolution in 1979. Even the United States had a youth bulge that peaked in 1968, the year of the country's strongest social protests since the Great Depression. In the case of the Arab world, this up-heaval has taken the form of a religious resurgence.

FAREED ZAKARIA, from *The Future of Freedom:*
Illiberal Democracy at Home and Abroad

INTEGRATING QUOTATIONS INTO YOUR PARAGRAPHS

You have learned how to present the words of others accurately and with ap-propriate citations. Now you must learn to incorporate quotations smoothly into your paragraphs, supporting—not preempting—your own ideas.

Using Quotations

1. **Quotations generally belong in the body of the paragraph, not at the very beginning as a replacement for the topic sentence.**

   The topic sentence should establish—in your own words—what you are about to explain or prove. *The quotation should appear later in the paragraph, as supporting evidence.*

2. **Let the quotation make its point; your job is to explain or interpret its meaning, not to translate it word for word.**

   Once you have presented a quotation, it is usually not necessary to provide an exact repetition of the same idea in your own words, making the same point twice. Instead, follow up a quotation with an *explanation* of its relevance to your paragraph or an *interpretation* of its meaning. Make sure that your commentary does more than echo the quotation.

In the following student example, the quotation used in the development of the paragraph is no more or less important than any of the other supporting sentences. The quotation adds interest to the paragraph because of the shift in tone and the shift to a sharper, narrower focus.

Some parents insist on allowing their children to learn through experi-ence. Once a child has actually performed a dangerous action and realized its consequences, he will always remember the circumstances and the possible ill effects. Yvonne Realle illustrates the adage that experience is the best teacher by describing a boy who was slapped just as he reached for a hot iron. The child, not realizing that he might have been burned, had no idea why he had been slapped. An observer noted that "if he had learned by experience, if he'd suffered some discomfort in the process, then he'd know enough to avoid the iron next time." In the view of parents like Yvonne Realle, letting a child experiment with his environment will result in a stronger lesson than slapping or scolding the child for trying to explore his surroundings.

Instead of looking at a completed paragraph that includes a quotation, let's reverse the process by starting with a simple quotation and seeing how it is used in the development of a paragraph. In an article on shopping written for the *Guardian*, a British newspaper, Jess Cartner-Morley is asserting the following thesis:

> Men tend to view shopping as a chore, a necessary way of obtaining things they need; for women, it is a leisure activity and a reward.

Cartner-Morley intends to include a quotation by Charles Revson, a major figure in the cosmetics industry:

> "In the factory we make cosmetics; in the store we sell hope."

The connection between the thesis and the quotation can be found in the words "reward" and "hope." So Cartner-Morley establishes a topic sentence—as well as a follow-up, explanatory sentence—that establishes the connection in general terms:

> Certainly, it is clear that in a consumer society, shopping has come to stand for much more than just buying things. It is your ticket to an idealized self.

Shopping as "reward" has led to shopping as a "ticket to an idealized self," and that, in turn, leads to Revson's compact and catchy sentence—well worth quoting—about cosmetics as a symbol of "hope."

To introduce the quotation, Cartner-Morley uses an explanatory citation identifying Revson:

> Charles Revson, who founded Revlon in 1932, figured this out long ago, saying, "In the factory, we make cosmetics; in the store we sell hope."

And then Cartner-Morley completes the paragraph by building on "long ago" in the citation and contrasting 1932 with 2004:

But it is in recent years that the culture of shopping has become increasingly about image rather than substance.

Now she is ready to move on and discuss the way the idealized image of self is developed and marketed. The paragraph is only four sentences long—short and easy to follow—but it makes its point clearly by working toward the quotation and then away from it. The quotation strongly supports Cartner-Morley's thesis, but can do so only because it is embedded in a strong paragraph.

Read through the complete paragraph and see how well it hangs together:

Certainly, it is clear that in a consumer society, shopping has come to stand for much more than just buying things. It is your ticket to an idealized self. Charles Revson, who founded Revlon in 1932, figured this out long ago, saying, "In the factory, we make cosmetics; in the store we sell hope." But it is in recent years that the culture of shopping has become increasingly about image rather than substance.

Academic writers often deal with more complex topics, but they use precisely the same techniques for incorporating quotations—the evidence of authoritative sources—into their paragraphs. Here is a paragraph from Dick Teresi's *Lost Discoveries: The Ancient Roots of Modern Science—From the Babylonians to the Maya.* Teresi is a science writer who bridges academic and popular audiences. Here, he is beginning a chapter on the origins of the science of geology:

topic sentence	Prehistoric peoples must have had intimate knowledge of the qualities of the stones they depended on in order to live. Neanderthal
example	humans in the Middle Pleistocene crafted stone tools of a specific form known as Mousterian.[1] They used two methods: by chipping
closer focus	at the stone core to create the tool, and by using the chips them-
support: authority (quotation)	selves as the tools.[2] Geologist Gordon Childe says that "both procedures demand both great dexterity and considerable familiarity with the properties of the stone utilized. Just bashing two stones together is not likely to yield a useable flake or core tool. To produce either the blow must be struck with precisely the right force
shift in focus to the present	and at the correct angle on a flat surface."[3] Modern geology students who have attempted to make their own tools in this fashion can vouch for the difficulty involved. One student told me she spent a full
support: brief anecdote	morning trying to make a stone cutting tool from two pieces of flint she found on the beach.

[1] Kenneth F. Weaver, "The Search for Our Ancestors," *National Geographic* 168 (Nov. 1985): 616.

[2] Gordon Childe, "The Prehistory of Science: Archaeological Documents," in Guy S. Metraux and François Crouzet (eds.), *The Evolution of Science: Readings from the*

History of Mankind (New York: New American Library, Mentor Books, 1963), pp. 39, 40.
    [3]Ibid.

Notice that Teresi's paragraph contains three footnotes to document the sources of his information as well as the quotation. Cartner-Morley is writing for a newspaper and is not expected to do more than identify sources by name and, if appropriate, provide some background. Complete information about when and how to document sources can be found in Chapter 10.

EXERCISE 12: INTEGRATING QUOTATIONS INTO A PARAGRAPH

The following student paragraph is taken from an essay, "The Compulsive Gambler." The second passage comes from *The Psychology of Gambling* by Edmund Bergler.

Choose one appropriate supporting quotation from the Bergler passage, decide where to place it in the student paragraph, and insert the quotation correctly and smoothly into the paragraph. Remember to lead into the quotation by citing the source.

Student Paragraph

One obvious reason for gambling is to make money. Because some gamblers are lucky when they play, they never want to stop. Even when quite a lot of money has been lost, they go on, assuming that they can get rich through gambling. Once a fortune is made, they will feel really powerful, free of all dependency and responsibilities. Instead, in most cases, gambling becomes a daily routine. There is no freedom, no escape.

Source

Every gambler gives the impression of a man who has signed a contract with Fate, stipulating that persistence must be rewarded. With that imaginary contract in his pocket, he is beyond the reach of all logical objection and argument.

The result of this pathologic optimism is that the true gambler never stops when he is winning, for he is convinced that he must win more and more. Inevitably, he loses. He does not consider his winnings the result of chance; to him they are a down payment on that contract he has with Fate which guarantees that he will be a permanent winner. This inability to stop while fortune is still smiling is one of the strongest arguments against the earnest assumption, common to all gamblers, that one can get rich through gambling.

AVOIDING PLAGIARISM

Quoting without quotation marks is called *plagiarism*. Even if you cite the source's name somewhere on your page, a word-for-word quotation without quotation marks would still be considered a plagiarism.

Plagiarism is the unacknowledged use of another writer's words or ideas. The only way to acknowledge that you are using someone else's actual words is through citation and quotation marks.

Chapter 10 discusses plagiarism in detail. At this point, you should understand that:

- If you plagiarize, you will never learn to write.

- Literate people consider plagiarism to be equivalent to theft.

- Plagiarists eventually get caught!

It is easy for an experienced reader to detect plagiarism. Every writer, professional or amateur, has *a characteristic style or voice* that readers quickly learn to recognize. In a few paragraphs or pages, the writer's voice becomes familiar enough for the reader to notice that the style has changed and there is a new, unfamiliar voice. When there are frequent acknowledged quotations, the reader simply adjusts to a series of new voices. When there are unacknowledged quotations, *the absence of quotation marks* and *the change of voices* usually suggest to an experienced reader that the work is poorly integrated and probably plagiarized.

Instructors are well aware of style and are trained to recognize inconsistencies and awkward transitions. A revealing clue is the patched-together, mosaic effect. The next exercise will improve your own perception of shifting voices and encourage you to rely on your own characteristic style as the dominant voice in everything that you write.

EXERCISE 13: IDENTIFYING PLAGIARISM

The following paragraphs contain several plagiarized sentences. Examine the language and tone of each sentence, as well as the continuity of the entire paragraph. Then underline the plagiarized sentences.

A. The Beatles' music in the early years was just plain melodic. It had a nice beat to it. The Beatles were simple lads, writing simple songs simply to play to screaming fans on one-night stands. There was no deep, inner meaning to the lyrics. Their songs included many words like I, and me, and you. As the years went by, the Beatles' music became more poetic. Sergeant Pepper is a stupefying collage of music, words, background noises, cryptic utterances, orchestral effects, hallucinogenic bells, farmyard sounds, dream sequences, social observations, and apocalyptic vision, all masterfully blended together on a four-track tape machine over nine agonizing and expensive months. Their music was beginning to be more philosophical, with a deep, inner, more secret meaning. After it was known that they took drugs, references to drugs were seen in many songs. The "help" in Ringo's "A Little Help from My Friends" was said to have meant pot. The songs were poetic, mystical; they emerged from a self-contained world of bizarre carnival colors; they spoke in a language and a musical idiom all their own.

B. Before the Civil War, minstrelsy spread quickly across America. Americans all over the country enjoyed minstrelsy because it reflected something of their own point of view. For instance, Negro plantation hands, played usually by white actors in blackface, were portrayed as devil-may-care outcasts and minstrelmen played them with an air of comic triumph, irreverent wisdom, and an underlying note of rebellion, which had a special appeal to citizens of a young country. Minstrelsy was ironically the beginning of black involvement in the American theater. The American people learned to identify with certain aspects of the black people. The Negro became a sympathetic symbol for a pioneer people who required resilience as a prime trait.

·4·

Paraphrasing Sources

Some passages are worth quoting for the sake of their precise or elegant style or their distinguished author. But many sources that you will use in your college essays are written in more ordinary language or by more ordinary writers. Rather than quoting undistinguished material, you should provide your readers with a clear paraphrase.

> *Paraphrase is the point-by-point recapitulation of another person's ideas, expressed in your own words.*

When you paraphrase, you retain everything about the original writing but the words.

USING PARAPHRASE IN YOUR ESSAYS

Paraphrasing helps your readers to gain a detailed understanding of sources that they may never have read and, indirectly, to accept your own thesis as valid. There are two major reasons for using paraphrase in your essays.

1. Use paraphrase to present information or evidence whenever there is no special reason for using a direct quotation.

Many sources don't have sufficient authority or a distinctive enough style to justify your quoting their words. The following illustration, from a *New York Times* article, paraphrases a report written by an anonymous group of "municipal auditors" that was not considered worth quoting. Note the initial reference to the source of the information ("a report issued yesterday") and the follow-up reminders ("they said"; "the auditors said").

> A city warehouse in Middle Village, Queens, stocked with such things as snow shovels, light bulbs, sponges, waxed paper, laundry soap and tinned herring, has been found to be vastly overstocked with some items and lacking in others. Municipal auditors, in a report issued yesterday, said that security was fine and that the warehouse was quicker in delivering goods to city agencies than it was when the auditors made their last check, in August, 1976. But in one corner of the warehouse, they said, nearly 59,000 paper binders, the 8½-by-11 size, are gathering dust, enough to meet the city's needs for nearly seven years. Nearby, there is a 10½-year supply of cotton coveralls.
>
> Both the overstock and shortages cost the city money, the auditors said. They estimated that by reducing warehouse inventories, the city could save $1.4 million, plus $112,000 in interest. . . .

2. Use paraphrase to give your readers an accurate and comprehensive account of ideas taken from a source—ideas that you intend to explain, interpret, or disagree with in your essay.

The first illustration comes from a *Times* article about the data and photographs provided by *Voyager 2* as it explored the farthest reaches of the solar system. In summarizing a press conference, the article paraphrases various scientists' descriptions of what *Voyager* had achieved during its journey near Triton, one of the moons of the planet Neptune. Note the limited use of carefully selected quotations within the paraphrase.

> Out of the fissures [on Triton], roughly analogous to faults in the Earth's crust, flowed mushy ice. There was no eruption in the sense of the usual terrestrial volcanism or the geyser-like activity discovered on Io, one of Jupiter's moons. It was more of an extrusion through cracks in the surface ice.
>
> Although scientists classify such a process as volcanism, Dr. Miner said it could better be described as a "slow-flow volcanic activity." A somewhat comparable process, he said, seemed to have shaped some of the surface features of Ariel, one of the moons of Uranus.
>
> Dr. Soderblom said Triton's surface appeared to be geologically young or "millions to hundreds of millions of years old." The absence of many impact craters was the main evidence for the relatively recent resurfacing of the terrain with new ice.

The next example shows how paraphrase can be used more briefly, to present another writer's point of view as the basis for discussion. Again, the writer of this description of a conference on nuclear deterrence has reserved quotation to express the precise point of potential dispute:

Scientists engaged in research on the effects of nuclear war may be "wasting their time" studying a phenomenon that is far less dangerous than the natural explosions that have periodically produced widespread extinctions of plant and animal life in the past, a University of Chicago scientist said last week. Joseph V. Smith, a professor of geophysical sciences, told a conference on nuclear deterrence here that such natural catastrophes as exploding volcanoes, violent earthquakes, and collisions with comets or asteroids could produce more immediate and destructive explosions than any nuclear war.

Using Paraphrase as Preparation for Reading and Writing Essays

Paraphrase is sometimes undertaken as an end in itself to improve your understanding of a complex passage. When you grasp an essay at first reading, when its ideas are clearly stated in familiar terms, then you can be satisfied with annotating it or writing a brief summary. But when you find an essay hard to understand, writing down each sentence in your own words forces you to stop and make sense of what you have read, helping you work out ideas that may at first seem beyond your comprehension.

Paraphrase can also be *a means to an end*, a preparation for writing an essay of your own. When you take notes for an essay based on one or more sources, you should mostly paraphrase. Quote only when recording phrases or sentences that clearly merit quotation. All quotable phrases and sentences should be transcribed accurately in your notes, with quotation marks separating the paraphrase from the quotation.

Writing a Good Paraphrase

In a good paraphrase, the sentences and the vocabulary do not duplicate those of the original. *You cannot merely substitute synonyms for key words and leave the sentences otherwise unchanged; that is plagiarism in spirit, if not in fact;* nor does word-for-word substitution really demonstrate that you have understood the ideas.

The level of abstraction within your paraphrase should resemble that of the original: it should be neither more general nor more specific. If you do not understand a sentence, do not try to guess or cover it up with a vague phrase that slides over the idea. Instead:

- Look up difficult words.
- Think of what they mean and how they are used together.

- Consider how the sentences are formed and how they fit into the context of the entire paragraph.
- Then, to test your understanding, write it all out.

Remember that a good paraphrase makes sense by itself; it is coherent and readable, without requiring reference to the original essay.

When a paraphrase moves completely away from the words and sentence structure of the original text and presents ideas in the paraphraser's own style and idiom, then it is said to be "free." A free paraphrase is as acceptable as the original—provided that the substance of the source has not been altered, disguised, or substantially condensed. Because a free paraphrase can condense repetitious parts of the original text, it may be somewhat briefer than the original, but it will present ideas in much the same order.

Guidelines for a Successful Paraphrase

- A paraphrase must be accurate.
- A paraphrase must be complete.
- A paraphrase must be written in your own voice.
- A paraphrase must make sense by itself.

Here, side by side with the original, is a free paraphrase of an excerpt from Machiavelli's *The Prince*. This passage exemplifies the kind of text—very famous, very difficult—that really benefits from a comprehensive paraphrase. *The Prince* was written in 1513. Even though the translation from the Italian used here was revised in this century, the paraphraser has to bridge a tremendous gap in time and in style to present Machiavelli in an idiom suitable for modern readers. Note that the paraphraser has no choice but to quote the five-word phrase that everyone knows.

Original Version	*Paraphrase*
It is not, therefore, necessary for a prince to have [good faith and integrity], but it is very necessary to seem to have them. I would even be bold to say that to possess them and always to observe them is dangerous, but to appear to possess them is useful. Thus it is well to seem merciful, faithful, humane, sincere,	It is more important for a ruler to give the impression of goodness than to be good. In fact, real goodness can be a liability, but the pretense is always very effective. It is all very well to be virtuous, but it is vital to be able to shift in the other direction whenever circumstances require it. After all, rulers,

religious, and also to be so; but you must have the mind so disposed that when it is needful to be otherwise you may be able to change to the opposite qualities. And it must be understood that a prince, and especially a new prince, cannot observe all those things which are considered good in men, being often obliged, in order to maintain the state, to act against faith, against charity, against humanity, and against religion. And therefore, he must have a mind disposed to adapt itself according to the wind, and as the variations of fortune dictate, and . . . not deviate from what is good, if possible, but be able to do evil if constrained.

A prince must take great care that nothing goes out of his mouth which is not full of the above-mentioned five qualities, and to see and hear him, he should seem to be all mercy, faith, integrity, humanity, and religion. . . . Everyone sees what you appear to be, few feel what you are, and those few will not dare to oppose themselves to the many, who have the majesty of the state to defend them; and in the actions of men, and especially of princes, from which there is no appeal, the end justifies the means. Let a prince therefore aim at conquering and maintaining the state, and the means will always be judged honorable and praised by every one, for the vulgar are always taken by appearances and the issue of the event; and the world consists only of the vulgar, and the few who are not vulgar are isolated when the many have a rallying point in the prince.

especially recently elevated ones, have a duty to perform which may absolutely require them to act against the dictates of faith and compassion and kindness. One must act as circumstances require and, while it's good to be virtuous if you can, it's better to be bad if you must.

In public, however, the ruler should appear to be entirely virtuous, and if his pretense is successful with the majority of people, then those who do see through the act will be outnumbered and impotent, especially since the ruler has the authority of government on his side. In the case of rulers, even more than for most men, "the end justifies the means." If the ruler is able to assume power and administer it successfully, his methods will always be judged proper and satisfactory; for the common people will accept the pretense of virtue and the reality of success, and the astute will find no one is listening to their warnings.

Paraphrase and Summary

To clarify the difference between paraphrase and summary, here is a paragraph that *summarizes* the excerpt from *The Prince.*

> According to Machiavelli, perpetuating power is a more important goal for a ruler than achieving personal goodness or integrity. Although he should act virtuously if he can, and always appear to do so, it is more important for him to adapt quickly to changing circumstances. The masses will be so swayed by his pretended virtue and by his success that any opposition will be ineffective. The wise ruler's maxim is that "the end justifies the means."

To make the distinction between summary and paraphrase entirely clear, here is a recapitulation of the guidelines for writing a brief summary:

1. *A summary is comprehensive.* Like the paraphrase, the summary of *The Prince* says more than "the end justifies the means." While that is probably the most important idea in the passage, it does not by itself convey Machiavelli's full meaning. For one thing, it contains no reference at all to princes and how they should rule—and that, after all, is Machiavelli's subject.

2. *A summary is concise.* It should say exactly as much as you need—and no more. The summary of *The Prince* is considerably shorter than the paraphrase.

3. *A summary is coherent.* The summary links together the passage's most important points in a unified paragraph that makes sense on its own. The ideas need not be presented in the same sequence as that of the original passage, as they are in the paraphrase.

4. *A summary is independent.* What is most striking about the summary, compared with the paraphrase, is the writer's attitude toward the original text. While the paraphraser has to follow closely Machiavelli's ideas and point of view, the summarizer does not. Characteristically, Machiavelli's name is cited in the summary, calling attention to the fact that it is based on another person's ideas.

You can use either summary or paraphrase to refer to this passage in an essay. Which you would choose to use depends on your topic, on the way you are developing your essay, and on the extent to which you wish to discuss Machiavelli.

- In an essay citing Machiavelli as only one among many political theorists, you might use the four-sentence summary; then you might briefly comment on Machiavelli's ideas before going on to summarize (and perhaps compare them with) another writer's theories.

- In an essay about a contemporary politician, you might analyze the way in which your subject does or does not carry out Machiavelli's strategies; then you probably would want to familiarize your readers with *The Prince* in some detail through paraphrase. You might include the full paraphrase, interspersed, perhaps, with an analysis of your present-day "prince."

Comparing Paraphrase and Summary

Paraphrase	*Summary*
▪ Reports your understanding to your reader	▪ Reports your understanding to your reader
▪ Records a relatively short passage	▪ Records a passage of any length
▪ Records every point in the passage	▪ Selects and condenses, recording only the main ideas
▪ Records these points in their original order	▪ Changes the order of ideas when necessary
▪ Includes no interpretation	▪ Explains and (if the writer wishes) interprets

Writing an Accurate Paraphrase

The basic purpose of paraphrase is to present a source's ideas as they appear in the original text. When paraphrase fails to convey the substance of the source, there are three possible explanations:

1. *Misreading*: The writer genuinely misunderstood the text.
2. *Projecting*: The writer insisted on reading his or her own ideas into the text.
3. *Guessing*: The writer had a spark of understanding and constructed a paraphrase centered around that spark, but ignored too much of the original text.

Read Christopher Lasch's analysis of the changing role of the child in family life. Then examine each of the three paraphrases that follow, deciding whether it conveys Lasch's principal ideas and, if not, why it has gone astray. Compare your reactions with the analysis that follows each paraphrase.

Original

The family by its very nature is a means of raising children, but this fact should not blind us to the important change that occurred when child-rearing ceased to be simply one of many activities and became the central concern—one is tempted to say the central obsession—of family life. This development had to wait for the recognition of the child as a distinctive kind of person, more impressionable and hence more vulnerable than adults, to be treated in a special manner befitting his peculiar requirements. Again, we take these things for granted and find it hard to imagine anything else. Earlier, children had been clothed, fed, spoken to, and educated as little adults; more specifically, as servants, the difference between childhood and servitude having been remarkably obscure throughout much of Western history. . . . It was only in the seventeenth century in certain classes that childhood came to be seen as a special category of experience. When that happened, people recognized the enormous formative influence of family life, and the family became above all an agency for building character, for consciously and deliberately forming the child from birth to adulthood.

from "Divorce and the Family in America," *Atlantic Monthly*

Paraphrase A

> The average family wants to raise children with a good education and to encourage, for example, the ability to read and write well. They must be taught to practice and learn on their own. Children can be treated well without being pampered. They must be treated as adults as they get older and experience more of life. A parent must build character and the feeling of independence in a child. No longer should children be treated as kids or servants, for that can cause conflict in a family relationship.

This paraphrase has very little in common with the original passage. True, it is about child rearing, but the writer chooses to give advice to parents, rather than present the contrast between early and modern attitudes toward children, as Lasch does. Since the only clear connection between Lasch and this paragraph is the reference to servants, the writer was probably confused by the passage, and (instead of slowing down the process and paraphrasing it sentence by sentence) guessed—mistakenly—at its meaning. There is also some projection of the writer's ideas about family life. Notice how assertive the tone is; the writer seems to be admonishing parents rather than presenting Lasch's detached analysis.

Paraphrase B

> When two people get married, they usually produce a child. They get married because they want a family. Raising a family is now different from the way it used to be. The child is looked upon as a human being, with feelings and thoughts of his own. Centuries ago, children were treated like robots, little more than hired help. Now, children are seen as people who need a strong, dependable family background to grow into persons of good character. Parents are needed to get children ready to be the adults of tomorrow.

This paragraph also seems to combine guessing (beginning) and projection (end). The middle sentences do present Lasch's basic point, but the beginning and the end move so far away from the main ideas that the paraphrase as a whole does not bear much resemblance to the original text. It also includes an exaggeration: are servants "robots"?

Paraphrase C

> Though the family has always been an important institution, its child-rearing function has only in recent centuries become its most important activity. This change has resulted from the relatively new idea that children have a special, unique personality. In the past, there was little difference seen between childhood and adulthood. But today people realize the importance of family life, especially the family unit as a means of molding the personalities of children from childhood to adulthood.

Although this paraphrase is certainly the most accurate of the three, it is too brief to be a complete paraphrase. In fact, the writer seems to be summarizing, not paraphrasing. Lasch's main idea is there, but the following points are missing:

1. There is a tremendous difference between pre-seventeenth-century and twentieth-century perceptions of childhood.
2. Before the seventeenth century, it was difficult to distinguish between the status and treatment of children and that of servants.
3. Child rearing has now become of overriding ("obsessive") importance to the family.
4. Children are different from adults in that they are less hardened and less experienced.

The author of Paraphrase C has done a thorough job of the beginning and the end of Lasch's passage, and evidently left the middle to take care of itself. But a paraphrase cannot be considered a reliable "translation" of the original text unless all the supporting ideas are given appropriate emphasis. The omission of Point 2 is particularly important.

Here is a more comprehensive paraphrase of the passage:

> Though the family has always been the institution responsible for bringing up children, only in recent times has its child-raising function become the family's overriding purpose and its reason for being. This striking shift to the child-centered family has resulted from the gradual realization that children have a special, unique personality, easy to influence and easy to hurt, and that they must be treated accordingly. Special treatment for children is the norm in our time; but hundreds of years ago, people saw little or no difference between childhood and adulthood, and, in fact, the child's role in the family resembled that of a servant. It was not until the seventeenth century that people began to

regard childhood as a distinctive stage of growth. That recognition led them to understand what a powerful influence the family environment must have on the child and to define "family" as the chief instrument for molding the child's personality and moral attitudes.

EXERCISE 14: IDENTIFYING A GOOD PARAPHRASE

The next passage is followed by a group of paraphrases. Examine each one and decide whether it conforms to the guidelines for paraphrasing. Ask yourself whether the paraphrase contains any point that is not in the original passage and whether the key points of the original are *all* clearly presented in the paraphrase. For more practice in paraphrase, check the *Writing from Sources* Web site at bedfordstmartins.com/writingfromsources.

> Violence is often seen as primitive or immature. And yet, the reality is that even in this era of gun-toting 12-year-olds, murderous violence is distressingly mature: Overwhelmingly, it is adult behavior. It is also easily triggered. When Marvin Wolfgang conducted extensive interviews with convicted killers in Philadelphia, he was able to identify 12 categories of motive. Far and away the largest, accounting for fully 37 percent of all murders, was what he designated "altercation of relatively trivial origin; insult, curse, jostling, etc." In such cases, people got into an argument at a bar over a sporting event, who paid for a drink, an off-hand remark, or a hastily uttered insult.
>
> To die over something so inconsequential as a casual comment or a dispute about some distant event seems the height of irony and caprice. But in a sense, disputes of that sort are not trivial, for they reflect the evolutionary past, when personal altercations were the stuff upon which prestige and social success—leading ultimately to biological success—were based. It is not surprising, therefore, that young men today will fight and die over who said what to whom, whose prestige has been challenged, and so forth.
>
> DAVID BARASH, from "Evolution, Males, and Violence,"
> *The Chronicle of Higher Education*

1. These days, young kids are quite capable of killing someone because of an unimportant matter, just as grownups do. It's very easy for someone to die simply because he said the wrong thing. Still, it's part of human nature to make a big deal out of a small remark, and it always has been that way since the beginning of the human race. Men fight because their egos depend on looking good among their peers. It's a question of image.

2. When a preteen commits murder, he is acting just like a grownup. When they are violent, adults are behaving immaturely. According to a survey,

most murders take place for silly, unimportant reasons. Like children, the murderers become offended by the wrong word said at the wrong time. To die for nothing is really tragic. Even though men have always been ready to pick a fight to impress their rivals and attract women, it's wrong for them to risk lives for no good reason.

3. The young have no monopoly on violent behavior. Grown men are as likely as preteens to shoot off a gun for insufficient reasons. A survey found that, among the 12 reasons for committing murder, the most common was a fight over some unintended offense—a word or a gesture that provoked an argument or a fight, out of all proportion to the cause. Dying for no good reason might seem random and senseless. But such readiness to act and to kill was the way primitive man established his ascendancy over other men and ultimately survived. It's built into the genes of today's young men, who still fight to prove they're macho.

Paraphrasing a Difficult Text

Since translating another writer's idiom into your own can be difficult, a paraphrase is often written in two stages.

- In your first version, you work out a *word-for-word substitution*, staying close to the sentence structure of the original, as if you are writing a translation. This is the *literal paraphrase*.
- In your second version, you work from your own literal paraphrase, turning it into a *free paraphrase* by reconstructing and rephrasing the sentences to make them more natural and more characteristic of your own writing style.

Writing a Literal Paraphrase

To write a paraphrase that is faithful to the original text is impossible if you are uncertain of the meaning of any of the words. To write a literal paraphrase of a difficult passage:

- Use a dictionary, especially if the passage contains obsolete or archaic language.
- Write down a few possible synonyms for each difficult word, making sure that you understand the connotations of each synonym.
- Choose the substitute that best fits the context of your literal paraphrase.

Too often, the writer of a paraphrase forgets that there *is* a choice and quickly substitutes the first synonym in the dictionary. Even when appropriate synonyms have been carefully chosen, the literal paraphrase can look peculiar and sound dreadful. While the old sentence structure has been retained, the key words have been yanked out and new ones plugged in.

To illustrate the pitfalls of this process, here is a short excerpt from Francis Bacon's essay "Of Marriage and Single Life," written around 1600. Some of the phrasing and word combinations are archaic and may sound unnatural, but nothing in the passage is too difficult for modern understanding *if* the sentences are read slowly and carefully.

> He that hath wife and children hath given hostages to fortune; for they are impediments to great enterprises, either of virtue or mischief. Certainly, the best works and of greatest merit for the public have proceeded from the unmarried or childless men: which both in affection and means have endowed the public.

The passage's main idea is not too difficult to establish: *Unmarried men, without the burden of a family, can afford to contribute to the public good.* But by now you must realize that such a brief summary is not the same as a paraphrase, for it does not fully present Bacon's reasoning.

Paraphrase A

He who has a wife and children has <u>bestowed</u> <u>prisoners</u> to <u>riches</u>; for they are <u>defects</u> in huge <u>business</u> <u>organizations</u> either for <u>morality</u> or <u>damage</u>.

Paraphrase B

He who has a wife and children has <u>given</u> a <u>pledge</u> to <u>destiny</u>; for they are <u>hindrances</u> to large <u>endeavor</u>, either for <u>good</u> or for <u>ill</u>.

Neither sentence sounds very normal or very clear; but the second has potential, while the first makes no sense. Yet, in *both* cases, the inserted words are synonyms for the original vocabulary. In Paraphrase A the words do not fit Bacon's context; in Paraphrase B they do. For example, it is misleading to choose "business organizations" as a synonym for "enterprises," since the passage doesn't actually concern business, but refers to any sort of undertaking requiring freedom from responsibility. "Impediment" can mean either "defect" (as in speech impediment) or "hindrance" (as in impediment to learning); but—again, given the context—it is the latter meaning that Bacon has in mind.

A phrase like "hostages to fortune" offers special difficulty, since it is a powerful image expressing a highly abstract idea. No paraphraser can improve on the original wording or even find an equivalent phrase. However, expressing the idea is useful: a bargain made with life—the renunciation of future independent action in exchange for a family. Wife and children become a kind of bond ("hostages") to ensure one's future social conformity. The aptness and singularity of Bacon's original phrase are measured by the difficulty of paraphrasing three words in less than two sentences!

Writing a Free Version of the Literal Paraphrase

Correct though the synonyms may be, the passage from Bacon cannot be left as it is in Paraphrase B, for no reader could readily understand this stilted, artificial sentence. It is necessary to rephrase the paraphrase, ensuring that the meaning of the words is retained, but making the sentence sound more natural. The first attempt at "freeing up" the paraphrase stays as close as possible to the literal version, leaving everything in the same sequence, but using a more modern idiom:

Paraphrase C

Married men with children are hindered from embarking on any important undertaking, good or bad. Indeed, unmarried and childless men are the ones who have done the most for society and have dedicated their love and their money to the public good.

The second sentence (which is simpler to paraphrase than the first) has been inverted here, but the paraphrase is still a point-by-point recapitulation of Bacon. Paraphrase C is acceptable, but can be improved, both to clarify Bacon's meaning and to introduce a more personal voice. What exactly *are* these unmarried men dedicating to the public good? "Affection and means." And what is the modern equivalent of means? Money? Effort? Time? Energy?

Paraphrase D

A man with a family has obligations that prevent him from devoting himself to any activity that pleases him. On the other hand, a single man or a man without children has a greater opportunity to be a philanthropist. That's why most great contributions of energy and resources to the good of society are made by single men.

The writer of Paraphrase D has not supplied a synonym for "affection," which may be too weak a motivation for the philanthropist as he is described here.

Paraphrase E

The responsibility of a wife and children discourages a man from taking risks with his money, time, and energy. The greatest social benefactors have been men who have adopted the public as their family.

The second sentence here is the only one of the five versions that approaches Bacon's economy of style. "Adopted the public" is not quite the same as "endowed the public" with one's "affection and means"; but nevertheless, this paraphrase is successful because it speaks for itself. It has a life and an importance of its own, independent of Bacon's original passage, yet it makes the same point that Bacon does.

> ## *Guidelines for Paraphrasing a Difficult Passage*
>
> 1. Look up in a dictionary the meanings of all the words of which you are uncertain. Pay special attention to the difficult words, considering the context of the whole passage.
>
> 2. Write a literal paraphrase of each passage by substituting appropriate synonyms within the original sentence structure.
>
> 3. Revise your literal paraphrase, keeping roughly to the same length and number of sentences as the original, but using your own sentence style and phrasing throughout. You may prefer to put the original passage aside at this point, and work entirely from your own version.
>
> 4. Read your free paraphrase aloud to make sure that it makes sense.

ASSIGNMENT 2: PARAPHRASING A DIFFICULT PASSAGE

Paraphrase one of the following passages, using the guidelines in the box above. (Your instructor may assign a specific paragraph for the entire class to paraphrase; you may be asked to work together with one or more of your classmates.)

1. Today, toys are designed to slot children into the dominant role in affluent societies: consumption. The function of modern toys is to turn children into brainless consumers, the impulsive buyers of tomorrow. Toys are little ideological bundles that inculcate a totally materialistic understanding of desire and satisfaction, enjoyment and happiness. It is the task of children to get Mom and Dad to divert an extraordinary amount of their income into buying toys.

   ZIAUDDIN SARDAR, from "Tyranny of Toys," *Resurgence*

2. Food was the basis of the earliest class system. Superior nourishment is the most primitive form of privilege, and originally quantity mattered more than quality.
   The gigantic appetite has normally commanded prestige in almost every society, partly as a sign of prowess and partly, perhaps, as an indulgence accessible only to wealth. Gluttony may be a sin but it has never been classed as a crime. On the contrary, big appetites stimulate production and generate surplus—leftovers on which lesser eaters can feed.

   FELIPE FERNANDEZ-ARMESTO, from "Food, Glorious Food,"
   The Guardian

3. It is somewhat ironic to note that grading *systems* evolved in part because of [problems in evaluating performance]. In situations where reward and recog-

nition often depended more on who you knew than on what you knew, and lineage was more important than ability, the cause of justice seemed to demand a method whereby the individual could demonstrate specific abilities on the basis of objective criteria. This led to the establishment of specific standards and public criteria as ways of reducing prejudicial treatment and, in cases where appropriate standards could not be specified in advance, to the normal curve system of establishing levels on the basis of group performance. The imperfect achievement of the goals of such systems in no way negates the importance of the underlying purposes.

WAYNE MOELLENBERG, from "To Grade or Not to Grade— Is That the Question?"

4. The price which society pays for the law of competition, like the price it pays for cheap comforts and luxuries, is also great; but the advantages of this law are also greater still than its cost—for it is to this law that we owe our wonderful material development, which brings improved conditions in its train. . . . While the law may be sometimes hard for the individual, it is best for the race, because it ensures the survival of the fittest in every department.

ANDREW CARNEGIE, from "Wealth," *North American Review* (1889)

5. Inducing soldiers to comply with dangerous orders, in short, is mostly an emotional game with mirrors, requiring psychological sleight of hand. At the decisive moments, effective leadership consists in persuasively redefining the situation, reconstructing the soldiers' sense of reality, so that what initially seems a foolhardy or even suicidal course of action comes to seem possible, even indispensable.

MARK J. OSIEL, from *Obeying Orders: Atrocity, Military Discipline and the Law of War*

USING PARAPHRASE WITH QUOTATION AND SUMMARY

The paraphrased ideas of other writers should never dominate your essay, but should always be subordinate to *your* ideas. When you insert a paraphrased sentence or a brief paraphrased passage (rather than a quotation) into one of your paragraphs, you minimize the risk that the source material will dominate your writing. *Most academic writers rely on a combination of quotation, paraphrase, and summary to present their sources and to support their theses.*

To illustrate the way in which these three techniques of presentation can be successfully combined, here is an extract from an article by Conor Cruise O'Brien that depends on a careful mixture of paraphrase, summary, and quotation. In

"Violence—And Two Schools of Thought," O'Brien gives an account of a medical conference concerned with the origins of violence. Specifically, he undertakes to present and (at the end) comment on the ideas of two speakers at the conference.

from VIOLENCE—AND TWO SCHOOLS OF THOUGHT*
Conor Cruise O'Brien

summary   The opening speakers were fairly representative of the main   1
schools of thought which almost always declare themselves when violence is discussed. The first school sees a propensity to aggression as biological but capable of being socially conditioned into patterns of acceptable behavior. The second sees it as essentially created by social conditions and therefore capable of being removed by benign social change.

quotation   The first speaker held that violence was "a bio-social phenome-   2
non." He rejected the notion that human beings were blank paper "on which the environment can write whatever it likes." He de-
paraphrase   scribed how a puppy could be conditioned to choose a dog food it did not like and to reject one it did like. This was the creation of conscience in the puppy. It was done by mild punishment. If human beings were acting more aggressively and anti-socially, despite the advent of better social conditions and better housing, this might be because permissiveness, in school and home, had checked the process of social conditioning, and therefore of conscience-building. He favored the reinstatement of conscience-building, through the use of
quotation   mild punishment and token rewards. "We cannot eliminate violence," he said, "but we can do a great deal to reduce it."

summary   The second speaker thought that violence was the result of stress;   3
in almost all the examples he cited it was stress from overcrowding. The behavior of apes and monkeys in zoos was "totally different"
paraphrase/   from the way they behaved in "the completely relaxed conditions in
quotation   the wild." In crowded zoos the most aggressive males became leaders and a general reign of terror set in; in the relaxed wild, on the other
paraphrase/   hand, the least aggressive males ruled benevolently. Space was all: "If
quotation   we could eliminate population pressures, violence would vanish."

summary   The student [reacting to the argument of the two speakers] pre-   4
ferred the second speaker. He [the second speaker] spoke with

*In its original format in *The Observer*, the article's paragraphing, in accordance with usual journalistic practice, occurs with distracting frequency; the number of paragraphs has been reduced here, without any alteration of the text.

ebullient confidence, fast but clear, and at one point ran across the vast platform, in a lively imitation of the behavior of a charging ape. Also, his message was simple and hopeful. Speaker one, in contrast, looked sad, and his message sounded faintly sinister. Such impres-

author's comment sions, rather than the weight of argument, determine the reception of papers read in such circumstances.

summary/ paraphrase Nonetheless, a student queried speaker two's "relaxed wild." He seemed to recall a case in which a troop of chimpanzees had completely wiped out another troop. The speaker was glad the student had raised that question because it proved the point. You see, where that had occurred, there had been an overcrowding in the jungle, just as happens in zoos, and this was a response to overcrowding. Condi-

author's comment tions in the wild, it seems, are not always "completely relaxed." And when they attain that attributed condition—through the absence of overcrowding—this surely has to be due to the "natural controls," including the predators, whose attentions can hardly be all that relaxing, or, indeed, all that demonstrative of the validity of the proposition that violence is not a part of nature. Speaker two did not allude to predators. Nonetheless, they are still around, on two legs as well as on four.

5

Although we do not have the texts of the original papers given at the conference to compare with O'Brien's description, this article seems to present a clear and comprehensive account of a complex discussion. In the first paragraph, O'Brien uses brief summaries to help us distinguish between the two speakers; next, he provides us with two separate, noncommittal descriptions of the two main points of view.

The ratio of quotation to paraphrase to summary works very effectively. O'Brien quotes for two reasons: *aptness of expression* and *the desire to distance himself from the statement*. For example, he chooses to quote the *vivid image* of the blank paper "on which the environment can write whatever it likes." And he also selects points for quotation that he regards as *open to dispute*—"totally different"; "completely relaxed"; "violence would vanish." Such strong statements are

---

Reasons to Use Quotation

- You can find no words to convey the economy and aptness of phrasing of the original text.

- A paraphrase might alter the statement's meaning.

- A paraphrase would not clearly distinguish between your views and the author's.

often quoted so that writers won't be accused of either toning down or exaggerating the meaning in their paraphrases.

In the last two paragraphs, it is not always easy to determine where O'Brien's paraphrase of the speakers' ideas ends and his own opinions begin. In Paragraph 4, his description of the student's reactions to the two speakers appears objective. At the end of the paragraph, however, we learn that O'Brien is scornful of the criteria that the student is using to evaluate these ideas. But at first we cannot be sure whether O'Brien is describing the *student's observation* or giving *his own account* of the speaker's platform maneuvers. It would be clearer to us if the sentence began: "According to the responding student, the second speaker spoke with ebullient confidence. . . ." Similarly, the last sentence of Paragraph 4 is undoubtedly O'Brien's opinion, yet there is nothing to indicate the transition from the student to O'Brien as the source of commentary.

This confusion of point of view is especially deceptive in Paragraph 5 as O'Brien moves from his paraphrased and neutral account of the dialogue between student and speaker to his own opinion that certain predators influence behavior in civilization as well as in the wild. It takes two readings to notice the point at which O'Brien has stopped paraphrasing and begins to speak in his own voice. Such confusions could have been clarified by inserting citations—the name of the source or appropriate pronoun—in the appropriate places.

EXERCISE 15: DISTINGUISHING BETWEEN QUOTATION, PARAPHRASE, SUMMARY, AND COMMENTARY

1. Read "Does Class Count in Today's Land of Opportunity?" by Felicia R. Lee, a staff reporter for the *New York Times*.

2. In the margin, indicate where the author uses quotation (Q), paraphrase (P), summary (S), and commentary (C).

3. In class discussion, be prepared to evaluate the use of quotation, paraphrase, and summary, and to indicate those places in the article where, in your opinion, one of the techniques is inappropriately or unnecessarily used, where the transition from one technique to the other is not clearly identified, or where the source is not clearly cited.

DOES CLASS COUNT IN TODAY'S LAND OF OPPORTUNITY?

Felicia R. Lee

As the maid Marisa Ventura in the new film "Maid in Manhattan," Jennifer Lopez 1
uses charm and hard work to vault the growing chasms between the rich, the poor
and the getting-by (managing to snag the cute, rich guy along the way).

Popular culture has always embraced the notion of America as a nation of porous 2
class lines. But as one of the most prosperous 20-year periods in American history ends, the question of just how important class has become has gained a new

immediacy. Critics accuse President Bush of skewing his $64 billion, 10-year economic plan to help the rich, while he counters that opponents are engaging in un-American "class warfare."

Sociologists, of course, have argued for decades about how to define "social class." Yet even the latest research has produced contradictory conclusions. 3

When it comes to class, is income all that matters? Is your college alma mater important? Or knowing how to use a fingerbowl? And where does race fit in? 4

"There is a big academic debate on social class as opposed to income," said David B. Grusky, director of the Center for the Study of Inequality at Cornell and a professor of sociology. "There are sociologists who argue that social class is in decline in regard to lifestyle, consumption factors and politics as coherent, meaningful groups." 5

Searching for answers, Professor Grusky and Kim Weeden, an assistant professor of sociology at Cornell, turned to 30 years of data collected by the federal government and the National Opinion Research Center, affiliated with the University of Chicago. Together, the two surveys contained information on a representative group of about 760,000 Americans, from their political attitudes to their reading and television habits. 6

The professors concluded that lumping people into big groups like the "working" or "middle" class on the basis of their incomes ultimately had little to do with what they bought, what they watched or whom they voted for. Rather, cultural and political similarities are more likely to be found among people who are in the same profession or do the same type of work, reinforced first by educational training and then by work experiences. 7

Sociologists, for instance, are mostly politically liberal while economists are mostly conservative, they said. 8

Even big occupation groupings can hide differences, Professor Grusky said. Consider an issue like abortion. Among service workers, bartenders tended to support legalized abortion while cooks and cleaners tended to oppose it. 9

"Classes are as weak as they ever were," Professor Grusky said. "There is nothing shared in the big classes. Social scientists were always off the mark in talking about these big classes." 10

Paul W. Kingston, a professor of sociology at the University of Virginia and the author of "The Classless Society: Studies in Social Inequality" (Stanford University Press, 2000), agrees. He says that people who share a common economic position "do not 11 significantly share distinct, life-defining experiences." And he further argues that economic inequality alone does not imply the existence of classes.

"The empirical issue is how would you recognize a class when you saw one," Professor Kingston said in an interview. "Does a blue-collar worker have a certain outlook, background, cultural disposition? The general impression is, there was a greater class structure 50 years ago. There is a lot of generational class mobility." 12

Professor Kingston says his research shows that habits in voting and tastes in music, television and recreation fail to correlate significantly with income. Class in the old-fashioned sense is arbitrary, he declares. 13

"Lots of people play golf, lots of people play tennis," he said, referring to two sports once seen as the province of the affluent. "Very few people go to the opera, and very few people discuss modern art. There are few of these things that speak to class." 14

In every era, some Americans work on their knees and some don't.

The public's readiness to swallow Ms. Lopez's glamorous ascent from maid to mogul is just a small indicator of how deeply ingrained the idea of social mobility is in America. Charges of class warfare often fail to resonate because many people believe they have the chance to occupy the rich end of the income scale—despite the ever-widening income gap. 15

Robert Perrucci, a sociologist at Purdue University, explains this attitude by saying, "People accept inequality if they think there is opportunity." But he, like a number of other sociologists, maintains that class counts for more now than ever. 16

"Paul Kingston views class in cultural terms," Professor Perrucci said. "I look at it in economic terms. As a sociologist, I am concerned about the volatility of a society where 80 percent of the people are frozen out of possibilities. No one is saying we all have to be equal." 17

The average annual salary in America, expressed in 1998 dollars, went from $32,522 in 1970 to $35,864 in 1999. In the same period, according to *Fortune* magazine, the average real annual compensation of the top 100 C.E.O.'s went from $1.3 million—40 times the pay of an average worker—to $37.5 million, or over 1,000 times the average worker's pay. 18

Professor Perrucci, along with Earl Wysong, at Indiana University of Kokomo and David W. Wright at Wichita State University, compared the incomes and occupations of 2,749 fathers and sons from the 1970's to the late 1990's. Their conclusion? That class mobility has decreased. 19

From the upper to the lower levels, the researchers found that sons retained 20
the same levels of income and occupational prestige as their fathers. At the upper
level, affluent sons gained prestigious positions—like doctors and lawyers—even
more frequently than their fathers did 30 years ago.

"What has happened in the last 25 years is that a large segment of American 21
society has become more vulnerable," said Professor Perrucci, who is co-author
of "The New Class Society: Goodbye American Dream?" (Rowman & Littlefield,
2002) with Professor Wysong. "Twenty years ago, going to college was enough.
Now, it has to be an elite school. The American dream is being sorely tested."

The new reality, he said, is a society in which one-fifth of Americans are privileged, 22
with job security, high wages and strong skills. The other 80 percent belong to a
"new working class," he said, that despite great variability within the group lacks
the same security and high wages.

Professor Perrucci and his colleagues proposed four measures to determine 23
where one lands on the class scale. They are: social capital (whom you know); credential capital (like where you received your degree); income or consumption capital; and investment capital (stocks and bonds). The last category is the one most
affected by Mr. Bush's new economic program and tax laws.

Minorities, Professor Perrucci added, are far more likely than whites, especially 24
white males, to lack elite educational credentials and social capital.

Although the black middle class roughly doubled in the last 20 years, about 30 25
percent of blacks (compared with 8 percent of whites) are poor by government
standards. Numerous studies also show that continued discrimination in housing
and jobs stymies black economic mobility, as does the perception that minorities
have different values and behavior from whites.

Erik Olin Wright, a sociology professor at the University of Wisconsin in Madi- 26
son, argues that race is one of the factors that mute the expression of class conflict.

"To say there's no class is to imply that the workers at Enron and the owners at 27
Enron have no built-in conflict, no different outcomes," said Professor Wright, who
is also the author of "Class Counts: Comparative Studies in Class Analysis" (Cambridge University Press, 1997).

But it is "simple-minded," he said, to argue, as some sociologists have done, that 28
the absence of open hostilities means there are no real social classes with similar
interests.

Race divisions, for example, could discourage people from similar classes to come 29
together and push for better health care or schools, Professor Wright said. Or people may be too "demoralized and resigned," he added, to organize movements that
pit working people against rich people.

"It may be the triumph of one class," he said, "one class that is so hegemonic 30
that people feel defeated."

Citing Your Paraphrased Sources

In academic writing the clear acknowledgment of the source is not merely a matter of courtesy or clarity; it is an assurance of the writer's honesty.

When you paraphrase another person's ideas, you must cite the author's name, as you do when you quote, or else risk being charged with plagiarism. Borrowing ideas is just as much theft as borrowing words.

You omit the quotation marks when you paraphrase, but you must not omit the citation. The name of the source should be smoothly integrated into your sentence, following the guidelines used for citation of quotations. The source's name need not appear at the beginning of the sentence, but it should signal the beginning of the paraphrase:

Not everyone enjoys working, but most people would agree with Jones's belief

that work is an essential experience of life.

The writer of the essay is responsible for the declaration that "not everyone enjoys working" and that most people would agree with Jones's views; but the belief that "work is an essential experience of life" is attributed to Jones. Here, the citation is well and unobtrusively placed; there are no quotation marks, so presumably Jones used a different wording.

Citing Sources

- When you *quote*, there can never be any doubt about where the borrowed material begins and where it ends: the quotation marks provide a clear indication of the boundaries.

- When you *paraphrase*, although the citation may signal the *beginning* of the source material, your reader may not be sure exactly where the paraphrase *ends*. There is no easy method of indicating the end of paraphrased material. (As you will see in Chapter 10, the author's name or a page number in parentheses works well if you are using that method of documentation.) You can signal the end of a paraphrase simply by starting a new paragraph. However, you may want to incorporate more than one person's ideas into a single paragraph. *When you present several points of view in succession, be careful to acknowledge the change of source by citing names.*

WRITING A PARAGRAPH THAT INCORPORATES PARAPHRASE AND QUOTATION

Now, let's look at the writing process in reverse again. Instead of observing the finished product and analyzing how a writer has used sources, you'll see exactly how one source can be used to support one paragraph of an essay.

The topic of the essay is *soldiers and the code of war*. The student writer is working with the following thesis: Given the nature of modern warfare, soldiers find it difficult to think of themselves as heroes. One relevant source is *Jarhead*, a memoir about Anthony Swofford's training as a Marine and his experiences during the first Gulf War. Here is an excerpt.

from JARHEAD

Anthony Swofford

As we drive in the tactical convoy toward the airfield, we occasionally pass a POW internment area, nothing more than a few-hundred-foot circle of concertina wire, and in the center a mass of surrendered men, constrained with plastic thumb cuffs. Marines walk the perimeter with Ml6s. We drive close enough to the wire so that I see the faces of the POWs, and the men look at us and smile. Occasionally an embarrassing scene of thanks unfolds as a detainee is processed, the detainee kneeling in front of his once enemy and now jailor, weeping and hugging the marine's legs. I suspect the performances are equal parts genuine and dramatic, men genuinely happy at the prospect of not dying and smart enough to please their fierce and potentially deadly jailors with an act of supplication. 1

It's easier to surrender than to accept surrender. The men who surrender do so with blind faith in the good hearts and justice of the men and the system they surrender to. They are faithful and faith is somewhat easy. Those who accept the surrendering men must follow the rules of justice. This requires not faith, but labor and discipline. 2

I feel more compassion for the dead Iraqi soldiers I witnessed yesterday than I do for these men, alive and waving the propaganda pamphlets with vigor and a smile as they await processing. These live men were my enemy just before surrendering, while the dead men are quite simply dead. Moments before surrendering, these incarcerated men might have tried to kill me, so until very recently they were capable of receiving my bullets. The dead men have been incapable of killing me for days or weeks or at least hours and so I would not have shot them. When I'd considered my enemy in the past, I'd been able to imagine them as men similar to me, similarly caught in a trap of their own making, but now that I see these men breathing and within arm's reach, witness them smiling and supplicating and wanting to be my friend, *my friend*, even as I am on my way to kill their fellow soldiers, I no longer care for the men or their safety or the cessation of combat. The enemy are caught in an unfortunate catch-22, in that I care for them as men and fellow 3 unfortunates as long as they are not within riflesight or they're busy being dead, but as soon as I see them living, I wish to turn upon them my years of training and suffering, and I want to perform some of the despicable acts I've learned over the prior few years, such as trigger-killing them from one thousand yards distant, or gouging their hearts with my sharp bayonet.

How do you write a paragraph that conveys Swofford's testimony about a soldier's life and links it to the proposed thesis of the essay? Here are four versions of a possible paragraph:

First Version

Soldiers are so caught up in the tension of battle and the fear of being killed that they can't suddenly feel compassion for the enemy when they are defeated and become prisoners. A soldier may feel more comfortable with a dead man than with a live prisoner of war. You can't kill the enemy one day and be expected to regard them as nice people the next day.

This is a reasonable *summary* of the Swofford passage. Unfortunately, there is no mention of the source. The reader has no idea that Swofford's experience is being described, and the writer is moving very close to *plagiarism*.

Second Version

In *Jarhead*, Anthony Swofford tells us about the time he came to a prisoner of war camp during the Gulf War and sees an embarrassing scene of thanks as prisoners weep and clutch their captors' legs. Swofford concludes that the prisoners have an easier time than their jailors since it's easier to surrender than to accept surrender. He can't understand how they can want to be his friend when he's performed so many despicable acts and has killed so many of their fellow soldiers.

This version cites Swofford as the source but plagiarizes his words. The writer is not *paraphrasing*, but, rather, stringing together bits of Swofford's phrases. The paragraph also lacks a *topic sentence* that explains why Swofford is being cited.

Third Version

It's easy for soldiers fighting a brutal war to lose their sense of humanity. Anthony Swofford's *Jarhead* tells us about an incident that happened to him when he was a Marine fighting in the first Gulf War. He sees a group of prisoners trying to placate their captors, and that makes him examine his own resentment at the fact that they are alive and happily trying to stay alive. Swofford can't bring himself to see them as human beings. After all, later that day he might have to kill men just like them in the enemy's army.

This is a good presentation of the source because it provides just enough material from Swofford to support the point of the topic sentence. But the writer could and should have used *quotation* to give some immediacy to Swofford's experience.

Fourth Version

Soldiers are trained to kill routinely, and to do that efficiently they can't let themselves think of the enemy as people like themselves. In *Jarhead*, Anthony Swofford describes his disgust at an "embarrassing scene of thanks" at a prisoner of war camp during the first Gulf War. Feeling ambivalent, he wants to think of the enemy "as men similar to me," but finds it hard to endure the sight of the prisoners carrying on the business of life by trying to please their captors. The enemy dead don't cause as much moral conflict for him as the living enemy. Swofford's conclusion is that "it's easier to surrender than to accept surrender" (227). It takes a lot of effort and self-control for a soldier to kill one day and be expected to take care of the enemy the next day. Swofford's experience helps me to understand what happened in Abu Ghraib jail.

The writer makes a point in the topic sentence and then convincingly uses *paraphrase* and *quotation* to support that point. The citation to Swofford is clear, and the quoted material is appropriate. Equally important, the writer doesn't just recount Swofford's experience but makes comments that link the source to the writer's own purposes in writing the essay. Finally, notice that the writer *documents* the source not only by citing the author's name and the work but also by inserting after the second quotation the page number where the paraphrased and quoted material can be found. You'll learn about the formal documentation of sources in Chapter 10.

EXERCISE 16: WRITING A PARAGRAPH THAT INCORPORATES PARAPHRASE AND QUOTATION

1. Read the following excerpt from *The Uses of Enchantment* by Bruno Bettelheim. Bettelheim was a noted psychologist who specialized in issues related to child development. *The Uses of Enchantment* analyzes the way children respond to fairy tales.
2. Assume that you're working on an essay about *the abused child in fairy tales* or about *the misery of sibling rivalry*. (Or make up a comparable topic of your own.) Write a paragraph that supports one of these topics and uses Bettelheim as a source. Remember to include appropriate and accurate citations to the author and, if your instructor requests it, provide the page number in parentheses.

from THE USES OF ENCHANTMENT
Bruno Bettelheim

No other fairy tale renders so well as the "Cinderella" stories the inner experiences of the young child in the throes of sibling rivalry, when he feels hopelessly outclassed by his brothers and sisters. Cinderella is pushed down and degraded by her stepsisters; her interests are sacrificed to theirs by her (step)mother; she is expected to do the dirtiest work and although she performs it well, she receives no credit for it; only more is demanded of her. This is how the child feels when devastated by the miseries of sibling rivalry. Exaggerated though Cinderella's tribulations and degradations may seem to the adult, the child carried away by sibling rivalry feels, "That's me; that's how they mistreat me, or would want to; that's how little they think of me." And there are moments—often long time periods—when for inner reasons a child feels this way even when his position among his siblings may seem to give him no cause for it.

When a story corresponds to how the child feels deep down—as no realistic narrative is likely to do—it attains an emotional quality of "truth" for the child. The events of "Cinderella" offer him vivid images that give body to his overwhelming but nevertheless often vague and nondescript emotions; so these episodes seem more convincing to him than his life experiences.

The term "sibling rivalry" refers to a most complex constellation of feelings and their causes. With extremely rare exceptions, the emotions / aroused in the person subject to sibling rivalry are far out of proportion to what his real situation with his sisters and brothers would justify, seen objectively. While all children at times suffer greatly from sibling rivalry, parents seldom sacrifice one of their children to the others, nor do they condone the other children's persecuting one of them. Difficult as objective judgments are for the young child—nearly impossible when his emotions are aroused—even he in his more rational moments "knows" that he is not treated as badly as Cinderella. But the child often feels mistreated, despite all his "knowledge" to the contrary. That is why he believes in the inherent truth of "Cinderella," and then he also comes to believe in her eventual deliverance and victory. From her triumph he gains the exaggerated hopes for his future which he needs to counteract the extreme misery he experiences when ravaged by sibling rivalry.

Note: Originally, this passage appeared on pages 237–238 of *The Uses of Enchantment*. A slash in the second sentence of the third paragraph indicates the page break.

PRESENTING SOURCES: A SUMMARY OF PRELIMINARY WRITING SKILLS

1. **Annotation: underlining the text and inserting marginal comments on the page.**

   The notes can explain points that are unclear, define difficult words, emphasize key ideas, point out connections to previous or subsequent paragraphs, or suggest the reader's own reactions to what is being discussed.

2. **Paraphrasing: recapitulating, point by point, using your own words.**

   A paraphrase is a faithful and complete rendition of the original, following much the same order of ideas. Although full-length paraphrase is practical only with relatively brief passages, it is the most reliable way to make sense out of a difficult text. Paraphrasing a sentence or two, together with a citation of the author's name, is the best method of presenting another person's ideas within your own essay.

3. **Quotation: including another person's exact words within your own writing.**

   Although quotation requires the least amount of invention, it is the most technical of all these skills, demanding an understanding of conventional and complex punctuation. In your notes and in your essays, quotation should be a last resort. If the phrasing is unique, if the presentation is subtle, if the point at issue is easily misunderstood or hotly debated, quotation may be appropriate. When in doubt, paraphrase.

4. **Summary: condensing the text into a relatively brief presentation of the main ideas.**

   Unlike annotation, a summary should make sense as an independent, coherent piece of writing. Unlike paraphrase, a summary includes only main ideas. However, the summary should be complete in the sense that it provides a fair representation of the work and its parts.

Part III

WRITING FROM SOURCES

The previous four chapters have described some basic ways to understand another writer's ideas and present them accurately and naturally, as part of your own writing. Until now, however, you have been working with forms of writing that are brief and limited—the sentence and the paragraph. Now you can start to use the skills that you practiced in Parts I and II to develop your own ideas in a full-length essay based on sources.

When you write at length from sources, you must work with *multiple points of view*—your own and those of the authors you're writing about. You therefore have a dual responsibility: you must do justice to your own ideas, and you must do justice to each source by fairly representing that author's ideas. But blending the ideas of two or more people within the same essay can create confusion. Who should dominate? How much of yourself should you include? How much of your sources? Moreover, in academic and professional writing you may also have to consider the perspective of your instructor or supervisor, who may assign a topic or otherwise set limits and goals for your work.

Chapter 5 discusses two approaches to writing based on a *single source*. Each demonstrates a way to reconcile the competing influences on your writing and blend the voices that your reader ought to hear:

- You can distinguish between your source and yourself by writing about the two separately, first the source and then yourself, and, in the process, developing an argument that supports or refutes your source's thesis.

- You can use your source as the basis for the development of your own ideas by writing an essay on a similar or related topic.

In the end, *your voice should dominate*. It is you who will choose the thesis and control the essay's structure and direction; it is your understanding and judgment that will interpret the source materials for your reader. When you and your classmates are asked to write about the same reading, your teacher hopes to receive, not an identical set of essays, but rather a series of individual interpretations with a common starting point in the same source.

Combining your own ideas with those of others inevitably becomes more difficult when you begin to work with *a group of sources* and must represent several authors. This is the subject of Chapter 6. It is more than ever vital that your own voice dominate your essay and that you do not simply summarize first one source and then the next, without any perspective of your own.

Blending together a variety of sources is usually called *synthesis*. You try to look beyond each separate assertion and, instead, develop a broad generalization that will encompass your source material. Your own generalized conclusions become the basis for your essay's thesis and organization, while the ideas of your sources serve as the evidence that supports those conclusions.

Chapter 6 emphasizes the standard methods of presenting multiple sources:

- Analyzing each source in a search for common themes
- Establishing common denominators or categories that cut across the separate sources and provide the structure for your essay
- Evaluating each source's relative significance as you decide which to emphasize
- Citing references from several different sources in support of a single point

You will start to practice synthesis first by working with material taken from interviews and surveys and then by beginning to analyze how writers use written sources to present their ideas and their research.

▪5▪

The Single-Source Essay

When you write from a source, you must understand another writer's ideas as thoroughly as you understand your own. The first step in carrying out the strategies described in this chapter is to read carefully through the source essay, using the skills for comprehension that you learned about in previous chapters: annotation, paraphrase, and summary. Once you can explain to your reader what the source is all about, you can begin to plan your analysis and rebuttal of the author's ideas; or you can write your own essay on a similar topic.

STRATEGY ONE:
ARGUING AGAINST YOUR SOURCE

The simplest way to argue against someone else's ideas is *complete separation between the source and yourself*. The structure of your essay breaks into two parts, with the source's views presented first, and your own reactions given equal (or greater) space immediately afterward. Instead of treating the reading as evidence in support of your point of view and blending it with your own ideas, you write an essay that first *analyzes* and then *refutes* your source's basic themes. Look, for example, at Roger Sipher's "So That Nobody Has to Go to School If They Don't Want To." Roger Sipher, a faculty member in the history department at the State University of New York at Cortland, has a special interest in educational standards.

SO THAT NOBODY HAS TO GO TO SCHOOL
IF THEY DON'T WANT TO

Roger Sipher

A decline in standardized test scores is but the most recent indicator that American education is in trouble.   1

One reason for the crisis is that present mandatory-attendance laws force many to attend school who have no wish to be there. Such children have little desire to learn and are so antagonistic to school that neither they nor more highly motivated students receive the quality education that is the birthright of every American.   2

The solution to this problem is simple: Abolish compulsory-attendance laws and allow only those who are committed to getting an education to attend.   3

This will not end public education. Contrary to conventional belief, legislators enacted compulsory-attendance laws to legalize what already existed. William Landes and Lewis Solomon, economists, found little evidence that mandatory-attendance laws increased the number of children in school. They found, too, that school systems have never effectively enforced such laws, usually because of the expense involved.   4

There is no contradiction between the assertion that compulsory attendance has had little effect on the number of children attending school and the argument that repeal would be a positive step toward improving education. Most parents want a high school education for their children. Unfortunately, compulsory attendance hampers the ability of public school officials to enforce legitimate educational and disciplinary policies and thereby make the education a good one.   5

Private schools have no such problem. They can fail or dismiss students, knowing such students can attend public school. Without compulsory attendance, public schools would be freer to oust students whose academic or personal behavior undermines the educational mission of the institution.   6

Has not the noble experiment of a formal education for everyone failed? While we pay homage to the homily, "You can lead a horse to water but you can't make him drink," we have pretended it is not true in education.   7

Ask high school teachers if recalcitrant students learn anything of value. Ask teachers if these students do any homework. Quite the contrary, these students know they will be passed from grade to grade until they are old enough to quit or until, as is more likely, they receive a high school diploma. At the point when students could legally quit, most choose to remain since they know they are likely to be allowed to graduate whether they do acceptable work or not.   8

Abolition of archaic attendance laws would produce enormous dividends.   9

First, it would alert everyone that school is a serious place where one goes to   10
learn. Schools are neither day-care centers nor indoor street corners. Young people who resist learning should stay away; indeed, an end to compulsory schooling
would require them to stay away.

Second, students opposed to learning would not be able to pollute the educa-   11
tional atmosphere for those who want to learn. Teachers could stop policing recalcitrant students and start educating.

Third, grades would show what they are supposed to: how well a student is learn-   12
ing. Parents could again read report cards and know if their children were making
progress.

Fourth, public esteem for schools would increase. People would stop regarding   13
them as way stations for adolescents and start thinking of them as institutions for
educating America's youth.

Fifth, elementary schools would change because students would find out early   14
that they had better learn something or risk flunking out later. Elementary teachers would no longer have to pass their failures on to junior high and high school.

Sixth, the cost of enforcing compulsory education would be eliminated. Despite   15
enforcement efforts, nearly 15 percent of the school-age children in our largest
cities are almost permanently absent from school.

Communities could use these savings to support institutions to deal with young   16
people not in school. If, in the long run, these institutions prove more costly, at
least we would not confuse their mission with that of schools.

Schools should be for education. At present, they are only tangentially so. They   17
have attempted to serve an all-encompassing social function, trying to be all things
to all people. In the process they have failed miserably at what they were originally formed to accomplish.

Presenting Your Source's Point of View

Sipher opposes compulsory attendance laws. On the other hand, suppose
that you can see advantages in imposing a very strict rule for attendance. In order to challenge Sipher convincingly, you incorporate both his point of view
and yours within a single essay.

Since your objective is to respond to Sipher, you begin by *acknowledging his
ideas and presenting them to your readers*. State them as fairly as you can, without
pausing to argue with him or to offer your own point of view about mandatory
attendance.

At first it may seem easiest to follow Sipher's sequence of ideas (especially
since his points are so clearly numbered). But Sipher is more likely to dominate if you follow the structure of his essay, presenting and answering each of
his points one by one; for you will be arguing on *his* terms, according to *his*

conception of the issue rather than yours. Instead, make sure that your reader understands what Sipher is actually saying, see if you can find any common ground between your points of view, and then begin your rebuttal.

1. Briefly summarize the issue and the reasons that prompted the author to write the essay.

You do this by writing a brief summary, as explained in Chapter 2. Here is a summary of Sipher's article:

> Roger Sipher argues that the presence in the classroom of unwilling students who are indifferent to learning can explain why public school students as a whole are learning less and less. Sipher therefore recommends that public schools discontinue the policy of mandatory attendance. Instead, students would be allowed to drop out if they wished, and faculty would be able to expel students whose behavior made it difficult for serious students to do their work. Once unwilling students were no longer forced to attend, schools would once again be able to maintain high standards of achievement; they could devote money and energy to education, rather than custodial care.

You can make such a summary more detailed by paraphrasing some of the author's arguments and, if you wish, quoting once or twice.

2. Analyze and present some of the basic principles that underlie the author's position on this issue.

In debating the issue with the author, you will need to do more than just contradict his main ideas: Sipher says mandatory attendance is bad, and you say it is good; Sipher says difficult students don't learn anything, and you say all students learn something useful; and so on. This point-by-point rebuttal shows that you disagree, but it provides no *common context* so that readers can decide who is right and who is wrong. You have no starting point for your counterarguments.

Instead, ask yourself why the author has taken this position, one that you find so easy to reject.

- What are the foundations of his arguments?
- What larger principles do they suggest?
- What policies is he objecting to? Why?
- What values is he determined to defend?
- Can these values or principles be applied to issues other than attendance?

You are now examining Sipher's specific responses to the practical problem of attendance in order to *analyze his premises* and *infer some broad generalizations* about his philosophy of education.

Although Sipher does not specifically state such generalizations in this article, you would be safe in concluding that Sipher's views on attendance derive from a *conflict of two principles*:

1. The belief that education is a right that may not be denied under any circumstances, and
2. The belief that education is a privilege to be earned.

Sipher advocates the second position. Thus, after your summary of the article, you should analyze Sipher's implicit position in a separate paragraph.

> Sipher's argument implies that there is no such thing as the right to an education. A successful education can only depend on the student's willing presence and active participation. Passive or rebellious students cannot be educated and should not be forced to stay in school. Although everyone has the right to an opportunity for education, its acquisition is actually the privilege of those who choose to work for it.

Through this analysis of Sipher's position, you have not only found out more about the issue being argued, but you have also established a common context—*eligibility for education*—within which you and he disagree. There is little room for compromise here; it is hard to reconcile the belief that education should be a privilege with the concept of education as an entitlement. Provided with a clear understanding of the differences between you, your reader now has a real basis for choosing between your opposing views. At the same time, your reader is being assured that this point and no other is the essential point for debate; thus, you will be fighting on ground that *you* have chosen.

You might also note that Sipher's argument is largely *deductive*: a series of premises that derive their power from an appeal to parents' concerns that their children (who faithfully attend) will have their education compromised by the unwilling students (who don't). His *supporting evidence* consists of one allusion to the testimony of two economists and one statistic. Both pieces of evidence confirm the subsidiary idea that attendance laws haven't succeeded in improving attendance. His third source of support—the adage about leading a horse to water—does deal more directly with the problem of learning; but can it be regarded as serious evidence?

Presenting Your Point of View

3. *Present your reasons for disagreeing with your source.*

Once you have established your opponent's position, you may then plan your own counterarguments by writing down your reactions and pinpointing the exact reasons for your disagreement. (All the statements analyzed in this section are taken from such preliminary responses; they are *not* excerpts from finished essays.) Your reasons for disagreeing with Sipher might fit into one of three categories:

- You believe that his basic principle is not valid (Student B).
- You decide that his principle, although valid, cannot be strictly applied to the practical situation under discussion (Student C).
- You accept Sipher's principle, but you are aware of other, stronger influences that diminish its importance (Student E).

Whichever line of argument you follow, it is impossible to present your case successfully if you wholly ignore Sipher's basic principle, as Student A does:

Student A

Sipher's isn't a constructive solution. Without strict attendance laws, many students wouldn't come to school at all.

Nonattendance is exactly what Sipher wants: he argues that indifferent students should be permitted to stay away, that their absence would benefit everyone. Student A makes no effort to refute Sipher's point; he is, in effect, saying to his source, "You're wrong!" without explaining why.

Student B, however, tries to establish a basis for disagreement:

Student B

If mandatory attendance were to be abolished, how would children acquire the skills to survive in an educated society such as ours?

According to Student B, the practical uses of education have become so important that a student's very survival may one day depend on having been well educated. Implied here is the principle, in opposition to Sipher's, that receiving an education cannot be a matter of choice or a privilege to be earned. What children learn in school is so important to their future lives that they should be forced to attend classes, even against their will, for their own good.

But this response is still superficial. Student B is confusing the desired object—*getting an education*—with one of the means of achieving that object—*being present in the classroom*; attendance, the means, has become an end in itself. Since students who attend but do not participate will not learn, mandatory attendance cannot by itself create an educated population.

On the other hand, although attendance may not be the *only* condition for getting an education, the student's physical presence in the classroom is certainly important. In that case, should the decision about attendance, a decision likely to affect much of their future lives, be placed in the hands of those too young to understand the consequences?

Student C

The absence of attendance laws would be too tempting for students and might create a generation of semi-illiterates. Consider the marginal student who, despite general indifference and occasional bad behavior, shows some promise and capacity for learning. Without a policy of mandatory attendance, he might choose the easy way out instead of trying to develop his abilities. As a society, we owe these students, at whatever cost, a chance at a good and sound education.

Notice that Student C specifies a "chance" at education. Here is a basic accommodation between Student C's views and Sipher's. *Both agree in principle that society can provide the opportunity, but not the certainty, of being educated.* The distinction here lies in the way in which the principle is applied. With his argument based on a sweeping generalization, Sipher makes no allowances or exceptions: there are limits to the opportunities that society is obliged to provide. Student C, however, believes that society must act in the best interests of those too young to make such decisions; for their sake, the principle of education as a privilege should be less rigorously applied. Students should be exposed to the conditions for (if not the fact of) education, whether they like it or not, until they become adults, capable of choice.

Student D goes even further, suggesting that not only is society obliged to provide the student with educational opportunities, but schools are responsible for making the experience as attractive as possible.

Student D

Maybe the reason for a decrease in attendance and an unwillingness to learn is not that students do not want an education, but that the whole system of discipline and learning is ineffective. If schools concentrated on making classes more appealing, the result would be better attendance, and students would learn more.

In Student D's analysis, passive students are like consumers who need to be encouraged to take advantage of an excellent product that is not selling well. To encourage good attendance, the schools ought to consider using more attractive marketing methods. Implicit in this view is *a transferral of blame from the student to the school.* Other arguments of this sort might blame the parents, rather than the schools, for not teaching their children to understand that it is in their own best interests to get an education.

Finally, Student E accepts the validity of Sipher's view of education, but finds that the whole issue has become subordinate to a more important problem.

Student E

We already have a problem with youths roaming the street, getting into serious trouble. Just multiply the current number of unruly kids by five or ten, and you will come up with the number of potential delinquents that will be hanging around the streets if we do away with the attendance laws that keep them in school. Sipher may be right when he argues that the quality of education would improve if unwilling students were permitted to drop out, but he would be wise to remember that those remaining inside school will have to deal with those on the outside sooner or later.

In this perspective, *security becomes more important than education.* Student E implicitly accepts and gives some social value to the image (rejected by Sipher) of school as a prison, with students sentenced to mandatory confinement.

Student E also ignores Sipher's tentative suggestion (in paragraph 16) that society provide these students with their own "institution," which he describes only in terms of its potential costs. What would the curriculum be? Would these institutions be "special schools" or junior prisons? And when these students "graduate," how will they take their place in society?

A reasonably full response, like those of Students C and E, can provide the material for a series of paragraphs that argue against Sipher's position. Here, for example, is Student E's statement analyzed into the basic topics for a four-paragraph rebuttal within the essay. (The topics are on the left.)

Student E

danger from dropouts if Sipher's plan is adopted (3) **custodial function of school (2)** **concession that Sipher is right about education (1)** **interests of law and order outweigh interests of education (4)**	We already have a problem with youths roaming the street, getting into serious trouble. Just multiply the current number of unruly kids by five or ten, and you will come up with the number of potential delinquents that will be hanging around the streets if we do away with the attendance laws that keep them in school. Sipher may be right when he argues that the quality of education would improve if unwilling students were permitted to drop out, but he would be wise to remember that those remaining inside school will have to deal with those on the outside sooner or later.

Here are Student E's four topics, with the sequence reordered, in outline format. The student's basic agreement with Sipher has become the starting point.

I.   Sipher is right about education.
    A.   It is possible that the quality of education would improve if unwilling students were allowed to drop out.

II.   School, however, has taken on a custodial function.
    A.   It is attendance laws that keep students in school.

III.   If Sipher's plan is adopted, dropouts might be a problem.
    A.   Youths are already roaming the streets, getting into trouble.
    B.   An increase in the number of unruly kids hanging out in the streets means even greater possibility of disorder.

IV.   The interests of law and order outweigh the interests of education.
    A.   Educators will not be able to remain aloof from the problems that will develop outside the schools if students are permitted to drop out at will.

Student E can now write a brief essay, with a summary and analysis of Sipher's argument, followed by four full-length paragraphs explaining each point. If a longer essay is assigned, Student E should go to the library to find supporting evidence—statistics and authoritative testimony—to develop these paragraphs. A starting point might be the issue that Sipher omits: how do these nonattenders fare later on when they look for work? What methods have been successful in persuading such students to stay in school?

Guidelines for Writing a One-Source Argument

- Present your source's point of view.
  1. Briefly summarize the issue and the reasons that prompted the author to write the essay.
  2. Analyze and present some of the basic principles that underlie the author's position on this issue.
- Present your point of view.
  3. Present your reasons for disagreeing with (or, if you prefer, supporting) your source.

An Argument Based on a Single Source

Here is one student's essay written in response to—and arguing against—a single source. Jana Dunn read Leon Botstein's "Let Teenagers Try Adulthood," and disagreed with his proposal to curtail the four years of high school and have students go out into the world at sixteen. Read Botstein's essay and then Dunn's response, and consider how well she argues her case.

LET TEENAGERS TRY ADULTHOOD
Leon Botstein

Note: *Leon Botstein is the president of Bard College and the conductor of the American Symphony Orchestra.*

The national outpouring after the Littleton shootings has forced us to confront something we have suspected for a long time: the American high school is obsolete and should be abolished. In the last month, high school students present and past have come forward with stories about cliques and the artificial intensity of a world defined by insiders and outsiders, in which the insiders hold sway because of superficial definitions of good looks and attractiveness, popularity and sports prowess.

The team sports of high school dominate more than student culture. A community's loyalty to the high school system is often based on the extent to which varsity teams succeed. High school administrators and faculty members are often former coaches, and the coaches themselves are placed in a separate, untouchable category. The result is that the culture of the inside elite is not contested by the adults in the school. Individuality and dissent are discouraged.

But the rules of high school turn out not to be the rules of life. Often the high school outsider becomes the more successful and admired adult. The definitions of masculinity and femininity go through sufficient transformation to make the game of popularity in high school an embarrassment. No other group of adults young or old is confined to an age-segregated environment, much like a gang in which individuals of the same age group define each other's world. In no workplace, not even in colleges or universities, is there such a narrow segmentation by chronology. 3

Given the poor quality of recruitment and training for high school teachers, it is no wonder that the curriculum and the enterprise of learning hold so little sway over young people. When puberty meets education and learning in modern America, the victory of puberty masquerading as popular culture and the tyranny of peer groups based on ludicrous values meet little resistance. 4

By the time those who graduate from high school go on to college and realize what really is at stake in becoming an adult, too many opportunities have been lost and too much time has been wasted. Most thoughtful young people suffer the high school environment in silence and in their junior and senior years mark time waiting for college to begin. The Littleton killers, above and beyond the psychological demons that drove them to violence, felt trapped in the artificiality of the high school world and believed it to be real. They engineered their moment of undivided attention and importance in the absence of any confidence that life after high school could have a different meaning. 5

Adults should face the fact that they don't like adolescents and that they have used high school to isolate the pubescent and hormonally active adolescent away from both the picture-book idealized innocence of childhood and the more accountable world of adulthood. But the primary reason high school doesn't work anymore, if it ever did, is that young people mature substantially earlier in the late twentieth century than they did when the high school was invented. For example, the age of first menstruation has dropped at least two years since the beginning of this century, and not surprisingly, the onset of sexual activity has dropped in proportion. An institution intended for children in transition now holds young adults back well beyond the developmental point for which high school was originally designed. 6

Furthermore, whatever constraints to the presumption of adulthood among young people may have existed decades ago have now fallen away. Information and images, as well as the real and virtual freedom of movement we associate with adulthood, are now accessible to every 15- and 16-year-old. 7

Secondary education must be rethought. Elementary school should begin at age 4 or 5 and end with the sixth grade. We should entirely abandon the concept of the middle school and junior high school. Beginning with the seventh grade, there 8 should be four years of secondary education that we may call high school. Young people should graduate at 16 rather than 18.

They could then enter the real world, the world of work or national service, in which they would take a place of responsibility alongside older adults in mixed company. They could stay at home and attend junior college, or they could go away to college. For all the faults of college, at least the adults who dominate the world of colleges, the faculty, were selected precisely because they were exceptional and different, not because they were popular. Despite the often cavalier attitude toward teaching in college, at least physicists know their physics, mathematicians know and love their mathematics, and music is taught by musicians, not by graduates of education schools, where the disciplines are subordinated to the study of classroom management. 9

For those 16-year-olds who do not want to do any of the above, we might construct new kinds of institutions, each dedicated to one activity, from science to dance, to which adolescents could devote their energies while working together with professionals in those fields. 10

At 16, young Americans are prepared to be taken seriously and to develop the motivations and interests that will serve them well in adult life. They need to enter a world where they are not in a lunchroom with only their peers, estranged from other age groups and cut off from the game of life as it is really played. There is nothing utopian about this idea; it is immensely practical and efficient, and its implementation is long overdue. We need to face biological and cultural facts and not prolong the life of a flawed institution that is out of date. 11

Jana Dunn

Ms. Janet Reed

ENGL 299-01

October 3, 2002

FIXING THE AMERICAN HIGH SCHOOL SYSTEM

Leon Botstein wastes no time in expressing his opinion of the American high school in his essay "Let Teenagers Try Adulthood." Botstein uses harsh words, stating that "the American high school is obsolete and should be abolished." He claims students are isolated from the real world and allowed to establish their own rules in an existence where athletes and "insiders" hold all the power in an "age-segregated environment." According to Botstein, abolishing the high school system and introducing teenagers to the adult world at the age of sixteen is the answer for today's troubled teenagers. However, what he does not acknowledge are the implications of being a teenager forced to make adult decisions at such a young age.

I agree with Botstein's assertion that the American high school institution is in dire need of attention and that the system is not meeting teenagers' needs, but abolishing high school as an institution is not the easy fix he wants us to believe. Botstein believes that teenagers are already subject to adult influences; therefore, graduating them into the adult world at a younger age is both logical and natural. Sure, teenagers are exposed to much more mature experiences today than in previous years; however, just because they are exposed to adult situations does not mean they know how to make adult decisions. Adolescent transitions are difficult. Getting rid of the middle school and introducing teenagers to an adult world two years early would send a mixed message to young people. They are already confused about the way adults want them to *act* like an adult, but expect them to accept being *treated* like a child. Teenagers need the transitional time provided by the high school system to successfully move from adolescence to adulthood; therefore, we need to focus on fixing the system, not abolishing it.

Botstein correctly touches on the problems in the high school system that need attention. One issue is "the poor quality of recruitment and training for high school teachers." In my high school, the algebra teacher held industrial arts credentials and was originally hired to be a full-time shop teacher. He often came to class with alcohol on his breath. His idea of teaching algebra was putting examples on the board and allowing the class to work on the problems together. My friend, who sat next to me in class, was my teacher. Because of the teacher's deficiencies, I have had to compensate for a lack of algebra skills throughout my college experience. Too many unqualified, uncaring people, like my algebra teacher, are filling the teaching positions in the high school system because our society does not respect the teaching profession enough to demand stellar performance from its teachers. Not until teachers are respected as professionals, given back the power to control students, and compensated appropriately will we see more qualified professionals teaching America's teenage population.

Another problem that Botstein discusses is the issue of wasted time for high school students. He states: "Most thoughtful young people suffer the high school environment in silence and in their junior and senior years mark time waiting for college to begin." I was one of those students. I went through the motions my last couple of years, just waiting for the college experience; however, I was not prepared for that experience once I graduated. Part of the problem was my guidance counselor, who did nothing but bring a few college recruiters in to talk to interested students. Nothing was done to creatively get our minds thinking about what motivates us and then learn how to turn those motivations into goals. High school students need to spend more time researching those areas they are interested in, and they need to be encouraged to do so. Too many students find themselves after graduation flailing around and wondering what to do next. Junior and senior year classes should be geared toward preparing teenagers for that next step, whether it be college or entering the work force. Taking the last two years of high school to properly prepare teenagers for the transition into adulthood is a better solution than abolishing the last two years and leaving them on their own.

Finally, Botstein introduces the idea that adults "don't like adolescents," so they use high schools "to isolate the pubescent and hormonally active adolescent away from both the picture-book idealized innocence of childhood and the more accountable world of adulthood." In other words, we don't know what to do with them while they are going through all these changes, so let's put them in a group of their own and hope for the best. I agree that many adults find it hard to deal with their teenage children; they don't always know where to go for help. Therefore, they tend to give up and just pray their children grow out of it. High school needs to be a place where teenagers feel free to ask questions, learn subjects other than the basic core curriculum, and learn to feel comfortable with who they are. Programs need to be developed to ensure these needs are met. Abolishing high school will not take care of the issues that need to be addressed; it will only skip the transitional time needed for teenagers and force them to become adults overnight.

Even though Botstein's solution misses the mark by a long shot, he does reveal the need for changes in the way our society deals with teenagers. I believe most parents and school administrators understand there is a problem, but they just do not know how to effect change. Botstein's theory of graduating students at the age of sixteen could possibly work, but only after society deals with the core problems, and only if the transitional needs of teenagers have been met. Parents, teachers, and students need to come together to make the high school institution a positive learning experience for all teenagers so that they will spend the time wisely to ensure their preparedness for adulthood.

ASSIGNMENT 3: WRITING AN ARGUMENT BASED ON A SINGLE SOURCE

Read "What Our Education System Needs Is More F's," "Forcing Greek Organizations to Go Coeducational Won't Lead to Greater Diversity," "Now, for Tonight's Assignment . . . ," and "Falling on Deaf Ears." As the starting point for an essay, select one source with which you disagree. (Or, with your instructor's permission, bring in an essay that you are certain you disagree with, and have your instructor approve your choice.)

1. Write a two-part summary of the essay, the first part describing the author's position and explicitly stated arguments, the second analyzing the principles underlying that position.
2. Then present your own rebuttal of the author's point of view.

The length of your essay will depend on the number and complexity of the ideas that you find in the source and the number of counterarguments that you can assemble. The minimum acceptable length for the entire assignment is two printed pages (approximately 500–600 words).

WHAT OUR EDUCATION SYSTEM NEEDS IS MORE F'S

Carl Singleton

Note: *Carl Singleton, a faculty member at Fort Hays State University, is the editor of* The Sixties in America, *a three-volume encyclopedia.*

I suggest that instituting merit raises, getting back to basics, marrying the university to industry, and . . . other recommendations will not achieve measurable success [in restoring quality to American education] until something even more basic is returned to practice. The immediate need for our educational system from pre-kindergarten through post-Ph.D. is not more money or better teaching but simply a widespread giving of F's. 1

Before hastily dismissing the idea as banal and simplistic, think for a moment about the implications of a massive dispensing of failing grades. It would dramatically, emphatically, and immediately force into the open every major issue related to the inadequacies of American education. 2

Let me make it clear that I recommend giving those F's—by the dozens, hundreds, thousands, even millions—only to students who haven't learned the required material. The basic problem of our educational system is the common practice of giving credit where none has been earned, a practice that has resulted in the sundry faults delineated by all the reports and studies over recent years. Illiteracy among high-school graduates is growing because those students have been passed rather than flunked; we have low-quality teaching because of low-quality teachers who never should have been certified in the first place; college students have to take basic reading, writing, and mathematics courses because they never learned those skills in classrooms from which they never should have been granted egress. 3

School systems have contributed to massive ignorance by issuing unearned passing grades over a period of some 20 years. At first there was a tolerance of students who did not fully measure up (giving D's to students who should have received firm F's); then our grading system continued to deteriorate (D's became C's, and B became the average grade); finally we arrived at total accommodation (come to class and get your C's, laugh at my jokes and take home B's). 4

Higher salaries, more stringent certification procedures, getting back to basics will have little or no effect on the problem of quality education unless and until we insist, as a profession, on giving F's whenever students fail to master the material. 5

Sending students home with final grades of F would force most parents to deal with the realities of their children's failure while it is happening and when it is yet possible to do something about it (less time on TV, and more time on homework, perhaps?). As long as it is the practice of teachers to pass students who should not be passed, the responsibility will not go home to the parents, where, I hope, it belongs. (I am tempted to make an analogy to then Gov. Lester Maddox's statement some years ago about prison conditions in Georgia—"We'll get a better grade of prisons when we get a better grade of prisoners"—but I shall refrain.) 6

Giving an F where it is deserved would force concerned parents to get themselves away from the TV set, too, and take an active part in their children's education. I realize, of course, that some parents would not help; some cannot help. However, Johnny does not deserve to pass just because Daddy doesn't care or is ignorant. Johnny should pass only when and if he knows the required material. 7

Giving an F whenever and wherever it is the only appropriate grade would force principals, school boards, and voters to come to terms with cost as a factor in improving our educational system. As the numbers of students at various levels were increased by those not being passed, more money would have to be spent to accommodate them. We could not be accommodating them in the old sense of passing them on, but by keeping them at one level until they did in time, one way or another, learn the material. 8

Insisting on respecting the line between passing and failing would also require us to demand as much of ourselves as of our students. As every teacher knows, a failed student can be the product of a failed teacher. 9

Teaching methods, classroom presentations, and testing procedures would have to be of a very high standard—we could not, after all, conscionably give F's if we have to go home at night thinking it might somehow be our own fault. 10

The results of giving an F where it is deserved would be immediately evident. There would be no illiterate college graduates next spring—none. The same would be true of high-school graduates, and consequently next year's college freshmen—all of them—would be able to read. 11

I don't claim that giving F's will solve all of the problems, but I do argue that unless and until we start failing those students who should be failed, other suggested solutions will make little progress toward improving education. Students in our 12 schools and colleges should be permitted to pass only after they have fully met established standards; borderline cases should be retained.

The single most important requirement for solving the problems of education   13
in America today is the big fat F, written decisively in red ink millions of times in schools and colleges across the country.

FORCING GREEK ORGANIZATIONS TO GO COEDUCATIONAL WON'T LEAD TO GREATER DIVERSITY
Billie Wright Dziech

Note: *Billie Wright Dziech, a faculty member at the University of Cincinnati, is the co-author of two books about sexual harassment at colleges.*

The recent decision by the Board of Trustees of Dartmouth College to make   1
the institution's Greek organizations "substantially coeducational" reflects a commitment to the principle of inclusiveness. Whether it also demonstrates understanding of the male and female students who will live out that principle is another matter.

President James Wright told a *Chronicle* reporter that single-sex organizations are   2
"not providing the fuller environment the trustees would like to have." Judging by the outcry the decision has caused, the majority of students do not agree. In protest, the College Fraternity Sorority Council at Dartmouth canceled all Greek-sponsored events during February's Winter Carnival, and a survey by the student newspaper indicated strong support for the current system, which provides much of the social life for both Greeks and non-Greeks on the isolated New Hampshire campus. Slightly more than half of Dartmouth's sophomores, juniors, and seniors are affiliated with the residential houses, although most Greek parties are open to all.

If students—and parents—who pay more than $20,000 a year in tuition and fees   3
to attend Dartmouth are satisfied with single-sex organizations; if alumni are, as reported, enraged about the proposed change, why not leave well enough alone?

It is understandable that Dartmouth is concerned about the impact of the Greek   4
system on the campus. While the trustees have not indicated that they plan to move beyond coeducation to eliminate Greek societies entirely, observers speculate that they may be contemplating such a step. Not surprisingly, many other colleges and universities—with their predominantly single-sex fraternities and sororities—are closely watching Dartmouth.

From an institutional point of view, valid reasons exist to oppose the Greek sys-   5
tem. Colleges and universities must devote significant resources to supervising the Greeks, and ultimately run a legal risk if drinking or hazing infractions occur. Although fraternities and sororities are far less elitist than in the past, they still maintain selection processes that exclude young people at an emotionally vulnerable point in their lives. And the money that it can take to join a Greek society can

limit membership to the affluent, or to those who are willing to compromise their educations by working to pay dues.

On the other hand, a compelling case can also be made in defense of the Greeks. On many campuses, they provide a significant portion of available housing, and are often the nucleus of campus activities and social life. Despite the reputation students in fraternities and sororities have for partying, they generally maintain higher grade-point averages and are more likely to pursue postgraduate education than are non-Greeks. Later, Greeks become more loyal, and financially supportive, alumni of their institutions. And, in attempting to improve their organizations' image, they partici-pate in service projects that have raised millions of dollars for charity over the past few decades.

Depending upon the situation on individual campuses, and on one's own predis-position, the cases for and against the Greek system are equally strong. Strong, that is, until one tries to argue against the system on the basis of a need for diver-sity. There, I believe, the weight is on the side of the Greeks—and that is what the trustees of Dartmouth and institutions contemplating similar changes have failed to recognize.

Problems of exclusivity will not be solved by forcing the Greeks to become co-educational. I suspect that the Dartmouth trustees and administrators have in-voked the general principle of diversity without thinking through whether enforcing coeducational fraternities and sororities genuinely promotes that goal.

Having spent decades as both a trainee and a trainer in programs designed to pro-mote diversity in educational institutions, I believe that the aim of such programs is to encourage dissimilar groups of people to recognize and respect differences in others—not to promote assimilation and sameness. That is as true for gender dif-ferences as it is for racial, ethnic, or class differences. A major impetus behind the women's movement, for example, was to establish women's rights to separate re-alities and different ways of knowing from those of men. Many of us believe that inclusiveness benefits everyone; in exploring our differences, we also discover our commonalities and achieve greater self-knowledge.

I am unsure how we moved from the original intent of diversity training to one that assumes that appreciation of diversity can be accomplished by depriving stu-dents of the right to choose their own social and living arrangements. What I do know from my own research and teaching is that denying men and women the op-portunity to bond in single-sex environments will not insure that members of either group realize their full potential. It will not enhance their college experience, will not better prepare them for the world of work, and will not improve relations between the sexes.

Twenty years ago, when I first became interested in issues of gender in litera-ture, like many others I was a true believer in an androgynous future. In the class I taught on sex roles in American literature, I was loquacious in analyzing conflicts that arose when characters acted according to gender scripts. I soliloquized about

6

7

8

9

10

11

a not-so-distant future when social conditioning would end, men and women would lay down those scripts, and gender warfare would cease as we all became as one.

Meanwhile, in discussion my students were yelling, "You just don't understand!" at one another—long before the sociolinguist Deborah Tannen made the phrase popular; my son was at home wrapping bandages stained with red paint around the doll we had given him, so that it would look like a casualty of football or war; and I was increasingly dividing males and females into segregated groups when I was called in to consult on sexual harassment in divisive work or academic environments.   12

Back in the 1970s, it was possible to attribute dissimilarities in gendered behavior entirely to psychosocial conditioning, but recent advances in endocrinology, neurology, genetics, and anthropology suggest that, however much males and females are similar, they also exhibit minute behavioral contrasts that can have serious consequences in everyday life. Some of those contrasts help to explain why same-sex bonding is important to the process of maturation, and why it is folly to assume that college students will be well served by denying them such experience. The bottom line (as my linear-minded male colleagues are fond of saying) is that Dartmouth could handcuff male and female students to one another for an entire academic year, and in most cases their communication styles, responses to stress, interests, and life styles still would differ so significantly that the experience would leave them less rather than more tolerant of one another.   13

If the aim of making the Greek system coeducational is to insure interaction between men and women, some reassessment of current conditions on the campus is in order. Coeducational institutions like Dartmouth provide countless means for males and females to socialize and work with one another. Students attend class and work together on projects that mirror the workplace. Campus clubs, publications, honor societies, and governance organizations rely on cooperation and contributions from both sexes. Intramural sports and social activities bring large numbers of men and women together; open Greek social events create additional opportunities. Except at single-sex institutions, in fact, there are few facets of college life—other than sororities and fraternities—that are not coeducational.   14

Changing the Greek system would destroy a unique opportunity for male and female students to bond with others of the same sex—all in the name of replicating conditions that already dominate the campus. And how would day-to-day collegiate existence be improved? More so than students in most dormitories, Greeks consider themselves members of quasi-families. The fact that they spend long periods of time together makes personal compatibility and shared interests and values essential.   15

Does anyone seriously believe that a young woman in the middle of a difficult emotional relationship or an academic trauma would benefit from having a group of her "brothers" engage in the typically male behavior of telling her what to do to solve her problem? Do we honestly believe that young men would be content listening to their "sisters" endlessly work their way through problems? How would   16 romantic partners who were not members react to the constant "togetherness" required of Greeks? And how would the Greek house cope with the internal sexual tensions that would inevitably surface? Date rape is already a crisis on the American campus. Could we trust coeducational sororities and fraternities to diminish the threat? Isn't it reasonable to assume that the emphasis on group cohesiveness in Greek houses would only exacerbate all of the problems that exist in coeducational dormitories?

In consulting and speaking on college and university campuses, I have found that   17
Greek organizations help students to explore confusing and personal health, safety, and lifestyle concerns with members of their own sex. Greek dinners and retreats routinely feature speakers on such issues, and the societies often require members to attend relevant campus lectures.

It is no secret, for example, that men and women approach the matter of sexual   18
harassment—as well as the issues of rape, sexually transmitted diseases, alcohol and substance abuse, eating disorders, and body image—from divergent perspectives. They have a right to engage in discussion, and to build self-esteem, within the privacy and security of environments they themselves have chosen. It would be insensitive to suppose that a female student who is having a problem with her weight—with anorexia or with overeating—would be comfortable discussing it in the presence of male students. Nor is it rational to assume that the initial education about date rape that students receive would be effective if men were too embarrassed by the presence of women to ask questions or express concerns.

More important, can we be certain that coeducational houses will further grad-   19
uates' job prospects? One of the most significant advantages of Greek membership lies in the contacts it provides. For women, the sophisticated data banks and sites on the World Wide Web that sororities have maintained have provided invaluable networking resources and job information. What will happen if the Dartmouth plan prevails across the country? Are we so naïve that we can believe that women will gain from men's access to women's resources? And are we so indifferent to men that we would deny them their own same-sex resources?

Higher education today is controlled by those who reached maturity in the 1960s   20
and 1970s. I suspect that the vast majority were not Greeks and view the characters depicted in *Animal House* as accurate models of the sorority-fraternity experience. That is not an entirely fair assessment. Further, if the Greek system does not address such problems as its excessive costs and demands on students' time, it will eventually die of its own weaknesses anyway. If Dartmouth's trustees cannot wait for that to happen, and are simply invoking diversity and inclusion to rid the campus of the Greeks, they have a responsibility to be forthright about their motivation.

If, on the other hand, the proposal for coeducational fraternities and sororities de-   21
rives from the passion for social engineering that so many of us learned in the '60s and '70s, we may need to recall that such passion often tempts us to oversimplify the complex and to disregard the interests of others. Respect for diversity is an

essential and achievable goal, but gender is a complicated issue, and we must take care that we do not allow our eagerness to improve the world to overcome common sense and respect for the rights of others.

Unlike us, the students to whom we are preaching gender equality have heard the message from birth. Arbitrarily forcing them on one another will not increase gender sensitivity or understanding.   22

Back in the days when we were first evolving our understanding of diversity, when we truly believed that we could change the world, everyone seemed to be reading Kahlil Gibran's *The Prophet*. It may not be great literature, but its observations about the young are nevertheless memorable: "Though they are with you yet they belong not to you. . . . For their souls dwell in the house of tomorrow, which you cannot visit, not even in your dreams."   23

We have given our students a vision of the ways in which men and women should relate to one another. It will be their responsibility, not ours, to determine how that vision will be realized in the future. Now we must allow them the freedom to begin living the ethic in their own ways.   24

NOW, FOR TONIGHT'S ASSIGNMENT . . .

Jonathan Rauch

Note: *Jonathan Rauch writes for the* Atlantic Monthly *(where this essay appeared), the* National Journal, *and other periodicals. His most recent book is about gay marriage.*

Suppose I told you that I knew of an education reform guaranteed to raise the achievement levels of American students; that this reform would cost next to nothing and would require no political body's approval; and that it could be implemented overnight by anybody of a mind to undertake it. You would jump at it, right? But Americans haven't jumped at it. They rarely even talk about it.   1

In 1983 I began my reporting career covering education for a North Carolina newspaper. Then—as now—everyone talked about reforming schools, but I became convinced that one of the key ingredients of successful schooling was being mostly overlooked. Learning depends on what educators call "time on task," which is what the rest of us call attending class and studying.   2

American schools are remarkably parsimonious with time. The school year is fixed at or below 180 days in all but a handful of states—down from more than 190 in the late nineteenth century, when Saturday-morning sessions were common. The instructional day is only about six hours, of which much is taken up with nonacademic matters. In 1994 a national commission calculated that in four years of high school a typical American student puts in less than half as much time on academic subjects as do students in Japan, France, and Germany.   3

Extending the school day or the school year can get expensive and complicated, and reducing nonacademic electives and gym brings hollers from parents and kids.   4

But there is one quite cheap and uncomplicated way to increase study time: add more homework.

You may not be shocked to learn that homework raises student achievement, at least in the higher grades. For young children homework appears not to be particularly helpful. Even among older students it is hard to be sure of the extent to which more homework causes higher achievement, because higher achievement also leads to more homework (brighter or harder-working kids will take more-demanding courses). Still, no one doubts that, as all kinds of studies have found, older kids learn more if they study more. Surveying the evidence in 2001, Harris Cooper, an educational psychologist, wrote, "For high school students the effect of homework can be impressive. Indeed, relative to other instructional techniques and the costs involved in doing it, homework can produce a substantial, positive effect on adolescents' performance in school." 5

You may also not be shocked to learn that, for the most part, American students don't do much homework. Nowadays homework loads among the Ivy-bound super-elite can be downright inhumane, but they are the exception. In 1999, according to the National Assessment of Educational Progress, two thirds of seventeen-year-olds did less than an hour of homework on a typical night (in other words, only about ten minutes per subject). Forty percent did no homework at all—up from 34 percent in 1984. In 1995 the Third International Mathematics and Science Survey asked high school seniors (or their equivalents) in twenty countries about study time. "Of twenty nations," says a recent report by the Brookings Institution's Brown Center on Education Policy, "the U.S. ranked near the bottom, tied for the next-to-last position." 6

I asked Tom Loveless, the director of the Brown Center, what might happen to achievement if students did more homework. "Let's say we took the forty percent who do no homework and they suddenly did an hour a night," he replied. "I think it would go up a lot. That's a hundred and eighty more hours of schoolwork"—assuming these kids studied only on school nights. For a reality check I called Raymond J. Pasi, the principal of Yorktown High School, in Arlington, Virginia, not far from where I live. He and his guidance counselors estimate that 25 to 30 percent of their students do no homework. "I believe if the average student spent twenty more minutes on homework—and by homework I would even include reviewing the day's notes—you'd see an increase in achievement of that student," Pasi told me. 7

It seems peculiar that in a country that chatters obsessively about its educational shortcomings, the word "homework" goes all but unspoken. In vain have I waited for governors and presidents to give speeches about homework, for states to audit and emphasize homework, for programs to identify and assist and prod students who don't study. 8

Why the silence? Perhaps because no one stands to earn billions of dollars on homework; perhaps because people resent politicians' and schools' intrusions into home life. I suspect that the biggest reason, however, is reluctance to use or even hint at the L-word in reference to American kids. 9

The country's schools certainly need plenty of fixing. But it is also the case that   10
many American students are lazy (there, I said it!). Just ask them. In 2001, 71 percent
of high school and middle school students agreed with the proposition that most
students in their school "[did] the bare minimum to get by." A minority described
themselves as "trying [their] best to do well in school," and 56 percent said they
"could try a little harder."

Americans like to view their children as passive recipients of education—as prod-   11
ucts of the schools. If the product is defective, fix the factory. You will know that
Americans are finally serious about education reform when they begin to talk not
just about how the schools are failing our children but also about how our children are failing their schools.

FALLING ON DEAF EARS
Pat Hagan

Note: *Pat Hagan is a British medical journalist who writes for the* New Scientist *(where
this article appeared). Unlike the other essays in this group, "Falling on Deaf Ears" presents both sides of an issue; you are free to support either one.*

Philip Aiello has been deaf since 1943. He was just three months old when his   1
hearing was destroyed by meningitis. More than half a century later, medicine had
advanced to the point where a tiny device called a cochlear implant could help.
The implant is no instant cure for deafness, but it can restore some degree of hearing. For Aiello, by this time 55, the chance was too good to miss.

In June 1998, he underwent surgery to have the device implanted. The first thing   2
he heard was the soft hum of the electrodes warming up. The second was his wife
Myrna saying hello.

But if the joy of hearing her voice for the first time is etched on his memory, so   3
too are the reactions he received. While he was still learning to use the implant,
Aiello went to Texas to attend a deaf congress. Aiello, from Wheaton, Maryland,
recalls what happened when people started noticing the implant's distinctive wire
and hearing-aid type headpiece. "They would finish the conversation to run and
tell their friends," he says.

People began to keep their distance. Or they'd creep up behind him and make   4
noises—if he didn't hear them, they'd tell their friends that the implant didn't work.
Aiello felt like he no longer belonged in the deaf community.

His ostracism demonstrates just how polarized opinions are on the treatment   5
of deafness. As cochlear implants and other devices become increasingly sophisticated, scientists are getting closer to "curing" deafness. But they are on a collision
course with large sections of the deaf community who believe they are not sick
and do not need curing. To some, it's a personal right to remain deaf.

But the current conflicts are nothing to the furor set to erupt when more ef- 6
fective and permanent treatments for deafness become available. Scientists believe
that within the next decade or so they may be able to completely restore deaf
people's hearing. Various high-tech strategies are being investigated, including gene
therapy and stem cell therapy. But to some deaf people, such approaches are akin to
eugenics. "We consider such research an appalling waste of money," says Paddy
Ladd, a lecturer in deaf studies at the University of Bristol, who has been deaf from
birth. "Do they really think we are damaged and deficient people who are simply
a biological mistake?"

About 5 percent of people in the west have significant hearing problems, and 7
just under 1 percent are profoundly deaf. Causes include genetics, infections in the
womb or during childhood, certain drugs, chronic exposure to loud noise, or simply the aging process.

Many people who have been profoundly deaf from an early age immerse them- 8
selves in the deaf community, where sign language is the primary communication
tool. The UK signing community has long fought for official recognition of British
Sign Language (BSL) as an indigenous language, arguing that about 70,000 people in
the UK use it as their first or preferred form of communication. Last year they
achieved this aim, when the government granted BSL official recognition. But the
deaf community argues this must be translated into better provision of interpreters
and video phones, and funding for teaching of BSL.

Many in the signing community reject the popular notion that they are "dis- 9
abled," arguing they are simply a minority with their own rich culture and language.
"These people were born deaf and they want to be deaf and the rest of us have
to come to terms with that," says Pamela Morrisey, head of fund-raising for the
British Deaf Association.

These battles have far-reaching implications for the way that doctors treat deaf- 10
ness, or whether they treat it at all. In particular, they will determine whether it is
ethically defensible to restore, or refuse, hearing to a deaf child too young to decide for themselves.

In many cases of deafness, the problem lies with the cochlea, the snail-shaped cav- 11
ity in the inner ear whose job is to convert sound waves into nerve impulses [see
figure on next page]. In the functioning ear, sound waves striking the eardrum trig-
ger movement of fluid inside the cochlea, stimulating auditory hair cells on its lining
to produce electrical signals; these travel along the auditory nerve to the brain. But
the hair cells are particularly vulnerable to damage, and cannot be regenerated.

A cochlear implant is an electrode that is embedded within the cochlea, where 12
it stimulates the auditory nerve directly, bypassing the hair cells. The user wears a
microphone on the back of the ear, which picks up sound waves and transmits
them to the implant. To avoid passing a wire through the skin, they are transmitted via radio waves.

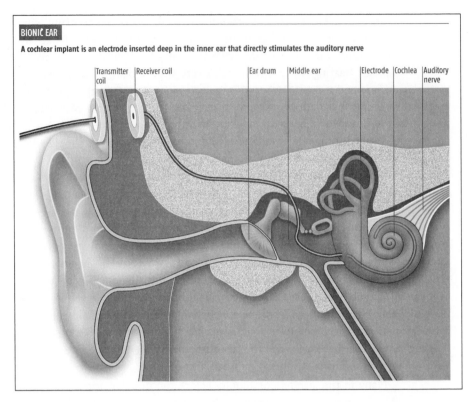

BIONIC EAR

A cochlear implant is an electrode inserted deep in the inner ear that directly stimulates the auditory nerve

Transmitter coil | Receiver coil | Ear drum | Middle ear | Electrode | Cochlea | Auditory nerve

Bionic ear

Cochlear implants by no means restore hearing to normal. The sounds produced have an artificial, tinny quality, and it can take months of effort for people to get used to them, with varying degrees of success. Children in particular need a lot of support. Some people never really succeed with the device. What's more, a cochlear implant can destroy any remaining natural hearing a person might have, because the surgery kills off any hair cells that are still functioning.   13

Despite these drawbacks, many people find the implants hugely beneficial. The device significantly improves lip-reading in most people and about 10 percent of users end up being able to communicate through sound alone. To date, an estimated 65,000 people worldwide have had a cochlear implant.   14

Debate rages among deaf people about the pros and cons of the device. Many members of the signing community argue they have no need to undergo invasive surgery that yields less-than-wonderful results. "Deaf people see themselves as not in need of 'cures,'" says Ladd, who is author of *Understanding Deaf Culture*.   15

Most contentious, however, is what happens with children. Nearly 90 percent of deaf children have hearing parents, who often see implants as a logical choice. But numerous deaf associations, including ones in Britain, the United States and Aus-   16 tralia, condemn cochlear implants for children. Implants, says Ladd, "cast [deaf children] adrift in a world in which they are an inferior version of a hearing person, rather than as a first-class deaf citizen."

Equally, deaf parents who reject implants for their deaf children also draw flak. 17
One deaf couple recently came under heavy fire when they took this a step further and deliberately conceived a deaf child through IVF.

The decision on whether to give a child a cochlear implant cannot be put off for 18
long. The first six years of life are crucial for language acquisition. Many centers advocate carrying out the surgery on children of two, or even younger. Recent research seems to support this approach. For example, a study published in May in the journal *Otology & Neurotology* followed 10 congenitally deaf infants fitted with implants between the ages of 6 and 18 months. Within one to four months of the surgery, the previously silent babies started babbling—the first stage of speech development. The younger they were when the device was implanted, the sooner this occurred.

The debate has been muddied by concerns that the implants raise the risk of the 19
potentially fatal brain infection meningitis, perhaps due to the surgery or simply the presence of a foreign object in the inner ear. Worldwide there have been 91 known cases of meningitis in people with implants, including 17 deaths. New implant recipients are now vaccinated, but passions on this issue run high. At a Manchester conference on cochlear implants two years ago, members of a group called the Deaf Liberation Front staged a protest with banners saying "Better deaf than dead."

If controversy surrounds cochlear implants, what would happen if a complete cure 20
for deafness became available? Many groups of scientists around the world are investigating other strategies to restore hearing, including gene therapy and stem cell therapy. The research is still at an early stage, but few doubt that eventually a cure will emerge.

In the late 1980s, researchers found that unlike mammals, birds can regenerate auditory hair cells. The new hair cells are derived from cells in the cochlea called supporting cells, which have a maintenance role. 21

In the developing embryo, both supporting cells and hair cells are descendants 22
of the same precursor cells. The ones that are destined to become hair cells start expressing a gene called *Math1*, whose protein product turns on a suite of other genes characteristic of hair cells.

Researchers at the University of Michigan have used gene therapy to turn supporting cells into hair cells in mammals (*The Journal of Neuroscience*, vol 23, p 4395). 23
They introduced the *Math1* gene into guinea pigs' supporting cells. Within two months they looked like hair cells. "They started changing their identity," says Yehoash Raphael, who led the research. The team is now seeing if the new hair cells can transmit signals to the auditory nerve.

But gene therapy is not the only possible approach. Last year, researchers at 24
Harvard Medical School found that small numbers of stem cells exist in the inner ear

of adult mice. Unfortunately these were in the balance organs of the inner ear, not the cochlea. But the balance organs contain hair cells that are very similar to those in the cochlea.

The team showed that when prodded with two biological signaling molecules,   25
the stem cells gave rise to what appeared to be new hair cells, both in the test tube and when put into the developing cochleae of chicken embryos. The researchers' next goals are to repeat the feat in mice embryos, then adult animals, and assess if the new cells function properly. "That's the ultimate test," says cell biologist Stefan Heller, who leads the team.

The finding has galvanized researchers in the field, for three reasons. First, it is   26
possible that inner ear stem cells could be taken from people who donate organs after death. Second, studying inner ear stem cells in the lab should make it much easier to work out how to push embryonic stem cells along the road to becoming hair cells. Third, it suggests that stem cells could also be present in the cochlea itself. Perhaps with the right chemical cues, they could be persuaded to form new hair cells without the need for any invasive surgery. "That's the hope of the whole field," says Heller. "To find a drug that brings back hearing."

Unsurprisingly, members of the signing community are less than impressed. "Sci-   27
entists are patronizing the deaf by assuming they need 'curing,'" says Lori Fuller, a deaf advocate for the campaigning group Deaf Empowerment, based in Wisconsin in the United States. "It's hearing people who have a problem with hearing loss, not deaf people."

Ladd slates the scientists involved in this research. "They do not care about us,   28
only about their own salaries or careers," he says. "None of these people has any sustained contact with deaf communities."

Not all deaf people feel the same way of course. The research is welcomed by   29
Richard Roehm, a leading deaf activist based in Irvine, California, although he acknowledges that "the majority of the adult deaf would perceive this as some sort of genocide."

Few would argue that adults have the right to decide for themselves if they want   30
medical treatment, but as with cochlear implants, the fiercest battles are likely to be fought over children. When the day eventually comes, as it surely will, that a safe cure for deafness becomes available, many hearing parents of deaf children will want to use it. To the deaf community, this is a challenge to their very right to exist, and must be resisted.

It's a viewpoint that most hearing people find hard to understand. Deaf people   31
"have to accept that there are now real treatments," says Heller. But to those who are sceptical of the deaf community's viewpoint, Ladd suggests the following thought experiment: "Had [gene therapy] emerged in the 1950s, there would have been immense social pressure to use this technology to remove homosexuality," he says. "Fifty years later, we can imagine the magnitude of the crime that would have been committed in society's name."

STRATEGY TWO: DEVELOPING AN ESSAY BASED ON A SOURCE

This strategy gives you the freedom to develop your own ideas and present your own point of view in an essay that is only loosely linked to the source. Reading an assigned essay helps you to generate ideas and topics and provides you with evidence or information to cite in your own essay; but the thesis, scope, and organization of your essay are entirely your own.

1. Finding and Narrowing a Topic

As always, you begin by studying the assigned essay carefully, establishing its thesis and main ideas. As you read, start brainstorming: noting ideas of your own that might be worth developing. You need not cover exactly the same material as the source essay. What you want is a *spin-off* from the original reading, not a summary.

Here is one student's preliminary list of topics for an essay based on Blanche Blank's "A Question of Degree." (Blank's essay can be found on pp. 11–14.) Notice that, initially, this student's ideas are mostly personal.

- "selling college": how do colleges recruit students? how did I choose this college? has my college experience met my expectations?

- "practical curriculum": what are my courses preparing me for? what is the connection between my courses and my future career? why am I here?

- "college compulsory at adolescence": what were my parental expectations? teachers' expectations? did we have any choices?

- "employment discrimination based on college degrees": what kinds of jobs now require a B.A.? was it always like that? what other kinds of training are possible—for clerks? for civil servants? for teacher's aides?

- financing college: how much is tuition? are we getting what we pay for? is education something to be purchased, like a winter coat?

- "dignity of work": job experience/work environment

- "joylessness in university life": describe students' attitudes—is the experience mechanical? is the environment bureaucratic?

- "hierarchical levels": what do the different college degrees mean? should they take as long as they do? should a B.A. take four years?

If you read a source a few times without thinking of a topic or if you can't see how your ideas can be developed into an essay, test some standard strategies, applying them to the source essay in ways that might not have occurred to the original author. Here, for example, are some strategies that generate topics for an essay based on "A Question of Degree."

Process

You might examine in detail one of the processes that Blank describes only generally. For example, you could write about your own experience to explain the ways in which teenagers are encouraged to believe that a college degree is essential, citing high school counseling and college catalogues and analyzing the unrealistic expectations that young students are encouraged to have. Or, if you have sufficient knowledge, you might describe the unjust manipulation of hiring procedures that favor college graduates or the process by which a college's liberal arts curriculum gradually becomes "practical."

Illustration

If you focused on a single discouraged employee, showing in what ways ambition for increased status and salary have been frustrated, or a single disillusioned college graduate, showing how career prospects have failed to measure up to training and expectations, your strategy would be an illustration proving one of Blank's themes.

Definition

Definition often emerges from a discussion of the background of an issue. What should the work experience be like? What is the function of a university? What is a good education? By attempting to define one of the components of Blank's theme in terms of the ideal, you are helping your reader to understand her arguments and evaluate her conclusions more rationally.

Cause and Effect

You can examine one or more of the reasons why a college degree has become a necessary credential for employment. You can also suggest a wider context for discussing Blank's views by describing the kind of society that encourages this set of values. In either case, you will be accounting for, but not necessarily justifying, the nation's obsession with degrees. Or you can predict the consequences, good or bad, that might result if Blank's suggested legislation were passed. Or you might explore some hypothetical possibilities and focus on the circumstances and causes of a situation different from the one that Blank describes. What if everyone in the United States earned a college degree? What if education after the eighth grade were abolished? By taking this approach, you are radically changing the circumstances that Blank depicts, but still sharing her concerns and exploring the principles discussed in her essay.

Problem and Solution

If Cause and Effect asks "why," then Problem and Solution explains "how." Blank raises several problems that, in her view, have harmful social consequences. What are some solutions? What changes are possible? How can we effect them? How, for example, can we change students' expectations of education and make them both more realistic and more idealistic? Note that exploring such solutions means that you are basically in agreement with Blank's thesis.

Comparison

You can alter the reader's perspective by moving the theme of Blank's essay to another time or place. Did our present obsession with education exist a hundred years ago? Is it a problem outside the United States at this moment? Will it probably continue throughout the twenty-first century? Or, focusing on contemporary America, how do trends in education and employment compare with trends in other areas of life—housing, finance, recreation, child rearing, or communications? With all these approaches, you begin with a description of Blank's issue and contrast it with another set of circumstances, past or present, real or hypothetical.

Before choosing any of these speculative topics, you must first decide:

- What is practical in a brief essay
- Whether the topic requires research
- Whether, when fully developed, the topic will retain some connection with the source essay

For example, there may be some value in comparing the current emphasis on higher education with monastic education in the Middle Ages. Can you write such an essay? How much research will it require? Will a discussion of monastic education help your reader better to understand Blank's ideas? Or will you immediately move away from your starting point—and find no opportunity to return to it? Do you have a serious objective, or are you simply making the comparison "because it's there"?

2. Taking Notes and Writing a Thesis

Consider how you might develop an essay based on one of the topics suggested in the previous section. Notice that the chosen topic is expressed as a question.

Topic: What is the function of a university today?

- After thinking about your topic, start your list of notes *before* you reread the essay, to make sure that you are not overly influenced by the author's point of view and to enable you to include some ideas of your own in your notes.

- Next, review the essay and add any relevant ideas to your list, *remembering to indicate when an idea originated with the source and not with you.*

Here is a complete list of notes for an essay defining the function of a university for our time. The paragraph references, added later, indicate which points were made by Blank and where in her essay they can be found. The thesis, which follows the notes, was written after the list was complete.

WHAT THE UNIVERSITY SHOULD DO

1. increase students' understanding of the world around them

   e.g., to become more observant and aware of natural phenomena (weather, for example) and social systems (like family relationships)

2. help students live more fulfilling lives

   to enable them to test their powers and know more and become more versatile; to speak with authority on topics that they didn't understand before

3. help students live more productive lives

   to increase their working credentials and qualify for more interesting and well-paying jobs (B.B., Paragraphs 3–9)

4. serve society by creating better informed, more rational citizens not only through college courses (like political science) but through the increased ability to observe and analyze and argue (B.B., Paragraphs 3, 14)

5. contribute to research that will help to solve scientific and social problems (not a teaching function) (B.B., Paragraphs 3, 14)

6. serve as a center for debate to clarify the issues of the day

   people should regard the university as a source of unbiased information and counsel; notable people should come to lecture (B.B., Paragraphs 3, 14)

7. serve as a gathering place for great teachers

   students should be able to regard their teachers as worth emulating

8. allow students to examine the opportunities for personal change and growth

   this includes vocational goals, e.g., career changes (B.B., Paragraph 4)

WHAT THE UNIVERSITY SHOULD NOT DO

9. it should not divide the haves from the have-nots

   college should not be considered essential; it should be possible to be successful without a college degree (B.B., Paragraphs 8, 10)

10. it should not use marketing techniques to appeal to the greatest number
    what the university teaches should be determined primarily by the faculty
    and to a lesser extent by the students; standards of achievement should
    not be determined by students who haven't learned anything yet

11. it should not ignore the needs of its students and its community by clinging
    to outdated courses and programs

12. it should not cooperate with business and government to the extent that it
    loses its autonomy (B.B., Paragraphs 6, 9)

13. it should not be an employment agency and vocational center to the exclu-
    sion of its more important functions (B.B., Paragraphs 6, 9, 16)

Thesis: As Blanche Blank points out, a university education is not a commodity
    to be marketed and sold; a university should be a resource center for those
    who want the opportunity to develop their intellectual powers and lead more
    productive, useful, and fulfilling lives.

3. Deciding on a Strategy

As a rule, you would consider strategies for your essay as soon as you
have established your thesis. In this case, however, the choice of strategy—definition—was made earlier when you chose your topic and considered several
possible strategies. The notes, divided into what a university should and
should not do, already follow a definition strategy, with its emphasis on
differentiation.

4. Structuring Your Essay

Having made all the preliminary decisions, you are ready to plan the structure of your essay.

- Mark those portions of the reading that you will need to use in support of
  your thesis. Your essay will be based on both your own ideas and the ideas
  of your source.

- Check whether your notes accurately paraphrase the source, and decide
  how many source references you intend to make so that you can write a
  balanced outline.

- Double-check to make sure that you are giving the source credit for all
  paraphrased ideas.

- If appropriate, include some examples from your own experience.

Organize your notes by arranging them in a logical sequence, which is usually called an *outline*. Some outlines use numbers and letters; some don't. But *all outlines represent the relationship of ideas by their arrangement on the page*: major points at the margin, supporting points and evidence underneath and slightly to the right.

- Organize your notes in groups or categories, each of which will be developed as a separate paragraph or sequence of related paragraphs.
- Decide the order of your categories (or paragraphs).
- Incorporate in your outline some of the points from Blanche Blank's essay that you intend to include. Cite the paragraph number of the relevant material with your outline entry. If the source paragraph contains several references that you expect to place in different parts of your outline, use a sentence number or a set of symbols or a brief quotation for differentiation.

Here is one section of the completed outline for an essay on "Defining a University for the New Millennium." This outline incorporates notes 3, 13, 9, and 8 from the list on pages 196–197.

I. The university should help students to live more productive lives, to increase their working credentials, and to qualify for more interesting and well-paying jobs. (Paragraph 6—last sentence)

   A. But it should not be an employment agency and vocational center to the exclusion of its more important functions. (Paragraph 9— "servicing agents"; Paragraph 12—"joylessness in our university life"; Paragraph 16)

   B. It should not divide the haves from the have-nots; success without a college degree should be possible. (Paragraph 2—"two kinds of work"; Paragraph 17)

II. The university should allow students to examine the opportunities for personal growth and change; this includes vocational goals, e.g., career changes. (Paragraph 4—"an optional and continuing experience later in life")

5. Writing the Essay

When you write from sources, you are engaged in a kind of partnership. You strive for an appropriate balance between your own ideas and those of your source. *It is your voice that should dominate the essay*. You, after all, are writing it; you are responsible for its contents and its effect on the reader. For this reason, all the important "positions" in the structure of your essay should be filled by you. The topic sentences of the paragraphs, as well as the essay's introduction and conclusion, should be written in your own words and should stress your views, not those of your author. On the other hand, your reader should not be allowed to lose sight of the source essay; it should be treated as a form of evidence and cited whenever it is relevant, but always as a context in which to develop your own strategy and assert your own thesis.

Here is the completed paragraph based on Points I and IA in the outline:

> To achieve certain goals, all of us have agreed to take four years out of our lives, at great expense, for higher education. What I learn here will, I hope, give me the communication skills, the range of knowledge, and the discipline to succeed in a career as a journalist. But, as Blanche Blank points out, a college education may not be the best way to prepare for every kind of job. Is it necessary to spend four years at this college to become a supermarket manager? A computer programmer? A clerk in the social security office? If colleges become no more than high-level job training or employment centers, or, in Blank's words, "servicing agents" to screen workers for business, then they lose their original purpose as centers of a higher form of learning. Blank is rightly concerned that, if a college degree becomes a mandatory credential, I and my contemporaries will regard ourselves "as prisoners of economic necessity," alienated from the rich possibilities of education by the "joylessness in our university life."

6. Revising the Essay

Your work isn't finished until you have reviewed your essay carefully to ensure that the organization is logical, the paragraphs are coherent, and the sentences are complete. To gain some distance and objectivity, most people put their work aside for a while before starting to revise it. You can also ask someone else to read and comment on your essay, but make sure that you have reason to trust that person's judgment and commitment to the task. It isn't helpful to be told only that "paragraph three doesn't work" or "I don't get that sentence"; your reader should be willing to spend some time and trouble to pinpoint what's wrong so that you can go back to your manuscript and make revisions. Problems usually arise in three areas.

Overall Structure

If you follow your outline or your revised list of notes, your paragraphs should follow each other fairly well. But extraneous ideas—some of them good ones—tend to creep in as you write, and sometimes you need to make adjustments to accommodate them. As you look carefully at the sequence of paragraphs, make sure that they lead into each other. Are *parallel points* presented in a series or are they scattered throughout the essay? Sometimes, two paragraphs need to be *reversed*, or two paragraphs belong together and need to be *merged*. In addition, your reader should be guided through the sequence of paragraphs by the "traffic signals" provided by *transitional phrases*, such as "in addition" or "nevertheless" or "in fact." The transitions need not be elaborate: words like "also," "so," and "too" keep the reader on track.

Paragraph Development

The paragraphs should be of roughly comparable length, each containing a *topic sentence* (not necessarily placed at the beginning), *explanatory sentences, details or examples* provided by your source or yourself, and (possibly) *quotations from your source*. It's important to have this mix of general material and detail to keep your essay from being too abstract or too specific. Make sure that every sentence contributes to the point of the paragraph. Look for sentences without content, or sentences that make the same point over again. If, after such deletions, a paragraph seems overly brief or stark, consider what illustrations or details might be added to support and add interest to the topic. Check back to the source to see if there are still some points worth paraphrasing or quoting.

Sentence Style

Your writing should meet a basic acceptable standard. Is the *sentence style* monotonous, with the same pattern repeated again and again? Look for repetitions, and consider ways to vary the style, such as starting some sentences with a phrase or subordinate clause. Are you using the same *vocabulary* again and again? Are too many of your sentences built around "is" or "are"? Search for stronger verbs, and vary your choice of words, perhaps consulting a thesaurus. (But think twice about using words that are totally new to you, or you'll risk sounding awkward. Use a thesaurus to remind yourself of possible choices, not to increase your vocabulary.) Finally, consider *basic grammar and punctuation*. Are the sentences complete? Eliminate fragments or run-ons. Check for apostrophes, for subject-verb agreement, for quotation marks. Don't let careless errors detract from your hard work in preparing and writing this essay. And use a spellchecker!

ASSIGNMENT 4: WRITING AN ESSAY BASED ON A SINGLE SOURCE

A. Read "An Army of One," "The Pillars of the Temple of Liberty," and "The End of Courtship." One of these three essays will serve as the starting point for an essay of your own. Assume that the essay you are planning will be approximately three pages long, or 600–900 words. Using Steps 1 and 2 in the guidelines on page 201, think of *three* possible topics for an essay of that length, and submit the most promising (or, if your teacher suggests it, all three) for approval.

B. Plan your essay by working from notes to an outline. Be prepared to submit your thesis and outline of paragraphs (with indications of relevant references to the source) to your teacher for approval.

Guidelines for Writing a Single-Source Essay

1. Identify the source essay's thesis; analyze its underlying themes, if any, and its strategy; and construct a rough list or outline of its main ideas.

2. After brainstorming, decide on two or three possible essay topics based on your work in Step 1, and narrow down one of them. (Be prepared to submit your topics for your teacher's approval and, in conference, to choose the most suitable one.)

3. Write down a list of notes about your own ideas on the topic, being careful to distinguish between points that are yours and points that are derived from the source.

4. Write a thesis of your own that fairly represents your list of ideas. Mention the source in your thesis if appropriate.

5. If you have not done so already, choose a strategy that will best carry out your thesis; it need not be the same strategy as that of the source essay.

6. Mark (by brackets or underlining) those paragraphs or sentences in the source that will help to develop your topic.

7. Draw up an outline for your essay. Combine repetitious points; bring together similar and related points. Decide on the best sequence for your paragraphs.

8. Decide which parts of the reading should be cited as evidence or refuted; place paragraph or page references to the source in the appropriate sections of your outline. Then decide which sentences of the reading to quote and which to paraphrase.

9. Write the rough draft, making sure that, whenever possible, the topic sentence of each paragraph expresses your views, introduces the material that you intend to present in that paragraph, and is written in your voice. Later in the paragraph, incorporate references to the source, and link your paragraphs together with transitions. Do not be concerned about a bibliography for this single-source essay. Cite the author's full name and the exact title of the work early in your essay. (See pp. 115–119 for a review of citations.)

10. Write an introduction that contains a clear statement of your thesis, as well as a reference to the source essay and its role in the development of your ideas. You may also decide to draft a conclusion.

11. Review your first draft to note problems with organization, transitions, or language. Proofread your first draft very carefully to correct errors of grammar, style, reference, and spelling.

12. Prepare the final draft. Even if you use a computer spellcheck, proofread once again.

C. Write a rough draft after deciding which parts of the essay should be cited as evidence, distributing references to the source among appropriate sections of your outline, and determining which parts of the reading should be quoted and which should be paraphrased.

D. Write a final draft of your essay, and then proofread the draft before submitting the final version to your instructor.

AN ARMY OF ONE

Christopher Clausen

Note: *Christopher Clausen, a faculty member at Penn State University, writes essays for the* American Scholar *and other literary journals. His most recent book is* Faded Mosaic: The Emergence of Post-Cultural America.

A few years ago I received an odd letter from a stranger. He said that he had read my capsule biography in *Contemporary Authors* and noticed it made no mention of military service in the Vietnam War. I had been of the right age to serve. Why hadn't I been drafted? There was no explanation of why the writer was interested in me, or whether he regularly scanned reference books for information about the military histories of little-known authors. He said nothing about himself. The letter was brief and entirely to the point.

In answering his somewhat aggressive question, I said truthfully that I had no idea why I had not been drafted. I had been ordered to report for a physical in 1965 but was immediately granted an occupational deferment. I was twenty-three and had just accepted a job teaching composition at the University of Hawaii. My deferment lapsed three years and two jobs later, at the height of the war, after which I was classified 1-A with eight more years of eligibility according to the law then in force. My draft board always knew where I was, yet it never bothered me again. In 1973 the draft ceased to operate, and, like most other young American males, I heaved a sigh of relief.

I could have said a great deal more, but how much information does one owe a stranger who writes out of the blue—especially a stranger who presumably supported the Vietnam War and suspects (correctly) that his addressee was opposed to it? I could have told him I still have the draft card my local board sent me after I registered at the age of eighteen, complete with a nine-digit number and an immature but recognizable version of my signature. I could have told him that in 1967, along with an unknown number of other draft-eligible men spending the summer in Europe, I signed a pledge saying that if called, I would refuse to be inducted as long as the Vietnam War continued. I could have told him that none of my three brothers and hardly any of my friends were drafted either. I could have told him to get lost.

Like most people my age, I had thought very little about this ancient history for almost thirty years when, as war against Saddam Hussein began to seem probable in the fall of 2002, a scattering of liberal Congressmen and columnists called for restor-

1

2

3

4

ing the draft in order, ostensibly, to distribute the potential burden of combat more equitably. Most were men in their sixties or seventies who had served in earlier wars. One of them was Representative Charles Rangel, a Korean War veteran who noted that few members of the House or Senate had children of their own in the armed forces. As he explained in a *New York Times* op-ed column:

> Service in our nation's armed forces is no longer a common experience. A disproportionate number of the poor and members of minority groups make up the enlisted ranks of the military, while the most privileged Americans are underrepresented or absent.
>
> We need to return to the tradition of the citizen soldier—with alternative national service for those who cannot serve because of physical limitations or reasons of conscience.

This plea aroused momentary attention but no immediate action. The Pentagon announced that the all-volunteer forces were working fine, while most commentators dismissed what they saw as a transparent ploy to make waging war prohibitively difficult.

Because young men subject to the draft had provided such a reservoir of anti-war opinion during the Vietnam era, proponents seemed to calculate that reviving the eligibility of their sons today would make almost any armed conflict politically impossible. Rangel hinted as much in his article. Adding their daughters to the mixture—a possibility about which he was silent—would create even greater havoc with public opinion. Women have never been subject to conscription in the United States. When the Carter administration asked Congress to reinstate registration (but not the draft itself) in 1980, it proposed requiring both sexes to comply. Congress refused to go along, and since that time men alone have had to register when they reach the age of eighteen. This durable form of sex discrimination would probably not survive judicial review if it ever became consequential again. The result would be upwards of four million new recruits, male and female, every year—a number that would wreak chaos on the Defense Department, which currently manages an active-duty force of 1.4 million uniformed personnel and about half as many civilian employees. Even in the peak year of the Vietnam War draft, 1966, the armed forces inducted only 343,000 men, a fraction of those eligible.   5

Having threatened indiscriminate jeopardy for the young, those who were proposing a new draft not surprisingly found that their natural audience, the peace movement, had minimal interest in it, and even before the war in Iraq began, it fell back out of public consciousness.   6

As James C. Miller III, a University of Virginia economist and future director of the Office of Management and Budget, wrote in 1968, "The volunteer army is an issue that cuts across political and foreign-policy lines; it counts among its supporters 'hawks' and 'doves,' liberals and conservatives, Democrats and Republicans." He added presciently, "It is an issue that is coming to the fore of American life."   7

Any serious proposal to restore conscription thirty years after its suspension   8
would dramatically expose splits not just between but among liberals and conservatives. People who in a former life had supported the Vietnam War would find
themselves on both sides, grouped in each case with people who had passionately
opposed it. Advocates of conscription usually argue, like Rangel, that equity demands
universal liability to military service; that the volunteer force disproportionately
(though not predominantly) attracts the poor and the nonwhite; and that the upper middle class should not be permitted to avoid the dangers faced by members
of the enlisted ranks in time of war. Of course, the conscript army as it existed in the
1960s was vulnerable to precisely the same charges—witness my deferment and that
of my brothers. Many of the criticisms now made of the volunteer army are nearly
identical to those formerly made of the draft. In order to avoid such inequalities, a
new draft would presumably offer few deferments of any kind. For purists, universal liability would mean universal service. More likely, a lottery system would reduce the actual recruits to a manageable number. In order for the armed forces to
mirror American society with any degree of fidelity, volunteering for the enlisted
ranks would probably have to be forbidden, in which case a professional officer
corps would preside over an ever-changing mass of short-term conscripts.

On the other side of the question, even many firm believers in equality are du-   9
bious about involuntary servitude to the government, whether actual or potential,
especially when it involves the risk of death. (In fact, being a commercial fisherman
or a taxi driver is more dangerous than being an American soldier, but no one is
coerced into those occupations by law.) Many Americans, both liberals and conservatives, feel a genuine commitment to individual liberty. In addition, many liberals consider the values of the military establishment so undemocratic that not even
a firm belief in what Rangel called "shared sacrifice" can make them enthusiastic
about conscription. While conservatives more often admire the armed forces and
what they stand for, their preference for voluntarism tends to outweigh their commitment to social equality. On yet another hand, conservatives tend to believe that
the responsibilities of citizenship are as important as rights. The ideological per-
mutations are nearly endless.

The terms of this intermittent debate have changed hardly at all since Vietnam.   10
In a 1971 op-ed piece for the *New York Times*, Senator Edward Kennedy wrote: "Although I share with many of my colleagues a deep and abiding respect for the concept of voluntarism in a democratic society, I cannot believe it should be raised
above the demands of social justice. For that reason, I remain unalterably opposed
to a volunteer army in wartime." Explicitly tying the continuation of the unpopular
draft to his hope of ending American participation in Vietnam, Kennedy also complained that a volunteer army "would mean that the economically disadvantaged
would form the bulk of the entries into the armed forces under the inducement
of higher pay." To make the draft more equitable, he proposed a random selection
system that would abolish student deferments, though he said nothing about the

messier question of deferments for people in what the Military Selective Service Act called occupations "found to be necessary for the public health, safety, or interest." A lottery system similar to what Kennedy proposed was in fact briefly instituted before the draft ended.

The moral argument against the draft, then as now, was usually based on traditional concepts of civil liberties in a country that until 1940 had known conscription only for brief periods during the Civil War and World War I, and had in both cases abolished it soon after the emergency ended. The idea that even a reformed draft could contribute to social equality was ridiculed by, among others, the distinguished pacifist A. J. Muste. At the height of World War II, Muste wrote: "The argument that compulsory military training will level barriers between economic groups will not bear a moment's scrutiny. Has that been, save in isolated individual cases, the effect of conscription and militarization in the countries like Germany and France where these have been tried out most fully?" He asked scornfully, "When have men ever looked, except in brief moments of revolution, to armies for anything but preservation of the status quo or reaction?" Subjecting the whole male population to military training would only indoctrinate them more efficiently in nationalistic and militaristic attitudes. 11

Much of Muste's argument was echoed during the Vietnam-era debate. In 1969, John W. Swomley, a writer for *The Nation*, repeated that the draft could never be made equitable and went on to make the fundamental point that united its growing number of opponents on the left and right: "The power to reach into every family, to take a boy from his home and subject him to complete military discipline for months or years, is the most serious limitation America places on freedom. In the final analysis, the issue is freedom, rather than equality under compulsion." An argument that probably carried more weight in Congress was the prospect that, compared with the draftees of the late sixties, an all-volunteer force would be better trained, more capable, and more committed to the service. 12

At eighteen I already knew that nature had not designed me to be a soldier but was not sure the army or the Selective Service System would agree. Youth hosteling in France a few years later, I discovered that the only males my age who were exempt and unworried were the British, whose country had abolished conscription in 1960. "England is the only democratic country in the world," I remember an Alsatian youth saying regretfully as he took one last vacation before reporting for duty. The sense of an impending and onerous obligation weighed on all the rest of us. It forged a strong international bond between young men and carried with it a widespread, usually unspoken envy of young women's freedom that would probably surprise most feminists today. Despite their longtime reluctance to engage in military conflict, the countries of Western Europe lagged far behind the United States in doing away with conscription. France, whose revolution gave rise to the concept of "the nation in arms," ended its draft only in 2001. Spain, Portugal, and Italy soon 13 announced they would follow suit. Switzerland and the Scandinavian countries, however, practice conscription to this day. Perhaps the oddest case of all is Germany, a country whose contemporary self-image is based on rejecting militarism in all its guises. In early 2003, the German government successfully defended its continuing policy of male-only conscription in the European Court of Human Rights against a charge of sex discrimination. (Ironically, the same court had recently ordered the all-volunteer British armed forces to admit homosexuals.) Perhaps realizing how out of step Germany has become with most other free countries, and also feeling the need for a more effective professional force, in recent years German commentators have increasingly called for an end to the conscription practiced in their country for nearly two centuries.

Like many other late-nineteenth-century immigrants, my male ancestors on both sides came to the United States to avoid a European military draft. In my paternal great-grandfather's case, Prussia wanted him, an eighteen-year-old Dane from newly conquered Schleswig-Holstein, to do his bit in the Franco-Prussian War. My maternal grandfather, on the other hand, was a Romanian Jew who had no desire to fight for a country in which his career options were so limited by prejudice. Both took refuge in the New York garment industry. My paternal grandfather, born in the slums of lower Manhattan, volunteered for the Seventh Cavalry in 1905 and served creditably in a time of peace. Although probably the most warlike Clausen in living memory, he soon left the army and spent the rest of a long life as a traveling pharmaceutical salesman. He continued to voice the extreme reverence for American institutions so often found among the successful children of immigrants, but I suspect he was too strong-willed to have flourished for long in uniform. His own sons, a sociologist and a botanist, held deferments throughout World War II. My father, the sociologist, spent most of those four years working for the War Department on a massive study of the American soldier. One of my earliest childhood memories is of driving with my parents to his office at the newly opened Pentagon on a rainy day near the end of the last great war of massed conscript armies, a war in which the United States drafted some ten million men.

Suspended after the war, the draft was reinstated in 1948 and lasted for twenty-five years. It was during this period that being "in the service" came to be accepted as a routine hurdle on the track to manhood. Few of my high school contemporaries regarded it as a major injustice, let alone an outrage. It was just a fact of life, like so many other burdens that adults placed on the young. Even Elvis Presley submitted to a GI haircut and served his time without protest. If a boy dropped out of high school, he almost invariably joined the service at seventeen, since doing so gave him a greater choice of branch and specialty than if he waited around to be drafted. Navy and air force uniforms were considered more glamorous than the army's drab olive green. On the other hand, the enlistment period was longer. If one were drafted, one would serve two years on active duty in the army, followed by four more in the reserves. Healthy young men who graduated from high school but didn't

14

15

volunteer or go immediately to college could expect to be called up sooner or later, we were told, sometime before their twenty-sixth birthday. They became eligible at eighteen and a half but might not actually be needed for years. Meanwhile, they had to notify their draft board every time they moved and ask its permission if they wished to leave the country. For those of us who went to college, the uncertainty dragged out even longer, potentially well into our thirties. Contrary to popular opinion a generation later, the National Guard was not an especially attractive alternative. It involved the same six years of liability, and its members might be called to active service at any time.

This stoical attitude toward not being in full possession of one's life survived the Korean War but changed rapidly with Vietnam. At least it changed rapidly among those of us who had gone to elite colleges, thought we were well informed, and were now at an age when acceptance of adult dictates came less readily than it had in high school. How much of this change really derived from opposition to the Vietnam War is debatable. Perhaps longer-term trends in American life merely coincided with a war that has come to be tactfully described as "unpopular." 16

There was a story one used to hear in the late 1960s about a brilliant graduate student, a friend of a friend, who had been drafted out of Harvard or Columbia, maybe Berkeley, before he could finish his Ph.D. He might have claimed to be a conscientious objector, but he was too honest. After basic training, he had immediately been sent to Vietnam. There, in the last week of his tour of duty, he had been caught in an ambush, or stepped on a mine, and suffered irreversible brain damage. A vegetable, he had been sent home to a Veterans Administration hospital. Fortunately, he had died. Such a waste. 17

The point of the story was not that some dropout from Harlem or the West Virginia hollows should have gone to Vietnam instead. The point was that nobody should have had to go. Once that conclusion had been reached about Vietnam, it inevitably condemned the draft as a whole, on principle. Conscientious objection to Vietnam in particular, or to any specific war, was impossible for potential draftees. According to the law, you had to be a religious pacifist of long standing, universally opposed to conflict, and the evidence for your claim was rigorously scrutinized. Eventually, many clergymen who opposed the war themselves were willing to lie in order to help young men of no particular religious convictions stay out of the army. I had an activist friend in New York, a Jewish atheist, who managed to get testimonials from a number of impeccable sources, including the Protestant chaplain of Yale. But most young men had neither the connections nor the stamina to pursue such a complicated procedure. Becoming a clergyman oneself, and thereby exempt from the draft, seemed even more dubious to members of a generation that congratulated itself on its contempt for hypocrisy. Inspired by the professional football star Joe Namath, who was classified 4-F, many searched for cooperative doctors who would attest to a disqualifying medical condition. If all else failed, for those who were utterly determined to avoid both the army and prison, there was Canada. 18

The war showed no sign of ending, and I opposed it in such futile ways as were   19
available to me: demonstrating outside Pearl Harbor, relentlessly hectoring anyone
who would listen, writing shrill letters, raising money for Vietnamese war orphans,
giving at least a C to most of the students who told me that a failing grade would
send them to Vietnam, supporting Eugene McCarthy for president in 1968. Late
one night, a friend and I Scotch-taped an antiwar petition to the Confederate soldier monument in Pearisburg, Virginia. When President Johnson announced an end
to his run for re-election that year, it seemed as though the stalemate might soon
be over after all. Then came the assassinations of Martin Luther King and Robert
Kennedy, followed by the election of Richard Nixon. At that point I decided to spend
a year in England. Then, worn out with resisting, I moved to Canada to begin my long-
deferred Ph.D. In all this turmoil my draft board never seems to have given me a
thought once it had reclassified me, proving again the advantages of total obscurity.

　　With its long, open border, liberal immigration policies, and no draft of its own—   20
in fact, with no significant armed forces—Canada was the obvious refuge for American opponents of the war. It was the only foreign country where Americans could
usually pass for natives, since few Canadians could distinguish them by their speech.
Better still, beginning in 1968, it welcomed draft dodgers. From then on, Canada
figured in the mythology of draft resisters much as the underground railroad had for
escaped slaves. Some people were bitterly offended by the thought of having to take
refuge in another country. I remember hearing a Washington friend of my grandmother's, an official af the Bureau of Standards, tell his son, who was far too young
to be drafted, that he should never let the warmongers drive him out of his own
country. But what if (as seemed increasingly possible) the war was going to drag
on until the end of time and the only alternative was jail? Perhaps thirty to forty
thousand draft evaders and deserters—there is no official estimate—did cross the
border and begin new lives above the forty-ninth parallel. After a few years, their enforced exile ended when the Carter administration, in one of its first acts, proclaimed an amnesty for Vietnam-era draft evaders. By then many of them had
become so used to living in Canada that they stayed on permanently.

　　Unlike the draft dodgers I soon met at Queen's University and in Toronto, I was   21
in a position to cross the border as many times as I liked in both directions. No border inspector ever so much as asked about my draft status. This freedom gave my
exile a very odd character. Canadians, particularly Canadian academics, greeted
me as a refugee from oppression and sympathized vastly with all I had suffered.
But I rather spoiled the effect by going home every few months. How could they
imagine me as a Jew on the run from Nazi Germany—a favorite comparison of the
time—if I spent vacations in Munich or Baden-Baden? Up to a point, my trips across
the border made me seem even braver, for surely I ran the risk of being arrested
for my opposition to the war, or beaten up, or shot by one of the many Americans
who carried guns? When I explained that none of these things was likely, some of my
Canadian acquaintances concluded I was hopelessly naïve. Perhaps in some respects

I was, but going back and forth led me unintentionally to make a series of running comparisons between life in the two countries. While in many respects this comparison showed Canada to advantage, it was not as one-sided as my Canadian friends, few of whom regularly visited the States, would have expected. I was weighing a humane, enlightened nation whose complacency disguised a marked lack of self-confidence against a great world power that was tearing itself apart in an evil time. Neither country knew much about the other, but while Americans who were not attempting to escape the war seldom gave Canada a thought, to its northern neighbor the United States was a permanent obsession.

It was hard to credit the fantasies of some Canadian professors and students   22
about the United States. Its major cities were in ruins because of perpetual racial strife. The country was gearing up for civil war or possibly a military coup. And for good measure, at any moment the United States government might fulfill the goal of invading and annexing Canada that it had cherished since 1812. Eventually I gave up trying to reassure Canadians that this picture was wildly exaggerated, and in particular that nobody in the United States had the slightest intention of invading Canada. Many of them did not wish to be reassured. So much of the Canadian national identity, for intellectuals at least, seemed to be based on not being American. America was warlike and aggressive; Canada was a peaceful friend of all the world. (Never mind that Canada depended entirely on the United States for its defense.) Most Americans were violent racists; Canadians never so much as raised their voices except to denounce the prejudices of others. Canada had an expanding array of social programs, including a new scheme of national health insurance; the United States remained mired in social Darwinism. A well-published senior literary scholar explained to me patiently that one had to expect "such a young country" as the United States to behave like an adolescent on the world stage. (This from a native of a confederation created by an act of the British Parliament in 1867.) Although I agreed with my Canadian colleagues' positions on Vietnam and many other things, their uninformed sense of moral superiority eventually alienated me even more from them than from my own country.

I should emphasize that I enjoyed living in Canada, and I profited enormously from   23
studying there during the brief heyday of Canadian higher education. At the same time, the net effect was to make me more tolerant of American flaws and less indulgent toward neighbors who were frequently too timid or incurious to visit the United States and see what things were really like. I felt more and more like Quentin Compson, the Harvard freshman in William Faulkner's novel *Absalom, Absalom!* who tried to explain the American South to his uncomprehending Canadian roommate and was ultimately reduced to saying, "You would have to be born there." By my last year in graduate school, influential Canadian academics were loudly complaining that Americans had taken over the Canadian economy, bought up the best Canadian land, polluted Canadian culture, even taken all the best jobs in Canadian universities. Stung by what seemed to have become a perpetual whine, I wrote a

letter on the subject to the *Toronto Star* near the end of my stay. As a result, I was invited on a national TV program to debate three buffoonish nationalists from an organization called the Committee for an Independent Canada. With truculent monotony they accused Americans of buying everything in Canada worth having. When, in the heat of the moment, I pointed out we weren't buying anything that wasn't for sale, it finally dawned on me that I would never become a Canadian.

Really, that decision had been made without my quite knowing it the previous year, when I finished my degree and began to think about the future. My Ph.D. committee included an Australian, a South African, an Englishman, and an American. It was a distinguished group, but not a very positive sign that I was joining the Canadian way of life. The world was starting to look different again. I had just turned thirty. The likelihood of my ever being drafted seemed very small. South of the border, George McGovern was running for president. Canada offered many advantages and much generosity, but every week I felt more like a foreigner. It was evidently time to go.   24

At a time when many Vietnam veterans were also coming home, I crossed the border at Buffalo for the last time in a blinding snowstorm, driving a rental car that was crammed to the roof with my possessions. The American customs and immigration inspector looked about my own age. "How long have you been in Canada?" he asked blandly. "Three and a half years," I answered. "You buy anything there?" I pointed to the back of the car. He laughed and waved me through. "Welcome home," he said.   25

The draft has been dormant now for almost as long as it lasted during its entire sporadic existence in America. It seems in retrospect a thoroughly antique institution, like the kind of warfare for which it was devised in the first place. Looking back on the first half of a mostly fortunate life, I can hardly believe that conscription bedeviled my entire youth and that of so many others born between the 1920s and the 1950s. Yet it did. Except possibly during World War II, it was always more significant as a social institution, a largely disruptive one for the poor and affluent alike, than as an effective means to create armies and fight wars. Some found a career or learned a trade in the army. The vast majority simply served out their time. When the draft was still in force, most of its supporters admitted it was a moral imposition, thoroughly inconsistent with the values on which the country was based, but argued that it was necessary for defending those same values in a dangerous world.   26

While the world obviously remains dangerous today, the argument for the draft has become almost the opposite of what it used to be. Now, those who support restoring it do so almost entirely on the basis of other moral considerations— equity, discipline for the well-off, and a sometimes unacknowledged pacifism—while conceding that a new draft would be immensely expensive in dollars and liberty without being essential, or even helpful, for any military purposes the United States   27 is ever likely to have. Whatever one thinks of American foreign policy then or now, the morale of an army composed of losers in a lottery is not hard to imagine. A system whose original purpose was to make large-scale warfare possible would now be used to discourage American participation in any military action not wholly defensive. Whether it would actually have that effect is anybody's guess. The remembered image of youthful crowds burning draft cards and chanting "Hell no, we won't go" may still be vivid, but it belongs to another world. Those who long for its return are probably deceiving themselves.

Because a universal military draft would be neither practicable nor useful, most present-day enthusiasts for conscription propose forms of "national service" that would not necessarily be military. This idea, which goes back to William James, has been debated on and off since the 1940s. It seems to combine liberal egalitarianism and echoes of the New Deal with conservative ideals of responsibility and social obligation, of "giving something back," which is no doubt why both liberals and conservatives support it. Such a plan would not, however, solve the problem of who should fight our wars. If "national service" allowed for other options besides the armed forces—most people who propose it seem to envision something like the Civilian Conservation Corps, carrying out public-works projects in national parks or teaching inner-city children to read—then the job of combat would remain exactly where it is today, in the hands of volunteers. Moreover, a draft for these purposes would impose mass compulsion without even the justification of necessity that supporters of the old draft were able to offer. Some of the same journalists and public figures who complain most loudly that the War on Terror is destroying civil liberties simultaneously propose to abolish the freedom of every young American for a year or two, or however long it would take to make their point.   28

The wave of hedonism and individualism that began sweeping through every Western society in the 1960s would have crested even if Vietnam had never existed. Both its causes and its effects are immensely complicated, but one thing it did was make certain kinds of demands on individuals—by the state or by "society," one of the vaguest words in the English language—seem illegitimate. Even the most regimented organizations had to come to terms with this change in attitude. At present, the Defense Department seems to have adapted more successfully than many of its critics. Its most memorable recruiting slogan is "An army of one," a phrase that many listeners find ironic, since—in all sorts of obvious respects—belonging to an army drastically reduces one's individuality. But the phrase demonstrates brilliantly just how discipline, initiative, *esprit de corps*, and other military values can be marketed in the seemingly adverse context of contemporary America. "One's-Self I sing, a simple separate person," wrote Walt Whitman a few years after the Civil War, "Yet utter the word Democratic, the word En-Masse." The effort to square this circle, to reconcile the prized values of individual choice and opportunity with solidarity in an extended family, is one of the major themes of American history. The effectiveness and evident self-confidence of the volunteer   29 armed forces thirty years after Vietnam suggest that the Pentagon has learned a great deal about the society it exists to protect.

The Selective Service System still exists, with a handsome Web site and a budget of more than twenty-five million dollars a year, waiting for something to do besides encourage males to obey the law by registering within thirty days of their eighteenth birthdays. But so far as anyone can reasonably predict, the draft itself is gone forever, and good riddance. Except during the gravest emergencies, it was an intolerable policy for a free society. If nothing else, the fact that eighteen-year-olds can now vote makes its resurrection unlikely. Those who want to bring it back seem, like the man who wrote to ask about my military career, to be still refighting the Vietnam War. People who live in the past should not expect the rest of us to join them there.   30

THE PILLARS OF THE TEMPLE OF LIBERTY
Diana Schaub

Note: *Diana Schaub, a faculty member at Loyola College, serves on the President's Council on Bioethics. She has written articles on American political philosophy for various journals and has published a book on Montesquieu.*

> *At what point shall we expect the approach of danger? By what means shall we fortify against it? Shall we expect some transatlantic military giant, to step the Ocean, and crush us at a blow? Never! All the armies of Europe, Asia and Africa combined, with all the treasure of the earth (our own excepted) in their military chest; with a Buonaparte for a commander, could not by force, take a drink from the Ohio, or make a track on the Blue Ridge, in a trial of a thousand years.*
>
> Abraham Lincoln, Address before the Springfield
> Young Men's Lyceum, 1838

Are we to think that September 11 proved Lincoln wrong? Certainly, there are many Americans who now feel vulnerable. In losing their sense of security, they may also have lost their sense of American exceptionalism. While it might have been true that America was once geographically blessed, our moated fortress is no longer unbreachable. Nature's gift has been undone by our own technological ingenuity. It does not even require an intercontinental ballistic missile to "step the Ocean"—an airplane will do. A few foresighted observers had long (and unavailingly) warned that the advances of modernity might be turned against us by anti-modern crusaders who would take a sick delight in the irony of such death-dealing. It seems that in the future our protection will depend more on ourselves than on Providence, and will largely be a matter of defending ourselves against the vicious application of our own inventions, devices, appliances, and agents.   1

At the start of the Lyceum Address—the most profound meditation we have on the perpetuation of our political institutions—Lincoln says that each post-founding   2 generation has two tasks: to transmit the possession of "this goodly land . . . unprofaned by the foot of an invader" and to transmit the "political edifice of liberty and equal rights . . . undecayed by the lapse of time, and untorn by usurpation." The attack on September 11 was a profanation. By the standards of world history, it was a minor one, but not so in the American collective consciousness. Yet the fact that we can express the sum total of our experience of foreign attack with such concision—December 7 and September 11—is a testament still to American exceptionalism. No enemy is marching along the Blue Ridge and, I daresay, none will be. Thus, it seems to me that Lincoln is still essentially correct. There is no American equivalent of the Fall of France, the Battle of Britain, the Siege of Stalingrad, or the Austrian Anschluss. What we have are two infamous days—days that stir us to such anger and overwhelming counterattack that they are not soon repeated. Moreover, it is worth remembering that the Islamic militants do not have in view a takeover of America; they left a footprint intended to insult and panic us, but have no plan (or at least no reasonable expectation) of placing a jackboot on our supine neck forever. Their tyrannical aspirations are directed closer to home where they are engaged in an intra-Islamic struggle. If they hoped to provoke our withdrawal from the Arabian Peninsula, they chose a singularly stupid tactic that may well prove suicidal not just for the bombers but for the movement as a whole. The enshrinement of suicide at the heart of an enterprise is likely to become a self-fulfilling prophecy.

Lincoln believed that the task of maintaining "the political edifice of liberty and equal rights" against the twin threats of "time" and "usurpation" was a much more daunting task than that of protecting the land from invaders. Here is what he says:

> At what point then is the approach of danger to be expected? I answer, if it ever reach us, it must spring up amongst us. It cannot come from abroad. If destruction be our lot, we must ourselves be its author and finisher.

In the immediate wake of September 11, there was a worry that we would harm ourselves (and grant the terrorists a victory) if we allowed the fear of further attack to alter our way of life. We were cautioned against curtailing either our civil liberties or our spending habits (hence, zero-percent financing on a new car to "Keep America Rolling"). This attitude of hardy disdain has much to recommend it. It was the first reaction of Londoners to the Blitz. In *Their Finest Hour*, Churchill says that "everybody went about his business and pleasure and dined and slept as he usually did. The theatres were full, and the darkened streets were crowded with casual traffic." Although the wisdom of taking sensible precautions soon became apparent, Churchill describes that initial refusal to admit disruption as "a healthy reaction," far superior to "the frightful squawk which the defeatist elements in Paris had put up on the occasion when they were first seriously raided."

Civil libertarians want to tough it out as well. What they fear more than loss of American lives is that certain forms of self-defense will grant a lasting and insidious victory to the enemy. They worry about self-inflicted damage to the system— a kind of home-front equivalent of "friendly fire." It is already obvious that the terrorists know how to manipulate our political system (especially the freedom to travel and the protections of the person against arbitrary search, seizure, and arrest), just as they know how to manipulate our technology. They would use liberty to undermine liberty. Hitler's exploitation of legality to bring about the collapse of the Weimar regime is the classic example of democracy's liability to subversion. Must we accept that this is a vulnerability inseparable from our form of government? In the name of liberty, must we allow liberty to be abused? Or can we defend liberty without sacrificing or sullying the end for which we are fighting by the means that unscrupulous enemies make necessary?

Given that Lincoln was himself willing to use strong measures against saboteurs, it does not seem that his fears of self-inflicted damage were the same as the ACLU's. It is good to remember what Lincoln said in defense of his suspension of the privilege of the writ of habeas corpus (in accord with Article I, section 9 of the Constitution which explicitly allows for such suspension "when in Cases of Rebellion or Invasion the public Safety may require it"). Lincoln compared the measure, in his strikingly homely fashion, to an emetic. He did not anticipate any permanent damage from the use of emergency powers, since he didn't believe either individuals or nations develop a taste for foul medicines:

> Nor am I able to appreciate the danger . . . that the American people will, by means of military arrests during the rebellion, lose the right of public discussion, the liberty of speech and the press, the law of evidence, trial by jury, and Habeas corpus, throughout the indefinite peaceful future which I trust lies before them, any more than I am able to believe that a man could contract so strong an appetite for emetics during temporary illness, as to persist in feeding upon them through the remainder of his healthful life.

Lincoln may be right, but what gives one pause with respect to the creation of the Office of Homeland Security is that it does not seem to be conceived as a temporary wartime measure. It has all the trappings of a permanent establishment. If Americans are now to understand themselves as under a lasting and indefinite threat, with the home front indistinguishable from the front line, it really would mean a sea change. While a few of the preparedness measures (e.g., better training and coordination of emergency personnel) are probably smart things to do, I nonetheless suspect that we could (and should) abandon many of the costly and time-consuming security measures, which are both ineffective and insulting. Instead of treating every citizen like a potential terrorist, why not trust the eagle eyes of the flying public? The necessary virtue is courage—a virtue that does not flourish in overly bureaucratized, overly policed states.

Leaving aside questions about the intended scope and tenure of the Office of Homeland Security, I wonder about the wisdom of pressing into service the term "homeland." It is a word that comes into currency when national survival is at stake and will, I believe, under more normal circumstances, sound overheated. Indeed, even in times of national danger, it is not a term that leaps naturally to the American tongue, perhaps because in a nation of immigrants "homeland" could never have quite the resonance that it has for older, more homogeneous peoples. Even for second-, third-, and fourth-generation Americans, the homeland is the place one's ancestors left. Certainly, "fatherland" and "motherland" have a distinctly un-American ring to them. Filial piety may contribute to American patriotism, but it is not its foundation. Accordingly, American patriotic songs rhapsodize as much about the flag as about the land (witness especially "The Star-Spangled Banner" and "You're a Grand Old Flag"). When they do celebrate the land, it is in unique ways, as in the remarkable verse "This is my country! Land of my choice!" I doubt that a survey of anthems from around the world would produce any equivalent.

Other nations emphasize autochthony: "Thou art the gentle mother of the children of this soil, Beloved land, Brazil" or "Think, beloved fatherland, that heaven gave you a soldier in each son" (Mexico) or "Indonesia, my native land, my place of birth, where I stand guard, over my motherland." America being such a vast, geographically diverse land produces other unusual effects. Lyrical tributes often catalogue the variety: "From the mountains, to the prairies, to the oceans white with foam" or "From California to the New York Islands, from the Redwood Forests to the Gulf Stream waters, this land is made for you and me." The United States could have no equivalent of "Edelweiss." Yes, "Edelweiss" was written by Rodgers and Hammerstein for *The Sound of Music*; nonetheless, it perfectly captures the rooted character of patriotism in a small, alpine nation. By contrast, American songs convey a bird's-eye view of the whole "from sea to shining sea." The diversity of the land is matched, of course, by the diversity of individuals who choose this land as their own. Woody Guthrie's line "this land is made for you and me" implies that America is broad enough (physically and metaphysically) to accommodate both "you" and "me." What transforms you and me into "us" is not a shared nativity, but our pledged allegiance to the flag "and to the republic for which it stands." 8

Since September 11, there has been a phenomenal resurgence of flag-waving. The symbolic stand-in for the republic stands proud and upright, but how about the republic itself. How—and for what—does the republic stand? Perhaps not as sturdily or as undivided as one would hope. This was Lincoln's worry in 1838 and must still be ours today to the extent that Americans are confused about, ignorant of, contending over, and (whether consciously or not) departing from the founding principles of the republic. 9

There have been painful recent reminders of our self-division. Witness the flap over the proposed memorial to the New York firefighters who lost their lives at the World Trade Center. The commissioned statue was to be based on the widely circulated photo, first published in the Bergen County *Record*, of three firemen raising an American flag at Ground Zero—a photo strikingly reminiscent of the even more famous photo of six American servicemen raising the flag at Iwo Jima. The 10

World War II photo was translated into bronze, becoming the U.S. Marine Corps Memorial. The Fire Department of New York wanted a similarly monumental rendering of the image and moment of its heroism. Before casting the scene into bronze, however, it made a decision to change the cast of characters. Instead of the three white firemen of the photo, there were to be one white, one black, and one Hispanic. The recasting, however, met with objections, and then the objections to the recasting met with objections, and soon enough everyone was offended. The most flattering light in which to put the incident would be to say that Americans of all complexions love their flag so much they fight over the honor of raising it (and the honor of dying for it). A less flattering light would reveal how many of our judgments are filtered and distorted by racially polarizing lenses.

I see no reason to doubt that most of those who object to the photo's alteration do so on principle. They want the statue to reflect the grim and glorious reality of that moment. Those were real men acting in real time. They don't want a gussied up, public relations version. Such "diversity" (which pretends to an inclusiveness and racial proportionality that does not in fact exist in the FDNY) might be fine for recruiting brochures, but the appeal of the photo was in the way it bodied forth inner qualities. It was the soulfulness of the picture that captured the nation's attention. If the flag-raisers had been all black or all female, I trust that the advocates of historical memory would be demanding the same fidelity to the moment and that the photo (despite its superficial unrepresentativeness) would still be regarded as a natural for commemoration. Yet, under the current ideological dispensation, one is not allowed simply to see character. The eye is arrested by the surface. It is color that must be seen. If the rainbow isn't there, it must be added.   11

Since it is the expression of dedication and heroism that counts, one might ask what difference a little "artistic license" makes. The argument of "artistic license," however, seems stretched since the reason for the change is not aesthetic but political. Those who corrected the photo say they wished to pay tribute to all the firefighters who died, some of whom were African American and Hispanic. Presumably the firefighters were also of varying religion, marital status, sexual orientation, height, handedness, and moral quality. Why is race the relevant category? And if racial designations are so important, must artistic and symbolic renditions be accurate, neither over- nor underrepresenting the 24 martyred firemen, out of 343, who were minorities?   12

Perhaps it would help if we remembered that the purpose of any memorial is to honor the dead, not necessarily to depict them. The photo was of living firemen captured in a spontaneous act of honoring their fallen brothers. It was one degree removed or abstracted from the actual event. By what reasoning must the honor guard mirror the racial composition of the honored dead? If the brotherhood is real, what matters the race of the honorer? It would be suggestive of segregation rather than integration if a black fireman had to be added in order to deliver honor to the fallen black firefighters, since the governing presumption would then be that one   13 can honor only those of one's own hue. It would certainly give new meaning to the term "color guard."

Perhaps what generated most offense was the implication that there was some-   14
thing wrong with the event as it actually transpired. Being airbrushed (or firehosed) out of the picture cannot help but be perceived as a denigration of the individuals in-volved and, by extension, of white firemen in general (since what was wrong was their race). If the racial homogeneity of the original group constituted an insuper-able objection, then the idea of using the photo should have been dropped to avoid the Orwellian insult.

The opponents of political correctness have found some unlikely allies among   15
black commentators. Clarence Page, columnist for the *Chicago Tribune*, has argued that a multiracial memorial would serve only to "mask patterns of discrimination that fire departments have practiced for decades." Since this is a department that is 94 percent white, the monochrome of the photo was not accidental. For the Fire Department of New York to offer a retouched self-presentation, driven by bad conscience, in which minority representation swells from 6 percent to 66 per-cent is mendacious. Thus, the call for historical accuracy cuts in different direc-tions. The picture that seemed so right—because so expressive of sacrifice and bravery—is now bedimmed and just as likely to be interpreted as evidence of on-going institutional racism. There are those who would reinstate the white-guy orig-inals not for their originality but for their whiteness. Thereby the memorial would become "exhibit A" in the court of racial opinion, where there is no protection against self-incrimination.

Although as a nation we are often greatly divided on racial matters, rarely is   16
there a straight black/white divide. For that, I suppose, we should be thankful. De-spite predictions of eventual "race war" from commentators the likes of Thomas Jefferson and Alexis de Tocqueville, America's racial battles have not, in the main, been racial in the sense of being fought out between the races. They have instead been contests between the holders of alternative understandings of justice and al-ternative visions of what conduces to racial accord. Like so much else in America, the disputes are fundamentally doctrinal. Happily enough—happy at least for those who believe in the freedom of the mind—race, sex, and class do not turn out to be reliable proxies for viewpoint.

Lincoln, of course, became a protagonist in the greatest of these doctrinal dis-   17
putes. Already in 1838, well before the rent in the Union became manifest, he warned of the danger of self-destruction: "As a nation of freemen, we must live through all time, or die by suicide." Freedom is invulnerable to all but self-inflicted wounds. It is for this reason that Lincoln agrees with the ancient authors who argued for the priority of domestic over foreign affairs. Again, even more against the mod-ern bias, Lincoln did not regard economic matters as the essence of domestic affairs. If the "body politic" can be said to have a soul, then the alimentary is elemental, but subordinate. Subscribing to the "statecraft as soulcraft" school, Lincoln elevated

virtue above security (whether economic or physical) and education above defense. Or, rather, he saw virtue and education as the only true means of defense against the twin threats of "time" and "usurpation." Similarly, when *The New Criterion* sponsors an inquiry into the "survival of culture," it expresses a concern not for survival but for culture, or not simply for survival but rather for the survival of a thing that transcends mere survival. As Aristotle noted of the political community, "while it comes into being for the sake of living, it exists for the sake of living well"—"well" being defined as living by law and justice, living nobly rather than richly.

For Lincoln, the perpetuation of our political institutions depends decisively on   18 the rightness of our self-understanding. Indeed, in 1855, Lincoln said he was prepared to withdraw his allegiance should our divarication from orthodoxy go much further. In a letter to a slave-owning friend, he closed with these mordant lines:

> Our progress in degeneracy appears to me to be pretty rapid. As a nation, we began by declaring that "*all men are created equal.*" We now practically read it "all men are created equal, *except negroes.*" When the Know-Nothings get control, it will read "all men are created equal, except negroes, *and foreigners, and catholics.*" When it comes to this I should prefer emigrating to some country where they make no pretence of loving liberty—to Russia, for instance, where despotism can be taken pure, and without the base alloy of hypocracy.

Unlike Jefferson, who wrote so sanguinely of "the progress of the human mind," Lincoln concluded that the mind, or at any rate the American mind, was more likely to retrogress and digress. Principles that had been clearly understood in the beginning (despite their frequent violation in practice) were being lost to sight, covered over, distorted, repudiated, and forgotten (perhaps because of their too-long-permitted violation).

In the Lyceum Address, Lincoln diagnosed the decay brought about by "the lapse   19 of time." His metaphor was architectural. He spoke of "the temple of liberty," originally supported by "pillars," now "crumbled away." Those pillars were "the *passions* of the people" or more precisely the sound form which the passions assumed as a result of the impress of "the interesting scenes of the revolution." During the fight for liberty, the people's worst passions were either suppressed (as were "jealousy, envy, and avarice") or redirected outward against the enemy (as was the case with "hate" and "revenge"). Once the fight was over, however, and more especially once the memory of the fight had faded, the base passions lost their structural and supportive form. Lincoln declares that "[p]assion has helped us; but can do so no more. It will in future be our enemy." Lincoln recommends the crafting of wholly new pillars, "hewn from the solid quarry of sober reason."

Although Lincoln's aim is the perpetuation of our political institutions, his method   20 is not that of a historic preservationist. He does not strive to repair or reproduce the original pillars. Perpetuation can be achieved only by a fundamental improvement: the substitution of imperishable reason for perishable passion. Lincoln's depreciation of passion leads him to expect little from the study of history. There can be no lasting appeal to "the scenes of the revolution." The history books cannot inspire patriotism. What rendered those scenes once powerful was the "*living history*" of the men who figured in them,

> a history bearing the indubitable testimonies of its own authenticity, in the limbs mangled, in the scars of wounds received . . . —a history, too, that could be read and understood alike by all, the wise and the ignorant. . . . But *those* histories are gone. They *can* be read no more forever. They *were* a fortress of strength; but, what invading foemen could *never do*, the silent artillery of time *has done.*

In keeping with his choice of reason over passion, Lincoln emphasizes the texts that perdure (the Declaration, Constitution, and laws) rather than the vanishing "scenes of the revolution." He favors the word over the spectacle. His discipline is political philosophy, not history.

Lincoln's new pillars would demand much more of the people. While the passions of the people were sufficient to erect the political edifice, its maintenance will depend on "their judgment." Self-government begins with the self. A well-ordered state cannot be formed out of disordered individuals. Here again, Lincoln runs counter to the modern claim that private vice can conduce to public benefits if only the vices be ingeniously arrayed. From Machiavelli to Kant, we have been promised that moderation will be the automatic, systemic consequence of immoderate, competitive interaction—no need for the old-fashioned version of moderation which consisted in the habit of saying no to the desires. 21

Lincoln's paean to the rulership of reason in the individual soul calls for reason to be molded into three qualities: "*general intelligence, sound morality* and, in particular, *a reverence for the constitution and laws.*" The last of these, which allies reason with reverence, is the most intriguing. Whereas scenes and spectacles fade over time, words and texts can acquire greater force, taking on an almost scriptural status. It is as if religious feeling is transposed onto the plane of politics. While some might consider reverence a passion, Lincoln describes it as crafted from the material of "cold, calculating, unimpassioned reason." In this he seems to disagree with Madison who, as Father of the Constitution, was also very keen on reverence. Although Madison admits that "in a nation of philosophers . . . a reverence for the laws would be sufficiently inculcated by the voice of an enlightened reason," he suspects that ordinary nations will discover reverence to be a salutary public prejudice, dependent on factors other than the abstract rightness of obedience to law. Reverence is more a function of the stability (and hence antiquity) of the government. In Federalist 49, Madison recommends that this conservative prejudice be carefully encouraged, primarily by not involving the people too often in large and troublesome questions that would disturb their tranquility. 22

In Lincoln's day, public tranquility (the key ingredient of non-philosophic rever-   23
ence) was already compromised "by the operation of this mobocratic spirit, which
all must admit, is now abroad in the land." Under the circumstance of "increasing disregard for law," Lincoln could not trust time to settle the inflammation. He had to
address the public on the most significant and sensitive issue and he had to do so
through reason alone. His speeches are remarkable for the non-impassioned, almost
mathematical spareness and rigor of their argumentation. Lord Charnwood, in his
biography of Lincoln, says that "[h]e put himself in a position in which if his argument
were not sound nothing could save his speech from failure as a speech." This willingness to trust to the compulsion of logic was a great act of faith in the capacities
of the people. If self-government is a real possibility, then even a mob must have
its "better angels." Perhaps Lincoln's democratic faith helps explain how these same
speeches are often suffused with religious language and culminate in moments of
deep but restrained reverence. Think of the final paragraphs of the Lyceum Address,
the Cooper Union Address, and the First Inaugural, as well as virtually the whole
of the Gettysburg Address and the Second Inaugural.

Lincoln's speeches are in themselves demonstrations of how "reverence for the   24
constitution and laws" can proceed from reason alone. The efforts he made to reduce his thoughts to the cleanest, most crystalline formulations were in the service of a recovery of orthodox constitutionalism. It was Lincoln's conviction that the
Constitution, properly understood and venerated, offered the only hope for a solution to the slavery crisis—a solution that would do justice to all, South as well
as North, and achieve justice for all, black as well as white. If slavery could be once
again placed where the Founders had placed it—namely "where the public mind
shall rest in the belief that it was in the course of ultimate extinction"—then all
might yet be well. To prove it, Lincoln undertook patient, textual explications of
the principles informing the founding charters and equally patient elaborations of
the public policy implications of those principles.

In one sense, Lincoln failed miserably. His attempt to engraft these new pillars   25
seemed to shake the edifice itself. The election of the man most dedicated to reason provoked an unreasoning rebellion. The faded scenes of the revolution were replaced with fresh (but unwholesome) scenes of civil war, where hate and revenge
turned inward.

Yet the conflict issued in something sublime: the Union was saved and refounded   26
on the fundamental principle of emancipation. And all understood that this was
Lincoln's achievement. Walt Whitman described the culmination of the war of secession in the martyrdom of Lincoln as "that seal of the emancipation of three million slaves—that parturition and delivery of our at last really free Republic, born
again, henceforth to commence its career of genuine homogeneous Union, compact,
consistent with itself." According to Whitman, the death of Lincoln provided

a cement to the whole people, subtler, more underlying, than any thing in written constitution, or courts or armies—namely, the cement of a death identified

thoroughly with that people, at its head, and for its sake. Strange, (is it not?) that battles, martyrs, agonies, blood, even assassination, should so condense—perhaps only really, lastingly condense—a Nationality.

Whitman emphatically sides with history and the commemorative muse of poetry. If Lincoln's analysis in the Lyceum Address is correct, however, then the scenes of the Civil War, including its murderous climax—what Whitman calls "its highest poetic, single, central, pictorial denouement"—will fade. So too all subsequent American scenes of moral grandeur. We live right now on the cusp of the loss of the "living history" of World War II—the history that bears "the indubitable testimonies of its own authenticity, in the limbs mangled, in the scars of wounds received." The recent tributes to "the greatest generation," fitting though they are, will not prevent the action of "the all-resistless hurricane" of time.

There is a direct connection between these perils of "time" and that other danger mentioned by Lincoln: "usurpation." Because the very passions that proved a pillar of liberty at the time of the nation's framing will, in later days, become instruments for demagogic manipulation and demolition, only new pillars "hewn from the solid quarry of sober reason" could succeed in upholding liberty. Reason prepares the people to resist usurpation by teaching them how to recognize it. Unlike invasion by an avowed enemy (which in all but the most debilitated nations would prompt self-defense), usurpation can occur imperceptibly, particularly when it is ideological rather than personal in character. Mistaken understandings insinuate themselves into the public mind and become habitual. To usurp means literally "to take possession of by use," and that is precisely how false philosophy comes to seize public opinion. (Of course, if false philosophy goes far enough, it can blind a nation to external threats as well and weaken self-preservative reflexes.) Resistance to usurpation begins with the ability to recognize what is pernicious, to understand which streams of thought are dangerously at odds with the principles of republican self-government. 27

Aware that reflection must supersede reflex, Lincoln dedicated his entire political career to educating Americans in the meaning of their original charters. It was an education conducted by means of electoral contests with the usurpers (or their progeny), from John C. Calhoun—the man who began what Lincoln termed "an insidious debauching of the public mind"—to Stephen A. Douglas, whose doctrine of "popular sovereignty" effected a reinterpretation of the Declaration that left it "without the *germ* or even the *suggestion* of the individual rights of man," thereby rendering it "mere rubbish" and "old wadding." Even Lincoln's prosecution of the war entailed teaching—namely, "teaching men that what they cannot take by an election, neither can they take it by a war." Bullets were far from the only weapons employed to defend the sanctity of the ballot. As much as the rebel army, it was the rebel argument about the legitimacy of secession that had to be defeated. Lincoln did so by revealing the articulation of the principle of free elections, the doctrine of the social compact, and the original truth of human equality, at each point contrasting it with the counter-trinity of secession, state rights, and slavery. 28

The inscription on the Lincoln Memorial reads: "In this temple, as in the hearts   29
of the people, for whom he saved the Union, the memory of Abraham Lincoln is
enshrined forever." Despite those words, we must wonder whether there is anything
imperishable in Lincoln's statesmanship, never forgetting that in Lincoln's own estimation, memory by itself is insufficient. This is true even in the First Inaugural, where
he famously refers to "mystic chords of memory, stretching from every battlefield,
and patriot grave, to every living heart and hearthstone, all over this broad land." Lincoln goes on to say, however, that the mystic chords of memory must be activated or
sounded by something else within us, namely "the better angels of our nature," which
I take to mean intellect and understanding—after all, the whole of the First Inaugural is a carefully argued logical appeal which waxes poetic only in its final lines.
Once again, it is reason that stirs reverence; it is dialectics that "will yet swell the chorus of the Union." (The cosmos operates the same way: without mathematics there
would be no music of the spheres.) The lesson I would draw is that the memory
of Lincoln is vitalized only when we think the thoughts he thought. Accordingly,
the Lincoln Memorial rightly includes, on flanking walls, the full texts of the Gettysburg Address and the Second Inaugural—texts that in turn direct the reader to
other texts: the Declaration of Independence, the Constitution, and the Bible. As the
Gettysburg Address tells us, it is fitting to grieve and pay our respects to the dead,
but the only complete commemoration is for the living to dedicate themselves to the
same "cause" and "unfinished task," so that the dead "shall not have died in vain."

Since it is a rare thing to encounter politicians capable of serving as preceptors   30
of the people, the task of citizen education falls heavily upon the schools. To the
extent that they have even bothered with it, their approach has been historical—
tending to err either in the direction of hagiography or in a debunking revisionism
that essentially criminalizes the nation's founding. It has not worked. And I don't
believe it can work. Students are much more receptive to a philosophic approach—
one that puts reason before reverence (or irreverence). Such an approach, in fact,
fits well with many of their predispositions and allergies. Being inclined toward
cynicism, they are suspicious of pious story telling. At the same time, despite having been exposed to a lot of "feet-of-clay" historiography, they long to have America's past—and especially the idea of America—restored to respectability (so long
as it can be done without a whitewash). While I have focused almost exclusively
on Lincoln here, one would proceed very differently in a course, substituting dialectics for exhortation. Students would read works by Calhoun, Douglas, and the
abolitionists (especially Frederick Douglass), in addition to Lincoln. Unlike so many
other intellectual projects, this one grabs them because it is connected with their
sense of self. They want to know how they ought to regard their nation. They
want to know how to think about equality and liberty.

Despite the best efforts of the deconstructionists, young people often venerate   31
the Constitution. When they encounter the debate between Jefferson and Madison on the desirability of regular change in the laws, they all immediately side with

Jefferson (since "laws and institutions must go hand in hand with the progress of the human mind"), but when they realize that Jefferson wanted a Constitutional Convention every twenty years, these supposed partisans of the new are horrified. It is as Madison had hoped: undisturbed longevity has produced veneration. The problem, however, is that the veneration is often devoid of any knowledge, and so the content of their political ideas is frequently at odds with the documents they claim to respect. Respecting a document is not as straightforward as respecting a person. Without philosophic literacy, it is easy for public opinion to be shanghaied.

To give an example: when affirmative action was adopted more than a generation ago, it was widely understood to be a violation of the fundamental principle of color blindness. It was justified as a temporary expedient to reverse the effects of discrimination and exclusion. In other words, it was thought to be a necessary evil—desirable in the circumstances, but not desirable in and of itself. Privilege and preference, once established, however, are not readily relinquished. To make the policy permanent a new rationale was needed: hence the call for "diversity," which makes race-consciousness a positive good. "Diversity" dismisses the old standard of color-blindness, declaring it not only impossible, but also undesirable. This movement from affirmative action to diversity parallels the transformation in antebellum thought which began by recognizing slavery as a necessary evil and ended by hailing it as a positive good (the better to maintain race-based privileges). I don't mean to suggest that the injustice of quotas is on a par with the injustice of slavery, but I do mean to say that the doctrine of the equality of rights-bearing individuals would condemn both. It makes no difference which group—white or black, majority or minority—is arguing for (or being benefited by) the permanence of race-based preferences. If it were understood that the genealogy of the "diversity" argument owes more to Calhoun (who pioneered the shift from the constitutional protection of individual rights to group rights) than to the Declaration's assertion of natural human equality, then the generous lip-service paid to the notion might become less fashionable. Well-intentioned idiocy can be almost as detrimental as malice aforethought. 32

A better understanding of natural right would improve the quality of public reflection (and the resultant public policy) not just on race, but on a whole range of issues, from foreign policy to genetic engineering and cloning, not to mention our contemporary equivalent of "the crisis of the house divided": abortion. Although such an education can be readily accomplished through the study of the Founders and Lincoln, there are all sorts of other ways to do it as well, since it is not fundamentally an historical enterprise, but a philosophic one. However it's done, it must challenge the usurping ideas that have slipped in over time—which turn out to be closely related (though not identical) to those Lincoln confronted. I am not suggesting a civic catechism (which is likely to be about as efficacious as the religious version). 33

What Americans need is a searching exploration of the meaning of the founding charters, and that would include an examination of the most powerful dissenting views. Moreover, as Lincoln understood, the recovery of old insights would not 34 mean a return to square one, but an ascent—a "new birth of freedom." The aim is not to get back to the past, but "back to the future." Fundamentalism and progress are conjoined. Orthodoxy can be the most creative stance. No one, particularly not democratic man, wants to feel like an epigone. The example of Lincoln shows us how our pride can be satisfied, not through departures and deconstruction, but through fidelity and humility. It is by means of a refreshed and deepened understanding of self-government—by means of the building of new pillars—that we might make the bold claim of having secured for ourselves "the blessings of liberty."

from "THE END OF COURTSHIP"
Leon R. Kass

Note: *Leon R. Kass, a faculty member at the University of Chicago and a fellow of the American Enterprise Institute, is a molecular biologist who has written extensively about biomedical ethics. He is Chairman of the President's Council on Bioethics. As this is a very long essay, the last section has been omitted.*

In the current wars over the state of American culture, few battlegrounds have seen more action than that of "family values"—sex, marriage, and child rearing. Passions run high about sexual harassment, condom distribution in schools, pornography, abortion, gay marriage, and other efforts to alter the definition of "a family." Many people are distressed over the record-high rates of divorce, illegitimacy, teenage pregnancy, marital infidelity, and premarital promiscuity. On some issues, there is even an emerging consensus that something is drastically wrong: Though they may differ on what is to be done, people on both the left and the right have come to regard the breakup of marriage as a leading cause of the neglect, indeed, of the psychic and moral maiming, of America's children. But while various people are talking about tracking down "dead-beat dads" or reestablishing orphanages or doing something to slow the rate of divorce—all remedies for marital failure—very little attention is being paid to what makes for marital success. Still less are we attending to the ways and mores of entering into marriage, that is, to wooing or courtship.

There is, of course, good reason for this neglect. The very terms—"wooing," "courting," "suitors"—are archaic; and if the words barely exist, it is because the phenomena have all but disappeared. Today, there are no socially prescribed forms of conduct that help guide young men and women in the direction of matrimony. This is true not just for the lower or under classes. Even—indeed especially—the elite, those who in previous generations would have defined the conventions in these matters, lack a cultural script whose denouement is marriage. To be sure, there are still exceptions, to be found, say, in closed religious communities or among new immigrants from parts of the world that still practice arranged marriage. But for most of America's middle- and upper-class youth—the privileged college-educated and graduated—there are no known explicit, or even tacit, social paths directed at marriage. People still get married—though later, less frequently, more hesitantly, and, by and large, less successfully. People still get married in churches and synagogues—though often with ceremonies of their own creation. But, for the great majority, the way to the altar is uncharted territory: It's every couple on its own bottom, without a compass, often without a goal. Those who reach the altar seem to have stumbled upon it by accident.

Then and Now

Things were not always like this; in fact, one suspects things were never like this, not here, not anywhere. We live, in this respect as in so many others, in utterly novel and unprecedented times. Until what seems like only yesterday, young people were groomed for marriage, and the paths leading to it were culturally well set out, at least in rough outline. In polite society, at the beginning of [the twentieth] century, our grandfathers came a-calling and a-wooing at the homes of our grandmothers, under conditions set by the woman, operating from strength on her own turf. A generation later, courting couples began to go out on "dates," in public and increasingly on the man's terms, given that he had the income to pay for dinner and dancing. To be sure, some people "played the field," and, in the pre-war years, dating on college campuses became a matter more of proving popularity than of proving suitability for marriage. But, especially after the war, "going steady" was a regular feature of high-school and college life; the age of marriage dropped considerably, and high-school or college sweethearts often married right after, or even before, graduation. Finding a mate, no less than getting an education that would enable him to support her, was at least a tacit goal of many a male undergraduate; many a young woman, so the joke had it, went to college mainly for her MRS. degree, a charge whose truth was proof against libel for legions of college coeds well into the 1960s.[1]

In other respects as well, the young remained culturally attached to the claims of "real life." Though times were good, fresh memory kept alive the poverty of the recent Great Depression and the deaths and dislocations of the war; necessity and the urgencies of life were not out of sight, even for fortunate youth. Opportunity was knocking, the world and adulthood were beckoning, and most of us stepped forward into married life, readily, eagerly, and, truth to tell, without much pondering. We were simply doing—some sooner, some later—what our parents had done, indeed, what all our forebears had done.

Not so today. Now the vast majority goes to college, but very few—women or men—go with the hope, or even the wish, of finding a marriage partner. Many do not expect to find there even a path to a career; they often require several years of post-graduate "time off" to figure out what they are going to do with themselves. Sexually active—in truth, hyperactive—they flop about from one relationship to another; to the bewildered eye of this admittedly much-too-old but still romantic observer, they manage to appear all at once casual and carefree and grim and humorless about getting along with the opposite sex. The young men, nervous

3

4

5

predators, act as if any woman is equally good: They are given not to falling in love with one, but to scoring in bed with many. And in this sporting attitude they are now matched by some female trophy hunters.

But most young women strike me as sad, lonely, and confused; hoping for some-   6
thing more, they are not enjoying their hard-won sexual liberation as much as lib-
eration theory says they should.[2] Never mind wooing, today's collegians do not even make dates or other forward-looking commitments to see one another; in this, as in so many other ways, they reveal their blindness to the meaning of the passing of time. Those very few who couple off seriously and get married upon graduation as we, their parents, once did are looked upon as freaks.

After college, the scene is even more remarkable and bizarre: singles bars,   7
personal "partner wanted" ads (almost never mentioning marriage as a goal), men practicing serial monogamy (or what someone has aptly renamed "rotating polygamy"), women chronically disappointed in the failure of men "to commit." For the first time in human history, mature women by the tens of thousands live the entire decade of their twenties—their most fertile years—neither in the homes of their fathers nor in the homes of their husbands; unprotected, lonely, and out of sync with their inborn nature. Some women positively welcome this state of affairs, but most do not; resenting the personal price they pay for their worldly in-
dependence, they nevertheless try to put a good face on things and take refuge in work or feminist ideology. As age 30 comes and goes, they begin to allow themselves to hear their biological clock ticking, and, if husbands continue to be lacking, single motherhood by the hand of science is now an option. Meanwhile, the bachelor herd continues its youthful prowl, with real life in suspended animation, living out what Kay Hymowitz, a contributing editor of *City Journal*, has called a "post-
modern postadolescence."

Those women and men who get lucky enter into what the personal ads call   8
LTRs—long-term relationships—sometimes cohabiting, sometimes not, usually to discover how short an LTR can be. When, after a series of such affairs, marriage happens to them, they enter upon it guardedly and suspiciously, with prenuptial agree-
ments, no common surname, and separate bank accounts. Courtship, anyone? Don't be ridiculous.

Recent Obstacles to Courtship

Anyone who seriously contemplates the present scene is—or should be—filled   9
with profound sadness, all the more so if he or she knows the profound satisfactions of a successful marriage. Our hearts go out not only to the children of failed- or non-marriages—to those betrayed by their parents' divorce and to those deliberately brought into the world as bastards—but also to the lonely, disappointed, cyn-
ical, misguided, or despondent people who are missing out on one of life's greatest adventures and, through it, on many of life's deepest experiences, insights, and joys. We watch our sons and daughters, our friends' children, and our students bumble

along from one unsatisfactory relationship to the next, wishing we could help. Few things lead us to curse "o tempore, o mores" more than recognizing our impotence to do anything either about our own young people's dilemmas or about these melancholy times.

Some conservatives frankly wish to turn back the clock and think a remoralization 10 of society in matters erotic is a real possibility. I, on the other hand, am deeply pessimistic, most of the time despairing of any improvement. Inherited cultural forms can be undermined by public policy and social decision, but once fractured, they are hard to repair by rational and self-conscious design. Besides, the causes of the present state of affairs are multiple, powerful, and, I fear, largely irreversible. Anyone who thinks courtship can make a comeback must at least try to understand what he is up against.

Some of the obstacles in the way of getting married are of very recent origin; 11 indeed, they have occurred during the adult lifetime of those of us over 50. For this reason, one suspects, they may seem to some people to be reversible, a spasm connected with the "abnormal" sixties. But, when they are rightly understood, one can see that they spring from the very heart of liberal democratic society and of modernity altogether.

Here is a (partial) list of the recent changes that hamper courtship and mar- 12 riage: the sexual revolution, made possible especially by effective female contraception; the ideology of feminism and the changing educational and occupational status of women; the destigmatization of bastardy, divorce, infidelity, and abortion; the general erosion of shame and awe regarding sexual matters, exemplified most vividly in the ubiquitous and voyeuristic presentation of sexual activity in movies and on television; widespread morally neutral sex education in schools; the explosive increase in the numbers of young people whose parents have been divorced (and in those born out of wedlock, who have never known their father); great increases in geographic mobility, with a resulting loosening of ties to place and extended family of origin; and, harder to describe precisely, a popular culture that celebrates youth and independence not as a transient stage en route to adulthood but as "the time of our lives," imitable at all ages, and an ethos that lacks transcendent aspirations and asks of us no devotion to family, God, or country, encouraging us simply to soak up the pleasures of the present.

The change most immediately devastating for wooing is probably the sexual rev- 13 olution. For why would a man court a woman for marriage when she may be sexually enjoyed, and regularly, without it? Contrary to what the youth of the sixties believed, they were not the first to feel the power of sexual desire. Many, perhaps even most, men in earlier times avidly sought sexual pleasure prior to and outside of marriage. But they usually distinguished, as did the culture generally, between women one fooled around with and women one married, between a woman of easy virtue and a woman of virtue simply. Only respectable women were respected; one no more wanted a loose woman for one's partner than for one's mother.

The supreme virtue of the virtuous woman was modesty, a form of sexual self-control, manifested not only in chastity but in decorous dress and manner, speech and deed, and in reticence in the display of her well-banked affections. A virtue, as it were, made for courtship, it served simultaneously as a source of attraction and a spur to manly ardor, a guard against a woman's own desires, as well as a defense against unworthy suitors. A fine woman understood that giving her body (in earlier times, even her kiss) meant giving her heart, which was too precious to be bestowed on anyone who would not prove himself worthy, at the very least by pledging himself in marriage to be her defender and lover forever.   14

Once female modesty became a first casualty of the sexual revolution, even women eager for marriage lost their greatest power to hold and to discipline their prospective mates. For it is a woman's refusal of sexual importunings, coupled with hints or promises of later gratification, that is generally a necessary condition of transforming a man's lust into love. Women also lost the capacity to discover their own genuine longings and best interests. For only by holding herself in reserve does a woman gain the distance and self-command needed to discern what and whom she truly wants and to insist that the ardent suitor measure up. While there has always been sex without love, easy and early sexual satisfaction makes love and real intimacy less, not more, likely—for both men and women. Everyone's prospects for marriage were—are—sacrificed on the altar of pleasure now.   15

Sexual Technology and Technique

The sexual revolution that liberated (especially) female sexual desire from the confines of marriage, and even from love and intimacy, would almost certainly not have occurred had there not been available cheap and effective female birth control—the pill—which for the first time severed female sexual activity from its generative consequences. Thanks to technology, a woman could declare herself free from the teleological meaning of her sexuality—as free as a man appears to be from his. Her menstrual cycle, since puberty a regular reminder of her natural maternal destiny, is now anovulatory and directed instead by her will and her medications, serving goals only of pleasure and convenience, enjoyable without apparent risk to personal health and safety. Woman on the pill is thus not only freed from the practical risk of pregnancy; she has, wittingly or not, begun to redefine the meaning of her own womanliness. Her sexuality unlinked to procreation, its exercise no longer needs to be concerned with the character of her partner and whether he is suitable to be the father and co-rearer of her yet-to-be-born children. Female sexuality becomes, like male, unlinked to the future. The new woman's anthem: Girls just want to have fun. Ironically, but absolutely predictably, the chemicals devised to assist in family planning keep many a potential family from forming, at least with a proper matrimonial beginning.   16

Sex education in our elementary and secondary schools is an independent yet related obstacle to courtship and marriage. Taking for granted, and thereby ratifying,   17 precocious sexual activity among teenagers (and even preteens), most programs of sex education in public schools have a twofold aim: the prevention of teenage pregnancy and the prevention of venereal disease, especially AIDS. While some programs also encourage abstinence or noncoital sex, most are concerned with teaching techniques for "safe sex"; offspring (and disease) are thus treated as (equally) avoidable side effects of sexuality, whose true purpose is only individual pleasure. (This I myself did not learn until our younger daughter so enlightened me, after she learned it from her seventh-grade biology teacher.) The entire approach of sex education is technocratic and, at best, morally neutral; in many cases, it explicitly opposes traditional morals while moralistically insisting on the equal acceptability of any and all forms of sexual expression provided only that they are not coerced. No effort is made to teach the importance of marriage as the proper home for sexual intimacy.

But perhaps still worse than such amorality—and amorality on this subject is itself morally culpable—is the failure of sex education to attempt to inform and elevate the erotic imagination of the young. On the contrary, the very attention to physiology and technique is deadly to the imagination. True sex education is an education of the heart; it concerns itself with beautiful and worthy beloveds, with elevating transports of the soul. The energy of sexual desire, if properly sublimated, is transformable into genuine and lofty longings—not only for love and romance but for all the other higher human yearnings. The sonnets and plays of Shakespeare, the poetry of Keats and Shelley, and the novels of Jane Austen can incline a heart to woo, and even show one whom and how. What kind of wooers can one hope to cultivate from reading the sex manuals—or from watching the unsublimated and unsublime sexual athleticism of the popular culture? 18

Decent sex education at home is also compromised, given that most parents of today's adolescents were themselves happy sexual revolutionaries. Dad may now be terribly concerned that his daughter not become promiscuous in high school or college, but he probably remains glad for the sexual favors bestowed on him by numerous coeds when he was on campus. If he speaks at all, he will likely settle for admonitions to play it safe and lessons about condoms and the pill. And mom, a feminist and career woman, is concerned only that her daughter have sex on her own terms, not her boyfriend's. If chastity begins at home, it has lost its teachers and exemplars. 19

Crippled by Divorce

The ubiquitous experience of divorce is also deadly for courtship and marriage. Some people try to argue, wishfully against the empirical evidence, that children of divorce will marry better than their parents because they know how important it is to choose well. But the deck is stacked against them. Not only are many of them frightened of marriage, in whose likely permanence they simply do not believe, but they are often maimed for love and intimacy. They have had no successful models to 20 imitate; worse, their capacity for trust and love has been severely crippled by the betrayal of the primal trust all children naturally repose in their parents, to provide that durable, reliable, and absolutely trustworthy haven of permanent and unconditional love in an otherwise often unloving and undependable world. Countless students at the University of Chicago have told me and my wife that the divorce of their parents has been the most devastating and life-shaping event of their lives.[3] They are conscious of the fact that they enter into relationships guardedly and tentatively; for good reason, they believe that they must always be looking out for number one. Accordingly, they feel little sense of devotion to another and, their own needs unmet, they are not generally eager for or partial to children. They are not good bets for promise keeping, and they haven't enough margin for generous service. And many of the fatherless men are themselves unmanned for fatherhood, except in the purely biological sense. Even where they dream of meeting a true love, these children of divorce have a hard time finding, winning, and committing themselves to the right one.

It is surely the fear of making a mistake in marriage, and the desire to avoid a later divorce, that leads some people to undertake cohabitation, sometimes understood by the couple to be a "trial marriage"—although they are often one or both of them self-deceived (or other-deceiving). It is far easier, so the argument goes, to get to know one another by cohabiting than by the artificial systems of courting or dating of yesteryear. But such arrangements, even when they eventuate in matrimony, are, precisely because they are a trial, not a trial of marriage. Marriage is not something one tries on for size, and then decides whether to keep; it is rather something one decides with a promise, and then bends every effort to keep. 21

Lacking the formalized and public ritual, and especially the vows or promises of permanence (or "commitment") that subtly but surely shape all aspects of genuine marital life, cohabitation is an arrangement of convenience, with each partner taken on approval and returnable at will. Many are, in fact, just playing house—sex and meals shared with the rent. When long-cohabiting couples do later marry, whether to legitimate prospective offspring, satisfy parental wishes, or just because "it now seems right," post-marital life is generally regarded and experienced as a continuation of the same, not as a true change of estate. The formal rite of passage that is the wedding ceremony is, however welcome and joyous, also something of a mockery: Everyone, not only the youngest child present, wonders, if only in embarrassed silence, "Why is this night different from all other nights?" Given that they have more or less drifted into marriage, it should come as no great surprise that couples who have lived together before marriage have a higher, not lower, rate of divorce than those who have not. Too much familiarity? Disenchantment? Or is it rather the lack of wooing—that is, that marriage was not seen from the start as the sought-for relationship, as the goal that beckoned and guided the process of getting-to-know-you? 22

Feminism against Marriage

That the cause of courtship has been severely damaged by feminist ideology and attitudes goes almost without saying. Even leaving aside the radical attacks on traditional sex roles, on the worth of motherhood or the vanishing art of homemaking, and sometimes even on the whole male race, the reconception of all relations between the sexes as relations based on power is simply deadly for love. Anyone who has ever loved or been loved knows the difference between love and the will to power, no matter what the cynics say. But the cynical new theories, and the resulting push toward androgyny, surely inhibit the growth of love.   23

On the one side, there is a rise in female assertiveness and efforts at empowerment, with a consequent need to deny all womanly dependence and the kind of vulnerability that calls for the protection of strong and loving men, protection such men were once—and would still be—willing to provide. On the other side, we see the enfeeblement of men, who, contrary to the dominant ideology, are not likely to become better lovers, husbands, or fathers if they too become feminists or fellow-travelers. On the contrary, many men now cynically exploit women's demands for equal power by letting them look after themselves—pay their own way, hold their own doors, fight their own battles, travel after dark by themselves. These ever so sensitive males will defend not a woman's honor but her right to learn the manly art of self-defense. In the present climate, those increasingly rare men who are still inclined to be gentlemen must dissemble their generosity as submissiveness.[4]   24

Even in the absence of the love-poisoning doctrines of radical feminism, the otherwise welcome changes in women's education and employment have also been problematic for courtship. True, better educated women can, other things being equal, be more interesting and engaging partners for better educated men; and the possibility of genuine friendship between husband and wife—one that could survive the end of the child-rearing years—is, at least in principle, much more likely now that women have equal access to higher education. But everything depends on the spirit and the purpose of such education, and whether it makes and keeps a high place for private life.   25

Most young people in our better colleges today do not esteem the choice for marriage as equal to the choice for career, not for themselves, not for anyone. Students reading *The Tempest*, for example, are almost universally appalled that Miranda would fall in love at first sight with Ferdinand, thus sealing her fate and precluding "making something of herself"—say, by going to graduate school. Even her prospects as future Queen of Naples lack all appeal, presumably because it depends on her husband and on marriage. At least officially, no young woman will admit to dreaming of meeting her prince; better a position, a salary, and a room of her own.   26

The problem is not woman's desire for meaningful work. It is rather the ordering of one's loves. Many women have managed to combine work and family; the difficulty is finally not work but careers, or, rather, careerism. Careerism, now an   27 equal opportunity affliction, is surely no friend to love or marriage; and the careerist character of higher education is greater than ever. Women are under special pressures to prove they can be as dedicated to their work as men. Likewise, in the work place, they must do man's work like a man, and for man's pay and perquisites. Consequently, they are compelled to regard private life, and especially marriage, homemaking, and family, as lesser goods, to be pursued only by those lesser women who can aspire no higher than "baking cookies." Besides, many women in such circumstances have nothing left to give, "no time to get involved." And marriage, should it come for careerist women, is often compromised from the start, what with the difficulty of finding two worthy jobs in the same city, or commuter marriage, or the need to negotiate or get hired help for every domestic and familial task.

Besides these greater conflicts of time and energy, the economic independence of women, however welcome on other grounds, is itself not an asset for marital stability, as both the woman and the man can more readily contemplate leaving a marriage. Indeed, a woman's earning power can become her own worst enemy when the children are born. Many professional women who would like to stay home with their new babies nonetheless work full-time. Tragically, some cling to their economic independence because they worry that their husbands will leave them for another woman before the children are grown. What are these women looking for in prospective husbands? Do their own career preoccupations obscure their own prospective maternal wishes and needs? Indeed, what understanding of marriage informed their decision to marry in the first place? 28

Not Ready for Adulthood

This question in fact represents a more subtle, but most profound, impediment to wooing and marriage: deep uncertainty about what marriage is and means, and what purpose it serves. In previous generations, people chose to marry, but they were not compelled also to choose what marriage meant. Is it a sacrament, a covenant, or a contract based on calculation of mutual advantage? Is it properly founded on eros, friendship, or economic advantage? Is marriage a vehicle for personal fulfillment and private happiness, a vocation of mutual service, or a task to love the one whom it has been given me to love? Are marital vows still to be regarded as binding promises that both are duty-bound to keep or, rather, as quaint expressions of current hopes and predictions that, should they be mistaken, can easily be nullified? Having in so many cases already given their bodies to one another—not to speak of the previous others—how does one understand the link between marriage and conjugal fidelity? And what, finally, of that first purpose of marriage, procreation, for whose sake societies everywhere have instituted and safeguarded this institution? For, truth to tell, were it not for the important obligations to care for and rear the next generation, no society would finally much care about who couples with whom, or for how long. 29

This brings me to what is probably the deepest and most intractable obstacle to courtship and marriage: a set of cultural attitudes and sensibilities that obscure and even deny the fundamental difference between youth and adulthood. Marriage, especially when seen as the institution designed to provide for the next generation, is most definitely the business of adults, by which I mean, people who are serious about life, people who aspire to go outward and forward to embrace and to assume responsibility for the future. To be sure, most college graduates do go out, find jobs, and become self-supporting (though, astonishingly, a great many do return to live at home). But, though out of the nest, they don't have a course to fly. They do not experience their lives as a trajectory, with an inner meaning partly given by the life cycle itself. The carefreeness and independence of youth they do not see as a stage on the way to maturity, in which they then take responsibility for the world and especially, as parents, for the new lives that will replace them. The necessities of aging and mortality are out of sight; few feel the call to serve a higher goal or some transcendent purpose. 30

The view of life as play has often characterized the young. But, remarkably, today this is not something regrettable, to be outgrown as soon as possible; for their narcissistic absorption in themselves and in immediate pleasures and present experiences, the young are not condemned but are even envied by many of their elders. Parents and children wear the same cool clothes, speak the same lingo, listen to the same music. Youth, not adulthood, is the cultural ideal, at least as celebrated in the popular culture. Yes, everyone feels themselves to be always growing, as a result of this failed relationship or that change of job. But very few aspire to be fully grown-up, and the culture does not demand it of them, not least because many prominent grown-ups would gladly change places with today's 20-somethings. Why should a young man be eager to take his father's place, if he sees his father running away from it with all deliberate speed? How many so-called grown-ups today agree with C. S. Lewis: "I envy youth its stomach, not its heart"? 31

Deeper Cultural Causes

So this is our situation. But just because it is novel and of recent origin does not mean that it is reversible or even that it was avoidable. Indeed, virtually all of the social changes we have so recently experienced are the bittersweet fruits of the success of our modern democratic, liberal, enlightened society—celebrating equality, freedom, and universal secularized education, and featuring prosperity, mobility, and astonishing progress in science and technology. Even brief reflection shows how the dominant features of the American way of life are finally inhospitable to the stability of marriage and family life and to the mores that lead people self-consciously to marry. 32

Tocqueville already observed the unsettling implications of American individualism, each person seeking only in himself for the reasons for things. The celebration of equality gradually undermines the authority of religion, tradition, and custom, 33 and, within families, of husbands over wives and fathers over sons. A nation dedicated to safeguarding individual rights to liberty and the privately defined pursuit of happiness is, willy-nilly, preparing the way for the "liberation" of women; in the absence of powerful non-liberal cultural forces, such as traditional biblical religion, that defend sex-linked social roles, androgyny in education and employment is the most likely outcome. Further, our liberal approach to important moral issues in terms of the rights of individuals—e.g., contraception as part of a right to privacy, or abortion as belonging to a woman's right over her own body, or procreation as governed by a right to reproduce—flies in the face of the necessarily social character of sexuality and marriage. The courtship and marriage of people who see themselves as self-sufficient, rights-bearing individuals will be decisively different from the courtship and marriage of people who understand themselves as, say, unavoidably incomplete and dependent children of the Lord who have been enjoined to be fruitful and multiply.

While poverty is not generally good for courtship and marriage, so neither is   34 luxury. The lifestyles of the rich and famous have long been rich also in philandering, divorce, and the neglect of children. Necessity becomes hidden from view by the possibilities for self-indulgence; the need for service and self-sacrifice, so necessary for marriage understood as procreative, is rarely learned in the lap of plenty. Thanks to unprecedented prosperity, huge numbers of American youth have grown up in the lap of luxury, and it shows. It's an old story: Parents who slave to give their children everything they themselves were denied rarely produce people who will be similarly disposed toward their own children. Spoiled children make bad spouses and worse parents; when they eventually look for a mate, they frequently look for someone who will continue to cater to their needs and whims. Necessity, not luxury, is for most people the mother of virtue and maturity.

The progress of science and technology, especially since World War II, has played   35 a major role in creating this enfeebling culture of luxury. But scientific advances have more directly helped to undermine the customs of courtship. Technological advances in food production and distribution and a plethora of appliances—refrigerators, vacuum cleaners, washing machines, dryers, etc.—largely eliminate the burdens of housekeeping; not surprisingly, however, homemaking itself disappears with the burdens, for the unburdened housewife now finds outside fish to fry. More significantly, medical advances have virtually eliminated infant mortality and deadly childhood diseases, contributing indirectly to the reduction in family size. The combination of longer life-expectancy and effective contraception means that, for the first time in human history, the child-bearing and child-rearing years occupy only a small fraction (one-fifth to one-fourth) of a woman's life; it is therefore less reasonable that she be solely prepared for, and satisfied by, the vocation of motherhood. Lastly, medical advances quite independent of contraception have prepared the drive toward our recently permitted sexual liberation: For the triumph of the sexual is a clearly predictable outcome of the successful pursuit, through medicine, of the young and enduringly healthy human body.

In fact, in his *New Atlantis*, Francis Bacon foresaw that the most likely social outcome of medical success would be a greatly intensified eroticism and promiscuous sexuality, in which healthy and perfected bodies seek enjoyment here and now without regard to the need for marriage, procreation, and child-rearing. Accordingly, to counter these dangers, Bacon has his proposed utopian society establish the most elaborate rituals to govern marriage; and it gives its highest honor (after those conferred on the men of science) to the man who has sired over 30 living descendants (of course, within conventional marital boundaries). In the absence of such countervailing customs, as Bacon clearly understood, the successful pursuit of longer life and better health leads—as we have seen in recent decades—to a culture of protracted youthfulness, hedonism, and sexual license.

Technology aside, even the ideas of modern science have hurt the traditional understanding of sex. Modern science's rejection of a teleological view of nature has damaged most of all the teleological view of our sexuality. Sure, children come from the sex act; but the sex act no longer naturally derives its meaning or purpose from this procreative possibility. After all, a man spends perhaps all of 30 seconds of his sexual life procreating; sex is thus about something else. The separation of sex from procreation achieved in this half-century by contraception was worked out intellectually much earlier; and the implications for marriage were drawn in theory well before they were realized in practice. Immanuel Kant, modernity's most demanding and most austere moralist, nonetheless gave marriage a heady push down the slippery slope: Seeing that some marriages were childless, and seeing that sex had no necessary link to procreation, Kant redefined marriage as "a life-long contract for the mutual exercise of the genitalia." If this be marriage, the reason for its permanence, exclusivity, and fidelity vanishes.

With science, the leading wing of modern rationalism, has come the progressive demystification of the world. Falling in love, should it still occur, is for the modern temper to be explained not by demonic possession (Eros) born of the soul-smiting sight of the beautiful (Aphrodite) but by a rise in the concentration of some still-to-be-identified polypeptide hormone in the hypothalamus. The power of religious sensibilities and understandings fades too. Even if it is true that the great majority of Americans still profess a belief in God, He is for few of us a God before whom one trembles in fear of judgment. With adultery almost as American as apple pie, few people appreciate the awe-ful shame of *The Scarlet Letter*. The sexual abominations of Leviticus—incest, homosexuality, and bestiality—are going the way of all flesh, the second with religious blessings, no less. Ancient religious teachings regarding marriage have lost their authority even for people who regard themselves as serious Jews or Christians: Who really believes that husbands should govern their wives as Christ governs the church, or that a husband should love

36

37

38

his wife as Christ loved the church and should give himself up to death for her (Ephesians 5:24–25)?

The Natural Obstacle

Not all the obstacles to courtship and marriage are cultural. At bottom, there is also the deeply ingrained, natural waywardness and unruliness of the human male. Sociobiologists were not the first to discover that males have a penchant for promiscuity and polygyny—this was well known to biblical religion. Men are also naturally more restless and ambitious than women; lacking woman's powerful and immediate link to life's generative answer to mortality, men flee from the fear of death into heroic deed, great quests, or sheer distraction after distraction. One can make a good case that biblical religion is, not least, an attempt to domesticate male sexuality and male erotic longings, and to put them in the service of transmitting a righteous and holy way of life through countless generations.

39

For as long as American society kept strong its uneasy union between modern liberal political principles and Judeo-Christian moral and social beliefs, marriage and the family could be sustained and could even prosper. But the gender-neutral individualism of our political teaching has, it seems, at last won the day, and the result has been male "liberation"—from domestication, from civility, from responsible self-command. Contemporary liberals and conservatives alike are trying to figure out how to get men "to commit" to marriage, or to keep their marital vows, or to stay home with the children, but their own androgynous view of humankind prevents them from seeing how hard it has always been to make a monogamous husband and devoted father out of the human male.

40

Ogden Nash had it right: "Hogamus higamus, men are polygamous; higamus hogamus, women monogamous." To make naturally polygamous men accept the conventional institution of monogamous marriage has been the work of centuries of Western civilization, with social sanctions, backed by religious teachings and authority, as major instruments of the transformation, and with female modesty as the crucial civilizing device. As these mores and sanctions disappear, courtship gives way to seduction and possession, and men become again the sexually, familially, and civically irresponsible creatures they are naturally always in danger of being. At the top of the social ladder, executives walk out on their families and take up with trophy wives. At the bottom of the scale, low-status males, utterly uncivilized by marriage, return to the fighting gangs, taking young women as prizes for their prowess. Rebarbarization is just around the corner. Courtship, anyone?

41

Why It Matters

Given the enormous new social impediments to courtship and marriage, and given also that they are firmly and deeply rooted in the cultural soil of modernity, not to say human nature itself, one might simply decide to declare the cause lost. In fact, many people would be only too glad to do so. For they condemn the old ways as re-

42

pressive, inegalitarian, sexist, patriarchal, boring, artificial, and unnecessary. Some urge us to go with the flow; others hopefully believe that new modes and orders will emerge, well-suited to our new conditions of liberation and equality. Just as new cultural meanings are today being "constructed" for sexuality and gender, so too new cultural definitions can be invented for "marriage," "paternity and maternity," and "family." Nothing truly important, so the argument goes, will be lost.

New arrangements can perhaps be fashioned. As Raskolnikov put it—and he should know—"Man gets used to everything, the beast!" But it is simply wrong that nothing important will be lost; indeed, many things of great importance have already been lost, and, as I have indicated, at tremendous cost in personal happiness, child welfare, and civic peace. This should come as no surprise. For the new arrangements that constitute the cultural void created by the demise of courtship and dating rest on serious and destructive errors regarding the human condition: errors about the meaning of human sexuality, errors about the nature of marriage, errors about what constitutes a fully human life. 43

Sexual desire, in human beings as in animals, points to an end that is partly hidden from, and finally at odds with, the self-serving individual: Sexuality as such means perishability and serves replacement. The salmon swimming upstream to spawn and die tell the universal story: Sex is bound up with death, to which it holds a partial answer in procreation. This truth the salmon and the other animals practice blindly; only the human being can understand what it means. According to the story of the Garden of Eden, our humanization is in fact coincident with the recognition of our sexual nakedness and all that it implies: shame at our needy incompleteness, unruly self-division, and finitude; awe before the eternal; hope in the self-transcending possibilities of children and a relationship to the divine.[5] For a human being to treat sex as a desire like hunger—not to mention as sport—is then to live a deception. 44

Thus how shallow an understanding of sexuality is embodied in our current clamoring for "safe sex." Sex is by its nature unsafe. All interpersonal relations are necessarily risky and serious ones especially so. And to give oneself to another, body and soul, is hardly playing it safe. Sexuality is at its core profoundly "unsafe," and it is only thanks to contraception that we are encouraged to forget its inherent "dangers." These go beyond the hazards of venereal disease, which are always a reminder and a symbol of the high stakes involved, and beyond the risks of pregnancy and the pains and dangers of childbirth to the mother. To repeat, sexuality itself means mortality—equally for both man and woman. Whether we know it or not, when we are sexually active we are voting with our genitalia for our own demise. "Safe sex" is the self-delusion of shallow souls.[6] 45

It is for this reason that procreation remains at the core of a proper understanding of marriage. Mutual pleasure and mutual service between husband and wife are, of course, part of the story. So too are mutual admiration and esteem, especially where the partners are deserving. A friendship of shared pursuits and pastimes enhances any marriage, all the more so when the joint activities exercise deeper 46 human capacities. But it is precisely the common project of procreation that holds together what sexual differentiation sometimes threatens to drive apart. Through children, a good common to both husband and wife, male and female achieve some genuine unification (beyond the mere sexual "union" that fails to do so): The two become one through sharing generous (not needy) love for this third being as good. Flesh of their flesh, the child is the parents' own commingled being externalized, and given a separate and persisting existence; unification is enhanced also by their commingled work of rearing. Providing an opening to the future beyond the grave, carrying not only our seed but also our names, our ways, and our hopes that they will surpass us in goodness and happiness, children are a testament to the possibility of transcendence. Gender duality and sexual desire, which first draws our love upward and outside of ourselves, finally provide for the partial overcoming of the confinement and limitation of perishable embodiment altogether. It is as the supreme institution devoted to this renewal of human possibility that marriage finds its deepest meaning and highest function.

There is no substitute for the contribution that the shared work of raising children makes to the singular friendship and love of husband and wife. Precisely because of its central procreative mission, and, even more, because children are yours for a lifetime, this is a friendship that cannot be had with any other person. Uniquely, it is a friendship that does not fly from, but rather embraces wholeheartedly, the finitude of its members, affirming without resentment the truth of our human condition. Not by mistake did God create a woman—rather than a dialectic partner—to cure Adam's aloneness; not by accident does the same biblical Hebrew verb mean both to know sexually and to know the truth—including the generative truth about the meaning of being man and woman.[7]   47

Marriage and procreation are, therefore, at the heart of a serious and flourishing human life, if not for everyone at least for the vast majority. Most of us know from our own experience that life becomes truly serious when we become responsible for the lives of others for whose being in the world we have said, "We do." It is fatherhood and motherhood that teach most of us what it took to bring us into our own adulthood. And it is the desire to give not only life but a good way of life to our children that opens us toward a serious concern for the true, the good, and even the holy. Parental love of children leads once wayward sheep back into the fold of church and synagogue. In the best case, it can even be the beginning of the sanctification of life—yes, even in modern times.   48

The earlier forms of courtship, leading men and women to the altar, understood these deeper truths about human sexuality, marriage, and the higher possibilities for human life. Courtship provided rituals of growing up, for making clear the meaning of one's own human sexual nature, and for entering into the ceremonial and customary world of ritual and sanctification. Courtship disciplined sexual desire and romantic attraction, provided opportunities for mutual learning about one another's character, fostered salutary illusions that inspired admiration and devotion, and, by   49 locating wooer and wooed in their familial settings, taught the inter-generational meaning of erotic activity. It pointed the way to the answers to life's biggest questions: Where are you going? Who is going with you? How—in what manner—are you both going to go?

The practices of today's men and women do not accomplish these purposes, 50 and they and their marriages, when they get around to them, are weaker as a result. There may be no going back to the earlier forms of courtship, but no one should be rejoicing over this fact. Anyone serious about "designing" new cultural forms to replace those now defunct must bear the burden of finding some alternative means of serving all these necessary goals. . . .

[1] A fine history of these transformations has been written by Beth L. Bailey, *From Front Porch to Back Seat: Courtship in Twentieth Century America* (Baltimore: Johns Hopkins University Press, 1988).

[2] Readers removed from the college scene should revisit Allan Bloom's profound analysis of relationships in his *The Closing of the American Mind* (New York: Simon & Schuster, 1987). Bloom was concerned with the effect of the new arrangements on the possibility for liberal education, not for marriage, my current concern.

[3] In years past, students identified with Hamlet because of his desire to make a difference in the world. Today, they identify with him because of his "broken home"—the death of his father and the too-hasty remarriage of his mother. Thus, to them it is no wonder that he, like they, has trouble in his "relationships."

[4] Truth to tell, the reigning ideology often rules only people's tongues, not their hearts. Many a young woman secretly hopes to meet and catch a gentleman, though the forms that might help her do so are either politically incorrect or simply unknown to her. In my wife's course on Henry James's *The Bostonians*, the class's most strident feminist, who had all term denounced patriarchy and male hegemonism, honestly confessed in the last class that she wished she could meet a Basil Ransom who would carry her off. But the way to her heart is blocked by her prickly opinions and by those of the dominant ethos.

[5] See my "Man and Woman: An Old Story," *First Things*, November, 1991.

[6] This is not to say that the sole meaning of sexuality is procreative; understood as love-making, sexual union is also a means of expressing mutual love and the desire for a union of souls. Making love need lose none of its tenderness after the childbearing years are past. Yet the procreative possibility embedded in eros cannot be expunged without distorting its meaning.

[7] I recognize that there are happily monogamous marriages that remain childless, some by choice, others by bad luck, and that some people will feel the pull of and yield to a higher calling, be it art, philosophy, or the celibate priesthood, seeking or serving some other transcendent voice. But the former often feel cheated by their childlessness, frequently going to extraordinary lengths to conceive or adopt a child. A childless and grandchildless old age is a sadness and a deprivation,

even where it is a price willingly paid by couples who deliberately do not procreate. And for those who elect not to marry, they at least face the meaning of the choice forgone. They do not reject, but rather affirm, the trajectory of a human life, whose boundaries are given by necessity, and our animal nature, whose higher yearnings and aspirations are made possible in large part because we recognize our neediness and insufficiency. But, until very recently, the aging self-proclaimed bachelor was the butt of many jokes, mildly censured for his self-indulgent and carefree, not to say profligate, ways and for his unwillingness to pay back for the gift of life and nurture by giving life and nurturing in return. No matter how successful he was in business or profession, he could not avoid some taint of immaturity.

·6·

The Multiple-Source Essay

Until now, most of your writing assignments have been based on information derived from a *single* source. Now, as you begin to work with *many* different sources, you will need to understand and organize a wider range of materials. You will want to present the ideas of your sources in all their variety while at the same time maintaining your own perspective.

- How can you describe each author's ideas without taking up too much space for each one?
- How can you fit all your sources smoothly into your essay without allowing one to dominate?
- How can you transform a group of disparate sources into an essay that is yours?

Many of the sources used in this chapter have their equivalents in professional writing. Lawyers, doctors, engineers, social workers, and other professionals often work from notes taken in interviews and surveys to prepare case notes, case studies, legal testimony, reports, and market research.

SELECTING INFORMATION
FOR A MULTIPLE-SOURCE ESSAY

In academic writing, you do not usually find the materials for an essay in a neatly assembled package. The first stage of a research project is traditionally working in the library or on the computer to find and select sources, with a topic to explore and questions to ask. This information will later be interpreted, sifted, and synthesized into a finished essay.

To demonstrate this process, assume that you have been assigned the following project, which calls for a narrow range of research:

> Read an entire newspaper or news magazine published on a day of your choice during the past century (such as your birthday), and write a summary describing what life was like on that day. Your sources are the articles and advertisements in that day's paper.

Given the amount and variety of information contained in the average newspaper, you must first *narrow the topic* by deciding what and how much to include. You would look for two kinds of *evidence*—major events that might have altered the fabric of most people's lives, and more ordinary happenings that might suggest how people typically spent their days. While these events may have taken place before your birth, not having been there may give you the advantage of perspective: as an outsider, you can more easily distinguish between stories of lasting historic importance and those that simply reflect their era.

To begin this project, follow these steps:

1. Read rapidly through the entire newspaper. Then read the same issue again more slowly, jotting down your impressions of important *kinds* of events or *characteristics* of daily life. Search for a pattern, a thesis that sums up what you have read.

2. Review your notes, and isolate a *few main ideas* that seem worth developing. Then read the issue a third time, making sure that there really is sufficient evidence for the points that you wish to make. Note any additional information that you expect to use, and write down the page number next to each reference in your notes. Remember that you are not trying to use up all the available information.

3. Plan a series of paragraphs, *each focusing on a different theme* that is either significant in itself or typical of the day that you are describing. Spend some time choosing a *strategy for a sequence of paragraphs* that will not only introduce your reader to the world that you are describing, but also make apparent the pattern of events—the thesis—that seems to characterize that day.

Drawing Conclusions from Your Information

Through your essay, you should interpret the significance of the information for your readers. The evidence should not be expected to speak for itself. Consider the following paragraph:

> Some popular books in the first week of 1945 were *Brave Men* by Ernie Pyle, *Forever Amber* by Kathleen Winsor, and *The Time for Decision* by Sumner Welles. The average price of these new, hardcover books was about three dollars each. The price of the daily *Times* was three cents, and *Life* magazine was ten cents.

What is probably most interesting to your reader is how little the reading material cost. This evidence would be very informative in a paragraph devoted to the cost of living or the accessibility of information through the media. Here, however, the emphasis is on the books. Can you tell why they were popular? Do they seem typical of 1945's bestseller list? If you don't have sufficient knowledge to answer questions like these, you will do better to focus on some other aspect of daily life that the paper describes in greater detail.

In contrast, another student, writing about a day shortly after the end of World War II, built a paragraph around a casualty list in the *New York Times*. What seemed significant about the list was the fact that, by the end of the war, casualties had become so routine that they assumed a relatively minor place in daily life. Notice that the paragraph begins with a topic sentence that establishes the context and draws its conclusion at the end.

> For much of the civilian population, the worst part of the war had been the separation from their loved ones, who had gone off to fight in Europe, Africa, and the Pacific. Even after the end of the war, they still had to wait for the safe arrival home of the troops. In order to inform the public, the *New York Times* ran a daily list of troop arrivals. However, not everyone was destined to return, and the *Times* also ran a list of casualties. On September 4, that list appeared at the very bottom of page 2, a place where it would be easily overlooked except by those interested in finding a particular name.

Another paragraph about May 6, 1946, informs the reader that the postwar mid-forties were a transitional period.

> The process of switching over from a wartime to a peacetime economy was not without its pains. Then, as now, there was a high rate of unemployment. The *Times* featured a story about the million women production workers who

had recently lost their jobs in war industries. Returning male and female veterans were also flooding the job market. Some working wives were waiting to see how their husbands readjusted to postwar jobs. If their ex-GI husbands could bring home enough money to support the family, they could return to their roles as housewives. If their husbands chose to continue their education or vocational training under the GI Bill, they would expect to stay on the job as long as they could.

This paragraph appears to be a straightforward account of the transition from a wartime economy, as expressed in the topic sentence; but the writer is, in fact, summarizing information taken from *several* articles in that day's newspaper. (Notice that, while the source of the information—the *Times*—is cited, the names of the reporters are not considered significant in this very general summary.) The suggestion of a personal comment—unemployment, one gathers, is a recurring problem—adds immediacy and significance to a topic that might otherwise be remote to today's readers.

Finally, it is not always necessary to present your conclusion in a topic sentence at the *beginning* of your paragraph. Here is one in which the evidence is presented first:

> The July 30, 1945, issue of *Newsweek* lists three bills that were going before Congress. The first, the Burton-Ball-Hatch Bill, proposed that all industries institute a labor management mediation system. The second, the Kilgore Bill, proposed providing $25 a week in unemployment for a period of 26 weeks. And the third, the Mead Bill, proposed raising the minimum wage from 40 cents to 65 cents. It is obvious from these three bills that a great deal of attention was being focused on employment, or the lack of it. Here we have another clue about the lifestyle of 1945. The majority of the working class must have been greatly dissatisfied with economic conditions for their congressmen to have proposed these improvements. These bills were also in keeping with the late President Roosevelt's New Deal policy, which was primarily directed toward the improvement of economic conditions. From these bills, it is safe to assume that the cost of living may have been rising, that unemployment was still something of a problem, and that strikes by workers were becoming so prevalent that a mediation system seemed necessary.

This paragraph explicitly links together three related points, suggests their possible significance, and provides a historical context (the New Deal) in which to understand them.

EXERCISE 17: SELECTING AND PRESENTING INFORMATION

Read the following student essay, a description of life taken from the *New York Times* of September 21, 1967. Analyze each paragraph and be prepared to discuss the following questions:

1. What are the writer's reasons for building a paragraph around that piece of information? (Use your own knowledge of the contents of the average newspaper today to estimate the range of choices that the writer might have had.)
2. How clear is the presentation of the information?
3. Do the topic sentences interpret the information and suggest its significance for the reader?
4. How is the essay organized: the relationship between paragraphs; the sequence of paragraphs; the unity within each paragraph; the transitions between paragraphs?
5. What is the thesis and how well does the author characterize September 21, 1967, as typical of its era and as a contrast to her own era?

According to the *New York Times*, on September 21, 1967, there was considerable violence and unrest in the United States, much of it in response to the United States' involvement in the Vietnam War. The United States had increased its bombing of Vietnam in an attempt to cut off the port of Haiphong from contact with the rest of the world. As a result, a group opposed to President Johnson's Vietnam policy began an "anti-Johnson" campaign. They were a coalition of Democrats who hoped to block his reelection. Meanwhile, seventy female antiwar demonstrators were arrested outside the White House. Later, to protest their arrest, 500 members of Women Strike for Peace marched to the White House and clashed with police.

There was not only civil unrest on this day, but also a conflict between President Johnson and the House Ways and Means Committee over the president's proposed tax increase. The committee would not approve the increase without a 5 billion dollar cut in spending. The Senate proposed the following cuts: a 2 billion dollar decrease in defense spending; a 1 billion dollar decrease in "long-range research"; and a 2 billion dollar decrease in other civilian services. However, aid to the poor and to cities was not to be cut. In defense of the president's request, Secretary of Commerce Trowbridge said that a tax increase would be necessary because of inflation.

Throughout the rest of the country, there was much racial tension and violence. There had been days of fighting in Dayton, Ohio's West Side, which had

1

2

3

a large black population. A rally took place there to protest the killing of a black Social Security Administration field-worker. There was also a supermarket fire in Dayton, which resulted in $20,000 of damage. In the end, twenty teenagers were arrested. In the Casa Central Outpost, a Puerto Rican neighborhood in Chicago, Governor Romney of Michigan, a would-be presidential candidate, was given a hostile welcome. His visit to the Outpost was blocked by its director, Luis Cuza, who handed him a two-page press release claiming that the governor was only touring these poor neighborhoods for political gain. Governor Romney expressed outrage at the accusation and the fact that the Outpost had not informed him earlier that he would not be welcome. In the meantime, the streets of Hartford, Connecticut's North End were quiet after three days of racial violence. Civil rights demonstrators were marching against housing discrimination in the South End, a predominantly middle-class Italian neighborhood. There were 66 arrests, mainly of young blacks. To control the violence, five to ten policemen were posted at every intersection, and the mayor asked for a voluntary curfew.

On the local level, a protest against traffic conditions took place in the Bronx, at 149th Street and Courtlandt Avenue. The protesters, four clergymen and dozens of neighbors, wanted Courtlandt Avenue to be one way. Two men refused to leave after police tried to disperse the crowd.   4

There was not only racial unrest in the country on this day, but also many labor disputes and strikes. Seventeen thousand Prudential Insurance Company of America agents threatened to strike if no contract was agreed on in four days. They could not accept any of the proposals previously given to them. Also, the steelhaulers' strike in Chicago was spreading east, and had already resulted in a violent confrontation in Pittsburgh. Finally, on strike were the 59,500 New York public school teachers, whose refusal to enter the classrooms had kept more than a million students out of school for eight days. The teachers' slogan was "no contract, no work."   5

Even the weather was in turmoil. Hurricane Beulah, in Texas, had winds estimated at 80 miles per hour at the center of the storm and 120–150 miles per hour at its peak. Eighty-five percent of Port Isabel, a town at the southern tip of Texas, was destroyed, and four people were killed by the record number of twenty-seven tornadoes spawned by Beulah. All the Gulf states experienced heavy rain in Beulah's aftermath. Meanwhile, rain and thunderstorms also battered the east coast.   6

ASSIGNMENT 5: WRITING AN ESSAY FROM FACTUAL INFORMATION

Choose one of the following:

1. At the library or on the Internet, examine the issue of the *New York Times* that was published on the day that your mother or father was born. Select the articles that seem most interesting and typical of the period, and use them as evidence for an account of what it was like to live on that day. This essay should not merely be a collection of facts; you should suggest the overall significance of the information that you include. Remember that your reader was almost certainly not born on that date, and that your job is to arouse that reader's interest. If you like, draw some parallels with the present time, but don't strain the comparison. The essay should not run much more than 1,000 words: select carefully and refer briefly to the evidence.

2. Use a newspaper or magazine published this week and try to construct a partial portrait of what it is like to live in America (or in your city or town) right now. Don't rely entirely on news stories, but, instead, draw your evidence as much as possible from advertisements and features (like TV listings, classifieds, announcements of all sorts). Try, if you can, to disregard personal knowledge; pretend you are a Martian if that will enable you to become detached from your familiar environment. Don't offer conclusions that the evidence does not substantiate, and don't try to say *everything* that could possibly be said. The essay should not run much more than 1,000 words: select carefully and refer briefly to the evidence.

GENERALIZING FROM EXAMPLES

Summarizing the contents of a newspaper can be difficult because newspaper stories often have little in common except that they all happened on the same day. By contrast, in academic writing a common theme often links apparently dissimilar ideas or facts. *The writer has to find that common theme and make it clear to the reader through generalizations that cover several items in the sources.*

Assume that you have been asked to consider and react to seven different but related situations, and then formulate *two* generalizations.

A. In a sentence or two, write down your probable reaction if you found yourself in each of the following situations.* Write quickly; this exercise calls for immediate, instinctive responses.

1. You are walking behind someone. You see him take out a cigarette pack, pull out the last cigarette, put the cigarette in his mouth, crumple the package, and nonchalantly toss it over his shoulder onto the sidewalk. What would you do?

*Adapted from "Strategy 24" in Sidney B. Simon et al., *Values Clarification* (New York: Hart, 1972).

2. You are sitting on a train and you notice a person (same age, sex, and type as yourself) lighting up a cigarette, despite the no smoking sign. No one in authority is around. What would you do?

3. You are pushing a shopping cart in a supermarket and you hear the thunderous crash of cans. As you round the corner, you see a two-year-old child being beaten, quite severely, by his mother, apparently for pulling out the bottom can of the pile. What would you do?

4. You see a teenager that you recognize shoplifting at the local discount store. You're concerned that she'll get into serious trouble if the store detective catches her. What would you do?

5. You're driving on a two-lane road behind another car. You notice that one of its wheels is wobbling more and more. It looks as if the lugs are coming off one by one. There's no way to pass, because cars are coming from the other direction in a steady stream. What would you do?

6. You've been waiting in line (at a supermarket or gas station) for longer than you expected and you're irritated at the delay. Suddenly, you notice that someone very much like yourself has sneaked in ahead of you in the line. There are a couple of people before you. What would you do?

7. You've raised your son not to play with guns. Your rich uncle comes for a long-awaited visit and he brings your son a .22 rifle with lots of ammunition. What would you do?

B. Read over your responses to the seven situations and try to form two general statements (in one or two sentences each), one about *the circumstances in which you would take action* and a second about *the circumstances in which you would choose to do nothing*. Do not simply list the incidents, one after the other, divided in two groups.

You form your generalizations by examining the group of situations in which you *do* choose to take action and determining what they have in common. (It is also important to examine the "leftovers," and to understand why these incidents did not warrant your interference.) As a first step, you might try looking at each situation in terms of either its *causes* or its *consequences*. For example, in each case there is *someone to blame*, someone who is responsible for creating the problem—except for number 5, where fate (or poor auto maintenance) threatens to cause an accident.

As for consequences, in some of the situations (littering, for example), there is *little potential danger,* either to you or to the public. Do these circumstances discourage action? In others, however, the possible victim is oneself or a member of one's family. Does self-interest alone drive one to act? Do adults tend to intervene in defense of children—even someone else's child—since they cannot stand up for themselves? Or, instead of calculating the consequences of not intervening, perhaps you should imagine *the possible consequences of interference*. In which situations can you expect to receive abuse for failing to mind your own business? Would this prevent you from intervening?

The list of examples has two characteristics worth noting:

1. Each item is intended to illustrate a specific and very different situation. Thus, although it does not include every possible example, the list as a whole constitutes a *set* of public occasions for interfering with a stranger's conduct.

2. Since you probably would not choose to act in every situation, you cannot use the entire list as the basis for your generalization. Rather, you must establish *a boundary line*, dividing those occasions when you would intervene from those times when you would decide not to act. The exact boundary between intervention and nonintervention will probably differ from person to person, as will the exact composition of the list of occasions justifying intervention. Thus, there is no one correct generalization.

This exercise results in a set of guidelines for justifiably minding other people's business. You formulate the guidelines by applying your own standards to a sampling of possible examples.

Broad concepts offer a great deal of room for disagreement and ambiguity and therefore allow a great many interpretations. You can clarify your ideas and opinions about any important abstract issue by inventing a set of illustrations, marking off a subgroup, and then constructing a generalization that describes what is *inside* the boundary: the common characteristics of the contents of the subgroup. Thus, in the previous problem, one person might consider the set of seven examples and then decide to intervene only in Situations 3 (the child beaten in a supermarket), 5 (the wobbly wheel), and 7 (the gift of a gun). What makes these three cases different from the others? They and they alone involve protecting some person from physical harm.

This process of *differentiation*, followed by *generalized description*, is usually called "definition"; it can serve as an essay strategy in its own right or form the basis for a comparison, classification, argumentation, or evaluation essay.

ANALYZING MULTIPLE SOURCES

When you write from sources, your object is not to establish a single "right" conclusion but rather to present a thesis statement of your own that is based on your examination of a variety of views. Some of these views may conflict with your own and with each other. Because of this diversity, organizing multiple sources is more difficult than working with a series of examples, with the contents of a newspaper, or with even a highly complex single essay.

The writing process for multiple sources begins with *the analysis of ideas.*

Analysis is first breaking down a mass of information into individual pieces and then examining the pieces.

As you underline and annotate your sources, you look for similarities and distinctions in meaning, as well as the basic principles underlying what you read.

Only when you have taken apart the evidence of each source to see how it works can you begin to find ways of putting everything back together again in your own essay.

To illustrate the analysis of sources, assume that you have asked five people what the word *foreign* means. You want to provide a reasonably complete definition of the word by exploring all the shades of meaning (or connotations) that the five sources suggest. If each one of the five gives you a completely different answer, then you will not have much choice in the organization of your definition. In that case, you would probably present each separate definition of *foreign* in a separate paragraph, citing a different person as the source for each one. But responses from multiple sources almost always overlap, as these do. Notice the common meanings in this condensed list of the five sources' responses:

John Brown: "Foreign" means unfamiliar and exotic.

Lynne Williams: "Foreign" means strange and unusual.

Bill White: "Foreign" means strange and alien (as in "foreign body").

Mary Green: "Foreign" means exciting and exotic.

Bob Friedman: "Foreign" means difficult and incomprehensible (as in "foreign language").

Planning your essay depends on finding common meanings, not writing down the names of the five sources. That is why the one-source-per-paragraph method should hardly ever be used (except on those rare occasions when all the sources completely disagree).

When you organize ideas taken from multiple sources, never devote one paragraph to each page of your notes, simply because all the ideas on that page happen to have come from the same source.

If you did so, each paragraph would have a topic sentence that might read, "Then I asked John Brown for his definition," as if John Brown were the topic for discussion, instead of his views on "foreign." And if John Brown and Mary Green each get a separate paragraph, there will be some repetition because both think that one of the meanings of "foreign" is "exotic." "Exotic" should be the topic of one of your paragraphs, not the person (or people) who suggested that meaning.

Analyzing Shades of Meaning

Here is a set of notes, summarizing the ideas of four different people about the meaning of the word *individualist*. How would you analyze these notes?

Richard Becker: an "individualist" is a person who is unique and does not "fall into the common mode of doing things"; would not follow a pattern set by society. "A youngster who is not involved in the drug scene just because his friends are." A good word; it would be insulting only if it referred to a troublemaker.

Simon Jackson: doing things on your own, by yourself. "She's such an individualist that she insisted on answering the question in her own way." Sometimes the word is good, but mostly it has a bad connotation: someone who rebels against society or authority.

Lois Asher: one who doesn't "follow the flock." The word refers to someone who is very independent. "I respect Jane because she is an individualist and her own person." Usually very complimentary.

Vera Lewis: an extremely independent person. "An individualist is a person who does not want to contribute to society." Bad meaning: usually antisocial. She first heard the word in psych class, describing the characteristics of the individualist and "how he reacts to society."

At first glance, all the sources seem to say much the same thing: the individualist is different and "independent." However, it is worthwhile to examine the context in which the four sources are defining this word. First, *all the responses define the individualist in terms of other people*, either the "group," or the "flock," or "society." Oddly enough, it is not easy to describe the individualist as an individual, even though it is that person's isolation that each source is emphasizing. Whatever is "unique" about the individualist—what is described as "independent"—is defined by *the gap between that person and everyone else*. (Notice that both "unique" and "independent" are words that also suggest a larger group in the background; after all, one has to be independent of something!)

Having found a *meaning that is common to all four sources* ("independence") and, just as important, having established the *context for a definition* ("from the group"), you must now look for differences. Obviously, Lois Asher thinks that to be an individualist is a good thing; Vera Lewis believes that individualism is bad; and the other two suggest that both connotations are possible. But simply describing the reactions of the four sources stops short of defining the word according to those reactions.

Richard Becker and Lois Asher, two people who suggest a favorable meaning, describe the group from which the individual is set apart in similar and somewhat disapproving terms: "common"; "pattern set by society"; "follow the flock." Becker and Asher both seem to suggest *a degree of conformity or sameness that the individualist is right to reject*, as Becker's youngster rejects his friends' drugs. But Vera Lewis, who thinks that the word's connotation is bad, sees the individualist in a more benign society, with which the individual ought to identify himself and to which he ought to contribute. To be antisocial is to be an undesirable person—from the point of view of Lewis and society. Simon Jackson (who is ambivalent about the word) uses the phrases "by yourself" and "on your own," which suggest the isolation and the lack of support, as well as the admirable independence, of the individualist. In Jackson's view, the individualist's self-assertion becomes threatening to all of us in society ("antisocial") only when the person begins to rebel against authority. Probably for Jackson, and certainly for Vera Lewis, the ultimate authority should rest with society as a whole, not with the individualist. Even Richard Becker, who admires independence, draws the line at allowing the individualist complete autonomy: when reliance on one's own authority leads to "troublemaking," the term becomes an insult.

EXERCISE 18: ANALYZING SHADES OF MEANING IN MULTIPLE SOURCES

Analyze the following set of notes for a definition of the word *conservative*. Then explore some ways to organize these notes by following these steps:

A. Find the important terms or concepts that can lead to a context for defining *conservative*.

B. Write two generalizations that might serve as topic sentences for a two-paragraph essay. (Do not use "favorable" and "unfavorable" as your two topics.)

Bill Flanders: trying to keep things as they are; opposed to change; living in the past; hostile to new ideas: "He was too conservative to live in the twenty-first century."

Howard Gaines: traditional, proper, respectable; nothing flashy or new: "His wardrobe was very conservative; he never paid attention to more casual styles."

Hannah Marciano: holding on to what is tried and true; trying to maintain high standards; believing in strong values: "Conservative people tend to have strong religious beliefs; they understand the importance of faith in God and the need for stability in family life."

Regina Riley: holding on to what you've got; not buying more than your budget allows; not getting into debt: "You should be conservative in your spending if you want to be financially independent and plan for retirement."

LaShawn Simmons: never taking chances; never trying anything new or daring; never growing or changing over time; maintaining the status quo; keeping people in their place: "Conservative people resist change because they don't want to lose what they've got."

ASSIGNMENT 6: WRITING A DEFINITION ESSAY FROM MULTIPLE SOURCES

All the words in the following list are in common use and have either more than one usual meaning or a meaning that can be interpreted both favorably and unfavorably. Choose one word from the list as the topic for a definition essay. (Or, if your instructor asks you to do so, select a word from a dictionary or a thesaurus.)

shrewd	justice	self-interest
curiosity	ordinary	respectable
capitalism	power	smart
bias	flamboyant	polite
progress	eccentric	obedience
habit	politician	ambition
credit	genius	duty
ladylike	failure	poverty
royalty	competition	sophisticated
masculine	peace	humility
cautious	welfare	solitude
bias	immature	spiritual
dominance	culture	sentimental
revolution	aggression	glamorous
passive	modern	self-confidence
influential	feminine	passionate
criticism	imagination	impetuous
jealousy	romantic	successful
small	workman	smooth
cheap	privilege	intrigue
fashion	enthusiast	normal
pompous	mercenary	criticize
obligation	shame	freedom
control	idealistic	artificial
ambition	ethical	perfection

1. Clarify your own definition of the word by writing down your ideas about its meaning.

2. Interview five or six people, or as many as you need, to get a variety of reactions. The purpose of the *survey* is to become aware of several ways of using your word. Take careful and complete notes of each reaction that you receive.

3. Each person should be asked the following questions:

   ▪ What do you think X means? Has it any other meanings that you know of?

   ▪ How would you use this word in a sentence? (Pay special attention to the way in which the word is used, and note down the differences.

Two people might say that a word means the same thing and yet use it differently.)

- Is this a positive word or a negative word? In what situation could it possibly seem favorable or unfavorable?

In listening to the answers to these questions, do not hesitate to ask, "What do you mean?" It may be necessary to make people think hard about a word that they use casually.

4. As you note reactions, consider how the meaning of the word changes and try to identify the different circumstances and usages that cause these variations. Be alert, for example, for a difference between the *ideal* meaning of the word and its *practical* application in daily life.

5. If one person's reaction is merely an echo of something that you already have in your notes, you may summarize the second response more briefly, but keep an accurate record of who (and how many) said what.

6. Although your notes for each source may run only a few sentences, plan to use a separate sheet for each person.

7. Your notes should include not only a summary of each reaction, but also, if possible, a few quotations. If someone suggests a good definition or uses the word in an interesting way, try to record the exact words; read the quotation back to the speaker to make sure that what you have quoted is accurate; put quotation marks around the direct quotation.

8. Make sure that the names of all your sources are accurately spelled.

9. Analyze your notes and make an outline of possible meanings and contexts.

10. Write a series of paragraphs, first explaining *the most common meaning attributed to the word*, according to your sources. Be sure to cite different examples of this common usage. Then, in successive paragraphs, review the other connotations, favorable and unfavorable, always trying to trace the relationships and common contexts among the different meanings.

There is no set length for this essay. Contents and organization are governed entirely by the kind and extent of the material in your notes. *Your notes should be handed in with your completed essay.*

SYNTHESIZING MULTIPLE SOURCES

Once you have analyzed each of your sources and discovered their similarities and differences, you then reassemble these parts into a more coherent whole. This process is called *synthesis*. Although at first you may regard analysis and synthesis as contradictory operations, they are actually overlapping stages of a single, larger process.

To illustrate the way in which analysis and synthesis work together, let us examine a set of answers to the questions: "Would you buy a lottery ticket? Why?" First, read through these summaries of all seven responses.

Mary Smith: She thinks that lottery tickets were made for people to enjoy and win. It's fun to try your luck. She looks forward to buying her ticket, because she feels that, for one dollar, you have a chance to win a lot more. It's also fun scratching off the numbers to see what you've won. Some people don't buy tickets because they think the lottery is a big rip-off; but "a dollar can't buy that much today, so why not spend it and have a good time?"

John Jones: He would buy a lottery ticket for three reasons. The first reason is that he would love to win. The odds are like a challenge, and he likes to take a chance. The second reason is just for fun. When he has two matching tickets, he really feels happy, especially when he thinks that dollars can be multiplied into hundreds or thousands. "It's like Russian roulette." The third reason is that part of the money from the lottery goes toward his education. The only problem, he says, is that they are always sold out!

Michael Green: He has never bought a lottery ticket in his life because he doesn't want to lose money. He wants to be sure of winning. Also, he says that he isn't patient enough. The buyer of a lottery ticket has to be very patient to wait for his chance to win. He thinks that people who buy tickets all the time must enjoy "living dangerously."

Anne White: Buying a lottery ticket gives her a sense of excitement. She regards herself as a gambler. "When you win two dollars or five dollars you get a thrill of victory, and when you see that you haven't, you feel the agony of defeat." She thinks that people who don't buy tickets must be very cautious and noncompetitive, since the lottery brings "a sense of competition with you against millions of other people." She also knows that the money she spends on tickets goes toward education.

Margaret Brown: She feels that people who buy tickets are wasting their money. The dollars spent on the lottery could be in the bank, getting interest. Those people who buy tickets should expect to have thrown out their money, and should take their losses philosophically, instead of jumping up and down and screaming about their disappointment. Finally, even if she could afford the risk, the laws of her religion forbid her to participate in "any sort of game that is a form of gambling."

William Black: He would buy a lottery ticket, because he thinks it can be fun, but he wouldn't buy too many, because he thinks it's easy for people to get carried away and obsessed by the lottery. He enjoys the anticipation of wanting to win and maybe winning. "I think that you should participate, but in proportion to your budget; after all, one day you might just be a winner."

Elizabeth Watson: She wouldn't buy a lottery ticket because she considers them a rip-off. The odds are too much against you, 240,000 to 1. Also, it is much too expensive, "and I don't have the money to be throwing away on such foolishness." She thinks that people who indulge themselves with lottery tickets become gamblers, and she's against all kinds of gambling. Such people have no sense or self-control. Finally, "I'm a sore loser, so buying lottery tickets just isn't for me."

Making a Chart of Common Ideas

Since you are working with seven sources with varying opinions, you need a way to record the process of analysis. One effective way is to make a *chart of commonly held views*. To do so, follow these two steps, which should be carried out *simultaneously*:

1. Read each statement carefully, and identify each separate reason that is being cited for and against playing the lottery by writing a number above or next to the relevant comment. When a similar comment is made by another person, use *the same number* to provide a key to the final list of common reasons. In this step, you are analyzing your sources. Here is what the first two sets of notes might look like once the topic numbers have been inserted:

Mary Smith: She thinks that lottery tickets were made for people to enjoy and win. It's fun to try your luck. She looks forward to buying her ticket, because she feels that, for one dollar, you have a chance to win a lot more. It's also fun scratching off the numbers to see what you've won. Some people don't buy tickets because they think the lottery is a big rip-off; but "a dollar can't buy that much today, so why not spend it and have a good time?"

John Jones: He would buy a lottery ticket for three reasons. The first reason is that he would love to win. The odds are like a challenge, and he likes to take a chance. The second reason is just for fun. When he has two matching tickets, he really feels happy, especially when he thinks that dollars can be multiplied into hundreds or thousands. "It's like Russian roulette." The third reason is that part of the money from the lottery goes toward his education. The only problem, he says, is that they are always sold out!

2. At the same time as you number each of your reasons, also write a list or chart of reasons on a separate sheet of paper. Each reason should be assigned *the same number* you wrote next to it in the original statement. Don't make a new entry when the same reason is repeated by a second source. Next to each entry on your chart, put the names of the people who have mentioned that reason. You are now beginning to *synthesize* your sources. (This process is also known as *cross-referencing*.)

Here's what your completed list of reasons might look like:

Reason	Sources
1. People play the lottery because it's fun.	Smith; Jones
2. People play the lottery because they like the excitement of taking a chance and winning.	Smith; Jones; Green; White; Black
3. People don't play the lottery because they think it's a rip-off.	Smith; Watson
4. People play the lottery because they are contributing to education.	Jones; White
5. People don't play the lottery because they have better things to do with their money.	Green; Brown; Watson
6. People play the lottery because they like to gamble.	White; Brown; Watson
7. People who play the lottery and those who refuse to play worry about the emotional reactions of the players.	Green; White; Brown; Black; Watson

The process of synthesis starts as soon as you start to make your list. The list of common reasons represents the reworking of seven separate sources into a single new pattern that can serve as the basis for an essay.

Distinguishing between Reasons

One of the biggest problems in synthesis is deciding, in cases of overlapping, whether you actually have one reason or two. Since overlapping reasons were deliberately not combined, the preceding list may be unnecessarily long.

For example, Reasons 1 and 2 reflect the difference between the experiences of *having fun* and *feeling the thrill of excitement*—a difference in sensation that most people would understand. You might ask yourself, "Would someone play the lottery just for fun without the anticipation of winning? Or would someone experience a thrill of excitement without any sense of fun at all?" If one sensation can exist without the other, you have sufficient reason for putting both items on your chart. Later on, the similarities, not the differences, might make you want to combine the two; but, at the beginning, it is important to note down exactly what ideas and information are available to you.

The distinction between the *thrill of excitement* (2) and the *pleasure of gambling* (6) is more difficult to perceive. The former is, perhaps, more innocent than the latter and does not carry with it any of the obsessive overtones of gambling.

Resenting the lottery because it is a *rip-off* (3) and resenting the lottery because the players are *wasting their money* (5) appear at first glance to be similar reactions. However, references to the rip-off tend to emphasize the "injured victim" whose money is being whisked away by a public agency. In other words, Reason 3 emphasizes *self-protection from robbery*; Reason 5 emphasizes *the personal virtue of thrift*.

Reason 7 is not really a reason at all. Some comments in the notes do not fit into a tidy list of reasons for playing, yet they provide a valuable insight into human motivation and behavior as expressed in lottery playing. An exploration of the emotions that characterize the player and the nonplayer (always allowing for the lottery preference of the source) might be an interesting way to conclude an essay.

Deciding on a Sequence of Topics

The topics in your chart appear in the same random order as your notes. Once the chart is completed, you should decide on *a more logical sequence of topics* by ordering the entries in the list. You can make an indirect impact on your reader by choosing a logical sequence that supports the pattern that you discovered in analyzing your sources.

Here are two possible ways to arrange the "lottery" reasons. Which sequence do you prefer? Why?

1. fun	1. fun
2. excitement	2. rip-off
3. gambling	3. excitement and gambling
4. education	4. misuse of money
5. rip-off	5. education
6. misuse of money	6. personality of the gambler
7. personality of the gambler	

The right-hand sequence *contrasts the advantages and disadvantages* of playing the lottery. Moving back and forth between paired reasons calls attention to the relation between opposites and, through constant contrast, makes the material interesting for the reader. The left-hand sequence places all the advantages and disadvantages together, providing an opportunity to *explore positive and negative reactions to the lottery separately* without interruption, therefore encouraging more complex development. Both sequences are acceptable.

EXERCISE 19: IDENTIFYING COMMON IDEAS

This exercise is based on a set of interview notes, answering the question "Would you give money to a beggar?"

A. Read through the notes. (1) Identify distinct and different reasons by placing numbers next to the relevant sentences. (2) As you number each new reason, add an entry to the chart. (The first reason is already filled in.)

Reason   Sources

  1. I can afford to give to beggars.

  2.

  3.

  4.

  5.

  6.

  7.

  8.

  9.

 10.

B. Arrange the numbered reasons in a logical sequence. If it makes sense to you, combine those reasons that belong together. Be prepared to explain the logic behind your sequence of points. If you can find two possible sequences, include both, explaining the advantages of each.

Would You Give Money to a Beggar?

Jonathan Cohen: When asked for money on the street, I often apply a maxim of a friend of mine. He takes the question, "Have you got any spare change?" literally: if he has any loose change, he hands it over, without regard for his impression of what the money's for, since he doesn't think ulterior motives are any of his business. Since I can always afford the kind of contribution that's usually asked for—fifty cents or a dollar—or am at least less likely to miss it than the person asking me for it, I usually take the request as the only qualification of "need." I'm more likely to give out money if I don't have to go into my billfold for it, however, and would rather give out transit tokens or food, if I have them. But I want to be sympathetic; I often think, "There but for the grace of God go I."

Jennifer Sharone: I hate to think about what people who beg have to undergo; it makes me feel so fortunate to be well dressed and to have good food to eat and a home and a job. Begging seems kind of horrifying to me—that in this country there are people actually relying on the moods of strangers just to stay alive. I give to people who seem to have fallen on hard times, who aren't too brazen, who seem embarrassed to be asking me for money. I guess I do identify with them a lot.

Michael Aldrich: If a person meets my eye and asks plainly and forthrightly (and isn't falling-down drunk), I try to empty my pocket, or at least come up with a quarter or two. If the person has an unusually witty spiel—even if it's outlandish—I give more freely. I don't mind giving small change; it's quick and easy. I try not to think about whether or not the person really "needs" the money—how could you ever know? On some level, I think that if someone's begging, they need the money. Period. There's an old guy who stands on my corner—he's been there for years. I always give him money, if I have the change. If I don't have it, he says a smile will do. I would hate to think of him going without a meal for a long time or having to sleep out in the rain. He reminds me of my father and my uncle.

Marianne Lauro: I used to give people money, but frankly, I'm too embarrassed by the whole process. It seems to me that folks who really couldn't be all that grateful for somebody's pocket change still make an effort to appear grateful, and then I'm supposed to get to feel magnanimous when I really feel ridiculous telling them they're welcome to a couple of coins that don't even amount to carfare. So the whole transaction seems vaguely humiliating for everyone concerned. Really, the city or the state or the federal government should be doing something about this—not expecting ordinary people, going home from work, or whatever, to support people who have mental or physical impairments or addictions, especially when you're never sure what their money will be used for. But maybe I'm just rationalizing now—maybe the most "humane" thing about these kinds of transactions is the mutual embarrassment.

Donald Garder: I try, when possible, to respond to the person approaching me, by looking at them, perhaps even making eye contact, which frequently lends some dignity to the moment. But then I don't always reach into my pocket. I often give to people with visible physical handicaps, but rarely to someone who's "young and able-bodied." Sometimes I feel guilty, but I'm never sure if the person is for real or not—I've known people who swindled people out of money by pretending to be homeless, so I have a nagging doubt about whether or not a beggar is legitimate.

Darrin Johnson: I never give on the subway—I hate the feeling of entrapment, of being held hostage. The "O.K., so I have you until the next stop so I'm going to wear you down with guilt until I get the money out of you." I really resent that. I flatly refuse to give under those circumstances because it just pisses me off. I might give to somebody just sitting on the street, with a sign and a cup or something—someone who isn't making a big scene, who leaves it up to me whether I give or not. But I hate feeling coerced.

Jenny Nagel: I never give to people on the streets anymore—there are places where people who are really in need can go if they're really starving or need drug treatment or something. Someone once told me, after I'd given money to some derelict looking guy, that he'd probably buy rubbing alcohol or boot polish and melt it down for the alcohol content—that my money was just helping him kill himself. After that I never gave to anyone on the street. I'd rather make a contribution to a social agency.

Paul O'Rourke: I used to give money or if asked I'd give a cigarette. But one day a beggar let loose with a stream of obscenities after I gave him some money. A lot of these people are really messed up—the government should be looking after them, doing more to help them; if they keep getting money from people off the street, they'll just keep on begging. So now I volunteer once a month at a food shelf, and give to charitable organizations, rather than hand out money on the street.

ORGANIZING MULTIPLE SOURCES

Playing the lottery is not a subject that lends itself to lengthy or abstract discussion; therefore, charting reasons for and against playing the lottery is not difficult. The article that follows defines an educational and social problem without taking sides or suggesting any solutions. The reporter's sources simply cite aspects of the problem and express baffled concern.

Twenty students were asked to read the article and to offer their opinions; these are presented following the article. As you read the article and the student opinions, assume that you plan to address the issue and synthesize the opinions in an essay of your own.

from RULE TYING PUPIL PROMOTION TO READING SKILL STIRS WORRY
Gene I. Maeroff

A strict new promotion policy requires the public schools to hold back seventh-grade pupils until they pass the reading test. The difficulty will be compounded this year by a requirement that new seventh graders also pass a mathematics test. 1

"I am frightened that we may end up losing some of these kids, creating a whole new group of dropouts who leave school at junior high," said Herbert Rahinsky, principal of Intermediate School 293, on the edge of the Carroll Gardens section of Brooklyn. 2

Students like Larry, who is 16 years old and in the seventh grade at I.S. 293, are repeating the grade because they scored too low on the reading tests last June to be promoted. If Larry does not do well enough on the test this spring, he will remain in the seventh grade in the fall. 3

An analysis by the Board of Education has shown that about 1,000 of the 8,871 students repeating the seventh grade are already 16 years of age or older. At least one 18-year-old is repeating the seventh grade. 4

Normally, a seventh grader is 12 years old. 5

When the promotion policy, which threatened to hold back students with low reading scores in the fourth and seventh grades, was implemented in 1980, it was hailed by many observers as a welcome effort to tighten standards. 6

But as the program has continued, certain students have failed to show adequate progress. These youngsters are in jeopardy of becoming "double holdovers" in the seventh grade. Some were also held back at least once in elementary school. . . . 7

Authorities theorize that these youngsters form a hard core of poor readers for whom improvement is slow and difficult. Such students often were not held back in prior years because it was easier to move them along than to help them. 8

Educators now wonder whether repeated failure will simply lessen the likelihood of students persisting in school long enough to get a regular diploma. 9

Student Opinions

Diane Basi: If these students are pushed through the system and receive a diploma, not being able to read beyond a seventh-grade level, we will be doing them and society a grave injustice. What good will it do to have a diploma if you cannot read or write? In the end, the students will be hurt more if they are just promoted through the system.

Jason Berg: A student should not be repeatedly held back on the basis of one test. A student's overall performance should be taken into consideration, such as classwork, participation, and attitude. If a student is not up to par for some reason on the day of the test, all the work and effort that was put into school during the year goes down the drain.

Rafael Del Rey: This strict rule has unfortunate consequences. The students who are being forced out don't comprehend what is being taught to them. Exasperated and feeling like social outcasts and inferior beings, it is no wonder that many drop out without skills or goals. Low reading scores mean that students have been neglected by the school system. Educators should be interested in more than just test scores.

Anita Felice: It is extremely embarrassing to be a sixteen-year-old in a class of twelve-year-olds. Such poor students should be promoted to a special program with other students who have the same problems. In time, there should be some improvement in their reading scores. Being held back will only cause frustration and eventually cause them to drop out. Test scores should be a lot less important than they are now.

Joe Gordon: By enforcing a rigid standard, the schools are actually promoting an increased dropout rate and, by doing so, are harming the student and society. What about the teachers? Sometimes students fail a teacher, and for that reason fail the class.

Margaret Jenkins: After two tries, a student should be able to pass a test. It's to the child's advantage to learn and keep learning while moving upward in school. Holding them back is for their own good.

Rachel Limburg: It isn't fair to those students who can do the work just to push these students along. It also isn't fair to the kids who can't pass the test because eventually they are going to have to earn a living. We should look for new ways to help them find their talents and prepare them to face the future.

Barbara Martin: It's a hard question, but I think you have to look at the cost in terms of money, as well as frustration and embarrassment. I'm sorry for kids who are left back, but it's only going to be a problem for everyone later when they can't get a job. Work today is increasingly technical, and everyone needs basic skills. This policy is tough love, and it's necessary.

Len McGee: This policy isn't good enough because it doesn't deal with the individual student; it deals with seventh-graders as a whole. The individual's problems and motivation are not taken into consideration. Sometimes exam pressure defeats intelligence. If left back, the student is trapped in a revolving door and is likely to lose interest in school.

Tina Pearson: It's a mistake to pass students solely on the basis of the reading score. It may show they have learned to read well. But it doesn't mean they learned well in their other classes. Perhaps they worked especially hard on reading and English but just coasted along in their other subjects.

Julius Pena: Automatic promotion is a guarantee that the weak student will face future problems. Making the student repeat is for his own good. Imagine how frustrating it would be for someone who can't fill out a job application. Of course, you shouldn't just throw the student back into the class, but give as much encouragement as possible.

Mark Pullman: We must have certain standards in our educational system. This is a challenge for these students, and repeating the course may encourage them to try harder, making them smarter and better prepared to face life's challenges.

Anthony Raviggio: Strict standards are best for the student. In the long run, individuals who really want the college degree will be glad to remember the ordeal they went through in junior high. It's better to make them keep trying and succeed than to let them think it's okay to fail.

Vivian Ray: If a child has been held back in elementary school and held back again in junior high, it should become quite apparent to teachers and parents that the child has a problem. Being slow to learn is not sufficient reason to hold back a child. The child should be promoted and put in a slower class with more students like himself.

Bernice Roberts: I think there's too much concern for the feelings of the "poor" student and too little concern for the needs of society. Eighteen-year-olds who can't read are likely candidates for welfare. I don't want to have the responsibility of carrying some illiterate kid who couldn't be bothered to learn when he was in school.

Althea Simms: The tough standards are good for these students because they will be motivated to become more serious about doing well. There are kids who don't care whether or not they study for their exams since they know they're going to be promoted to the next grade anyway. Knowing that you may be held back is a strong motivator to study harder.

Patricia Sokolov: Not all students are intellectually gifted, nor is the progress of the nation solely dependent on the effort of intellectuals. Laborers and blue-collar workers have been credited throughout our history for their great contribution to the wealth and progress of our country. Educators should be more concerned with nurturing students' individual potential and less concerned with passing tests.

Matthew Warren: What's the point of promoting a student who won't be able to keep up in his new classes, much less perform his job properly when he's out in the working world? Standards should be enforced regardless of age. What's age? It's just a number.

Michael Willoughby: Educators should recognize that some students don't have the capacity, for whatever social, genetic, or psychological reasons, to fulfill the educators' traditional expectations. An alternative effort must be made, emphasizing vocational skills and also basic reading and math, that will permit students to progress at their own pace.

Betty Yando: I am concerned about the large number of dropouts and their dismal prospects. Why should a student, despite obvious learning disabilities, be forced to continue in an exasperating educational process in which he is making little or no progress? The standards by which we determine whether an individual will make a good worker and a good citizen are too high.

Organizing Multiple Sources

1. **Summarize the facts of the issue.**
   Write a brief, objective summary of the issue under discussion (in this case, the problem described in the article). Your summary of this article should convey both the *situation* and the *two key ideas* that are stressed. Try structuring your paragraph to contrast the conflicting opinions.

2. **Establish your own point of view.**
   End your summary with a statement of your own reaction to suggest a possible direction for your essay.

   This step is more important than it might at first seem. Once you begin to analyze a mass of contradictory opinion, you may find yourself being completely convinced by first one source and then another, or you may try so hard to stay neutral that you end up with no point of view of your own at all. You need to find a vantage point for yourself from which to judge the validity of the statements that you read. Of course, you can (and probably will) adjust your point of view as you become more familiar with all the arguments and evidence that your sources raise. Do not regard your initial statement of opinion as a thesis to be proven, but rather as a *hypothesis to be tested, modified, or even abandoned.*

3. **Synthesize your evidence.**

Label your set of opinions and *establish categories*. The statements following the article are all personal reactions to withholding promotion because of poor performance and the issue of maintaining standards versus individual needs. For each statement, follow these steps:

A. *Read each statement carefully and think about its exact meaning*. First, get a rough idea of what each statement says—do a mental paraphrase, if you like. You will naturally notice which "side" the author of each statement is on. There is a tendency to want to stop there, as if the authors' positions are all that one needs to know. But your object is not only to find out which side of an issue each person prefers, but also to understand why that side was chosen.

B. *Try to pick out the chief reason put forth by each person, or, even better, the principle that lies behind each argument*. Sum up the reasoning of each person in a word or phrase.

C. When you have labeled the statements, the final stage of synthesis becomes easier. *Review your summarizing phrases to see if there is an abstract idea, used to describe several statements, that might serve as a category title*. (Some change in the wording may be necessary.) Once two or three categories become obvious, consider their relationship to each other. Are they parallel? Are they contrasting? Then attempt to see how the smaller categories fit into the pattern that is beginning to form.

How the Three Steps Work

Following is one student's exploration of the article on promotion and the twenty student opinions.

1. **Summarizing.** Here the student identifies the article to which he and his sources are responding, summarizing the issue and the nature of the conflict.

In the *New York Times*, Gene I. Maeroff reported that seventh-grade students, who formerly would pass into the eighth grade despite failing their reading tests, are now required to repeat the year until they can pass the test. Some repeaters in the seventh grade are now older than sixteen. The school system adopted this new rule in order to maintain standards for promotion. But the students most affected apparently don't have the skills to meet those standards.

Some educators, questioning the change in policy, are concerned that such students may not stay "in school long enough to get a regular diploma."

2. **Hypothesizing** (stating your own point of view). Here the student expresses an opinion that suggests the possible direction for an essay. At this point, the student has not studied the group of opinions that accompanies the article.

School authorities have a dilemma. On the one hand, it's in society's interest to produce graduates who have mastered basic skills. Students who pass the reading test will benefit from the rest of their education and then qualify for and hold down good jobs. But, in many cases, the inability to pass the test does not mean that the students didn't try to the best of their capabilities. Holding them back again and again won't ensure that they pass. Later on, when no one wants to hire them, society will have to support them through welfare programs. Perhaps a new vocational track could be developed with less rigorous testing to accommodate children who can't learn well.

3. **Labeling your set of opinions and establishing categories.** In this step, the student moves away from the article to examine the opinions of others who have read the article, determining first *the position of each respondent and then the reasoning behind the position.* Here, the statements of the twenty respondents are repeated, with a summarizing label following each statement.

Student Opinions

Diane Basi: If these students are pushed through the system and receive a diploma, not being able to read beyond a seventh-grade level, we will be doing them and society a grave injustice. What good will it do to have a diploma if you cannot read or write? In the end, the students will be hurt more if they are just promoted through the system.

Basi: literacy necessary for employment; otherwise, individual and society both suffer

Jason Berg: A student should not be repeatedly held back on the basis of one test. A student's overall performance should be taken into consideration, such as classwork, participation, and attitude. If a student is not up to par for some reason on the day of the test, all the work and effort that was put into school during the year goes down the drain.

Berg: test scores less important than individual potential

Rafael Del Rey: This strict rule has unfortunate consequences. The students who are being forced out don't comprehend what is being taught to them. Exasperated and feeling like social outcasts and inferior beings, it is no wonder that many drop out without skills or goals. Low reading scores mean that students have been neglected by the school system. Educators should be interested in more than just test scores.

Del Rey: test scores less important than individual self-esteem

Anita Felice: It is extremely embarrassing to be a sixteen-year-old in a class of twelve-year-olds. Such poor students should be promoted to a special program with other students who have the same problems. In time, there should be some improvement in their reading scores. Being held back will only cause frustration and eventually cause them to drop out. Test scores should be a lot less important than they are now.

Felice: test scores less important than individual self-esteem

Joe Gordon: By enforcing a rigid standard, the schools are actually promoting an increased dropout rate and, by doing so, are harming the student and society. What about the teachers? Sometimes students fail a teacher, and for that reason fail the class.

Gordon: society suffers if high standards lead to dropping out

Margaret Jenkins: After two tries, a student should be able to pass a test. It's to the child's advantage to learn and keep learning while moving upward in school. Holding them back is for their own good.

Jenkins: enforcing tough standards builds character

Rachel Limburg: It isn't fair to those students who can do the work just to push these students along. It also isn't fair to the kids who can't pass the test because eventually they are going to have to earn a living. We should look for new ways to help them find their talents and prepare them to face the future.

Limburg: fairness requires that both good and bad students get an education

Barbara Martin: It's a hard question, but I think you have to look at the cost in terms of money, as well as frustration and embarrassment. I'm sorry for kids who are left back, but it's only going to be a problem for everyone later when they can't get a job. Work today is increasingly technical, and everyone needs basic skills. This policy is tough love, and it's necessary.

Martin: literacy necessary for employment; otherwise, individual and society both suffer

Len McGee: This policy isn't good enough because it doesn't deal with the individual student; it deals with seventh-graders as a whole. The individual's problems and motivation are not taken into consideration. Sometimes exam pressure defeats intelligence. If left back, the student is trapped in a revolving door and is likely to lose interest in school.

McGee: society suffers if high standards lead to dropping out

Tina Pearson: It's a mistake to pass students solely on the basis of the reading score. It may show they have learned to read well. But it doesn't mean they learned well in their other classes. Perhaps they worked especially hard on reading and English but just coasted along in their other subjects.

Pearson: promotion should be based on a variety of skills

Julius Pena: Automatic promotion is a guarantee that the weak student will face future problems. Making the student repeat is for his own good. Imagine how frustrating it would be for someone who can't fill out a job application. Of course, you shouldn't just throw the student back into the class, but give as much encouragement as possible.

Pena: enforcing standards builds character; but offer more help

Mark Pullman: We must have certain standards in our educational system. This is a challenge for these students, and repeating the course may encourage them to try harder, making them smarter and better prepared to face life's challenges.

Pullman: enforcing tough standards builds character

Anthony Raviggio: Strict standards are best for the student. In the long run, individuals who really want the college degree will be glad to remember the ordeal they went through in junior high. It's better to make them keep trying and succeed than to let them think it's okay to fail.

Raviggio: enforcing tough standards builds character

Vivian Ray: If a child has been held back in elementary school and held back again in junior high, it should become quite apparent to teachers and parents that the child has a problem. Being slow to learn is not sufficient reason to hold back a child. The child should be promoted and put in a slower class with more students like himself.

Ray: provide alternate track

Bernice Roberts: I think there's too much concern for the feelings of the "poor" student and too little concern for the needs of society. Eighteen-year-olds who can't read are likely candidates for welfare. I don't want to have the responsibility of carrying some illiterate kid who couldn't be bothered to learn when he was in school.

Roberts: the problem is lack of effort, not lack of ability; it's not society's problem

Althea Simms: The tough standards are good for these students because they will be motivated to become more serious about doing well. There are kids who don't care whether or not they study for their exams since they know they're going to be promoted to the next grade anyway. Knowing that you may be held back is a strong motivator to study harder.

Simms: the problem is lack of effort, not lack of ability

Patricia Sokolov: Not all students are intellectually gifted, nor is the progress of the nation solely dependent on the effort of intellectuals. Laborers and blue-collar workers have been credited throughout our history for their great contribution to the wealth and progress of our country. Educators should be more concerned with nurturing students' individual potential and less concerned with passing tests.

Sokolov: test scores less important than individual potential

Matthew Warren: What's the point of promoting a student who won't be able to keep up in his new classes, much less perform his job properly when he's out in the working world? Standards should be enforced regardless of age. What's age? It's just a number.

Warren: literacy necessary for employment

Michael Willoughby: Educators should recognize that some students don't have the capacity, for whatever social, genetic, or psychological reasons, to fulfill the educators' traditional expectations. An alternative effort must be made, emphasizing vocational skills and also basic reading and math, that will permit students to progress at their own pace.

Willoughby: provide alternate track

Betty Yando: I am concerned about the large number of dropouts and their dismal prospects. Why should a student, despite obvious learning disabilities, be forced to continue in an exasperating educational process in which he is making little or no progress? The standards by which we determine whether an individual will make a good worker and a good citizen are too high.

Yando: individual suffers if high standards lead to dropping out

From this list, the student can establish eight *categories* that cover the range of topics. Here is the list of categories:

Category	Source	Notes
Literacy is necessary for employment	Warren	
	Basi Martin	Otherwise, individual and society both suffer.
The problem is lack of effort, not lack of ability	Simms	
	Roberts	If students can't meet standards, it's not society's fault.
Society suffers if high standards lead to dropping out	Gordon McGee Yando	
Enforcing tough standards builds character	Jenkins Pullman Raviggio	
	Pena	Society should also offer more help to the individual student.
Test scores are less important than individual potential	Sokolov	
	Berg Pearson	Promotion should be based on a variety of skills.
Test scores are less important than individual self-esteem	Del Rey Felice	
Society owes an education to bad students as well as good ones	Limburg	
Society should offer an alternative track for failing students	Ray Willoughby	

EVALUATING SOURCES

Although you are obliged to give each of your sources serious and objective consideration and a fair presentation, synthesis also requires a certain amount of *selection*. Certainly, no one's statement should be immediately dismissed as trivial or crazy; include them all in your chart. *But do not assume that all opinions are equally convincing and deserve equal representation in your essay.*

The weight of a group of similar opinions can add authority to an idea. If most of your sources hold a similar view, you will probably give that idea appropriate prominence in your essay. However, majority rule should not govern the structure of your essay. Your own perspective determines the thesis of your essay, and you must use your understanding of the topic to evaluate your materials, analyze the range of arguments provided by your sources, and determine for your reader which have the greatest validity.

- Review the hypothesis that you formulated before you began to analyze the sources. *Decide whether that hypothesis is still valid* or whether, as a result of your full exploration of the subject, you wish to change it or abandon it for another.

- Sift through all the statements and decide which ones seem *thoughtful and well-balanced*, supported by convincing reasons and examples, and which seem to be thoughtless assertions that rely on stereotypes, catch phrases, and unsupported references. Your evaluation of the sources may differ from someone else's, but you must assert your own point of view and assess each source in the context of your background, knowledge, and experience.

You owe it to your reader to evaluate the evidence that you are presenting, partly through what you choose to emphasize and partly through your explicit comments about flawed and unconvincing statements.

In synthesis, your basic task is to present the range of opinion on a complex subject. But you must also offer a valid thesis, an overall view of the competing issues to present to your reader. Your original hypothesis, either confirmed or altered in the light of your increased understanding, becomes the *thesis* of your essay.

WRITING A SYNTHESIS ESSAY

Spend some time planning your sequence of ideas and considering possible strategies. Do your topic and materials lend themselves to a cause-and-effect structure, or definition, or problem and solution, or comparison, or argument? In writing about the issue of school promotion, you might want to use an overall *problem-solution* strategy, at the same time *arguing* for your preferred solution.

Next, before starting to write each paragraph, review your sources' statements. By now, you should be fully aware of the reasoning underlying each point of view and the pattern connecting them all. But because your reader does not know as much as you do, you need to explain your main ideas in enough detail to make all the complex points clear. Remember that your reader has neither made a list nor even read the original sources. It is therefore important to include *some explanation in your own voice*, in addition to quoting and paraphrasing specific statements.

If possible, you should present your sources by using all three methods of reference: *summary, paraphrase*, and *quotation*. (See the paragraph in Exercise 20 as an appropriate model.) Remember that, as a rule, paraphrase is far more effective than quotation. But the first sentence presenting any new idea (whether the topic sentence of a new paragraph or a shift of thought within a paragraph) should be written entirely in your own voice, as a generalization, without any reference to your sources.

Citing Sources in a Synthesis Essay

- *Cite the source's full name*, whether you are quoting or not.

- *Try not to begin every sentence with a name*, nor should you introduce every paraphrase or quotation with "says."

- *Each sentence should do more than name a person*; don't include sentences without content: "Mary Smith agrees with this point."

- If possible, *support your general points with references from several different sources*, so that you will have more than one person's opinion or authority to cite.

- When you have several relevant comments to include within a single paragraph, *consider carefully which one should get cited first—and why.*

- You need not name every person who has mentioned a point (especially if you have several almost identical statements); however, *you may find it useful to sum up two people's views at the same time,* citing two sources for a single paraphrased statement:

  Mary Smith and John Jones agree that playing the lottery can be very enjoyable. She finds a particular pleasure in scratching off the numbers to see if she has won.

- *Cite only one source for a quotation*, unless both have used exactly the same wording. In the example above, the first sentence would not make sense if you *quoted* "very enjoyable."

- If an idea under discussion is frequently mentioned in your sources, *convey the relative weight of support* by citing "five people" or "several commentators." Then, after summarizing the common response, cite one or two specific opinions, with names. But try not to *begin* a paragraph with "several people"; remember that, whenever possible, the topic sentence should be a generalization of your own, without reference to the supporting evidence.

- *Discuss opposing views within a single paragraph as long as the two points of view have something in common.* Radically different ideas should, of course, be explained separately. Use transitions like "similarly" or "in contrast" to indicate the relationship between contrasting opinions.

To summarize, your essay should include the following elements:

- *Topic sentence*: Introduce the category or theme of the paragraph, and state the idea that is the common element tying this group of opinions together.

- *Explanation*: Support or explain the topic sentence. Later in the paragraph, if you are dealing with a complex group of statements, you may need a connecting sentence or two, showing your reader how one reason is connected to the next. For example, an explanation might be needed in the middle of the "enforcing tough standards builds character" paragraph as the writer moves from the need for "tough love" to the obligation of society to offer more help.

- *Paraphrase or summary*: Present specific ideas from your sources in your own words. In these cases, you must of course *acknowledge your sources* by citing names in your sentence.

- *Quotation*: Quote from your sources when the content or phrasing of the original statement justifies word-for-word inclusion. In some groups of statements, there may be several possible candidates for quotation; in others, there may be only one; often you may find no source worth quoting. For example, read the statements made by Sokolov, Berg, and Pearson once again. Could you reasonably quote any of them? Although Berg and Pearson both take strong positions well worth presenting, there is no reason to quote them and every reason to use paraphrase. You might want to quote Sokolov's first sentence, which is apt and well-balanced.

As you analyze the opinions of your sources in the body of your essay, *you should remain neutral*, giving a fair presentation of each point of view. It is also your responsibility to use the final paragraphs of your essay to present your own conclusions, in your own voice, about this issue—to argue for maintaining society's standards or nurturing the individual student, or to recommend ways to accommodate both sides.

EXERCISE 20: ANALYZING A PARAGRAPH BASED ON SYNTHESIS OF SOURCES

Read the following paragraph and decide which sentences (or parts of sentences) belong to each of these categories: topic sentence, explanation, summary, paraphrase, quotation. Insert the appropriate category name in the left margin, and bracket the sentence or phrase illustrating the term. Be prepared to explain the components of the paragraph in class discussion.

Reading test scores may not always be a valid basis for deciding whether students should be promoted or made to repeat the seventh grade. According to Jason Berg, Tina Pearson, and Patricia Sokolov, proficiency in reading is just one factor among many that should count toward promotion. Pearson points out that students with high scores in reading don't necessarily excel in other subjects. In her view, it is unfair to base the decision on just one area of learning. Berg finds it equally unfair that one test should be valued more highly than a year's achievements. But the issue here is not limited to academic competence. Both

Berg and Sokolov attach more importance to a student's character and potential than to intellectual attainments. Berg's definition of "overall performance" includes general contributions to the class that demonstrate a positive attitude. For Berg, the context is the classroom; for Sokolov, it is the nation. In her view, intellect alone won't make the nation thrive: "Laborers and blue-collar workers have been credited throughout our history for their great contribution to the wealth and progress of our country." Our primary concern should be to educate good citizens rather than good readers.

CITING SOURCES FOR SYNTHESIS

When you yourself have interviewed people as part of a survey, you may feel a particular obligation to indicate who they are and what they represent. To illustrate a particularly deft use of citation in synthesizing a group of interviews, here is an excerpt from *Moral Freedom* by Alan Wolfe, a sociologist who has published several books exploring American national identity. Based on interviews with ordinary Americans, *Moral Freedom* attempts to define an era in which moral certainties are eroding. In this section, Wolfe is recording opinions about the disappearance of loyalty in everyday life.

As you read, notice that each paragraph begins with a sentence or two in which Wolfe sums up and comments on what his interviewees have told him. Then he introduces Quincy Simmons, Kellie Moss, Laverne Eaton, and Caroline Bowen, one at a time, each with a brief biographical description that moves seamlessly—within the same sentence—into a paraphrase or quotation expressing their views. (In this excerpt, the citations have been italicized.) The transitions—where Wolfe moves from person to person or from paraphrase to commentary—are extremely clear. You're never in doubt whose voice you're hearing. This is an excellent model for the presentation of oral evidence.

from MORAL FREEDOM:
TILL CIRCUMSTANCES DO US PART
Alan Wolfe

No other institution in American life provokes such bittersweet reflections of loyalty lost as the business corporation. Quincy Simmons, who is now forty-seven years old, came to America from one of the Caribbean islands and eventually settled in the Hartford area. A small businessman who makes his living painting and remodeling, *Mr. Simmons remembers* that "in the old days you got a job and for both the company and the employee it would be different." *He is struck* by these differences between then and now. Then, "you go back home and at the same time the company will see that you get reasonable pay or whatever for the work you do. But now it goes back to greed, everybody's thinking about the money."

Mr. Simmons's views are surely influenced by the wave of downsizings that took place in his city. Known as the home of the American insurance industry, Hartford was hit hard by managed care, a rationalization of health care costs that, for a time, cut into the profits of such large insurers in the area as Aetna or the Hartford. Given the traumatic effects of economic consolidation on the region, *Mr. Simmons's lament was repeated* by so many of his neighbors, and in words so close to his, as to constitute a kind of folk truth. Since the big companies started merging, as *Kellie Moss, a retired bank clerk, puts it*, "there's no heart. It takes the heart and soul out of a company. They make more money—and it all comes down to money—but they don't take care of it. Everything is merging, merging, merging. Push this one out, buy this one out, get him out." *Laverne Eaton, a fifty-five-year-old grandmother, could see* the changes in her own life. She worked for the same company for thirty-two years before retiring. "They cared about us; we cared about them; we would work ourselves silly because it was important to the company, and the company always showed in kind that they cared about us," *she recalls. Her son now works for the same firm, and his experiences are entirely different.* For him, "there's no loyalty and people don't care about doing the job that they're hired to do."

Those who write about the declining importance of loyalty in American life generally chastise individuals for no longer believing in such old-fashioned virtues, downplaying in the process any role that powerful institutions like business corporations might play in its loss. By contrast, many of those in a community like Hartford see themselves as virtuous people trying to live by old-fashioned rules, yet unable to do so given the reward system of contemporary capitalism. *Few of those with whom we spoke felt this way with quite the passion of Caroline Bowen*, a thirty-seven-year-old buyer for a chemical company in nearby Fall River, Massachusetts, once a thriving mill town, but now better known for the factories sitting empty near the waterfront. Mrs. Bowen, who grew up in Fall River, is a fierce loyalist to her friends, her family, and the coparishioners of her Catholic church. Reflecting the characteristics of what sociologists call "urban villagers," *she believes* that corporations need to be loyal to workers, while workers have no particular obligation to be loyal to companies. That is because "companies are here, they're institutions. They're going to be around a long time." Employees, by contrast, "are living lives. Companies don't live lives." Because people have lives to lead, things happen to them: childbirth and sickness, to take just two examples. "I think that the company has to learn to adjust and be loyal to and help their employees get through those periods and in turn make them a loyal employee as well."

ASSIGNMENT 7: WRITING AN ESSAY SYNTHESIZING MULTIPLE SOURCES

Read the following essay by Todd Gitlin.

1. Write a summary of the point at issue, and then write a brief explanation of your opinion of this issue.
2. Use the statements that follow as a basis for a synthesis essay. These statements were written in response to the question: *Should college instructors distribute their lecture notes to students?* Analyze each statement, label each kind of reason, and organize all the categories in a chart. Then write an essay that presents the full range of opinion, paraphrasing and, if desirable, quoting from representative sources.

DISAPPEARING INK

Todd Gitlin

Hearing that a new Internet company is now posting free notes for core courses at 62 universities threw me back to a time in the 1980's when I was teaching a large class in a lecture hall at the University of California at Berkeley. The student government had approved a note-taking service called, for some arcane reason, Black Lightning. With the professor's approval, a graduate student would attend lectures, take notes and type them up, whereupon Black Lightning would duplicate the notes and offer them to students for a nominal fee (and to the professor for free).   1

With some trepidation, I agreed. Students wanted the service. I read the first few sets of notes and was reasonably impressed. The graduate student in question evidently knew what he was doing. My thinking looked tidier in his transcription than in my own notes. In fact, a professor who wanted to regurgitate the same notes year after year could use those nicely printed notes the next time and the next.   2

But I soon saw that class attendance was down. Not drastically down, but down. I also became aware that questions in class were slacking off. I have long encouraged students to interrupt lectures with questions, partly to raise the plane of comprehension, partly to keep them thinking, partly to generate arguments. Enough students normally did pipe up, during an 80-minute period, to enliven the class. But now that the notes were available in cold black type, the students were less available in spirit.   3

So when that semester was over, I stopped giving permission to Black Lightning. Some students weren't pleased. But I didn't and don't think that the University of California had hired me to please. Needless to say, in an age when the Bill of Rights seems to begin with the right to nonstop entertainment, this is a controversial belief.   4

Now it may well be argued that universities are already shortchanging their students by stuffing them into huge lecture halls where, unlike at rock concerts or   5 basketball games, the lecturer can't even be seen on a giant screen in real time. If they're already shortchanged with impersonal instruction, what's the harm in offering canned lecture notes?

The amphitheater lecture is indeed, for all but the most engaging professors, a lesser form of instruction, and scarcely to be idealized. Still, Education by Download misses one of the keys to learning. Education is a meeting of minds, a process through which the student educes, draws from within, a response to what a teacher teaches. 6

The very act of taking notes—not reading somebody else's notes, no matter how stellar—is a way of engaging the material, wrestling with it, struggling to comprehend or to take issue, but in any case entering into the work. The point is to decide, while you're listening, what matters in the presentation. And while I don't believe that most of life consists of showing up, education does begin with that—with immersing yourself in the activity at hand, listening, thinking, judging, offering active responses. A download is a poor substitute. 7

I can't comment on the quality of the notes posted at StudentU.com, the new, advertising-supported Internet venture. When I tried to register yesterday a message came back that my ZIP code in lower Manhattan was unrecognizable to the machine in charge. 8

Perhaps the server is located on Mars, or is suffering the death of a thousand hackers. No matter. The quality of the notes isn't the point. Glitches will be deglitched, and similar sites will follow as surely as advertisers follow a market. No doubt someone is about to register the Internet addresses Notes!.com and CollegeforDummies.com. 9

I.P.O.'s won't be far behind. And higher education may be as virtual as black lightning. 10

Agnes Adams: The professor may want and expect students to take an interest in his lecture and ask questions. But if the lecture is deadly dull, everyone will be asleep. In that case, you might as well distribute notes so people will know what they slept through.

Ronald Blitzstein: The object of going to college is to learn. It doesn't matter how you learn—through lectures, through taking notes, through reading notes. I would support the most effective way of mastering the material. Reading canned notes isn't necessarily the way I'd prefer to learn, but it might be preferable to sitting in a huge lecture hall, where it's too crowded to learn much anyway.

Brook Borne: If we can buy notes, why do we need lectures? I personally don't mind lectures if the professor makes the material interesting. But it would certainly be tempting to get the core material summarized so I could pay more attention to the presentation and not have to sit there scribbling. If you can buy *Cliffs Notes* for great works of literature, why can't you buy lecture notes? Faculty are ostriches if they don't realize that students will get help from wherever they can.

Cathy Cadiz: Neither lectures nor canned notes are what I came to college for. Learning is more than receiving knowledge from on high. College courses should be small discussion sections or seminars, where material can be discussed and the students can develop their ideas. But for those courses that are purely information based, you might as well receive the information in written form.

Wendy Chin: If some graduate student writes up the lectures for the professor, they will end up being carved in stone. The professor will end up working from the notes and delivering the same lecture year after year. That's not what I'm paying tuition for. I came to college to receive the best possible education, and I expect the faculty to stimulate my mind by making the material interesting, even entertaining. I don't expect singing and dancing, but I am entitled to an original and unique delivery of the material.

Don DiCarlo: I think lectures are okay. It's good to be face to face with the professors. We don't have that many opportunities to see them; so many courses are taught by graduate students. College can be a very isolating experience, and lectures add to the sense that you're anonymous, so it would be helpful if the professor in a large lecture hall devised some way to get to know some of the students.

Elihu Eisenberg: We're paying our money to get the professor's point of view, not the opinions of some graduate students. I admit it would be easier to use canned notes, but I'd rather not get my information at second hand. If students want to skip lectures and learn from notes, why didn't they choose distance learning so they could stay in their pajamas all the time?

Noriko Hashimoto: I don't see why you can't have lectures and notes. The notes would serve as a supplement, a reminder of what the professor said. During the lecture, I could concentrate more on the material if I didn't have to write things down.

Philip Jenkins: I'm sure that, if notes were provided, some students would stop coming to lectures. But there are ways around that. The college could always make attendance mandatory. Or, after the first time around, the professor could start putting extra material in his lectures that wasn't in the notes to penalize those who didn't bother to come and reward those who did.

Lauren Marks: I actually don't mind taking notes. It helps me to absorb what's being said; it helps me to concentrate. Laptops make it much easier to take notes—you don't have to read your own handwriting. I don't see what the problem is. Lectures mean learning directly from someone who's an authority. That's what college is about.

Eduardo Martinez: My college is famous for its distinguished faculty. It's their knowledge and expertise that made me come here; it's what I'm paying tuition for. I'd rather listen and take notes during a lecture than rely on what some half-baked graduate student has to say.

Blake Morrison: A good professor will personalize the lecture. You can get a lot out of the way it's presented, the words and the images he uses, even the body language. The material seems more real. I think that experience is an important part of college, and it's preferable to a stack of impersonal notes written by someone who's not an authority on the subject.

Jason McGiver: Canned notes are one step away from research papers bought on the Internet. I suppose that if everyone agreed that it was okay to use canned notes (or even to use canned papers), that would be okay with me. But the college would have to approve. And it would have to be across the board—you shouldn't be given canned notes for one course and be expected to attend and take your own notes for another. That's not fair.

Jamal Peters: I learn best when I'm involved in the process. Discussion courses are best, but lecture courses are okay if the professor is reasonably lively. It can be a nuisance to take notes when I want to concentrate on the subject, but I find it useful to have my own take on the material.

Suzie Quintana: The solution to this problem would be to do away with large lecture courses. Personal contact enhances learning. I don't want to be an anonymous person among a hundred or more students in a large hall. I want to know the professor and have him or her know me. Lectures are not what college is about. Lectures are really no different from taking college courses on the Internet—which is a good deal cheaper!

Michael Rollafson: Canned notes are essentially a shortcut, a quick fix. They're great for students who don't want to make an effort to learn. It's the lazy person's kind of education. I'm earning part of the money for my tuition, and I want to get the most out of college. So I go to lectures and I take notes, and I don't think it's fair if the person down the hall is allowed to use canned notes. Also, if the notes cost students money over and above tuition, that becomes an economic issue.

Bernie Singer: The point about taking notes is what you put in and leave out. You're not supposed to write down every word of the lecture. You're supposed to make decisions about what's important. That's part of the learning experience. In a way, it's an ungraded test of your ability; it teaches you to focus and to summarize, which is important when you take exams.

Rose Szybrowski: Lecture classes are too big. If the college doesn't have respect for students and doesn't treat them like individuals, then the students won't respect the faculty. There's no point in going to a lecture when I can find out exactly the same information—and more quickly—from notes. I've got better things to do with my time.

Ralph Tedesco: In some courses, the professors make you buy their textbooks. What's the difference between that and buying canned notes? Is it okay only if the professor makes a profit? There's no particular advantage to having material read to you. Lectures are a waste of time.

Helen Young: I think that it's useful to have the professor's own view of the material. It helps to clarify difficult points. If it's possible to ask questions, so much the better. It would be best if a substantial part of the class were devoted to questions and discussion. That way, new ideas might get introduced. Students who didn't bother coming to class would be the losers—especially if that material appeared on the exam.

ASSIGNMENT 8: WRITING AN ARGUMENT FROM MULTIPLE SOURCES

Read the excerpt from "When Doctors Slam the Door," by Sandeep Jauhar.

1. Write a brief response to the issue raised by Jauhar: *when is it appropriate for doctors to turn away patients?* Submit your response to your instructor.

2. When you receive the group of responses provided by your class, prepare labels and a chart, according to the guidelines on page 264, and then write an essay that explores both sides of the issue but also establishes your own thesis. Make sure that you use summary, paraphrase, and quotation to present the views of your sources.

from WHEN DOCTORS SLAM THE DOOR

Sandeep Jauhar

When can a doctor refuse to treat a patient? Not surprisingly, there are rules. In 1987, Dr. John Bower, a kidney specialist at the University of Mississippi Medical Center, was sued after dismissing from his practice a patient who regularly missed dialysis appointments, verbally abused nurses and even threatened to kill Bower and a hospital administrator. Bower cited medical noncompliance and violent threats as grounds for terminating care. The Fifth Circuit Court of Appeals, in New Orleans, agreed with him, ruling that doctors can refuse to treat violent or intransigent patients as long as they give proper notice so that the patient can find alternative care. Forcing doctors to treat such patients, the court said, would violate the 13th Amendment, which prohibits involuntary servitude.

Sometimes doctors can refuse to treat on the basis of conscience. I once took care of a man in his 50's who had metastatic tongue cancer and respiratory failure requiring a ventilator. His family refused to turn off the machine and let him die, choosing instead to escalate treatment with even more aggressive interventions. Medicine is a stochastic science—no doctor can predict the future—but in this case the outcome was never in doubt. Advanced cancer patients who end up on ventilators die during their hospitalizations. Life support was futile, and continuing to insert catheters and tubes into this man seemed inhumane. After the attending physician and I consulted with the hospital's ethics committee, we told the family that we could no longer obey their wishes. We gave them the option of transferring the patient to another hospital. They didn't want to do that; treatment was scaled back, and the man died a few days later.

In rare cases, doctors have objected to treatment on moral grounds. In February 2001, it was reported that surgeons in Melbourne, Australia, were refusing to provide heart and lung transplants, coronary-bypass surgery and lung-reduction surgery to smokers. At one hospital, surgeons insisted that patients be free of nicotine, alcohol and other drugs for at least six months before going into the operating room. "Why should taxpayers pay for it?" one surgeon asked. "It is consuming resources for someone who is contributing to their own demise." The policy predictably drew an outcry from human rights organizations and many doctors. The Australian Medical Association said it was "unconscionable" for a surgeon to take a moral stand on treating a patient. Ethicists said it was discriminatory because lifestyle could be blamed for many illnesses, including obesity and certain types of cancer.   3

In the last decade, there has emerged a new, unexpected impetus for denying treatment to patients. Consider the case of P., a jovial, heavyset man in his 50's with a weakness for chocolate and cheesecake. In his mid-30's, P. had a heart infection that required surgery to replace a damaged valve with one from a pig. About 10 years later, his kidneys failed for unknown reasons, and he had to start getting dialysis treatments. A religious man, he took it all in stride as the will of God.   4

Now a cardiac catheterization showed severe limitations in blood flow to several parts of his heart. P.'s coronary arteries looked like sausage links, sectioned off by numerous tight blockages. During the catheterization, fluid filled his lungs, and he had to be treated with intravenous morphine and nitroglycerin and emergency dialysis. Once his condition stabilized, he was scheduled for coronary-bypass surgery.   5

In the hospital, P. continued to have severe chest pains—small heart attacks, really—that were inadequately relieved by medications. One morning, he nearly doubled over while washing up. Because of his medical conditions, a surgeon decided that P. was a "high risk" surgical candidate and should be transferred to an affiliated hospital to have his operation.   6

The surgeon said that agencies monitoring surgical outcomes had been putting tremendous pressure on surgeons to produce good results. He was referring to "report cards" on cardiac surgeons. Over the past decade, while surgeons with higher-than-expected mortality statistics have lost operating privileges, others with lower-than-predicted rates have taken to advertising on the radio. Because the surgeon and his colleagues had been aggressive about treating very sick patients like P., they had incurred higher mortality rates and had been penalized by the state department of health. This was an insult he could no longer countenance, and so he had decided that all high-risk surgeries would be transferred to another hospital.   7

And so P. was transferred. A few days later, after his operation, he died. . . .   8

WHEN NOT TO SYNTHESIZE

Synthesis is a method; it is not an end in itself. Some works do not lend themselves to synthesis, which tends to *emphasize similarities* at the expense of interesting differences between sources.

The academic writer needs to distinguish between material that is appropriate for synthesis and material whose individuality should be recognized and preserved. One example of the latter is fiction; another is autobiography. Assume that three writers are reminiscing about their first jobs: one was a clerk in a drugstore, the second a telephone operator, and the third plowed his father's fields. In their recollections, the reader can find several similar themes: accepting increased responsibility; sticking to the job; learning appropriate behavior; living up to the boss's or customers' or father's expectations. But, just as important, the three autobiographical accounts *differ* sharply in their context and circumstances, in their point of view and style. You cannot lump them together in the same way that you might categorize statements about the lottery or opinions about begging, for they cannot be reduced to a single common experience. The three are not *interchangeable*; rather, they are *comparable*.

Comparison and synthesis both involve analyzing the ideas of several sources and searching for a single vantage point from which to view them. However, there is an important difference. *The writer of a synthesis constructs a new work out of the materials of the old; the writer of a comparison tries to leave the sources intact throughout the organizational process, so that each retains its individuality.*

When you are assigned an essay topic, and when you assemble several sources, you are not likely to want to *compare* the information that you have recorded in your notes; rather, you will *synthesize* the material into a complete presentation of the topic. One of your sources may be an encyclopedia; another a massive survey of the entire subject; a third may devote several chapters to a scrutiny of that one small topic. In fact, these three sources are really not comparable, nor is your primary purpose to distinguish between them or to understand how they approach the subject differently. You are only interested in the results that you can achieve by using and building on this information. In contrast, the appropriate conditions for comparison are more specific and rare. *For comparison, you must have two or more works of similar length and complexity that deal with the same subject and that merit individual examination.*

SYNTHESIZING SOURCES IN ACADEMIC ESSAYS

So far, all the sources that you have worked with in this chapter have been transcripts of interviews, originating as informal statements of opinion. But unless you're including interviews or a survey as part of your research, when you write an essay for your college courses, you'll be using mostly *written* sources: published documents in print or electronic form. Written sources vary enormously, not only in their length and their targeted audience, but also in their treatment of the topic and in their reliability. In Chapter 8, you'll learn how to choose written sources and how to integrate different types into your essay.

In a way, your relationship with your sources changes as they grow in number. When you worked with a single source, you were essentially engaging in a conversation with one person. When you work with multiple sources, you're like the *moderator of a roundtable discussion* in which you choose who speaks and which points each speaker is allowed to make. In the excerpt from Alan Wolfe's *Moral Freedom* on page 274, he is managing the "discussion" quite easily because he has interviewed the sources, asking the questions and setting the agenda. None of his sources is going beyond the limits he has set. The role of the moderator becomes more challenging when you are working with written sources or other kinds, like films, that all have agendas of their own and aren't even aware of your questions.

To illustrate this process, let's look at an excerpt from Jeffrey Rosen's *The Naked Crowd*. Rosen teaches law at George Washington University and frequently writes about the legal aspects of issues like privacy. In *The Naked Crowd*, he is concerned with Americans' lack of security—on many levels—since 9/11. In this excerpt, he is developing some theories about the way in which we express our fears through stigmatizing others.

The notes in the margin point to Rosen's use of sources. But even without these comments, you can easily track the way in which Rosen embeds his sources into the structure of his argument, both as evidence for what he wants to say and as a spur toward the development of new ideas. Because this is an academic work (although published for a general audience), Rosen is using formal documentation: endnotes. (The three basic methods of documentation, including endnotes, will be explained at length in Chapter 10.) You can find out about Rosen's sources by checking the endnotes at the back of his book (or, in this case, at the end of the excerpt).

As you read, notice that, while some sources get cited only by endnote, others get cited by endnote and also by name within the text. (Rosen is using a variant of the usual endnote form, so you will see some differences between his notes and the models in Chapter 11.) When he's dealing with *facts or statistics*, Rosen has to acknowledge where he found the information, but there's no need to cite the person who produced the document. Hence, he provides an endnote, but no citation in the text. When he's dealing with *ideas*, he is back to conducting that roundtable discussion, and each participant has to be acknowledged as a *source* (in the endnote) and as a *person* (in the citation within the text). This distinction is important to the smooth and effective presentation of research. Finally, *anything that isn't endnoted or named in the text can be attributed to Rosen and Rosen alone*. As you read through the passage, try to pinpoint the places where Rosen stops using a source and advances the analysis or argument himself. Also, see if you can find the one place where he includes an unacknowledged source.

from THE NAKED CROWD
Jeffrey Rosen

One of the most salient features of stigma is fear. But today, we   1
fear different attributes than our twentieth-century predecessors
did. Instead of fearing unfamiliar races, nations, or religions, people in
a more individualistic and egalitarian world are hesitant to make
moral judgments about others but we have no hesitation about
showing an obsessive concern about the visible signs of our own
marketability, such as personal hygiene, physical fitness, health, and
sexual attractiveness. We increasingly focus, therefore, on medical
risks rather than moral risks. As Alan Wolfe has argued, "When

names Wolfe
3 times: quotation
and summary

nonjudgmental people make judgments, they often defer to the scientific and medical authorities whom they cite in avoiding making
judgments in other situations."[7] Wolfe explores the ways that we
medicalize our moral judgments—cloaking our opposition to smoking in the purported health risks of secondhand smoke rather than
in our disapproval of the smoker's lack of self-control, for example—
and the ways that we try to explain away our moral disapproval of
self-destructive behavior by chalking it up to addiction rather than
choice. In contrast to the moralistic Victorian era, Wolfe suggests,
America has "entered a new era in which virtue and vice are redefined in terms of public health and addiction." Smoking and obesity

Stearns cited in
footnote: summary

are attacked as symbols of a failure of discipline that used to be associated with a failure of moral character.[8] And conditions or diseases that are feared to be contagious may lead the tainted
individuals or places to be stigmatized with a ruthlessness that the
ancient Greeks would have recognized.

Today, individuals and objects can become stigmatized not merely   2
because they are infected with a contagious disease, but because
they are symbolically contaminated in a way that others fear might
be contagious. Paul Rozin of the University of Pennsylvania has stud-

names Rozin
3 times:
paraphrase and
brief quotation

ied the ways that fear of contagion can lead individuals to avoid even
the briefest contact with an object that poses no actual health risk.
Rozin gives the following example: You are about to drink a glass of
juice, when a friend drops a cockroach in it. You refuse to drink it, on
the grounds that cockroaches are dirty and might carry disease.
The friend pours a new glass of juice and drops a dead sterilized
cockroach into it, ensuring that there is no longer a safety issue.
You refuse to drink again, confessing that the drink has been spoiled
because it has been "cockroached" by brief contact with a disgusting
object: What motivates you to spurn the juice is not a rational fear

of disease, but a visceral reaction that is best described as being grossed out. The health risk turns out to be a masquerade for a psychological aversion that is harder to justify in rational terms.

The response to the cockroach, Rozin argues, illustrates what he calls "the law of contagion."[9] Because we respond more emotionally to negative than positive images, even the briefest physical contact with an object that is perceived to be contaminated can lead a person or an object to be perceived as contaminated as well. Once an object or a person has been spoiled or stigmatized, it may be very hard to remove the stigma: The cockroached juice remains objectionable even if the cockroach has been sterilized. And if there are psychological or moral fears lurking behind a medicalized fear, no amount of reassurance about physical risks will remove the stigma: This is why there is widespread reluctance to touch people with AIDS. The result may be the permanent shunning of individuals who are not, in fact, contagious but who engage our deep and ineradicable fears of contagion, which are rooted in a disgust that we dare not publicly express.

government Web site cited: summary of event

After 9/11, the most dramatic illustration of the principle of contagion was America's response to fears of anthrax. Four letters containing anthrax were mailed to congressional and media leaders in October 2001, leading to twenty-three cases of anthrax infections and five deaths by the end of November. But the disruption that resulted was wildly disproportionate to the actual risk: The Hart Senate Office Building was closed for months and decontaminated at a cost of $22 million. After traces of anthrax were found in its mailroom, the U.S. Supreme Court evacuated its courtroom for the first time since the building opened in 1935, and held a special session down the street at the U.S. Court of Appeals for the D.C. Circuit. When traces of spores were found at almost two dozen off-site mail facilities that served federal buildings throughout Washington, including the White House, the CIA, and the State Department and the Justice Department, mail to all federal government offices was shipped to Ohio to be decontaminated, delaying its delivery for months. The postmaster general told Congress that the total cost of the anthrax attacks could exceed $5 billion.[10]

news article cited: summary

After the anthrax attacks, many citizens reported increased levels of fear. During the month of October, the FBI investigated 2,500 reports of suspected anthrax attacks, many of which turned out to involve harmless substances such as talcum powder. There was a surge in purchases of gas masks and Cipro, the anthrax antibiotic. Three out of ten people surveyed in a Gallup Poll at the end of

3

4

5

October said they had thought about buying a gas mask or Cipro, and more than half said they were considering handling their mail more cautiously.[11] In another poll, half said they had some concern about contracting anthrax, although the other half had little or no concern.[12] More than a third of Americans reported washing their hands after opening Christmas cards.[13] Whether this behavior should be interpreted as a limited panic by an irrational minority or as "reluctance to panic"[14] by the calmer majority is open to debate; but it demonstrates a level of concern vastly disproportionate to the actual threat of infection.

More striking than the fluctuating polls were the rituals that the government adopted in order to expunge the stigma of a mail system that had been tainted in just the way that Rozin's experiments with cockroaches suggest. Once the postal service had been marked in the public mind as a bearer of contamination, even the most remote possibility of contact with a letter that had passed through one of the facilities where a few anthrax spores had been detected became a source of public fear and disgust. Soon after the attacks, on the advice of the Centers for Disease Control and Prevention, universities and other private employers advised their employees to wash their hands after handling mail and to wear latex gloves when opening envelopes. Months after the attacks, the post office adopted elaborate procedures for the permanent irradiation, in off-site facilities, of letters addressed to federal offices, resulting in substantial delays. And a post office report issued in March 2002 promised to implement a "multi-layered, multi-year Emergency Preparedness Plan" to protect customers and employees from exposure to biohazardous material and safeguard the mail system from future attacks. The plan includes the deployment of technology to identify and track all retail mail in the United States; to scan each letter for possible contamination; to sanitize mail addressed to targeted groups; and to expand the use of "e-beam and X-ray irradiation" of contaminated mail. It aspires in the next few years to develop an "intelligent mail system" that would allow "capturing and retaining data to enable tracking and tracing of mail items, data mining to allow forensic investigation, and positive product tracking to eliminate anonymous mail." Within four years of its implementation, the program is estimated to cost up to $2.4 billion a year.[15]

Recall that these extraordinary rituals, which have permanently changed the way mail is delivered in America, were triggered by an attack that claimed only five lives. But the rituals were designed not to purify the mail but to eliminate the stigma that has attached itself

[margin annotations]

news articles cited: summaries

Glass & Schoch-Spana cited: brief quotation

names Rozin: reminder/ no endnote

government report cited: summary

6

7

to the American postal system. Like the early Christians who understood stigmata as bodily signs of holy grace, and thus transformed the symbols of Christ's ultimate sacrifice into symbols of divine favor, we are attempting to purge the stigma of anthrax by reenacting a ritual of reassurance. In this sense, the scanning of envelopes for anthrax is similar to the rituals that require us to remove our shoes at the airport or to use plastic knives in the sky. Like a religious rite, its purpose is psychological rather than empirical. Just as people take Communion to remind themselves that Jesus died on the Cross and sacrificed Himself for their sins, so people remove their shoes to give themselves the illusion of being protected from future shoe bombers. Like believers taking the leap of faith, they are more concerned about ritualized expressions of safety than about safety itself.

Our response to the anthrax attacks after 9/11 is only one example of the tendency of crowds to think in terms of emotional images rather than reasoned arguments, which helps to explain why different groups respond differently to unfamiliar risks. In a Gallup Poll taken soon after September 11, 69 percent of the women surveyed said they were "very worried" that their families might be victimized by terrorist attacks. Only 46 percent of the men were *names Slovic twice: paraphrase* similarly concerned. Paul Slovic's work suggests that in thinking about a range of risks—from the hazards of nuclear waste to the possibility of being victimized by crime and violence—men tend to judge the risks as smaller and less threatening than women.[16] Better educated, richer people perceive themselves to be less at risk than their poorer counterparts. People of color tend to be more fearful of risk than white people. And white men consistently perceive risks to be lower than everyone else, including white women and men and women of color.

When Slovic examined the data more closely, however, he found that not all white men are less fearful than everyone else. The "white male effect," he discovered, seemed to be caused by about 30 percent of the white men surveyed, who judged risks to be extremely low. The rest of the white men didn't perceive risks very differently from all the other groups.[17] What distinguished the 30 percent of less fearful white men from everyone else? They shared certain characteristics that had more to do with their worldview than with their sex. The calmer white men tended to be less egalitarian than everyone else: A majority agreed with the proposition that America has gone too far in pursuing equal rights. They tended to display more trust in authorities, agreeing that government and industry could

8

9

be relied on to manage technological risks. By wide margins, they felt very much in control of risks to their own health, and they agreed that if a risk was small, society could impose it on other individuals without their consent. They believed that individuals should be able to take care of themselves. In short, they were more politically conservative, more hierarchical, more trusting of authority, and less egalitarian than most of their fellow Americans.

One reason that relatively conservative white men seem to be   10 less concerned about risk than their fellow citizens is that people are most fearful of risks they perceive as beyond their ability to control. Many Americans preferred to drive rather than to fly in the months following September 11, even though their risks of being killed in a car crash were greater than their risks of being killed in another terrorist attack. At the wheel of a car, people have an illusion of control that they can't achieve as passengers on a plane, and, therefore, they tend to underestimate the risk of driving and overestimate the risk of flying. It isn't easy to imagine yourself in situations you haven't personally experienced, which means that people have a hard time making decisions about unfamiliar and remote risks. This is why people fear most being a victim of those crimes that they are, in fact, least likely to experience. Women worry most about violent crime, even though they have the lowest risk of being victims, while young men worry the least, even though they have the highest risk. Because of their physical differences, men have a greater illusion of control over their ability to respond to violent crime than women do. In areas where women feel more in control than men, however, they are more likely to engage in risky behavior. When it comes to social risks—such as asking strangers for directions—women turn out to be more intrepid than men. Because men are more reluctant than women to risk the humiliation of appearing foolish before strangers, they perceive the ordeal to be more socially risky.

In the case of terrorism after 9/11, in fact, men and women appear to be equally at risk. But the best explanation for why men   11 perceive the risk of future terrorist attacks to be lower than women do is that men tend to be angrier than women about the 9/11 at-

study cited: tacks, while women tend to be more fearful. In a study of 1,000
summary Americans conducted a few weeks after 9/11, a group of scholars at Carnegie Mellon University found that women believed they had a greater chance of being hurt in a future terrorist attack than men did. Eighty-one percent of the difference between men's and women's perception of risk could be explained by the fact that

women reported lower degrees of anger about the attacks, and higher degrees of fear.[18] Fear is more likely to arise in people who feel uncertain and unable to control future events, while anger is more likely to arise in people who are more confident of their ability to control their environment. Because angrier people have a greater sense of personal control than fearful ones, they tend to be less pessimistic about the possibility of future attacks.

Despite these gender differences, both men and women dramatically overestimated the risks of a future attack after 9/11: The respondents saw a 20 percent chance that they would be personally hurt in a terrorist attack within the next year, and a nearly 50 percent chance that the average American would be hurt. Thankfully, these predictions proved to be wrong, and there was no attack comparable to those on the World Trade Center in the twelve months following 9/11. But the predictions seemed alarmist even when they were made: They could have come true only if an attack of similar magnitude occurred nearly every day for the following year. This shows how liable people are to exaggerate the risk of terrorism because of their tendency to evaluate probabilities in emotional rather than empirical terms.

Behavioral economists and psychologists have found that in making decisions about unfamiliar events, people rely on mental shortcuts, or heuristics, that often lead them to miscalculate the probability of especially dreaded hazards. People believe that they are most likely to be victimized by the threats of which they are most afraid. They imagine that they are more likely to be harmed by nuclear accidents, terrorism, and radioactive pollution than by less dreaded accidents involving power mowers, railroads, or skiing, even though the less dreaded accidents are, in fact, more likely to occur. Terrorism, in this regard, is among the risks that are so horrific to contemplate and hard to control that people's judgments about its probability are likely to be especially clouded by their fear of the outcome. Acts of terrorism are dreaded in the extreme: Their effects are inequitably distributed, they unfairly burden victims without any compensating benefits, and they are hard to predict and hard to understand. This means that relatively minor acts of terrorism can cause fear that greatly exceeds the immediate injuries they cause or the probability that they will recur.

names Slovic: paraphrase One reason that people have difficulty coolly appraising the risks of especially frightening threats reflects a phenomenon that Slovic calls the "affect heuristic"—that is, the tendency of people to make judgments about risk based on emotional feelings and intuitions about whether something is good or bad, rather than on a dispassionate calculation of costs and benefits. Affective judgments are holistic rather than analytic; they focus on pleasure and pain rather than logic, on free associations rather than deductive connections. They take the form of images, metaphors, and narratives—all of which are deeply embedded in our therapeutic and democratic culture—rather than of abstract symbols, words, and numbers. They justify themselves—on the theory that "experiencing is believing"—rather than requiring justification by logic and evidence.[19] In evaluating the risk of flying, for example, people don't tally up the number of plane accidents versus auto accidents; instead, they ask themselves broadly whether they like airplanes, whether they feel comfortable in them, and whether they think they are safe and good. Because our judgments about risks and benefits are guided by seat-of-the-pants emotional impressions about whether we like or dislike an activity, all things considered, we tend not to be swayed by empirical evidence. This makes us especially vulnerable to overestimating the risks of hazards that we fear, even when experts tell us to calm down.

15

The tendency of crowds to make judgments about risks based on visual images rather than on reasoned arguments results in another mental shortcut that leads us to overestimate the probability of especially dramatic risks. People fixate on the hazards that catch their attention, which means those that are easiest to imagine and recall. As Gustave Le Bon recognized in *The Crowd*, a single memorable image will crowd out less visually dramatic risks in the public mind and will lead people wrongly to imagine that they are more likely to be victims of terrorism than of mundane risks, like heart disease. The Nobel Prize winners Amos Tversky and Daniel Kahneman have called this the "availability heuristic,"[20] which they define as the tendency to assume that an event is likely to recur if examples of it are easy to remember. . . . For the same reason, people overestimate the frequency of deaths from dramatic disasters such as tornadoes, floods, fire, and homicide and underestimate the frequency of deaths from diabetes, stomach cancer, stroke, and asthma.[21]

names Le Bon: no endnote

names Tversky & Kahneman: quotation and summary

16

When presented with two estimations of risk—one high and the other low—people tend to believe the high risk estimation regardless of whether it comes from government or industry.[22] This bias toward the worst-case scenario is another example of the fact that crowds, when their emotions are intensely engaged, tend to focus on the vividness of a particularly unpleasant risk rather than on its likelihood. This phenomenon, which Cass Sunstein calls "probability neglect,"[23] can lead to behavioral changes that strike experts as

article cited: summary

Sunstein named: brief quotation

irrational, such as buying gas masks and Cipro and canceling flights while continuing to drive and eat Big Macs. The print and electronic media play an important role in contributing to this behavior, but it is a role that can't be separated from the demands of the public itself. Most journalists can tell stories of editors who have pressured them to describe worst-case scenarios, in order to scare the audience into thinking that the story in question is somehow relevant to their lives.

Tocqueville named: paraphrase and quotation

As Tocqueville noted in his discussion of why American writers are bombastic, citizens in democratic societies spend most of their time contemplating themselves, and can be tempted to stop gazing at their navels only when they are confronted with the largest and most gripping of subjects. Writers, therefore, have an incentive to attract the attention of the crowd by exaggerating the significance of every topic: If they report that things aren't as bad as they might be, the public won't pay attention. Because of this unfortunate dynamic, Tocqueville reported, "the author and the public corrupt one another at the same time."[24]

When reporting on essentially random risks, there is especially great pressure on reporters to exaggerate the scope and probability of the danger, in order to make more people feel that they, too, could be victims. Joel Best of Southern Illinois University has examined the "moral panics" about dramatic new crimes that seized the public attention in the 1980s and 1990s, such as freeway violence in 1987, wilding in 1989, stalking around 1990, children and guns in 1991, and so forth. In each of these cases, Best writes, the television media seized on two or three incidents of a dramatic crime, such as freeway shooting, and then claimed that it was part of a broader trend. By taking the worst and most infrequent examples of criminal violence and melodramatically claiming they were typical, TV created the impression that everyone was at risk, thereby increasing its audience. Although the idea of random violence appeals to our democratic sensibilities—if violence is random, then everyone is equally at risk—Best points out that "most violence is not patternless, is not pointless, nor is it increasing in the uncontrolled manner we imagine."[25] After purported trends failed to pan out in most of the cases described above, the media spotlight moved on in search of new and even more melodramatic threats.

Best named 3 times: quotation and paraphrase

17

[7]Alan Wolfe, *Moral Freedom: The Search for Virtue in a World of Choice* (New York: W. W. Norton, 2001), p. 88.

[8]Peter N. Stearns, *Battleground of Desire: The Struggle for Self-Control in Modern America* (New York: NYU Press, 1999), p. 325.

[9]Paul Rozin, "Technological Stigma: Some Perspectives from the Study of Contagion," in *Risk, Media and Stigma*, pp. 31–35.

[10]See <http://www.usps.com/news/2001/press/mailsecurity/allfaq.htm>.

[11]Richard Benedetto, "Poll Finds Anthrax Fear but No Panic," *USA Today*, October 23, 2001, p. A4.

[12]J. Mozingo, "Poll: Floridians Not Panicked," *The Miami Herald*, October 25, 2001, p. 3B.

[13]Tom Pelton, "36% of Americans Wash Up after Handling Mail," *The Baltimore Sun*, December 18, 2001, p. 8A.

[14]See generally Thomas A. Glass and Monica Schoch-Spana, "Bioterrorism and the People: How to Vaccinate a City against Panic," in *Confronting Biological Weapons*, CID, January 15, 2002.

[15]See generally *U.S. Postal Service Emergency Preparedness Plan for Protecting Postal Employees and Postal Customers from Exposure to Biohazardous Material and for Ensuring Mail Security against Bioterror Attacks*, March 6, 2002, available at <http://www.usps.com/news/2002/epp/welcome.htm>.

[16]Paul Slovic, "Trust, Emotion, Sex, Politics and Science: Surveying the Risk-Assessment Battlefield," in Paul Slovic, *The Perception of Risk* (Sterling, Va.: Earthscan, 2000), p. 396.

[17]Ibid., pp. 398–99.

[18]Jennifer S. Lerner, Roxana M. Gonzalez, Deborah A. Small, and Baruch Fischoff, "Effects of Fear and Anger on Perceived Risks of Terrorism: A National Field Experiment," *Psychological Science* (2002).

[19]Paul Slovic, Melissa Finucane, Ellen Peters, and Donald G. MacGregor, "The Affect Heuristic," in *Heuristics and Biases: The Psychology of Intuitive Judgment*, eds. T. Gilovich, D. Griffin, and D. Kahneman (Cambridge: Cambridge University Press, 2002), pp. 397, 400.

[20]See Amos Tversky and Daniel Kahneman, "Availability: A Heuristic for Judging Frequency and Probability," 5 *Cognitive Psychology* 207 (1973).

[21]Ibid., p. 107.

[22]W. Kip Viscusi, "Alarmist Decisions with Divergent Risk Information," 107 *Ec. Journal* 1657 (1997).

[23]Cass Sunstein, "Probability Neglect: Emotions, Worst Cases, and Law," 112 *Yale L.J.* 61 (2002).

[24]Alexis de Tocqueville, *Democracy in America*, eds. Harvey C. Mansfield and Delba Winthrop, vol. 2, part 1, ch. 18 (Chicago: University of Chicago Press, 2000), p. 464.

[25]Joel Best, *Random Violence: How We Talk about New Crimes and New Victims* (Berkeley: University of California Press, 1999), p. 10.

EXERCISE 21: INTEGRATING THREE ACADEMIC SOURCES

In 2000, the *Chronicle of Higher Education* asked three academic scholars with a special interest in animal life for statements explaining *why there was a sudden vogue for animal prints in women's clothing.*

Read the three statements, analyze the common themes, and write two or three paragraphs, based on these sources, that account for the popularity of animal prints. For the purposes of this exercise, you may limit your documentation to citing the names of the three scholars; no formal documentation is needed. Note: Do not discuss one source per paragraph!

I see the interest in animal prints as Marie Antoinette setting up her peasant hut at Versailles, rather than a real interest in the characteristics or attributes of wild animals. It's not about any kind of love of the wild or love of the sexy—I think it's the love of the fake.

The animal-print thing is a subcategory of the love of the cool. A lot of cool people love the fake right now. It's not like the fake is a new thing; it's been in fashion for centuries. But cool people today don't hide the fact that they absolutely love fakeness. They like synthetic fabrics, chartreuse or international orange, Lycra, weird jewelry; they let their roots show, they wear wacko colors on their lips, they wear shiny sprinkles on their skin.

Clothes aren't about serious work but serious decoration. You don't have to really go out and help wild animals, you can just wear the fake skins. You get to quote nature in a safe way, in the context of the mall or the club or the urban scene. You get to combine your indulgence in a fashion trend with feeling morally superior in an easy way.

It's part of the tremendous appetite to appropriate anything and everything out there. I don't think there's passionate meaning attached to it. It's not romantic. It's not longing for the wild, for the jungle; it's quoting them. Animal prints are symbols of wildness filtered through a contemporary retro taste for the 50's—when rock 'n' roll was still innocent, and everyone necked passionately in drive-ins but didn't go all the way. Combine it with Lycra and lots of exposed flesh, and you see people pushing sexiness, but in this culture of so much exposure, it's desperate. People with nothing to say make fashion statements. We're dragging animal patterns and fakery into fashion because we're bored.

LAURIE FENDRICH

The basis of all fashion is animal in nature. In general, animal patterns serve three purposes in the natural world: to attract, repel, or disguise. To attract: that would be the most obvious way, with certain colors, shapes, and forms. To repel: a certain anti-aesthetic like punk serves as a double negative, to attract while repelling.

To disguise: with certain kinds of uniform-like fashions, like interchangeable blue-polyester suits, the point is to blur into a mass, which would be the function of zebra stripes—to eliminate a particular target from a predator.

Animals serve a totemic function, and by appropriating certain animal patterns, shapes, or even parts of the animal, you take on some of that animal's properties. In some ways, that's like a photograph. Even if it's imaginary, you have this linkage to the animal itself.

What's particularly interesting is the shift from fur to fake fur, to synthetic animals. Fake fur takes the use of the animal into another interesting realm. If you pursue the analogy of photography, fake fur is like a movement into digital imaging, which similarly eliminates the reference without ever having taken the photograph. Now, with the notion of a synthetic animal, you don't know where you are in relationship to modernity.

With animal patterns, clearly there is a sign also of having triumphed over the animal, and the animal pattern serves in fashion as a trophy as well. In the same way that you have the bearskin rugs and the deer heads as trophies, wearing the animal is a sign of having killed the animal, so it serves as a mark of power.

AKIRA MIZUTA LIPPIT

We have a lot of cultural uses of animals that are dangerous to them. Even fake furs and animal prints are dangerous. It makes sense that leopard prints make it easier for people to wear furs; it blurs the continuum. When we appropriate animal images and commodify them, we almost always do it ironically and condescendingly, out of a sense of superiority. We call a car a Chevy Impala, but antelopes don't pollute and don't kill 50,000 people a year. All these perversions of animal images, including naming sports teams after animals and animal-print clothing, are culturally dangerous, because they blind us to the reality of the real animals. They convince us that animal names, images, and patterns are ours for the taking. They're gimmicks for us to use in our entertainment and fashions.

The real tiger, zebra, leopard, antelope is something very different. Real creatures have habitats, and we're destroying their habitats heedlessly, precisely because when we think of animals, we don't think of their realities, because they've been through this cultural meat-grinder. We excise little pieces—the spots, the stripes. Culture subtly coerces us to minimize animal reality, because our factories can keep churning out zebra prints. The prints testify to our ability to rip nature out of nature. And this is something, perversely, that we enjoy doing a lot.

RANDY MALAMUD

ASSIGNMENT 9: SYNTHESIZING ACADEMIC SOURCES

Read Bill Coplin's "Lost in the Life of the Mind" and Marshall Gregory's "A Liberal Education Is Not a Luxury." Then review Blanche Blank's "A Question of Degree" (pp. 11–14) and Shannon French's "When Teaching the Ethics of War Is Not Academic" (pp. 80–85).

Using at least three of these sources, write an essay on the following topic: *Who, if anyone, needs to have a liberal education?* As you analyze your sources and explore their common themes and their differences, develop a thesis that responds to the topic. Follow the guidelines for writing a synthesis essay, and cite the sources appropriately within your paragraphs. If your instructor asks you to use formal documentation, consult Chapter 10 as well as the forms in Chapter 12. The essay should be three pages long.

Like Shannon French and Blanche Blank, Marshall Gregory and Bill Coplin are academics. The former teaches English at Butler University; the latter teaches public affairs at Syracuse University.

LOST IN THE LIFE OF THE MIND

Bill Coplin

"Bait and switch" is usually used to describe the sleazy telephone sales rep who starts, "This is your lucky day. You are the winner of a free vacation in the Bahamas." Schnooks take the bait only to find out the hidden costs.   1

I felt like a schnook after my second week as an undergraduate in 1956 at Washington College in Chestertown, Md. After a year, I transferred to the Johns Hopkins University, where the switch was even more apparent. My parents, relatives, high-school teachers, and guidance counselor had said, "You are college material," so I thought I'd go to college and live happily ever after.   2

However, I quickly realized that I had been a victim of a gigantic conspiracy on the part of colleges that was unwittingly supported by the rest of society in the name of the American dream, unfettered social mobility. I took the bait that college would lead to a high-paying and rewarding job. Once there, the switch was on. My role was to please the faculty by showing them I wanted to learn everything they loved to learn. It wasn't until getting my Ph.D. in international relations from American University that I was told by a wise professor, "A college degree and four quarters will get you a dollar."   3

I thought taking English meant improving my writing skills, that taking Spanish meant that when I went to Mexico I'd be able to converse, that studying history would be an exercise in learning about the past. Wrong on all three counts!   4

English courses at that time were about appreciating literature. (Now many are about deconstructing text and going off on ideological rants.) Spanish taught language that would permit me to read great Spanish novelists and thinkers, not close   5 a deal. History was a study of the study of history—discussion, for instance, of Charles Beard's economic interpretation of the Constitution rather than of what the founding fathers actually did.

I was impressed by my English professor's passion and excitement. Wish I could have been as excited about Chaucer, or even figured out what the hell he was saying. If you haven't had the pleasure, here is a short quote out of *Bartlett's Familiar Quotations*: "feeld hath eyen, and the wode has eres." 6

The first thing that strikes you is that if you had this on Microsoft Word, there would be red squiggles under half of it. I had to learn a foreign language called 14th-century English. The professor subjected me to this because he was a professional scholar saying, in essence, "Be like me." 7

I could not blame him for his missionary zeal because that is why he went into academe in the first place, and what his Ph.D. trained him for. However, I was plenty angry at a system that treated all students as if they were in college to learn for the sake of learning when in fact the vast majority wanted college to prepare them for a successful career. I wanted to learn about life; they wanted me to lose myself in the life of the mind. 8

Not much has changed over the past 48 years, and with devastating results, if a recent conversation I had with Joe, let's call him, is any indication. I met Joe in the late 1980s when he was 12 years old in a program in which my undergraduates worked with at-risk youth. Joe adopted me as his mentor because, despite a serious speech impediment, he liked to argue politics. He didn't want to end up, like many of his friends had, in jail or dead, and he didn't want to be on welfare like his parents were. 9

However, Joe could not pass the New York State standardized tests required for graduation. He went into the Job Corps, where he got his GED, became a professional house painter, joined the Army, completed basic training at the top of his class, served overseas, and eventually left the military. He decided he wanted to be a policeman and did OK on the civil-service exam. 10

He called me in 2003 to tell me that he was in a local community college to study criminal justice and get an associate degree. During the course of the conversation, he said, "Coplin, how come I got to learn the MLA, the APA, and the Chicago style? Can't they make up their minds?" 11

I told Joe that the college curriculum, even at a community college serving students who don't necessarily want to go on to a four-year liberal-arts degree, was designed to prepare professional scholars. Moreover, the inability to select one citation form was evidence that college faculty members can't reach a consensus on even the most trivial of educational goals. I advised him to play the game. He said, "No problem, I learned to do that in the Army." 12

Joe would have been far better served if he had spent his time learning to write and speak more clearly and with better grammar. It's tempting to dismiss him as an example because of his socioeconomic background and the faults of the public-school system. But poor oral and written communication skills are rampant 13 no matter what the educational background of the student or the ranking of the college.

According to employers, college students are not prepared for the work force because they lack the skills and character needed to succeed. Our best and brightest students might take statistics in college and score A's on the tests that measure their ability to solve some abstract problem about white and black Ping-Pong balls, but cannot figure out how to set up a bar graph to display real-world data. They learn calculus, but they can't make budget projections. 14

They learn shortcuts to jump the academic hurdles with a minimum of effort, but not much about honesty and work ethic. A director of sales and marketing for a media company wrote me: "What I found from my hiring—the higher the GPA and the more prestigious the school, the less prepared for the real world the grad was. I was amazed at the basics that these 22- and 23-year-olds lacked. Real basic—like how about we wake up every day and show up for work on time!" 15

Liberal-arts leaders have no choice but to continue setting the bait. It's a matter of economic survival. Most students and their parents will pay as much as $160,000 only if they believe a college experience will lead to a better economic future. 16

The important question is to what degree colleges will deliver what they promise. Teaching critical thinking and fostering intellectual well-roundedness are important goals, but too general and self-serving. Faculties need to take more responsibility for helping students acquire the skills employers want. The list needs to be specific enough so that professors can assess skill levels but general enough so that the skills cut across all academic programs. 17

Those skills include dependability, attention to detail, teamwork, obtaining and analyzing information, problem solving, and writing clearly. Such a list can be found in my recent book *10 Things Employers Want You to Learn in College*. Similar lists can be found in a study in 2002 that the National Association of Colleges and Employers based on surveys of 457 employers, or in work from the early 1990s by the Department of Labor's Secretary's Commission on Achieving Necessary Skills, or in the 2003 Business–Higher Education Forum report, "Building a Nation of Learners." 18

The focus on general professional skills would allow liberal-arts faculties to have their cake and eat it too. On one hand, they would be free to choose whatever curricular content they want. On the other, they would provide students with the opportunity to practice and improve the skills employers expect. Professors just need to keep their eye on the target and to be as rigorous about students' skills as they are about their own research. Whatever content they teach should be applicable beyond the confines of their disciplines. They can do that by incorporating more fieldwork and active learning into their courses. 19

For example, students from a class studying *The Canterbury Tales* could rewrite one of them in a modern setting (active learning) or present one to a 12th-grade English class in a local high school (fieldwork). Instructors teaching methods in various social sciences could require students, as I have since 1979 in my methods course, to complete a client survey for a community agency serving youth. 20

Liberal-arts professors will have to accept the implicit social contract with their   21
students. They need to treat undergraduates as clients who learn not only from
what is said, assigned, and tested, but also from the professor's own behavior. For
their part, students must recognize professors' expertise in their subjects, but also
their importance as professional-skills coaches. That means seeking constructive
criticism rather than worrying only about grades, and working hard to master the
material rather than cramming before tests.

Over the past 30 years, service learning, internships, computer-based instruc-   22
tion, team projects, and problem-based interdisciplinary courses have become more
widespread. However, they remain the exceptions, helping admissions officers better set the bait. Liberal-arts institutions overall need to embrace a skills perspective to minimize the switch.

A LIBERAL EDUCATION IS NOT A LUXURY
Marshall Gregory

A couple of years ago, in one of the "idea of the university" seminars that I regu-   1
larly direct for professional staff members, I spoke with a recruiter from the admissions office who enthusiastically agreed with everything I had to say about the aims
and practices of liberal education but who reported that she hardly mentioned the
nature of liberal education in her standard pitch to prospective students and their
parents. When I asked why not, she hemmed and hawed and then blurted out: "If we
had the luxury of really explaining liberal education to prospective students the way
you are explaining it to us, we'd do it—but we just don't have that luxury. What our
students want to hear about is not liberal education, but jobs!"

As we sat there a moment, silently, the line that Emperor Joseph II repeats in   2
the movie *Amadeus* kept running through my head: "Well, there it is." So helping
students get jobs is a necessity, but helping them get a liberal education is a luxury?
If that is the case, I thought, then there's not much difference between liberal education and sports teams, exercise centers, campus movies, and ice cream in the cafeteria, is there? Are we willing to live with that trivialization of higher education?

Those of us who spend our careers putting our hearts and souls into liberal ed-   3
ucation sometimes fail to realize that the most potent threat to the mission we
love comes not from outside enemies but from the proponents of liberal education themselves. At universities that focus on the bottom line—and what university these days does not?—supporters of liberal education have been on the
defensive for so long, they no longer know how to fight prevailing trends. They don't
challenge the current orthodoxy that the modern university must go along to get
along, especially in relation to marketplace practices and values. Their friends' support is only lukewarm, sometimes no more than lip service, and would vanish if
liberal education became powerful enough to threaten others' resources.

The liberal-education rhetoric that developed in the last century is subtly and qui-   4
etly accommodationist. Often, in fact, it is a rhetoric of silence. It implicitly concedes

the strongest ground in any discussion of educational aims to faculty members from professional and preprofessional programs, who love to insist that students' progress should be measured exclusively by grades and skills, and who seem to believe that making lots of money is an imperative somehow woven into the fabric of the universe itself. Such people almost always talk in narrow, instrumental terms about what a student is to do, rather than talk in broad terms about who that student is to be.

The proper response is to point out that students' overriding concern with post-graduation employment is simply misguided. The real danger is not that students will miss out on a job, but that they will miss out on an education. In 35 years of teaching, I have never seen a student who really wanted a job fail to get one after graduation, regardless of his or her major. (The best predictor of students' future incomes is not their college major; it is their parents' incomes.) But I have seen many students fail to get an education because they were fixated on the fiction that one particular major or another held the magical key to financial success for the rest of their lives.

Students' overriding concern should be how to develop as fully as possible their basic human birthright: their powers of imagination, aesthetic responsiveness, introspection, language, rationality, moral and ethical reasoning, physical capacities, and so on. Those are the powers that students must cultivate if they wish to strive for excellence. Moreover, those are the powers that higher education is especially suited to help students hone.

But while many faculty members talk twaddle about accommodating liberal and vocational education—by which they mean to "accommodate" liberal education all the way outside the city limits where it won't bother anyone—we liberal educators too often make no response or, worse, make small, meek noises that suggest we will be content with any moldy corner in the university as long as we can, please heaven, just have that corner. I cannot remember the last time I heard any liberal educator bluntly and emphatically challenge the presumptions behind the preprofessional rhetoric of narrow utilitarianism, which always paints itself as simply being realistic (a rhetorical strategy that condescendingly marks liberal educators as people with no proper grasp of reality).

Accommodationist rhetoric began as a coping mechanism to allow liberal education to coexist with burgeoning professional and preprofessional programs. However, coping mechanisms that stay around too long run the risk of becoming dysfunctional. Liberal educators have tried immensely hard to avoid giving offense to the futurists and instrumentalists who increasingly control university programs today. And we have succeeded. We are nothing if not inoffensive. However, our rhetoric of accommodation also makes us seem irrelevant and hopelessly old-fashioned, like the crocheted doilies that my grandmothers placed on every armchair in their homes.

Liberal education should not be about going along to get along. It's not about a genteel frosting of humane learning—like knowing that Bizet, despite composing *Carmen*, was French, not Spanish. It's not merely about being well rounded, whatever that cliché means, nor is it about being able to discuss a variety of entertaining topics at cocktail parties. Con men can be well rounded, and fools can be entertaining.

Liberal education is the pursuit of human excellence, not the pursuit of excel-   10
lent salaries and excellent forms of polish and sophistication. Liberal education is not even about excellent intellectual achievements. Its goal is more ethical than intellectual: It focuses on the development of individuals as moral agents, and it teaches students how to reflect both analytically and evaluatively on the fact that the choices we make turn us into the persons we become.

If the enterprise I have just described is a luxury, then I cannot begin to define a   11
necessity. What could be more necessary for any human being than learning how to claim, develop, enjoy, and put to public use the distinctive advantages of our nature—to be able, first, to choose the kind of person that we turn out to be and, second, to influence the kinds of persons that others turn out to be? If liberal education is a luxury, then so is truth in a courtroom, love in marriage, or kindness in response to suffering.

I regret that I must contradict the young recruiter in my staff seminar. She was, af-   12
ter all, only reflecting accurately and conscientiously the views and pressures that she receives from her usual audience of prospective students and their parents. But challenging those views, no matter who expresses them, is crucial for liberal educators. No matter what career we choose, the single job that every human being has to work at is the job of deciding what kind of person he or she will become. That is a requirement grounded in the existential conditions of human life. What are discretionary are goals that have little to do with the pursuit of human excellence. And when those discretionary pursuits begin to define all of education, as they threaten to do in academe today, then true education becomes trivialized. Most of the professional and technical training that people need for their jobs actually takes place on the job, and valuing that training above education comes perilously close to making colleges and universities minor-league farm clubs for the world's corporations and bureaucracies.

Liberal education represents the last and best—but least understood and least ap-   13
preciated—mechanism for achieving the fullest development of human potential. Today's universities too often pander to, rather than challenge, students' educational utilitarianism. But who is better equipped to help cure that problem than liberal educators? Surely we can make a strong case for liberal education instead of using accommodationist rhetoric that gives the store away before students have a chance to see what's on the shelves. Without our assistance, students may never understand that they get the profits from buying the wares of liberal education, and that those wares appreciate in value as students use them in a lifetime pursuit of human excellence.

Part IV

WRITING THE RESEARCH ESSAY

Most long essays and term papers in college courses are based on library research. Sometimes, an instructor will expect you to develop and present a topic using preassigned sources only; but for many other assignments, you will be asked to formulate your own opinion and then to validate and support that opinion by searching for and citing authorities. Whether your essay is to be wholly or partly substantiated through research, you will still have to base your essay on sources.

Your research essay (or extended multiple-source essay) will present you with several new problems, contradictions, and decisions. On the one hand, you will probably be starting out with no sources, no thesis, and only a broad topic to work with. Yet as soon as you go to the library and start your research, you will find yourself with a multitude of sources—books and articles in the library and on the Internet from which you will have to make your own selection of readings. Locating and evaluating sources are complex skills, calling for quick comprehension and rapid decision making.

- *In the electronic databases* and *computer catalogs*, you have to judge which books and periodicals are worth locating.
- *At the shelves* and *on the computer screen*, you have to skim a variety of books, articles, and Web sites rapidly to choose the ones that may be worth reading at length.
- *At the library tables* and *on the computer screen*, you have to decide which information should be written up as part of your notes and which pages should be duplicated or printed out.

In Chapters 7, 8, and 9, you will be given explicit guidelines for using the library, choosing sources, and taking notes.

As you have learned, in order to write a multiple-source essay, you have to establish a coherent structure that builds on your reading and blends together your ideas and those of your sources. In Chapter 9, you will find a stage-by-stage description of the best ways to organize and write an essay based on complex sources. But here, again, is a contradiction.

Even as you gather your materials and synthesize them into a unified essay, you should also keep in mind the greatest responsibility of the researcher—accountability. *From your first efforts to find sources at the library and at your computer, you must carefully keep track of the precise source of each of the ideas and facts that you may use in your essay.* You already know how to distinguish between your ideas and those of your sources and to make that distinction clear to your readers.

Now, you also have to make clear which source is responsible for which idea and on which page of the source that information can be found—without losing the shape and coherence of your own paragraphs.

To resolve this contradiction between writing a coherent essay and accounting for your sources, you will use a system that includes the familiar skills of *summary, quotation, paraphrase,* and *citation of authors,* as well as the skills of *documentation* and *compiling a bibliography.* This system is explained in Chapter 10.

What should your essay look like when it's completed? For reference, in Chapter 11 you can examine three essays that demonstrate how to write a persuasive, analytical research essay, each one using one of the three most common methods of documentation.

▪7▪

Finding Sources

Chapter 7 shows you the many ways to develop a topic for a research essay as you search for information in the library and on the Internet. You can use databases and search engines to identify and locate a range of books, periodical articles, and Web sites that are appropriate for academic research. At the same time, you'll learn to transform these sources into a formal bibliography.

TOPIC NARROWING

When you start your research, sometimes you will know exactly what you want to write about, and sometimes you won't. Your instructor may assign a precise topic. Or you may start with a broad subject and then narrow the focus. Or you may develop an idea that you wrote about in your single- or multiple-source essay.

Ask yourself these practical questions as you think about your topic and before you begin collecting material for your essay:

- How much time do I have?
- What information is available to me?
- How long an essay am I being asked to write?
- How complex a project am I ready to undertake?

305

The box below contains some approaches to topic narrowing that work well for students starting their first research project.

Narrowing Your Topic

1. Whether your instructor assigns a broad topic for your research paper or you are permitted to choose your own topic, do some preliminary searching for sources to get background information.
2. As you see what's available, begin to break down the broad topic into its components. Try thinking about a specific point in time or the influence of a particular event or person if your topic is *historical* or *biographical*. Try applying the standard strategies for planning an essay (see pp. 194–195 in Chapter 5) if you're going to write about a *contemporary* issue. Try formulating the reasons for and against if you're going to write an *argument*.
3. Once you have some sense of the available material, consider the *scope* of your essay. If the scope is too broad, you run the risk of presenting a superficial overview. If the scope is too narrow, you may run out of material.
4. As you read, consider *your own perspective* and what interests you about the person, event, or issue. If you really want to know more about the topic, your research will go smoothly and you're more likely to get your essay in on time.
5. Formulate a few *questions* that might help you to structure your reading and research. As you read, you'll increasingly want to stay within that framework, concentrating on materials that add to your understanding of the topic, skimming lightly over those that don't.
6. As answers to these questions emerge, think about a potential *thesis* for your essay.

Topic Narrowing: Biographical and Historical Subjects

Biographical and historical topics have an immediate advantage: they can be defined and limited by space and time. Events and lives have clear beginnings, middles, and ends, as well as many identifiable intermediate stages. You are probably not ready to undertake the full span of a biography or a complete historical event, but you could select a specific point in time as the focus for your essay.

Writing about People

Assume, for example, that by choice or assignment your broad subject is *Franklin Delano Roosevelt*, who was president of the United States for thirteen

years—an unparalleled term of office—from 1933 until 1945. You begin by reading *a brief overview of FDR's life.* An encyclopedia article of several pages might
be a starting point. This should give you enough basic information to decide
which events in FDR's life interest you enough to sustain you through the long
process of research. You might also read a few articles about the major events
that formed the background to FDR's career: the Great Depression, the New
Deal, the changing role of the president.

Choosing a Point in Time: Now, instead of tracing *all* the incidents and related events in which he participated during his sixty-three years, you might
decide to describe FDR at the point when his political career was apparently ru-
ined by polio. Your focus would be the man in 1921, and your essay might develop a thesis drawing on any or all of the following topics—his personality, his
style of life, his physical handicap, his experiences, his idea of government—at
that point in time. Everything that happened to FDR after 1921 would be relatively unimportant to your chosen perspective. Another student might choose a
different point in time and describe the new president in 1933 against the background of the Depression. Yet another might focus on an intermediate point in
FDR's presidency and construct a profile of the man as he was in 1940, at the
brink of America's entry into World War II, when he decided to run for an unprecedented third term in office.

Finding a Focus: The topic might be made even more specific by focusing on
a single event and its causes. For example, the atomic bomb was developed during FDR's presidency and was used in Japan shortly after his death:

- What was FDR's attitude toward atomic research?
- Did he advocate using the bomb?
- Did he anticipate its consequences?
- How has sixty years changed our view of the atomic bomb and FDR's role
  in its development?

Or you might want to study Roosevelt in the context of an important political
tradition:

- How did he influence the Democratic party?
- How did the party's policies influence his personal and political decisions?
- What role did Roosevelt play in the establishment of the United States as a
  "welfare state"?
- How has the Democratic party changed since his time?

This kind of profile attempts to describe a historical figure, explore his or her
motives and experiences, and, possibly, apply them to an understanding of current issues. In effect, your overriding impression of character or intention becomes the basis for the thesis, the controlling idea of your essay.

Writing about Events

You can also view a *historical event* from a similar specific vantage point. Your broad topic might be the Civil War, which lasted more than four years, or the Berlin Olympics of 1936, which lasted a few weeks, or the Los Angeles riots of 1991, which lasted a few days. Rather than cover a long span of time, you might focus on an intermediate point or stage, which can serve to illuminate and characterize the entire event.

The *Battle of Gettysburg*, for example, is a broad topic often chosen by those interested in the even broader topic of the Civil War. Since the three-day battle, with its complex maneuvers, can hardly be described in a brief narrative, you would want to narrow the focus even more. You might describe the battlefield and the disposition of the troops, as a journalist would, at a single moment in the course of the battle. In this case, your thesis might demonstrate that the disposition of the troops at this point was typical (or atypical) of tactics used throughout the battle, or that this moment did (or did not) foreshadow the battle's conclusion.

Finding a Focus: In writing about history, you also have to consider your own point of view. If, for example, you set out to recount an episode from the Civil War, you first need to *establish your perspective*: Are you describing the Union's point of view? the Confederacy's? the point of view of the politicians of either side? the generals? the civilians? industrialists? hospital workers? slaves in the South? black freedmen in the North? If you tried to deal with *all* these reactions to a chosen event, you might have difficulty in settling on a thesis.

The "day in the life" approach can also be applied to *events that had no specific date*.

- When and under what circumstances were primitive guns first used in battle?
- What was the reaction when the first automobile drove down a village street? When television was first introduced into American homes?

Rather than describe the effects of a new invention, you might focus on *a social institution that has changed radically*.

- What was it like to shop for food in Paris in 1810?
- In Chicago in 1870?
- In any large American city in 1945?

Instead of attempting to write a complete history of the circus from Rome to Ringling, try portraying *the particular experience of a single person*.

- What was it like to be an equestrian performer in Astley's Circus in London in 1805?
- A chariot racer in Pompeii's Circus Maximus in 61 BC?

Setting a tentative target date helps you to focus your research, giving you a practical way to judge the relevance and the usefulness of each of your sources.

Establishing a Thesis and a Strategy

As you narrow your topic and begin your reading, watch for your emerging thesis—a *clear impression of the person or event* that you wish your reader to receive. Whether you are writing about a sequence of events, like a battle or a flood, or a single event or issue in the life of a well-known person, you will still need both a *thesis* and a *strategy* to shape the direction of your essay. A common strategy for biographical and historical topics is the *cause-and-effect sequence*—reasons why a certain decision was made or an event turned out one way and not another.

- Why did the United States develop the atomic bomb before Germany did?
- Why did President Truman decide to use the atomic bomb against Japan as the war was ending?

Your thesis may contain your own view of the person or event that you're writing about:

- "FDR had no choice but to support the development of the atomic bomb."
- "The development of the supermarket resulted in major changes to American family life."
- "The imposition of term limits for the presidency after FDR's fourth term in office was [or was not] good for the United States [or for democracy in the United States or for political parties in the United States or for politicians in the United States]."

Finally, do not allow your historical or biographical portrait to become an exercise in creative writing. Your evidence must be derived from and supported by well-documented sources, not just your imagination. The "Napoleon might have said" or "Stalin must have thought" in some biographies and historical novels is often a theory or an educated guess that is firmly rooted in research—and the author should provide documentation and a bibliography to substantiate it.

Topic Narrowing: Contemporary Subjects

If you chose to write about the early history of the circus, you would find a limited assortment of books describing many traditional kinds of circus activity, from the Roman arena to the Barnum and Bailey big top. But these days an enormous amount of information is available. Reviews and features are printed—and preserved for the researcher—every time Ringling Brothers opens in a new city. Your research for an essay about the circus today might be endless and the results unmanageable unless, quite early, you focus your approach.

Finding a Focus: The usual way is to analyze a topic's component parts and select *a single aspect* as the tentative focus of your essay. Do you want to write about circus acts? Do you want to focus on animal acts or, possibly, the animal rights movement's opposition to the use of animals for circus entertainment? Or the dangers of trapeze and high-wire acts? What does the trend to small, one-ring circuses tell us about people's taste today? Or the advent of the "new age" Cirque de Soleil? Or you could write about the logistics of circus management—transport, for example—or marketing. Or consider larger issues: Why are circuses still so popular in an age of instant electronic entertainment? How has modern entertainment (e.g., TV) altered the business of circuses?

One practical way to begin narrowing a topic is to do a *computer search*. Many of the guides, indexes, and online databases contain not only lists of sources but also a useful directory of subtopics. As you'll see later in this chapter, descriptors and keywords can suggest possibilities for the direction of your essay.

Yet another way to narrow your perspective is to apply different strategies to possible topics. Suppose that *food* is your broad topic. Your approach might be *descriptive*, analyzing *causes and effects*: you could write about some aspect of nutrition, discussing what we ought to eat and the way in which our nutritional needs are best satisfied. Or you could deal with the production and distribution of food—or, more likely, a specific kind of food—and use *process description* as your approach. Or you could analyze a different set of *causes*: Why don't we eat what we ought to? Why do so many people have to diet, and why aren't diets effective? Or you could plan a *problem-solution* essay: What would be the best way to educate the public in proper nutrition?

Within the narrower focus of *food additives*, there are numerous ways to develop the topic:

- To what degree are additives dangerous?
- What was the original purpose of the Food and Drug Act of 1906?
- What policies does the Food and Drug Administration carry out today?
- Would individual rights be threatened if additives like artificial sweeteners were banned?
- Can the dangers of food additives be compared with the dangers of alcohol?

On the other hand, your starting point could be *a concrete object*, rather than an abstract idea: you might decide to write about the Big Mac. You could describe its contents and nutritional value; or recount its origins and first appearance on the food scene; or compare it to best-selling foods of past eras; or evaluate its relative popularity in different parts of the world. All of these topics require research.

It is desirable to have a few approaches in mind before you begin intensive reading. Then, as you start to compile your preliminary bibliography, you can begin to distinguish between sources that are potentially useful and sources that will probably be irrelevant. You will probably start to develop a *hypothesis*, a theory that may or may not be true, depending on what you find in your research. What you *cannot* do at this stage is formulate a definite thesis. Your thesis will probably answer the question that you asked at the beginning of your research. Although, from the first, you may have your own theories about the answer, you cannot be sure that your research will confirm your hypotheses. Your thesis should remain tentative until your reading has given your essay content and direction.

Topic Narrowing: Issues for Argument

Most people want to argue about an issue that has significance for them. If no issue immediately occurs to you, try *brainstorming*—jotting down possible ideas in a list. Recall conversations, news broadcasts, class discussions that have made you feel interested, even argumentative. Prepare a list of possible topics over a few days, and keep reviewing the list, looking for one that satisfies the following criteria:

- *Your topic should allow you to be objective.* Your reader expects you to present a well-balanced account of both sides of the argument. Too much emotional involvement with a highly charged issue can be a handicap. If, for example, someone close to you was killed in an incident involving a handgun, you are likely to lose your objectivity in an essay on gun control.

- *Your topic should have appropriate depth.* Don't choose an issue that is too trivial: "Disney World is better than Disneyland." For a general audience, don't choose an issue that is too specialized: "The Rolling Stones were a more influential band than the Beatles," or "*2001: A Space Odyssey* is the most technically proficient science-fiction film ever made." And don't choose an issue that is too broad or too abstract: "Technology has been the bane of the modern world" or "A life without God is not worth living." Your topic should be definable in terms that your reader can understand and, perhaps, share. Finally, your topic should lend itself to a clear, manageable path of research. Using the keywords "god" and "life" in a database search will produce a seemingly unending list of books and articles. Where will you begin?

- *Your topic should have appropriate scope.* Consider the terms of your instructor's assignment. Some topics can be explored in ten pages; others require more lengthy development. Some require extensive research; others can be written using only a few selected sources. Stay within the assigned guidelines.

- *Your topic should have two sides.* Some topics are nonissues: it would be hard to get anyone to disagree about them. "Everyone should have the experience of work" or "Good health is important" are topics that aren't worth arguing. (Notice that they are also far too abstract.) Whatever the issue, the opposition must have a credible case.

- *Your topic can be historical.* There are many issues rooted in the past that are still arguable. Should President Truman have authorized dropping the atomic bomb on Japan? Were there better alternatives to ending slavery than the Civil War? Should Timothy McVeigh have been executed?

- *Your topic should be practical.* It may be tempting to argue that tuition should be free for all college students, but, in the process, you would have to recommend an alternative way to pay for the cost of education—something that state and federal governments have yet to figure out.

- *Your topic should have sufficient evidence available to support it.* You may not know for sure whether you can adequately defend your argument until you have done some research. A local issue—Should a new airport be built near our town?—might not have attracted a substantial enough body of evidence.

- *Your topic should be within your range of understanding.* Don't plan an essay on "the consequences of global warming" unless you are prepared to present scientific evidence, much of which is written in highly technical language. Evidence for topics in the social sciences can be equally difficult to comprehend, for many depend on surveys that are hard for a nonprofessional to evaluate. Research on literacy and teaching methods, for example, often includes data (such as reading scores on standardized tests) that require training in statistics.

Many of these criteria also apply to choosing a historical narrative or a contemporary subject. What's important in writing any essay—especially one involving a commitment to research—is that the topic interest you. If you are bored while writing your essay, your reader will probably be just as bored while reading it.

EXERCISE 22: NARROWING A TOPIC

A. Here are ten different ways of approaching the broad topic of *poverty in America*. Decide which questions would make good starting points for an eight- to ten-page research essay. Consider the practicality and the clarity of each question, the probable availability of research materials, and the likelihood of being able to answer the question in approximately nine pages. Try rewriting two of the questions that seem too broad, narrowing the focus.

1. How should the nation deal with poverty in its communities?

2. What problems does your city or town encounter in its efforts to make sure that its citizens live above the poverty level?

3. What are the primary causes of poverty today?

4. Whose responsibility is it to help the poor?

5. What effects does a life of poverty have on a family?

6. What can be done to protect children and the aged, groups that make up the largest proportion of the poor?

7. Does everyone have the right to freedom from fear of poverty?

8. Which programs for alleviating poverty have been particularly successful, and why?

9. Should all those receiving welfare funds be required to work?

10. What nations have effectively solved the problem of poverty, and how?

B. Make up several questions that would help you to develop the broad topic of *restricting immigration to America* for an eight- to ten-page research essay.

EXERCISE 23: PROPOSING A TOPIC

The following topic proposals were submitted by students who had been given a week to choose and narrow their topics for an eight- to ten-page research essay. Consider the scope and focus of each proposal, and decide which ones suggest *practical* topics for an essay of this length. If the proposal is too broad, be prepared to offer suggestions for narrowing the focus.

Student A

Much of the interest in World War II has been focused on the battlefield, but the war years were also a trying period for the public at home. I intend to write about civilian morale during the war, emphasizing press campaigns to increase the war effort. I will also include a description of the way people coped with brown-outs, shortages, and rationing, with a section on the victory garden.

Student B

I intend to deal with the role of women in feudal life, especially the legal rights of medieval women. I would also like to discuss the theory of chivalry and its effects on women, as well as the influence of medieval literature on society. My specific focus will be the ideal image of the medieval lady.

Student C

I have chosen the Lindbergh kidnapping case as the subject of my essay. I intend to concentrate on the kidnapping itself, rather than going into details about the lives of the Lindberghs. What interests me is the planning of the crime, including the way in which the house was designed and how the kidnapping was carried out. I also hope to include an account of the investigation and courtroom scenes. Depending on what I find, I may argue that Hauptmann was wrongly convicted.

Student D

I would like to explore methods of travel one hundred and fifty years ago, and compare the difficulties of traveling then with the conveniences of traveling now. I intend to stress the economic and social background of the average traveler. My focus will be the Grand Tour that young men used to take.

Student E

I'd like to explore quality in television programs. Specifically, I'd like to argue that popular and critically acclaimed TV shows of today are just as good as comparable programs ten and twenty years ago and that there really hasn't been a decline in popular taste. It may be necessary to restrict my topic to one kind of television show—situation comedies, for example, or coverage of sports events.

Student F

I would like to do research on several aspects of adolescent peer groups, trying to determine whether the overall effects of peer groups on adolescents are beneficial or destructive. I intend to include the following topics: the need for peer acceptance; conformity; personal and social adjustment; and peer competition. I'm not sure that I can form a conclusive argument, since most of the information available on this subject is purely descriptive; but I'll try to present an informed opinion.

LOCATING SOURCES

Preliminary research takes place in three overlapping stages:

- Identifying and locating possible sources.
- Recording or saving basic facts about each source.
- Noting each source's potential usefulness—or lack of usefulness—to your topic (and, when possible, downloading or copying extracts from the useful ones).

It's rare that you'll be able to locate all your sources first, and then record all your basic information, and after that choose those that are worth including in your essay. Research isn't that tidy. At a later stage of your work, you may come across a useful database and find new materials that must be reviewed, recorded, and included in your essay even after you've written a draft.

The three most common kinds of sources are *books*, *periodicals* (including magazines, newspapers, and scholarly journals), and *Web sites*. Most books and periodicals are published in print form; you can hold them in your hands (or read articles by inserting microfilm or microfiche into reading machines). Web sites and some periodicals are located in cyberspace on the Internet and appear only on your computer screen. And, increasingly, some periodical articles can be found both in print and on the Web (although sometimes the print and Web versions are not exactly the same).

Databases

Searching for sources is best done through *electronic databases* that enable you to sit at a computer terminal at home or in the library and, using a menu that appears on the screen, retrieve information about your topic. Increasingly, databases for books and periodical articles are *online*, accessible through the Internet; sometimes the information is stored on *CD-ROMs* (compact disk, read-only memory), which you obtain in the library and insert in a computer. Since databases generally list books or periodical articles, but not both, you'll have to engage in at least two separate searches to find a full range of materials. And searching for information on the Web requires using yet another kind of database, known as a *search engine*. All databases are periodically updated to include the most current listings.

Are Libraries Obsolete?

If you have a personal computer connected to the Internet (and, preferably, to your college's information system), you can do a good deal of research without ever entering the library. Certainly, you can obtain information about potential sources for your topic; you can download Web material for later use; you can find the complete texts of many periodical articles and even some books—all on your computer screen. But you'll still need to use the library:

- To obtain most books
- To read periodical articles that aren't available on the Internet
- To look for older articles in print indexes
- To use microfilm and microfiche machines
- To obtain and use CD-ROMs
- To get assistance from reference librarians

The last reason is probably the most important one. Librarians can provide you with all the information you need to carry out your research successfully. They'll show you how the library is organized, how to navigate the stacks of books, how the online catalogs and databases work, and how to do a computerized search. Much of this information will be available on the home page of your library's Web site; but it's hard to improve on having your questions answered by a real person in real time.

Computer Searches

Databases and search engines have to manage huge amounts of information. If they added a new subject to their indexes every time a book, article, or Web site appeared, they would soon have overflowing lists and unmanageable systems. Instead, each new work is scanned and then listed only under those *subject headings* (often called *descriptors*) that are relevant to its content. This key organizing principle is called *cross-referencing*: a method of obtaining a standardized, comprehensive list of subject headings that can be used to index information. One example of such a list, used by many libraries as an index for books, is the *Library of Congress Subject Headings,* or LCSH.

One way to start a computer search is to check the database's or search engine's own list of descriptors for one or more that correspond to your topic. Google, for example, provides a subject directory, organized into categories, which you can search. Or you can begin to narrow down your topic by considering just what it is that you want to find and then expressing it briefly, in a

---

What Is Boolean Searching?

Boolean searching, named after George Boole, a nineteenth-century mathematician, is a method of focusing your topic to get the best possible results from your computer search. If you are too broad in your wording, you'll get an exceedingly long list of sources, which will be unmanageable; if you're too specific in your wording, you'll get a very short list, which can bring your research to a dead halt.

To carry out a Boolean (or advanced) search, you refine your topic by *combining words*, using *phrases* to express complex subjects, and inserting "operators"—AND, OR, NOT—between keywords. (Sometimes, the operators are symbols, such as +, rather than words.) In effect, you must ask yourself what you do and what you don't want to know about your topic. Let's apply these guidelines to a database search for information about Lawrence of Arabia.

"Lawrence of Arabia" is your subject expressed as a phrase: the search will include only those sources in which the entire phrase is found and omit all those in which both "Lawrence" and "Arabia" appear only separately.

"Lawrence of Arabia" AND "guerrilla warfare" limits the search to those sources that contain *both* phrases. A book that mentions Lawrence but not guerrilla warfare won't appear in the results list, and vice versa.

"Lawrence of Arabia" OR "T. E. Lawrence" expands the search by expressing the topic two ways and potentially multiplying the number of sources found.

"Lawrence of Arabia" NOT "motion picture" limits the search by excluding sources that focus on the film rather than the man.

word or phrase. Following a series of commands from a menu on the screen, you type the words—known as *keywords*—in the designated slot. In an "advanced" or "guided" search, using two or more keywords, sometimes along with words like "and" and "not," will further break down and limit your topic. (Every database and search engine has its own techniques for formulating keywords; for an efficient search, it's worth taking the time to check the "Help" page or the "About . . ." page attached to the database that you're using.) This do-it-yourself process, usually called *Boolean searching*, will be explained and illustrated in the remainder of this chapter.

Searching for Lawrence of Arabia

Let's assume that you've decided to write about *Lawrence of Arabia*. T. E. Lawrence was a key figure in the Middle East campaigns of World War I, a British scholar fascinated by the desert, whose guerrilla tactics against the Turks succeeded partly because he chose to live like and with the Bedouin tribes that fought with him. You've enjoyed the 1962 award-winning movie about Lawrence, but you'd like to find out whether it accurately represents his experience. Here are some issues and questions about Lawrence's life that might intrigue you:

- Acclaimed as a hero after the war, Lawrence chose to enlist in the Royal Air Force at its lowest rank, under an assumed name. Why?
- He died at the age of forty-six in a mysterious motorcycle crash. Was this an accident?
- He contributed to the development of a new kind of military tactics. Why was his kind of guerrilla warfare so effective?
- He hoped to gain political independence for the Bedouin tribes. What prevented him?

Starting with an Encyclopedia: One place to begin your search about Lawrence of Arabia is an *encyclopedia*, which will provide you with a brief overview of his life and so help you to narrow down your topic. There are twenty general encyclopedias listed in the Google directory (under "reference"), some of which are free to use. (Exercise caution if you use *Wikipedia*, the free online encyclopedia "that anyone can edit," since the articles are written and edited by readers and the information may not be authoritative.) The best choices—*Encyclopedia Britannica Online* or *Encarta*—are pay-to-view only. Access the one that is available through your library's online link.

If you consult *Encarta*, you'll be prompted to type in a question or keyword. So, you type "Lawrence of Arabia." Why use quotation marks? They identify your keyword as a single *phrase*, so your results will be restricted to information about the Lawrence you're looking for. Without quotation marks, Lawrence of Arabia will be interpreted as a request for information about anyone or anything named Lawrence and any material about Arabia. Throughout your searching, you should submit the request as a phrase in quotation marks, unless the search procedure offers another mechanism specifically for phrase searching.

In its response, *Encarta* offers you a choice: an article about Lawrence of Arabia (adventurer) or an article about *Lawrence of Arabia* (motion picture). At this stage, you'll probably want to click on and read both; you're interested in comparing the movie version with Lawrence's actual experiences. In fact, clicking on the entry for Lawrence of Arabia (adventurer) gives you more choices. There are subheadings for references to Lawrence in other articles:

Assistance to Faisal I
Guerrilla tactics
Role in the Arab revolt against Turkey during World War I

Choosing and reading any of these articles can help you decide what aspect of Lawrence's life you want to write about.

Carrying out research is all about choices. You type in a request in a database, and you receive a list of topics or sources to choose from. You read an article about your subject, and at the end you find a list of additional articles headed "Bibliography" or "Further Reading." You look at a Web site, and throughout the text you see *hyperlinks*—underlined words, phrases, or Web addresses— that will lead you to related Web pages. Finding sources is not difficult; the real challenge is deciding which ones to read first.

Using Computer Searches to Locate Books

Databases that contain books are usually place-specific. In other words, each library produces a computerized database that lists all the books housed in its building or group of buildings. The library in the next town will have a different database for its holdings. *Your own college library almost certainly has such a database listing all the books on its shelves, organized and searchable by author, by title, and by subject.* You can also search comparable databases for other libraries in the area or major libraries across the globe. If you want to examine a full range of the books in existence on Lawrence of Arabia, you can look up that topic in the database of the Library of Congress or the New York Public Library, both of which are available online. If you locate a book that seems important for your research and your own library does not have it, your librarian can probably arrange for an *interlibrary loan* from a library that does.

Searching a Database: Let's search the Library of Congress Online Catalog (http://catalog.loc.gov/) for books about Lawrence of Arabia. On the catalog home page, click "Guided Search." Figure 7-1 shows you the interactive screen on which you begin your search.

- After you've clicked on "Guided Search," you type in *Lawrence of Arabia*. For this search, you don't have to use quotation marks to indicate that your keyword is a phrase; further along the line, there's a drop-down menu that lets you choose among "any of these," "all of these," or "as a phrase."

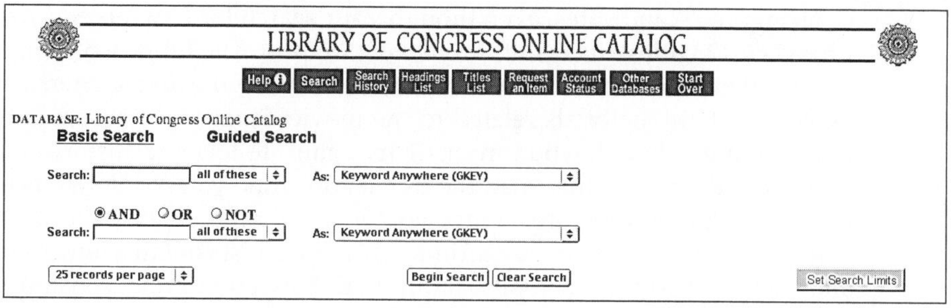

Figure 7-1. Library of Congress Online Catalog Search Form

(This means that you can choose to search for items categorized under either *Lawrence* or *Arabia*, those categorized under both *Lawrence* and *Arabia*, or those categorized under the specific phrase *Lawrence of Arabia*.)

- You highlight and click "as a phrase."
- In a second menu, you're given the option to do a Boolean search by choosing to pair *Lawrence of Arabia* with an operator (AND, OR, or NOT) and another word or phrase. You decide not to exercise this option yet, and just click "Begin Search."

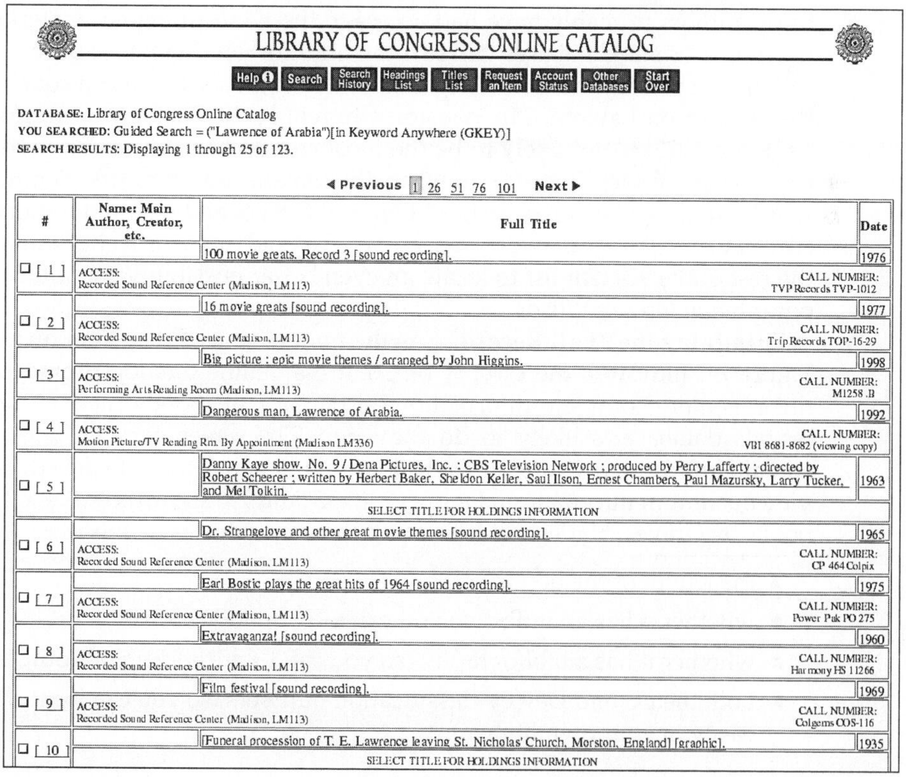

#	Name: Main Author, Creator, etc.	Full Title	Date
[1]		100 movie greats. Record 3 [sound recording].	1976
	ACCESS: Recorded Sound Reference Center (Madison, LM113)	CALL NUMBER: TVP Records TVP-1012	
[2]		16 movie greats [sound recording].	1977
	ACCESS: Recorded Sound Reference Center (Madison, LM113)	CALL NUMBER: Trip Records TOP-16-29	
[3]		Big picture : epic movie themes / arranged by John Higgins.	1998
	ACCESS: Performing Arts Reading Room (Madison, LM113)	CALL NUMBER: M1258 .B	
[4]		Dangerous man, Lawrence of Arabia.	1992
	ACCESS: Motion Picture/TV Reading Rm. By Appointment (Madison LM336)	CALL NUMBER: VBI 8681-8682 (viewing copy)	
[5]		Danny Kaye show. No. 9 / Dena Pictures, Inc. : CBS Television Network ; produced by Perry Lafferty ; directed by Robert Scheerer ; written by Herbert Baker, Sheldon Keller, Saul Ilson, Ernest Chambers, Paul Mazursky, Larry Tucker, and Mel Tolkin.	1963
	SELECT TITLE FOR HOLDINGS INFORMATION		
[6]		Dr. Strangelove and other great movie themes [sound recording].	1965
	ACCESS: Recorded Sound Reference Center (Madison, LM113)	CALL NUMBER: CP 464 Colpix	
[7]		Earl Bostic plays the great hits of 1964 [sound recording].	1975
	ACCESS: Recorded Sound Reference Center (Madison, LM113)	CALL NUMBER: Power Pak PO 275	
[8]		Extravaganza! [sound recording].	1960
	ACCESS: Recorded Sound Reference Center (Madison, LM113)	CALL NUMBER: Harmony HS 11266	
[9]		Film festival [sound recording].	1969
	ACCESS: Recorded Sound Reference Center (Madison, LM113)	CALL NUMBER: Colgems COS-116	
[10]		[Funeral procession of T. E. Lawrence leaving St. Nicholas' Church, Morston, England] [graphic].	1935
	SELECT TITLE FOR HOLDINGS INFORMATION		

Figure 7-2. Library of Congress Online Catalog: Search Results

As Figure 7-2 indicates, even though your search for Lawrence of Arabia has produced 123 titles, the results aren't very helpful. The Library of Congress has media other than print in its collections, and none of the first ten items listed are books; most are materials related to the movie. Since the first search took less than a minute, though, you can easily try again. To focus on historical information about the man rather than the movie, this time you try "Lawrence of Arabia" NOT "motion picture." Once you've been more explicit about what you want, the results are more rewarding. This Titles List contains fewer items (92), and most of them are actually about T. E. Lawrence. Now you must decide which are worth looking at.

Choosing Books to Review: Figure 7-3 shows a sequence of twenty-four books from the middle of the list. Looking carefully at the titles and dates of publication enables you to exclude quite a few. Some are fiction (Eden's *Murder of Lawrence of Arabia*); some deal with very narrow topics (Allen's *Medievalism of Lawrence of Arabia*); one is about "the female Lawrence of Arabia" (Gertrude Bell's *Desert and the Sown*); and some are duplicates. *Repetition* is a recurring problem in computerized searches. The same book can appear as a reprint (with the same contents, but a new cover, possibly paperback) or in a new edition (with revisions or with new material, such as a preface). As the entries for Winston Churchill indicate, each version receives a separate line in the catalog.

Another way to narrow down this list is to *choose the most recent books* since those authors probably have had access to the widest range of material about Lawrence. (Some databases will sort the titles for you in reverse order of publication, most recent first.) Looking at the titles on this list, you can conclude that the chapter on Lawrence in Winston Churchill's 1937 collection (reprinted in 1971 and 1973) is not likely to be the most comprehensive or objective among these titles. In fact, items 19 to 42 really contain only two titles immediately worth pursuing: books by Richard Perceval Graves and H. Montgomery Hyde. And since they're both over twenty-five years old, it's worth checking through the rest of the 92-item list to locate an even better possibility: an authorized biography by Jeremy Wilson.

Examining the "Full Record": As the underlining of each item on the list in Figure 7-3 indicates, the Library of Congress Online Catalog provides hyperlinks to more complete information about each of its holdings, and your library's database is likely to do the same. The screen for any book should contain an icon labeled "Full Record" or "Full View" that, if clicked, will provide maximum information. Figures 7-4, 7-5, and 7-6 show the *full records* of the books by Graves, Hyde, and Wilson. Each computer screen specifies:

- the length of the book,
- whether it has an index (so you can look up topics easily),
- whether it has a bibliography (so you can locate additional sources), and
- both the LC and Dewey classification numbers (so you can locate the book easily in your own library).

☐ [19]	Allen, M. D. (Malcolm Dennis), 1951-	Medievalism of Lawrence of Arabia / M.D. Allen.	1991
	ACCESS: Jefferson or Adams Bldg General or Area Studies Reading Rms		CALL NUMBER: D568.4.L45 A64 1991
☐ [20]	Armitage, Flora.	Desert and the stars; a biography of Lawrence of Arabia. Illustrated with photos.	1955
	ACCESS: Jefferson or Adams Bldg General or Area Studies Reading Rms		CALL NUMBER: D568.4.L45 A68
☐ [21]	Arnold, Julian Biddulph, 1863-	Lawrence of Arabia [by] Julian Biddulph Arnold.	1935
	ACCESS: Rare Book/Special Collections Reading Room (Jefferson LJ239)		CALL NUMBER: D568.4.L45 A7
☐ [22]	Baxter, Frank C. (Frank Condie), 1896-1982.	Annotated check-list of a collection of writings by and about T. E. Lawrence, Lawrence of Arabia, with many other things collateral to the story of his military, literary, and personal life and to the history of the Arab revolt and the Palestine campaign	1968
	ACCESS: Jefferson or Adams Bldg General or Area Studies Reading Rms		CALL NUMBER: Z8491.5 .B3
☐ [23]	Bell, Elise. [from old catalog]	Fall of Constantinople. [Sound recording]	
	LIBRARY OF CONGRESS HOLDINGS INFORMATION NOT AVAILABLE		
☐ [24]	Bell, Elise. [from old catalog]	Lawrence of Arabia. [Phonodisc]	
	LIBRARY OF CONGRESS HOLDINGS INFORMATION NOT AVAILABLE		
☐ [25]	Bell, Gertrude Lowthian, 1868-1926.	Desert and the sown : the Syrian adventures of the female Lawrence of Arabia / by Gertrude Bell ; new introduction by Rosemary O'Brien ; with frontispiece by John Sargent.	2001
	SELECT TITLE FOR HOLDINGS INFORMATION		
☐ [26]	Blackmore, Charles.	In the footsteps of Lawrence of Arabia / Charles Blackmore.	1986
	ACCESS: Jefferson or Adams Bldg General or Area Studies Reading Rms		CALL NUMBER: D568.4.L45 B54 1986
☐ [27]	Broughton, Harry.	Lawrence of Arabia and Dorset; compiled by Harry Broughton.	1966
	ACCESS: Jefferson or Adams Bldg General or Area Studies Reading Rms		CALL NUMBER: DA670.D7 B75 1966
☐ [28]	Browne, Maurice, 1884-1961.	[Notebook on T.E. Lawrence].	1900
	ACCESS: Jefferson or Adams Bldg General or Area Studies Reading Rms		CALL NUMBER: D568.4.L45 B75 1900z Rosenwald Coll
☐ [29]	Burbidge, William Frank.	Mysterious A.C. 2, a biographical sketch of Lawrence of Arabia, by Wm. F. Burbidge ...	1943
	ACCESS: Jefferson or Adams Bldg General or Area Studies Reading Rms		CALL NUMBER: D568.4.L45 B8
☐ [30]	Carrington, Charles Edmund, 1897-	T. E. Lawrence (of Arabia) by Charles Edmonds [pseud.]	1936
	ACCESS: Jefferson or Adams Bldg General or Area Studies Reading Rms		CALL NUMBER: D568.4.L45 C3 1936
☐ [31]	Churchill, Winston, Sir, 1874-1965.	Great contemporaries.	1973
	ACCESS: Jefferson or Adams Bldg General or Area Studies Reading Rms		CALL NUMBER: D412.6 .C5 1973
☐ [32]	Churchill, Winston, Sir, 1874-1965.	Great contemporaries.	1971
	ACCESS: Jefferson or Adams Bldg General or Area Studies Reading Rms		CALL NUMBER: D412.6 .C5 1971
☐ [33]	Churchill, Winston, Sir, 1874-1965	Great contemporaries. by the Rt. Hon. Winston S. Churchill, C.H., M.P. With 21 portraits.	1937
	ACCESS: Jefferson or Adams Bldg General or Area Studies Reading Rms		CALL NUMBER: D412.6 .C5 1937a
☐ [34]	Crawford, Fred D.	Richard Aldington and Lawrence of Arabia : a cautionary tale / Fred D. Crawford.	1998
	ACCESS: Jefferson or Adams Bldg General or Area Studies Reading Rms		CALL NUMBER: D568.4.L45 A633 1998
☐ [35]	Disbury, David George William.	T. E. Lawrence (of Arabia) -- a collectors booklist; compiled by David G. Disbury.	1972
	ACCESS: Jefferson or Adams Bldg General or Area Studies Reading Rms		CALL NUMBER: Z8491.5 .D57
☐ [36]	Ebert, Richard.	Lawrence of Arabia / by Richard Ebert ; ill. by Roy Schofield.	1979
	LIBRARY OF CONGRESS HOLDINGS INFORMATION NOT AVAILABLE		
☐ [37]	Eden, Matthew.	Murder of Lawrence of Arabia : a novel / by Matthew Eden.	1979
	SELECT TITLE FOR HOLDINGS INFORMATION		
☐ [38]	Glen, Douglas.	In the steps of Lawrence of Arabia, by Douglas Glen.	1940
	ACCESS: Jefferson or Adams Bldg General or Area Studies Reading Rms		CALL NUMBER: DS207 .G6 1940
☐ [39]	Graves, Richard Perceval.	Lawrence of Arabia and his world / Richard Perceval Graves.	1976
	ACCESS: Jefferson or Adams Bldg General or Area Studies Reading Rms		CALL NUMBER: D568.4.L45 G68 1976b
☐ [40]	Graves, Richard Perceval.	Lawrence of Arabia and his world / Richard Perceval Graves.	1976
	ACCESS: Jefferson or Adams Bldg General or Area Studies Reading Rms		CALL NUMBER: D568.4.L45 G68 1976
☐ [41]	Hyde, H. Montgomery (Harford Montgomery), 1907-	Solitary in the ranks : Lawrence of Arabia as airman and private soldier / by H. Montgomery Hyde.	1978
	LIBRARY OF CONGRESS HOLDINGS INFORMATION NOT AVAILABLE		
☐ [42]	Hyde, H. Montgomery (Harford Montgomery), 1907-	Solitary in the ranks : Lawrence of Arabia as airman and private soldier / [by] H. Montgomery Hyde.	1977
	ACCESS: Jefferson or Adams Bldg General or Area Studies Reading Rms		CALL NUMBER: D568.4.L45 H92 1977

Figure 7-3. Library of Congress Online Catalog: Links to Additional Sources

Most important, the screen includes a list of "subjects" as a clue to the specific contents of each book. How would you decide which book to examine first?

Lawrence of Arabia and His World (Figure 7-4) is brief, with a brief bibliography. In addition to the basic subject that all the books have in common—T. E. Lawrence—Graves emphasizes World War I (and, specifically, the Middle East campaign) as well as Lawrence's experiences as an orientalist, archaeologist, and soldier. That's a lot of coverage for a hundred or so pages of text. If the book were more recent than 1976, you might want to read it as a supplementary overview to the *Encarta* article, but you have no special reason for making it a priority.

Solitary in the Ranks (Figure 7-5) is longer, with a longer bibliography, and has a more specific focus: Lawrence's career as a private soldier in the RAF after the war. If you want to explore the enigma of Lawrence's reenlistment, this would obviously be a crucial source. But if you want to make comparisons with the motion picture, Hyde would be of peripheral interest.

Lawrence of Arabia: The Authorised Biography of T. E. Lawrence (Figure 7-6) is "authorised," which usually means that the subject, or his heirs, or his estate, has had enough confidence in this biographer to provide access to material not otherwise available. Wilson's work will undoubtedly be an important resource.

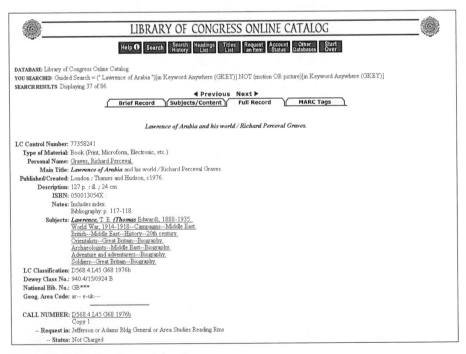

Figure 7-4. Catalog Record for Graves

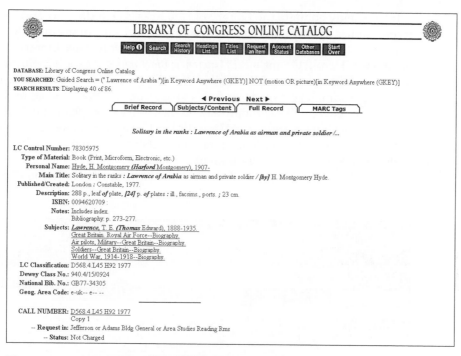

Figure 7-5. Catalog Record for Hyde

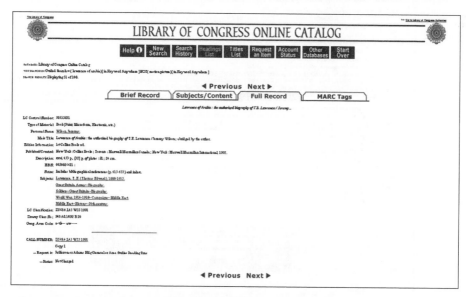

Figure 7-6. Catalog Record for Wilson

Interestingly enough, the Library of Congress search does not turn up some recent studies of Lawrence that may be very useful. One of the items found in a search for "Lawrence of Arabia" in the Columbia University Library database (CLIO) was Harold Orlans's *T. E. Lawrence: Biography of a Broken Hero*, published in 2002. Notice that the CLIO "Full View" (Figure 7-7) includes a table of contents and a summary (which, since it's taken from the book jacket, may not be considered reliable). It's certainly a good idea to try more than one database.

Following Cross-Referenced Hyperlinks: Cross-referencing in an electronic database provides you with one more set of choices. Each of the subjects listed in the "Full Record" of a work is an underlined hyperlink, which means an opportunity to click on any one of them for more information. If you choose the

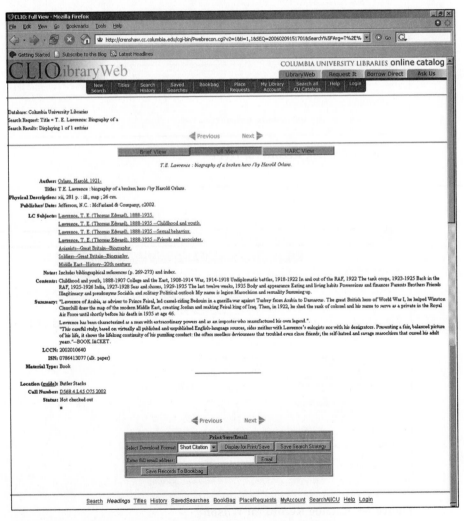

Figure 7-7. Columbia University Library Record for Orlans

first and most basic subject, "Lawrence, T. E. (Thomas Edward), 1888–1935," your screen will display numerous subtopics related to Lawrence, ranging from his death and burial to his psychology. If, for example, you click on "Military leadership," you're referred to Oliver Butler's *The Guerrilla Strategies of Lawrence and Mao*, which compares the military exploits of Lawrence—especially in guerrilla warfare—with those of Mao Zedong, the Chinese Communist leader. And the screen for the Butler book also contains another hyperlinked subject list, including guerrilla warfare, that would allow you to continue your search for this topic.

Searching Bibliographies: In carrying out your computerized search for books on Lawrence, don't neglect a more traditional way of identifying sources: looking in the *bibliographies* of standard works on the subject, like Wilson's. This allows you to add to your own bibliography some of the titles that the authors of these works used in their research. The books on Lawrence will probably be shelved together in your library stacks, and you'll want to examine the *table of contents*, *index*, and *bibliography* of several before deciding which ones merit your time.

Using Computer Searches to Locate Periodical Articles

Finding appropriate periodical articles is more complicated than looking for books. Each issue of a periodical contains a dozen or so articles; each year, thousands of periodicals appear in English alone; many of the best ones have been publishing for decades, a few for centuries. There are huge numbers of items to catalog, and, as a result, there is no single database that includes every possible newspaper, magazine, and journal article on a specific topic.

Moreover, most computerized databases limit their coverage to periodicals published within the last ten years. The online version of the *New York Times Index*, for example, goes back only to 1996. If you're working on a historical topic or you simply want to find a wide range of information, you may need to move among several databases, possibly including printed volumes listing the contents year by year. Academic databases are still in the process of transferring their print listings for earlier years to an electronic format.

The best approach is to search in more than one database. First, check the *periodical database in your campus library*, which should list all the articles in all the newspapers, magazines, and journals that the library owns. It will probably be cross-referenced so you can search using your keyword phrase, "Lawrence of Arabia." Your library will also have a listing of the *other periodical databases available to you online and on CD-ROM*. For example, under the heading "Humanities and History," Columbia University lists 94 online databases, ranging from the broadly useful (the *Oxford English Dictionary* or the *Dictionary of National Biography*) to the discipline-based (*Humanities Abstracts* or *Handbook of Latin American Studies*), to the highly specialized (*Koryosa*—which deals with the history of the Koryo dynasty in China). The *Social Sciences Index* and the *Humanities Index* are often good starting points for topics within those broad disciplinary areas. Be aware that most databases have restricted access and require a fee for use—which means you may have to do your searching at a computer in your college library's reference room.

Searching Databases: Databases don't all provide the same sort of information:

- Some databases provide only bibliographical listings of articles (sometimes called *citations*) and leave you to find the periodical in bound volumes on your library shelves, in another electronic database, or on microfilm.

- Other databases provide *abstracts* of the articles that they list. An abstract is a brief summary of an article—a sentence or two—that helps you to decide whether you want to locate and read the entire article.

- Some databases include *extracts*—samples from the article.

- A few databases will produce the *full text*, sometimes for a fee.

Like databases for books, electronic databases for periodicals often allow you to choose between a *basic search* and an *advanced search*. The advanced search allows you to limit the range of sources (only history? or the social sciences? or all available journals?); to refine your search with Boolean connectives; and to restrict your search to articles that have been *peer reviewed*. That means that a journal requires each of its articles to be read and approved by authorities in the field before it's accepted for publication. Peer review is, in effect, a guarantee of reasonable quality.

Many databases also provide you with a choice between *browse* and *search*. Browsing enables you to review what's available on your specific topic by clicking through the subject categories that exist within the database. It's useful to browse before searching since it may help you to define what you're looking for and devise more precise keywords.

Searching for Popular Periodicals: Some databases focus on popular periodicals rather than scholarly journals:

- The *Readers' Guide to Periodical Literature* or *Periodical Abstracts* can be useful for research on current issues, but should not be the *only* databases that you consult in preparing an academic essay.

- *Pro Quest* is a comprehensive database of more than 33,000 general interest periodicals and professional journals, unfortunately limited to the last few years. A search for "Lawrence of Arabia" in *Pro Quest*'s Periodical Abstracts Research database resulted in eighteen listings, mostly reviews of recently published books on Lawrence.

- *Factiva* provides business information based on several thousand sources.

- The *New York Times Index* is an excellent source of information on events and issues, both historical and contemporary, containing a century and a half's worth of listings from the *Times*. If you read a few articles in the *Times* starting with those from 1915, when Lawrence's exploits began to be widely known, you will be able to include in your essay a contemporary view of Lawrence's successes and failures. Archival articles from the *Times* can be found on the *Historical Newspapers Online* database.

- A wide range of newspapers across the country can be found at www.newspapers.com.

Searching for Scholarly Journals: Increasingly, online databases, established by universities or commercial companies, provide listings of scholarly articles across the disciplines, with abstracts of their contents or, in some cases, the full text of articles. Again, most allow access only through university-sponsored computer systems (which have paid for their use). The number of journals in these databases varies from a few hundred (*Project Muse* or *Jstor*) to well over a thousand (*Science Direct*) to thirty thousand (*Ingenta*). On the other hand, the size of the database won't necessarily make your search easier. Frequently, the list resulting from your search will contain numerous articles that are only tangentially related to your topic. Lawrence of Arabia may be mentioned once— as a comparison or a type of hero—or an article about British foreign policy or Arab democracy will include his name in a historical summary. That's why it's important to click on and read the abstract before you waste time finding the article.

An *Ingenta* search for "Lawrence of Arabia," limited to 1995–2004, resulted in twenty-four listings; an expanded search, back to 1989, increased the number to forty (largely because a new print of the movie was released in 1989, generating a new wave of film reviews). Figure 7-8 shows the beginning of the listings from the latter search. Notice that some of the articles are book reviews: the name of the book's author is contained on the title line. Others are far too specialized to be useful—focusing on Lawrence's Brough motorcycle in *Cycle World*, for example (8). But if you click on the summary of *First Person a Desert Engagement* (11), the abstract tells you that Michael Asher "retraces the steps of Lawrence of Arabia and discovers his greatness owes as much to his many weaknesses as his strengths," which makes this an article worth reviewing as background for any of the Lawrence essay topics under consideration. Similarly, Don Belt's article in *National Geographic* (12) discusses how and why Lawrence became involved in the Arab revolt against the Ottoman empire, useful material for essays with an emphasis on politics.

One rule of database searching is never to assume that the first few listings are the most important, even if they're the most recent, and so ignore the rest. A *Cineaste* article, listed as number 19, in which Michael Wilson describes how he wrote the screenplay for *Lawrence of Arabia*, is essential reading for an essay about the film's authenticity. In fact, although the *Ingenta* database doesn't include it, the very next article in that issue of *Cineaste* is an account by Robert Bolt, Wilson's coauthor, of *his* approach to the film. Another rule of database searching is that no single database contains all the material you'll need. It always pays to look a little further.

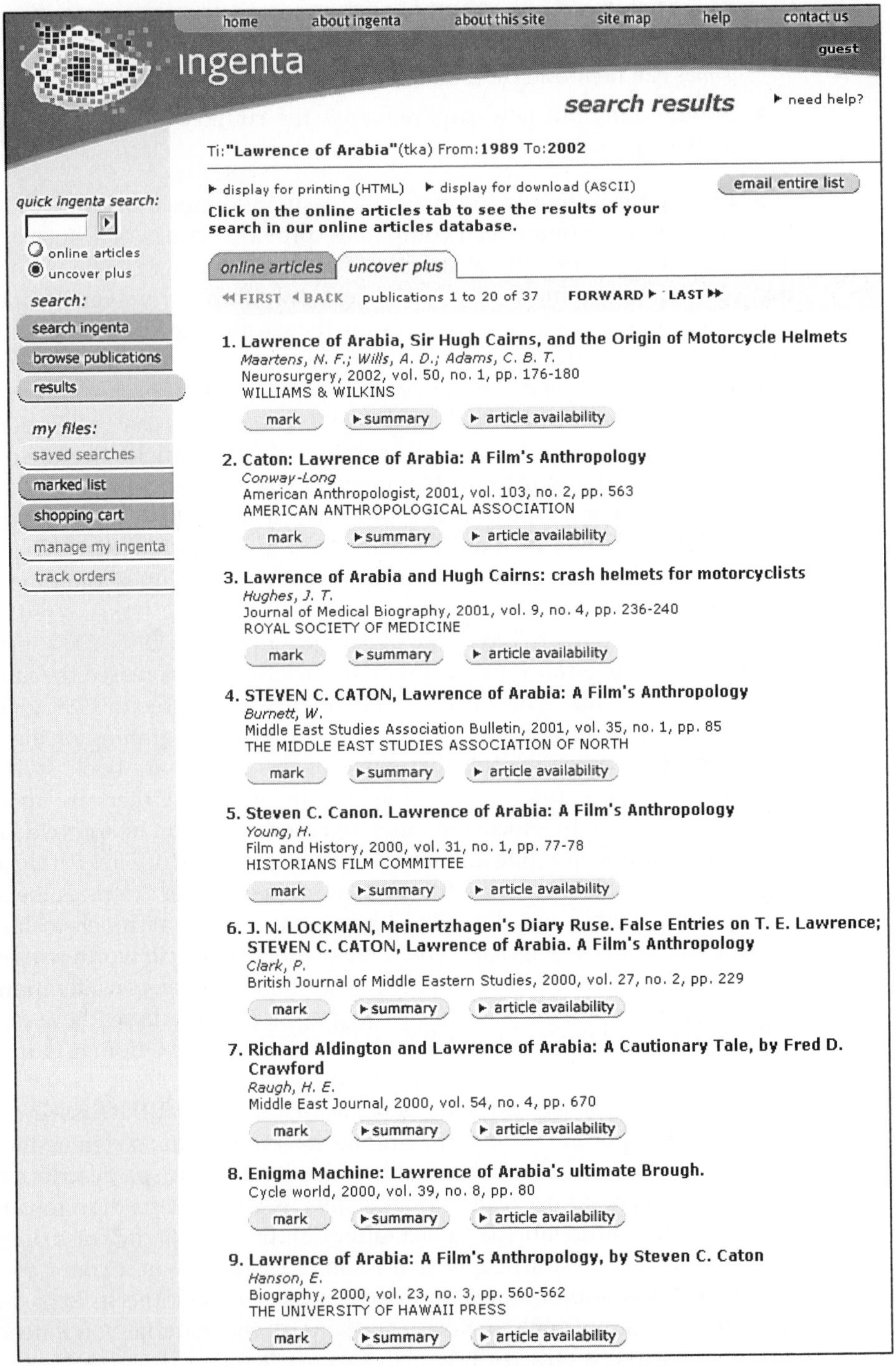

Figure 7-8. Ingenta Journal Search

10. **Standing in the light.**
Peachment, Chris
New statesman, 1999, vol. 12, no. 546, pp. 35

(mark) (▸ summary) (▸ article availability)

11. **First Person a Desert Engagement.**
Asher, Michael
Geographical, 1999, vol. 71, no. 2, pp. 20

(mark) (▸ summary) (▸ article availability)

12. **Lawrence of Arabia.**
Belt, Don
National geographic, 1999, vol. 195, no. 1, pp. 38

(mark) (▸ summary) (▸ article availability)

13. **Kit Carson, John C. Fremont, Manifest Destiny, and the Indians; Or, Oliver North Abets Lawrence of Arabia.**
Canfield, J. Douglas
American indian culture and research journal, 1998, vol. 22, no. 1, pp. 137

(mark) (▸ summary) (▸ article availability)

14. **On Films: Cinema Scope: A restored Lawrence of Arabia is fresher than two new films, The Myth of fingerprints and Going All The Way.**
Kauffmann, Stanley
The new republic, 1997, vol. 217, no. 14, pp. 28

(mark) (▸ summary) (▸ article availability)

15. **Lawrence of Arabia as Archaeologist.**
Tabachnick, Stephen E.
The Biblical archaeology review, 1997, vol. 23, no. 5, pp. 40

(mark) (▸ summary) (▸ article availability)

16. **Casualties of Amour.**
Glass, Charles
Premiere, 1996, vol. 10, no. 4, pp. 96

(mark) (▸ summary) (▸ article availability)

17. **Lawrence of Arabia, Designer and Printer.**
Graalfs, Gregory T.
Print, 1996, vol. 50, no. 6, pp. 56

(mark) (▸ summary) (▸ article availability)

Figure 7-8. *(continued)*

Using Computer Searches to Locate Web Sites

Once you have an Internet account through your college or with a local server, you will have access to the millions of sites available on the *World Wide Web*. Web sites can be created by anyone who wants to set one up: governmental agencies, schools, businesses, nonprofit organizations, and individuals. Because they are ideal for distributing up-to-date information to a worldwide audience, many Web sites are maintained by corporations for advertising purposes. That's one reason why you need to make doubly sure that information for research obtained through the Web is accurate and objective. As you'll learn in Chapter 8, not all Web sites are reliable or worth citing in your essay. Before you take notes or print out material, get some sense of the author's credentials and the material's validity.

The distinctive qualities of the Web—the speed with which it can be updated and searched, and the huge amount of information it contains—are both its strength and its weakness. Web sites change and disappear without any notice, and the information that you thought you had on Monday may be unavailable by Friday. The Web contains lots of material about today's issues, but rarely goes back more than a few years. It is huge, but indiscriminate. You can search for anything, but often find nothing useful for your purpose. Unless you're very focused in your search requirements, you're likely to receive a list of sites that seem randomly chosen and ranked. As Danny O'Brien wrote in "The Fine Art of Googling," search engines "may know the contents of all Web pages, but they know the meaning of none." Good research does not start and end with point and click.

Using Search Engines

To help you navigate the Internet and view Web sites, you must first access a *Web browser*, usually Netscape Navigator or Microsoft Internet Explorer. Then, to find the information that you want, you choose a *search engine*: a huge database containing indexes of keywords and phrases gathered from millions of Web sites. Search engines trawl the Web for new sites, organizing their contents into categories or cross-referenced indexes. You can tap into that information by visiting the engine's home page and starting a keyword search. Once you make your keyword request, the computer searches through its index, locates the addresses of Web sites that include those words, presents you with a list of results, and allows you to visit the sites by clicking on a link. Alternatively, if the search engine features a *directory of subject categories*, you can browse through the list of sites and click on those related to your topic.

Search engines are divided into two broad groups. *Web crawlers* use computers ("spiders") to compile, collate, and rank information mechanically, according to a formula or algorithm. *Hierarchical indexes* (also known as *Web directories*) employ staff to scan and categorize individual Web sites. In theory, human intelligence should do a better job of sorting, ranking, and avoiding duplication than a set formula does; but, in fact, practically all search engines—crawlers or indexes—can produce a hodgepodge of results, irrelevant to the topic you're searching for. One disadvantage of all search engines, whether humanly or mechanically generated, is that the descriptions come directly from the sites' owners and may or may not be accurate summaries of the contents.

Crawlers have very large databases and provide long lists of results, but do very little rational sorting. The sheer numbers of Web sites listed can be overwhelming if you search too broadly; but if you know precisely what you're looking for, you'll get a fast answer. One highly regarded crawler is *Google*, which does rank sites—according to their relative popularity—by calculating the number of hyperlinks that lead to them. Figure 7-9 shows Google's Advanced Search page set for a search for the phrase "Lawrence of Arabia." Notice that the operators (AND, OR, and NOT) are replaced by self-explanatory phrases ("with *all* of

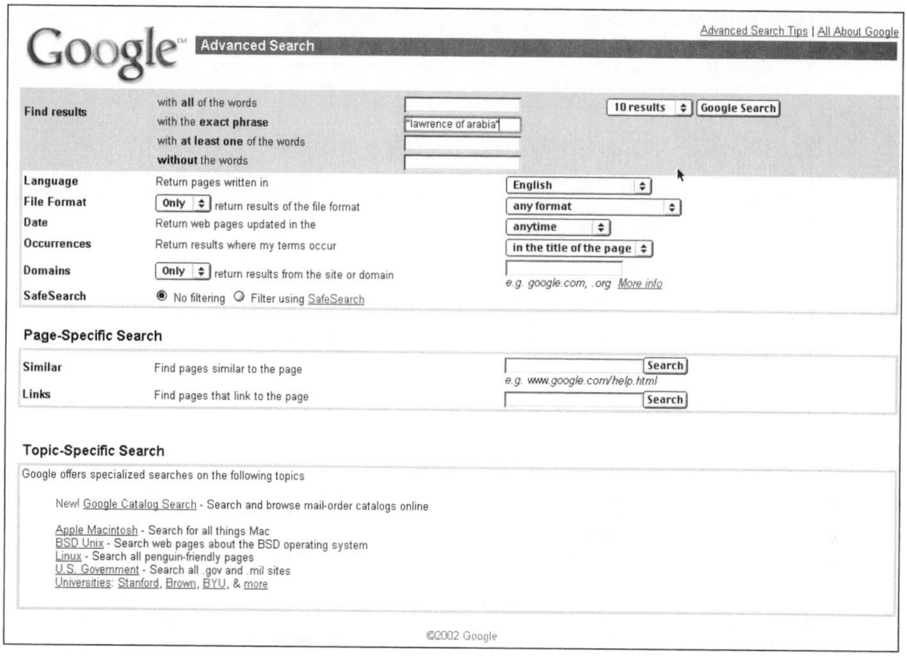

Figure 7-9. Google Advanced Search

the words," "with the *exact phrase*," "with *at least one* of the words," "*without* the words"). You can also use the "Occurrences" menu and either limit your search to sites that explicitly focus on Lawrence and therefore mention him in the title, or accept those that refer to him anywhere in the site. Even restricting the search to title references and excluding "movies," this search produced a list of 121,000 sites (known as "hits"). And, to illustrate the aberrations of Web searching, exactly the same Google search three weeks later increased the number of hits to over 126,000.

It's often said that search engines have cataloged less than 1 percent of what's really available on the Web. For this reason, no single search engine can achieve a truly exhaustive search. You usually have to carry out several searches before receiving a plausible results list. In fact, if your first few searches have been unsuccessful, you may want to cover as much ground as you can by using a *meta search engine*: a super-crawler that covers large tracts of Web material by scanning the contents of several other search engines. But to achieve such wide coverage, you have to provide a broad, unrefined topic, so meta engines don't always work well with complex searches.

One highly regarded meta search engine is Clusty (www.clusty.com), which relies on a relatively small number of search engines and which attempts to sort the results into useful categories. The same "advanced" search for Lawrence of Arabia—again excluding references to the movie—resulted in fewer hits than

Figure 7-10. Google Scholar Search for Lawrence of Arabia

did the Google search: the "top 182 results" were shown, out of some 88,000 retrieved by the search. Despite the exclusion, numerous sites related directly to the motion picture. However, once you eliminate the trivial, irrelevant, or duplicated sites, you do end up with about ten from the first three pages of the search that have a reasonable chance of advancing your research. There is no point in proceeding past those first three pages, as the quality of the sites listed deteriorates dramatically after that.

Finally, there is also a growing number of "academic" search engines, many sited at a university, that serve the same function for Web sites as databases do for periodicals and books. Database/search engines like the *Librarians' Index to the Internet* and the *Internet Public Library* have only a modest number of sites in their indexes, numbering in the thousands, not the millions. But the sites are read and selected by librarians or faculty (a form of peer review); they are objectively described and rationally ranked; and they are often accompanied by helpful hyperlinks or even bibliographies. *Google Scholar* also presents itself as an academic search engine with the results drawn from articles in scholarly journals. As you can see from the first ten hits of a "Lawrence of Arabia" search (Figure 7-10), Google Scholar does use scholarly journals, but the references to Lawrence are often peripheral and there are few sites that you would be likely to cite in a mainstream essay.

[BOOK] **Lawrence of Arabia**: An Encyclopedia
SE Tabachnick - 2004 - dx.doi.org
Greenwood Publishing Group. **Lawrence of Arabia**: An Encyclopedia Tabachnick, Stephen E. This encyclopedia,
the first work of its kind ...
Web Search - Library Search

Lawrence of Arabia, Sir Hugh Cairns, and the Origin of Motorcycle Helmets.
NFSN Maartens, AD Wills, CB Adams, M Ch - Neurosurgery, 2002 - neurosurgery-online.com
January 2002, 50:1 > Lawrence of Arabia, Sir Hugh Cairns,... ... **Lawrence of Arabia**, Sir Hugh Cairns, and the Origin
of Motorcycle Helmets. ...
Web Search - neurosurgery-online.com - ncbi.nlm.nih.gov

[BOOK] Megiddo 1918: Lawrence, Allenby, and the March on Damascus
B Perrett - 2004 - dx.doi.org
... As depicted in the great film **Lawrence of Arabia**, General Allenby planned a swift campaign that would knock
Turkey out of World War I. His Desert Mounted Corps ...
Web Search - Library Search

The role of suggestions and personality characteristics in producing illness reports and desires for ...
MA Lindberg - J Psychol, 2002 - ncbi.nlm.nih.gov
... Half the participants were met by a confederate student who claimed to be cleaning up the remains of a production of
"**Lawrence of Arabia**," and the other half ...
Web Search

On Being a Patient
BS Goldman, BS Goldman, BS Goldman - Pacing and Clinical Electrophysiology, 2004 - blackwell-synergy.com
... down; however, after getting through the maze of hospital corridors and elevators, into the car and home, I easily identified
with **Lawrence of Arabia** on that ...
Web Search - ncbi.nlm.nih.gov

John Adams
NC Durham - Am J Psychiatry, 2002 - dx.doi.org
... and fervor of Martin Luther (4) as well as the militant nonviolence of Gandhi (5). John Mack delved into the complex psyche
of **Lawrence of Arabia** (6). More ...
Web Search - ajp.psychiatryonline.org - ajp.psychiatryonline.org

Figure 7-10. *(continued)*

Managing Computer Searches

- Choose a *search engine* that's appropriate for your topic: a *Web directory* when you want a few well-focused sites for a broad topic; a *Web crawler* when you want the maximum number of links for a concrete topic; a *meta search engine* when you want the widest possible range of information.

- Take time to read the search engine's "Help" section. The more precise your search instructions, the greater the number of meaningful responses.

- Refine your search by choosing an "advanced" or "guided" search page and using exact phrases and other "operators" to limit the results. You can specify a range of dates by using two dots: "Lawrence of Arabia" 1915..1918 will restrict the results to Lawrence's wartime activities. Or you can limit the search to sites sponsored by academic institutions by attaching site:edu to the keyword.

- Use more than one search engine, as necessary. If one turns up little of interest, try another.

- Don't waste more than ten minutes on any search engine if the results seem unpromising. Try other engines, or use a database, or go to the library.

- If your search yields a list of a thousand sites, look at the first twenty. If there's nothing at all worthwhile, refine your search with more operators, or try another search engine.

- Avoid commercial sites selling products. They rarely contain material appropriate for academic research.

- Don't settle for the first sites you find that seem remotely connected to your topic. Keep on searching until the information is solid.

- Watch out for dead links: Web sites that were indexed months or even years ago and are no longer being maintained by their owners.

- Don't just add interesting possibilities to your "Favorites" or "Bookmarks" for later reading. The material will pile up. If you read (or, at least, skim) as you go along, you'll learn enough about your topic to give some direction to your search.

- Don't be tempted to open every link you come to and pursue stray pieces of information just because they're there. Before you click on a link, consider whether this information is likely to be useful to your present project. Surfing isn't research.

- Maintain concrete and reasonable expectations for your search. Decide what you want to get out of each session on the Internet, and concentrate on that goal. Search with a purpose.

Using Computer Searches to Locate Images

You can sometimes complement the effectiveness of your research essay by including pictures. A historical topic—biography or event—often benefits from a presentation that includes images of people or places. But you can also use images to support the analysis of a contemporary issue.

How to choose and document appropriate images is discussed in Chapter 9 (page 451). At a point in your research when your thesis has already begun to take shape, you may want to look at a few image databases (or "galleries") to see what kinds of pictures are available and whether they will suit your purpose.

Google's basic search page includes an icon labeled "Images" that will transfer you to a search page exclusively for images. A search for "Lawrence of Arabia" yields a large number of photographs, most of which are stills or posters from the motion picture. But there are also several images of T. E. Lawrence on each screen of photos, including the last photograph of him taken before his death, showing Lawrence astride his Brough motorcycle (Figure 7-11). In fact, the picture comes from the Web site for Brough Superior Motorcycles, which contains some useful material about Lawrence as both hero and motorcyclist.

The last known photograph of Lawrence.
Clouds Hill 1935

[Home] [More]

Brough Superior Motorcycles

Figure 7-11. Lawrence of Arabia

A number of Web sites feature databases of photos appropriate for academic work. Although many allow you to download pictures for free, most require some sort of registration. Here are a few useful sites to try:

- http://thefreesite.com/Free_Graphics/Free_photos/
  A clearinghouse with links to free image galleries.
- www.artstor.com
  A collection focusing on art history, containing a large selection of prints and posters.
- http://ap.accuweather.com/apphoto/
  A searchable multimedia archive with 500,000 images covering 160 years, including photos, text, audio, and graphics. A search for VJ Day 1945 produced three very different photographs of Times Square on the day World War II ended. Downloading an image from this site would require a fee, so you should connect through your library's link.
- www.memory.loc.gov
  The Web site of American Memory: Historical Collections for National Digital Library, sponsored by the Library of Congress. This collection, presented

by theme—cities, culture, environment, sports, and so on—includes images. For an essay on early aviation, for example, you can find photos of airplanes used by the Wright brothers.

- www.bbcmotiongallery.com
  Cosponsored by CBS. This site contains seventy years of motion imagery, including clips of news events, natural history, and culture. Of course, you would need access to appropriate media to make the clips available to your instructor and classmates.

Finding Other Sources on the Internet

E-mail enables people to communicate with each other, develop their own computer networks, and exchange information electronically, all over the world, in minutes. E-mail can also be used to get assistance in exploring a research topic. If you know the e-mail address of an expert in that field, you can send a message, asking questions or requesting specific information. Keep in mind, though, that academic and professional authorities have little time to answer unsolicited e-mail and, as the number of e-mail inquiries has increased, many are less willing to participate in students' research. If the person you plan to e-mail has already written a book or article on the subject, try consulting that instead. If you do send an e-mail, make sure that you are courteous in making your request. At the very least, you should be sufficiently familiar with the expert's work so that your inquiry will seem serious and warrant a response. Remember that any information obtained through e-mail that is subsequently used in an essay must have its source cited.

Listserv® subscriptions are another way to gain information through e-mail. These are, basically, e-mail exchanges between people interested in a particular subject. When your address is added to the mailing list, you receive e-mail from members of the group and can send e-mail in return. Large mailing lists are usually automated, with a computer (called a listserv) receiving and distributing e-mail to and from you and the other group members. You may also have access to previous "discussions" and messages through the archives. Not all listservs are open to the public, and some are moderated: volunteers screen all messages to ensure that they are appropriate for distribution. Remember, too, that material obtained through e-mail or, indeed, from the Internet in general, has not been validated for accuracy to the same extent as works that have gone through the selection processes used by publishers of books and periodicals. You can search for listservs at www.liszt.com or www.lsoft.com/catalist.html.

Usenet newsgroups provide a similar means of access to information, through a worldwide network of electronic bulletin boards, each devoted to a particular subject. Using your Web browser, you can post messages to one or more newsgroups, read messages other people have posted, and reply to those messages. Unlike postings to listservs, those to newsgroups do not come to your own e-mail; you need to go to the bulletin board to see them and to respond or to post messages of your own. Older postings are removed from the bulletin board periodically, although many newsgroups now archive their old messages for a certain time. You can find archived Usenet messages in searchable engines such as Google or Yahoo, or try www.tile.net. Be aware that the same concerns about reliability and accuracy of Internet information apply to Usenet groups.

INTERVIEWING AND FIELD RESEARCH

As well as books, articles, films, videos, Web sites, and other research materials, personal interviews and field research can provide worthwhile information for your research essay. A well-conducted interview with an expert in the field, if it is carefully focused on your topic, can give you information unavailable from any other source. A personal interview can also enrich your essay with details, based on actual experience, that will capture and hold your audience's interest. Similarly, your own observation of an event or environment can be a source of valuable information. Through close observation of the river flowing past a sewage treatment plant or of the behavior of people during a political demonstration, you can collect data to support your thesis, to supplement the texts you have read, and to suggest alternative interpretations of the issues and ideas developed in your essay.

Interviewing

You will want to interview experts or authorities who are both knowledgeable and appropriate sources of information about your specific topic. First, consider the faculty on your campus, not only as direct sources of information but as sources of referrals to other experts in the field at nearby colleges and universities. If your general topic is the Holocaust, for example, you may want to interview a faculty member with that specialization in your college's history, sociology, or Judaic studies department. You may, in fact, come across the names of appropriate faculty at your college in the course of your library research.

An entirely different source of direct information is a person who has had personal experience with some aspect of your essay topic. As you talk about your research on the Holocaust, one of your friends might tell you about an aunt living nearby, someone who, for example, survived the concentration camps at Auschwitz. That woman's recollections can be just as appropriate and important an addition to your essay as a professor's more theoretical comments, lending it human drama or highlighting a particular issue that interests you.

Some essays can be enhanced by interviewing several sources. For example, if you were preparing a report on an environmental issue in your town—let's say, the purity of its water supply—you would want to learn about the impact of the new sewage treatment plant on the local environment. Of course, you would want to talk to the plant's manager; but you might also consult the managers of local businesses to determine some of the economic implications, and to some public health officials to learn about the kinds of health hazards the plant is intended to avoid. In this case, a single source would not cover the possible spectrum of responses.

Planning an Interview

You are more likely to get someone to consent to an interview if you write or phone first to make an appointment. Arrange your appointments as soon as possible once you have focused your topic and identified candidates for interviews. Since your potential subjects are likely to have busy schedules, allow enough time to make initial contact and then to wait a week or two, if necessary, until the person has enough time to speak with you at length. This way you can avoid having your initial conversation turn into an interview before you are quite prepared for it—which can be awkward if you don't have your questions ready.

When you call or write to those whom you hope to interview, politely identify yourself; then briefly describe your topic and the special focus of your essay. Ask for an interview of 20 to 30 minutes at a later time convenient for the subject. If appropriate, mention the name of the person who suggested this source, or refer to the publication in which you saw the subject's name. Your objective is to convey your own serious interest in the topic and in your subject's knowledge of the topic. Be friendly, but professional. If someone is reluctant to be interviewed, you should retreat gracefully. At the same time, don't hesitate to ask for a referral to someone else who might be in a better position to provide helpful information.

Preparing for an Interview

Because your interview, whether in person or on the phone, will probably be brief, you need to plan in advance what you intend to say and ask so that you can use the time effectively. Careful preparation is also a compliment to your interview subjects and shows respect for their expertise.

Reviewing your research notes, make a focused list of questions in writing beforehand, tailoring them to your specific paper topic and to your source's area of knowledge. If, for example, you are going to interview the manager of a sewage treatment plant on the Hudson River about the effective removal of PCBs from the water, you don't want to use up ten minutes asking about plant management. It can be helpful to prepare a questionnaire, leaving space between the questions for you to take notes. You can use the same questionnaire, with variations, for a whole series of personal interviews.

Recording Information during an Interview

If you plan to use a tape recorder, make sure you ask your subject's permission in advance; test the equipment beforehand (especially if it's borrowed for the occasion); and know how to operate it smoothly. Bring it to the interview with the tape already loaded in the machine, and be sure the batteries are fresh. (Bring along a second tape in case the first one jams or breaks, and carry extra batteries.) When the interview is about to begin, check again to see if your subject has any objection to your recording the conversation. Then, to avoid making your subject self-conscious, put the tape recorder in an unobtrusive place. After that, don't create a distraction by fiddling with the machine.

Even if you plan to tape-record the interview, come prepared to take careful notes; bring notebook and pens, as well as your list of questions or questionnaire. One way of preparing for detailed note taking—the kind that will provide you with accurate direct quotations to use in your essay—is to rehearse. Pair off with a classmate who is also preparing for an interview, and practice interviewing and note taking (including handling the tape recorder). If your subject presents a point so well that you know you'll want to quote it, write it down rapidly but carefully, and—then and there—read it back to make sure that you have transcribed the statement correctly.

Conducting the Interview

Briefly remind your subject of the essay topic and your reason for requesting the interview. Then get right down to your "script": ask each question clearly, without hurrying; be alert to recognize when the question has been fully answered (there is usually a pause); and move briskly on to the next question. Otherwise, let your subject talk freely, with minimum interruption. Remember that you are the receiver, not the provider, of information, and let your subject do almost all the talking.

Sometimes, a particular question will capture your subject's interest, and you will get a more detailed answer than you expected. Be aware of the time limit for the interview; but if you see a promising line of questioning that you didn't anticipate, and your subject seems relaxed and willing to prolong the conversation, take advantage of the opportunity and ask follow-up questions. What if your subject digresses far away from the topic of your essay? At the first opportunity, ask whether there is a time constraint. If there is, politely indicate that you have three or four more questions to ask and you hope that there will be enough time to include them.

No matter how careful your preparations, a good interview won't go exactly as you planned. You should aim to participate in a conversation, not direct an interrogation. At the end, your subject should, ideally, offer to speak with you again, if necessary, to fill any gaps. To maintain that good impression, be sure to send a brief note of thanks to your subject no longer than a day or two after the interview. Later on, you may want to send a copy of the completed essay.

Using Interview Sources in Your Essay

Since the purpose of the interview is to gather information (and to provide yourself with a few apt quotations), you need to have clear notes to work from as you organize your essay. If you used a tape recorder, you should transcribe the interview as soon as you can; if you took notes, you should go over them carefully, clarify confusing words, and then type a definitive version. Otherwise, you may find yourself deciphering your almost-illegible notes at a later time or searching through the entire tape to find a specific sentence that you want to quote. Transcribe the interview accurately, without embroidering or revising what your subject actually said. Keep the original notes and tapes; your instructor may want to review them along with your essay.

Working with notes from an interview is almost exactly the same as working with notes from library research. As you organize your essay (following the process described in Chapter 9), you cross-reference your notes with a list of the topics for your essay, choosing information from the interview that might be cited to support the major points in your outline. Remember that it is the well-chosen and carefully placed source that carries authority, not the number of words quoted. Finally, document each use of material taken from your interview, whether it is ideas or words, with a parenthetical reference. (See Chapter 12 for the appropriate bibliographical entry.)

Field Research

Like interviewing, field research is a way of supplementing the material you take from texts and triggering new ideas about your topic. When you engage in field research, you are gathering information directly, acting as an observer, investigator, and evaluator within the context of an academic or professional discipline. If you are asked by your anthropology instructor to describe and analyze a family celebration as an ethnographer would, your observations of Thanksgiving dinner at home would be regarded as field research.

In many of your college courses, you will be expected to engage in field research. When, for example, the nursing program sends students to a nearby hospital for their clinical practice and asks for a weekly report on their work with patients, these students are doing field research. Other students may participate in a cooperative education program involving professional internships in preparation for potential careers; the reports these interns prepare on their work experiences are based on field research. Whatever the course, your instructor will show you how to connect your field research activities to the theories, procedures, and format characteristic of that discipline. Still, there are certain practices common to most kinds of field research that you need to know from the beginning. Let's follow that process from assignment to essay as you develop a simple topic based on field research.

Your sociology professor has suggested that, although college students like to think of themselves as unique individuals, certain patterns clearly underlie their characteristic behavior. As an example, he asserts that both male and female students prefer to work and relax with members of the opposite sex. He is asking each of you to test this hypothesis by choosing a place on campus to observe students as they go about their daily routine, keeping in mind two questions: Are there patterns one can observe in these students' behavior? What might be the significance of these patterns? If you were assigned this project, your work would fall into three stages: gathering the information, analyzing that information, and writing the essay.

Gathering Information

According to your instructor's guidelines for this essay based on field research, you will need to perform at least six separate observations for 20 to

30 minutes each at a site of your choice and, later, be prepared to hand in copies of your accumulated observation notes along with your essay. So your first important decision concerns the location for gathering information about students' behavior: the cafeteria? the library? a particular class? the student union? the college bookstore? a classroom or another place on campus where students congregate? You decide to observe students gathered at the row of benches outside Johnson Hall, the busiest classroom building, extending from the bookstore on the right to the student union building on the left; these benches also face a field where gym classes meet and the baseball team practices. Since this area is an important junction on the campus, you can assume that enough students will appear to provide basic information for your field research.

Planning the Observations: To conform to your instructor's requirements and obtain all the information you need for your essay, you should prepare for your observation sessions quickly and carefully. First, establish a schedule that will fulfill the guidelines for the assignment. Since your first class in Johnson Hall is at 11 a.m., and you are free before that, you decide to schedule your observations for the half hour before class, that is, from 10:30 to 11:00 a.m. on Monday, Wednesday, and Friday, for the next two weeks.

You will need to set aside a separate notebook for recording your observations. For each session, start a fresh page, and indicate the date and the times when you begin and end your sessions. Such specific information is what establishes your authority as a field researcher. Before your first session, consider making a diagram of the site, roughly sketching in the location of the buildings, placing the seven benches correctly, and assigning each a number.

As with interviewing, a list of prepared questions will help you to spend your time profitably. This time, however, your object is not to ask for information, but to set up a framework for your observations and, possibly, a potential structure for your essay. For this assignment, you are basically trying to find out:

- How many students are spending time at this site?

- Where are they and what are they doing?

- Do they stay for the whole observation period, or do they come and go?

Engaging in Observation: Your work consists of careful observing and precise note taking. You are not trying to write a narrative or, at this point, understand the significance of what you are seeing; you are only trying to record your subjects' activities accurately to provide notes for future reflection.

Some people may feel self-conscious to have an observer watching them closely and writing down everything they do. To avoid potential questions or confrontations, try to do your observing and note taking unobtrusively, without staring too hard at any one person. If someone asks what you are doing, be prepared to say that you are working on an assignment for a college class, that you aren't going to identify anyone by name, and that you would be grateful for the person's cooperation. As with interview subjects, you will find that most subjects of field research are sympathetic and helpful. If someone speaks to you, take advantage of the opportunity to combine observations with a little formal interviewing, and possibly gain a useful quotation for your essay. If someone objects to being included in your study, however, you should immediately turn your attention elsewhere, or move on and try again at another time.

A portion of your notes for one session might look like that shown in Figure 7-12.

After a couple of sessions, you may feel that you have a general idea of the range of students' behavior at the site, so you can begin to look specifically for repeated instances of certain activities: studying together or individually, eating, relaxing. But you will need to keep an open mind and eye about what you might observe. Again, as with interviewing, your subjects' behavior may not absolutely conform to your planned questions, so you may need to add new questions as the sessions progress. For example, you may not have realized until your third session that students sitting on the benches closest to the playing field are focusing on the sports activities there; from then on, you will be looking for that behavior.

For this assignment, you would continue observing until you complete the number of observations specified; but for your own field research in a project for a course in your major field, you might conduct observations for most of a semester. As a professional researcher (like Margaret Mead when she was

> Monday, April 3; 10:30 am.
>
> 3 students at bench 3 -- 1 male & 2 females. Females sitting on bench. Male, between them, standing with 1 foot up on bench, smoking. They're talking quietly. About 5 minutes later, another male arrives on bike & stands, straddling bike, in front of the bench. Conversation continues, now with 4 participants. At 10:50, females get up & walk into Johnson, along with 1st male. 2nd male rides off toward library.
>
> At benches 4 & 5, 2 people at each. At 4, 1 male reads book, stopping now and then to use a highlighter. 1 female has bunch of 3x5 cards, & she looks at each one for a second, then flips it, then goes to next one. At 10:35, another male comes over to her, she gets up, & they both go to bench 6, where no one is sitting. There she continues going through her cards, but now she seems to read something from each card, as male responds with a word or 2. They continue to do this for another 10 minutes.

Figure 7-12

observing Pacific Island adolescents for her classic book *Coming of Age in Samoa*), you might even live with a tribe, studying their culture for a year or more.

Analyzing Your Information

When you have all your observations recorded, you are ready to move on to the next stage: reviewing your notes to understand what you have seen, and analyzing what you have learned. You have probably noticed that this overlaps with the previous observation stage; as you watched students in front of Johnson Hall, you were already beginning to group their activities into several categories: studying, casual conversations, watching sports, eating, sleeping.

Once you establish these categories, you pull out of your notes the specific references that match the category, noting the date and time of each instance. So now you have several new pages that look like those shown in Figure 7-13.

> Studying
>
> girl and guy with flash cards 4/6 10:35
> group of 5 with science notes 4/8 10:30 - 10:58
>   (they told me about their 11 am quiz --
>   all in same class)
> guy with book and highlighter 4/6
>   10:30 - 10:45

> Sports watching
>
> observations 2, 4, 5, 6: groups of 2 - 5 guys at
>   benches 1, 2, 3 (facing sports field).
>   Groups generally talked, pointed,
>   laughed, while gym classes did
>   aerobics.
>
> observations 4, 5: during baseball team
>   practice, guys in small groups
>   cheered, pointed; several stood up
>   and walked over to edge of path
>   that overlooks field.
>
> female pairs watching sports
>   during 4, 5, but no groups.
>
> observations 1, 2: no sports scheduled
>   then; few people on benches 1, 2,
>   and 3.

Figure 7-13

You may want to chart your observations to represent at a glance such variables as these: How many students studied, or watched sports, or socialized? Which activities were associated with males or with females? If your sessions took place during different times of the day, the hour would be another variable to record on your chart.

As you identify categories, you need to ask yourself some questions to help you characterize each one and define the differences among some of your subjects' behaviors. For example: Are these differences determined by gender, as with the sports watchers, or by preferred methods of learning, like solitary or group study? As you think through the possible conclusions to be drawn from your observations, record them in your notebook, for these preliminary analyses will later become part of your essay.

Writing the Essay

An essay based on field research generally follows a format appropriate to the particular discipline. Your instructor will provide detailed guidelines and, perhaps, refer you to an article in a professional journal to use as a model. For the essay analyzing student behavior, you might present your findings according to the following outline:

Purpose: In the first section, you state the problem—the purpose of your field research—clearly indicating the question(s) you set out to investigate.

Method: Here, you explain your choice of site, the times and number of your observation sessions, and the general procedure for observation that you followed, including any exceptions to or deviations from your plan.

Observations: Next, you record the information you gathered from your observations, not as a list of random facts, but as categories or groupings that make the facts coherent to the reader. In many disciplines, this kind of information can be presented through charts, graphs, or tables.

Analysis: The heart of your essay, here is where you explain to your readers the significance of your observations. If, for example, you decided that certain activities were gender related, you would describe the basis for that distinction. Or you could discuss your conclusion that students use the benches primarily as a meeting place to socialize. Or you might make the connection between studying as the most prevalent student activity outside Johnson Hall and the scheduling of midterms during the time of your observations.

Conclusions: At the end of your essay, you remind your readers—and the instructor who is evaluating your work—that your purpose throughout has been to answer the questions and clarify the problems posed in the first paragraph. What did you discover that can illuminate your response to your professor's assertions about students' behavior?

Using Field Research

There are several important points to remember about using field research:

1. In actual practice across the curriculum, field research is usually combined with library research. As part of your investigation, you will often be asked to include in an early section of your essay a "review of the literature," that is, a summary of some key articles on your topic. This summary shows that you are familiar with an appropriate range of information and, especially, the major work in the field.

2. Whether you emphasize library or field research depends on the purpose and nature of your essay. If field research is integral to your topic, you will be acting as the principal investigator and interpreter of new data, and the library research will serve only as a supplement to your field research. Otherwise, you should integrate your field research into your essay as you would any other source of information.

3. For field research, careful documentation is especially important since you are asking your reader to trust the data that you yourself have gathered and upon which your speculations and conclusions are based. You can create this trust by making careful and repeated observations, recording them in detail and accurately, and presenting them in a clear and logical manner.

4. The methods of analyzing data obtained through field research are, in most cases, specific to particular disciplines. So you should indicate to your readers, by reference to authorities or models, that you are observing the conventions of the field you are working in. It is especially important that, after consultation with your instructor, you use the appropriate method of documenting both your field research and your library research, so that a reader can clearly distinguish the work of the previous investigators who are your secondary sources from your own primary contributions.

ASSIGNMENT 10: WRITING AN ESSAY BASED ON INTERVIEWS OR FIELD RESEARCH

A. Choose a topic from the following list; or think of a question that might stimulate a wide range of responses, and submit the question for your teacher's approval. Try to avoid political issues and very controversial subjects that may make it difficult for you to control the interview and prevent you from getting a well-balanced set of notes. You want a topic in which everyone you interview can take an interest, without becoming intensely partisan.

Suggestions for Topics

Is "traditional" dating still desirable today?

Does it matter whether an elementary-school child has a male or female teacher?

Is there a right age to get married?

What are the ingredients for a lasting marriage?

Should children be given the same first names as their parents?

Is it better to keep a friend by not speaking your mind or risk losing a friend by honesty?

Should community service become a compulsory part of the high school curriculum?

Should English be made the official language of the United States?

Are laws requiring the wearing of seat belts an infringement of individual rights?

Is graffiti vandalism?

Should animals be used in laboratory research?

Should colleges ban drinking alcohol on campus and in fraternity houses?

How should ethics be taught in the schools?

How should the commandment "honor thy parents" be put into practice today?

What, if anything, is wrong with the nuclear family?

Are students forced to specialize too soon in their college experience?

Should schools stay in session all year round?

Should citizens have to pay a fine for not voting?

Should movies have a rating system?

Should children's TV time be rationed?

Should parents be held legally or financially responsible for damage done by their children?

At what age is it acceptable for children to work (outside the family)?

Should high school students be tested for drug use?

Should hosts who serve alcohol be held responsible if their guests later are involved in auto accidents?

Should students have to maintain passing grades in order to participate in school athletics?

How should society deal with homeless people?

When should parents cease to be financially responsible for their children?

1. Once your topic is decided (and, if necessary, approved), interview at least six people, or as many as you need to get a variety of reactions for your survey. (Some of your sources should be students in your class.) If you wish, use the following format for conducting each interview:

Name: (first and last: check the spelling!)

Do you think . . . . ?

Why do you think so? What are some of your reasons? (later) Are there any other reasons?

Why do you think people who take the opposite view would do so?

Do any examples come to your mind to illustrate your point?

Quotation:

2. Take careful and complete notes of the comments that you receive. (*You will be expected to hand in all your notes, in their original form, with your completed essay.*) Keep a separate sheet for each person. If one of your sources says something worth quoting, write down the exact words; read them back to make sure that what you have quoted is what the speaker meant to say; then put quotation marks around the direct quotation. Otherwise, use summary or paraphrase.

3. List the ideas from your notes and arrange the points in a sequence of your choice.

4. Write a summary of your notes that presents the full range of opinion, paraphrasing and (occasionally) quoting from representative sources. After analyzing the arguments of your sources, conclude with one or two paragraphs explaining which point of view, in your opinion, has the most validity, and why.

B. Select a topic appropriate for engaging in field research on your campus, in your dormitory, or in your workplace. For example, you might want to learn about how students occupy their time during large lecture courses; by auditing two or three lecture classes over a period of time and taking notes about students' behavior, you could test Todd Gitlin's thesis (see p. 276) about the wisdom of providing printed lecture notes. Present your topic to your instructor for approval, and after carrying out your research, organize your notes and prepare your essay according to the instructions on page 344.

SAVING AND RECORDING INFORMATION FOR YOUR BIBLIOGRAPHY

As you scan the sources that you find, you have to decide which ones may be worth including in your essay as well as the best way to save them. Before the computer and the copying machine were invented, a researcher had to make immediate and firm choices, *taking notes* from useful material and rejecting everything else. Later on, those notes would become the basis for the essay. There are definite advantages in taking and working from notes. You gain a firm grasp of the topic; you will develop ideas of your own as you summarize and paraphrase what you read; and you can more easily estimate the progress of your research, deciding whether you have enough sources to support your essay.

But the twenty-first century does provide some convenient alternatives. Even if you take notes, it makes sense to copy key pages from books and articles so that, as you write, you can check your version of the material against the actual text. Having that text discourages inadvertent plagiarism since it will be very clear which ideas and language are the source's and which are yours. Copies also make it possible to write comments in the margin and circle or highlight key points. As you organize your essay, you can cut and paste text or interleave copied pages from different sources in a sequence corresponding to your outline.

Once you have located and briefly examined a book or periodical article or a Web site and decided that it is worth including in your essay, you should not only copy pages, but also write a few preliminary notes about the source's probable usefulness. Jot down your opinion of the work's scope and contents, strong or weak points, and relevance to your topic, as well as any impressions about the author's reliability as a source. Often, you can make these tentative judgments just by examining the table of contents and leafing or scrolling through the pages. If you forget to note down your reactions, you'll find it more difficult to prioritize your reading when you're pressed for time at a later stage of your research.

Notes are also useful for your bibliography and essential if you're asked to submit an annotated bibliography. *A bibliography is a complete list of all the works that you use in preparing your essay.* What's included in a bibliography can differ at various stages of your work:

- A *preliminary* or *working* bibliography consists of all the sources that you find worth recording and saving as you do your research.

- A *final* bibliography (sometimes called "Works Cited" or "References") consists of the material that you have actually used in writing your essay.

- An *annotated* bibliography includes a sentence or two after each item, describing the work's scope and specific focus and suggesting its relevance and usefulness to the development of your topic. An example of an annotated bibliography is provided on pages 351–353.

Copying and Recording Print Material

If you copy pages from books or periodicals, keep in mind that you may not always remember how that extract fit into the author's sequence of ideas. Provide yourself with a brief explanation of context at the top of the first copied page: the focus of the chapter, the author's previous point. Otherwise, you may have to go back to the library while writing your essay and find the original source. It can be helpful to copy some or all of the bibliography in the back of a key text.

Place the book carefully in the copier to avoid cutting off material at the top, bottom, or sides of the page; days or weeks later, if you want to quote, it may be difficult to reconstruct missing language. You should make especially sure that the page numbers show on the copies, since those numbers are crucial in the citation of your sources.

To record basic publication information about a book and keep the details legible and accurate, copy the title page and the copyright page (the back of the title page) at the same time that you copy extracts. For a periodical article, copy the cover of the magazine or journal and the table of contents. Of course, if you used a database to identify books and periodical articles, most of the information that you need will be included in the results list. (That's one reason why it's useful to download or print the results pages of your database searches.) But even if you have those lists saved on your computer, the information that you'll need will be scattered over a number of downloaded files. At some point, you'll have to put it all together in a single file.

Start the computer file or notebook list for your working bibliography early in the research process, and every time you find a source you're likely (but not necessarily certain) to use, add it to the list. Transcribe the information from the databases that you've downloaded and the stack of title pages that you've copied. Or, if you use a word processing program (like Nota Bene) or a bibliographic software program (like Research Assistant) that automatically prepares a bibliography in any of the standard formats, enter the data about each new source into the fields of the database. It's important to be accurate and consistent in recording each entry. Check the spelling of the author's name. Don't abbreviate unless you're sure you'll remember the significance of each symbol. Make it clear whether the place of publication was Cambridge, Massachusetts, or Cambridge, England. Leave blank spaces if, for example, you've forgotten to include the publisher's name or the journal's volume number.

The majority of college research essays use MLA (Modern Language Association) style for documentation. To prepare a final bibliography in MLA style (or, indeed, in most other styles), you should include the following facts in your preliminary list:

For Print Books

- the full name of the author(s)
- the exact title, italicized
- the name of the editor(s) (for an anthology) or the name of the translator (for a work first written in a foreign language)
- the date and place of publication and the name of the publisher
- the original date of publication and the date of the new edition or reprint, if the book has been reissued
- the inclusive page numbers and any other information for a specific chapter or other section (such as the author and title of an introduction or of a selection within an anthology)
- the volume number, if the book is part of a multivolume work
- the call number, so that you will not need to return to the catalog if you decide to locate the book again
- the medium of publication ("Print")

For Print Articles

- the full name of the author(s)
- the title of the article, in quotation marks
- the exact title of the periodical, italicized
- the volume and issue numbers (if any) and the date of the issue
- the inclusive page numbers of the article
- the call number of the periodical, so that you will not need to return to the database if you decide to locate the article again
- the medium of publication ("Print")

Copying and Recording Web Material

Downloading material from the Web is the equivalent of copying print texts. If you click on a document and can't make up your mind whether it's worth saving, you can "bookmark" it, or include it among the "favorites" on your browser. Once you're sure it's a solid source, click "Save As" on the File menu, choosing a name that will be easily recognizable and (if you want to save space on your hard drive) selecting a "text only" option rather than saving the complete document, graphics and all. If the document is large, you may want to highlight extracts and then copy and paste them to a file in your word processing program. (Since the content of a Web site can change from day to day—or the site itself can disappear—it's a good idea to download if you have any inclination at all to use the source.) Early on in your research, create a new folder named for your paper topic and, after that, save all Web material to that folder, so it won't be scattered all over your hard drive.

Printing out a Web document is also helpful. Web graphics can be distracting; computer screens are hard on the eyes. In addition, having a print copy allows you to put comments in the margins and highlight important points. Actually, once you've downloaded a document, you can always add your own notes on the screen, without printing it, inserting brackets between paragraphs or within the text, or using a tracking program included in your word processing software.

It's particularly important to keep a running record of *URLs*—the Web addresses—so that if you want to go back to a page you can do so easily. (Be careful with the spelling of Web addresses.) Don't assume that you'll remember a URL. If you've downloaded Web material, saving it under a convenient name, you may have to search hard to reconstruct its address. Often, by checking the "history" list on your browser you can locate the Web page you used a few days or weeks ago. On the whole, though, it's safest to have a single file that records all your sources, with complete bibliographic information. And save it! And back it up by copying it to a disk or CD or external drive!

To compile your working bibliography, you need to add information about Web sources to the file where you're storing data about print sources. Many Web documents were previously or simultaneously published in print; in those cases, include both the print and the electronic data. (If you read the material on the Web, you must cite the Internet source, not the print source, in your bibliography.) On many sites, the kind of bibliographic information shown in print sources is not provided or is difficult to find. Look for and record any of the following items that you can identify:

For Web Material

- the name of the author(s) of the article or other document and of the person(s) or sponsor(s) who created the site
- the title of the article or other document, in quotation marks
- the title of the book or periodical or of the site, italicized, or a description, such as *Home page*
- any volume number, issue number, or other identifying number
- any print publication information, including the date
- the date of publication on the Web, or of the most recent update
- the range or total number of pages, paragraphs, or other sections, if they are numbered on the site
- the name of the database (if applicable)
- the date of access: when you downloaded the site or took notes from it
- the Web address (URL), so that you can return to the site if you need to
- the medium of publication ("Web")

Obviously, this information can vary depending on the kind of document you're intending to use. An individual's home page, for example, would require nothing more than the author's name, the indication that it is a home page, the sponsor of the site (often the individual), and the date of access. But serious research is much more likely to depend on Web sites with academic or professional (or even commercial) sponsorship, and it's necessary to indicate all those details in the bibliography. Examples of bibliographical entries for citing Web sources can be found in Chapter 12.

Presenting an Annotated Bibliography

Here's how you put together some of the information you've recorded about Lawrence of Arabia and turn it into an *annotated bibliography* (following MLA style):

The Myth of Lawrence of Arabia in the Movies:

An Annotated List of Sources Consulted

Butler, Oliver J. *The Guerrilla Strategies of Lawrence and Mao:*
An Examination. Houston: Butler, 1974. Print. Useful background
for understanding the success of Lawrence's campaigns against the
Turks and evaluating the movie's accuracy, particularly the bombing
of the train.

Hodson, Joel C. *Lawrence of Arabia and American Culture: The Making of a Transatlantic Legend.* Westport: Greenwood, 1995. Print. This book focuses on the impact the Lawrence myth had on American culture. The last part is particularly useful in analyzing the movie's presentation of Lawrence, especially his alleged homosexuality.

Kauffmann, Stanley. "On Films: The Return of El Aurans. *Lawrence of Arabia* Reissued, Restored to Its Original Length." *New Republic* 20 Feb. 1989: 26–28. Print. One of the most eminent film critics reassesses the significance of the film.

"Last Known Photograph of Lawrence." 1935. *dropbears.com.* dropbears .com, 1997–2010. Web. 12 May 2010. <www.dropbears.com/m/ models/brough/players.htm>.

Lawrence, T. E. *The Letters of T. E. Lawrence of Arabia.* Ed. David Garnett. 1938; London: Spring, 1964. Print. This is a comprehensive collection of Lawrence's correspondence, which provides an especially detailed and moving picture of his later years in the RAF.

---. *The Seven Pillars of Wisdom.* London: Pike, 1926. Print. Lawrence's own interpretation of what happened in the campaign against the Turks is written in a flowery and sometimes opaque style. Nevertheless, it's essential reading.

Waters, Irene. "The Lawrence Trail." *Contemporary Review* 272.1587 (1998): 205–10. *General OneFile.* Web. May 2010. This is little more than a personal narrative following Lawrence's path through the desert in the 1917 campaign. Useful only for local color.

Williams, Sian. Home page. Sian Williams, 2 July 2001. Web. 16 Dec. 2003. <http://www.ouphrontis.co.uk/>. Although rather dramatic in style, this site is very useful, especially for its links to other Web pages about Lawrence (man and film) that don't appear on any search results lists.

Wilson, Jeremy. *Lawrence of Arabia: The Authorised Biography of T. E. Lawrence.* London: Heinemann, 1989. Print. Although not the most recent, this is the most comprehensive of the biographies of Lawrence and covers every aspect of his life. The bibliography could be more helpful.

---. *T. E. Lawrence Studies.* Castle Hill Press, Apr. 2009. Web. 10 Feb. 2010. <http://www.telawrence.info>. This is a superb, searchable

Web site containing information about Lawrence, maps and chronology, bibliography, and a link to the journal *T. E. Lawrence Studies*.

Wilson, Michael. "Lawrence of Arabia: Elements and Facets of the Theme." *Cineaste* 21.4 (1995): 30–32. Print. This article, though brief, provides interesting insights into how the screenwriter thought he was representing Lawrence's life.

How Much Research Is Enough?

Research is open-ended. You can't know in advance how many sources will provide adequate support for your topic. Your instructor may stipulate that you consult at least five authorities, or ten, or fifteen; but that is probably intended to make sure that everyone in your class does a roughly equal amount of research. Quantity is not the crucial issue. There's little point in compiling the required number of source materials if the works on your list are minor, or trivial, or peripheral to the topic. Your bibliography could contain hundreds of sources—whole sections of a database or whole pages of an index—but would that be the basis for a well-documented essay?

At various stages of your research, you may think that you have located enough sources. When that happens, try asking yourself these questions:

- Do my sources include a few of the "standard" books on my topic by well-known authorities? The most recent books? Contemporary accounts (if the topic is historical)?

- Have I checked databases and indexes to find the most authoritative periodical articles, whether in print or on the Web? Have I included the best ones among my sources?

- Does Web material supplement my research, rather than dominate it?

- Have I discussed any questions about my research with my instructor or with a librarian?

- Have I taken notes of my own ideas and thoughts about the topic?

- Without consulting sources, can I talk about the subject convincingly and fluently? Have I succeeded in doing this with a friend?

- Is a point of view or thesis emerging from my research?

- Have I gathered a critical mass of information, copied excerpts, and downloaded material so that my essay has the prospect of substantial support?

- Do I feel ready to start writing my essay?

EXERCISE 24: COMPILING A WORKING BIBLIOGRAPHY

Here are three topics for a research essay dealing with the broad subject of *advertising*, followed by a bibliography of eighteen articles, arranged in order of their publication dates. Each item in the bibliography is followed by a brief description of its contents.

Examine the bibliography carefully and choose a set of possible sources, appropriate for a preliminary bibliography, for each of the three essay topics. Depending on the topic, which ones should you read? You are not expected to locate and read these articles; use the notes to help you make your decisions.

List the numbers of the articles that you select underneath each topic. You will notice that some of the articles can be used for more than one topic.

Topics

A. Feminists have argued that the image of women created by the advertising industry remains a false and objectionable one. Is that claim valid?

B. How do advertising agencies go about manipulating the reactions of consumers?

C. To what extent does advertising serve the public? harm the public?

1. Hitchon, Jacqueline C., and Chingching Chang. "Effects of Gender Schematic Processing on the Reception of Political Commercials for Men and Women Candidates." *Communication Research* 22.4 (1995): 430–58. Print. A scholarly survey focusing on the appeal to gender in the marketing of commercials for political candidates.

2. Tauchi, Teresa. "Truth in Advertising." *HaasWeek*. UC Berkeley Haas School of Business, 30 Oct. 1995. Web. 13 Oct. 2004. <http://haas.berkeley.edu/~haasweek/issues/XXII_10/index.html>. A chatty little story about tasteless ads, often offensive to women, and the need for more responsible behavior on the part of advertising executives.

3. Lafky, Sue, Margaret Duffy, Mary Steinmaus, and Dan Berkowitz. "Looking through Gendered Lenses." *Journalism & Mass Communication Quarterly* 73.2 (1996): 379–88. Print. Full of jargon, this article describes a study of gender-role stereotyping. High school students were given magazine ads to show how quickly they are influenced by stereotypes of gender.

4. Miller, Molly. "The Color of Money." *Mother Earth News* Feb.–Mar. 1996: 78–89. Print. The subject is environmental protection, and the false claims about their environmental policies that some companies have made in their advertisements.

5. Pratt, Charlotte A., and Cornelius B. Pratt. "Nutrition Advertisements in Consumer Magazines." *Journal of Black Studies* 26.4 (1996): 504–23. *General*

OneFile. Web. 17 Dec. 2004. The authors focus on claims made about potential benefits to health in advertisements for various foods.

6. McFadden, Daniel L., and Kenneth E. Train. "Consumers' Evaluation of New Products." *Journal of Political Economy* 104.4 (1996): 683–703. *JSTOR.* Web. 17 Dec. 2004. This is a technical article about how people accept new products through their own or other people's experiences, and how that process can be word-of-mouth information; the authors map out a step-by-step process evaluation that might be helpful to advertisers.

7. Attas, Daniel. "What's Wrong with 'Deceptive' Advertising?" *Journal of Business Ethics* 21.1 (1999): 49–59. *JSTOR.* Web. 17 Dec. 2004. This is essentially a defense of deceptive advertising, examining the responsibility of the advertiser and the responsibility of the consumer. It is written in sociological jargon.

8. Nordlinger, Pia. "Taste: Anything Goes." *Wall Street Journal* 15 Sept. 2000: W17. Print. This focuses on the proliferation of semi-pornographic ads in magazines, and the questionable standards set by the editors. The author is clearly disapproving of the "prurient" images.

9. White, Candace, and Katherine N. Kimmick. "One Click Forward and Two Clicks Back: Portrayal of Women Using Computers in Television Commercials." *Women's Studies in Communication* 23.3 (2000): 392–412. *Academic OneFile.* Web. 17 Dec. 2004. Based on a survey of 351 TV commercials, this article shows that the image of women in computer ads is definitely more menial than that of men, confirming the usual stereotypes.

10. Smith, April. "In TV Ads, the Laugh's on Men . . . Isn't It?" *Los Angeles Times* 24 Oct. 2000: E1. Print. This describes images of men in commercials, concluding that they are just as stereotyped as those of women—except the image is that of beer-drinking, dopey sports fans. The point is that male viewers don't get offended by such ads.

11. Harker, Debra, and Michael Harker. "The Role of Codes of Conduct in the Advertising Self-Regulatory Framework." *Journal of Macromarketing* 20.2 (2000): 155–66. *Sage Journals Online.* Web. 17 Dec. 2004. This article discusses whether or not the advertising industry is capable of self-regulation in dealing with offensive or misleading advertising. Its findings are based on an Australian survey.

12. Gardner, Marilyn. "Slim But Curvy—the Pursuit of Ideal Beauty." *Christian Science Monitor* 24 Jan. 2001: 16. Print. The author writes about idealized images of women in advertisements, exploring the connection between extreme thinness on the page and increasing obesity among the readers. According to the author, these ideals of beauty are unrealistic.

13. Vranica, Suzanne. "Sirius Ad Is Best Bet for Most Sexist." *Wall Street Journal* 1 Apr. 2004: B6. Print. This article is about the award given each year for advertising's most sexist commercial or advertisement and describes the various tasteless finalists. Although some advertising people think that higher standards of decency will eventually be imposed, others say that "edgy" ads appeal to young consumers.

14. Klempner, Geoffrey. "Ethics and Advertising." *CCELS Publications Online.* Cardiff Centre for Ethics, Law and Society, June 2004. Web. 3 Mar. 2005 <www.ccels .cardiff.ac.uk/pubs/klempnerpaper.html>. In a philosophical article (with references to Plato and Wittgenstein), this "professional metaphysician" attempts to "deconstruct the dream world of advertising" and the ways in which advertisers seduce us, and concludes that advertising is only as moral as the consumers it serves.

15. Drumwright, Minette E., and Patrick Murphy. "How Advertising Practitioners View Ethics: Moral Muteness, Moral Myopia, and Moral Imagination." *Journal of Advertising* 33.2 (2004): 7–25. *Expanded Academic ASAP.* Web. 4 June 2005. <www.gale.cengage.com/ExpandedAcademic/>. This article describes a study that concluded that a large proportion of advertising professionals have a blind spot— "moral myopia"—about ethical issues when they arise. They believe that, if the consumers will accept it, then an advertising practice has to be morally acceptable and there's no need for concern.

16. Vagnoni, Anthony. "Ads Are from Mars, Women Are from Venus." *Print: America's Graphic Design Magazine* 59.2 (2005): 52–56. *Factiva.* Web. 9 Aug. 2005. <http://www.factiva.com>. An advertising executive believes that ads targeted at women tend to be tasteless and even offensive, and, in return, women are ignoring most ads. The article contrasts strategies presently used to attract male and female consumers, but does not attempt to solve the problem.

17. Singer, Emily. "They Know What You Want." *New Scientist* 31 July 2004: 36. *Factiva.* Web. 18 May 2005. <http://www.factiva.com>. Singer describes "neuromarketing," a new kind of technology that scans consumers' brains while they are shopping and comparing products. Advertisers hope to learn more about the origins of brand preference and brand loyalty so that they can better predict customer behavior.

18. Edwards, Jim. "The Seifert Code." *Adweek* 18 July 2005: 12. *Factiva.* Web. 10 Aug. 2005. <http://www.factiva.com>. An advertising executive convicted of financial fraud was required, as part of her sentence, to write a code of ethics for the industry. This article doesn't describe the ethical code, but reports the reactions of some advertising professionals.

EXERCISE 25: FINDING AND SELECTING SOURCES

Each of the historical figures on the following list has been the subject of a motion picture. (The dates and, where necessary, titles of the films are in parentheses.) Choose one figure and then compile a preliminary bibliography for an essay that sets out to determine to what extent the film is authentic. (Since this is a *preliminary* bibliography and you're not being asked to write the essay, you need not have seen the film in order to start the research process.)

Using databases and search engines, search for sources that are clearly linked to your topic. Print out a list of the first twenty or thirty items from each search, eliminate those that are obviously commercial or trivial, and choose those that might appropriately be included in a preliminary bibliography. You do not have to examine the books, articles, or Web sites in order to make your selection; base your choices on the descriptions, summaries, or abstracts provided by the database or search engine. If you don't find sufficient material in your first search, keep trying.

Your preliminary bibliography should contain at least ten items, with a balance of one-third books, one-third print periodical articles, and one-third Web material. Hand in the results lists from your searches with the appropriate choices marked. If your instructor requests it, also prepare a formal bibliography using MLA format.

Alexander the Great
(*Alexander* 2004)
Alfred Kinsey (*Kinsey* 2004)
Benito Juarez (*Juarez* 1939)
Charlie Chaplin (*Chaplin* 1992)
Charles Gordon (*Khartoum* 1966)
Charles Lindbergh (*Spirit of St. Louis* 1957)
Cleopatra (1963)
Cole Porter (*Night and Day* 1946; *De-Lovely* 2004)
Dian Fossey (*Gorillas in the Mist* 1988)
El Cid (1961)
Eleanor of Aquitaine (*The Lion in Winter* 1968)
Emma Hamilton (*That Hamilton Woman* 1941)
Erwin Rommel (*The Desert Fox* 1951)
Eva Peron (*Evita* 1996)
Frida Kahlo (*Frida* 2002)
Gandhi (1982)
George III (*The Madness of King George* 1994)

George Patton (*Patton* 1970)
Hans Christian Andersen (1952)
Helen Keller (*The Miracle Worker* 1962)
Howard Hughes (*The Aviator* 2004)
Isadora Duncan (*Isadora* 1968)
Jackson Pollack (*Pollack* 2000)
Jim Morrison (*The Doors* 1991)
Kurt Cobain (*Last Days* 2005)
Lillian Hellman (*Julia* 1977)
Larry Flynt (*People vs Larry Flynt* 1996)
Lenny Bruce (*Lenny* 1974)
Marie Curie (*Madame Curie* 1943)
Loretta Lynn (*Coal Miner's Daughter* 1992)
Marie Antoinette (1938)
Michael Collins (1996)
Mikhail Kutuzov (*War and Peace* 1956)
Mozart (*Amadeus* 1984)
Muhammad Ali (*Ali* 2001)
Oscar Wilde (1998)
Queen Victoria (*Mrs. Brown* 1997)

Ray Charles (*Ray* 2004)
Richard Nixon (*Nixon* 1995)
T. S. Eliot (*Tom and Viv* 1994)
Thomas Jefferson (*Jefferson in Paris* 1995)
Tina Turner (*What's Love Got to Do with It?* 1993)
Ty Cobb (*Cobb* 1994)

Vincent Van Gogh (*Lust for Life* 1956)
William Gilbert or Arthur Sullivan (*Topsy Turvy* 1999)
William Randolph Hearst (*Citizen Kane* 1941)
William Wallace (*Braveheart* 1995)
Wyatt Earp (*My Darling Clementine* 1946)

ASSIGNMENT 11: PREPARING A TOPIC PROPOSAL FOR A RESEARCH ESSAY

A. Choose a broad topic that, for the next few weeks, you will research and develop into an extended essay of ten or more pages.

- If you have a *person or an event* in mind, but do not have sufficiently detailed knowledge to decide on a focus and target date, wait until you have done some preliminary reading. Start with an encyclopedia article or an entry in a biographical dictionary; then use the online databases and search engines, as well as any bibliographies that you find along the way.

- If you select a *contemporary subject or issue for argument*, search for books, journal and newspaper articles, and Web sites that will help you to formulate a few questions to be explored in your essay.

B. Compile a preliminary bibliography, based on your search results. At this point, you need not examine all the sources, take notes, or plan the organization of your essay. Your purpose is to assess the *amount* and, as much as possible, the *quality* of the material that is available. Whether or not your instructor asks you to hand in your preliminary bibliography, make sure that the publication information that you record is accurate and legible. Indicate which sources your library has available and which may be difficult to obtain.

C. Submit a topic proposal to your instructor, describing the probable scope and focus of your essay. (If you are considering more than one topic, suggest a few possibilities.) Be prepared to change the specifics of your proposal as you learn more about the number and availability of your sources.

▪8▪

Evaluating Sources

Locating sources comes before *choosing* sources. In the first step, you look for possible material, promising material, from print sources and from the Web. That becomes your preliminary bibliography. In the second step, you decide which of the possibilities are worth including in your essay. Those will be the contents of your final bibliography. In this chapter, you'll learn more about the process of choosing sources.

LEARNING MORE ABOUT YOUR SOURCES

Few of us know enough about most subjects to write about them from our own knowledge and experience. We have to rely on the evidence of others, usually in written form, published in print or on the Web. If the evidence isn't valid, then the work that depends on it will lose its credibility. For this reason, it's essential that—before you start writing—you evaluate each potential source to determine whether it's solid enough to support your essay or so shoddy as to discredit it.

Evaluating sources doesn't have to take a great deal of time. You do have to read enough of each text to make some judgments about its *substance* and its *tone*. You have to understand what kind of work it is—whether it's *plausible*, whether it's *appropriate* for the essay that you're writing. You need to be sure it's *relevant* to your topic. And since a good source should be *authoritative,* you must explore the author's claims to your serious consideration.

EVALUATING PRINT SOURCES

Let's assume that you've begun research for an essay on *animal rights*. You've often wondered about the motivations of vegetarians. As a meat-eater yourself, you're curious about the arguments used by animal rights advocates to discourage the slaughter of living creatures for the table. You are also aware of an ongoing controversy about the use of animals in medical experiments.

Your library holds many of the books and periodicals that have turned up in your database searches. How do you determine which ones to read seriously? How do you weigh one source of evidence against another and decide which ideas should be emphasized in your essay? Since all the books and articles have been chosen for publication, each one has presumably undergone some form of selection and review. Would it have been published if its author's authority was questionable? Why is it necessary to inquire further?

Credentials

At the most basic level, you want to find out whether the author of a book or article about animal rights can be trusted to know what he or she is writing about. Here's where the person's education and professional experience become relevant. Is the writer an academic? If so, what's the field of specialization?

- A *psychologist* might provide insights into the personal beliefs motivating vegetarians, but would probably be less concerned with the ideology of the animal rights movement.

- A *philosopher* will present theoretical arguments, but the analysis may be too abstract to provide you with concrete examples for developing your thesis.

- An *economist* might seem to be an unlikely source to support this topic, but the movement toward vegetarianism has had serious consequences for the agricultural economy as well as the retail world of the supermarket.

What about *home economists*? Any database search on "'animal rights' AND vegetarianism" will include a number of cookbooks and helpful guides for good nutrition, but the authors of such books are much less likely to possess academic qualifications. Does that matter? More important, do you want to include that kind of material in your essay? What kind of essay are you writing, anyway? One that stresses the theoretical arguments behind the animal rights movements? The practical motivation? The economic consequences? Evaluating sources can give your essay focus and direction.

How can you find out about an author's background?

- Check a book's *preface* (including acknowledgments), which will often contain biographical information.

- Read the *blurb* on the jacket cover—often laudatory—which should include some basic facts among the hype.

- Look for *thumbnail biographies* at the beginning or end of periodical articles, or grouped together somewhere in the issue. Be aware that such brief biographies (often written by the authors themselves) can be vague or even misleading. "A freelance writer who frequently writes about this topic" can describe a recognized authority or an inexperienced amateur.

- Do a *Web search* using the author's name. See what other books and articles the author has published.

- Consult one of the many *biographical dictionaries and encyclopedias* available on the Web.

- Check the *Book Review Index* on the Web. If the book is a recent one, there will probably be many reviews available.

- Routinely check the level and extent of the *documentation* that the author provides. Footnotes or parenthetical notes and a comprehensive bibliography usually indicate a serious commitment to the subject.

Peter Singer is the author of *Animal Liberation: A New Ethics for Our Treatment of Animals*. After a database search turns up this title, you find the book on the library shelves, note that it was published in 1975 (but revised in 1990), and wonder whether it's worth delving into a book that's more than thirty years old. So you search for his name in the *Encarta* encyclopedia and find the following:

> Singer, Peter (1946–), Australian philosopher and bioethicist. Born in Melbourne, Australia, Singer studied at the University of Melbourne and at the University of Oxford, in England. He began his career lecturing ethics [sic] at Oxford from 1971 to 1973. He subsequently worked at various universities in North America and Australia. In 1977, he became a professor of philosophy at Monash University in Melbourne. Singer also became closely associated with the university's Centre for Human Bioethics, which is dedicated to the study of the moral implications of biomedical discoveries. . . . In 1999 he became a professor at Princeton University's Center for Human Values.

The article goes on to describe Singer as a *rationalist,* who views ethical issues from a utilitarian point of view and so advocates actions that result in the greatest good for the greatest number of people. He has written, cowritten, or edited twenty-four books, the most recent in 2006, some in areas of pure philosophy (*Hegel; Marx*) but most dealing with matters of ethical choice.

What do you learn from this information? Singer holds impeccable academic credentials and has had a long and estimable academic career. As a philosopher, he is likely to root his work on animal rights in abstract arguments. As an ethicist, he is likely to provide plenty of concrete examples to illustrate his arguments.

So far, *Animal Liberation* seems like a certain choice for your preliminary bibliography and, quite probably, your final bibliography. Is there anything more that you need to know about it?

Impartiality

Sometimes you have to consider an author's personal interest in a subject, especially if it's a contentious one like animal rights. In the simplest terms, a declared vegetarian is likely to support the arguments against using animals for food and may present those arguments in a way that's less than impartial. There's nothing intrinsically wrong with having one's own point of view. Few people succeed in being totally detached or objective, whether about their beliefs or their areas of professional expertise. But there's a big difference between an acknowledged personal interest and an underlying prejudice.

The issue here is *bias*: the special interest or personal angle that might affect an author's opinion or treatment of a subject. The existence of bias isn't necessarily wrong or bad, and it needn't prevent you from using and citing a source. It's simply one factor that can affect your understanding of an author's ideas. A *dogmatic* writer may want to convert you at all costs. A *narrow-minded* writer will ignore or downplay opposing points of view. You may conclude that either is too biased to be credible. But a third author, who also cares passionately about a subject, may argue the issue in the strongest terms and yet remain credible. Such writers are usually aware of and acknowledge their bias—and seek to persuade or convince rather than bludgeon their readers into submission. Don't reject an interesting source just because you believe that the writer may have a special interest in the subject. Either disregard the bias as harmless, or adjust your judgment to allow for its influence, or—if the bias is really prejudice in disguise—reject the source as not worth your time.

Looking further at the *Encarta* profile, you notice that Peter Singer's books tend to have strong titles, urging action: *Animal Liberation, In Defence of Animals, Ethics into Action, Democracy and Disobedience.* Clearly, he's not an ivory tower philosopher, and so, curious to learn more about his activities, you do a Web search. You don't have to click on any of the thirty-three items on the results lists to learn that Singer has been called the world's "most controversial ethicist" and that a petition was started to protest his appointment to a named chair at Princeton. There are references to his "infanticide excesses" and "utilitarian horrors" as well as comparisons with Hitler's Nazism. On the other hand, there are other Web sites that support his views and praise his reasoned defense of his ethical beliefs.

Since these searches have taken only a few minutes, you try one more, and find a four-page article in *Current Biography* that provides an analysis of reactions by reviewers to many of Singer's works. Focusing on those that deal with *Animal Liberation*, you find praise for his documentation and for his "unhysterical and engaging" style. He is referred to as a propagandist, and he is apparently a successful one, since *Animal Liberation* is described by one reviewer as "one of the most thoughtful and persuasive books that I have read in a long time."

What can you conclude now? That the present controversy over Singer may or may not concern his 1975 work, which is the one that's most relevant to your research. That he has his detractors and his supporters, which is understandable given his contentious subject. That you should judge for yourself by reading *Animal Liberation*, while being alert for the possibility of a biased presentation.

Style and Tone

Writers aim their work at particular audiences and adjust the content and style accordingly. A children's book about kindness to animals would be an unlikely candidate for inclusion in a research paper; both style and content would be too simplified to be taken seriously. At the other extreme, technical papers in the sciences and social sciences are often written in a dense style, with a vocabulary incomprehensible to someone outside the discipline; essentially, one academic is writing for an audience of peers. You would probably want to avoid reading—and citing—a journal article that focuses on the methodology for a survey of animal rights activists or analyzes the chemical basis of nutrients needed in a vegetarian diet.

Nonfiction books are often categorized as:

Popular: intended to attract the widest possible audience and, therefore, be accessible to people with a wide range of educational backgrounds. A popular treatment of a serious subject is likely to emphasize colorful detail rather than abstractions and complexities.

General interest: intended for an audience that is interested in a subject but has no special grounding in it. General interest books provide a thorough introduction, with some level of complexity, but without a lot of technical description.

Academic: intended for a limited audience in the field. An academic book is usually published by a university press and contains a level of scholarship and depth of analysis that might well be beyond the comprehension of the general public.

To determine whether a book may be useful for your research, look at the table of contents, the introduction, and a sample from a middle chapter that will give you a sense of style and tone. Also check the index to see how often your topic appears. Does the book have a bibliography? Footnotes or other documentation?

Periodicals also serve a wide range of readers. Most have a marketing "niche," appealing to a specific audience with well-defined interests and reading habits. Since readership varies so greatly, articles on the same subject in two different periodicals are likely to differ widely in their content, point of view, and presentation. A newsmagazine like *Time* or *Newsweek* might provide factual information on an animal rights demonstration; the article would be short and lively, filled with concrete illustrations and quotations. It would not have the same purpose, nor cite the same kinds of evidence, nor use the same vocabulary as a longer article on the animal rights movement in a general interest periodical like *Psychology Today*. And that, in turn, would have little in common with an essay in a scholarly journal on the moral basis of the contractarian argument supporting the rights of animals. Researchers must allow for this wide variation in style and tone when they select and use their sources.

Journals in the social sciences frequently include articles intended for a narrow audience, using a conventional structure and professional terminology that can sometimes seem like jargon. At the beginning of such articles, you're likely to find a *"review of the literature"*: a summary of the contributions that other sociologists or psychologists have made to an understanding of the topic. Here's a typical paragraph taken from "Social Work and Speciesism," an article by David B. Wolf in the journal *Social Work*:

> There are many connections between our treatment of animals and environmental integrity; these touch on issues such as hunger, poverty, and war. Toffler (1975) suggested that the most practical hope for resolving the world's food crisis is a restriction of beef eating that will save billions of tons of grain. Ehrlich and Ehrlich (1972) reported that production of a pound of meat requires 40 to 100 times as much water as the production of a pound of wheat. Altschul (1964) noted that in terms of calorie units per acre, a diet of grains, vegetables, and beans will support 20 times as many people as a diet of meat. . . .

In effect, Wolf is summarizing the evidence of his sources in the topic sentence and then citing them, one by one. This pattern of presentation should not be imitated in an essay written for a basic writing course, *nor is it usually a good idea to include such a "review of the literature" as a source within your essay.* You would be quoting or paraphrasing Wolf, who is paraphrasing Toffler or Altschul. Better to eliminate the middleman (Wolf) and go directly to the source (Altschul or Toffler).

You can often decide to dismiss or pursue an article just by considering the title of the periodical. In an *Ingenta* search for articles on "animal rights," the results list (152) included periodicals ranging from *Chemical and Engineering News* to *Broiler Industry* to *Restaurant Business* to *Vegetarian Times*. It's highly unlikely that articles in any of those four periodicals would be suitable for a research essay on "animal rights." What about *Gender and Society*? If you're especially interested in gender issues and wonder whether activism on behalf of animals may be gender-specific, that might be an excellent article to include in your preliminary bibliography. *Animal Law*? That depends on the technical level of the article. You'd have to see it to decide whether the issues are presented in accessible language or in professional "legalese." *Audubon*? Here, again, the issue is audience. Is the article intended to appeal to a limited group of nature lovers, or will its content interest a broader audience?

The style and tone of a book or article should be appropriate for your level of research. If you find a source too erudite, then you'll have difficulty understanding it and presenting it to your readers. If you find that a source is written in a superficial, frivolous, or overly dramatic style, then it's not serious or authoritative enough to include in your essay.

In the case of Peter Singer's *Animal Liberation,* you've already found out from the *Current Biography* summary that his style is regarded as accessible; according to one reviewer, it was "intended for the mass market." Something can also be learned about the style and tone of a book just by considering the *publisher.* Most of Singer's books come from Oxford University Press or Cambridge University Press, but *Animal Liberation* was published by Random House, a "general interest" house eager to sell books to the general public. Finally, you open the book to a chapter that particularly interests you and glance at a few sentences:

> Becoming a vegetarian is not merely a symbolic gesture. Nor is it an attempt to isolate oneself from the ugly realities of the world, to keep oneself pure and so without responsibility for the cruelty and carnage all around. Becoming a vegetarian is the most practical and effective step one can take toward ending both the killing of nonhuman animals and the infliction of suffering upon them.

The language is clear; the sentences compelling. You hope that Singer will at some point present the arguments of the nonvegetarian and realize that, if he does not, it will be your job to find the appropriate sources and do so.

Currency

One indication of a work's usefulness for your purpose is its *date.* Only in the last few years has animal rights emerged as an issue of international importance. As a rule, in the sciences and social sciences, the most recent sources usually replace earlier ones. Unless you're interested in providing a historical review of attitudes toward animals, your research would probably focus on representative works published over the last ten or twenty years. An article about vegetarianism as practiced in the 1930s would probably be of little value to you. On the other hand, Singer's 1975 *Animal Liberation* is now regarded as a seminal work—a key influence on later writers about animal rights—and would therefore not lose currency.

For research on historical and biographical topics, you need to know the difference between *primary* and *secondary* sources.

> **A primary source *is a work that is itself the subject of your essay or (if you are writing a historical research essay) a work written during the period that you are writing about that gives you direct or primary knowledge of that period.***

"Primary source" is frequently used to describe an original document—such as the Constitution—or memoirs and diaries of historical interest, or a work of literature that, over the years, has been the subject of much written commentary. Your interview or survey notes are primary sources.

A secondary source can be any commentary written both after and about the primary source.

A history textbook is usually a secondary source. So are most biographies. While you generally study a primary source for its own sake, the secondary source is important—often, it only exists—because of its primary source.

- If you are asked to write an essay about *Huckleberry Finn,* and your instructor tells you not to use any secondary sources, you are to read only Mark Twain's novel and not consult any commentaries.

- T. E. Lawrence's *Seven Pillars of Wisdom* is a secondary source if you are interested in guerrilla warfare, but a primary source if you are studying Lawrence.

- If you read the *New York Times* to acquire information about Lawrence's desert campaign in World War I, you are using the newspaper as a primary source since it was written during the period you are studying. But when you look up a *Times* movie review of *Lawrence of Arabia,* then you are locating a secondary source in order to learn more about your primary subject.

Currency is not always essential for research about historical and biographical subjects, which usually includes primary sources. Even out-of-date secondary sources can be useful. Lowell Thomas's 1924 biography of T. E. Lawrence is still of moderate interest in part because Thomas was present during the desert campaigns and could provide firsthand (although not necessarily unbiased) information. Nevertheless, because research is always unearthing new facts about people's lives, Thomas's work has long been superseded by new biographies providing a broader range of information. *For a biographical or historical essay, you should consult some primary sources, one or two secondary sources written at the time of the event or during the subject's lifetime, and the most recent and reliable secondary sources.* It is the sources in the middle—written a few years after your target date, without the perspective of distance—that often lack authenticity or objectivity.

Evaluating books and articles shouldn't dominate your research process. If you're building a lengthy preliminary bibliography—ten or more sources—and you're writing an essay in which you anticipate that no single source will be emphasized, don't waste time looking up every author. On the other hand, if you're likely to be working with only a few key sources, invest some time in finding out about these authors and their qualifications.

EVALUATING WEB SOURCES

Finding out about *print sources*—books and periodical articles—can strengthen your research. It is useful to do so, but not always essential. Finding out about *Web sources* can be crucial to the credibility of your essay. It should become a routine part of your research practice.

You need to evaluate Web sources for two reasons:

- *An overabundance of information.* The profusion of material on the Web far exceeds the number of available print articles and books. What do you do when the keyword "animal rights" in a Yahoo search produces 137,000 Web sites? First, you narrow down your search; next, you evaluate what's left and decide which sites to access and examine.

- *An absence of editorial or peer review.* When a book or article is submitted for print publication, editors or specialist reviewers judge its quality, accuracy, and timeliness, based on their knowledge of comparable material. If the work is published, the reader can assume that it meets a reasonably high standard. There is no comparable process for reviewing most material appearing on the Web. No one at Google or Yahoo is qualified to make choices or is in charge of maintaining standards. Each of the 137,000 Web sites on animal rights is presented as equal to the rest. Even search engines that claim to rank responses do not actually do so in a meaningful way. The basis for ranking—if any—tends to be commercial, not intellectual.

One way to avoid the quagmire of endless results lists is to start your search with *academic databases that include Web material.* When a college library compiles or endorses a database, the contents are likely to be reliable. That is by no means true of databases that are compiled randomly or those that accept payment from sites in return for inclusion in search engine lists. If, initially, you don't know which databases are academic or if your access is limited to general search engines, that's all the more reason to narrow down your topic with an advanced Boolean search. Then, scan the search engine's results list looking for *Web sites sponsored by academic institutions or governmental agencies* and accessing them first. Remember that you can limit searches to sites sponsored by academic institutions if you attach site:edu to the keyword. One or two reliable, comprehensive sites can lead you, via hyperlinks, to the best material about your subject on the Web. For example, one of the links in the 137,000-hit Yahoo search on animal rights led to a Google Directory that, in turn, listed four sites, all sponsored by governmental or academic institutes, which serve as clearinghouses for Web sites about animal rights. One, from the University of British Columbia, provides thirty-four links to relevant and credible sites. Some are appropriate for a college-level essay; some are not. But they're all worth examining.

Since the Web is still a new medium and there are very few rules or standard procedures, evaluating Web sites can be a hit-or-miss process. But the categories are the same as those for evaluating works in print: credentials, impartiality, style and tone, and currency.

Credentials

As with print sources, the material's credibility greatly depends on the author's *qualifications*. If the name of the author (or *owner*) appears on the site, then you must try to find out about that person's background and credentials and determine his or her likely credibility in your area of research.

- What else has the owner published?
- Is there a section of the site specifically about the owner (often called "About Me")?
- Does the site contain a link to the owner's home page?
- Does he appear in other writers' bibliographies?
- Has she any professional experience in a discipline appropriate to this subject?

Much of the time, you'll find no single author taking responsibility for the site. Instead, there will be a *sponsoring organization*, which will probably include an "About Us" section, describing the group's collective purpose or "mission." If there's no "About" link, then it may be possible to do a Web search for more information about the sponsor.

- Is the organization commercial or nonprofit? (The "com" and "org" in the URL used to distinguish between the two, but that's no longer the rule.)
- What's the reason for creating a site about this topic?
- Is there a political or cultural agenda?
- If the sponsor is commercial, what's the motive for expending resources on this Web site?

A second element to look for is *documentation*. Appropriate documentation tells you that the author or sponsor understands the basic requirements for presenting academic scholarship; seeing bibliographical references or endnotes gives you some assurance that the information contained in the site is reliable. Documentation found in Web pages will probably consist of hyperlinks to other Web sources; you will want to click on some of these, to evaluate the quality of the linked sources and perhaps add them to your bibliography.

Impartiality

You should keep in mind that people and organizations usually create Web sites not to provide a fair, well-balanced account of an issue, but to sell something: a product, a cause, a point of view, a lifestyle. Bias isn't to be avoided on the Web; it's considered a legitimate basis for self-presentation. So you do have to scrutinize what you find, searching for the larger context behind narrow reasoning and imagining rebuttals for one-sided arguments.

As you begin to read a Web page, consider the *nature of the content*. Is it personal opinion? Is it self-serving? Is it advocacy? commercial? ideological? academic? Does the owner apparently have an ax to grind? Does the site present fact or opinion? Or does it present opinion as fact? Are you the target of propaganda for a cause or advertising for a product? Can you tell the difference between the site of a pet food company with a feature on animal welfare, that of an advocacy group organizing a rally against cruelty to animals, and that of a university veterinary department publishing a report on the use of animals in experiments?

Whatever the degree of bias, worthwhile Web material should provide reasonable support for its assertions. As you begin to read, consider the following:

- Does the site have a discernible thesis or point, or was it put on the Web purely to indulge the owner's desire for self-revelation?
- Is there a clear context established for the material?
- Does the author make an initial statement of intention, purpose, and scope?

Many sites are the spatial equivalent of a soundbite. Their authors don't engage in complex analysis and argument.

- Is there supporting evidence?
- Is there a logical sequence of ideas or just a series of claims?
- Is there a convincing level of fact and detail?
- Does the author anticipate and deal with potential objections to opinions?
- Is the evidence mostly anecdotal, depending on stories ("It happened to me")?
- Are examples and anecdotes relevant to the topic?

Don't assume that you should automatically exclude poorly supported or one-sided Web material (or print sources) from your bibliography. Rather, you should make yourself aware of the flaws in your sources and, if you choose to include them in your essay, compensate for their deficiencies by finding stronger or complementary sources so that your essay will become well balanced and well supported.

Style and Tone

In a free-wheeling medium like the Web, there are few rules about *style* or *tone*. Many sites, particularly home pages developed by individual owners or blogs, which serve as personal journals, will be presented informally, as if the writer were delivering a monologue or holding a one-sided conversation. This lack of rigor or purpose should raise some doubts as soon as you click on and start reading the site.

- Is the material *clearly focused* and *coherent*?
- Is the *tone* dispassionate, or conversational, or hysterical?
- Is the *language* inflammatory? Overly enthusiastic? Frivolous? Is it full of superlatives?

- Is the *argument* presented in neutral language, or are there slurs or innuendoes about those holding opposing views?

- Does the writer follow the basic rules of *grammar*?

- Can the material be summarized or paraphrased? Be particularly wary with blogs, as the uncredentialed blogger is likely to post self-indulgent, opinionated blather.

As with print material, it is helpful to consider the intended *audience*. Web sites frequently target niche audiences. What sort of user does a specific Web page hope to attract?

- Is the site intended for the general public? Then the content may be worth your consideration.

- Is it aimed at juveniles? If so, the approach and style are probably too simplistic to be useful for an academic essay.

- Does the author assume that the reader shares a common religious background or political assumptions? A reader unfamiliar with these beliefs or causes may find the contents hard to understand or accept.

- Is the sponsor a local group that's appealing to a grassroots audience? The site's purpose and level of detail may be so narrow that it is likely to interest only those who live in that area.

The *appearance of the site* itself can help you to evaluate the content.

- Is there any logic to its construction? Is it well designed? Easy to use? Or is it sprawling and hard to follow?

- Does it have a plan or method of organization? If it's a large site, are there links—on the home page and elsewhere—that enable you to go directly to pages that interest you?

- Are additions and updates integrated into existing material, or left dangling at the end?

- Are there graphics? Do they help your understanding of the site, or do they distract you?

Currency

In print sources, currency is estimated in *decades*; in Web sources, it's often a matter of *months or even days*. If you don't download or print material quickly, you may not have access to that information when you actually need it. The site may have disappeared from the Web. Other sites, however, will linger on even when they have lost their currency. The owners are no longer taking responsibility for regular maintenance and updating. If the subject of your essay is a current issue and you need to find and use up-to-the-minute sources, you should be very careful about checking the date at the end of each Web site. And, whatever the subject, you should note the date of the site's last update to include a complete reference to the site in your bibliography.

EVALUATING WEB SOURCES ABOUT ANIMAL RIGHTS

To demonstrate some of these evaluative criteria, let's look at a few of the hundreds of Web sites found in Google and Clusty searches using the keywords "animal rights." As is usually the case, the results list includes several commercial sites selling products totally unrelated to the subject of the search. Most of the others are sponsored by organizations or individuals actively advocating the cause of equal rights for animals and urging the public to join in protesting various instances of "speciesism." Such sites are typically crammed with news stories about animal exploitation; links to like-minded organizations; offers for products and services (often supporting vegetarianism); and invitations to participate in online discussions, attend rallies and events, and register for membership—often requiring fees or contributions—in the common cause. The range of links found in one site includes "The Joy of Adopting an Older Animal," "Featured Shelter of the Month," "Ways to Help Animals without Leaving Your Computer," "Dogs in Heaven," and "Tiny Tim—a Kitten's Story."

The home page of In Defense of Animals (Figure 8-1) is typical. Crowded with lists and choices, the site is busy and difficult to navigate. The links and

Figure 8-1. In Defense of Animals Web Site

options are all intended to educate the reader about the plight of animals and encourage participation in their defense. On the home page, pictures of animal-loving celebrities compete for space with lists of news releases and "action alerts." Various news items have been selected to inspire, inform, and touch the hearts of site visitors: the "Men and Their Cats" contest solicits inspirational essays from male cat guardians; the article "America's Vegan Bodybuilder" urges readers to overcome their dependence on animal products. There's a section for vegan nutrition, and a heartwarming story about Quentin the Dog, who escaped death at an animal shelter. The Cat Therapist will provide advice for your "feline friend." The site seems aimed at an intellectually unsophisticated audience: although some of the links are useful, most of the information on the site itself is not appropriate for research into the issues surrounding animal rights.

One of the strengths of In Defense of Animals is its emphasis on *local interests*. You're invited to join campaigns all over the world and be kept informed about activities where you live. As a medium of communication, the Web is particularly suited to this kind of grassroots appeal. It provides an international pulpit for anyone with a cause, even if the cause itself affects a relatively small number of people. In effect, the Web is serving as a community bulletin board. That's why the "animal rights" search result includes so many sites devoted to the activities of local groups. Students for Ethical Animal Treatment, for example, is the home page for a student group at Knox College; it provides details of fundraising bake sales and vegan potluck suppers. Sites like these, while admirable as grassroots operations, are little more than a distraction for researchers looking for more broadly based information.

Animal rights is a provocative topic that lends itself to a hard sell and offers no amnesty to opposing views. In fact, there are very few sites dealing with this issue that take a neutral stance. What varies is the tone in which the propaganda is presented. Consider, for example, the content and presentation of the Americans for Medical Progress (AMP) Web site (Figure 8.2). The home page contains a large picture of a pig instead of a "guardian" kissing his cat, but the overall effect of the page is less busy and confusing. Prominently featured is a straightforward statement about the organization and its purpose: to make the public aware that, "thanks to scientists' responsible and humane work with research animals, there are new advances in the prevention, diagnosis and treatment of disease and injury." There are numerous links to press releases and studies describing the medical progress that has resulted from animal research, as well as to government documents such as the "Public Health Service Policy on Humane Care and Use of Animals." The site's content has a temperate and accommodating tone.

Nevertheless, AMP doesn't rely entirely on an appeal to reason and social conscience. Understanding the emotional impact of a human interest story, the organization includes one section devoted to profiles of people—and animals—whose lives have been lengthened and transformed by animal research. Sabrina the cat, for example, recovers from cancer thanks to chemotherapy techniques

Figure 8-2. Americans for Medical Progress Web Site

developed, in part, by using animals. Whether or not Sabrina's story is suitable for citation in a research paper is open to doubt.

Although the AMP site includes a section on how to become an active advocate for animal research, it avoids the abstract question of whether violent actions are appropriate in defense of animal rights. (Some pro animal rights sites express fewer doubts.) If you intend to make this issue the focus of your research, you might gain some helpful material by clicking on the links provided on the AMP site—as long as you remain aware of the underlying bias and make an effort to balance your presentation.

Before going further, you should also click on the link "About AMP" to find out more about the *sponsoring organization*. It's reassuring that the sponsors provide an address and phone number at the bottom of the home page (many sites do not). The site's credibility is enhanced by a listing of the Board of Directors that includes some Nobel laureates; but there are also several representatives of the pharmaceutical industry, which stands to benefit a great deal from continuing to use animals in developing new drugs. On balance, this is a site that merits some cautious exploration.

Some Web sites fail to identify any author, owner, or sponsor; others do so unconvincingly. Brian Carnell at Animalrights.net tells us that he's been "following and reporting the animal rights movement for the past 8 years. Beyond that, I don't have any special credentials." Stephen Ronan's credentials for establishing a list of animal rights links on the site of the WWW Virtual Library are presented as follows: "Stephen Ronan lives in the USA. His companions of other species are, for the most part, rabbits."

In contrast, Chris MacDonald, who prepared a comparable list of links for the Center for Applied Ethics, provides a two-page biography (plus picture) that includes his academic qualifications, professional experience, research, and Web sites. Whose links are likely to inspire more confidence, Ronan's or MacDonald's? It's significant that the Center for Applied Ethics is affiliated with the University of British Columbia, while the WWW Virtual Library is described as "the oldest catalog of the web . . . run by a loose confederation of volunteers" who develop Web sites in their particular areas of expertise. The description includes an offer to anyone who's interested to prepare a site for the Virtual Library—no credentials requested or apparently required. It's this casual approach to competency that makes research on the Web so risky.

Without a doubt, it takes time and patience to evaluate Web sources. You have to inspect each site to make sure it's reliable before downloading it. Is it authoritative? Is it at an appropriate level? Will it make a contribution to your essay? And however scrupulous you may be about selecting Web sources, your research can't stop there.

> *If you want your essay to be successful and receive a commensurate grade, don't get all or even most of your sources from the Internet.*

Many important authors still publish their work only in traditional print forms. If you don't include these sources in your research, your essay will lack balance and completeness.

How will your instructor realize that your research is exclusively from the Web? In "How the Web Destroys the Quality of Students' Research Papers," Professor David Rothenberg says that "it's easy to spot a research paper that is based primarily on information collected from the Web," partly because no books are included in the bibliography. Most disturbing to Professor Rothenberg is the mindlessness of the Web research process:

> You toss a query to the machine, wait a few minutes, and suddenly a lot of possible sources of information appear on your screen. Instead of books that you have to check out of the library, read carefully, understand, synthesize and then tactfully excerpt, these sources are quips, blips, pictures, and short summaries that may be downloaded magically to the dorm-room computer screen. Fabulous! How simple! The only problem is that a paper consisting of summaries of summaries is bound to be fragmented and superficial, and to demonstrate more of a random montage than an ability to sustain an argument through 10 to 15 double-spaced pages.

There are no shortcuts to thorough research. Use the Internet as you would use any tool available to you, but try to resist its facile charms.

INTEGRATING SOURCES

So far, we've been looking at ways to evaluate sources one by one, making sure that each is worth including in your research. But sources won't appear in your essay one at a time, each in splendid isolation. They must work well together. They must be *compatible*.

Authors write for different audiences. Their work varies in tone, in style, in level of detail. As we've seen, the sources that you find on the Web or in the library may have nothing at all in common but their subject. Before you can decide which ones belong together in your essay, you need to be able to describe them. As you glance through a book, or an article, or Web material, ask yourself:

- Does the content seem primarily theoretical or practical?

- How often does the author offer concrete evidence to support conclusions? What kind of evidence? Facts? Examples? Anecdotes? Documentation?

- Does the author's thesis depend on a series of broad propositions, logically linked together?

- What is the scope of the work? Does it include many aspects of your broad subject, or does it focus on one?

- How abstract or technical is the language? Do you have difficulty understanding the sentences or following the argument?

In the end, the sources that you include in your essay should be at roughly the same *level of difficulty*. This does not mean that they should be identical: the same range of ideas, the same length, the same style and depth of evidence. But it does mean you should be able to move from one to the other easily as you write about them; you should be able to integrate them into your own approach to the subject.

Let's look at three different sources—all books—dealing with the subject of animal rights:

1. The first is an extended consideration of the arguments for and against strict enforcement of animal rights that relies heavily on philosophical abstractions to make its points; the author supports the use of animals in medical experiments.

2. The second recounts the history of the animal rights movement, taking a neutral stance. The authors rely on concrete evidence to demonstrate that animal rights campaigners are often the products of their culture.

3. The third is a sociological study of animal rights activists and their motivations. The text relies heavily on interview transcripts.

Here are excerpts from these three sources:

1. A number of authors [have] contributed to an image of humans as the great despoilers, the beings who are always out of place and can do nothing right in the natural world. Some paint an idyllic and completely unrealistic picture of pristine,

peaceful nature, beyond our blundering rapacious hands. Others exclaim despairingly that the world would be a better place without humans. . . . What these ideas have in common is a nostalgia for simpler times and a veiled lament for a lost Edenic paradise. In fact, guilt and the need for repentance through self-punishment pervade much contemporary writing on the environment and our relationship to animals. The fable of the Fall of Man has now acquired a secular guise, and a group of righteous pop environmental philosophers and animal liberationists are the new self-appointed apostles of redemption.

MICHAEL ALLEN FOX, from *The Case for Animal
Experimentation: An Evolutionary and Ethical Perspective*

2. The meat and food industry has inadvertently contributed to the anthropomorphic intuitions that drive animal protection demands. At least since Charlie the Tuna, food commercials have thoroughly personified their own products. In one commercial, two anthropomorphic cows shoot at a Lea and Perrins bottle, "the steak sauce only a cow could hate." The only speaking parts in an ad for Roy Rogers' chicken club sandwich belong to two fast-talking goldfish. Talking chickens, fish, and other animals seem clever, but they also remind sensitive viewers of the origins of their food.

JAMES M. JASPER and DOROTHY NELKIN,
from *The Animal Rights Crusade: The Growth of a Moral Protest*

3. A quietly spoken public servant, Rhett decided some years ago to take the step to animal rights activism. He claims it was the inconsistency in our treatment of animals that was the catalyst for his activism and the cause of some tension in his personal relationships:

> But I can tell you that when I was a child, I was presented with an inconsistency which always stuck in my mind. And that was that my father would never eat fowl, and at Christmas time he would always have a chop or something like that. And the reason was that when he was a child, his father brought home some chickens. The kids had made pets of them, and then they were served up for Christmas dinner. He was so upset that he refused to participate in the killing of chooks [young birds]. . . . This was when I was quite young, and I could see that he was being inconsistent, but I'm grateful for the inconsistency because if I hadn't had that example of someone who was sensitive, I mean, who knows? It might have taken me ten more years or something. I don't know.

LYLE MUNRO, from *Compassionate Beasts:
The Quest for Animal Rights*

Can these three sources be integrated into the same essay? They aren't equivalent; in many ways, they aren't even similar. But each is relevant and interesting in its own way. What you *don't* want to do is to plunk down excerpts from these three sources side by side, in adjoining sentences. Remember that your sources are your evidence. You use them to illustrate *your* ideas, your understanding of the issues involved in the animal rights movement.

The excerpt from Fox is notably abstract. He hardly touches on the issues of animal exploitation, but rather tries to interpret the significance of this growing impulse to identify with the more natural environment represented by animals.

Jasper and Nelkin are more concerned with practical cause and effect: advertising strategies portraying animals as if they were human have encouraged people to identify with the animal rights movement. It's easy to follow the examples of Charlie the Tuna and the Roy Rogers goldfish.

Rhett's personal experiences are of a very different order. He doesn't have a thesis to prove; he doesn't provide you with a topic sentence that shows you where this excerpt might be placed in your essay. It's up to you to interpret his musings and determine how—or whether—they fit in with the other sources.

How you use these three sources depends on the kind of essay you intend to write. *Will your thesis be abstract?* If you intend to emphasize the political and philosophical premises underlying this issue—do animals have the same rights that humans do?—then you'll focus your attention on Fox's book, summarizing his arguments and, in the process, figuring out what you really believe. In this way, you determine your research priorities. As you develop your thesis, you'll go on to read other books like Fox's and find many of the same ideas with new arguments and new conclusions. You'll notice that authors writing on this abstract level tend to be familiar with each other's theories and argue with each other on paper. The same names will appear again and again. Your essay will become one more voice in an ongoing dialogue.

Or are you planning a *more practical thesis*? You might be more interested in the relatively rapid emergence of this movement. Why has animal rights become such a hot issue? Is it our affluence that enables us to express concern about the plight of animals? Is it our increasing urbanization? Or is it the absence of other compelling causes? This thesis would be more "popular" in its approach to the subject and would require less rigorous sources. That doesn't diminish its value for your essay. A popularization is no more than a simplification of a difficult subject. In a sense, a college research essay has to be "popular" since it serves as evidence of a student's understanding of the subject, not as a contribution to scholarly knowledge. Your thesis would be supported by *secondary sources* like Jasper and Nelkin or by *primary sources* like the evidence of activists like Rhett.

As you develop your thesis and decide whether or not to take the popular approach, remember to consider *the level of your course*. In an introductory course, you are expected only to grasp the broad concepts that are basic to the discipline; so your instructor will probably not want you to go out of your depth in hunting scholarly sources for your essay. In an advanced course, you are preparing to do your own research; so you need to demonstrate your understanding of the work of others as well as the methods that are commonly used in that field. In an advanced course, the popular approach can be regarded as superficial.

What's crucial is that you *include in your bibliography only sources that you yourself understand*. If you come across a difficult source that seems too important to leave out, do consult your instructor, or a librarian, or the staff of the writing center on your campus. But never cite sources whose writing makes no sense to you, no matter how eminent and qualified these authorities may be.

Another consideration is *the assigned length of your essay*. If you're writing fewer than ten pages, you would be wise to limit your sources to those that blend well together because they are of the same order of difficulty. The writers don't have to agree with each other, but their scope and approach should be roughly equivalent. But in a longer essay of ten pages or more, you'll have an opportunity for leisurely development, and you can position different kinds of sources in different parts of the essay, each where it is most appropriate and where it will have the most convincing effect.

There is actually a common theme that runs through the three excerpts on animal rights. Fox writes about our generalized feelings of guilt for having plundered our natural heritage; Jasper and Nelkin imply that our anthropomorphic identification with cartoon animals has made us into guilty vegetarians; and Munro's Rhett describes his father's ambivalence about eating chicken, which brings him close to guilt by association. All three excerpts support the following paragraph, which analyzes one of the more complex motivations underlying the animal rights movement. (Note that the sources are documented using MLA style; this process of documentation will be explained in Chapter 10.)

> Animal rights activists pursue their cause with great passion and intensity, as if the fate of the Earth depended on the success of their mission. They seem to be trying to compensate for or even undo all the harm that man has done to the natural environment and particularly to its living creatures. In Michael Allen Fox's view, their yearning to return to the Garden of Eden is linked to a sense of guilt and a compulsion to atone for our culture's crimes against nature. He refers, somewhat contemptuously, to a "nostalgia for simpler times" that seems unrealistic and sentimental (20). Fox seems to be saying that we wallow too easily in a kind of Disneyland view of animals. James M. Jasper and Dorothy Nelkin support that view when they describe the anthropomorphic world of commercials in which Charlie the Tuna and the Roy Rogers goldfish become our friends (149). It's also easy to read that kind of sentimentality into the personal experience of Rhett, an animal rights activist, whose father never got over the guilt of eating the chickens that had been his pets (Munro 95).

You will have noticed that this paragraph is essentially negative about the animal rights movement, reflecting Fox's bias. (Indeed, the paragraph relies heavily on Fox's ideas, which makes sense since he offers more of them than the other authors do.) Depending on your chosen thesis, you could build on the implication that animal rights is little more than sentimental claptrap, supplying further evidence; or you could rebut Fox's point, arguing that Rhett and his father are displaying an admirable sensitivity to the needs of living creatures. Where you take these ideas is up to you; it's your essay.

Choosing Sources

As you choose sources for your essay, consider the following:

- the author's background and qualifications to write on that subject;
- the date of the work, whether it is a primary or secondary source, and (if secondary) whether its information is still timely;
- the scope of the work and the extent to which it deals with your topic;
- the depth of detail, the amount and kind of evidence presented, the documentation of sources, and the level of analysis and theory;
- the degree to which you understand and feel comfortable with the author's language and style; and
- the way in which possible sources could be used together in your essay.

EXERCISE 26: EVALUATING INTERNET SOURCES

The following passages have been excerpted from the first few pages of Web sites found in an advanced Google search using the keywords "Battle of Wounded Knee" NOT "1973." (The search was focused on the 1890 battle, rather than the demonstration that took place at the same site in 1973.) The purpose of the search was to compile a preliminary bibliography for an essay examining the extent to which the U.S. government carried out an aggressive policy of extermination against Native Americans in the nineteenth century. The Web material in this exercise was not chosen at random but represents some of the typical noncommercial sites found in the search. The excerpts have not been edited.

Read through the eight passages. Making allowances for repetition, examine the way in which each writer presents information about the Battle of Wounded Knee, paying special attention to tone and style. Consider the probable audience for which each site was intended. Then decide which sites you would read through to the end and which ones, if any, you would be likely to include in a preliminary bibliography for a 10- to 12-page essay assigned in an introductory level course.

1. After Sitting Bull's death, Big Foot feared for the safety of his band, which consisted in large part of widows of the Plains wars and their children. Big Foot himself had been placed on the list of "fomenters of disturbances," and his arrest

had been ordered. He led his band toward Pine Ridge, hoping for the protection of Red Cloud. However, he fell ill from pneumonia on the trip and was forced to travel in the back of a wagon. As they neared Porcupine Creek on December 28, the band saw 4 troops of cavalry approaching. A white flag was immediately run up over Big Foot's wagon. When the two groups met, Big Foot raised up from his bed of blankets to greet Major Samuel Whitside of the Seventh Cavalry. His blankets were stained with blood and blood dripped from his nose as he spoke.

Whitside informed him of his orders to take the band to their camp on Wounded Knee Creek. Big Foot replied that they were going that way, to Pine Ridge. The major wanted to disarm the Indians right then but was dissuaded by his scout John Shangreau, in order to avoid a fight on the spot. They agreed to wait to undertake this until they reached camp. Then, in a moment of sympathy, the major ordered his army ambulance brought forward to accept the ill Minneconjou chief, providing a warmer and more comfortable ride. They then proceeded toward the camp at Wounded Knee Creek, led by two cavalry troops with the other two troops bringing up the rear with their Hotchkiss guns. They reached the camp at twilight.

2. The events at Wounded Knee (South Dakota) on December 29, 1890, cannot be understood unless the previous 400 years of European occupation of the *New World* are taken into consideration. As Dee Brown has pointed out in *Bury My Heart at Wounded Knee* (pp. 1–2):

> "'So tractable, so peaceable, are these people,' Columbus wrote to the King and Queen of Spain [referring to the Tainos on the island of San Salvador, so was named by Columbus], 'that I swear to your Majesties there is not in the world a better nation. They love their neighbors as themselves, and their discourse is ever sweet and gentle, and accompanied with a smile; and though it is true that they are naked, yet their manners are decorous and praiseworthy.'
>
> "All this, of course, was taken as a sign of weakness, if not heathenism, and Columbus being a righteous European was convinced the people should be 'made to work, sow and do all that is necessary and to *adopt our ways*.' Over the next four centuries (1492–1890) several million Europeans and their descendants undertook to enforce their ways upon the people of the New World."

Many accounts (from both sides: US Army and Lakota) of this shameful episode exist, and many of those can be found on the Internet. The following is a brief, edited description (from *The Great Chiefs* volume of Time-Life's *The Old West* series) of events. Links to further resources and descriptions follow.

3. Wounded Knee, A Wound That Won't Heal Did the Army Attempt To Coverup the Massacre of Prisoners of War?

Historical reference material from:
The Official Bulletin National Indian War Veterans U.S.A. Section One, Section Two, Section Three and Section Four.

The Medals of Wounded Knee

Medals of dis-Honor

. . . more Medals of dis-Honor

Medals of dis-Honor Campaign
An email campaign has been initiated so as to force the U.S. Government to rescind the twenty medals of dis-Honor awarded participants in the Massacre at Wounded Knee. Your help is solicited . . . an input form is provided for your convenience

Lieutenant Bascom Gets His Due

Rescindment Petition Comments

Senator McCain Responds to the Rescindment Petition

My Response to McCain

Wokiksuye Canpe Opi . . . a site dedicated to rescindment of the "medals of dis-Honor."

4. Eyewitness to a Massacre
Philip Wells was a mixed-blood Sioux who served as an interpreter for the Army. He later recounted what he saw that Monday morning:

"I was interpreting for General Forsyth *(Forsyth was actually a colonel)* just before the battle of Wounded Knee, December 29, 1890. The captured Indians had been ordered to give up their arms, but Big Foot replied that his people had no arms. Forsyth said to me, 'Tell Big Foot he says the Indians have no arms, yet yesterday they were well armed when they surrendered. He is deceiving me. Tell him he need have no fear in giving up his arms, as I wish to treat him kindly.' Big Foot replied, 'They have no guns, except such as you have found.' Forsyth declared, 'You are lying to me in return for my kindness.'"

5. The round up of the Lakota was in response to the growing fear and ignorance on the part of the US Govt. The white people did not know about the culture, beliefs, or lives of the Lakota and saw them as a threat to the society they were trying to preserve: the white society. The Lakota were seen as outsiders; the

"other" in a world where a person's looks and background determined who belonged here. Through much of American history, where a person was born also determined if they belonged. Ironically, the Native Americans were here on this land first, but were treated as though they were visitors. Their assumption was that because they look different or act different, they are not the same; they are not Americans. The white people refused to recognize the Lakota's right to the land and did everything in their power to remove them. This ignorance led to violence in an obvious act of proving power and control.

Col. James W. Forsyth ordered the Sioux people to be disarmed. A shot was fired and the fighting ensued. The federal troops fired on the Lakota with rifles and powerful, rapid-shooting Hotchkiss guns. Sioux casualties totaled 153 dead and 44 wounded, half of whom were unarmed women and children. Survivors were pursued and butchered by US troops. Cavalry losses totaled 25 dead and 39 wounded. Charges were brought against Col. Forsyth for his part in the bloodshed, but a court of inquiry exonerated him.

At the time, and continually after, people regarded the confrontation as a massacre. This terrible blow to the Lakota people proved to break down their strength in fighting back. To subsequent generations of Indians, it "symbolized the injustices and degradations inflicted on them by the US government" (Robert Utley). It later served as an inspiration for the 1973 occupation at Wounded Knee.

We must never forget this moment in US history of the horrific destruction of human life and liberty. For many, the picture of US history is filled with tales of brave rebels, fighting for a belief in equality, such as the ideals which started and founded the nation. However, not many recognize the hypocritical actions of the nation which went against this idea of equality. This is just another example where the question of "Who belongs?" and "Who has a right to 'American' liberties?" is tested. The Lakota were never allowed a place in the nation, forced to give up their land and suffered immensely in loss of lives and rights. The Wounded Knee massacre serves as a reminder to a time when those people seen as "foreigners" were exterminated and refused their rights as Americans.

6. No one knows what caused the disturbance, no one claims the first shot, the Wounded Knee Massacre began fiercely with the Hotchkiss guns raining fragmentation shells into the village at a combined rate of 200 or more rounds a minute. The 500 well armed Cavalry Troopers were well positioned using crossing fire to methodically carry out what is known as the Wounded Knee Massacre.

Almost immediately most of the Sioux Indian men were killed. A few Sioux Indians mustered enough strength barehanded to kill 29 soldiers and wound 39 more. The bravery of these people was to no avail for as long as an Indian moved, the guns kept firing. Unarmed Sioux Indian Women and children were Mercilessly

Massacred. A few ran as far as three miles only to be chased by the long knives of the Cavalry and put to death.

Of the original 350 Indians one estimate stated that only 50 survived. Almost all historical statistics report over 200 Indians being killed on that day but government figures only reported the Indian dead as 64 men, 44 women and girls, and 18 babies. All of the bodies were buried in one communal grave.

If the Battle of the Little Big Horn had been the beginning of the end, Wounded Knee was the finale for the Sioux Indians. This was the last major engagement in American history between the Plains Indians and the U. S. Army. Gone was the Indian dream, pride and spirit.

7. The James W. Forsyth Papers document the career of a nineteenth-century military officer in the American West and, in particular, his service in the Wounded Knee campaign. The collection spans the dates 1865–1932, but the bulk of the material falls in the period 1870–98.

The collection is arranged in six series with oversize material housed at the end. Series I, Correspondence, contains letters to and from Forsyth arranged chronologically with two letterpress copybooks of similar material. Series II, Wounded Knee Papers, consists of printed papers and manuscripts documenting the actions taken on December 29 and 30, 1891. Series III, Military Papers, contains documents by and about James W. Forsyth, his son-in-law, son, and other military officers. Carte-de-visites and cabinet photographs collected by Forsyth can be found in Series IV, Photographs. Series V, Forsyth Family Papers, consists of a few items belonging to Forsyth's two daughters as well as personal papers of James W. Forsyth. Series VI, Dennison Family Papers, contains financial receipts of Governor William Dennison's family (James W. Forsyth's in-laws) and a book belonging to the governor.

8. "Sometimes dreams are wiser than waking," says Black Elk, Oglala Sioux Indian who took part in the Ghost Dance Religion during the late 19th century. The Wounded Knee epidemic took place in December 29, 1890 between the U.S. government and the Sioux Indians in South Dakota. Primarily, the outbreak occurred at Wounded Knee in part result of the growing support of the Ghost Dance Religion. Army leaders feared the religion would lead to an Indian uprising and called for troops to be sent to keep things under control. Thus, the hostilities that drug out between the U.S. government and the Sioux Indians in South Dakota are an important historical event that unfolded in U.S. western history. When reviewing the Wounded Knee battle, it is of utmost importance for various teachers who want to gain more knowledge of this epidemic that took place to fully understand insights about when, where, what, and why this battle occurred in 1890 in South Dakota. Furthermore, the Sioux Ghost Dance Religion

played a crucial role in "triggering" the hostilities and events that lead up to the Wounded Knee battle.

First, before going into depth about the history of Wounded Knee Creek battle, it is important to understand the need for history. Why do we study and need to know history? Well, David E. Kyvig and Myron A. Marty believe history is an essential part of human development: We all need to know who we are, how we have become what we are, and how to cope with a variety of situations in order to conduct our own lives successfully. We also need to know what to expect from people and institutions around us. Organizations and communities require the same self understanding in order to function satisfactorily. For individuals and groups alike, experience produces a self-image and a basis for deciding how to behave, manage problems, and plan ahead. We remember sometimes accurately, sometimes not-what occurred, the causes of certain responses or changes, and learn reactions to different circumstances. These memories, positive and negative, help determine our actions.

EXERCISE 27: CHOOSING INTERNET SOURCES

The following list of fifteen Web sites has been compiled from searches using the keywords "TV Violence." Assume that you are preparing a preliminary bibliography for an essay examining *the links between violence on television and violent crimes in American schools.* Review the list of Web sites and choose those sites that you would definitely want to explore. Be prepared to give your reasons for including or excluding each site.

Your instructor may ask you to click on some or all of the sites before you do your ranking. If many of the sites are no longer being maintained, you may be asked to do a new search on the same topic, choosing a group of sites (preferably noncommercial) and indicating those that, in your opinion, seem relevant and reliable.

1. Sociology and Philosophy Essays: TV & Violence
   http://www.magicdragon.com/EmeraldCity/Nonfiction/socphil.html
   Essays by Jonathan Vos Post, on various topics, including one on the correlation between television and violence.

2. APA HelpCenter: Warning Signs of TV Violence
   http://www.apahelpcenter.org/featuredtopics/feature.php?id=38
   The American Psychological Association and MTV team up to get important information to the nation's youth about warning signs of violent behavior, including violence in schools.

3. Children and television violence
   http://www. abelard.org/tv/tv.htm
   Abelard's front page. Violence on television affects children negatively, according to psychological research.

4. National Television Violence Study
   http://www.ccsp.ucsb.edu/ntvs.htm
   The National Television Violence Study is the "largest ongoing scientific study of television violence ever undertaken." Sponsored by the University of California at Santa Barbara.

5. The context of violence
   http://www.dailybruin.ucla.edu/db/issues/96/10.16/news.tv
   .html - 5.2KB - UCLA
   A news report in the UCLA student newspaper about a study of violence on network television conducted by the university's Center for Communication Policy.

6. TV and Film Violence
   www.cybercollege.com/violence.htm
   A brief report on the CyberCollege Internet Web site outlining the relationship between exposure to TV violence and acts of aggressiveness later in life.

7. UNESCO International Clearing House on Children and Violence on the Screen
   http://www.nordicom.gu.se/clearinghouse.php
   The Clearinghouse is to contribute to and effectivize knowledge on children, young people and media violence, seen in the perspective of the UN Convention on the Rights of the Child. Our prime task is to make new knowledge and data known to prospective users all over the world.

8. Information Packet: Violence and the Media
   http://interact.uoregon.edu/medialit/JCP/resources/violence.html
   Includes: Video Resources, Media Violence and Media Literacy, Bibliography: Children and Media, and Bibliography: Violence and Media. Source: Jesuit Communication Project, Toronto.

9. Impact of Television Violence
   http://www.ksu.edu/humec/fshs/faculty/lifespan/murray/kulaw.htm
   Questions about the effects of television violence have existed since the earliest days of this medium. Source: John P. Murray, Kansas State University.

10. Children and TV Violence
    http://www.parenthoodweb.com/articles/phw247.htm
    Children and TV Violence article from the American Academy of Child and Adolescent Psychiatry.

11. Does TV Kill?
    http://www.pbs.org/wgbh/pages/frontline/teach/tvkillguide.html
    PBS Study guide to the Frontline production of "Does TV Kill?"

12. Children and Television Violence
    http://www.allsands.com/kids/childtelevision_twd_gn.htm
    An essay on television violence and children. Copyright by Pagewise.

13. Does TV Violence Harm Youth?
    http://wildcat.arizona.edu/~wildcat/papers/old-wildcats/fall94/
    September/September1,1994/02_2_m.html

The disruptive viewings, of violence and carnage on television, can eventually take a toll on a person and the way they view life someday.

14. Telecommunications Act of 1996
    http://www.fcc.gov/telecom.html
    Full text of the Telecommunications Law is available via FTP. Source: Pub Docs US Congress.

15. Violent Media is Good for Kids
    http://www.motherjones.com/reality_check/violent_media.html
    Author Gerard Jones argues that violence in videogames and other media give [sic] children a tool to master their rage.

EXERCISE 28: EVALUATING SOURCES

Each of the following passages has been extracted from an article, Web site, or book on the general subject of *flag burning*. Many of these excerpts refer to the so-called Johnson case: during a 1984 anti–Reagan administration march in Dallas, demonstrators burned an American flag. The trial of Gregory Lee Johnson for violating a Texas law against desecrating "venerated objects" led ultimately to the 1989 Supreme Court decision that permitted flag burning as a kind of political protest. Neither a proposed act of Congress to bar flag burning nor a proposed amendment to the Constitution (1990) was successful.

A. Carefully examine the distinctive way in which each passage presents its information, noting especially:
   - the amount and kind of evidence that is cited, and how it is documented
   - the expectations of the reader's knowledge and understanding
   - the relative emphasis on generalizations and abstract thinking
   - the characteristic tone and vocabulary
   - the date of publication

B. The authors' credentials have not been provided. Take into consideration what you may already know about some of these periodicals, books, or Web sites and the audience for each. Then decide how—or whether—you would use these sources together in a single research essay exploring the symbolism of the American flag and the reactions to flag burning.

C. Write a tentative thesis for such an essay, and then decide which sources you would definitely use in writing your essay. Be prepared to justify your choice.

Note that these are *extracts* from books, articles, and Web sites: many of them may begin abruptly since space does not permit providing their full context.

1. Under what is now the prevailing view of the First Amendment, . . . men retain the right to speak as they please, regardless of the consequences of their speech, because the government is forbidden to weigh those consequences or take them

into account. Just as Congress may not make any law favoring religion, especially one religion over another, so it may not favor, or put the weight of its authority behind, one or another view of republican government. Accordingly, while Americans, out of habit, might continue to "pledge allegiance to the flag of the United States of America, and to the Republic for which it stands," the Republic itself stands for nothing in particular, which means that the flag stands for nothing in particular. This, of course, was not the view of those who designed it. For them the flag, and its ceremonies, was one of the means of promoting patriotism.

The flag carried by the Continental army in January 1776 had thirteen stripes and the British ensign in the upper left-hand corner; but, after we declared our independence in July of that year, the Continental Congress resolved that "the flag of the thirteen United States be thirteen stripes, alternate red and white: that the union be thirteen stars, white in a blue field, representing a new constellation," which is to say, a new and different kind of country. Congress later declared the "Star-Spangled Banner" to be the national anthem, and June 14 to be Flag Day, and, later still, John Philip Sousa's "Stars and Stripes Forever" was designated the national march. As Madison indicated, republican government especially requires public-spiritedness, and Congress obviously intended the celebration of the flag—on Flag Day, for example—to be one of the means of promoting it. 2

In due course, the governments of the United States and forty-eight of the fifty states enacted statutes forbidding the burning (and, generally, the desecration) of the flag. They saw it as the symbol of this new country, this *novus ordo seclorum*, a country dedicated to the principles set down in the Declaration of Independence: liberty, equality of opportunity, and religious toleration. Its friends pledge allegiance to it and salute it, and its enemies burn it. (What better way to express contempt for the country than by burning its flag, or otherwise showing disrespect for it, for example, by spitting on it or by wearing it attached to the seat of one's trousers?) And when a person was tried and convicted under one of those statutes, the Supreme Court upheld the conviction, saying, "The state [of Nebraska] may exert its power to strengthen the bonds of Union, and therefore, to that end, may encourage patriotism and love of country among its people." 3

But this was said in 1907, before the new political theory took hold. In 1984, with his friends chanting, "America, the red, white, and blue, we spit on you," one Gregory Lee Johnson burned the American flag and was convicted under a Texas statute forbidding the desecration of a venerated object; and in 1989 the U.S. Supreme Court, by the narrowest of margins, declared the statute a violation of the First Amendment. Writing for the five-justice majority, Justice William Brennan said that Johnson's act was a form of expression, that the First Amendment protects the freedom of expression, that the Texas statute was not neutral insofar as it was aimed at this particular kind of expression, and, therefore, was unconstitutional. 4

This was sufficient to dispose of the case, but Brennan went on for another five   5
pages to argue that Johnson was convicted for exercising the "freedom that this
cherished emblem represents." Like the American Civil Liberties Union, Brennan believes that the flag stands, above all, for freedom of expression, which implies that, by prohibiting Johnson from expressing himself, the state of Texas,
not Johnson, had committed an offense against the flag. His argument, although
not stated as such, takes the form of a syllogism: the flag stands for the Republic, the Republic stands for freedom of expression, therefore the flag stands for
freedom of expression.

But the First Amendment protects freedom of speech, not expression, and,   6
whereas all speech may be expression of a sort, not all expression is speech,
and there is good reason why the framers of the First Amendment protected the
one and not the other. A person can express himself in isolation, or (and it
amounts to the same thing) by burning the flag or a draft card, by denouncing
Catholics, or by marching through a Jewish neighborhood brandishing swastikas.
But speech implies a listener—one speaks *to* someone—and, as well, the willingness to be a listener in return. In a word, speech implies conversation and, in
the political realm especially, deliberation. It is a means of arriving at a decision, of
bringing people together, which requires civility and mutual respect; and in a
polity consisting of blacks and whites, Jews, Muslims, and Christians, liberals and
conservatives, and peoples from every part of the globe, civility and mutual respect are a necessity. So understood, speech is good, which is why the Constitution protects it.

Even so, the flag and country obviously stand for more than freedom of speech   7
(to say nothing of freedom of expression). Even Johnson knew this. He was part
of a group gathered "to protest the policies of the Reagan administration and
of certain Dallas-based corporations," which, of course, he was entitled to do;
indeed, he would not have been arrested—not under the statute involved—had
he burned an effigy of Ronald Reagan. (Reagan may be venerated in some quarters, but he is not a "venerated object.") Instead, he burned the flag, evidently
because he wanted to show his contempt for it and, therefore, what it stands
for. If, however, the right to speak freely, or even to express oneself, is all it
stands for, he could not have shown his contempt for it by exercising the freedom
for which it stands. In that circumstance, he would be paying tribute to it; and
that, surely, is not what he intended to do.

I do not mean to belittle the importance of freedom of speech; as I suggested   8
above, it is an essential feature of republican government. I mean only to say
that the flag stands for *everything* the country stands for, and, therefore, that Brennan's understanding of it is partial or incomplete. As such, it cannot explain why
it is, as Brennan said it was, a "cherished emblem." It cannot explain why, for example, the Marines on Iwo Jima, where some six thousand of them died fighting
for their country, raised the flag on Mount Suribachi, in fact (as we know from the

famous photograph, and especially from the Marine Corps Memorial in the Arlington National Cemetery), struggled to raise it on the only staff available to them, a piece of battlefield pipe. Nor can it explain why it was thought appropriate to drape the flag over the body of the Marine sergeant killed in the 1998 bombing of our embassy in Nairobi, Kenya, or why the embassy staff—I'm quoting the Marine Corps report—"stood erect and silent as the body was removed from the rubble and placed in a waiting vehicle." The fact is, the flag is used to express what is in the hearts and minds of most Americans on such occasions. The chief justice said as much when, in his dissenting opinion in the *Johnson* case, he spoke of "the deep awe and respect for our flag felt by virtually all of us." We are, as the chief justice suggests, emotionally attached to it.

WALTER BERNS, from Making Patriots (2001)

2. As many readers will already have detected, I believe that the Supreme Court decided the flag desecration issue correctly in 1989–90. So that all readers can be fully alerted to detect and discount my biases, I believe that it is important to set out my own views on this contentious subject. From one perspective, the 1989–90 flag desecration controversy was surely one of the greatest examples of "much ado about nothing" in American, if not world, history. The United States was not overrun with mobs of flag burners in the 1980s; as the *Tampa Tribune* pointed out on June 28, 1989, "You are likely to live a lifetime, and never see a 'dissident' burn a flag, except on television where such events are greatly welcomed. All we know about flag-burners is that they are microscopically few and seriously deficient in public-relations skills." Furthermore, there is no evidence that flag desecration threatens the flag's symbolic value. Indeed, the reaction to the Supreme Court's *Johnson* ruling suggests that from the standpoint of promoting patriotism and mass flag waving, both verbal and actual, *Johnson*'s contribution was virtually unprecedented (and certainly unheralded).

Although tolerating flag desecration is hardly likely to threaten the flag's symbolic value (or anything else), forbidding flag burning as a means of peaceful political protest will surely diminish the flag's symbolic ability to represent political freedom. As Professor Arnold Loewy has written, "Perhaps the ultimate irony is that *Johnson* has done more to preserve the flag as a symbol of liberty than any prior decision, while the decision's detractors would allow real desecration of the flag by making it a symbol of political oppression." Although the particular incident involving *Johnson* was isolated and ultimately insignificant, the principle represented by the Supreme Court's decision was absolutely fundamental to the core values of a political democracy: the right to vigorous, vehement, and even highly offensive and upsetting peaceful dissent from government policy. As Justice William Brennan summed up this key point in his *Johnson* opinion, "If there is a bedrock principle underlying the First Amendment, it is that the Government may not prohibit the expression of an idea simply because society finds the idea itself offensive or disagreeable." Or as the late Supreme Court justice Robert Jackson declared in a 1942 case (in which the Court outlawed compulsory flag salutes and recitals of the Pledge of Allegiance in public schools), in what remains probably the most eloquent and apposite paean to democratic principles ever penned by the Court:

> Those who begin coercive elimination of dissent soon find themselves exterminating dissenters. Compulsory unification of opinion achieves only the unanimity of the graveyard. . . . The case is made difficult not because the principles of its decisions are obscure but because the flag involved is our own. . . . Freedom to differ is not limited to things that do not matter much. That would be a mere shadow of freedom. The test of its substance is the right to differ as to things that touch the heart of the existing order. If there is any fixed star in our constitutional constellation, it is that no official, high or petty, can prescribe what shall be orthodox in politics, nationalism, religion or other matters of opinion.[3]

As Justice Jackson suggests, much of the controversy over the *Johnson* ruling came not from the principles at issue but because it involved the flag, and "the flag involved is our own." No serious claim would likely be made that it should be unlawful for an opponent of the 1991 American war with Iraq to burn a newspaper copy of President George Bush's explanation for this policy. Although ultimately any flag is simply a piece of cloth or other substance with colors or designs imprinted on it, many Americans have clearly invested this fabric with highly emotionally charged values. But, again to quote Justice Jackson, "A person gets from a symbol the meaning he puts into it, and what is one man's comfort and inspiration is another's jest and scorn." If there is to be any meaning to freedom of expression in the United States, it can only be that if President Bush can wave the flag as he sends troops to Panama or Iraq, then dissenters can protest that action by burning the flag. As the great civil libertarian scholar Alexander Meiklejohn has written, the true meaning of freedom of expression is that if

> on any occasion in the United States it is allowable to say that the Constitution is a good document it is equally allowable . . . to say that the Constitution is a bad document. If a public building may be used in which to say, in time of war, that the war is justified, then the same building may be used in which to say that it is not justified. If it be publicly argued that conscription for armed service is moral and necessary, it may likewise be publicly argued that it is immoral and unnecessary. If it may be said that American political institutions are superior to those of England or Russia or Germany, it may, with equal freedom, be said that those of England or Russia or Germany are superior to ours. . . . When a question of policy is "before the house," free men choose it not with their eyes shut, but with their eyes open. To be afraid of ideas, any idea, is to be unfit for self-government.[4]

In the context of this eloquent explanation of the meaning of democracy, it cannot make any difference that a flag burner speaks symbolically rather than verbally. Common sense dictates that attempts have been made to ban flag desecration because the *message* the act conveys is disliked, not because the burning of one or even a thousand flags inflicts any concrete damage or that the government has, as Justice Brennan wrote in a 1982 Supreme Court case, an "esthetic property interest in protecting a mere aggregation of stripes and stars for its own sake." As Senator James McClure told his colleagues on July 18, 1989, the real offense committed by flag desecrators was that "no other act" could "enrage citizens of this country more during a protest situation."[5]

4

ROBERT GOLDSTEIN, from *Burning the Flag: The Great 1989–1990 American Flag Desecration* (1996)

[3] Arnold Loewy, "The Flag Burning Case: Freedom of Speech When We Needed It Most," *University of North Carolina Law Review* 68 (1989): 174; *Texas v. Johnson*, 491 U.S. 397, 414 (1989); *W.Va. Bd. of Education v. Barnette*, 319 U.S. 624, 641–42 (1943).

[4] *Barnette*, 632–33; Alexander Meiklejohn, *Free Speech and Its Relation to Self-Government* (New York: Harper, 1948), 27.

[5] *Kime v. U.S.*, 459 U.S. 949, 953 (1982); *CR* (1989), p. S8106.

3. The flag and reverence toward it are central to popular images of patriotic devotion. In spite of this tight association, it is evident that patriotism and flag-centered rituals are quite distinct phenomena. This is not to say that the flag may not play an important role for patriots, but concern for the flag and expressions of reverence for it are not the same as patriotism.

1

One might wonder why we need the flag at all and why there must be holidays and other ritualized occasions for the expression of patriotic feeling. This kind of anti-ritual challenge is not one that I would embrace. We need ways to express and affirm our public values. Rituals and holidays can serve to provide these occasions and to strengthen our sense of connectedness with people who share these values. Rituals can keep alive a sense of history and help us to rededicate ourselves to our ideals. Flags, monuments, and holidays can all play a role in expressing, sustaining, and transmitting worthwhile attitudes and ideals. Saluting the flag may help to instill a commitment to the values of "liberty and justice for all" and to assure them a central place in the country for which the flag stands.

2

Nonetheless, we know that rituals may become empty, mechanical, and meaningless. Because they are performed according to a schedule, they can become mere habits that are not so much expressions of attitudes as substitutes for them. They may come to lack the spontaneity that animates our most genuine expressions of feeling. In addition, because rituals can be performed apart from the feelings they are supposed to express, they can be performed insincerely.

3

They are subject to hypocrisy and to manipulation. As the visible signs of attitudes, they can be mistaken for the attitudes themselves and can lead us to lose sight of the values they are meant to affirm.

All these problems arise in connection with ritualized patriotism. Flag salutes, parades, and overt expressions of dedication to the country may come to take the place of genuine love and commitment. The result is an explosion of public avowals of patriotism that may or may not reflect genuine concern about the well-being of the country and its inhabitants. The visible signs of patriotic commitment may replace actual commitment.   4

To make these points is not to devalue patriotic rituals. We need publicly shared ways of expressing our values. Nonetheless, we need to be wary of both fake and shallow expressions of patriotism. Fake expressions are used by hypocrites who "wrap themselves in the flag," portraying themselves as patriots in order to advance their personal goals and interests. Shallow expressions are genuinely felt but are not backed by a willingness to promote the country's well-being when doing so requires personal sacrifice.   5

If we . . . equate patriotism with its ritualized expressions, then we can no longer differentiate genuine patriotism from fake and shallow patriotism. That such a distinction exists is quite evident, however, and provides a basis for arguing that ritualized patriotism is insufficient as a mark of genuine commitment to one's country.   6

STEPHEN NATHANSON, from *Patriotism, Morality, and Peace* (1993)

4. Patriots also increasingly turned to vigilante justice [during World War I]. "The   1
victims of mob violence were varied," recalled the IWW organizer Elizabeth Gurley Flynn, including: "Christian ministers, Negro and white, advocates of peace on religious, moral or political grounds; Socialists, IWWs, members of the Non-Partisan League . . . [and] friends of Irish freedom." Gurley also described how "inoffensive Germans, residents of this country for years, parents of American-born children, were suspected as potential 'spies' and attacked merely for being German."[62] Typical of individuals who took the law into their own hands, a Milwaukee marine placed a man in his own custody after hearing him make disparaging remarks about the flag.[63] Similarly, a group in Santa Cruz, California, made a man accused of "insult[ing] the colors" kneel on the sidewalk and "kiss the flag."[64] At a New York supper club, an angry crowd surrounded and attacked a former reporter for a socialist newspaper and two suffragists after they refused to stand when a band played the "Star-Spangled Banner." Later, the diners turned the three over to the police on charges of disorderly conduct.[65] Numerous states responded to the rise of such public incidents by dramatically stiffening their penalties for flag desecration. Texas passed a "disloyalty act" in 1918, raising its

prewar penalty of thirty days in jail for desecrating a flag to twenty-five years. No longer limited to actual acts of desecration, the new law applied to anyone who used "any language," privately or publicly, that "cast contempt" on the Stars and Stripes.[66]

Undivided loyalty became the watchword of "true Americans." The Department of Justice issued a warning to all new immigrants that they would be arrested immediately if they abused the American flag.[67] But the wrath of the courts was not directed solely at immigrants; it also extended to native-born, ethnic Americans. In a typical case, a New York judge sentenced a native-born man of German descent to twenty days in the county jail for "using profane language in reference to the American colors." The man's denial of disloyalty fell on deaf ears despite his four years of service in the U.S. army and his appearance in court wearing a U.S. flag on his jacket lapel.[68] In Illinois, vigilantes took people from their homes and forced them to publicly profess their loyalty, and a volunteer of the county council of defense in Tulsa, Oklahoma, shot a waiter for allegedly making pro-German statements. When the jury returned a not-guilty verdict at his trial, the courtroom broke into cheers. In Missouri, Robert Paul Prager, a German by birth, became another victim of patriotic murder after he talked to fellow miners about the merits of socialism. A mob went after Prager, stripped him of his clothes, and wrapped an American flag around his body. When the police rescued him, the mob simply broke into jail and hung Prager on the outskirts of town for allegedly being a German spy.[69]

In 1918, Kansas convicted Frederick Shumaker Jr. for insulting the Stars and Stripes while visiting a blacksmith's shop. Among the evidence marshaled against him was a witness's report that months earlier, when Shumaker had seen flags flying at half-mast, he had said, "What in hell is going on? I see you got the rags on the poles." The Kansas Supreme Court upheld his conviction on the grounds that any "man who uses such language" lacked the kind of respect "that should be found in the breast of every citizen."[70] The court maintained that the blacksmith's shop constituted a public space, and according to the Kansas flag statute, any language that "cast contempt" on the flag in public was against the law.[71] The exercise of political power through institutions of the nation-state increasingly took precedence over liberal ideas of individual freedom. Only a few years earlier, George M. Cohan had used the word *rag* in his wildly popular song "You're a Grand Old Rag." But by the time of Shumaker's trial the mood of the country had changed. Cohan himself briefly came under criticism when a theater critic complained about the song's title. Cohan promptly changed the wording and said that he had not intended it to be unpatriotic, but to describe how the flag had become "splendidly tattered after valiant service." But intent no longer mattered.[72]

The cult of the flag became the common sense of the nation. In a Socialist parade in Massachusetts, a red flag with the words "Finnish Socialist Branch" earned a man a prison sentence for violation of a state statute that prohibited parading with a red flag or carrying a placard with an inscription that could be construed as against the government.[73] In Montana, a court convicted E. V. Starr in 1918 for the crime of sedition after he refused to kiss an American flag. When attacked, Starr retorted, "What is this thing anyway? Nothing but a piece of cotton with a little paint on it and some other marks in the corner there. I will not kiss that thing. It might be covered with microbes." For his abusive language, the court sentenced him to the state penitentiary for up to twenty years of hard labor. When Starr appealed his case, Judge Bourquin reluctantly decided that he could not legally reverse the lower court's decision despite its "horrifying" sentence. The judge's sympathies went to the appellant, whom he believed "was more sinned against than sinning." In the judge's opinion, the mob had descended into the kind of "fanaticism" that "incited the massacre of St. Bartholomew, the tortures of the Inquisition, the fires of Smithfield, [and] the scaffolds of Salem."[74]

CECILIA O'LEARY, from *To Die For: The Paradox of American Patriotism* (1999)

[62] Elizabeth Gurley Flynn, *The Rebel Girl, an Autobiography: My First Life, 1906–1926*, new rev. ed. (New York: International Publishers, 1973), 229–30.

[63] "Marine Punishes Man," *Milwaukee Sentinel*, 24 April 1917, 1.

[64] "Insulter of Flag Is Made to Kiss It," *San Francisco Examiner*, 17 April 1917, 8.

[65] "Diners Resent Slight to the Anthem," *New York Times*, 7 April 1917, 3.

[66] The Texas "disloyalty act" remained in effect until 1973. During an anti–Viet Nam War protest, this law was used to sentence a man to a four-year prison term for burning a flag (Goldstein, *Saving "Old Glory,"* 80).

[67] "Aliens Warned against Desecrating American Flag," *New York Times*, 10 April 1917, 4.

[68] "Twenty Days for Insult to Flag," ibid., 8.

[69] Peterson and Fite, *Opponents of War*, 200–203.

[70] "The State v. Shumaker, 9 November 1918, no. 21,894," in *Reports of Cases Argued and Determined in the Supreme Court of the State of Kansas, April 7, 1918–December 31, 1918*, 103 (1919; Topeka: Kansas State Printing Office, 1919), 741–43.

[71] Rosenblatt, "Flag Desecration Statutes," 212–13; "The State v. Shumaker, 9 November 1918, no. 21,894," 741.

[72] John McCabe, *George M. Cohan: The Man Who Owned Broadway* (Garden City, N.Y.: Doubleday, 1973), 74–75.

[73] Curtis, *The Constitution and the Flag*, vol. 1, *The Flag Salute Cases*, xxiv–xxv.

[74] Ex parte Starr, District Court, D. Montana, 31 January 1920, no. 794, in *The Federal Reporter: Cases Argued and Determined in the Circuit Courts of Appeals and District Courts of the United States and the Court of Appeals of the District of Columbia, May–June, 1920*, 263 (St. Paul: West Publishing, 1920), 145–47.

5. Semiotics is the study of signs and the transmission of their meaning. While language appears to be the most conspicuous form of communication, semiotics directs attention to other types of signification in society and culture, assuming that *all* social actions are symbolic. From a semiotic point of view, a sign actually is not a *thing*; rather, it is a *representation* of something else. "By a sign is meant a three-termed relation formed when, for somebody, something (the signifier) stands in for something else (the signified) in some context (the ground)" (Mann, 1984:350; Eco, 1976; Gottdiener, 1995; C. S. Pierce, 1931; Saussure, 1966; Sperber, 1974). Culture serves as the context unifying the signifier with the signified, thus enabling the sign to be communicated clearly. More to the point for our analysis, it is through power relations in culture that meanings are constructed and manipulated (Barthes, 1967; Foucault, 1979). By the same cultural process, Barthes (1967) and Levi-Strauss (1963) demonstrate that myths, considered second-order systems of signification, also are shaped by the influence of power. The impact of semiotics on sociology is found in the work of Durkheim (1933 [1964]) who proposed that myths are compelling forces in social organization, particularly in the formation of collective representations of consciousness. Similarly, Marx (1867 [1967]) situated the role of myths in the construction of ideologies which are hierarchical symbolic systems propelled by political and economic imperatives, stratifying society into producers and consumers of culture (Gottdeiner, 1995; see Baudrillard, 1983; Derrida, 1976; Kevelson, 1990; Milovanovic, 1988).

At its most basic level of interpretation, the American flag signifies patriotism. Still, at a higher level of abstraction, Old Glory has been transformed from a secular object of nationalism into a sacred icon through an elaborate cultural process involving civil religion (see Bellah, 1988). As we shall explore further in Chapters 2 and 3, the Stars and Stripes is a cultural product of mythmaking and is embodied in such popular legends as Betsy Ross and General George Washington. Due to its sacred quality, the flag enjoys a degree of prestige not common in other national emblems, such as the bald eagle and the Statue of Liberty. It is precisely Old Glory's venerated status that makes its destruction such a potent form of protest and resistance; indeed, flag *desecration*—a religious term—often is likened to iconoclasm, the act of vandalizing holy symbols. According to Congressman Douglas Applegate:

> Yes, the flag is, in my estimation, an icon defined as an object of critical devotion. As such, it should not be destroyed for any reason by iconoclasts. . . . As a comparison, if one attempted to overthrow or destroy the Republic, we would be tried for treason and if found guilty, would be executed. While I do not suggest this punishment for those convicted of burning or desecrating the flag, I do expect some restitution or punishment that fits the crime that I believe it is. (*CR*, July 20, 1989:E2593)

In expanding our appreciation for a semiotic approach to vexillogy—the study   3
of flags the flag—let us also consider the ontological implications. As a branch
of metaphysics, ontology explores the nature of being, or essence, and in what
form things actually exist, if at all (Runes, 1968). Ontologically, the flag's essence
is significant because it is treated as much more than a mere symbol of American patriotism, liberty, and freedom. The crusade to protect the Old Glory has
struggled to transform the symbol into a *thing*, a process called reification. Political commentator Sidney Blumenthal insightfully observed, "The Republicans,
post-Reagan, adhere to a literalist faith in the power of elemental national symbols" (Blumenthal, 1990:13). Consider the thoughts by Representative Newt
Gingrich (GOP, Georgia) who argued: "It's a very real issue because symbols matter" (quoted in Blumenthal, 1990:13). Grasping to comprehend the Republican
party's ontology, Blumenthal concluded: "By this logic, an issue exists because a
sign exists, making the issue a projection of a symbol, not the symbol the reflection of an issue" (Blumenthal, 1990:13; see Hitchens, 1997).

MICHAEL WELCH, from *Flag Burning: Moral Panic*
and the Criminalization of Protest (2000)

6. Who can deny the exceptional importance of the national flag in the hearts   1
   and minds of contemporary Americans—or in their visible landscape? Indeed,
   "for many Americans the flag is literally a sacred object" ("Who Owns the Stars
   and Stripes?," *Time*, 1976:15), and "the flag . . . is a symbol so charged with emotion that people cannot look at and judge, even, whether or not the design
   is aesthetically good or bad" (Pullen, 1971:184). In part, as a prominent student
   of flag lore has suggested, this is because "our nation lacks both a royal family
   and a single dominant religion. Hence, in searching for an encompassing symbol, the majority have traditionally rallied around the flag. We invented—the first
   people to do so—an annual Flag Day. Our children pledge allegiance to the flag.
   . . . Unquestioning loyalty to the flag has been considered a fundamental American principle" (Whitney Smith as quoted in Wolfe, 1975:61). And among some
   segments of the population flag fetishism has gone well beyond the threshold
   of hysteria (Balch, 1890; L. Harris, 1971; Woelfly, 1914). Although we lack the
   detailed research to confirm the notion, I am inclined to accept the statement
   that "the flag has always occupied a much stronger place in American life and
   mythology than have flags in other countries" ("Who Owns the Stars and
   Stripes?," *Time*, 1976:15), except perhaps for the word "always." It may not be too
   extreme to argue that, as *the* organizing symbol of our nation-state and of the
   Americanism that is its civil religion, the flag has preempted the place, visually and
   otherwise, of the crucifix in older Christian lands.

   Is the United States unique among the countries of the world in its obses-   2
   sion with its national flag, and, specifically, in the propensity to display it in pub-

lic places? In lieu of published data or a methodical worldwide survey, any answer must be provisional. I have the impression that the combination of green, white, and red—the order in which they appear on the Italian flag—has been used with increasing frequency recently to denote things Italian in signs and advertisements within the United States. But from the scattered information and recollections available to me, my guess is that the only countries that rival America in the frequency with which the citizenry exhibit the flag of their own free will may be the Scandinavian (Lassen, 1985) and especially Sweden (Abler, 1983; Hägerstrand, 1984; Leighly, 1985), where the national colors (blue and yellow) are conspicuously presented on a great variety of objects. Many Swedish homes and vacation cottages are equipped with flagpoles from which the national flag is flown frequently, but rather more in the spirit of hospitality than nationalism (Hägerstrand, 1984). The Swedish flag code is almost as elaborate as the American, and flag display is prescribed for no fewer than sixteen holidays, religious as well as national. The incidence of national and provincial flags in Canada is significant, but well below the level of its southern neighbor. I recall seeing very few flags of any sort, except in government installations, in Mexico, Central America, Great Britain, and Ireland during my travels there; and I am told that the private display of the national flag in both Brazil (Schiller, 1982) and Australia (Albinski, 1985) is exceedingly uncommon. In the course of several thousand kilometers of highway and ship travel through Germany, France, Belgium, Switzerland, and Turkey during the summer of 1983, I took special pains to note flags along the way. In the case of West Germany, I did not observe a single national flag aside from those on naval and merchant ships and government buildings; and very few were visible in the other countries, with the single interesting exception of Switzerland. In that land a fair number of private residences fly the red-and-white national banner, but the frequency of such displays is well below the modest level to be seen in Canada and, presumably, Sweden.

WILBUR ZELINSKY, from *Nation into State: The Shifting Symbolic
Foundations of American Nationalism* (1988)

7. JOINT RESOLUTION

Proposing an amendment to the Constitution of the United States authorizing the Congress and the States to prohibit the physical desecration of the flag of the United States.

Whereas the flag of the United States of America is a national symbol of such stature that it must be kept inviolate;

Whereas the physical desecration of the flag should not be considered constitutionally protected speech; and

Whereas physical desecration may include, but is not limited to, such acts as burning, mutilating, defacing, defiling or trampling on the flag, or displaying the flag in a contemptuous manner: Now, therefore, be it

Resolved by the Senate and the House of Representatives of the United States of America in Congress assembled (two-thirds of each House concurring therein), That the following article is proposed as an amendment to the Constitution of the United States, which shall be valid to all intents and purposes as part of the Constitution when ratified by the legislatures of three-fourths of the several States within seven years after the date of its submission for ratification:

ARTICLE—

"The Congress and the States shall have power to prohibit the physical desecration of the flag of the United States."

> *Constitutional amendment sponsored by President Bush to legalize forbidding flag desecration in response to the Supreme Court's* Texas v. Johnson *ruling.*

SEC. 2. CRIMINAL PENALTIES WITH RESPECT TO THE PHYSICAL INTEGRITY OF THE UNITED STATES FLAG

(a) IN GENERAL.—Subsection (a) of section 700 of title 18, United States Code, is amended to read as follows:

"(a)(1) Whoever knowingly mutilates, defaces, physically defiles, burns, maintains on the floor or ground, or tramples upon any flag of the United States shall be fined under this title or imprisoned for not more than one year, or both.

"(2) This subsection does not prohibit any conduct consisting of the disposal of a flag when it has become worn or soiled."

(b) DEFINITION—Section 700(b) of title 18, United States Code, is amended to read as follows:

"(b) As used in this section, the term 'flag of the United States' means any flag of the United States, or any part thereof, made of any substance, of any size, in a form that is commonly displayed."

SEC. 3 EXPEDITED REVIEW OF CONSTITUTIONAL ISSUES

Section 700 of title 18, United States Code, is amended by adding at the end the following:

"(d)(1) An appeal may be taken directly to the Supreme Court of the United States from any interlocutory or final judgment, decree, or order issued by a United States district court ruling upon the constitutionality of subsection (a).

"(2) The Supreme Court shall, if it has not previously ruled on the question, accept jurisdiction over the appeal and advance on the docket and expedite to the greatest extent possible."

> *Text of the Flag Protection Act of 1989,*
> *Public Law No. 101-131, 103 Stat. 777*
> *(amending 18. U.S.C. §700 [Document One]).*

8. National symbols, once locked in place, are rarely judged for what they are. They are simply there, adopted or inherited, sometimes just tolerated, collective heirlooms that represent a country's unity, its identity, its memory and its ideals. 1

Or not—as the case may be. In Russia this month, the Parliament summarily dropped one national anthem adopted during democracy for another written under Communism, thus opening another chapter in the long debate over Russia's national identity. 2

"You can't judge a nation by one symbol, but you can make a judgment about competing symbols," said Richard Wortman, professor of history at Columbia University and author of "Scenarios of Power: Myths and Ceremony in Russian Monarchy" (Princeton University Press, 1995). The battle of Russia's two anthems—at this point, both of them wordless melodies—sum up conflicting attitudes toward Russia's Communist past. Some say the Soviet anthem should be stricken from official memory because of Communism's terrible crimes, while others say it should not be forgotten because of glorious moments like the victory over Hitler in World War II or Yuri A. Gagarin's first flight in space. That is a lot of meaning packed into one tune—albeit a great thumping one. 3

Of course, nations struggling to create a new identity or character are not the only ones where a hummable tune or a colorful scrap of material are endowed with such power. 4

No issue galvanized South Carolina politics quite as much in recent years as whether the Confederate flag should fly atop the State House in Columbia. Did it symbolize slavery, as many claimed, or was it a piece of benign memorabilia from Southern history, a proud emblem of states' rights, as others insisted? When the state legislature voted to remove it last May, some commentators said it was not because the issue was resolved but because politicians and their constituents had grown weary of the endless debate. 5

"Some of the most active debates we have had in recent years are struggles over what we want our symbols to represent, over how we want to remember our past," said Cecilia O'Leary, a professor of history at California State University at Monterey Bay and the author of "To Die For: The Paradox of American Patriotism" (Princeton University Press, 1999). American national symbols are particularly potent. "Unlike other countries, the question of national cohesion and identity has always been problematic," said Michael Frisch, professor of history and American studies at the State University College at Buffalo. "In America, national identity is more political than genetic, and thus the function of civil religion, which gives the country that identity, is extremely important." 6

Mr. Frisch compares Betsy Ross to the Virgin Mary in that, blessed by the father (George Washington), she gives birth to the American flag. "The flag itself was not quite powerful enough to shape the symbol," he said. "It was the coming together of the flag with the woman that gives it its unique power." 7

CELESTINE BOHLEN, from "O Say Can You See What That
Flag Means?" *New York Times* (12/16/2000)

9. The most sacred of sacred American cows is Old Glory—the American flag.   1
Indeed, it is more sacred than the Bible, the cross, or any other symbol of American piety. There are no major movements afoot to elevate religious symbols
above the First Amendment. But millions of Americans—and not a few oppor-
tunistic politicians—would like to see the Constitution amended to protect the
flag from desecration.

The flag is a symbol of patriotism, a supposed virtue that most people sel-   2
dom challenge. The question of one's patriotism rarely comes up except during
preparations for war. No one questions the patriotism of those willing to go to
war whenever the commander-in-chief deems it necessary. But in a climate of
war, exercising one's First Amendment right to disagree is considered dangerously unpatriotic. Paradoxically—and hypocritically—freedom of thought and
freedom of expression come to appear disgracefully anti-American.

To most Americans, the flag represents freedom and democracy. To others,   3
it stands for White supremacy, U.S. imperialism, aggressive militarism, and the like.
Frederick Douglass believed that though African Americans had done so much to
make America great, "every star in" the American flag "was against us."

Similarly, shortly after September 11, 2001, Katha Pollitt wrote a column in *The*   4
Nation in which she linked the flag to militarism and Christian fanaticism. She
would not allow her thirteen-year-old daughter to fly an American flag out their
living room window. Rabid pro-flag zealots harshly criticized Pollitt; some inun-
dated her daughter with unsolicited American flags. To many patriots, trying to
force patriotism down Americans' throats is both a wonderful virtue and a time-
honored practice.

In truth, America, like every other nation, has its good and bad points. It is a   5
land of great opportunity, scientific progress, impressive technology, athletic excellence, musical talent, and so on. However, it is also a land of poverty, discrimination, and police brutality. Most Americans love the nation despite its faults.
Others profess to hate it despite its strengths.

As quietly as it's kept, one might love the United States and hate the flag. One   6
need only look to the Christian religion to understand this. Most Christians apparently identify with the Cross or crucifix. Others, however, find the symbol distasteful. They say it is like hanging a small gun or a small electric chair around
one's neck to commemorate the loss of a loved one. Should Christians with such
views be deemed un-Christian? Similarly, if a person loves the United States but
associates the flag with injustice, is that person necessarily un-American?

Whether one accepts the flag is a very superficial way to determine one's com-   7
mitment to the United States. Love for and devotion to one's country is what being patriotic means. The flag might be a symbol of one's love for the United
States, but it is not the only symbol—nor is it necessarily the best.

NORM R. ALLEN, from "True Patriotism,"
in *Free Inquiry* (Jun./Jul. 2004)

10. Flag Burning and Other Acts Deemed Disrespectful of American Symbols

The Issue: Does the First Amendment allow the government to punish individuals who mutilate flags, burn draft cards, or engage in other acts deemed disrespectful of patriotic symbols?

Introduction

"Symbolic expression" is a phrase often used to describe expression that is mixed with elements of conduct. The Supreme Court has made clear in a series of cases that symbolic expression (or expressive conduct) may be protected by the First Amendment. Several of these cases have been highly controversial—perhaps none more so than *Texas vs Johnson* (1990) reversing the conviction of a man who expressed his strong displeasure with U.S. policy by burning an American flag.

It was a case involving the burning of another symbol, however, in which the Supreme Court announced the test it would use to analyze expressive conduct cases. Paul O'Brien's burning of his draft card led to his conviction for the "knowing destruction or mutilation" of a draft card. The Supreme Court, over only one dissent, affirmed O'Brien's conviction, but in so doing offered a test that would later be used to protect other protesters. Specifically, the Court said that a law regulating expressive conduct would be upheld only if it furthered an important governmental objective unrelated to the suppression of speech, was narrowly tailored to achieve the government's legitimate objective, and the law left open ample alternative means for expression. In O'Brien's case, the Court found the law to be narrowly tailored to its important objective of "smooth and efficient functioning of the selective service system." (Many commentators were critical of the Court's decision, arguing that the law was really an attempt to suppress a dramatic form of anti-war speech.) . . .

Finally, the Court addressed the highly emotional issue of flag burning. In *Texas vs Johnson*, it reversed Gregory Johnson's conviction for burning an American flag during the 1984 Republican National Convention. The Court concluded that the flag burning was "speech" and again determined that the flag desecration statute was aimed at the communicative impact of Johnson's message. The Court noted, however, that speech-neutral laws, such as those applicable to public burning generally, might be constitutionally applied against flag burners. The next term the Court again confronted the flag burning issue, this time to consider the constitutionality of the Federal Flag Protection Act of 1989, passed by a Congress unhappy with the Court's decision in *Johnson*. The Court again ruled for the protester, a man who set fire to a flag on the steps of the U.S. Capitol, finding that the act was an attempt to suppress unpopular speech. The Court's decisions in the flag burning cases has led to numerous attempts to pass a constitutional amendment authorizing punishment of flag burning and mutilation, but so far

1

2

3

the proposed amendment has fallen short of the two-thirds support necessary in the Senate.

"Exploring Constitutional Conflicts"
http://www.law.umkc.edu/faculty/projects/
ftrials/conlaw/flagburning.htm

11.

The Flag Burning Page

Before you go any further, you have to read this. And you have to understand it. Don't just click "OK" without reading it.   1

I'm not a flag burner. I don't plan to burn the flag. I respect the flag. I even agree with people who say that flag burning is ineffective, mis-directed, or "improper."   2

I'm not "Anti-America."   3

Some people choose to burn the flag. It is a controversial topic because some people are offended by that action. Supreme Court rulings have upheld that peaceful flag desecration is a form of political speech that should be protected by our Constitution. I agree.   4

So I'm not even trying to change anything. I like these laws the way they are. I'm not fighting, or rallying, or trying to mess things up. I'm trying to keep them "American."   5

Some people would like peaceful political protestors who burn the flag to be thrown in prison. That's not the kind of action that a "free country" takes.   6

The worst part of all is that we can't pass and enforce laws against flag burning unless we modify the U.S. Constitution and remove an important part of the First Amendment.   7

Some people are trying to do just that. And if the only reason is to stop a few "hippie protestors" from burning flags, it's a very mis-directed effort. They claim they want to "protect the flag," but the reason most flag-burning protestors burn the flag is to protest flag-burning laws. Very few people protest against wars and taxes by desecrating the flag. It's time our Senators just let the issue drop.   8

Allright. Now you know how I feel. I have put this site together as a resource for people who are doing research for school about Texas v Johnson, flag desecration, or the Supreme Court. It contains a lot of history, a bibliography, some essays and editorial cartoons, and a bunch of other stuff. It's for people who are interested in flag burning laws, the actions of the Senate, and whether they can legally throw away those little flags they bought for their car windows.   9

from http://www.esquilax.com/flag/

EXERCISE 29: COMPARING SOURCES

In the middle of the night of November 29, 1942, a Boston nightclub called the Cocoanut Grove burned down, resulting in the deaths of at least 300 people. Read the following three accounts of this disaster, and be prepared to discuss the differences in content, organization, tone, purpose, and point of view. What is the thesis of each article? Consider how you would use the three articles in a single research essay dealing with the Cocoanut Grove disaster. Are these three variations interchangeable?

NEW YORK TIMES, 30 NOVEMBER 1942

300 KILLED BY FIRE, SMOKE AND PANIC IN BOSTON RESORT— DEAD CLOG EXITS—Terror Piles Up Victims as Flames Suddenly Engulf Nightclub—Service Men to Rescue—Many of Them Perish—Girls of Chorus Leap to Safety—150 Are Injured

BOSTON, Sunday, Nov. 29—More than 300 persons had perished early this morning in flames, smoke and panic in the Cocoanut Grove Night Club in the midtown theatre district.   1

The estimate of the dead came at 2 a.m. from William Arthur Reilly, Fire Commissioner, as firemen and riggers searched the ruins for additional bodies. It was a disaster unprecedented in this city.   2

The chief loss of life resulted from the screaming, clawing crowds that were wedged in the entrance of the club. Smoke took a terrific toll of life and scores were burned to death.   3

At the Boston City Hospital officials said there were so many bodies lined up in corridors that they would attempt no identifications before daybreak.   4

Commissioner Reilly stated that an eyewitness inside the club said the fire started when an artificial palm near the main entrance was set afire.   5

Martial law was clamped on the entire fire area at 1:35 a.m. Sailors, Coast Guardsmen, shore patrolmen and naval officers dared death time and again trying to get at bodies that were heaped six feet high by one of the entrances.   6

Firemen said that many bodies were believed to have fallen into the basement after the main floor collapsed.   7

A chorus boy, Marshall Cook, aged 19, of South Boston, led three co-workers, eight chorus girls and other floor show performers totaling thirty-five to an adjoining roof from the second-floor dressing rooms and from there they dropped to the ground from a ladder.   8

Scores of ambulances from nearby cities, the Charlestown Navy Yard and the Chelsea Naval Hospital poured into the area, but the need for ambulances became so great that even railway express trucks were pressed into service to carry away   9 victims. At one time victims, many of them dead, lay two deep in an adjoining garage.

Many of the victims were soldiers, sailors, marines and Coast Guardsmen, some 10 of them junior officers, visiting Boston for a weekend of merrymaking. In the throng were persons who had attended the Holy Cross–Boston College football game.

Scores of dead were piled up in the lobbies of the various hospitals as the doc- 11 tors and nurses gave all their attention to the 150 injured.

A "flash" fire, believed to have started in the basement, spread like lightning 12 through the dance floor area, and the panic was on. All available nurses and priests were being called into the disaster area.

Among the dead were a marine and one who appeared to be a fireman. Casual- 13 ties were arriving at hospitals so rapidly that they were being placed in the corri- dors wherever a suitable place could be found.

It appeared probable that the greatest loss of life was in the newly opened lounge 14 of the night club in Broadway. Here, one policeman said, burned and suffocated per- sons were heaped to the top of the doors, wedged in death.

The night club was a one-and-a-half story building with a stucco exterior. The 15 blaze was said to have broken out in the basement kitchen at 10:17 p.m. just as the floor show performers were preparing for their next performance. Performers on the second floor were met by terrific smoke and flame as they started downstairs. Their stories were the only ones available, as those who had escaped the dance floor and tables were too hysterical to talk.

A temporary morgue and hospital were set up in the garage of the Film Exchange 16 Transfer Company at the rear of the club in Shawmut Street. At least fourteen per- sons, suffocated and lying in grotesque positions, were lying on the garage floor at one time, while scores of injuries were cared for by garage workers and others.

The city's Civilian Defense Workers were called to the scene to maintain order 17 and to give first aid to those suffering from burns and smoke inhalation. Every hos- pital in the area soon was loaded with the victims.

At least thirty-five performers and their friends were rescued by the quick actions 18 of Marshall Cook, a South Boston boy. He was met by a blast of flame as he started down stairs, went back to the dressing room and organized those caught there.

He then smashed his way through a window, carrying away the casing. Through 19 this opening he led a group to an adjoining room, where a small ladder was found. The ladder was not long enough to reach the street, but Cook and several other male performers held the top end over the roof's edge and guided the women over the side. They had to jump about 6 feet to reach the ground.

At the City Hospital bodies were piled on the floors, many so burned that there 20 was no attempt to identify them immediately. Many service men were among the victims, many of whom were partly identified through their uniforms.

Buck Jones, the film star, was believed to be one of the victims. 21

Among the first at the scene was the Rev. Joseph A. Marcus of Cranwell School, 22 Lenox, who administered the last rites for at least fifty persons. In the meantime, thirty or forty ambulances rushed to the fire, these coming from Lynn, Newton, and Brookline. Despite the hindrances caused by automobiles parked in the streets, some of the dead and injured were taken from nearby buildings, where they had been left covered only by newspapers.

Abraham Levy, a cashier at the Cocoanut Grove, said there were about 400 in the place, including many sailors. 23

Sailors saved many lives, pulling people through the doors and out of danger. A fireman said that he saw at least thirty bodies lying on the floor, and that he believed some of them were firemen. 24

Among the spectacular escapes were those of two of the eight chorus girls, who leaped from the second floor and were caught by two of the male dancers. They were Lottie Christie of Park Drive, Boston, and Claudia Boyle. They jumped into the arms of Andrew Louzan and Robert Gilbert. Louzan and Gilbert had climbed out of a window of their dressing room to an adjoining roof and then descended by ladder. 25

TIME, 7 DECEMBER 1942
CATASTROPHE: BOSTON'S WORST

Holy Cross had just beaten Boston College: downtown Boston was full of men & women eager to celebrate or console. Many of them wound up at Cocoanut Grove: they stood crowded around the dimly lighted downstairs bar, filled the tables around the dance floor upstairs. With them mingled the usual Saturday night crowd: soldiers & sailors, a wedding party, a few boys being sent off to Army camps. 1

At 10 o'clock Bridegroom John O'Neil, who had planned to take his bride to their new apartment at the stroke of the hour, lingered on a little longer. The floor show was about to start. Through the big revolving door, couples moved in & out. 2

At the downstairs bar, a 16-year-old busboy stood on a bench to replace a light bulb that a prankish customer had removed. He lit a match. It touched one of the artificial palm trees that gave the Cocoanut Grove its atmosphere; a few flames shot up. A girl named Joyce Spector sauntered toward the checkroom because she was worried about her new fur coat. 3

Panic's Start

Before Joyce Spector reached the cloakroom, the Cocoanut Grove was a screaming shambles. The fire quickly ate away the palm tree, raced along silk draperies, was sucked upstairs through the stairway, leaped along ceiling and wall. The silk hangings, turned to balloons of flame, fell on table and floor. 4

Men & women fought their way toward the revolving door; the push of bodies jammed it. Nearby was another door; it was locked tight. There were other exits, but few Cocoanut Grove patrons knew about them. The lights went out. There was nothing to see now except flame, smoke and weird moving torches that were men & women with clothing and hair afire. 5

The 800 Cocoanut Grove patrons pushed and shoved, fell and were trampled.   6
Joyce Spector was knocked under a table, crawled on hands & knees, somehow was
pushed through an open doorway into the street. A chorus boy herded a dozen
people downstairs into a refrigerator. A few men & women crawled out windows;
a few escaped by knocking out a glass brick wall. But most of them, including Bridegroom John O'Neil, were trapped.

Panic's Sequel

Firemen broke down the revolving door, found it blocked by bodies of the dead,   7
six deep. They tried to pull a man out through a side window; his legs were held tight
by the mass of struggling people behind him. In an hour the fire was out and firemen began untangling the piles of bodies. One hard bitten fireman went into hys-
terics when he picked up a body and a foot came off in his hand. They found a girl
dead in a telephone booth, a bartender still standing behind his bar.

At hospitals and improvised morgues which were turned into charnel houses for   8
the night, 484 dead were counted; it was the most disastrous U.S. fire since 571
people were killed in Chicago's Iroquois Theater holocaust in 1903. One Boston
newspaper ran a two-word banner line: BUSBOY BLAMED. But the busboy had not
put up the Cocoanut Grove's tinderbox decorations, nor was he responsible for
the fact that Boston's laws do not require nightclubs to have fireproof fixtures, sprin-
kler systems or exit markers.

BERNARD DEVOTO, *HARPER'S*, FEBRUARY 1943
THE EASY CHAIR

On the last Sunday morning of November, 1942, most inhabitants of greater   1
Boston learned from their newspapers that at about the time they had gone to bed
the night before the most terrible fire in the history of their city had occurred. The
decorations of a crowded night club had got ignited, the crowd had stampeded, the
exits had jammed, and in a few minutes hundreds of people had died of burns or
suffocation. Two weeks later the list of dead had reached almost exactly five hundred, and the war news was only beginning to come back to Boston front pages.
While the Allied invasion of North Africa stalled, while news was released that several transports engaged in it had been sunk, while the Russians and the Germans
fought monstrously west of Stalingrad and Moscow, while the Americans bombed
Naples and the RAF obliterated Turin and conducted the war's most widespread
raids over western Europe, while the Japs tried again in the Solomons and mowed
down their attackers in New Guinea, while a grave conflict of civilian opinion over
the use of Admiral Darlan developed in America and Great Britain, while the anniversary of Pearl Harbor passed almost unnoticed—while all this was going on the
Boston papers reported it in stickfuls in order to devote hundreds of columns to
the fire at the Cocoanut Grove. And the papers did right, for the community has

experienced an angry horror surpassing anything that it can remember. For weeks few Bostonians were able to feel strongly about anything but their civic disaster.

There is irony in such preoccupation with a minute carnage. In the same fort- 2 night thousands of men were killed in battle. Every day, doubtless, more than five hundred were burned to death, seared by powder or gasoline from bombed dumps, in buildings fired from the sky, or in blazing airplanes and sinking ships. If these are thought of as combatants meeting death in the line of duty, far more than five hundred civilians were killed by military action in Germany, Italy, France, Great Britain, Russia, China, Australia, and the islands of the Pacific. Meanwhile in two-thirds of the world civilians died of torture and disease and starvation, in prison camps and wire stockades and the rubble of their homes—they simply came to their last breath and died, by the thousand. At a moment when violent death is commonplace, when it is inevitable for hundreds of thousands, there is something grotesque in being shocked by a mere five hundred deaths which are distinguished from the day's routine only by the fact that they were not inevitable. When hundreds of towns are bombed repeatedly, when cities the size of Boston are overrun by invading armies, when many hundreds of Boston's own citizens will surely be killed in battle in the next few weeks, why should a solitary fire, a truly inconsiderable slaughter, so oppress the spirit?

That oppression provides perspective on our era. We have been so conditioned 3 to horror that horror must explode in our own backyard before we can genuinely feel it. At the start of the decade our nerves responded to Hitler's murdering the German Jews with the outrage properly felt in the presence of cruelty and pain. Seven years later our nerves had been so overloaded that they felt no such outrage at the beginning of a systematic effort to exterminate an entire nation, such as Poland. By progressive steps we had come to strike a truce with the intolerable, precisely as the body develops immunity to poisons and bacteria. Since then three years of war have made the intolerable our daily bread, and every one of us has comfortably adapted to things which fifteen years ago would have driven him insane. The extinction of a nation now seems merely an integral part of the job in hand. But the needless death of five hundred people in our home town strikes through the immunity and horrifies us.

The fire at the Cocoanut Grove was a single, limited disaster, but it exhausted 4 Boston's capacity to deal with an emergency. Hospital facilities were strained to the limit and somewhat beyond it. If a second emergency had had to be dealt with at the same time its victims would have had to wait some hours for transportation and a good many hours for treatment. If there had been three such fires at once, two-thirds of the victims would have got no treatment whatever in time to do them any good. Boston is an inflammable city and it has now had instruction in what to expect if a dozen hostile planes should come over and succeed in dropping incendiary bombs. The civilian defense agencies which were called on justified themselves and vindicated their training. The Nurses' Aid in particular did a memorable job;

within a few hours there was a trained person at the bed of every victim, many other Aids worked to exhaustion helping hospital staffs do their jobs, and in fact more were available than could be put to use. Nevertheless it was clearly demonstrated that the civilian agencies are nowhere near large enough to take care of bombings if bombings should come. There were simply not enough ambulances; Railway Express Company trucks had to be called on to take the injured to hospitals and the dead to morgues. The dead had to be stacked like cord wood in garages because the morgues could take no more; the dying had to be laid in rows in the corridors of hospitals because the emergency wards were full. The drainage of doctors into the military service had left Boston just about enough to care for as many victims as this single fire supplied. Six months from now there will be too few to handle an equal emergency; there are far too few now for one twice as serious. One plane-load of incendiaries would start more fires than the fire department and its civilian assistants could put out. There would be more injured than there are even the most casually trained first-aiders to care for. Hundreds would be abandoned to the ignorant assistance of untrained persons, in streets so blocked by rubble and so jammed with military vehicles that trained crews could not reach them even when trained crews should be free. Boston has learned that it is not prepared to take care of itself. One doubts if any community in the United States is.

Deeper implications of the disaster have no direct connection with the war. An   5
outraged city has been confronting certain matters which it ordinarily disregards. As a place of entertainment the Cocoanut Grove was garish but innocuous and on the whole useful. It has been called "the poor man's Ritz"; for years people had been going there to have a good time and had got what they were looking for. With the naive shock customary in such cases, the city has now discovered that these people were not receiving the minimum protection in their pleasures to which they were entitled and which they supposed they were receiving.

The name of the night club suggests the kind of decorations that cluttered it; the   6
public supposed that the law required them to be fireproof; actually they burned like so much celluloid. The laws relating to them were ambiguous and full of loopholes; such as they were, they were not enforced. The public supposed that an adequate number of exits were required and that periodic inspections were made; they were not. There were too few exits for the customary crowds, one was concealed, another could not be opened, and panic-stricken people piled up before the rest and died there by the score. The public supposed that laws forbidding overcrowding were applied to night clubs and were enforced; on the night of the fire the place was packed so full that movement was almost impossible, and it had been just as crowded at least once a week throughout the years of its existence. The public supposed that laws requiring safe practice in electric wiring and machinery were enforced; the official investigations have shown that the wiring was installed by unlicensed electricians, that a number of people had suspected it was faulty, and that in fact officials had notified the club that it was violating the law and had threatened to take ac-

tion—but had not carried out the threat. Above all, the public supposed that an adequate building code taking into account the realities of modern architecture and modern metropolitan life established certain basic measures of protection. It has now learned that the Boston building code is a patched makeshift based on the conditions of 1907, and that though a revision which would modernize it was made in 1937, various reasons have held up the adoption of that revision for five years.

These facts have been established by five official investigations, one of them made by the Commonwealth of Massachusetts in an obvious expectation that the municipal authorities of Boston would find convincing reasons to deal gently with themselves. They have turned up other suggestive facts. The Cocoanut Grove was once owned by a local racketeer, who was murdered in the routine of business. The present owners were so expertly concealed behind a facade of legal figureheads that for twenty-four hours after the fire the authorities were not sure that they knew who even one of them was and two weeks later were not sure that they knew them all. An intimation that financial responsibility was avoided by a technically contrived bankruptcy has not yet been followed up as I write this, and other financial details are still lost in a maze of subterfuges. It is supposed that some of the club's employees had their wagescale established by terrorism. Investigators have encountered, but so far have not published, the customary free-list and lists of those entitled to discounts. Presumably such lists contemplated the usual returns in publicity and business favors; presumably also they found a use in the amenities of regulation. Names and business practices of the underworld have kept cropping up in all the investigations, and it is whispered that the reason why the national government has been conducting one of them is the presence at the club of a large amount of liquor on which the latest increase in revenue taxes ought to have been paid but somehow had not been.

In short, Boston has been reminded, hardly for the first time, that laxity in municipal responsibility can be made to pay a profit and that there can be a remunerative partnership between the amusement business and the underworld. A great many Bostonians, now writing passionate letters to their newspapers and urging on their legislators innumerable measures of reform, have gone farther than that. They conclude that one of the reasons why the modernized building code has not been adopted is the fact that there are ways of making money from the looser provisions of the old code. They suppose that one reason why gaps and loopholes in safety regulations are maintained is that they are profitable. They suppose that one reason why laws and regulations can be disregarded with impunity is that some of those charged with the duty of enforcing them make a living from not enforcing them. They suppose that some proprietors of night clubs find that buying immunity is cheaper than obeying safety regulations and that they are able to find enforcement agents who will sell it. They suppose that civil irresponsibility in Boston can be related to the fact that a lot of people make money from it.

But the responsibility cannot be shouldered off on a few small grafters and a few underworld characters who have established business relations with them, and it

7

8

9

would be civic fatuousness to seek expiation for the murder of five hundred citizens in the passage of some more laws. The trouble is not lack of laws but public acquiescence; the damaging alliance is not with the underworld but with a communal reverence of what is probably good for business. Five hundred deaths in a single hour seem intolerable, but the city has never dissented at all to a working alliance between its financial interests and its political governors—a partnership which daily endangers not five hundred but many thousand citizens. Through Boston, as through every other metropolis, run many chains of interests which might suffer loss if regulations for the protection of the public's health and life were rigorously enforced. They are sound and enlightened regulations, but if they should be enforced then retail sales, bank clearings, and investment balances might possibly fall off. The corner grocery and the downtown department store, the banks and the business houses, the labor unions and the suburban housewife are all consenting partners in a closely calculated disregard of public safety.

Since the system is closely calculated it usually works, it kills only a few at a time,   10
mostly it kills gradually over a period of years. Sometimes however it runs into another mathematical certainty and then it has to be paid for in blocks of five hundred lives. At such times the community experiences just such an excess of guilt as Boston is feeling now, uncomfortably realizing that the community itself is the perpetrator of wanton murder. For the responsibility is the public's all along and the certain safeguard—a small amount of alertness, civic courage, and willingness to lose some money—is always in the public's hands. That means not the mayor's hands, but yours and mine.

It is an interesting thing to hold up to the light at a moment when millions of   11
Americans are fighting to preserve, among other things, the civic responsibility of a self-governing people. It suggests that civilians who are not engaged in the war effort, and who feel intolerably abased because they are not, could find serviceable ways to employ their energies. They can get to work chipping rust and rot from the mechanisms of local government. The rust and rot are increasing because people who can profit from their increase count on our looking toward the war, not toward them. Your town may have a police force of no more than four and its amusement business may be confined to half a dozen juke joints, but some percentage of both may have formed a partnership against your interests under cover of the war.

Certainly the town has a sewage system, a garbage dump, fire traps, a rudimen-   12
tary public health code, ordinances designed to protect life, and a number of Joe Doakes who can make money by juggling the relationship among them. Meanwhile the ordinary hazards of peace are multiplied by the conditions of war, carelessness and preoccupation increase, and the inevitable war pestilence is gathering to spring. The end-products do not look pleasant when they are seen clearly, especially when a community realizes that it has killed five hundred people who did not need to die.

▪9▪
Writing the
Research Essay

In Chapter 9, you take the evidence and information that you have found in your sources and transform them into an essay. At this stage of the writing process, you truly begin to make the sources your own—by taking notes; by developing a thesis; by deciding which information is relevant and important to that thesis; by organizing the material into a sequence of paragraphs in support of the thesis; and, finally, by expressing your ideas and presenting your evidence to the reader, as far as possible in your own words. Most of these steps have been explained in earlier chapters. Chapter 9 provides an overview of some of the key stages.

SAVING INFORMATION

Whatever the topic of your research, you will probably accumulate a large quantity of written notes that serve as the raw materials for your synthesis. Here, the term "notes" refers to any of the products of your research: your own summaries and paraphrases, quotations, photocopies of book pages and articles, printouts and downloaded copies of Web material, class lecture notes, stories clipped from newspapers and magazines, and jottings of your own ideas about the topic.

More specifically, research often requires you to "take notes": you read through a text, sometimes quickly and sometimes slowly, deciding as you go which information you probably will want to use in your essay and writing it down as summary, paraphrase, and quotation. Before the days of computers, notes were usually handwritten on index cards or lined pads, ready to be organized into a sequence that would become the outline of an essay. The text of books and articles was pared down to handwritten notes that, in turn, were rewritten into the sentences of an essay. Many students still prefer this slow but thorough way of absorbing ideas and information.

Now, technology offers an alternative. More often than not, text from a book goes through a copying machine and becomes a photocopied page; the words of the text remain the same. Online articles or Web sites get downloaded and appear in a file on your computer screen; the words of the text remain the same. Certainly, copying the original text can be useful: for example, you may want to include a small portion in your essay verbatim, as quotation. But, at some point, most of it will have to be rewritten in your own words, in your own voice. Otherwise, you will not be writing an essay; you will be compiling an anthology of quotations.

Downloading presents a particular temptation. The information is available right there, on your screen, and by clicking a few keys you can transfer it directly into the file you've created for your research essay. You can keep on cutting and pasting from other Web sites and database articles, and type in or scan some extracts from photocopies; and you'll end up with something that contains sentences and paragraphs and meets the minimum number of assigned pages. It may look like an essay—but will it read like an essay?

The cut-and-paste method of writing an essay involves no writing. Technically, you are presenting the results of your research by assembling an electronic scrapbook. Your instructor will easily observe that the writing component of the assignment hasn't been fulfilled and will grade the "essay" accordingly.

Learning to write essays means learning to speak for yourself. Learning to write research essays means using the skills of summary and paraphrase to present your sources. And you can't delay doing that until you're at the point of writing the essay. If you were dealing with only one or two authors, you might be able to move back and forth from the source file to the essay file (or have them both on a split screen) and write directly from your sources. But juggling a dozen or more authors, each on a different screen, you'll find it hard to achieve any kind of coherent structure for your essay. What's the solution? Take notes!

TAKING NOTES

If it's your preference or if your access to a computer is limited, by all means use the traditional method of taking *handwritten notes on index cards or a pad of paper*. There can be no more thorough or reliable bridge between your research and your essay. But if you opt for convenience, establish *a new computer file* at the onset of your research. This file will not be the one used for the writing of your essay; it will be exclusively for notes. As you start working with a new source, *open that file, put the bibliographical information about that source clearly at the start of a new section, and type in your version of the material that you may want to use.* Don't copy-type (except for the occasional quotation). Use your own words.

When you've finished your notes, you'll have one long file ready to be printed out and reorganized, or simply reorganized on the screen. Once you've synthesized your sequence of ideas, you can transfer your notes into your essay file. The difference is that, this way, you will be cutting and pasting your own work.

Here are some other guidelines for note taking:

1. *Wait to take notes*: Don't start taking notes until you have compiled most of your preliminary bibliography. Choosing materials to copy and to download will help you gradually to understand the possibilities of your subject and decide on a potential thesis. But if you start taking notes from the first few texts that you find, you may be wasting time pursuing an idea that will turn out to be impractical or that the evidence ultimately won't support. You may discover, for example, that there's very little documented information about the gunfight at the OK Corral, and so shift your focus to Billy the Kid.

2. *Use photocopies and printouts*: Unless it's prohibitively expensive, try to take notes from photocopies of books and articles, rather than the texts themselves; that way, you'll always have the copies to refer to if there's a confusion in your notes. (The copies will also be useful if your instructor asks you to submit some of your sources.) Print out downloaded material and work from the printed copy so that you don't have to keep shifting from file to file. It's hard to take good notes if you don't have the text in front of you as you write.

3. *Use paraphrase and summary*: As you learned in Chapter 4, quotation should be the exception, not the rule. Copying the author's language will make it more difficult for you to shift to your own writing style later on. You want to avoid producing an anthology of cannibalized quotations. The effort of paraphrasing and summarizing also helps you to understand each new idea. In your notes, always try to explain the author's exact meaning.

4. *Cite evidence*: Include evidence to support the broader ideas that you're writing about. If your topic is corruption in the Olympic games, don't simply allude to issues like the use of performance-enhancing drugs or the influence of network television in the scheduling of events. Cite facts to illustrate your point. You won't remember the range of evidence as you're writing the paper unless you include examples in your notes.

5. *Separate yourself from your source*: Differentiate your own ideas from those that you are paraphrasing. When you take notes, you're working slowly and concentrating on what you're reading. It's at that time that you're most likely to develop your own comments and ideas, spinning them off from the text. Be careful to indicate in your notes what's yours and what's the source's. Later on, you'll need to know which material to document. Using square brackets [like these] around your own ideas is a good way of making this distinction or use the tracking program on your word processor.

6. *Record page numbers*: Keep a running record of page references. You'll need to cite the exact page number for each reference, not an approximate guess. It isn't enough to write "pp. 285–91" after a few paragraphs of notes. Three weeks or three hours later, how will you remember on which page you found the point that you're about to cite in your essay? If you're quoting or paraphrasing a source in some detail, make a slash and insert a new page number to indicate exactly where you turned the page. Put quotation marks around all quotations *immediately*.

7. *Record bibliographical data*: Always include complete bibliographical information for each source. If you don't have a clear record of details like place of publication, volume number, or URL, you won't be able to hand in a complete bibliography. Either start a new file just for bibliography or include that information at the beginning of each section of your notes.

Taking Good Notes

1. Don't start taking notes until you have compiled most of your preliminary bibliography.
2. Try to take notes from photocopies of books and articles and printouts of sources, rather than the texts themselves.
3. Use paraphrase and summary, rather than quotation.
4. Include evidence to support the broader ideas that you're writing about.
5. Differentiate your own ideas from those that you are paraphrasing.
6. Keep a running record of page references.
7. Always include complete bibliographical information for each source.

Organizationally, you can take notes in either of two ways: *by source* or *by topic. Taking notes by source* is the more obvious way. You start your computer file (or your cards or pad) with the first source, presenting information in the order of its appearance. Then you go on to the second, the third, and so on. Figure 9-1 on p. 415 shows notes for an essay, organized by source, describing *the 1871 fire that devastated Chicago*. The source (described in detail earlier in the file) is the *New York Times* for October 15, 1871.

NY Times, 10/15/71, p. 1   Source J

1. city normal again
2. still martial rule; Gen. Sheridan in charge
3. citizens working at night to watch for new outbreak of fire
4. newspapers moved to other locations
5. estimate 1,000 dead
6. earlier reports of looting and loss of life not exaggerated
7. waterworks won't open until next day
8. two-thirds of the city still using candlelight
9. suffering mostly among "humbler classes"
10. businessmen are "buoyant"
11. bread is 8 cents
12. saloons are closed at 9:00 p.m. for one week

Figure 9-1. Notes Grouped by Source

- Each item in the list is assigned a number; this will be useful later on, when you are organizing your notes to write your essay.
- The source has also been assigned an identifying letter; if you have two sources with the same name (for example, the *Times* for two different dates), you'll be able to distinguish between them.

The disadvantage of taking notes by source is that your notes remain raw material, with no organizational pattern imposed on them. *Taking notes by topic* is a more sophisticated system.

- Decide on the basic events or issues that your essay will cover.
- Assign each of those topics a separate section of your notes file.
- Place each new piece of information under the relevant topic.

For example, early in the note-taking process, one student decided that she would definitely write about the aftermath of the Chicago fire; one section of her notes would be devoted to efforts to contain and put out the blaze. After that, every time she came across a new point about *firefighting*—no matter what the source—she scrolled through (or searched) her file, looking for the topic name and then adding that information. Similar sections were established to deal with *food supplies* and *looting*. Figure 9-2 shows a sample of her notes.

Organizing notes by topic makes it much easier to organize your essay. In fact, because your information is already categorized, you can often skip a whole stage in the process and begin to write your essay from your notes without much additional synthesis. But taking notes by topic does require you to make a list, either written or mental, of possible categories or note topics while

---

Firefighting

All engines and hose carts in city come (NYT 10/8, p. 5)
Water station on fire, with no water to put out small fires
    (Hall, p. 228)
all engines out there; fire too big to stop (NYT 10/8, p. 5)
fire department "demoralized"; bad fire previous night; men
were drinking afterward; fire marshal "habitually drunk"
    (NYT 10/23, p. 2)

Figure 9-2. Notes Grouped by Topic

you're still doing your research. And you may not be completely sure about your thesis and structure that early in the process. When you take notes by topic, it's also vital to make sure that *each* point is followed by its source and the relevant page number.

EXERCISE 30: TAKING NOTES ON TWO TOPICS

Reread the three articles dealing with the Cocoanut Grove fire of 1942 at the end of Chapter 8. Head one file "Causes of the Fire" and take a set of notes on that topic. Head another file "The Fire's Intensity and Speed" and take a second set of notes on the second topic. Each set of notes should make use of all three sources.

EXERCISE 31: TAKING NOTES ON THREE TOPICS

Assume that you are doing research on *celebrations in American culture* and that you have come across the following source in the library. After doing a preliminary evaluation of the passage, take a set of notes for an essay entitled "The Commercialization of Holidays," a second set of notes for an essay entitled "Origins of Our National Holidays," and a third set of notes for an essay entitled "The Recognition of Women as Mothers and Homemakers."

Note: *The founder of the Council on Contemporary Families, Stephanie Coontz teaches at Evergreen State College and has published several books on marriage and family life.*

THE CURIOUS HISTORY OF MOTHER'S DAY

The extent to which the right-wing analysis has permeated our understanding of women's changing roles is illustrated in the ritual lamentations we hear each year about the "debasement of Mother's Day." Most people believe that Mother's Day was originally a time for an intensely personal celebration of women's private roles and nuclear family relationships. In "the old days," we brought mom breakfast in bed to acknowledge all the meals she had made for us. We picked her a bouquet of fresh flowers to symbolize her personal, unpaid services to her family. "Traditional" Mother's Day images, whether on the front of greeting cards or in the back of our minds, are always set in the kitchen or at a child's bedside, emphasizing mother's devotion to her own family and ignoring her broader kin networks, social ties, and political concerns.

But as domestic work has been devalued and formerly private arenas of life drawn into the market, the story goes, the personal element in this celebration has been lost. Mother's Day has become just another occasion for making money—the busiest day of the year for American restaurants and telephone companies, the best single week of the year for florists. So every May, between the ads for "all-you-can-eat" Mother's Day buffets, we hear a chorus of pleas for Americans to rediscover "the true meaning of Mother's Day."   2

Last year, for example, my son carried home from school (along with three dinner coupons from local fast-food restaurants) a handout urging children to think of some "homemade" gift or service to express their appreciation for their mothers' "special" love. It was a nice sentiment, and I was delighted to receive the fantasy book my child pulled from his personal library and wrapped in a hand-drawn heart—but the historian in me was a little bemused. The fact is that Mother's Day originated to celebrate the organized activities of women *outside* the home. It became trivialized and commercialized only after it became confined to "special" nuclear family relations.   3

The people who inspired Mother's Day had quite a different idea about what made mothers special. They believed that motherhood was a *political* force. They wished to celebrate mothers' social roles as community organizers, honoring women who acted on behalf of the entire future generation rather than simply putting their own children first.   4

The first proposal of a day for mothers came from Anna Reeves Jarvis, who in 1858 organized Mothers' Work Days in West Virginia to improve sanitation in the Appalachian Mountains. During the Civil War, her group provided medical services for soldiers and civilians on both sides of the conflict. After the war, Jarvis led a campaign to get the former combatants to lay aside their animosities and forge new social and political alliances.[7]   5

The other nineteenth-century precursor of Mother's Day began in Boston in 1872, when poet and philanthropist Julia Ward Howe proposed an annual Mothers' Day for Peace, to be held every June 2:   6

> Arise then, women of this day! . . . Say firmly: "Our husbands shall not come to us, reeking with carnage. . . . Our sons shall not be taken from us to unlearn all that we have been able to teach them of charity, mercy and patience. We women of

one country will be too tender of those of another country to allow our sons to be trained to injure theirs."[8]

Howe's Mothers' Day was celebrated widely in Massachusetts, Pennsylvania, and other Eastern states until the turn of the century.

Most of these ceremonies and proposals, significantly, were couched in the plural, not the singular, mode: Mothers' Day was originally a vehicle for organized social and political action by all mothers, not for celebrating the private services of one's own particular mother.

When Anna Reeves Jarvis died in 1905, her daughter, also named Anna Jarvis, began a letter-writing campaign to have a special day set aside for mothers. But by this period, there was already considerable pressure to sever the personal meaning of motherhood from its earlier political associations. The mobilization of women as community organizers was the last thing on the minds of the prominent merchants, racist politicians, and antisuffragist activists who, sometimes to Jarvis's dismay, quickly jumped on the bandwagon.[9]

In fact, the adoption of Mother's Day by the 63rd Congress on May 8, 1914 represented a reversal of everything the nineteenth-century mothers' days had stood for. The speeches proclaiming Mother's Day in 1914 linked it to celebration of home life and privacy; they repudiated women's social role beyond the household. One antisuffragist leader inverted the original intent entirely when she used the new Mother's Day as an occasion to ask rhetorically: If a woman becomes "a mother to the Municipality, who is going to mother us?" Politicians found that the day provided as many opportunities for self-promotion as did the Fourth of July. Merchants hung testimonials to their own mothers above the wares they hoped to convince customers to buy for other mothers. A day that had once been linked to controversial causes was reduced to an occasion for platitudes and sales pitches.[10]

Its bond with social reform movements broken, Mother's Day immediately drifted into the orbit of the marketing industry. The younger Jarvis had proposed that inexpensive carnations be worn to honor one's mother. Outraged when the flowers began to sell for a dollar apiece, she attacked the florists as "profiteers" and began a campaign to protect Mother's Day from such exploitation. In 1923, she managed to get a political and commercial celebration of Mother's Day cancelled in New York (on grounds, ironically, of infringement of copyright), but this was her last victory. Jarvis spent the rest of her life trying to regain control of the day, becoming more and more paranoid about those who "would undermine [Mother's Day] with their greed." She was eventually committed to a sanitarium, where she died in 1948.[11]

The history of Mother's Day is a microcosm of the simultaneous sentimentalization and commercialization of private life over the past one hundred years and of the ways in which the market has penetrated every aspect of family relations. What paved the way for this transformation was not the women's rights movement, nor the growing entry of women into the paid labor force, but the metamorphosis of domestic roles in the Gilded Age.

For all its repressiveness, the early-nineteenth-century definition of woman's   12
sphere had given her moral responsibility beyond the household, a duty that shaded
easily into social activism. Women who participated in antislavery agitation, temperance, and welfare reform saw this work as essentially maternal in nature. Thus
the earliest proponents of honoring motherhood were people allied with such social reform movements. Toward the end of the nineteenth century, however, a major change occurred in the role and image of women.

The privatization of family values during the Gilded Age . . . meant that the roles   13
of wife and mother lost their transcendent moral and political significance. As historian Paula Fass notes, by the early twentieth century the middle-class family had
become much more emotionally expressive for its members but at the same time
"more and more separated from other social institutions and freed of direct responsibility to them." The growth of family privacy, historian Barbara Laslett argues, reduced "the sources of social support and satisfaction" for women's domestic
roles. As older political, social, and religious functions of the home were eroded, a
woman increasingly labored only for the personal comfort of her husband and children. A focus on individual fulfillment in the home meant for many women more
companionship with their husbands, but it divested motherhood of any larger social and political meaning.[12]

This ideological transformation of domesticity was connected to changes in the   14
organization and technology of production, in both the home and the economy.
These changes laid the groundwork for the increasing entry of women into paid employment during the twentieth century, a phenomenon largely independent of either
the suffrage movement of the early 1900s or the women's liberation movement of
the late 1960s. Indeed, the revival of feminism in the 1960s was more response
than impetus to women's integration into the labor force.

Certainly, feminism changed the terms on which women understood their work   15
and confronted its conditions; conversely, women's growing economic clout encouraged them to demand equality with men both on and off the job, including the
opportunity to seek fulfillment outside the family. For many women, new work opportunities *broadened* their commitment to others. To the extent that some
women, like some men, came to define self-fulfillment in terms of materialism, immediate gratification, and "me-first" individualism, the source of such values lay in
mainstream economic and cultural trends, not in feminism or any other dissident
movement of the 1960s or 1970s.

STEPHANIE COONTZ, from *The Way We Never Were:*
American Families and the Nostalgia Trap

[7] James Johnson, "Death, Grief, and Motherhood: The Woman Who Inspired
Mother's Day," *West Virginia History* 39 (1978); W. R. Higginbotham, "The Mother
of Mother's Day," *San Francisco Chronicle*, 12 May 1985; "Mother's Day Origins and
Tradition," *Triad Woman*, May 1985.

[8] Indira Clark, "Mother's Day," *Woman's Compendium*, May–June 1987, p. 15. See also Louise Tharp, *Three Saints and a Sinner: Julia Ward Howe, Loyisa, Annie, and Sam Ward* (Boston: Little, Brown, 1956), p. 351; Laura Richards, *Julia Ward Howe, 1819–1910* (Dunwoody, Calif.: N. S. Berg, 1970), pp. 319, 345; Deborah Pickman Clifford, *Mine Eyes Have Seen the Glory: A Biography of Julia Ward Howe* (Boston: Little, Brown, 1979), p. 187.

[9] James Johnson, "How Mother Got Her Day," *American Heritage* 30 (1979).

[10] *Proceedings of the Sixty-third Congress*, sess. 2, res. 10–13 (Washington, D.C., 1914), p. 770; Johnson, "How Mother Got Her Day"; *Ladies' Home Journal*, 7 May 1914, p. 28.

[11] E. Robert McHenry, ed., *Famous American Women: A Biographical Dictionary from Colonial Times to the Present* (New York: Dover, 1983), pp. 209–10; Jane Hatch and George Douglas, *The American Book of Days* (New York: Wilson, 1978), pp. 439–40; Johnson, "How Mother Got Her Day," pp. 20–21.

[12] Paula Fass, *The Damned and the Beautiful: American Youth in the 1920s* (New York: Oxford, 1977), p. 55; Barbara Laslett, "The Family as a Public and Private Institution: An Historical Perspective," *Journal of Marriage and the Family* 35 (1973): 482n4.

DEVELOPING A LIST OF TOPICS

Once you have all your notes in a computer file (or on cards or a pad), you need to organize them into a plan for your essay. (If you've already organized your notes by topic, you can skip this stage.) The first step is to *take inventory*: you search for ideas worth developing in your essay by (1) reviewing your notes and (2) identifying and writing down all the major topics that you have learned and thought about during your research.

Here's a list of topics taken from a set of notes about the Chicago fire of 1871:

Mrs. O'Leary's cow kicks over the lantern: did that start the fire?
Extent of the damage
Preventing panic
Feeding the homeless
Dealing with those trapped within buildings
Drought conditions the previous summer
Preventing looting
Beginning to rebuild the city
Mobilizing manpower to fight the fire
Improvising hospital conditions
Providing shelter
How the fire spread
Crowd control
Fighting the fire
Organizing the firefighters and police
Sounding the alarm

Since the subject of this essay is an event, the items on the list are factual and brief. An essay that deals with ideas rather than events is likely to have a preliminary list of topics with longer, more abstract entries. Notice that, at this point, the sequence of the entries doesn't matter; the points are in *random order*, just as they were found in the notes. Nor do you have to include supporting evidence at this stage. That's why the list is so skinny. You are extracting what's important from the mass of your notes; you are looking for the bones of your essay.

> ## *Taking Inventory of Your Notes and Forming Paragraph Topics*
>
> - *Do write down in any order the important ideas* that you find in your notes. At this point, the items don't have to be related to each other in sequence.
>
> - *Don't try to summarize* all your notes or even summarize each of your notes. At this point, you are working on organizing your topics, not summarizing your research.
>
> - *Don't try to link the ideas that you write down to specific sources.* At this point, there is no special reason to place the names of the sources next to your new list of ideas; not every statement in your new list will necessarily be included in your essay. Later, you will decide which source to use in support of which topic sentence.
>
> - *Do think about your own reactions* to the information that you have collected. Now you are deciding what is worth writing about.
>
> - *Do use your own words.* At this point, even if you only jot down a phrase, it should be your own version of the source's idea. Even if the information has appeared in ten different articles and you've included it ten different times in your notes, you are now, in some sense, making it your own.

PLANNING A STRATEGY

Essays about *events or people* tend to have a straightforward organization based on a time sequence, with a beginning, middle, and end. You certainly will have a thesis to support—"The rescue and rehabilitation efforts after the Chicago fire were competently carried out"—but the bulk of the essay will analyze what happened during and after the fire in sequential order.

Abstract topics, which are often *arguments*, require a more complex structure. The thesis is likely to be a general proposition that you intend to prove, citing your research as evidence.

In Chapter 1, you learned that most arguments are based on a combination of two kinds of logical reasoning:

- *Deductive reasoning*: You provide a series of linked premises, based on a general assumption that you and your reader share, that leads to a specific conclusion.

- *Inductive reasoning*: You provide a range of specific evidence from which you construct a general conclusion.

In practice, these two basic logical tools—the use of linked premises, and the use of evidence—are used together to develop the most common strategies: cause and effect and problem and solution.

The *cause-and-effect* essay establishes a causal link between two circumstances. The thesis usually answers the question "Why?" Let's assume that your general subject is *high school dropouts*. Why is the high school dropout rate as high as it is today? Here are a few typical answers:

Because class sizes are too large

Because students are poorly prepared to handle the work

Because many students are foreign-born and can't speak English well

Because local governments are not providing sufficient funding

Because family life is breaking down, leaving students without support and discipline

Clearly, this inventory list suggests many possible causes. You may initially be inclined to write about all of them, giving each one equal weight. If you do, your essay may be long and unmanageable, with a thesis that pulls the reader in many contradictory directions. But if you focus on only one cause, you run the risk of oversimplifying your argument. You need to consider which of these causes is *most responsible* for its effect—the high dropout rate—and which ones have a *contributing influence*.

Analyzing your list should also help you to determine *which causes work together*. For example, the problem of class size is probably linked to—caused by—the problem of inadequate funding. Here you have a smaller cause and effect embedded within the larger one:

Inadequate funding results in overly large classes, which, in turn, contribute to the dropout rate.

The links between causes—like funding and class size—form the *deductive* part of your argument. But the causes in the list above also lend themselves to *inductive* support. By the time you finish your research, you should be able to determine *whether your inductive evidence supports your deductive argument* about the reasons why students drop out. Assuming that it does, your essay will present factual evidence, including statistics, about class sizes, student preparedness, language difficulties, and diminished local budgets for education. The last point on your list—family breakdown—is the most abstract and so the most difficult to support. You would need to develop a series of deductive premises, along with evidence, to make a strong causal link between the decline of family life and the incidence of high school dropouts.

Let's assume that you decide on the following thesis:

The poor educational environment, resulting from inadequate funding, makes it hard for students to learn, so they drop out.

What kinds of *counterarguments* would you have to anticipate and rebut? While your research supports your thesis, you have also found authorities who argue that students from strong family backgrounds perform well and stay in school even in overcrowded, poorly funded districts. You can continue to defend your preferred thesis, but you must also acknowledge your opponents' views, while pointing out their limitations.

The *problem-and-solution* essay often incorporates the cause-and-effect essay, using five stages:

1. *Establish that a problem exists.* Explain why it is a problem, and anticipate the negative consequences if nothing is done.

2. *Analyze the causes of the problem.* Here, you can include a modified version of the cause-and-effect strategy: emphasize the major causes, but remind your reader that this is a complex issue, with a number of contributory influences working together. Provide some evidence, but not necessarily the full range of your research.

3. *Assert the best solution.* Using the evidence of your research, demonstrate why the preferred solution will work and indicate how you would go about implementing it.

4. *Anticipate counterarguments and answer them.* Your research has turned up authorities who have recommended different solutions. What are the advantages and disadvantages of those solutions? Is your solution better? Why?

5. *Conclude in a spirit of accommodation.* Assert your solution once again, but also consider acknowledging the complexity of the problem and making room for some of your opponents' ideas. Sometimes the arguments on either side of an issue are too evenly balanced for certainty, and you need to find a solution within common ground.

ARRANGING THE ORDER OF TOPICS

At some point in the process of organizing your essay, your skinny list of ideas becomes an outline. An *outline* is a list of the major and minor points supporting an essay's thesis, presented in a pattern that reflects their relative importance.

Their major points will probably all be *parallel* or of the same kind:

> the *reasons* why **x** is true,
> or the *ways* in which **y** happens,
> or the *differences* between **x** and **y**,
> or the chief *characteristics* of **z**.

These major points—the items on your inventory—are given the most prominent place in the outline, usually at the left-hand margin.

Secondary material—the ideas, information, or examples being used as supporting evidence—appears directly under each major point and slightly to the right.

If there are different kinds of evidence to support a point or a group of examples, each is listed on a separate line.

Traditionally, outlines are written in a standard format, with major and minor points assigned numbers and letters of the alphabet to keep them in order. But there is absolutely no need to create a formal outline, with its letters and numbers, unless your instructor requires it or you find it useful for organizing your information. You can indicate the relationships between ideas simply by the way you place them on the page.

What is important is that you *revise and expand your inventory of major topics*, making new lists out of old ones, adding and deleting ideas, changing the order to correspond to your strategy. When that inventory list is as good as you can make it, you have *a sequence that will roughly correspond to the sequence of paragraphs in your essay*.

How do you decide on the best order for your topic list? Outlining is all about priorities and relationships. Ask yourself the following questions:

- How are ideas linked together?
- Which is more important?
- What does your reader need to know first?
- What information does your reader need in order to understand a second, more complex point?
- How does one idea lead into another?

Look for an *organizing principle*. In a historical essay, the ordering principle is frequently time: the deployment of troops has to be described before the actual battle. In a personality profile, dominant qualities will take precedence over minor quirks. Problems get described before solutions; causes are analyzed in order to understand their effects. One rationale for your sequence might be "most compelling" to "least compelling" reason. But an even stronger rationale is "most fundamental" to "most complex": you start with your most basic point and demonstrate how everything else rests on that central idea.

In addition to rearranging the order of your topics, you also have to expand your inventory by *adding supporting evidence for each major topic*. (In effect, you are filling in the secondary tiers of your outline.) Under headings like "firefighting" and "medical care," you insert factual information demonstrating that the authorities in Chicago reacted to the fire as efficiently as circumstances allowed. Similarly, having established a linked set of the causes and subcauses that encourage a higher dropout rate, you distribute the material gathered in your research—statistics, surveys, anecdotes, theories—under the appropriate topics.

Arranging Your Order of Topics

1. *Evaluate your inventory list of important ideas.*

   - Notice which ideas are in the mainstream of your research, discussed by several of your sources, and which ones appear only in one or two sources.

   - Consider whether you have enough evidence to support all of your topics.

   - Think about eliminating topics that seem minor or remote from your subject and your thesis.

   - Look for and combine topics that restate the same point.

   - If you are developing an argument essay, make sure that each of the key points supporting your side, as well as your counterarguments to the opposition, is supported by your research.

2. *Think about the sequence of ideas on your final list and the possible strategies for organizing your essay.*

   - How does your list of ideas help to establish a thesis?

   - Are you working with a collection of reasons? Consequences? Problems? Dangers?

   - What kind of essay are you writing? Cause and effect? Problem and solution? Explanation of a procedure? Evaluation of reasons for an argument?

   If you are developing a historical or biographical topic:
   - Did the event fall into distinct narrative stages?

   - What aspects of the scene would an observer have noticed?

   - Which of your subject's activities best reveals his or her personality?

   If you are developing an argument:
   - Does your issue lend itself to a cause-and-effect or a problem-and-solution essay?

   - Do your main reasons require deductive or inductive support?

   - Which are your most compelling arguments?

3. *Arrange your list of topics in a sequence that has meaning for you, carries out your strategy, and develops your thesis in a clear direction.*

COMPLETING YOUR OUTLINE

Your final task is to organize your notes in accordance with your outline. This can be done either *directly on the computer,* working from your outline, or by *cross-referencing.* You may need to use a combination of both methods.

Using the Computer to Organize Your Essay

Let's assume that most of your notes are contained in a file on your computer. If you originally organized your notes *by topic,* you simply *rearrange your notes on the screen,* section by section, so that the topics correspond to the sequence of those in your outline. This is one time when cutting and pasting is a quick and acceptable method of getting your work done. (Alternatively, you can split the screen between your notes file and your essay file, establish your outline topics in your essay file, and drag portions of your notes from one file to the appropriate place in the other. But dragging can be a messy business, and it's possible to lose or misplace material in the process.) Be sure to safeguard your notes. Instead of cutting and pasting, try copying and pasting so that your original file of notes remains intact. Keep a backup version of both your note file and your essay file on a separate disk. Above all, *save your work at regular and frequent intervals.*

If you originally organized your notes *by source,* organizing your essay now becomes a more complex process. If your topic is straightforward and your essay is under ten pages, you can probably rearrange your notes directly on the computer, as described in the previous paragraph. You place your outline in your essay file, with wide gaps between the topics, and start to move items (copying and pasting) from one file to the other. Instead of transferring whole sections as you would if you had organized your notes by topic, you'll be *pulling out a quotation or a paragraph or an example from your notes and finding the right place for it* in your outline sequence. This can be tedious and painstaking work.

Be extremely careful to *make sure that the source of each piece of information is indicated next to it before you move it.* Otherwise, as you write your essay, you won't be able to document your sources. Without documentation of sources, your research efforts have no validity. This is why it saves time and effort to organize your notes by topic when you originally write them.

Using Cross-Referencing to Organize Your Essay

If you're working on a lengthy and complicated essay with a set of notes organized by source, or if a large portion of your notes is on paper rather than in a computer file, your best option is to use cross-referencing to complete your outline and organize your essay. Cross-referencing is used *before* physically moving material from file to file. Once again, you're working from two sets of material:

- *Your completed outline of topics.* The topics are listed either on the screen or on a long pad. Make sure to leave wide gaps between each item. Assign a number (preferably a Roman numeral), in sequence, to each topic in your outline.

- *Your notes.* It's easiest to have everything on paper, including printouts of any computer notes. Assign an identifying letter to each source (placing it at the top of each page of notes devoted to material from that source). If you have twelve sources, you'll be using A–L. Assign an Arabic numeral to each separate piece of information within the notes from a specific source.

Now, once again, slowly read through all your research notes, this time keeping your outline of topics in front of you. Every time you come across a point in your notes that should be cited in support of a topic on your outline, immediately:

1. Place the number of the outline topic (III) next to the reference in your notes.

2. Place the source's identifying letter (F) and the identifying number of the item in your notes (9) under the relevant topic in your outline.

For the system to work, you must complete both stages: notes must be keyed to the outline, and the outline must be keyed to each item in your research notes. The notes and the outline criss-cross each other; hence the term *cross-referencing*.

To illustrate cross-referencing, here is an example taken from the notes and outline for an essay on the Chicago fire. The outline was divided into three main sections: the *causes* of the fire, the *panic* during the fire, and *restoring order* after the fire. Figure 9–3 shows an excerpt from the *notes*, with Roman numerals written in the margins to indicate cross-references to three specific paragraph topics.

Source G

<u>Times</u>, October 11, "The Ruined City," p. 1

1. The fire has stopped and there has been some "blessed rain."

2. 20-30 people have died in their homes.

XI 3. Plundering everywhere – like a scene of war
    A. A thief suffocated while trying to steal jewelry from a store.
    B. People who were caught pilfering had to be released because the jail burned down.

X 4. Lake used for drinking water.

5. People dying of exposure.

IX 6. Little food: people searching the ruins

IX 7. Difficulties of transporting supplies

XI 8. Meeting of citizens at church to help protect what was left, to help homeless, and to provide water if further fires broke out

---

Figure 9-3. Cross-Referencing

Here are the topics, which come from the last section of the outline:

IX. Feeding the homeless *G6 / G7*

X. Providing basic services *G4*

XI. Protecting life and property *G3 / G8*

When you have finished cross-referencing:

- Your outline will have a precise list of sources to be cited for each major point, and
- Your research notes will have code numbers in most (but not necessarily all) of the margins.

Cross-referencing helps you to avoid time-consuming searches for references while you are writing the essay. When you start to work on the paragraph dealing with feeding the homeless, you consult your outline and immediately go to Source G, Items 6 and 7. (Later, references to other sources will also have been placed next to Item IX on your outline.) The accumulated information will become the basis for writing that paragraph.

A few of the items in the notes for Source G have no cross-references next to them. Some will be cross-referenced to other topics in this outline, and haven't yet been given their reference numbers. Items 2 and 5, for example, would probably come under the heading of Casualties, in the section on panic during the fire. On the other hand, not all the notes will necessarily be used in the essay. Some items simply won't fit into the topics chosen for the outline and will be discarded.

When you are developing a complex research topic, it is helpful to print out your outline and your notes, to identify outline topics and sections of your notes through numbers and letters, and to match up your notes with your outline by cross-referencing, using numbers and letters in the margins. Only when you are satisfied with your organization, and when the topics in your outline are fully supported by information from your notes, should you turn to the computer and copy and paste on the screen.

Organizing Your Essay

1. Read through your list of notes, thinking about your thesis and the appropriate strategy for your essay.
2. Write down a list of potential paragraph topics.
3. Revise the list, adding and deleting items, and indicating possible supporting evidence.
4. Rearrange the order of the items on the list until the topics are in logical sequence.
5. If necessary, cross-reference your notes and your outline.
6. Integrate your notes into your outline by pasting them into your essay file.

EXERCISE 32: WRITING AN OUTLINE WITH CROSS-REFERENCING

Read the following set of notes, organized by source, for an essay on immigration.

1. Write an outline of topics for an essay to be called "The Economic and Social Consequences of Immigration in the United States Today."
2. Cross-reference the notes with your outline.

As you consider the information in these notes, remember that, if this exercise were preparation for an assigned essay, you could return to any of the sources, if you wished, and add details or examples to develop a topic that does not have enough supporting information.

Source A

Borjas, George J. "Tired, Poor, On Welfare." *National Review* 13 Dec. 1993: 40–42. Print.

1. It's true that immigrants contribute more in taxes to the nation's economy than they consume in welfare payments.

2. But the cost of living in this country and of using services and facilities adds an enormous amount to the cost of their support. That isn't being considered in most pro-immigration arguments. In this regard, immigrants do potentially take more than they give.

3. In 1990, a greater percentage of immigrants than natives received welfare. Immigrants comprise 8% of the population; they receive 13% of the cash benefits distributed.

4. Recent immigrants are less skilled than their counterparts 100 years ago. (B. says he's not saying that immigrants come to this country expressly to live on welfare.)

5. Whether immigrants want to work or not isn't the point; they don't have the skills, so they go on welfare.

6. B. fears creation of a new underclass of the unskilled. "A welfare state cannot afford the large-scale immigration of less-skilled persons." (42)

Source B

Brimelow, Peter. "Time to Rethink Immigration?" *National Review* 22 June 1992: 30–46. Print.

1. Cites large numbers of recent immigrants. Between 1951 and 1990, about one-fifth of the population of Jamaica had immigrated to the U.S.

2. 85% of legal immigrants between 1971 and 1990 were from the Third World.

3. Consequence: "The American ethnic mix has been upset." (31) White population of U.S. fell by 13% from 1960–90. The projection: by 2020, whites would only be 61% of population.

4. U.S. birthrate has declined since big waves of immigration at turn of century; therefore, new immigrants now have greater opportunity to dominate.

5. Major historical influence on U.S. culture has been British and German.

6. Proponents of present immigration policy are urging "Americans to abandon the bonds of a common ethnicity and instead to trust entirely to ideology to hold together their state." (35) Historically, this bond of ideology hasn't been successful (e.g., USSR).

7. Melting pot tradition: "cultural synthesis . . . a pattern of swallowing and digestion" of immigrant groups (e.g., Irish immigrants eventually abandoned antisocial tendencies like dysfunctional families, alcoholism, disease). (36)

8. Economic argument: immigrants needed to perform jobs no one else will do. Instead, why not force unemployed Americans to work for their welfare? Or encourage a higher birthrate?

9. Cultural characteristics of each immigrant group predict whether that group will thrive or fail in new country. Cultural qualities of current major immigrant groups include unfortunate antisocial tendencies (like violence); this will have "economic consequences" for U.S.

10. Cites Borjas: welfare benefits to immigrants cost $1 billion more than they pay in taxes.

11. Hispanics in particular aren't being urged to assimilate; their tendency to support bilingualism and multiculturalism is deplorable.

Source C

Fonte, John. "Americanization Now: Getting Serious about Assimilation." *National Review Online*, National Review Online. 8 Nov. 2001. Web. 10 Mar. 2010. <http://www.nationalreview.com/comment/comment-fonte110801.shtml>.

1. A fair number of first- and second-generation immigrants may be doing well economically and learning English.

2. But that is not the same as fully integrating themselves into the idea of being American. For one middle-class Muslim family, "assimilation is not a goal."

3. One survey found that 80% of Muslim immigrants interviewed felt "more allegiance to a foreign country than to the United States." [Kambiz Ghaneabassiri]

4. An even more complete survey (5,000 interviewed) of the children of Mexican and Filipino immigrants also concluded that their sense of being American decreased after four years in American schools.

5. In the past, immigrants became patriotic Americans because the government and the culture expected it of them; assimilation was "institutionalized." "Civic assimilation, American style, is (as most of us agree) not based on adherence to particular ethnic customs, religious beliefs, cultural rituals, or culinary traditions, but on political loyalty to our democratic republic."

6. Instead of treating immigrants as clients who expect to receive services, the Immigration and Naturalization Service should treat them as "candidates" for future citizenship.

7. Emphasizing the Oath of Allegiance would unite new and old Americans instead of allowing them to become divided by race, ethnicity, and religion.

Source D
Fukuyama, Francis. "Immigrants and Family Values." *Commentary* 95.5 (1993): 26–32. Print.

1. "The symptoms of cultural decay are all around us, but the last people in the world we should be blaming are recent immigrants." (26)

2. Rejects Brimelow's argument that culture determines economic success for immigrants.

3. American identity doesn't derive from a specific culture; it's rooted in (a) ideals of democracy that transcend ethnicity, and (b) a consumer culture. Both are available to any immigrant group.

4. Do non-European immigrant groups threaten basic American values (e.g., nuclear family, success through hard work)? Decline of family structure and work ethic results from our declining postindustrialist society, not from values of new immigrants, who tend to have strong family loyalties (e.g., Asian immigrants: large families, economically successful).

5. Fear of immigration really directed at Hispanics: some Hispanics have had social problems, and many Americans lump together Hispanics with blacks as "a vast threatening underclass." (29)

6. F. cites diversity of Hispanics: some good, some bad. Problems really arise from poverty.

7. Reason for cultural disruption in U.S. has to do with economic and social change. Newly arrived immigrants didn't create sexual revolution, feminism, alienating workplace, single-parent households.

8. Clamor for multiculturalism comes more from leaders than from the average immigrant, for whom preserving ethnicity is not a primary goal.

9. Real issue: do we believe so strongly in our cultural heritage that we insist that all immigrants assimilate, or do we "carry respect for other cultures to the point that Americans no longer have a common voice with which to speak to one another"? (31)

Source E

Glazer, Nathan. "The Closing Door." *New Republic* 27 Dec. 1993. Rpt. in *Arguing Immigration*. Ed. Nicolaus Mills. New York: Simon, 1994. 37–47. Print.

1. Some immigrants (mostly Asians) come with better education and work skills than most Americans have. Some are less qualified than Americans (mostly Hispanics and Caribbean blacks).

2. Even within these groups, ability to work and support themselves varies.

3. The economic argument isn't the crucial one. Whether we import cheap labor or not isn't the point (Japan thrives on a low immigration rate).

4. Those who use the economic argument to propose restrictions are really responding to the perceived threat of a more diverse nation. But they shouldn't be called bigots or racists. The preference for people of one's own culture is natural. "There is a difference between recognizing those who are in some sense one's own, with links to a people and a culture, and a policy based on dislike, hostility, or racial antagonism." (44)

5. Why doesn't U.S. assimilate immigrants the way it used to? "It is a different country: less self-confident, less willing to impose European and American customs and loyalty as simply the best in the world." (44)

6. G. is very tolerant of the movement to restrict immigration. "They ask why the stream of immigration should be so unrepresentative of the nation that already exists." (45)

Source F

Krikorian, Mark. "Will Americanization Work in America?" *Freedom Review*. Center for Immigration Studies, Fall 1997. Web. 22 Aug. 2001. <http://www.cis.org/articles/1997/freedom_review.html>.

1. We've been experiencing the largest influx of immigrants in American history, with no end in sight. 900,000 green cards given to potential citizens in 1996.

2. Why has immigration become such a hot issue? Those who favor an open access policy say that opposition to immigration results from a fear of multiculturalism, which is likely to "weaken America's national identity." Krikorian questions this "romanticized and sanitized" myth.

3. There are other difficult issues. For example, the National Research Council has issued a report expressing fears that the increased rate of immigration is turning the U.S. into a nation of haves and have-nots. Some immigrants have skills that feed into our present economic needs; they are likely to benefit from emigrating to America. Unskilled workers—like those who didn't finish high school in their own country—will have little chance of managing on their own, let alone thriving economically.

4. Most of the newest wave of immigrants are likely to be uneducated. Far from contributing to the tax base, they will become a drain on our public services. [This is Krikorian's analysis of the arguments, not his opinion.]

5. The very fact that the number of immigrants is the largest in our history makes it unlikely that they will assimilate quickly (e.g., learn English). These groups are large enough to support their own cultural institutions, so they need not mingle with native-born Americans or other immigrant groups. (Example: Spanish-speaking radio and television stations. Univision (Los Angeles) is the fifth-largest TV network.)

6. This cultural "clustering" prevents true diversity. It also discourages intermarriage since few immigrants have the opportunity to meet people (except employers) outside their culture. Still, Krikorian asserts that most immigrant populations are, in fact, willing to marry outside their cultures, suggesting the "potential amalgamation of the immigrant stock."

7. Krikorian's major point is that America is finding it extremely difficult to encourage assimilation among immigrants because it can't itself decide on its own national identity. There are too many different versions of history. Who should be our hero—George Washington or Malcolm X? Which holiday should we celebrate—Lincoln's birthday or Cinco de Mayo?

8. A study of immigrant children in 1992 and again in 1995 showed a significant decline in identification with American heritage and values.

9. Our view that our society ought to be multicultural is too deep to be easily modified or reversed. Our present immigration population only encourages the breakup of our society into smaller, self-sustaining groups. It's unlikely that we will soon be able to return to a "common civic culture." [Note: Krikorian himself seems neutral on these issues.]

Source G

McCarthy, Kevin. "Immigration by the Numbers." *New York Times* 15 Oct. 1997: 28. Print.

1. McC. is a demographer who produces studies of the impact of immigrants on the California economy. Such statistics are used and sometimes distorted by proponents and opponents of present immigration policy. The issue is: does immigration have a positive effect on the national economy?

2. "No matter what ideologues on both sides say, immigration is neither absolutely good or evil."

3. On balance, California has gained more than it has lost from the availability of a low-wage immigrant work force.

4. But low-skilled workers (immigrant and native) are earning less and less.

5. Immigrants without skills aren't thriving.

6. The state is burdened by providing services to immigrants.

7. McC. suggests "modest" changes in policy: (a) scale back the number of immigrants admitted to halfway between present number and the number in the 1960s; and (b) try for a formula that favors immigrants with education and skills, rather than low-skilled immigrants who are being admitted to join family members already here.

Source H

Simon, Julian L. *The Economic Consequences of Immigration into the United States.* 2nd ed. Ann Arbor: U of Michigan P, 1999. Print.

1. Immigrants tend to work harder than "natives" both physically at their jobs and intellectually at school. This is because they have nothing at first and need to

support themselves and also because they have energy and initiative. After all, they had the drive and energy to make the big leap and leave their home countries.

2. A study [by Steinberg] concludes that more serious crimes are committed by natives than by immigrants.

3. It is not true that immigrants displace natives from available jobs. Rather, their willingness to work stimulates the local industries and the economy, creating more jobs for everyone.

4. If more immigrants are admitted into the country, everyone's income is likely to increase.

5. Everyone benefits from immigration. "American citizens even do well while doing good when admitting refugees."

WRITING INTEGRATED PARAGRAPHS

Writing a research essay resembles putting together a *mosaic*. Each paragraph has a basic design, determined by its topic sentence. To carry out the design, a paragraph might contain a group of reasons or examples to illustrate its main idea, *or* an extended explanation to develop that idea in greater detail, *or* a comparison between two elements introduced in the first sentence. These are the same paragraphing patterns that you use in all your writing. *What makes the research essay different is the fact that the materials are assembled from many sources.*

Imagine that the notes that you have taken from several different sources are boxes of tiles, each box containing a different color. You may find it easier to avoid mixing the colors and to work *only* with red tiles or *only* with blue, or to devote one corner of the mosaic to a red pattern and another to a blue. In the same way, you may find it both convenient and natural to work with only one source at a time and to avoid the decisions and the adjustments that must be made when you are combining different styles and ideas. But, of course, it is the design and only the design that dictates which colors should be used in creating the pattern of the mosaic, and it is the design or outline of your essay that dictates which evidence should be included in each paragraph.

When you present a topic in a given paragraph, you must work with all the relevant information that you have gathered about that topic, whether it comes from one source or from many. Of course, you may have too much material; you may find it impossible to fit everything into the paragraph without overloading it with repetition. These rejected pieces may not fit into another part of the essay; instead, they will go back into their boxes as a backup or reserve fund of information.

> ## Constructing Paragraphs in a Research Essay
>
> 1. *Each paragraph should possess a single main idea, usually expressed in the topic sentence, that supports the development of your essay's thesis.* That topic controls the arrangement of all the information in the paragraph. Everything that is included should develop and support that single idea, without digressions.
> 2. *The body of the paragraph should contain information taken from a variety of sources.* The number of different sources that you include in any one paragraph depends partly on the number of authors in your notes who have touched on its main idea and partly on the contribution each can make to the development of your topic.

The criteria for judging the quality of a paragraph remain the same—*clarity, coherence,* and *unity.*

- Do integrate your material so that your reader will not be distracted by the differing sources or made aware of breaks between the various points.
- Don't integrate your material so completely that you forget to provide appropriate acknowledgment of your sources.

Here is a paragraph from a student essay about the novelist F. Scott Fitzgerald, in which four different explanations of an incident are presented, each at suitable length. Formal documentation of the sources has been omitted; but, to emphasize the variety and complexity of the research, the names of the sources and the attributing verbs and phrases have been underlined. The writer is describing an affair between Fitzgerald's wife, Zelda, and Edouard Jozan, a young Frenchman.

> There is a lack of agreement about the details of the affair as well as its significance for the Fitzgeralds' marriage. According to one of Fitzgerald's biographers, Jozan and Zelda afterward regarded it as "nothing more than a summer flirtation." But Ernest Hemingway, in his memoirs, wrote much later that Scott had told him "a truly sad story" about the affair, which he repeated many times in the course of their friendship. Gerald and Sara Murphy, who were present that summer and remembered the incident very well, told of being awakened by Scott in the middle of a September night in order to help him revive Zelda from an overdose of sleeping pills. The Murphys were sure that this incident was related to her affair with Jozan. Nancy Milford, Zelda's biographer, believes that the affair affected Zelda more than Scott, who, at that time, was very engrossed in his work. Indeed, Milford's account of the affair is the only one that suggests that Zelda was so deeply in love with Jozan that she asked Scott for a divorce.

According to an interview with Jozan, the members of this triangle never engaged in a three-way confrontation; Jozan told Milford that the Fitzgeralds were "the victims of their own unsettled and a little unhealthy imagination."

This paragraph gives a brief but adequate account of what is known about the events of that summer of 1924. The writer does not try to rush through the four accounts of the affair, nor does he reduce each one to a phrase, as if he expected the reader to have prior knowledge of these people and their activities. In the context of the whole essay, the paragraph provides enough information for the reader to judge whose interpretation of the affair is closest to the truth.

ACCOMMODATING ARGUMENT IN YOUR PARAGRAPHS

When you write a paragraph based on *induction*, the topic sentence should clearly summarize the range of evidence being cited. Here is an example from Edward Tenner's *Why Things Bite Back*, a book about the dangers of technological progress:

> The startling wartime successes of penicillin created the dangerous myth of an antibiotic panacea. Even after the U.S. Food and Drug Administration began to require prescriptions in the mid-1950s, an antibiotic injection or prescription remained for many people the payoff of a medical encounter. They resisted the medical fact that antibiotics can do nothing against colds and other viral diseases. In many other countries, antibiotics are still sold legally over the counter to patients who may never get proper instructions about dosage or the importance of completing a course of treatment. Dr. Stuart B. Levy of Boston cites an Argentinian businessman who was cured of leukemia but died of an infection by the common bacterium *E. coli*. Ten years of self-medication had produced plasmids in his body that were resistant to every antibiotic used. Governments, too, have unintentionally promoted resurgence. Indonesian authorities have literally ladled out preventive doses of tetracycline to 100,000 Muslim pilgrims for a week at a time. Since the Mecca pilgrimage has historically been one of the great mixing bowls of microorganisms, it is especially disturbing to learn that half of all cholera bacilli in Africa are now resistant to tetracycline.

Paragraphs presenting inductive evidence tend to be long. Tenner makes his point about the "dangerous myth" of penicillin in the topic sentence, but he doesn't immediately cite evidence. He first explains the "danger" in the second sentence, and the "myth" in the third. Only then does he introduce his first supporting point—self-medication in countries without drug regulation—with Dr. Levy's example of the antibiotic-resistant Argentinian businessman. Signaled by the transitional word "too," Tenner's second example—the Mecca pilgrimage—increases the scale of potential danger.

In contrast to the specific examples of induction, an article on "Methods of Media Manipulation" starts in a *deductive* mode, with a series of premises:

> We are told by people in the media industry that news bias is unavoidable. Whatever distortions and inaccuracies are found in the news are caused by deadline pressures, human misjudgment, budgetary restraints, and the difficulty of reducing a complex story into a concise report. Furthermore—the argument goes—no communication system can hope to report everything, selectivity is needed.
>
> I would argue that the media's misrepresentations are not at all the result of innocent error and everyday production problems, though such problems certainly do exist. True, the press has to be selective, but what principle of selectivity is involved?
>
> Media bias usually does not occur in random fashion; rather, it moves in the same overall direction again and again, favoring management over labor, corporations over corporate critics, affluent whites over low-income minorities, officialdom over protesters. . . . The built-in biases of the corporate mainstream media faithfully reflect the dominant ideology, seldom straying into territory that might cause discomfort to those who hold political and economic power, including those who own the media or advertise in it.

The initial presentation of Michael Parenti's argument is based on a dichotomy—contrast—between the media's view of news bias and his own. There is a disputed primary premise (bias is or is not avoidable) and a disputed secondary premise (one can't print everything vs. one prints what pleases one's corporate masters). Parenti's premises are developed in more detail, and the article goes on to support those premises through induction, by citing evidence of such manipulative tactics as "suppression by omission" and "framing."

While the opening of Parenti's article presents the opposition's argument as well as his own, the tone is grudging, even hostile. He leaves no room for accommodation between the two points of view. Yet, whenever possible, *it is useful to acknowledge some merit in your opponents or in their argument*. Here are excerpts from two essays supporting opposite sides of the "wilderness preservation" issue. In the first, John Daniel is arguing that the advancement of science, if uncontrolled, can do harm to unspoiled land. He is careful, however, to distinguish between his allies and his enemies:

> I don't mean to indict science in general. Many of the foremost champions of wild nature are scientists, and their work has done much to warn us of the environmental limits we are transgressing. I am arguing only against interventionist science that wants to splice genes, split atoms, or otherwise manipulate the wild—science aimed more at control than understanding, science that assumes ownership of the natural mysteries. When technological specialists come to believe that nature is answerable to their own prerogatives, they are not serving but endangering the greater community.

In William Tucker's view, society has more compelling interests, to which the wilderness movement must sometimes defer. But, before stating his argument, he pays his dues to nature:

> I am not arguing against wild things, scenic beauty, pristine landscapes, and scenic preservation. What I am questioning is the argument that wilderness is a value against which every other human activity must be judged and that human beings are somehow unworthy of the landscape. The wilderness has been equated with freedom, but there are many different ideas about what constitutes freedom. . . .

Interestingly enough, Tucker then proceeds to move from his impeccably fair presentation to an argument that approaches *ad hominem*—a personal attack:

> It may seem unfair to itemize the personal idiosyncrasies of people who feel comfortable only in wilderness, but it must be remembered that the environmental movement has been shaped by many people who literally spent years of their lives living in isolation.

Citing John Muir, David Brower, and Gary Snyder, leaders of the Sierra Club who spent much time alone in the mountains, Tucker continues:

> There is nothing reprehensible in this, and the literature and philosophy that emerge from such experiences are often admirable. But it seems questionable to me that the ethic that comes out of this wilderness isolation—and the sense of ownership of natural landscapes that inevitably follows—can serve as the basis for a useful national philosophy.

Whatever his disclaimers, Tucker is rooting one of his key arguments against the wilderness movement in the personal preferences of three men. He does not, however, resort to using slanted, exaggerated, or dismissive language about his opponents. In contrast, here is Robert W. McChesney's attack on commercialism in the media:

> The commercial blitzkrieg into every nook and cranny of U.S. culture, from schools to sport to museums to movie theaters to the Internet, has lessened traditional distinctions of public service from commercialism.

The word *blitzkrieg* (literally, lightning battle) originally referred to the German army in World War II. It immediately conjures up an image of a mechanized, pitiless army rolling over everything in its path, a reference reinforced by the domestic, vulnerable image of "nook and cranny," used to describe U.S. culture, the victim. Without even articulating his point, McChesney has created a lingering association between corporations and Nazis. This is a clever use of language, but is it a fair argument? In the next example, Leslie Savan also uses emotionally charged language to attack a similar target:

> Advertising now infects just about every organ of society, and wherever advertising gains a foothold it tends to slowly take over, like a vampire or a virus.

The brutal swiftness of the blitzkrieg has been replaced by the slow insinuation of an infection, but both images are deadly and unyielding. (The allusion to a vampire must have been tempting—advertising leaves viewers bloodless and brainwashed—but it should not be placed in tandem with the insidious, slowly creeping image of infection.) Interestingly enough, McChesney and Savan are both adopting the tactics of the commercial media that they condemn: using powerful images in an attempt to force their readers into agreement.

Mistakes to Avoid When Summarizing an Argument

1. Don't be one-sided; present *both* sides of an argument.
2. Don't omit crucial parts of the source's reasoning; provide a complete account of the argument.
3. Don't quote ideas out of context: make sure that you—and your reader—understand whether the source really supports the idea that you are citing.
4. Don't twist the source's ideas to fit your own purpose; provide a fair presentation.

PRESENTING ARGUMENTS FAIRLY

Perhaps the greatest disservice that you can do your sources is to distort them so that your reader is left with a false impression of what they have said or written. Such distortion is most likely to happen when you are writing an argumentative essay.

1. Present both sides of the argument.

One way of shading an argument to suit your own ends is to *misrepresent the strength of the opposition.* Let us assume that you are working with a number of articles, all of which are effectively presented and worth citing. Some clearly support your point of view; others are openly opposed; and a few avoid taking sides, emphasizing related but less controversial topics. If your essay cites only the favorable and neutral articles, and avoids any reference to the views of the opposition, you have presented the issue falsely. A one-sided presentation will make you appear to be either biased or sloppy in your research. If the sources are available and if their views are pertinent, they should be represented and, if you wish, refuted in your essay.

2. **Provide a complete account of the argument.**

Sometimes, distortions occur accidentally, because you have presented only a *partial* account of a source's views. In the course of an article or a book, authors sometimes examine and then reject or accept a variety of views before making it clear which are their own conclusions. Or an author may have mixed opinions about the issue and see merit in more than one point of view. If you choose to quote or paraphrase material from only one section of such a work, then you must find a way to inform your reader that these statements are not entirely representative of the writer's overall views.

3. **Make sure that you—and your reader—understand whether the source really supports the idea that you are citing.**

Ideas can get distorted because of the researcher's misunderstanding, careless note taking, or hasty reading. Remember to check the entire section of the article or all your notes before you attribute an opinion to your source. Make sure that you are not taking a sentence out of context or ignoring a statement in the next paragraph or on the next page that may be more typical of the writer's thinking. Writers often use an argumentative strategy that sets up a point with which they basically disagree in order to shoot it down shortly thereafter. Don't confuse a statement made for the sake of argument with a writer's real beliefs.

4. **Provide a fair presentation.**

Occasionally, you may be so eager to uphold your point of view that you will cite any bit of material that looks like supporting evidence. To do so, however, you may have to twist the words of the source to fit your ideas. This is one of the worst kinds of intellectual dishonesty—and one of the easiest for a suspicious reader to detect: one has only to look up the source. If you cannot find sufficient arguments and if your sources' evidence does not clearly and directly support your side, then you should seriously consider switching sides or switching topics.

Here is a fairly clear instance of such distortion. In an essay on the need for prison reform, Garry Wills is focusing on the *deficiencies of our society's penal system*; he is not directly concerned with the arguments for or against the death penalty. But the student citing Wills in a research essay is writing specifically in support of capital punishment. To make Wills's argument fit into the scheme of this essay, the student must make some suspiciously selective references. Here is a paragraph from the research essay (on the left), side by side with the source.

Although the death penalty may seem very harsh and inhuman, is this not fair and just punishment for one who was able to administer death to another human being? A murderer's victim always receives the death penalty. Therefore, the death penalty for the murderer evens the score, or, as stated in the Bible, "an eye for an eye, and a tooth for a tooth." According to Garry Wills, "take a life, lose your life." Throughout the ages, society has demanded that man be allowed to right his wrongs. Revenge is our culture's oldest way of making sure that no one "gets away with" any crime. As Wills points out, according to this line of reasoning, the taking of the murderer's life can be seen as his payment to society for his misdeed.

The oldest of our culture's views on punishment is the *lex talionis,* an eye for an eye. Take a life, lose your life. It is a very basic cry—people must "pay" for their crimes, yield exact and measured recompense. No one should "get away with" any crime, like a shoplifter taking something unpaid for. The desire to make an offender suffer equivalent pain (if not compensatory excess of pain) is very deep in human nature, and rises quickly to the surface. What is lynching but an impatience with even the slightest delay in exacting this revenge? It serves our social myth to say that this impatience, if denied immediate gratification, is replaced by something entirely different—by an impersonal dedication to justice. Only lynchers want revenge, not those who wait for a verdict. That is not very likely. Look at the disappointed outcry if the verdict does not yield even delayed satisfaction of the grudge.

In the essay, the writer is citing only *part* of Wills's argument and thus makes him appear to support capital punishment. Wills is being misrepresented because (unlike the writer) he considers it fair to examine the views of the opposing side before presenting his own arguments. The ideas that the student cites are not Wills's, but Wills's presentations of commonly accepted assumptions about punishment. It is not entirely clear whether the writer of the research essay has merely been careless, failing to read past the first few sentences, or whether the misrepresentation is intentional.

INTEGRATING YOUR SOURCES: AN EXAMPLE

To illustrate the need for careful analysis of sources before you write your paragraphs, here is a group of passages, all direct quotations, which have been gathered for a research essay on college athletics. The paragraph developed from these sources must support the writer's *thesis:*

Colleges should, in the interests of both players and academic standards, outlaw the high-pressure tactics used by coaches when they recruit high school players for college teams.

The first three statements come from college coaches describing recruiting methods that they have observed and carried out; the last four are taken from books that discuss corruption in athletics.

I think in the long run, every coach must recognize this basic principle, or face the alumni firing squad. Recruiting is the crux of building a championship football team.

STEVE SLOAN, Texas Tech

Athletics is creating a monster. Recruiting is getting to be cancerous.

DALE BROWN, Louisiana State University

You don't out-coach people, you out-recruit them.

PAUL "BEAR" BRYANT, University of Alabama

It is an athletic maxim that a man with no special coaching skills can win games if he recruits well and that a tactician without talented players is a man soon without a job.

KENNETH DENLINGER

There is recruiting in various degrees in every intercollegiate sport, from crew to girls' basketball and from the Houston golf dynasty that began in the mid-50's to Southern California importing sprinters and jumpers from Jamaica.

J. ROBERT EVANS

The fundamental causes of the defects in American college athletics are too much commercialism and a negligent attitude towards the educational opportunity for which the college exists.

CARNEGIE FOUNDATION, 1929

[*Collier's* magazine, in 1905, reported that] Walter Eckersall, All-American quarterback, enrolled at Chicago three credits short of the entrance requirement and his teammate, Leo Detray, entered the school before he even graduated high school. In addition the University of Minnesota paid two players outright to play in a single game (Nebraska: 1902). A quarterback and an end also from Minnesota admitted shaving points during the 1903 Beloit game.

JOSEPH DURSO

Examining the Sources

Your paragraph will focus on *recruiting high school stars,* as opposed to developing students who enter college by the ordinary admissions procedure. Which of these ideas and observations might help to develop this paragraph? In other words, which statements should be represented by *paraphrase* or perhaps by *direct quotation?*

> I think in the long run every coach must recognize this basic principle, or face the alumni firing squad. Recruiting is the crux of building a championship football team.
>
> STEVE SLOAN

This very broad generalization seems quotable at first, largely because it sums up the topic so well; but, in fact, because it does no more than sum up the topic, it does not advance your argument any further. Therefore, you need not include it if your topic sentence makes the same point. (In general, you should write your own topic sentences rather than letting your sources write them for you.) The phrase "alumni firing squad" might be useful to quote in a later paragraph, in a discussion of the specific influence of alumni on recruiting.

> Athletics is creating a monster. Recruiting is getting to be cancerous.
>
> DALE BROWN

Coach Brown's choice of images—"cancerous" and "monster"—is certainly vivid; but the sentence as a whole is no more than a *generalized opinion about recruiting,* not an explanation of why the situation is so monstrous. Don't quote Brown for the sake of two words.

> You don't out-coach people, you out-recruit them.
>
> PAUL "BEAR" BRYANT

This is the first statement that has advanced a specific idea: the coach may have a *choice* between building a winning team through recruiting and building a winning team through good coaching; but recruiting, not coaching, wins games. Coach Bryant, then, is not just making a rhetorical point, as the first two coaches seem to be. His seven-word sentence is succinct, if not elaborately developed, and would make a good introduction to or summation of a point that deserves full discussion.

The remaining four statements suggest a wider range of approach and style.

> Walter Eckersall, All-American quarterback, enrolled at Chicago three credits short of the entrance requirement and his teammate, Leo Detray, entered the school before he even graduated high school. In addition, the University of Minnesota paid two players outright to play in a single game (Nebraska: 1902). A quarterback and an end also from Minnesota admitted shaving points during the 1903 Beloit game.
>
> JOSEPH DURSO

This passage is as much concerned with corruption as recruiting and indicates that commercialism is nothing new in college athletics. Although the information is interesting, it is presented as a list of facts, and the language is not worth quoting. You may, however, want to summarize the example in your own words.

> The fundamental causes of the defects in American college athletics are too much commercialism and a negligent attitude towards the educational opportunity for which the college exists.
>
> CARNEGIE FOUNDATION

This extract from the 1929 Carnegie Foundation study is phrased in abstract language that is characteristic of foundation reports and academic writing in general. The foundation presents its point clearly enough and raises an important idea: an athlete recruited to win games (and earn fame and fortune) is likely to ignore the primary reason for going to college—to acquire an education. Nevertheless, there is no compelling reason to quote this statement. Remember that you include quotations in your essay to enhance your presentation; the quotation marks automatically prepare the reader for special words and phrasing. But the prose here is too colorless and abstract to give the reader anything to focus on; a paraphrase is preferable.

> There is recruiting in varying degrees in every intercollegiate sport, from crew to girls' basketball and from the Houston golf dynasty that began in the mid-50's to Southern California importing sprinters and jumpers from Jamaica.
>
> J. ROBERT EVANS

This statement presents a quite different, more detailed level of information; it lists several sports, including some not known for their cutthroat recruiting practices. But details do not necessarily deserve quotation. Will these references be at all meaningful to the reader who is not familiar with the "Houston golf dynasty" or Jamaican track stars? To know that recruitment is not limited to cash sports, such as football, is interesting, but such specifics date quickly: in a few years, they may no longer be remembered by most readers.

> It is an athletic maxim that a man with no special coaching skills can win games if he recruits well and that a tactician without talented players is a man soon without a job.
>
> KENNETH DENLINGER

Largely because of parallel construction, the last comment sounds both sharp and solid. In much the same way as Coach Bryant's seven words, but at greater length, Kenneth Denlinger sums up the contrast between coaching and recruiting, and suggests which one has the edge. Because the statement gives the reader something substantial to think about and because it is well phrased, Denlinger is probably worth quoting.

Should the writer include the statements by Bryant and by Denlinger, both of which say essentially the same thing? While Bryant's firsthand comment is terse and authoritative, Denlinger's is more complete and self-explanatory. A solution might be to include both, at different points in the paragraph, with Bryant cited at the end to sum up the idea that has been developed. Of course, the other five sources need not be excluded from the paragraph. Rather, if you wish, all five may be referred to, by paraphrase or brief reference, with their authors' names cited.

Here is one way of integrating this set of statements into a paragraph. (Note that the sources are documented using MLA style; the bibliography has been omitted. MLA style is explained on pp. 465–472.)

In college athletics, what is the best way for a school to win games? Should a strong team be gradually built up by training ordinary students from scratch, or should the process be shortened and success be assured by actively recruiting players who already know how to win? The first method may be more consistent with the traditional amateurism of college athletics, but as early as 1929, the Carnegie Foundation complained that the focus of college sports had shifted from education to the material advantages of winning (Denlinger 22). Even earlier, in 1903, there were several instances of players without academic qualifications who were "hired" to guarantee victory (Durso 6). And in recent years excellence of recruiting has become the most important skill for a coach to possess. Kenneth Denlinger has observed, "It is an athletic maxim that a man with no special coaching skills can win games if he recruits well and that a tactician without talented players is a man soon without a job" (3). It follows, then, that a coach who wants to keep his job is likely to concentrate on spotting and collecting talent for his team. Coaches from LSU, Alabama, and Texas Tech all testify that good recruiting has first priority throughout college athletics (McDermott 17; Mano 41; Sloan 106). According to Bear Bryant of Alabama: "You don't out-coach people, you out-recruit them" (Mano 41).

WRITING AN INTRODUCTION

The introduction presents a *preview* of your essay, informing your reader about the topic and the method(s) you are likely to use (explanation or analysis or persuasion). Often, the introduction will include a statement of the thesis, although with some strategies (notably problem and solution), it can be preferable to indicate the problem at the beginning and allow the argument and evidence to set the stage for a presentation of the thesis toward the end of the essay.

The introduction also has a *marketing* function. You want to encourage your reader to move past the first paragraph or two and into the body of the essay. To do so, you need to do more than set out your wares; you have to make the shop window look attractive. Using compelling or intriguing language can catch the reader's attention. Including an example or (if not too long) an anecdote can make the reader feel interested in or sympathetic to the topic that you propose to explore.

Here are the introductions of two essays by professional authors. As you read, consider whether the author tells you what he is going to write about and whether—and why—he makes you want to continue reading.

David Brooks, a writer, editor, and commentator on public affairs, wrote "People Like Us" for the *Atlantic Monthly*. Michael Bérubé, who teaches English and Cultural Studies at Pennsylvania State University, has published essays in a variety of journals, including the *Chronicle of Higher Education*, where "How to End Grade Inflation" appeared.

> Maybe it's time to admit the obvious. We don't really care about diversity all that much in America, even though we talk about it a great deal. Maybe somewhere in this country there is a truly diverse neighborhood in which a black Pentecostal minister lives next to a white anti-globalization activist, who lives next to an Asian short-order cook, who lives next to a professional golfer, who lives next to a post-modern-literature professor and a cardiovascular surgeon. But I have never been to or heard of that neighborhood. Instead, what I have seen all around the country is people making strenuous efforts to group themselves with people who are basically like themselves.
>
> DAVID BROOKS, from "People Like Us"

> Last month, Princeton University announced it would combat grade inflation by proposing that A-minuses, A's and A-pluses be awarded to no more than the top 35 percent of students in any course. For those of us in higher education, the news has come as a shock, almost as if Princeton had declared that spring in central New Jersey would begin promptly on March 21, with pleasant temperatures in the 60's and 70's through the end of the semester. For until now, grade inflation was like the weather: it got worse every year, or at least everyone said so, and yet hardly anybody did anything about it.
>
> MICHAEL BÉRUBÉ, from "How to End Grade Inflation"

Brooks's introduction does everything that an introduction is supposed to do. You are quickly made aware of his topic and its scope (social diversity in America), his intention (analysis through contrast between good intentions and reality), and his thesis (we try to fool ourselves that we live in culturally diverse communities, but we do not). Brooks compels your attention with a striking, brief first sentence that makes you wonder what "the obvious" is going to be. Then he proceeds to attack what he regards as a national illusion, citing a string of concrete examples that, by its very length, makes you want to know what cultural type will be mentioned next. He finishes the paragraph—and his introduction—by asserting the other half of the contrast contained in his thesis: people really don't want diversity. By the end of that paragraph, Brooks's intended audience—the readers of the *Atlantic Monthly*—are likely to be hooked.

In contrast, Bérubé begins his introduction much more traditionally: he tells his readers about Princeton's decision to stop grade inflation and thus provides the context for his essay. We know the topic and scope (grade inflation in American universities), but we don't know much as yet about his intention and his thesis. What is striking in this introduction is the use of irony: by drawing an analogy between Princeton's proposal and ideal weather conditions, Bérubé lets us know just how unsatisfactory a situation (like a rainy spring) grade inflation is and how desirable (but unlikely) it would be to find a solution to the problem. Since his audience is his fellow academics, who probably share his concerns, his readers will want to know how Bérubé proposes to solve the problem.

Students introducing a research essay can provide just as comprehensive a preview of their topic, scope, intention, and thesis. What is often missing is the vivid example or the compelling choice of words to make the reader want to continue reading. Consider the following example:

> As more and more women in the United States work outside the home for longer hours, their children are often cared for by workers in day care centers or by babysitters. Some women work for economic reasons, because they are single mothers or because their families can't manage on a single salary. Many of these women would really like to stay home with their children, but feel they have no choice but to go out of the home to work. Others have experienced housewife blues or have come to believe, with the feminist movement, that they can't be fulfilled without a career. In fact, psychologists have studied the children of working mothers and have concluded that being deprived of a mother's care and attention can cause lasting adverse effects on children. What can a working mother do to prevent this from happening?

Here, we have a straightforward presentation of a problem that, presumably, the writer will attempt to solve—or, at least, analyze and clarify—in the body of the essay. We can expect to see statistics and studies cited as well as the opinions of experts in the field. This is likely to be a solid essay that makes its point convincingly. But does the introduction make you want to read it?

> My grandparents emigrated to this country from Italy. They were eager to take advantage of the opportunities America offered and, in exchange, tried to become good citizens in the community where they settled. In a very few years, they had become completely assimilated, speaking and behaving more American than the third-generation Americans around them. For my grandparents, Amer-

ica was a melting pot; for immigrants today, it is merely a host nation that provides the opportunity to have a better life without requiring or even encouraging them to give their cultural allegiance in return. Our immigration policy will never be successful, as it used to be, until there is the expectation that immigrants will leave their old cultures behind and think, speak, and act like their American neighbors.

This introduction is anchored by the personal example in the first few sentences, which leads into the contrast between immigration fifty years ago and immigration now, expressed as a thesis in the last sentence. Persuading readers to accept this thesis will surely require the citation of facts, statistics, and expert opinion, not just examples and anecdotal evidence. But the story of the writer's grandparents is compelling and makes the reader want to find out why—or whether—experiences like these have passed into history.

USING VISUALS AS SOURCES

You can present ideas and cite evidence visually as well as through words. Several of the professional essays in this book—mostly those originally published in newspapers or popular magazines—are accompanied by visuals. In addition, each of the three model research essays in Chapter 11 includes pictures. Let's consider how the presence of various kinds of visuals can give the reader a more vivid and immediate understanding of the author's meaning.

Understanding the Impact of Visuals

One way of using visuals is to present data through *tables and figures such as charts, graphs, and maps.* These kinds of visuals generally compare information in separate categories, at different times or in different places. In this way, visuals serve as supporting evidence, used to make a point succinctly. In "The Weight of the World" (p. 7), Don Peck finds it easier to use maps than words to raise complex issues about increasing obesity in the United States. Peck is dealing with two sets of variables: location (levels of obesity vary among the 48 states) and time (levels of obesity in each of the states varied between 1991 and 2000). By using three maps to provide snapshots over time and shading to indicate relative levels of obesity, Peck gets his point across visually.

Drawings or diagrams can help the reader to understand the details of a place or an object or a process. In "Falling on Deaf Ears" (p. 190), Pat Hagan is writing about the resistance among some profoundly deaf people to the possibility of a cure for their deafness; the controversy centers around attitudes toward disability, not the technical details of a cochlear implant. So the diagram of a cochlear implant may not be crucial to your understanding of the article. Still, Hagan devotes a good deal of her article to explaining the implant procedure and its medical implications, and, far from being a distraction, the diagram clarifies the process.

Photographs or moving images provide the reader with an instant impression of the author's point. Images can attract readers to the text, interest them in the topic, and encourage them to see how the thesis develops. Although Anne Hollander writes at length about the "subversive authority" and sexual attraction of the new male uniform of T-shirt and jeans (p. 8), her point is really made through a single picture of a slouching Marlon Brando. Photographs are especially useful to authors who are writing about historical topics and want to provide readers with a sense of the period. As a context for her description of 1950s shopping centers (p. 121), Lizabeth Cohen includes pictures of typical shoppers. We know that the pictures are authentic because the caption cites the R. H. Macy & Co., Inc., *1957 Annual Report* and, equally important, the archival collection where Cohen found that report.

In contrast to the relatively objective data contained in charts and graphs, photographs and moving images are likely to appeal to the emotions rather than merely to reason, with the reader subtly encouraged to accept the author's assumptions and conclusions. A great deal depends on the *choice* of picture. At the beginning of Eric Hoover's article about bad behavior at college athletic events (p. 70), we're shown a picture of a basketball player standing in front of spectators in the bleachers. The image of the larger figure of the player is set off by the mass of heads, open mouths, and extended arms ranged behind him. We don't really need the caption (or, in some ways, the article) to understand that the player is being taunted by the crowd. The image is both vivid and appropriate for the author's purpose.

The three pictures that accompany Felicia R. Lee's "Does Class Count in Today's Land of Opportunity?" (pp. 153–154) seem less effective. To illustrate the fact that "the rich and the poor are still very much there," we're shown a black woman wistfully looking at a piece of fruit (presumably sorting it rather than buying it), along with a lady's maid kneeling to put on her mistress's shoe. The original article also included an image of an equestrian jumping a fence flanked by elegant floral displays. Because these images of the barriers between classes are stereotypes, they do make their point instantly; but they come from an earlier period and do little to enhance Lee's description of contemporary attitudes.

While it may be helpful to use photos as a way of interesting readers and encouraging them to accept a thesis, *authors have an obligation to present both sides of an issue objectively*. They therefore must refrain from loading the dice through choosing blatantly partisan photos. The need to avoid the impression of bias is heightened when the topic is controversial and especially when the significance resonates with a particular ethnic, religious, or cultural group. At the beginning of the article "Debating How Best to Love Your Country" (p. 582), the *New York Times* shows, side by side, a clearly focused picture of an elderly black man reverently hoisting a crisp and clean flag in what seems to be a small-town park and a fuzzy picture of some poorly dressed youngish people in the act of burning a crumpled flag. These two pictures are presumably intended to illustrate the traditionally patriotic views of Norman Podhoretz, as described in the article, and the broader definition of patriotism—which includes protest—presented by Victor Navasky. Is Navasky's side of the debate fairly represented by these two pictures? Is there any bias here?

In an article about the work of nonprofit organizations (NPOs) during major disasters, should an author show pictures of victims being aided or victims deteriorating because no help has arrived? Obviously, the choice to some extent depends on the article's thesis. But the pictures should also be reasonably representative of the facts: if data indicate that NPOs used their available resources effectively in a particular relief effort, then that's what should be depicted. If the author wants to demonstrate that the NPOs were too underfunded or too incompetent to deliver sufficient aid—and if the facts support that view—then it would be reasonable to appeal to the reader's compassion by showing injured, untended earthquake victims or a village decimated by a tsunami.

Using Visuals in Your Essay

Now, let's look at ways of using visuals in college essays. Occasionally, visuals—usually photographs—will serve as the inspiration for your thesis.

- If you were writing about the effects of plastic surgery on teenagers with facial defects, you would make the greatest impact by including "before and after" *photographs.*

- If you were analyzing the effect of automobile commercials on consumer choices, you would want to show your reader some striking examples, perhaps by supplementing the text of your essay with a *CD-ROM* containing some filmed commercials (or *links* to the commercials if they are available on the Web and you are submitting your essay electronically).

- If you were advocating limits to be set on the height of buildings in your city, you would find *photographs*—or take them yourself—of the skyline as it is now, as well as preparing *diagrams* or *computer-generated images* showing the relative heights of the proposed new buildings juxtaposed among the old ones.

For most topics, you should be able to support your thesis successfully through the text alone, whether or not you provide images or charts or any other illustrative information. And you should certainly avoid including a picture simply for its own sake. Still, carefully chosen visuals can often increase the effectiveness of your essay as well as fully engage your reader's attention. David Morgan's account of the strange occurrence at Lake Tunguska is definitely enhanced by a map of the region (p. 538) and a picture of the blast site (p. 546). Many readers will instantly recognize the stills from the films—*The Cabinet of Dr. Caligari, Freaks,* and *Psycho*—discussed in Bethany Dettmore's essay about horror movies (p. 492). Dettmore uses these pictures to illustrate (in the first two films) her point about the ambiguous nature of "monster" figures—half-frightening, half-sympathetic—as well as the transition, in *Psycho,* to films in which "normal" people are actually the monsters. And the curious practices of cannibalism as analyzed in Lee Myers's essay (pp. 517 and 522) seem both more and less normal when we see them depicted in the accompanying illustrations.

Some of the research topics discussed in the earlier chapters of *Writing from Sources* would certainly benefit from the inclusion of visuals.

- It's easy to find photographs of *Lawrence of Arabia*. The one shown on page 334 would be appropriate if you were writing about Lawrence's later years, but not if you were exclusively concerned with his desert campaigns.

- An essay about *excessive drinking by college students* could be accompanied by tables or line graphs showing instances of emergency room treatment or assaults or class attendance over time, as linked to documented consumption of alcohol. The tabulated results of any surveys you might conduct for this essay would certainly need to be included as an appendix. Would you choose to include photographs of students after a hard night's drinking? Possibly, if the photographs are truly representative of the situation that you are analyzing in your essay, and if the people in the photograph have given their permission for the use of these images.

- Similar kinds of visuals could be used in an essay about *responses to beggars*. Here you would want to consider whether the pity evoked by a picture of an unkempt, emaciated beggar would enhance or detract from the effectiveness of your essay. Again, this depends on your thesis.

- If your topic were *animal rights*, you might find it hard to resist including a picture of a pathetic dog or cat to engage the reader's sympathies. But you can carry pathos too far: a laboratory specimen bristling with electrodes or twitching under torture might serve to repel rather than engage your reader's interests.

Integrating Visuals into Your Essay

Placement and appearance: If you are integrating the visuals into your essay electronically, put each one as near as possible to the related point in your text. Make sure that the font that you use for the tables or charts is readable, but don't use such a large font that it dominates your text. Photographs should be an appropriate size: the details should be clear, but, again, the pictures should not overwhelm the words.

Captions: Visuals that include data should be explained and interpreted, either in a caption or in the main text. Don't assume that the reader will understand all their implications and why you have included them. Photos, on the other hand, may be self-explanatory, requiring no more than an allusion to them in your text. But, at a minimum, every visual should be identified with a caption that documents its source.

Permission: Unless a visual is from a government or other public source, you will need to get permission from the source to include it in an essay that is go-

> ## Choosing Visuals
>
> - Are the data in each chart or graph relevant to your point? Do they serve as evidence to support your thesis? Or are they merely an interesting sidebar? Do they digress from your line of argument? Will extensive columns of tables and graphs bore your readers rather than convince them?
>
> - Can readers readily understand the information contained in the chart or graph? Are the data sufficiently explained in either the caption or the text?
>
> - How will your readers respond to the picture? Will it engage their interest? Is it attractive and pleasing? Or is it unpleasant? Will readers feel indifferent or horrified? Will any of these reactions make it difficult for them to accept your thesis?
>
> - What assumptions does the picture require? Is the cultural context familiar and does it reflect the world your readers are living in? Or is it so dated or remote from their knowledge or experience as to have little significance for them? Is it a cliché, a cultural icon that no longer resonates?
>
> - Are the appearance and style of the photograph (or cartoon) appropriate to the tone set by your text? Is it so controversial as to distract readers from following the development of ideas in your essay? Will it engage their interest or make them stop reading?

ing to be posted on the Web. In any case, for any visual, acknowledgment of the source in your caption and in your bibliography is essential.

Preparation: Prepare any visuals after you have completed a working draft of your essay and have chosen the information or images that you intend to include. Don't assume that you can produce a clear copy and incorporate it into your text at the last moment. If you are preparing your own data (such as the results of a survey), spend some time considering how to present the information, what to include and what to omit, what categories to use, whether a table or graph or chart is most appropriate. Then tabulate the data well in advance as you may run into difficulties formatting the information on your computer. Similarly, make sure that the photographs you have chosen are sharp and an appropriate size and, if you're including them within a page of the text, take time to position them appropriately. Unless you are submitting your essay electronically, make sure that your printer can handle the production of the photographs you've chosen.

ASSIGNMENT 12: ORGANIZING AND
WRITING THE RESEARCH ESSAY

1. Read through the essays in Appendix B. Your instructor will indicate whether to read Group A (periodicals), Group B (academic books), or the entire set. Check with your instructor about whether you may use additional sources. Develop a topic for a research essay using most or all of these sources.

2. Write down a tentative list of main ideas, based on these sources, that should be discussed in an essay dealing with your subject. Also include your own ideas on the subject.

3. Develop an outline based on your list of ideas, and consider possible theses for the essay and the strategy that will best fit your thesis and sources.

4. After you have compiled a substantial list of topics and developed a tentative thesis, reread the passages, cross-referencing the topics on your list with the relevant material from the essays. While you do not have to use up everything in all of the readings, you should include all relevant points.

5. Develop this outline into an eight- or ten-page essay.

▪10▪
Acknowledging Sources

When you engage in research, you continually come into contact with the ideas and the words of other writers; as a result, the opportunities to plagiarize—by accident or by intention—increase tremendously. You must therefore understand exactly what constitutes plagiarism.

Plagiarism is the unacknowledged use of another person's work, in the form of original ideas, strategies, and research, or another person's writing, in the form of sentences, phrases, and innovative terminology.

- Plagiarism is the equivalent of *theft*, but the stolen goods are intellectual rather than material.

- Like other acts of theft, plagiarism is against the law. The copyright law governing publications requires that authorship be acknowledged and (if the borrowed material is long enough) that payment be offered to the writer.

- Plagiarism violates the moral law that people should take pride in, as well as profit from, the fruits of their labor. Put yourself in the victim's place. Think about the best idea that you ever had, or the paragraph that you worked hardest on in your last paper. Now, imagine yourself finding exactly the same idea or exactly the same sentences in someone else's essay, with no mention of your name, with no quotation marks. Would you accept the theft of your property without protest?

■ Plagiarists are not only robbers, but also cheats. People who bend or break the rules of authorship, who do not do their own work, will be rightly distrusted by their classmates, teachers, or future employers, who may equate a history of plagiarism with laziness, incompetence, or dishonesty. One's future rarely depends on getting a better grade on a single assignment; on the other hand, one's lifelong reputation may be damaged if one resorts to plagiarism in order to get that grade.

Plagiarism is a bad risk for, as you observed in Exercise 13, an experienced teacher can usually detect plagiarized work quite easily. If you can't write your own essay, you are unlikely to do a good enough job of adapting someone else's work to your needs. Anyone can learn to write well enough to make plagiarism an unnecessary risk.

The excuse of "inadvertent plagiarism" is sometimes used to explain including undocumented material from the Internet in a research essay. Information from the Web may not (as yet) be fully subject to copyright laws, but using it without appropriate acknowledgment is a violation of academic law. As Maurice Isserman suggests in the *Chronicle of Higher Education* (2 May 2003), instructors are unlikely to buy "the argument that the invention of the Internet somehow makes our old notions of intellectual property obsolete." Borrowing from an Internet source is just as much plagiarism as borrowing from a published work.

Cutting and pasting material from Web sites may be an easy way of meeting a paper deadline, but it will inevitably invite a charge of plagiarism unless you include the sites in your bibliography. And even if you properly acknowledge your Internet sources, you must still paraphrase and/or quote the text that you're using rather than just pasting it in and leaving it unchanged. If there is any disparity in style, instructors can easily do a Google search to compare material in your essay with material available on the Web.

If you resort to using a paper-writing service instead of doing your own work, you are just as likely to get caught. Software that detects plagiarism—like that available at turnitin.com—enables instructors to back up their suspicions by submitting a dubious paper and checking it against a vast database of previously plagiarized essays. Nor should you use the excuse that borrowing words and ideas is increasingly common practice in the world of business or government. Here is Maurice Isserman again, speaking for the vast majority of instructors: "As learning communities, colleges and universities are governed by a different set of rules than those governing the worlds of politics and commerce. What we do is teach students to develop their own voices and establish ownership of the words they use."

Finally, you will not receive greater glory by plagiarizing. On the contrary, most instructors believe that students who understand the ideas of their sources, apply them to the topic, and express them in their own words deserve the highest grades for their mastery of the basic skills of academic writing. There are, however, occasions when your instructor may ask you not to use secondary sources. In such cases, you would be wise to do no background reading at all, so that the temptation to borrow will not arise.

DOCUMENTING INFORMATION

Acknowledging your sources—or *documentation*—means telling your reader that someone other than yourself is the source of ideas and words in your essay. Acknowledgment can take the form of *quotation marks* and *citation of the author's name*—techniques that are by now familiar to you—or more elaborate ways to indicate the source, which will be explained later in this chapter. There are guidelines to help you decide what can and what cannot safely be used without acknowledgment, and these guidelines mostly favor complete documentation.

By conservative standards, *you should cite a source for all facts and evidence in your essay that you did not know before you started your research*. Knowing when to acknowledge the source of your knowledge or information largely depends on common sense. For example, it is not necessary to document the fact that there are fifty states in the United States or that Shakespeare wrote *Hamlet* since these facts are common knowledge. On the other hand, you may be presenting more obscure information, like facts about electric railroads, which you have known since you were a child, but which may be unfamiliar to your readers. Technically, you are not obliged to document that information; but your audience will trust you more and will be better informed if you do so. In general, if the facts are not unusual, if they can be found in a number of standard sources, and if they do not vary from source to source or year to year, then they can be considered common knowledge, and the source need not be acknowledged.

Let's assume that you are preparing to document your essay about *Lawrence of Arabia*. The basic facts about the film—the year of release, the cast, the director, the technicians, the Academy Awards won by the film—might be regarded as common knowledge and not require documentation. But the cost of the film, the amount grossed in its first year, the location of the premiere, and the circumstances of production are relatively unfamiliar facts that you would almost certainly have to look up in a reference book. An authority on film who includes such facts in a study of epic films is expected to be familiar with this information and, in most cases, would not be expected to provide documentation. But a student writing on the same subject would be well advised to do so.

Similarly, if you are writing about the most recent World Cup and know who won a specific match because you witnessed the victory on television, then it would probably not be necessary to cite a source. Issues surrounding the World Cup—such as the use of steroids—are less clearly in the realm of common knowledge. You may remember news broadcasts about which athletes may or may not have taken steroids before a match, but the circumstances are hardly so memorable in their details that you would be justified in writing about them from memory. The articles that you consult to jog your memory would have to be documented.

DOCUMENTING IDEAS FOUND IN YOUR SOURCE

Your objective is both to acknowledge the source and to provide your reader with the fullest possible background. Let us assume that one of the ideas that you are writing about was firmly in your mind—the product of your own intellect—long before you started to work on your topic. Nevertheless, if you come across a version of that idea during your research, you should cite the source, even though the idea was as much your own as the author's. Of course, in your acknowledgment, you might state that this source is confirming *your* theories and indicate that you had thought of the point independently.

Perhaps, while working on an essay, you develop a new idea of your own, stimulated by one of your readings. You should make a point of acknowledging the source of inspiration and, perhaps, describing how and why it affected you. (For example: "My idea for shared assignments is an extension of McKeachie's discussion of peer tutoring.") The reader should be made aware of your debt to your source as well as your independent effort.

PLAGIARISM: STEALING IDEAS

If you present another person's ideas as your own, you are plagiarizing *even if you use your own words.* To illustrate, the paragraph on the left, by Leo Gurko, is taken from a book, *Ernest Hemingway and the Pursuit of Heroism*; the paragraph on the right comes from a student essay on Hemingway. Gurko is listed in the student's bibliography and is cited as the source of several quotations elsewhere in the essay. But the student does not mention Gurko anywhere in *this* paragraph.

Source	*Student Essay*
The Hemingways put themselves on short rations, ate, drank, and entertained as little as possible, pounced eagerly on the small checks that arrived in the mail as payment for accepted stories, and were intensely conscious of being poor. The sensation was not altogether unpleasant. Their extreme youth, the excitement of living abroad, the sense of making a fresh start, even the unexpected joy of parenthood, gave their poverty a romantic flavor.	Despite all the economies that they had to make and all the pleasures that they had to do without, the Hemingways rather enjoyed the experience of being poor. They knew that this was a more romantic kind of life, unlike anything they'd known before, and the feeling that everything in Paris was fresh and new, even their new baby, made them sharply aware of the glamorous aspects of being poor.

The *language* of the student paragraph does not require quotation marks, but unless Gurko is acknowledged, the student will be guilty of plagiarism. These impressions of the Hemingways, these insights into their motivation, would not have been possible without Gurko's biography—and Gurko deserves the credit for having done the research and for having formulated the interpretations. After reading extensively about Hemingway, the student may have absorbed these biographical details so thoroughly that he feels as if he had always known them. But the knowledge is still secondhand, and the source must be acknowledged.

PLAGIARISM: STEALING WORDS

When you quote a source, remember that the quoted material will require two kinds of documentation:

1. *The acknowledgment of the source of the information or ideas* (through a system of documentation that provides complete publication information about the source and possibly through the citation of the author's name in your sentence), and

2. *The acknowledgment of the source of the exact wording* (through quotation marks).

It is not enough to supply the author's name in parentheses (or in a footnote) and then mix up your own language and that of your sources. The author's name tells your reader nothing at all about who is responsible for the choice of words. Equally important, borrowing language carelessly, perhaps in an effort to use paraphrase, often garbles the author's meaning.

Here is an excerpt from a student essay about Henrik Ibsen, together with the relevant passage from its source:

Source	Student Essay
When writing [Ibsen] was sometimes under the influence of hallucinations, and was unable to distinguish between reality and the creatures of his imagination. While working on *A Doll's House* he was nervous and retiring and lived in a world alone, which gradually became peopled with his own imaginary characters. Once he suddenly remarked to his wife: "Now I have seen Nora. She came right up to me and put her hand on my shoulder." "How was she dressed?" asked his wife. "She had a simple blue cotton dress," he replied without hesitation. . . . So intimate	While Ibsen was still writing *A Doll's House*, his involvement with the characters led to his experiencing hallucinations that at times completely incapacitated his ability to distinguish between reality and the creations of his imagination. He was nervous, distant, and lived in a secluded world. Gradually this world became populated with his creations. One day he had the following exchange with his wife: Ibsen: Now I have seen Nora. She came right up to me and put her hand on my shoulder. Wife: How was she dressed?

had Ibsen become with Nora while at work on *A Doll's House* that when John Paulsen asked him why she was called Nora, Ibsen replied in a matter-of-fact tone: "She was really called Leonora, you know, but everyone called her Nora since she was the spoilt child of the family."

P. F. D. TENNANT,
Ibsen's Dramatic Technique

Ibsen: (without hesitation) She had a simple blue dress.
Ibsen's involvement with his characters was so deep that when John Paulsen asked Ibsen why the heroine was named Nora, Ibsen replied in a very nonchalant tone of voice that originally she was called Leonora, but that everyone called her Nora, the way one would address the favorite child in the family (Tennant 26).

The documentation at the end of the student's passage may refer the reader to Tennant's book, but it fails to indicate the debt that the student owes to Tennant's *phrasing* and *vocabulary*. Phrases like "distinguish between reality and the creatures of his imagination" must be placed in quotation marks, and so should the exchange between Ibsen and his wife. Arranging these sentences as dialogue is not adequate acknowledgment.

In fact, the problem here is too complex to be solved by inserting a few quotation marks. The student, who probably intended a paraphrase, has substituted some of her own words for Tennant's; however, because she keeps the original sentence structure and many of the original words, she has only succeeded in obscuring some of her source's ideas.

At times, the phrasing distorts the original idea: the student's assertion that Ibsen's hallucinations "incapacitated his ability to distinguish between reality and the creations of his imagination" is very different from "[Ibsen] was sometimes under the influence of hallucinations and was unable to distinguish between reality and the creatures of his imagination." Many of the substituted words change Tennant's meaning: "distant" does not mean "retiring"; "a secluded world" is not "a world alone"; "nonchalant" is a very different quality from "matter-of-fact." Prose like this is neither quotation nor successful paraphrase; it is doubly bad, for it both *plagiarizes* the source and *misinterprets* it.

Avoiding Plagiarism

You must acknowledge a source using an appropriate form of documentation whenever you summarize, paraphrase, or quote ideas or information derived from another person or organization's work.

You are obliged to use documentation whether the work has been published in print, has appeared on the Web, has been performed in public, has been communicated to you through an interview or E-mail, or exists as an unpublished manuscript.

EXERCISE 33: UNDERSTANDING WHEN
TO DOCUMENT INFORMATION

Here are some facts about the explosion of the space shuttle *Challenger*. Consider which of these facts would require documentation in a research essay—and why.

1. On January 28, 1986, the space shuttle *Challenger* exploded shortly after takeoff from Cape Canaveral.
2. It was unusually cold in Florida on the day of the launch.
3. One of the *Challenger's* booster rockets experienced a sudden and unforeseen drop in pressure 10 seconds before the explosion.
4. The explosion was later attributed to the failure of an O-ring seal.
5. On board the *Challenger* was a $100 million communications satellite.
6. Christa McAuliffe, a high school social studies teacher in Concord, New Hampshire, was a member of the crew.
7. McAuliffe's mission duties included conducting two classroom lessons taught from the shuttle.
8. After the explosion, classes at the high school were canceled.
9. Another crew member, Judith Resnick, had a Ph.D. in electrical engineering.
10. At the time of the explosion, President Ronald Reagan was preparing to meet with network TV news correspondents to brief them on the upcoming State of the Union address.
11. The State of the Union address was postponed for a week.

EXERCISE 34: UNDERSTANDING PLAGIARISM

In 2003, the *New York Times* reported that Brian VanDeMark, an associate professor of history at the U.S. Naval Academy (USNA), had been charged with plagiarizing the content and language of portions of books by four authors. More than 30 passages in VanDeMark's book about the origins of the atomic bomb were "identical, or nearly identical" to material published by the four authors, yet these passages contained neither acknowledgments nor quotation marks. In many instances, only a few words had been changed.

The *Chronicle of Higher Education* later reported that, as a result of these charges, the USNA had demoted VanDeMark, removed his tenure, and cut his salary. In effect, he was going to have to "re-establish his professional qualifications" as if he had just been newly hired.

Here, side by side, as published in the *Times*, are parallel excerpts from Van-DeMark's *Pandora's Keepers: Nine Men and the Atomic Bomb* on the left and from works by Robert S. Norris, William Lanouette, and Richard Rhodes on the right. Examine them and determine whether, in your opinion, VanDeMark has been guilty of plagiarism.

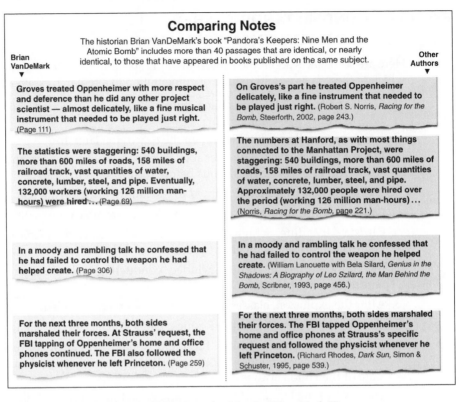

Figure 10-1. Evidence of plagiarism cited in the *New York Times*

EXERCISE 35: IDENTIFYING PLAGIARISM

There are two ways to plagiarize the work of a source: using ideas without attribution and using language without quotation marks.

A. The passage below, by John Lukacs, was one of the sources used for an essay titled "Has the Credit Card Replaced the Dollar Bill?" Compare this source with a paragraph taken from the student essay, and decide, sentence by sentence, whether the student has plagiarized Lukacs's work.

Source

The Modern Age has been the age of money—increasingly so, perhaps reaching its peak around 1900. During the Middle Ages, there were some material assets, often land, that money could not buy; but by 1900, there was hardly any material thing that money could not buy. But during the 20th century, the value of money diminished fast. One symptom (and cause) was inflation. By the end of the 20th century, the inflation of stocks and of other financial instruments became even more rapid than the inflation of money, at the bottom of which phenomenon another development exists, which is the increasingly abstract character of money—due, in part, to the increasing reliance on entirely electronic transactions and on their records.

JOHN LUKACS, "It's the End of the Modern Age,"
Chronicle of Higher Education, 4/26/02, p. B8

Student Essay

(1) For hundreds of years, we have lived in a society that worships money, believing that money can buy anything and everything. (2) A thousand years ago, during the Middle Ages, there were some things, like land, that money could not buy. (3) But by 1900, money could buy almost anything one could want. (4) That is no longer so true today. (5) John Lukacs observes that, over the last century, the value of money diminished quickly. (6) The same is true for stocks and other financial instruments. (7) In fact, our dependence on credit cards and other electronic means of transferring funds has made paper money almost irrelevant (B8).

B. The two passages below were among the sources used for an essay titled "Credentialing the College Degree." Compare these sources with a paragraph taken from the student essay, and decide, sentence by sentence, whether the student has plagiarized either of these sources.

Sources

Grade inflation compresses all grades at the top, making it difficult to discriminate the best from the very good, the very good from the good, the good from the mediocre. Surely a teacher wants to mark the few best students with a grade that distinguishes them from all the rest in the top quarter, but at Harvard that's not possible.

HARVEY C. MANSFIELD, "Grade Inflation: It's Time to Face the
Facts," Chronicle of Higher Education, 5 Apr. 2001, B24

Grade inflation subverts the primary function of grades. Grades are messages. They are means of telling students—and subsequently, parents, employers, and graduate schools—how well or poorly those students have done. A grade that misrepresents a student's performance sends a false message. It tells a lie. The point of using more than one passing grade (usually D through A) is to differentiate levels of successful performance among one's students. Inflating grades to please or encourage students is confusing and ultimately self-defeating.

RICHARD KAMBER AND MARY BIGGS, "Grade Conflation:
A Question of Credibility," Chronicle of Higher Education,
12 Apr. 2002, B14

Student Essay

(1) Some faculty are disturbed by what they regard as grade inflation. (2) They are concerned that grades will be awarded that are higher than students deserve, that will misrepresent a student's performance. (3) Kamber and Biggs, for example, believe that an inflated grade is the equivalent of a lie, for it sends a "false message." (4) Such faculty see themselves as differentiating between the different levels of successful performance, distinguishing, as Mansfield says, the best from the very good and the good from the mediocre. (5) In fact, they regard grades as a way of telling future employers how well or poorly these students have performed. (6) The emphasis is on providing students with credentials, not a successful learning experience.

USING DOCUMENTATION

In addition to using quotation marks and citing the author's name in your text, you also need to provide your reader with more detailed information about your sources. This documentation is important for two reasons:

1. *By showing where you found your information, you are providing proof that you did your research.* Including the source's *publication history* and the *specific page* on which you found the information assures your reader that you have not made up fictitious sources and quotations. The systems of documentation that are described in this chapter and in Chapter 12 enable your reader to distinguish your ideas from those of your sources, to know who was responsible for what, by observing the parenthetical notes or numbered notes.

2. *Documentation also enables your readers to learn more about the subject of your essay.* Methods of documentation originally developed as a way for serious scholars to share their findings with their colleagues—while making it entirely clear who had done the original research. The reader of your research essay should be given the option of going back to the library and locating the materials that you used in writing about the topic. Of course, the essay's *bibliography* can serve this purpose, but not even the most carefully annotated bibliography can guide readers to the book and the precise page that will provide the information that they need.

Using Parenthetical Notes

One widely accepted system of documentation is based on the insertion directly into your essay of the author's name and the page on which the information can be found, placed in parentheses. This style of documentation is called the Modern Language Association (MLA) style. It has replaced footnotes and endnotes as the most common form of documentation for undergraduates, and it will probably be the style you use in writing general research essays, especially those in the humanities. Documenting through parenthetical notes is much less cumbersome than preparing an additional page of endnotes or placing footnotes at the bottom of the page. MLA style also allows your reader to see the source's name while reading the essay, instead of having to turn to a separate page at the back. Readers who want to know more about a particular source than the author's name and a page number can turn to the "Works Cited" page, which provides all the necessary details of publication.

Another frequently used kind of parenthetical documentation is the one recommended by the American Psychological Association (APA) for research in the social and behavioral sciences. APA style is described on pages 549–559 of Chapter 12.

For those writing essays on a computer, many software packages (especially those, like Nota Bene, specializing in academic writing) provide documentation automatically, in a choice of styles—provided that basic information about each work cited has been entered into the computer.

Here is what an excerpt from a biographical essay about Ernest Hemingway would look like using MLA style. Notice that the parenthetical notes are meaningless unless the reader can refer to an accurate and complete bibliography placed at the end of the essay on a page titled "Works Cited."

> Hemingway's zest for life extended to women also. His wandering heart seemed only to be exceeded by an even more appreciative eye (Hemingway 102). Hadley was aware of her husband's flirtations and of his facility with women (Sokoloff 84). Yet, she had no idea that something was going on between Hemingway and Pauline Pfeiffer, a fashion editor for *Vogue* magazine (Baker 159). She was also unaware that Hemingway delayed his return to Schruns from a business trip in New York, in February 1926, so that he might spend more time with this "new and strange girl" (Hemingway 210; also Baker 165).

Works Cited

Baker, Carlos. *Ernest Hemingway: A Life Story.* New York: Scribner's, 1969. Print.

Hemingway, Ernest. *A Moveable Feast.* New York: Scribner's, 1964. Print.

Sokoloff, Alice Hunt. *Hadley: The First Mrs. Hemingway.* New York: Dodd, 1973. Print.

Many of the basic rules for using MLA style are demonstrated in the previous example. Here are some points to observe.

1. Format and Punctuation.

The placement of the parenthetical note within your sentence is governed by a set of very precise rules, established by conventional agreement. Like rules for quotation, these must be followed without any deviation.

a. *The parenthetical note is intended to be a part of your sentence, which should not end until the source has been cited.* For this reason, terminal punctuation (period or question mark) should be placed *after* the parenthetical note.

Incorrect

Unlike most American writers of his day, Hemingway rarely came to New York; instead, he spent most of his time on his farm near Havana. (Ross 17).

Correct

Unlike most American writers of his day, Hemingway rarely came to New York; instead, he spent most of his time on his farm near Havana (Ross 17).

b. *If the parenthetical note follows a quotation, the quotation should be closed before you open the parentheses.* Remember that the note is not part of the quotation and therefore has no reason to be inside the quotation.

Incorrect

Hemingway's farm consisted of "a domestic staff of nine, fifty-two cats, sixteen dogs, a couple of hundred pigeons, and three cows (Ross 17)."

Correct

Hemingway's farm consisted of "a domestic staff of nine, fifty-two cats, sixteen dogs, a couple of hundred pigeons, and three cows" (Ross 17).

c. *Any terminal punctuation that is part of the quotation* (like a question mark or an exclamation point) *remains inside the quotation marks.* Remember also to include a period at the end of the sentence, *after* the parenthetical note.

Incorrect

One critic reports that Hemingway said of *The Old Man and the Sea,* "Don't you think it is a strange damn story that it should affect all of us (me especially) the way it does" (Halliday 52)?

Correct

One critic reports that Hemingway said of *The Old Man and the Sea,* "Don't you think it is a strange damn story that it should affect all of us (me especially) the way it does?" (Halliday 52).

d. *When you insert the parenthetical note, leave one space before it and one space after it*—unless you are ending the sentence with terminal punctuation (period, question mark), in which case you leave no space between the closing parenthesis and the punctuation, and you leave the customary one space between the end of that sentence and the beginning of the next one.

Incorrect

Given Hemingway's intense awareness of literary tradition, style, and theory, it is strange that many critics and readers have found his work primitive(Cowley 47).

Correct

Given Hemingway's intense awareness of literary tradition, style, and theory, it is strange that many critics and readers have found his work primitive (Cowley 47).

2. Placement.

The parenthetical note comes at the end of the material being documented, whether that material is quoted, paraphrased, summarized, or briefly mentioned. By convention, your reader will assume that the *parenthetical note signals the end of the material from that source.* Anything that follows is either your own idea, independently developed, or taken from a new source that will be documented by the next parenthetical note later in the text.

One critic has remarked that it has been fashionable to deride Hemingway over the past few years (Cowley 50). However, though we may criticize him, as we can criticize most authors when we subject them to close scrutiny, we should never forget his brilliance in depicting characters having grace under the pressure of a sterile, valueless, painful world (Anderson 1036).

3. Frequency.

Each new point in your essay that requires documentation should have its own parenthetical note. Under no circumstances should you accumulate references to several different sources for several sentences and place them in a single note at the end of the paragraph. All the sources in the Hemingway paragraph cannot be covered by one parenthetical note at the end.

Incorrect

The sources of Hemingway's fiction have been variously named. One critic has said he is driven by "personal demons." Another believes that he is occupied by a desire to truly portray reality, with all its ironies and symbols. Finally, still another has stated that Hemingway is interested only in presenting "fragments of truth" (Cowley 51; Halliday 71; Levin 85).

Correct

The sources of Hemingway's fiction have been variously named. One critic has said he is driven by "personal demons" (Cowley 51). Another believes that he is occupied by a desire to truly portray reality, with all its ironies and symbols (Halliday 71). Finally, still another has stated that Hemingway is interested only in presenting "fragments of truth" (Levin 85).

4. Multiple Notes in a Single Sentence.

If you are using a large number of sources and documenting your essay very thoroughly, you may need to cite two or more sources at separate points in the same sentence.

Even at this early stage of his career, Hemingway seemed to have developed a basic philosophy of writing. His ability to perceive situations clearly and to capture the exact essence of the subject (Lawrence 93–94; O'Faolain 113) might have stemmed from a disciplined belief that each sentence had to be "true" (Hemingway 12) and that a story had to be written "as straight as you can" (Hemingway 183).

The placement of notes tells you where the writer found which information. The reference to Lawrence and O'Faolain must be inserted in mid-sentence because they are responsible only for the information about Hemingway's capacity to focus on his subject and capture its essence; Lawrence and O'Faolain are not responsible for the quoted material at the end of the sentence. The inclusion of each of the next two parenthetical notes tells you that a reference to "true" sentences can be found on page 12 of the Hemingway book and a reference to "straight" writing can be found on page 183.

5. Multiple Sources for the Same Point.

If you have two sources to document the same point, you can demonstrate the completeness of your research by placing both in the same parenthetical note. The inclusion of Lawrence and O'Faolain in the same note—(Lawrence 93–94; O'Faolain 113)—tells you that much the same information can be found in both sources. Should you want to cite two sources but emphasize only one, you can indicate your preference by using "also."

Hemingway's ability to perceive situations clearly and to capture the exact essence of the subject (Lawrence 93–94; also O'Faolain 113) may be his greatest asset as a writer.

There is, of course, a limit to how many sources you can cram into a single pair of parentheses; common sense will tell you what is practical and what is distracting to the reader. Usually, one or two sources will have more complete or better documented information; those are the ones to cite. If you wish to discuss the quality of information in your various sources, then you can use an explanatory endnote to do so (see p. 478 on explanatory notes).

6. Referring to the Source in the Text.

In the previous examples, the writer of the Hemingway essay has chosen not to name any sources in the text itself. That is why each parenthetical note contains a name as well as a page number. *If, however, you do refer to your source as part of your own presentation of the material, then there is no need to use the name twice; simply insert the page number in the parenthetical note.*

> During the time in Paris, Hemingway became friends with the poet Ezra Pound, who told Hemingway he would teach him how to write if the younger novelist would teach him to box. Noel Stock reports what Wyndham Lewis saw when he walked in on one of their boxing sessions:
>
> > A splendidly built young man [Hemingway] stript to the waist, and with a torso of dazzling white, was standing not far from me. He was tall, handsome, and serene, and was repelling with his boxing gloves—I thought without undue exertion—a hectic assault of Ezra's. (88)

Because Stock's name is cited in the text, it need not be placed in parentheses; the page number is enough. Stock's book would, of course, be included in the list of "Works Cited." Also notice that the parenthetical note works just as well at the end of a lengthy, *indented* quotation; but that, because the quotation is indented, and there are no quotation marks to signify its end, it terminates with a period placed *before* the parenthetical note, which follows separated by one space.

7. Including the Source's Title.

Occasionally, your bibliography will include more than one source by the same author or sources by different authors with the same last name. To avoid confusion and to specify your exact source, use an abbreviated title inside the parenthetical note. Had the author of the Hemingway essay included more than one work by Carlos Baker in the bibliography, the parenthetical note would look like this:

> Yet, she had no idea that something was going on between Hemingway and Pauline Pfeiffer, a fashion editor for *Vogue* magazine (Baker, *Life Story* 159).

If you are working from a newspaper or periodical article that does not cite an author, use an abbreviation of the article's title in your parenthetical note (unless you have referred to the title in your text, in which case you need only include the page number in your note).

8. Referring to a Whole Work.

Occasionally, you may refer to the overall theme of an entire work, citing the title and the author, but no specific quotation, idea, or page. If you refer to a work as a whole, no page numbers in parentheses are required.

> Hemingway's *The Sun Also Rises* focuses on the sterility and despair pervading modern culture.

9. Referring to a Source by More Than One Author.

Occasionally, you will need to refer to a book that is by two, or three, or even more authors. If you refer to a text by two or three authors, cite their last names, joined by "and." (If you have mentioned the authors' names in your text, just include a page reference in parentheses.) If you refer to a text by more than three authors and you have not mentioned them in your text, it is acceptable (and saves space) to cite the name of the first author followed by et al., unitalicized, and then the page number, all within parentheses. Et al. is Latin for "and others."

Two Authors

> We may finally say of the writer Hemingway that he was able to depict the turbulent, often contradictory, emotions of modern man in a style as starkly realistic as that of the sixteenth century painter Caravaggio, who, art historians tell us, seems to say, "Here is actuality . . . without deception or pretence . . ." (Janson and Cauman 221).

More Than Three Authors

> Hemingway did what no other writer of his time did: he captured the plight and total disenchantment of his age in vivid intensity (Spiller et al. 1300).

10. Referring to One of Several Volumes.

You may use a single volume from a set of several volumes. If so, refer to the specific volume by using an arabic numeral followed by a colon and a space if a page number follows. In your "Works Cited," be sure to list all the volumes. (See Chapter 12 for proper bibliographic entry of a set of volumes.)

> Perhaps Hemingway's work can be best summed up by Frederick Coppleston's comment concerning Camus: both writers prove that human greatness is not shown in escaping the absurdity of modern existence, but "in living in the consciousness of the absurd and yet revolting against it by . . . committing . . . [one]self and living in the fullest manner possible" (3: 393).

11. Referring to a Work of Literature.

If you refer to specific passages from a well-known play, poem, or novel, then you need not cite the author; the text's name is sufficient recognition. Use arabic numerals separated by periods for divisions such as act, scene, and line in plays and for divisions like books and lines in poems. For novels, cite the page number followed by a semicolon, "ch.," and the chapter number.

> *Play*
>
> Hemingway wished to show reality as truly as he could, even if he found man, as did King Lear, nothing but "a poor, bare, fork'd animal . . ." (3.4.106–7).
>
> *Poem*
>
> Throughout his career as a writer, Hemingway struggled to make sense of the human condition so powerfully and metaphorically presented in *The Waste Land*: "Son of man/ . . . you know only/ A heap of broken images" (2.21–23).
>
> *Novel*
>
> In *The Sun Also Rises*, toughness is an essential for living in the modern age, but even toughness has its limits in the novel; as Jake says, "It is awfully easy to be hard-boiled about everything in the daytime, but at night it is another thing" (34; ch. iv).

12. Referring to a Quotation from an Indirect Source.

When you quote a writer's words that you have found in a work written by someone else, you begin the citation with the abbreviation "qtd. in." This form shows the reader that you are quoting from a secondhand source, not the original.

In "Big Two-Hearted River," Hemingway metaphorically captures the pervasive atmosphere of his time in the tersest of descriptions: "There is no town, nothing . . . but the burned over country" (qtd. in Anderson 1027).

13. **Referring to Sources That Do Not Appear in Print.**

Sometimes you may cite information from nonprint sources such as interviews, films, or radio or television programs. If you do, be sure that the text mentions (for an interview) the name of the interviewer and/or the person being interviewed or (for a film) the name of the producer, director, and/or scriptwriter; these names should also appear in your list of "Works Cited." (For proper bibliographic form of nonprint sources, including the Internet, see Chapter 12.)

Interview

In an unpublished interview conducted by the writer of this essay, the poet Phil Arnold said that a lean style like Hemingway's may be just as artificial as an elaborate one.

Preparing to Document Your Essay

- Whether you take notes or use photocopies of your sources, remember always to write down the information that you will need for your notes and bibliography.
- Look at the front of each book or periodical and jot down or photocopy the publication information.
- When you move notes from one file to another on your computer, make sure that the source's name goes with the relevant material.
- As you work on the first draft of your essay, include the author's name and the relevant page number in parentheses after every reference to one of your sources, to serve as a guide when you document your essay. Even in this early version, your essay will resemble the finished product, with MLA documentation.
- Finally, when the essay is ready for final typing, read through it again, just to make sure that each reference to a source is covered by a correct and appropriate parenthetical note.

MLA Style: A Sample Page

<table>
<tr>
<td>

reference to
an article with
no author

reference to an
author with two
or more works
listed in the
bibliography

</td>
<td>

"Passive euthanasia" can be described as helping someone
to die by doing nothing and, according to *The Economist,*
"happens in hospitals all the time" ("Euthanasia War" 22). It
usually involves deliberate withholding of life-prolonging
measures (Keown, "Value" 6). Failing to resuscitate a patient
who has suffered a massive heart attack is one example of
passive euthanasia. Another is deciding not to feed termi-
nally ill patients who are unable to feed themselves. By con-
trast, removing the feeding tube from a patient who is being
fed that way would be considered active euthanasia.

</td>
</tr>
</table>

The distinction between active and passive euthanasia
is really about responsibility. In passive euthanasia, the
doctor or relative has done nothing directly to end the patient's life and so has less moral responsibility. An intermediate form of euthanasia—assisted suicide—is more
controversial. In assisted suicide, a doctor or other person
provides a terminally ill person with the means—pills, for
example—and the medical knowledge necessary to commit

Orentlicher refer-
ence contains
page number
only; author
mentioned in text

suicide. In the *Journal of the American Medical Association,*
Dr. David Orentlicher categorizes assisted suicide as a form
of passive euthanasia (1844). Derek Humphrey's *Final Exit,*

reference to an
entire work; no
page citation
needed

which describes ways to commit suicide painlessly, and the
organization Compassion in Dying, which helps terminally
ill patients to end their lives, are both sources of instruction

reference to two
sources contain-
ing similar infor-
mation; emphasis
on Belkin

in assisted suicide (Belkin 50; also Elliott 27).

The professional people who care for the sick and the
dying think that there is a great difference between active
euthanasia and passive euthanasia or assisted suicide. One

standard refer-
ence; author
mentioned in the
note

panel of distinguished physicians declared themselves in
favor, by a margin of 10 to 2, of doctor-assisted suicide for
hopelessly ill patients who request it (Orentlicher 1844).

Constructing a "Works Cited" Page

None of the parenthetical notes explained above would make complete sense without a "Works Cited" page. The technical forms for bibliographic entries according to MLA style are described in Chapter 12 on pages 549–559. Following is a sample "Works Cited" page for all of the parenthetical notes about Hemingway found earlier in this chapter.

Works Cited

Anderson, Charles W. Introduction. "Ernest Hemingway." *American Literary Masters.* Ed. Charles W. Anderson. New York: Holt, 1965. 1023–114. Print.

Arnold, Philip. Telephone interview. 3 Nov. 1993.

Baker, Carlos. *Ernest Hemingway: A Life Story.* New York: Scribner's, 1969. Print.

Copleston, Frederick. *Maine de Biran to Sartre.* New York: Doubleday, 1974. Print. Vol. 9 of *A History of Philosophy.* 9 vols. 1946–74.

Cowley, Malcolm. "Nightmare and Ritual in Hemingway." *Hemingway: Twentieth Century Perspectives.* Ed. Robert P. Weeks. Englewood Cliffs: Prentice, 1962. 40–51. Print.

Halliday, E. M. "Hemingway's Ambiguity: Symbolism and Irony." *Hemingway: Twentieth Century Perspectives.* Ed. Robert P. Weeks. Englewood Cliffs: Prentice, 1962. 52–71. Print.

Hemingway, Ernest. *A Moveable Feast.* New York: Scribner's, 1964. Print.

---. *The Sun Also Rises.* 1926. New York: Scribner's, 1964. Print.

Janson, H. W., and Samuel Cauman. *A Basic History of Art.* New York: Abrams, 1971. Print.

Lawrence, D. H. "In Our Time: A Review." *Hemingway: Twentieth Century Perspectives.* Ed. Robert P. Weeks. Englewood Cliffs: Prentice, 1962. 93–94. Print.

Levin, Harry. "Observations on the Style of Ernest Hemingway." *Hemingway: Twentieth Century Perspectives.* Ed. Robert P. Weeks. Englewood Cliffs: Prentice, 1962. 72–85. Print.

Ross, Lillian. "How Do You Like It Now, Gentlemen?" *Hemingway: Twentieth Century Perspectives.* Ed. Robert P. Weeks. Englewood Cliffs: Prentice, 1962. 17–39. Print.

Shakespeare, William. *King Lear. The Riverside Shakespeare.* Ed. Frank Kermode. Boston: Houghton, 1974. 1249–305. Print.

Spiller, Robert E., et al. *Literary History of the United States.* 3rd ed., rev. London: Macmillan, 1963. Print.

Stock, Noel. *The Life of Ezra Pound.* New York: Pantheon, 1970. Print.

EXERCISE 36: ACKNOWLEDGING SOURCES

Presenting sources in a research essay requires complete, appropriate documentation. If you are using MLA style, you must provide information about your source in a parenthetical note and (in some cases) include the source's name within your text. You must also present your source's ideas and words accurately, using quotation marks to indicate which words and phrases are taken directly from the source. See www.bedfordstmartins.com/wfs for more practice in documenting sources correctly.

Read the passage by Charles McGrath. Then read each of the four examples taken from student essays that use McGrath as a source. Consider the following questions:

1. Has the source been misquoted or misunderstood?

2. Have the source's ideas been acknowledged with sufficient and accurate documentation, according to MLA style?

3. Have quotations from the source been indicated with quotation marks?

Source

What is it with hockey? To begin with, it is a fast, physical game that encourages players and spectators alike to burn at a much higher emotional temperature than does baseball or even football, both of which have built-in cooling-off periods. And hockey is, of course, the only game in which—on the professional level, anyway—fistfights routinely break out and in which it is customary for every team to carry on its roster an "enforcer," whose main job is to intimidate the opposition. The game has underlying it a longstanding cult of toughness. What casual fans—and apparently many parents—don't understand, though, is that a lot of hockey fighting is ritualistic. There is more pushing and posturing than there is actual punching, and the whole show—the pointing, the snarling, the chest-bumping—may actually serve as a kind of safety valve.

CHARLES MCGRATH, "Ice Sturm," *The New York Times Magazine*, 20 Jan. 2002: 9

Student Essay A

Hockey is one of the roughest sports there is. Because it is so fast and physical, everyone, players and spectators, gets highly emotional, and there are no cooling-off periods, as there are in sports like baseball or even football.

Student Essay B

Hockey is one of the roughest sports there is. As Charles McGrath observes, the game depends on breakneck speed and constant physical contact, with no opportunity for players or audience to catch their breath and calm down.

The cult of toughness that underlies such a frenzied, belligerent sport would naturally encourage fighting in the stands and on the field. (McGrath, 9)

Student Essay C

Hockey is one of the roughest sports there is. But according to Charles McGrath, the "cult of toughness" associated with hockey, which makes the players seem so violent and dangerous, is largely "ritualistic," based upon menacing gestures and a pretense of belligerence (9).

Student Essay D

Hockey is one of the roughest sports there is. In contrast to games like baseball and football, players and spectators "burn at a high emotional level," which inevitably causes "fistfights to routinely break out." This "ritualistic pushing" and shoving is part of the "cult of toughness" that makes the game exciting (McGrath, p 9).

SIGNALING THE TRANSITIONS BETWEEN SOURCES

Once you have found and selected the right materials to support your ideas, you should use paraphrase and, where appropriate, include your sources' names in your sentences as a way of keeping them before your reader's eye.

In general, the citation of an author's name signals to your reader that you are starting to use **new** *source material; the parenthetical note signals the* **point of termination** *for that source.*

If the name is not cited at the beginning, readers may not be aware that a new source has been introduced until they reach the parenthetical note. Here is a brief passage from an essay that illustrates this kind of confusion:

The year 1946 marked the beginning of the postwar era. This meant the demobilization of the military, creating a higher unemployment rate because of the large number of returning soldiers. This also meant a slowdown in industry, so that layoffs also added to the rising rate of unemployment. As Cabell Phillips put it: "Motivation [for the Employment Act of 1946] came naturally from the searing experience of the Great Depression, and fresh impetus was provided by the dread prospect of a massive new wave of unemployment following demobilization" (292–93).

Here, the placement of the citation—"As Cabell Phillips put it"—creates a problem. The way in which the name is introduced into the paragraph firmly suggests that Cabell Phillips is responsible for the quotation and only the quotation. (The fact that the quotation is nothing more than a repetition of the first three sentences, and therefore need not have been included in the essay, may also have occurred to you.) Anyone reading the essay will assume that the reference to Phillips covers only the material that starts with the name and ends with the page number. The coverage is not expected to go back any farther than the beginning of the sentence. Thus, in this passage, *the first three sentences are not documented.* Although the writer probably took all the information from Phillips, his book is not being acknowledged as the source. "Probably" is not an adequate substitute for clear documentation. Phillips's name should be cited somewhere at the beginning of the paragraph (the second sentence would be a good place); alternatively, an "umbrella" note could be used (see pages 481–482).

You may need to insert a parenthetical note in midsentence if that single sentence contains references to *two* different sources. For example, you might want to place a note in midsentence to indicate exactly where the source's opinion leaves off and your own begins:

> These examples of hiring athletes to play in college games, cited by Joseph Durso (6), suggest that recruiting tactics in 1903 were not as subtle as they are today.

If the page number were put at the end of the sentence, the reader would assume that Durso was responsible for the comparison between 1903 and the present; but he is not. Only the examples must be documented, not the conclusion drawn from these examples. In this case, the *absence* of a parenthetical note at the end of the sentence signals to the reader that this conclusion is the writer's own.

Here is a passage in which the techniques of documentation have been used to their fullest extent and the transitions between sources are clearly indicated. This example is taken from Jessie Bernard's "The Paradox of the Happy Marriage," an examination of the woman's role in American marriage. At this point, Bernard has just established that more wives than husbands acknowledge that their marriages are unhappy:

> These findings on the wife's marriage are especially poignant because marriage in our society is more important for women's happiness than for men's. "For almost all measures, the relation between marriage, happiness and overall well-being was stronger for women than for men," one study reports (Bradburn 150). In fact, the strength of the relationship between marital and overall happiness was so strong for women that the author wondered if "most women are equating their marital happiness with their overall happiness" (Bradburn 159). Another study based on a more intensive examination of the data on marriage from the same sample notes that "on each of the marriage adjustment measures . . . the association with overall

happiness is considerably stronger for women than it is for men" (Orden and Bradburn 731). Karen Renne also found the same strong relationship between feelings of general well-being and marital happiness: those who were happy tended not to report marital dissatisfaction; those who were not, did. "In all probability the respondent's view of his marriage influences his general feeling of well-being or morale" (64); this relationship was stronger among wives than among husbands (63).[2] A strong association between reports of general happiness and reports of marital happiness was also found a generation ago (Watson).

> [2] Among white couples, 71 percent of the wives and 52 percent of the husbands who were "not too happy" expressed marital dissatisfaction; 22 percent of the wives and 18 percent of the husbands who were "pretty happy" expressed marital dissatisfaction; and 4 percent of the wives and 2 percent of the husbands who were "very happy" expressed marital dissatisfaction.

This paragraph contains *six* parenthetical notes to document the contents of seven sentences. Four different works are cited, and, where the same work is cited twice consecutively (Bradburn and Renne), the reference is to a different page. The material taken from page 64 of Renne covers a sentence and a half, from the name "Karen Renne" to the parenthetical note; the remainder of the sentence comes from page 63. Finally, there is no page reference in the note citing Watson, since Bernard is referring the reader to the entire article, not to a single part of it. Notice also that:

- Bernard quotes frequently, but she never places quotations from two different sources together in the same sentence.
- She is careful to use her own voice to provide continuity between the quotations.
- The reader is never in doubt as to the source of information.

Although Bernard does not always cite the name of the author, we are immediately told in each case that there is a source—"one study reports"; "the author wondered"; "another study based on a more intensive examination of the data on marriage from the same sample"; "Karen Renne also found." These phrases not only acknowledge the source but also provide vital transitions between these loosely related points.

USING EXPLANATORY NOTES

You will have noticed that, in the excerpt from Bernard above, following the second parenthetical reference to Renne, there is a number. This calls the reader's attention to a separate note appearing at the bottom of the paragraph. (In the actual essay, the note would appear either at the bottom of the page or, together with other notes, on a *separate sheet* at the end of the essay.) Jessie Bernard is using an *explanatory note* as a way of including information that does not quite fit into the text of her essay.

If your research has been thorough, you may find yourself with excess material. It can be tempting to use up every single point in your file and cram all the available information into your essay. But if you include too many extraneous points, your reader will find it hard to concentrate on the real topic of your paragraph. To illustrate this point, here are two paragraphs dealing with the domestic life of Charles Dickens: one is bulging; the other is streamlined. The first contains an analysis of Dickens's relationship with his sister-in-law; in the second, he decides to take a holiday in France.

Paragraph 1

Another good friend to Charles Dickens was his sister-in-law. Georgina had lived with the family ever since they had returned from an American tour in June 1842. She had grown attached to the children while the couple was away (Pope-Hennessy 179–80). She now functioned as an occasional secretary to Dickens, specifically when he was writing *A Child's History of England*, which Pope-Hennessy terms a "rather deplorable production." Dickens treated the history of his country in a very unorthodox manner (311). Dickens must have felt close to Georgina since he chose to dictate the *History* to her; with all his other work, Dickens always worked alone, writing and correcting it by himself (Butt and Tillotson 20–21). Perhaps a different woman would have questioned the relationship of her younger sister to her husband; yet Kate Dickens accepted this friendship for what it was. Pope-Hennessy describes the way in which Georgina used to take over the running of the household whenever Kate was indisposed. Kate was regularly too pregnant to go anywhere. She had ten children and four miscarriages in a period of fifteen years (391). Kate probably found another woman to be quite a help around the house. Pope-Hennessy suggests that Kate and her sister shared Charles Dickens between them (287).

Paragraph 2

In 1853, three of Dickens's closest friends had died (Forster 124),[5] and the writer himself, having become even more popular and busy since the publication of *David Copperfield* (Maurois 70), began to complain of "hypochondriacal whisperings" and also of "too many invitations to too many parties" (Forster 125). In May of that year, a kidney ailment that had plagued Dickens since his youth grew worse (Dickens, *Letters* 350), and, against the advice of his wife, he decided to take a holiday in Boulogne (Johnson 757).[6]

[5]The friends were Mr. Watson, Count d'Orsay, and Mrs. Macready.

[6]Tillotson, Dickens's doctor, who had been in Boulogne the previous October, was the one to encourage him to go there.

The first paragraph obviously contains too much information, most of which is unrelated to this topic. Pope-Hennessy's opinion of the history of England and the history of Kate's pregnancies are topics that may be worth discussing, but not in this paragraph. This extraneous material could be shifted to other paragraphs of the essay, placed in explanatory notes, or simply omitted.

The second, much shorter paragraph suggests that related but less important detail can usefully be put into explanatory notes where, if wanted, it is always available. Readers of the second paragraph are being given a choice: they can absorb the essential information from the paragraph alone, or they can examine the topic in greater depth by referring also to the explanatory notes.

Explanatory notes should be reserved for information that, in your view, is useful and to some degree relevant to the topic; if it is uninteresting and way off the point, simply omit it. If you indulge too often in explanatory notes, your notes may be longer than your essay. Also remember to find out whether including explanatory notes is acceptable to your instructor.

AVOIDING EXCESSIVE DOCUMENTATION

Numerous parenthetical notes were needed to document all the details found in the biographical essays about Charles Dickens. Here is a brief example:

> Dickens's regular work habits involved writing at his desk from about nine in the morning to two in the afternoon (Butt and Tillotson 19; Pope-Hennessy 248), which left a good deal of time for other activities. Some of his leisure each day was regularly spent in letter-writing, some in walking and riding in the open air (Pope-Hennessy 305, quoting Nathaniel Sharswell). Besides this regular routine, on some days he would devote time to reading manuscripts which Wills, his sub-editor on *Household Words*, would send to him for revision and comment (Forster 65; Johnson 702).

In this passage, three parenthetical notes are needed for three sentences because a different biography or pair of biographies is the source for each piece of information. To combine all the sources in a single note would confuse, rather than simplify, the acknowledgments. In addition, the writer of this essay is not only making it clear where the information came from, but is also providing the reader with a *choice of references*. The writer has come across the same information in more than one biography, has indicated the duplication of material in her notes, and has decided to demonstrate the thoroughness of her research by citing more than one reference. Since the sources are given equal status in the notes (by being placed in alphabetical order and separated by a semicolon), the reader can assume that they are equally reliable. Had the writer thought that one was more thorough or more convincing than another, she would either have omitted the secondary one or indicated its status by placing it after "also" (Johnson 702; also Forster 65).

But an abundance of parenthetical notes is not always appropriate. As the following example demonstrates, excessive documentation only creates clutter.

> In contrast to the Dickenses' house in London, this setting was idyllic: the house stood in the center of a large garden complete with woods, waterfall, roses (Forster 145), and "no end of flowers" (Forster 146). For a fee, the Dickenses fed on the produce of the estate and obtained their milk fresh from the landlord's cow (Forster 146). What an asset to one's peace of mind to have such a cooperative landlord as they had (Pope-Hennessy 310; Johnson 758; Forster 147) in the portly, jolly Monsieur Beaucourt (Forster 147)!

Clearly, this entire passage is taken from three pages in Forster's biography of Dickens, and a single note could document the entire paragraph. What information is contained in the sentence leading up to the triple parenthetical note that justifies citing three sources? And what does the last note document? Is it only Forster who is aware that Monsieur Beaucourt is portly and jolly? To avoid tiring and irritating his readers, the writer here would have been well advised to ignore the supporting evidence in Pope-Hennessy and Johnson, and use a single reference to Forster. The writer was undoubtedly proud of his extensive research, but he seems more eager to show off his hours in the library than to provide a readable text for his audience.

USING UMBRELLA NOTES

As in the previous example, sometimes the logical sequence of your ideas or information requires you to cite the same source for several sentences or even for several paragraphs at a stretch. Instead of repeating "Forster 146" again and again, you can use a single note to cover the entire sequence. These notes are sometimes called *umbrella notes*, because they cover a sequence of sentences as an umbrella might cover more than one person. Umbrella notes are generally used in essays where the sources' names are not often cited in the text, and so the reader cannot easily figure out the coverage by assuming that the name and the parenthetical note mark the beginning and ending points. An umbrella simply means that you are leaving the reader in no doubt as to how much material the note is covering.

An umbrella note consists of an explanation of how much material is being covered by a source. Such a note is too long to be put in parentheses within the text and generally takes the form of *an explanatory note placed outside the body of your essay*. Here is an example:

[2]The information in this and the previous paragraph dealing with Dickens's relationship with Wilkie Collins is entirely derived from Hutton 41–49.

Inside your essay, the superscript number 2 referring the reader to this note would follow right after the *last* sentence that uses material from Hutton to discuss Dickens and Wilkie Collins. In the list of Works Cited, the entry for Hutton would contain all of the bibliographic information documenting this source.

Of course, umbrella notes work only when you are using a single source for a reasonably long stretch. If you use two sources, you have to distinguish between them in parenthetical notes, and the whole point of the umbrella—to cut down on the number of notes—is lost.

Umbrella notes must also be used with caution when you are quoting. Because the umbrella provides the reference for a long stretch of material, the citation usually includes several pages; but how will the reader know on which page the quotation appears? Sometimes you can add this information to the note itself:

[2]The information in this and the previous paragraph is entirely derived from Hutton 41–49. The two quotations from Dickens's letters are from pages 44 and 47, respectively.

However, if you use too many umbrella notes, or if you expect a single note to guide your reader through the intricacies of a long paragraph, you will have abused the device. Your essay will have turned into a series of summaries, with each group of paragraphs describing a single source. That is not what a research essay is supposed to be.

THE FINAL BIBLIOGRAPHY

While the bibliography is always an essential part of the research essay, it becomes especially important when you use MLA documentation, since it is the only place where your reader can find publication information about your sources. Which works you include in your final bibliography may depend on the wording and intention of your assignment. There is an important difference between a list of works that you have *consulted* or *examined* and a list of works that you have *cited* or actually used in writing your essay. Many instructors restrict the bibliography to "Works Cited," but you may be asked to submit a list of "Works Consulted." Remember that one purpose of a "Works Consulted" bibliography is to help your readers to find appropriate background information, not to overwhelm them with the magnitude of your efforts. Don't present a collection of thirty-five titles if you actually cite only five sources in your essay.

An appropriate final bibliography of "Works Cited" for an undergraduate essay consists of all the sources that you used and documented, through parenthetical notes, in your essay.

If you consulted a book in the hope that it contained some relevant information, and if it provided nothing useful, should you include it in your final bibliography? You might do so to prevent your readers from consulting works with misleading titles in the belief that they might be useful, but only if your bibliography is *annotated* so that the book's lack of usefulness can be pointed out. Finally, if you have been unable to locate a source and have thus never examined it yourself, you may not ordinarily include it in your final bibliography, however tempting the title may be.

PREPARING THE ANNOTATED BIBLIOGRAPHY

Annotating your bibliography is an excellent way to demonstrate the quality of your research. But, to be of use, your brief annotations must be informative. The following phrases do not tell the reader very much: "an interesting piece"; "a good article"; "well-done"; "another source of well-documented information." What is well done? Why is it interesting? What is good about it? How much and what kind of information does it contain? A good annotated bibliography will answer some of these questions.

The bibliography on the following pages presents the basic facts about the author, title, and publication, as well as some *evaluative information*. If the annotations were omitted, these entries would still be perfectly correct, for they conform to the standard rules for bibliographical format. Without the annotation, one would simply have to change the heading to "Works Consulted" or "Works Cited."

HEMINGWAY IN 1924: AN ANNOTATED BIBLIOGRAPHY

Baker, Carlos. *Hemingway: A Life Story.* New York: Scribner's, 1969. Print. 563 pages of biography, with 100 pages of footnotes. Everything seems to be here, presented in great detail.

Donaldson, Scott. *Hemingway: By Force of Will.* New York: Viking, 1977. Print. The material isn't organized chronologically; instead, the chapters are thematic, with titles like "Money," "Sex," and "War." Episodes from Hemingway's life are presented within each chapter. The introduction calls this "a mosaic of [Hemingway's] mind and personality."

Gopnik, Adam, ed. *Americans in Paris: A Literary Anthology.* Library of America. New York: Literary Classics of the United States, 2004. Print. This anthology contains short excerpts from literary works and memoirs by contemporaries of Hemingway such as Faulkner, Cummings, Gertrude Stein, and Dos Passos, providing an account of what life was like in Paris in the '20s by people who were there at the time. The excerpt by Harry Crosby is particularly good at evoking atmosphere.

Griffin, Peter. *Less Than a Treason: Hemingway in Paris*. New York: Oxford UP, 1990. Print. Part of a multivolume biography. Covers Hemingway's life from 1921–1927, exclusively. Griffin says in the preface that his goal is not to "analyze this well examined life" but "to recreate it." Not surprisingly, it reads like a novel, with an omniscient narrator with access to Hemingway's emotions.

Gurko, Leo. *Ernest Hemingway and the Pursuit of Heroism*. New York: Crowell, 1968. Print. This book is part of a series called "Twentieth-Century American Writers": a brief introduction to the man and his work. After fifty pages of straight biography, Gurko discusses Hemingway's writing, novel by novel. There's an index and a short bibliography, but no notes. The biographical part is clear and easy to read, but it sounds too much like summary.

Hemingway, Ernest. *A Moveable Feast*. New York: Scribner's, 1964. Print. This is Hemingway's own version of his life in Paris. It sounds authentic, but there's also a very strongly nostalgic tone, so it may not be trustworthy.

"Hemingway Biography: The Paris Years." *Hemingway Resource Center*. Hemingway Resource Center, 1996–2008. Web. 12 Mar. 2010. Thorough discussion of Hemingway's time in Paris.

Hemingway, Leicester. *My Brother, Ernest Hemingway*. Cleveland: World, 1962. Print. For 1924–1925, L.H. uses information from Ernest's letters (as well as commonly known facts). The book reads like a third-hand report, very remote; but L.H. sounds honest, not as if he were making up things that he doesn't know about.

Hotchner, A. E. *Papa Hemingway*. New York: Random, 1955. Print. This book is called a "personal memoir." Hotchner met Hemingway in 1948, evidently hero-worshiped him, and tape-recorded his reminiscences. The book is their dialogue (mostly Hemingway's monologue). No index or bibliography. Hotchner's adoring tone is annoying, and the material resembles that of *A Moveable Feast*, which is better written.

Meyers, Jeffrey. *Hemingway: A Biography*. New York: Harper, 1999. Print. Includes several maps, and two chronologies: illnesses and accidents, and travel. Book organized chronologically, with every year accounted for, according to table of contents. Well-documented critical biography, with personal anecdotes taking a back seat to literary. Less gossipy, more circumspect in claims than Griffin.

Reynolds, Michael. *Hemingway: The Paris Years.* Vol. 2. Cambridge: Blackwell, 1989. Print. Second of three-volume biography. Includes a chronology covering December 1921–February 1926 and five maps ("Hemingway's Europe 1922–26," "France," "Switzerland," "Italy," and "Key points for Hemingway's several trips through France and Spain").

Sokoloff, Alice Hunt. *Hadley, the First Mrs. Hemingway.* New York: Dodd, 1973. Print. This is the Paris experience from Hadley's point of view, most of it taken from her recollections and from the standard biographies. (Baker is acknowledged.) It's a very slight book—102 pages—but there's an index and footnotes, citing letters and interviews that some of the other biographers might not have been able to use.

Weeks, Robert P., ed. *Hemingway: Twentieth Century Perspectives.* Englewood Cliffs: Prentice, 1965. Print. Contains many important essays on Hemingway's life and art. Offers a selected annotated bibliography.

Young, Philip. *Ernest Hemingway.* Minneapolis: U of Minnesota P, 1959. Print. A short psychobiography of Hemingway's life. Offers stimulating insights, but suffers from the limitations of psychoanalysis.

Guidelines for Bibliographical Entries

(Additional models can be found in Chapter 12)

1. The bibliography is always listed on a *separate sheet* at the *end* of your research essay. The title should be centered, one inch from the top of the page.

2. Each entry is *double-spaced,* with double spacing between entries.

3. Each bibliographical entry starts with *the author's last name at the margin*; the second line of the entry (if there is one) is indented *five spaces*. This format enables the reader's eye to move quickly down the list of names at the left-hand margin.

4. The bibliography is in *alphabetical order,* according to the last name of the author.

   ■ If there are two authors, only the first has the last name placed first: "Woodward, Robert, and Carl Bernstein."

   ■ If an author has more than one work included on your list, do not repeat the name each time: alphabetize the works according to

(continued)

(continued)

their titles; place the name at the margin preceding the first work; for the remaining titles, replace the name with three hyphens, followed by a period and one space.

Freud, Sigmund. *Civilization and Its Discontents*. London: Hogarth,

1930. Print.

---. *Moses and Monotheism*. New York: Knopf, 1939. Print.

- A work that has no author should be alphabetized within the bibliography according to the first letter of the title (excluding "A," "An," and "The"); the title is placed at the margin as the author's name would be.

5. A bibliographical entry for a book is read as a list of three items—author, title (italicized), and publication information—with *periods between each piece of information*. Each period is followed by *one* space. All the information should always be presented in exactly the same order that you see in the model bibliography on pp. 483–485. Place of publication comes first; a colon separates place and name of publisher; a comma separates publisher and date.

6. A bibliographical entry for a *periodical* starts with the author's name and the article title (in quotation marks), each followed by a period and one space. Then comes the name of the periodical, italicized, followed by one space (and no punctuation at all). What comes next depends on the kind of periodical you are citing.

- For *quarterly and monthly journals*, include the volume number, a period, no space, and the issue number, followed by a space, and then the year in parentheses, followed by a colon.

- For *weekly or biweekly journals*, include only the full date—day, month, and year—followed by a colon.

All periodical entries end with the inclusive pages of the article, first page to last, followed by a period.

Tobias, Sheila, and Carol Weissbrod. "Anxiety and Mathematics: An

Update." *Harvard Educational Review* 50.1 (1980): 61–67. Print.

Winkler, Karen J. "Issues of Justice and Individual's Rights Spur

Revolution in Political Philosophy." *Chronicle of Higher Education*

16 Apr. 1986: 6–8. Print.

7. Each entry of the bibliography ends with the medium ("Print") and a period.

EXERCISE 37: PREPARING THE BIBLIOGRAPHY

Correct the errors of form in the following bibliography:

Becker, Howard S, Geer, Blanche, and Everett C. Hughes. Making the Grade: New York (1968) Wiley.

Dressel, Paul L.. College and University Curriculum, Berkeley (California): McCutcheon, 1971, Print

(same)----Handbook of Academic Evaluation. San Francisco (California): Jossey-Bass: 1976.

J. F. Davidson, "Academic Interest Rates and Grade Inflation," Educational Record.   56, 1975, pp. 122–5, Print

(no author). "College Grades: A Rationale and Mild Defense." AAUP Bulletin, October 1976, 320–1.

New York Times. "Job Plight of Young Blacks Tied to Despair, Skills Lack," April 19, 1983: Section A page 14.

Milton Ohmer, Howard R. Pollio and James A. Eison. GPA Tyranny, Education Digest 54   (Dec 1988): 11–14. Print.

Leo, John. "A for Effort". Or for Showing Up. U.S. News & World Report, 18 Oct, 1993: 22. (Print)

Kennedy, Donald. *What Grade Inflation? The New York Times* June 13, 1994: All. Bretz, Jr., Robert D. "College Grade Point Average as a Predictor of Adult Success: a Meta-analytical Review and Some Additional Evidence" Public Personnel Management 18   (Spring 1989): 11–22.

PRESENTING YOUR ESSAY

A well-presented research essay must conform to a few basic mechanical rules:

1. Type your essay on a computer. Make sure that you use a letter-quality printer.
2. Double-space throughout the essay.
3. Use 8½-by-11-inch paper; leave 1½-inch margins on both sides as well as top and bottom.
4. Use only one side of the page.
5. Number each page in the upper right corner; include your name with the number (Doe 4).

6. Proofread your essay, and print out the revised version.

7. Include graphics or illustrations only with your instructor's permission.

8. Include your name, your instructor's name, the name of the course, and the date on the first page of the essay at the top left margin. Place the title of the essay, centered, a few lines below that information.

Check with your instructor for any other special rules that may apply to the assignment.

A Checklist for Revision

As you read and re-read your essay, keep the following questions in mind.

1. Does the essay have a single focus that is clearly established and maintained throughout?
2. Does the essay have a thesis or a consistent point of view about the events or issues being described?
3. If it is a narrative essay, does the narration have a beginning, middle, and end? If it is an argument essay, are all assumptions explained and defended, and are all obvious counterarguments accommodated or refuted?
4. Does the essay begin with an informative introduction?
5. Does the essay end on a conclusive note?
6. Does each paragraph have a clear topic sentence?
7. Does each paragraph contain one and only one topic? Should any paragraphs be merged or deleted?
8. Are the paragraphs long enough to be convincing? Is each point supported by facts and information?
9. Does the development of the essay depend entirely on a dry listing of facts and examples, or do you offer explanations and relevant commentary? Is there a good balance between generalization and detail?
10. Do you use transitions to signal the relationship between separate points?
11. Is there unnecessary repetition? Are there any sentences that lack content or add nothing to the essay?
12. Is the style appropriate for a formal essay? Do the sentences seem too conversational, as if you were sending an e-mail?
13. Does the reader get a sense of the relative importance of the sources being used?
14. Do you use one source for very long stretches at a time?

15. Is there an appropriate number of notes rather than too many or too few?
16. Is it clear how much material is covered by each note?
17. In essays containing endnotes, do notes provide important explanatory information?
18. Are the quotations well chosen?
19. Is paraphrase properly used? Is the style of the paraphrase consistent with your style?
20. Do you use enough citations? Does the text of the essay make it clear when you are using a specific source, and who that person is?
21. Have you proofread the essay (in addition to using a spellchecker)?
22. Is the essay convincing? Will your reader accept your analysis, interpretation, and arguments?

·11·

Three Research Essays

The following three student research papers, on three very different subjects, use three different kinds of documentation.

Bethany Dettmore uses the evidence of three films, various print and Internet sources, and her own survey to develop and support a theory about why audiences enjoy horror movies. After *describing* and *interpreting* the films' narratives and *analyzing* the expectations that viewers form about their experiences in the theater, she concludes that horror films both reflect and alleviate some of our society's deepest fears. Dettmore documents her sources with MLA documentation. She summarizes, paraphrases, or quotes her sources, using brief and unobtrusive parenthetical notes, generally at the ends of the sentences. Almost everything that she wants to say is said within the body of the essay, so there are only a few endnotes.

Lee Myers also explores a social issue, using *analysis* supported by evidence presented in *narrative* form. To find out why cannibalism remains one of society's strongest taboos, she *interprets* a series of real events, historical and recent, ordinary and exotic. She also *reviews* a number of the anthropological theories that attempt to explain these events. Finally, she attempts to *persuade* her readers that the Western attribution of cannibalism to "primitive peoples" and the Western stigma against it are, in many ways, part of a social and political agenda and that, in certain circumstances, the practice of cannibalism can be justified. This essay will help you to understand the usefulness of the traditional footnote or endnote and bibliographic form of documentation. Myers is working with a great deal of precise detail, frequently referring to a group of sources to support specific points. She also presents a great deal of background information that cannot be included in the body of her paper. The separate endnotes provide enough room to cite all the sources and explain some of the points they are making.

David Morgan also combines *narrative and analysis* by describing the aftermath of the strange event that happened in 1908 at Lake Tunguska, Siberia, and then analyzing some of the many theories that have been used to explain that event over the last hundred years. The bibliography for this essay contains relatively few sources, which are cited less frequently than the sources are in the first two essays. The writer's purpose is to help his readers understand what might have happened at Lake Tunguska and to clarify the scientific explanations. He is not using numerous sources to reconstruct the event in complete detail, or trying to convince his readers, by citing authorities, that his conclusions are the right ones. Like many essays in the social sciences, this paper uses a variation of the author-year method of parenthetical note documentation. (This variation, often called APA after the American Psychological Association, is described in Chapter 12, on pp. 559–566.) Having the date, as well as the author, included within the body of the essay is especially useful when you are reading about scientific theories developed over a span of one hundred years.

Bethany Dettmore

Professor xxx

English 102

Spring 2005

Looking at Horror Films

In the lobby of the movie theater, the walls are lined with posters advertising what is "Coming Soon" to the cinema. Between the photos of cute couples and strapping action heroes lurk the dark forms of screaming women, monsters, and ghostly mansions. These images represent the genre of horror, a staple of entertainment since the beginning of cinema. Year after year all through the 20th century, Hollywood has produced movies that have no other purpose than to evoke fear in their viewers. Nor has the genre's importance diminished in the 21st century: in 2004, Roger Ebert reported that he had reviewed fifteen different horror films. Although the vast majority of horror films have earned a poor critical reputation over the years, they have always been an excellent investment for Hollywood studios and a surefire attraction for audiences. This paper will explore some of the reasons for the popularity of horror films and consider whether they exist only to provide cheap thrills or whether, in some respects, they serve a legitimate social purpose.

For any movie to be successful, the audience has to enter into the experience unfolding on the screen, almost as if each person sitting in the theater is participating in the story and feeling the emotions of some of the characters. Far from being passive observers, moviegoers help to "create the experience [they] are enjoying" while the director must work to "activate the imaginations that reach out to meet his own" (Prawer 20). In doing so, the viewer is taking a risk. Will the experience be a good one? Or will some people in the audience respond so deeply to what is happening on screen that the emotions aroused become difficult to deal with? Viewing a horror film involves an even greater risk, for the audience is expected not just to undergo an experience, but also "to court a certain danger, to risk being disturbed, shaken up, assaulted" (Dickstein 68). It is as if, by buying a ticket for the film, the moviegoer agrees to participate in what Andrew Tudor calls a "collective nightmare" (3).

It is because seeing a horror movie can pose such a great emotional and psychological risk that moviegoers are sharply divided in their reactions to the genre. Some love horror movies so much that they make a point of seeing every one that opens; others refuse to enter a theater with a monster or a screaming woman on the poster. In a survey conducted for this paper with respondents from both sexes and spanning all age groups, over 46% of the respondents said that they watched horror films very often or some-times, while the remainder did so rarely (47%) or never (6%). One respondent described horror as nothing more than "bad acting, dark sets and leaves you empty afterwards." What keeps such viewers away is apparently not so much the blood and gore (which 11% of the respondents said was what scared them most about such films) or the villains and monsters (8%), but the ele-ment of suspense—leading to fear—built into the plot (62%). Interestingly enough, that same element—suspense—is also the reason cited by 42% of the respondents for why they enjoy horror films; it captures their interest and hooks them for the remainder of the film. One respondent wrote that horror films promise "a suspenseful plot that carries you on a mysterious rollercoaster." We can only conclude that some people like to be frightened!

Why, then, as Tudor describes it, do many thousands of people want to sit in a movie theater and feel the threat that something dire will happen (8)? Here, the survey provides us with a useful distinction between creating *suspense*, the quality that two-thirds of the respondents see as the essence of a horror film, and creating *fear*, the quality chosen by the other third. It seems likely that the two-thirds focusing on suspense are people who go to see horror films regularly. They don't want or expect to experience a lot of terror and dread; instead, they anticipate a certain amount of tension and nervous anxiety that—if the film is any good—will be resolved by the final shot. Such viewers expect that "fear will be aroused, then controlled" (Giles 39). There is always a time limit: the length of the movie. Their anxiety is "neutralized" and can even become pleasurable because it is experienced in safe surroundings (Dickstein 69).

The secure environment of the movie theater makes it possible for us to experience another emotion—catharsis, the feeling that can occur when you have been under an intense threat and then realize that it has gone away. Janet Maslin compares the emotion that we can experience during horror films to that of people gawking at highway accidents or watching TV dramas about fatal illnesses: "The knowledge that these things have befallen others provides a grim relief for those who have been spared." Other people's misfortunes—in real life or on the screen—act as our own shield against disaster. Using the "roller coaster" image again, the critic Linda Williams recalls the experience of seeing *Psycho* for the first time, describing it as a "roller coaster sensibility of repeated tension and release, assault and escape" (162). What she carried home with her was the release and the escape, not the tension and the assault. The viewers know that, however terrifying the situation may be in the movie, someone or something will intervene and put things right (Tudor 214–15) and they can leave the theater "drained and satisfied" (Dickstein 77).

But horror films also appeal to audiences on a more intellectual level. We don't just feel anxiety and terror; we also want to know how the story is going to work out. We admire the ingenuity of the writer and director as we wait for the ending when, we anticipate, all the mysteries of the plot will be logically revealed (Solomon 254). But, in a horror film, we don't just want to know what will happen next. The very weirdness of the characters, settings, and situations excites our curiosity. According to Noel Carroll in "The General Theory of Horrific Appeal," the central theme of horror movies is a voyage of discovery; their business is "proving, disclosing, discovering and confirming the existence of something that is impossible" (3). What beings could be more "impossible" than monsters and aliens? If the film is any good, we begin to focus less on the horribleness of these creatures and more on the logic behind their story. We wonder whether such creatures can really exist, and we want to find out how.

Our interest is also stimulated by the elements of myth in many horror films. Like popular epics such as *The Lord of the Rings* or *Star Wars*, a good horror movie often revolves around a group of people confronted with dire peril who must find strength that they didn't realize they possessed so that their cause will eventually triumph. Because the danger and the fear are so great, the heroism needed to overcome the danger must be equally great. R. H. W. Dillard describes the myth of the horror film in religious terms: "Like a medieval morality play, the horror film deals with the central issue of Christian life—the struggle between the spirits of good and evil for the possession of man's immortal soul" (36). Such themes are common to all societies because they speak to our deepest need to know who we are, why we are here, and what use we will make of our lives. Jonathan Crane insists that such needs go far beyond "the influence of everyday life": "When audience members engage with a horror film they are not enjoying visions that respond to everyday fears; they are responding to atavistic terrors nearly as old as the reptilian brain" (24–25). To explore some of these themes, I want to focus briefly on three landmark horror films: *The Cabinet of Dr. Caligari*, *Freaks*, and *Psycho*.

Regarded as the first classic horror film, *The Cabinet of Dr. Caligari* was made in Germany as a silent movie. In 1919, Hans Janowitz, a Czech poet, and Carl Mayer, an Austrian artist, wrote a script that told the story of a bizarre murder, in a terrifying dreamlike setting, based on a legend in Janowitz's home town. At the center of the narrative are the sinister hypnotist Dr. Caligari, who operates a fortune-telling booth at a fair, and his "creature" Cesare, a young man who, while hypnotized, looks into the future, tells fortunes, and on occasion commits brutal murders. One of the striking scenes of the film shows the entire population of the village chasing after Cesare, who has abducted and is likely to murder the heroine. As Figure 1 illustrates, this scene emphasizes what the extremely creepy appearance and behavior of Dr. Caligari and Cesare—weird even by silent-movie standards— have told the audience (Prawer 172): these are not normal humans but alien beings, who pose a threat to ordinary people and must be rooted out.

At the end of the movie, it is discovered that Dr. Caligari himself has actually been under the influence of an 18th century homicidal hypnotist who has been inhabiting his body. But an even more upsetting revelation is that, even while he—through Cesare—has been terrorizing the village, Dr. Caligari has simultaneously held the respectable post of director of an insane

Figure 1. The hypnotized Cesare flees with his intended victim through a nightmarish landscape. Still from *The Cabinet of Dr. Caligari*, dir. Robert Wiene, 1921 (Image Entertainment, 1997; DVD).

Dettmore 6

asylum some distance away. In effect, the madman has been in charge of the asylum.

If, as Stephen Prince describes, horror movies can be regarded as representations of our own psychic processes (118), then *The Cabinet of Dr. Caligari* is all about our fear of the alien in our midst. In *Caligari's Children*, S. S. Prawer analyzes the many roles that Dr. Caligari assumes in the audience's imagination. He is the "stranger who disrupts the normal lives of the inhabitants of a small town" (172), yet he plays a vital part in the life of the community as the person in charge of one of its important institutions (173). He is one of the first of a long line of mad scientists to dominate the genre, and yet he is also a "mystic" who understands ancient secrets (173). He controls the actions of the unfortunate Cesare, yet he himself is the victim of "demonic possession" (171). Most interesting, we are terrified by Caligari both because of and despite the fact that his odd way of walking makes him seem deformed and crippled (174). As Prawer puts it, all of these impressions of Caligari are intended "to suggest monsters arising from the subconscious" of the viewer (176), monsters that have long been suppressed by civilized society (Wood 10).

In the same way, Cesare is also a character on whom we can project our ambivalence about our "dark desires" (Prawer 181). He is a zombielike figure who commits acts forbidden to the culturally inhibited audience, yet who doesn't have to take responsibility because he is being controlled by the hypnotist. Prawer points out that Cesare is the first of a long line of horror film monsters who may seem horrifying but for whom we also feel pity and even affection (178; also Dillard 39).

However alien these monsters might appear, they are essentially like us:

> The vampires and werewolves, monsters and mummies are all human at source and are all personifications of that potentiality for evil and sin which is so much a part of us all. Hero and villain are much the same—both human, both flawed unto death. . . .
> (Dillard 41)

Casper Tybjerg makes a related point when he disputes with critics who believe that the standard source of fear in horror films has to be the inhuman "monster" figure: "Although Cesare and Caligari are certainly menacing, the real danger is in the threat of madness and of reality breaking down" (16; also Soren 30).[1] What keeps the audience interested here is the possibility of their own emotional or moral breakdown.

It is the ambiguity of *The Cabinet of Dr. Caligari* that makes it such a great horror film. We can recognize something of ourselves in these alien figures who should really repel us. The publicity campaign for the opening of *Caligari* in Berlin in 1920 captured the film's underlying horror: people were invited to come to see the movie with the assurance: "You must be a Caligari!" (Clarens 16–17).

As the title suggests, the characters in *Freaks*, a 1932 film by Tod Browning, are abnormal in a different way from Caligari and Cesare. Here, the immediate focus of horror is the physical deformity of the freaks in a circus sideshow, which is contrasted with the beauty of Cleopatra, the trapeze artist with whom one of the midgets, Hans, falls in love. (Figure 2 captures that contrast.) Although she agrees to marry him, Cleopatra is actually plotting (with Hercules, the Strong Man) to murder Hans for his money. When the rest of the freaks discover what Cleopatra and Hercules are trying to do, they hunt down, capture, and attack the two, mutilating her until she is "one of them"[2]—a "Hen Woman" suitable for viewing in a freak show.

One of the major selling points of the film—when Browning was trying to convince MGM to produce it and when MGM was attempting to market it—was that the freak characters were played not by professional actors but by real Siamese twins, bearded ladies, pinheads, dwarves, and so on. Browning went to a great deal of trouble to portray his characters sympathetically, with the freaks often shown behaving like normal people. In one scene, for example, two dwarves have a normal conversation in a setting with miniaturized furniture and props, so that everything seems quite familiar and ordinary to the audience—until a normal-sized person arrives on the scene (Clarens 70).[3] As Clarens puts it, "Freaks among themselves cease to be freaks" (71). They are also sympathetic because they make the best of their handicaps, with the pinhead flirting, the limbless worm lighting cigarettes,

Figure 2. When the "freaks" in a circus sideshow learn that the "normal" Cleopatra (standing at right) is planning to marry the midget Hans (on table) only to murder him for his money, they take a horrifying revenge. Still from *Freaks*, dir. Tod Browning, 1932 (Warner Home Video, 2004; DVD).

the armless woman drinking from a glass (Thomas 136). At the beginning, the freaks are very trusting of normal people, welcoming them into their society. In all these ways, the audience is encouraged to accept them as "normal." For example, in a key scene, when we first see the freaks from a distance, they appear to us as monstrous, misshapen creatures capering around in a bizarre kind of dance; but this impression changes in the next close-up shot as the freaks "are transformed from agents of terror to objects of compassion within moments" (Thomas 137).

     Here is the crucial issue of the film. To what extent will the audience actually sympathize with the freaks, accepting them as people like us, living in a little world that mirrors ours? On the one hand, we tend to have a reflex prejudice against deformity. Many in the audience will be turned off by the initial shot of the freaks dancing; the distorted figures will make them feel unsettled and afraid (Cantor and Oliver 55). According to Michael Grant, we inevitably feel a sense of revulsion for what we regard as lesser beings: "In the cruelty of our sarcasm, we look down upon them, and it seems that there is no way for the small protagonist, a being in the process of discovering the world's bitterness, to escape his fate when he can't even reach the door handle" (128). In this perversion of the "there but for the grace of God . . ." response, we are eager to disassociate ourselves from these images because they might suggest to us that freaks are humans like us and that we might also be like them. Certainly, some audiences in 1932 felt that revulsion: at a preview in San Diego, one woman ran up the aisle screaming; many movie theaters refused to show the film; and, in New York, thirty minutes of footage were cut by the censors (Clarens 70).[4]

On the other hand, audiences who stay with the movie will almost certainly sympathize with poor Hans, the victim of the greedy, unfeeling Cleopatra. If a horror film has to have a monster, surely it is the "normal" and beautiful Cleopatra, who is shown to have no redeeming qualities at all. As one reviewer on the Internet puts it, "You quickly realize who Browning intends to be the real freaks. It is the 'normal' people who display the worst human traits of deceit and greed. The 'freaks' are shown to be loyal to each other, having an unwritten code of honor" (Bright).

And yet, in the final twist, Browning seems to turn Cleopatra into the victim and the freaks into the monsters by having them take their ghastly revenge on her. The scene in which they hunt her down is easily the most terrifying in the film, as the previously rather charming freaks become grotesque and predatory before our eyes. Are we horrified by what they do to Cleopatra, or are we horrified by what the freaks have become? Or are we afraid that we might have the potential to become like freaks ourselves?

Clarens believes that, although we recognize that the freaks are entitled to their "just retribution," all along our sympathy for them has been no more than "intellectual," and we are naturally more concerned about the fate of Cleopatra and Hercules, who are more like us (71). Thomas, however, takes a broader view, recognizing the ambiguity that is so often at the center of the horror movie. He wonders whether the freaks can simultaneously "be seen both as objects of sympathy and as nightmarish incarnations of the nonhuman" (135). Does the grotesque ending undercut everything that Browning was trying to achieve in the film? Ultimately, Thomas concludes that Browning does succeed because so much sympathy has been created for the freaks during the course of the film that we will stifle our disgust at the ending: "We are horrified, but we are simultaneously ashamed of our horror; for we remember that these are not monsters at all but people like us, and we know that we have again been betrayed by our own primal fears" (137). If Thomas is right—and *Freaks* has always been a cult classic—then the horror film has once again enabled us to see the freakish monster within ourselves and—going a step further than Caligari—forgive ourselves for being human.

Psycho (1960) marks a shift from the traditional horror film in which terror is found in monster figures that are clearly alien or abnormal. According to some critics, through this one film, Alfred Hitchcock transformed the entire genre, allowing horror to be seen in the context of contemporary American society (Jancovitch 4). On the surface, the relationships between the characters in *Psycho* are quite ordinary: two sisters, mother and son, innkeeper and customer. Figure 3 shows us two average people in conversation; there's nothing monstrous about them. We certainly don't anticipate that Marian Crane, someone with a rather unsavory back story whom we accept as our heroine, will be savagely killed one-third of the way through the film. So we are unprepared for the famous shower scene at the Bates Motel: "We see an old woman with white hair pull back the shower curtain and stab Marian a half dozen times. The scene is back lit and we don't get a clear picture of the face of the murderer" (Ghani). We also don't anticipate that the murderer will turn out to be the amiable Norman Bates, almost cozy in his wooly cardigan. In a way, it would be easier on the audience if the murderer were an intergalactic intruder or a time-traveling Ice Age warrior, or some sort of freak or clairvoyant from a traveling circus. We know that such beings appear only in horror films, not in real life, and we can sit secure in our seats waiting for the end of the movie.

Dettmore 11

Figure 3. Anthony Perkins as Norman Bates and Janet Leigh as Marian Crane. Still from *Psycho (Collector's Edition)*, dir. Alfred Hitchcock, 1960 (MCA Home Video, 1998; DVD).

Once the audience understands that "the monster within" (Dickstein 74) lurks in ordinary people and in familiar social settings, and an apparently normal person can be transformed into a psychotic murderer without any warning (Tudor 221), that sense of security is gone forever from the horror film.[5] These new monsters

> do not come from outside our nebulous social networks; they do not arrive in our suburbs fresh from the remote Carpathian mountains; they are not created by . . . well-intentioned scientists who err as ambitious humans will. They are us, and we never know when we will act as monsters. (Crane 8)[6]

Throughout the early parts of *Psycho*, we are encouraged to have sympathy for Norman Bates, and, as Tudor points out, it is possible to retain some of that sympathy even after we realize that he is Marian's murderer. But, as with our response to the ending of *Freaks*, the collision between our revulsion and our sympathy makes us ambivalent and acutely uncomfortable. The ultimate effect is a kind of audience paranoia. Our perceptions are no longer reliable, and we can no longer trust the most "normal" of our friends and relations, for they might at any time attack us: "The world in which this kind of horror makes sense, then, is one which is fundamentally unreliable" (Tudor 221).

In recent years, for many film critics, horror has not been considered a legitimate genre. They regard post-*Psycho* horror films as worthless: imitative, predictable, sleazy, and much too concerned with blood and gore. As one writer in a college newspaper put it, such films are "dismissed by critics across the board . . . as a disgustingly stupid thing to enjoy" (Olson). The audience is so accustomed to the trite plot devices that they know exactly what will happen in the next scene—and announce it out loud—minutes before it occurs. Even the movie music sends clear signals to the audience (Scott). The chief attraction of the traditional horror film—suspense—is totally gone. Yet, according to the *Internet Movie Database*, horror films remain among Hollywood's top grossing movies. Leaving aside the teenage boys who wallow in the blood and gore, what continues to be the attraction? In my view, removing the element of suspense from horror films has restored to the audience the sense of security that they used to feel when the movie was populated by monsters that you were unlikely to meet in everyday life. If the nice guy whose locker is next to yours or the waitress at the diner is going to turn into a serial murderer, you'll only be able to stay within your comfort zone if you can predict the appearance of the ax in advance.

In place of suspense, the modern horror film provides excess: too much blood, too much violence, too much sex. The original horror films gained their interest from exploring the nature of evil and the psychology of madness; they didn't need buckets of gore to keep the audience's attention (Crane 4). Now, however, nothing is left to the imagination:

> There is no opportunity to view the monster as the embodiment of
> a community's fears, or as the darker side of man's nature, or as

anything other than a cryptic, single-minded creep. There's no time to identify with the characters, since they are killed off so quickly that they don't have time to impress themselves upon an audience. (Maslin)

The effect of all the blood and all the violence is to desensitize the audience; the gore serves as an anesthetic to prevent us from feeling anything at all. According to Aviva Briefel, those watching the ultra-bloody *Texas Chain Saw Massacre* find it hard to identify with anyone in the film: certainly not the sadistic killers, or even the masochistic victims, who allow themselves to become sitting ducks: "We may feel endangered by the images of violence on screen, but we are ultimately numb to the pain they represent" (19).

Horror films have always tended to "perfectly mirror the fears of contemporary society" (Soren 153) and have been especially popular in times of social disruption (Dickstein 66). Their function has always been to assure their audience of "man's ability to cope with and even prevail over the evil of life which he can never hope to understand" (Dillard 37). But each generation demands a different kind of horror movie, one that is (in the words of a Hollywood producer) "'in tune with the zeitgeist'" (qtd. in Shone). The time is over for what Tudor calls "secure horror": movies in which man's ingenuity invariably triumphs over monstrous evil. Such films belonged to an age that was "confident of its own capacity to survive all manner of threats" (220). Since 9/11, our confidence, public and private, has been shaken, perhaps irretrievably. So it is not surprising that, on the one hand, horror movies continue to draw huge audiences. People still need to view "imaginative and plausible encounters with evil and cosmic amorality [because] they help us ponder and respond emotionally to natural and deep worries about the nature of the world" (Freeland 193). But, given the enemy we face in the war on terror, an enemy that is "nebulous" and "wraith-like," that "regroups whenever you strike it" (Shone), it is no longer easy to believe that the monster will be vanquished at the end of the two-hour film. People are more on edge, more vulnerable to fear and terror. What they seek is the anesthetizing power of the contemporary horror film with all its formulaic predictability and gory special effects. Horror films can no longer compete on their own terms with the real terror existing in the world (Solomon 254).

Notes

[1]The famous Expressionist set designs for *Caligari* carry out the theme of the breakdown of reality. David Soren points out that "the sets are distorted, often jagged and harsh, indicators of the madness in which the characters are trapped" (30).

[2]One of the most frightening scenes in the movie shows the wedding festivities, with the freaks dancing around Cleopatra—she and Hercules are the only normal people attending—chanting: "We accept her, we accept her, gobble gobble, one of us, one of us."

[3]Given this focus on normality among the freaks, some critics conclude that *Freaks* is not actually a horror movie. Peter Hutchings argues that it "functions as a kind of anti-horror film" because it completely avoids any of the special effects typical of horror movies and derives its thrills simply from the contrast between the normal and the abnormal (27).

[4]Interestingly enough, in the United Kingdom, *Freaks* was banned for thirty years, not for fear of audience reaction, but because Browning was considered to have exploited his cast. Skal reports that some cast members did, indeed, feel degraded by its content. Olga Roderick, who played the role of the bearded lady, told reporters that the film was "an insult to all freaks everywhere" (156).

[5]During screenings of *Psycho*, there was an amazing amount of screaming and dashing up the aisles as members of the audience tried to get out. In certain scenes, people could hardly hear the soundtrack (Williams 164).

[6]Tom Shone points out that when "America's bogeymen no longer smacked of the supernatural, but hailed from your neighbor's backyard," Hollywood stopped calling these movies "horror films" and instead produced "psychological thrillers" and "suspense movies."

Works Cited

Briefel, Aviva. "Monster Pains: Masochism, Menstruation, and Identification in the Horror Film." *Film Quarterly* 58.3 (2005): 16–27. Print.

Bright, Gerry ["gerb"]. "Return of the Chicken Woman." *Dooyoo Review.* Dooyoo GmBH, 2 Oct. 2002. Web. 15 May 2005.

The Cabinet of Dr. Caligari. Dir. Robert Wiene. 1921. Image Entertainment, 1997. DVD.

Cantor, Joanne, and Mary Beth Oliver. "Developmental Differences in Responses to Horror." *Horror Films: Current Research on Audience Preferences and Reactions.* Ed. James B. Weaver III and Ron Tamborini. Mahwah: Erlbaum, 1996. 63–80. Print.

Carroll, Noel. "The General Theory of Horrific Appeal." *Dark Thoughts: Philosophic Reflections on Cinematic Horror.* Ed. Steven Jay Schneider and Daniel Shaw. Lanham: Scarecrow, 2003. 1–9. Print.

Clarens, Carlos. *An Illustrated History of Horror and Science-Fiction Films.* New York: Da Capo, 1967. Print.

Crane, Jonathan Lake. *Terror and Everyday Life.* Thousand Oaks: Sage, 1994. Print.

Dickstein, Morris. "The Aesthetics of Fright." *Planks of Reason: Essays on the Horror Film.* Ed. Barry Keith Grant. 1980. Metuchen: Scarecrow, 1984. 65–78. Print.

Dillard, R. H. W. "The Pageantry of Death." *Focus on the Horror Film.* Ed. Roy Huss and T. J. Ross. 1967. Englewood Cliffs: Prentice-Hall, 1972. 36–41. Print.

Ebert, Roger. "Movie Reviews: Carrie." *RogerEbert.com.* RogerEbert.com, 1 Jan. 1976. Web. 17 May 2005.

Freaks. Dir. Tod Browning. 1932. Warner Home Video, 2004. DVD.

Freeland, Cynthia. "Horror and Art-Dread." *The Horror Film.* Ed. Stephen Prince. New Brunswick: Rutgers UP, 2004. 189–205. Print.

Ghani, Cyrus. *My Favorite Films.* Washington: Mage, 2004. Print.

Giles, Dennis. "Conditions of Pleasure in Horror Cinema." *Planks of Reason: Essays on the Horror Film.* Ed. Barry Keith Grant. 1980. Metuchen: Scarecrow, 1984. 38–52. Print.

Grant, Michael. "On the Question of the Horror Film." *Dark Thoughts: Philosophic Reflections on Cinematic Horror.* Ed. Steven Jay Schneider and Daniel Shaw. Lanham: Scarecrow, 2003. 120–37. Print.

Hutchings, Peter. *The Horror Film.* Edinburgh: Pearson, 2004. Print.

Internet Movie Database. IMDb.com, 1990–2005. Web. 12 May 2005.

Jancovitch, Mark. Introduction. *Horror, The Film Reader.* Ed. Mark Jancovitch. London: Routledge, 2002. 1–9. Print.

Maslin, Janet. "Bloodbaths Debase Movies and Audiences." *New York Times* 21 Nov. 1982, Arts and Leisure: 1. Print.

Olson, Melissa. "Horror Films Are Like Broken Records." *Daily Trojan.* Univ. of Southern California, 8 June 2005. Web. 12 June 2005.

Prawer, S. S. *Caligari's Children.* Oxford: Oxford UP, 1980. Print.

Prince, Stephen. "Dread, Taboo, and *The Thing*: Toward a Social Theory of the Horror Film." *The Horror Film.* Ed. Stephen Prince. New Brunswick: Rutgers UP, 2004. 118–30. Print.

Psycho (Collector's Edition). Dir. Alfred Hitchcock. Perf. Anthony Perkins and Janet Leigh. 1960 MCA Home Video, 1998. DVD.

Scott, Kirsty. "Music + Chase Scenes = New Formula for Fear." *Guardian.co.uk.* Guardian News and Media, 5 Aug. 2004. Web. 10 May 2005.

Shone, Tom. "This Time It's Personal." *The Guardian* 25 Nov. 2005, Films and Music: 25. Print.

Skal, David J. *The Monster Show: A Cultural History of Horror.* New York: Macmillan, 2001. *Google Book Search.* Web. 21 May 2005.

Solomon, Robert. "Real Horror." *Dark Thoughts: Philosophic Reflections on Cinematic Horror.* Ed. Steven Jay Schneider and Daniel Shaw. Lanham: Scarecrow, 2003. 230–64. Print.

Soren, David. *The Rise and Fall of the Horror Film.* Baltimore: Midnight Marquee, 1997. Print.

Thomas, John. "Gobble, Gobble . . . One of Us!" *Focus on the Horror Film.* Ed. Roy Huss and T. J. Ross. Englewood Cliffs: Prentice-Hall, 1972. 135–38. Print.

Tudor, Andrew. *Monsters and Mad Scientists: A Cultural History of the Horror Movie.* Cambridge: Blackwell, 1989. Print.

Tybjerg, Casper. "Shadow-Souls and Strange Adventures: Horror and the Supernatural in European Silent Film." *The Horror Film.* Ed. Stephen Prince. New Brunswick: Rutgers UP, 2004. 15–39. Print.

Williams, Linda. "Learning to Scream." *Horror, The Film Reader.* Ed. Mark Jancovitch. London: Routledge, 2002. 163–68. Print.

Wood, Robin. Introduction. *American Nightmare: Essays on the Horror Film.* Ed. Andrew Britton et al. Toronto: Festival of Festivals, 1979. 7–28. Print.

Dettmore 18

The Horror Film Survey

Name_____

This survey includes four multiple-choice questions and two open-ended questions asking for short responses. Circle your answers to the multiple-choice questions, and respond to the open-ended questions in the spaces provided.

1. How often do you watch horror films?
   a. Very often 13.5%
   b. Some of the time 32.5%
   c. Not very often 47%
   d. Never 6%

2. Where do you watch horror films?
   a. In theaters 9%
   b. At home 46%
   c. Half in theaters and half at home 39%
   d. Nowhere 6%

3. What scares you most about horror films?
   a. The blood and gore 11%
   b. The suspense 62%
   c. The villains 8%
   d. Identification with the victims 18%

4. How would you best describe horror films?
   a. A cheap thrill 23.5%
   b. An art form 19%
   c. Trashy films 8.5%
   d. A legitimate genre 49%

5. What do you like/dislike about horror films?

   Like: Creates suspense 42%

   Dislike: Predictability 35%

                Scares me long after the movie 23%

6. How would you define a horror film?

   Any film that creates suspense 66%

   Any film that creates fear 33%

Lee Myers

Professor xxx

Anthropology 1

22 December 2004

Is Eating People Really Wrong?

In a 1957 Broadway revue, the comic duo Flanders and Swann sang about a young cannibal boy who defies his family, insisting:

> I don't eat people
>
> I won't eat people
>
> Eating people is wrong.

His puzzled father reasons with him:

> People have always eaten people
>
> What else is there to eat?
>
> If the Juju had meant us not to eat people
>
> He wouldn't have made us of meat.[1]

Yet, despite accusations of cowardice ("You're afraid of ending up in the pot yourself"), the boy continues to resist the temptation of "roast leg of insurance salesman."

Part of the song's humor comes from its reversal of expectations: it assumes that cannibalism is normal, that the boy's high moral tone is just squeamishness, and that there's no good reason not to eat human flesh. In "The Reluctant Cannibal" Flanders and Swann are tapping into the audience's horror of and fascination with one of the last remaining social taboos. We are being encouraged to wonder whether eating people really is wrong, an issue that is well worth exploring by examining the motivation for cannibalism in different cultures and different circumstances.[2] One can conclude that "survival cannibalism" caused by hunger is a reasonable course of behavior that should not be automatically condemned by Western morality and that even the various tribal customs known as "ritual cannibalism" can be better understood and even accepted within the context of their specific cultures.

Petrinovich suggests that such behavior in times of crop failure or flood or war should not be regarded as pathological but as quite sensible,

Myers 2

even natural, under the circumstances. During such disasters, normal moral constraints must be suspended: "It is as though the outer coverings of society have been peeled away to reveal the basic core of human nature."[3] Petrinovich describes the extreme consequences of starvation: everything within the body shrinks, including oxygen consumption, and strength and coordination weaken; but intellectual performance is not affected,[4] so presumably one can still make reasonable moral decisions.

Cannibalism would seem to be a reasonable choice in time of extreme famine. While the nutritional value of human flesh has been much debated, Garn and Block say that a man weighing fifty kilograms would provide sufficient protein for one day for sixty people, "skimpily." But if only one edible man was available in a week, the group wouldn't find the effort of killing him "nutritionally worthwhile."[5] During the Egyptian famine of 1201, when babies were sold "roasted or boiled," the Egyptians were horrified at first, but they grew used to it and some even "conceived such a taste for these detestable meats that they made them their ordinary provender, eating them for enjoyment and [thinking up] a variety of preparation methods."[6] In modern times, war has prompted outbreaks of cannibalism, particularly during sieges. In Paris, during the Franco-Prussian War, there was a butcher shop on the Ile St. Louis that was well known for supplying unusually fine meat.[7] During the siege of Leningrad in World War II, when one million people—one-third of the city's population—died, numerous "crimes-for-food" were committed.[8] According to Aleksandr Solzhenitsyn, in the prison camps of the Gulag Archipelago, hunger existed "to the point at which parents ate their own children."[9] As recently as the 1990s, extreme famine occurred in Russia and the Ukraine, which led to at least thirty documented murders in which bodies were sold for food.[10]

As these historical precedents suggest, anyone might engage in survival cannibalism if all sources of food disappeared. Perhaps the most well-publicized incident of this sort occurred in 1972, in the Andes, when the plane carrying a party of forty-five members of a Uruguayan rugby team with their families and friends crashed in bad weather. Injured and exposed to the bitter cold, the twenty-seven survivors existed on a daily ration of one square of chocolate, one teaspoon of jam, a bit of toothpaste, and a small mouthful of wine in a deodorant cap.[11] When these supplies ran out and search efforts had evidently been called off, the leader of the survivors, Roberto Canessa, argued that the group had a moral duty to stay alive, that they had been given the gift of life and were responsible for sustaining it. God wanted them to live, they concluded. He had spared them from the crash and had given them the dead bodies to eat. It would be wrong to reject this gift on the grounds of squeamishness[12] for "refus[ing] to live would be a form of suicide, a mortal sin."[13] Good Catholics, the survivors were very conscious of the sacrament of Holy Communion as they prepared the bodies,[14] and this theme was echoed by some of the Catholic priests who were sympathetic to them when, after seventy-two days, they returned to civilization:

> The body must have a worthy purpose, and in [this] case, this purpose was to serve as food for the survivors. The living who still have strength must preserve themselves, and this the survivors tried faithfully to do. Of course, one must treat the dead with respect—and one symbol of the survivors' respect was to choose them for food.[15]

Treating the dead with respect is important in understanding acts of cannibalism. The Andes party had certain advantages over most other survival groups: they all knew and cared for each other and could work together to survive.[16] (Indeed, they were finally rescued by their own initiative: the two strongest set out to walk out of the mountains and find help.) Throughout, they maintained a sense of charity and morality, made their decisions in relative harmony, and went about the dreadful business of cannibalism with some delicacy. For example, one group prepared each portion of meat and a different group consumed it, and none of the dead women were regarded as candidates for consumption. In addition, the Andes party, believing that they had done nothing wrong, decided when rescue was imminent not to hide the pieces of flesh that had been stockpiled. Of course, since so many had died in the crash, they had not had to make the dreadful decision to kill in order to survive.[17]

In 1846, when the Donner Party was stranded by blizzards in the Rocky Mountains, they had none of these advantages. Starting from Illinois

Myers 4

and intending to settle in California, this group of eighty-seven farmers and townspeople (most of whom were women and children), eventually joined by two Indians, was trapped by the onset of an unusually early winter. They were not used to camping or fending for themselves, nor could they forage for food or read a trail. Still, they were highly organized, holding meetings to make decisions. First they gradually abandoned their goods and their twenty ox-drawn wagons as they pushed on through the waist-deep snow. But most eventually decided to wait out the winter in two camps: sixty people (about half children) in three cabins and twenty-one (again about half children) in a single cabin at a nearby site. Ironically, they had shelter, warmth, and clothing, and they were relatively safe; they just had no food. Once the oxen were slaughtered, they had nothing.[18]

A party of five women and twelve men went off on improvised snowshoes to see if they could get through a pass and bring back help. On Christmas day, they huddled together in a blizzard, with blankets over them for communal warmth, until they were completely covered by snow; after thirty hours under the blankets, they were safe, but they were beginning to be delirious and demented. After several more days without food, they discussed struggling on until one of them died and then eating the corpse.[19] At this point, the all-important issue of a lottery also arose as they tried to find a way to decide "who should die to furnish food for the others."[20] After five days with no food at all, they did begin to eat the corpses of group members, roasting and drying the flesh so they could carry it further.[21] But a week later, this had been consumed, and they inevitably had to decide whether one of the women (who was slowing the party down) should be killed for food or whether, since she was a wife and mother, they should, instead, choose a widow. Fortuitously, at this point they stumbled across the two dying Indians, who had earlier left the party anticipating their probable fate, and it was decided to finish them off.[22] Stewart writes about the degeneration of the snowshoe group's moral sense:

> At first they had waited for a comrade who fell behind, and had
> flinched at drawing lots to see who should die, and had shrunk from
> cannibalism, even when it meant eating only a man already dead.

Then they had eaten the food which centuries of civilization had forbidden them. Then as the mania of starvation worked upon them,
they had plotted to kill men of another race, and then men or even
women of their own race. . . . Now they were ready to sink to a still
lower level.[23]

Of the seventeen in the snowshoe group, seven ultimately made it to
California.

Later in the winter, relief parties began to come back through the
pass, bringing food with them, often getting stuck themselves in the continuing blizzards and needing rescue. These relief parties would find a few
demented people, a few mangled corpses, and one or two survivors in their
right minds. Of the original Donner Party, forty-two died and forty-seven survived. Afterward, according to the television documentary *Snowbound*, newspaper accounts distorted the story, implying that the survivors had enjoyed
practicing cannibalism. The sensational treatment of the experience
ultimately stigmatized the survivors and even their descendants.

Three crucial issues, then, affect our understanding of survival cannibalism: eating human flesh, killing to obtain a supply of it, and choosing
who will be killed. In general, society has accepted eating human flesh "as a
reasonable solution to the problem of starvation" provided that no one is
killed for the purpose.[24] As Thomas Hodgkinson points out, "the crime is in
the murdering, not in the eating."[25] And the crime of killing for food can be
mitigated if a formal procedure—like a lottery—is used to ensure fairness.
Another kind of survival situation—the shipwreck—illustrates the perils of
choosing who is to die by lottery.

By the nineteenth century, shipwrecks happened frequently enough
for customary procedures to be developed for the conduct of cannibalism
when those on board were cast away. Otherwise, as hunger grew intense,
there would be a frenzy of wild killing and eating. In 1816, for example, the
survivors of the shipwreck of the *Medusa*, after consuming those already
dead, resorted to the worst excesses of cannibalism.[26] So, a customary order
developed for selecting who was to be killed and eaten when the food ran out:
dying people first, then slaves or other outsiders within the group, then male

passengers, then single (male) crew members. This sequence was based on the belief that, for the good of the whole group, the strong deserved to survive (and the weak to be eaten).[27] Still, it often happened that the survivors, huddled in a small rowboat, would all be crew members, making the choice more difficult. Under those circumstances, a lottery was supposed to take place to legitimize the decision.[28]

But holding an orderly lottery among starving men in an open boat required strong leadership and deference to the captain's authority, which easily eroded under the pressure of hunger and fear. Even if it was held, the lottery was often rigged. In the eighteenth-century shipwrecks of the *Peggy*, the *Dolphin*, the *Tyger*, and the *Zong*, it was invariably a slave or a foreigner who lost the lottery.[28] Indeed, in 1874, when the crew of the *Euxine* was set adrift in an open boat, the one "dark-skinned Italian boy" lost the lottery three times running.[30] Sometimes the crew didn't go through the motions of holding a lottery, but the survivors would swear that they had done so. In 1826, after no food at all for ten days, the twenty-one survivors of the *Francis Mary* eventually ate nine of their number. The six who were eventually rescued did not specify whether any were killed for food, and, as was usually the custom, no one asked them.[31]

The 1884 wreck of the *Mignonette* was unusual for several reasons and led to a public debate about cannibalism at sea.[32] The four crew members, stranded in an open dinghy, had only a couple of tins of turnips and resorted to drinking their own urine. As in other shipwrecks of this era, even if they had met a boat, it was unlikely to stop since the captain would be reluctant to share its limited supplies with four more men. After fifteen days, three of the crew discussed killing the seventeen-year-old cabin boy, who was near death,[33] and, after some disagreement, they did so.[34] (See Figure 1.)[35] Once they were picked up, Captain Tom Dudley was honest enough to admit that they had killed Richard Parker and that lots had not been drawn. In fact, they hadn't even bothered to throw the remains of Parker overboard when they saw the rescue boat coming. The result of their candor was that Dudley and his first officer were arrested and tried for murder. Although the public sympathized with them—even Parker's mother said

Myers 7

Figure 1. An engraving from *Illustrated Police News*, September 20, 1884, showing the killing of the *Mignonette*'s cabin boy by the other castaways. Reprinted in Neil Hanson, *The Custom of the Sea* (New York: Wiley, 1999; print; figure 5).

that she didn't blame these "poor, unfortunate men"[36]—the courts and the press took a high moral tone and found them guilty, sentencing them to hang. According to the *Spectator*, it was

> high time that the hideous tradition of the sea which authorizes starving sailors to kill and eat their comrades, should be exposed in a Court of Justice and sailors be taught once for all that the special dangers of their profession furnish no excuse for a practice as directly opposed to human as it is to divine law.[37]

What annoyed the Establishment was not that they had committed cannibalism but that they made no pretense about it and expressed no remorse.[38] Ultimately, they were pardoned, amid suggestions that exposure had made them mad and that they were not to be held to the normal standards of civilized behavior. In effect, the whole trial, sentence, and pardon were intended to make a point and set a precedent. Thereafter, when crews were cast away and had to resort to the "custom of the sea," they knew better than to confess as Dudley had.

Instances of survival cannibalism after shipwrecks still occur today. Recently, a survivor of the 1961 Bay of Pigs invasion of Cuba revealed that he and his comrades, stranded on a raft for sixteen days, had agreed, in extremity, to eat the bodies of those already dead.[39] In 1988, after twenty-eight days at sea in a leaky boat, a group of Vietnamese resorted to eating the dead and killing the dying. One man, Phung Quang Minh, took charge and made the decision to do this. Despite their gratitude at the time, the survivors later complained that Phung had taken advantage of their weakness and forced them into it, threatening that otherwise they'd be targeted next. Phung, however, insisted that he, too, thought cannibalism was wrong, but that there'd been no choice; now, he'd been scapegoated because the others didn't want to acknowledge their responsibility.

> I was only a member in a group of persons, so I didn't have the ability to force all of them to follow me. I was only a man who was thinking more clearly than the others. I had to do what I did to keep all the people living. We were at sea in huge waves. I had no other choice.[40]

And, in March 2001, sixty people, trying to cross the Caribbean from the Dominican Republic to Puerto Rico, had engine trouble and ran out of food and water. After twenty-two days, amid violent fights, they turned to cannibalism. One of the only two survivors insisted that he had not participated, but doctors say that he couldn't possibly have stayed alive without cannibalism.[41]

It is difficult to understand why people struggling for survival should be so severely stigmatized. Under less extreme situations, armies kill the enemy and police kill suspected criminals. Why is it so much worse to kill for food if one is starving? It is easy to share Stewart's compassionate view of the Donner Party's cannibalism: "Humanity may fall into many worse degradations."[42] So why did cannibalism become one of the most powerful cultural taboos in Western civilization? Probably because eating dead humans could so quickly degenerate into killing live humans, as it did among the Donner Party:

Once the taboo against cannibalism was broken, it became easier to engage in, harvesting members of the expedition became more efficient, and there seemed to be little moral revulsion to the practice. This initial resistance against engaging in cannibalism, followed by an unquestioning acceptance by most, is to be found in almost all of the instances of survival cannibalism.[43]

Anthropologists have, therefore, concluded that the potential for cannibalism is in all of us, whether we practice it or not.[44]

Despite—or because of—the powerful taboo, our fascination with cannibalism remains as strong as ever.[45] This attraction is often expressed in folk tales and myth[46] and in the arts and popular culture.[47] With few exceptions (such as "Cannibalism in the Cars" or the movie based on the Andes survivors), these entertainments are not concerned with the hardships and difficult choices of survival cannibalism, but focus on the violence and the horror of sociopathic cannibalism. According to Harris, "it is part of human nature to pay rapt attention to unusual sights and sounds such as blood spurting from wounds and loud shrieking and howling."[48] For decades, American audiences have flocked to see horror movies featuring cannibalism, from *The Night of the Living Dead*, in which "a young girl is transformed into a ghoul and then begins to dine on her mother,"[49] to the extremely bloody and violent *Hannibal*, which took in $58 million in its opening weekend.[50] Even serious academics who write about cannibalism tend to use narrative techniques and language that sensationalize the subject. Accounts of cannibalism are often fictionalized into stories, with use of the present tense, exotic details, and imaginary conversations to make the events seem more immediate and real. Anthropologists are particularly apt to do this when describing acts of ritual cannibalism among "primitive" tribes.[51]

In survival cannibalism, abnormal circumstances cause people to behave abnormally. In ritual cannibalism, eating people is normal behavior.[52] The classic figure in ritual cannibalism is the tribal warrior, wearing a feathered skirt and waving a hatchet while dancing around the cooking pot containing the captured enemy or an aged matriarch of the tribe. Exocannibalism—eating those outside the tribe—was practiced for political reasons (to terrorize enemies[53] and assimilate their strength[54]) and for spiritual reasons (to propitiate the gods). There were also practical reasons: when a warring group of tribesmen brought back captives to the village, there was rarely a surplus of provisions available to feed them. It made economic sense to regard the prisoner as food and "absorb him into the group."[55] The chief of the Miranha tribe was very pragmatic about this: "When I have killed an enemy it is better to eat him than let him go to waste. . . . The bad thing is not being eaten, but death. . . . You whites are really too dainty."[56] Nor was ritual cannibalism always the wild orgy of revenge depicted in missionaries' tales. It was an organized activity, integrated into the culture according to traditional rules. "To cannibals," says MacClancy, "the idea of unregulated man-eating—consuming anyone, anywhere, any time, anyhow—is as horrific as it is to us. If one is going to indulge in human meat, one must do it in the ritually prescribed manner."[57]

The basis for endocannibalism—eating members of one's own tribe— was respect for one's family and tribal elders that was demonstrated by making their tomb one's own living body: "Far better to be inside a warm friend than under the cold ground."[58] In the nineteenth century, a Mayoruna tribesman asked a European: "When you die, wouldn't you rather be eaten by your own kinsmen than by maggots?"[59] But children were not always eager to consume the flesh of their parents[60] and the motives for doing so were not always to the parents' advantage. Endocannibalism could be used as a form of population control, like infanticide, and the means of disposing of the aged were sometimes violent or vicious.[61]

Although anthropologists theorize that tribes have engaged in ritual cannibalism for at least two million years,[62] it has been very difficult to document specific instances. What information there is about prehistoric cannibalism comes from excavated bones that have been examined for intentional fractures and marks indicating where to cut, just as one would prepare an animal for eating.[63] There is evidence that Peking Man "roasted his victims and ate their brains" 500,000 years ago, that Cro-Magnon man "cracked leg bones and [broke] skulls" 30,000 years ago,[64] and that Neanderthal man removed the meat and marrow from bones 100–120,000 years ago.[65] Still, anthropologists are now being extremely careful about attributing cannibalism to prehistoric tribes.[66]

The issue of whether and what sort of ritual cannibalism occurred—or still occurs—has become a sensitive one, in part because of controversy over the allegations in William Arens's 1979 work, *The Man-Eating Myth*. In effect, Arens declared that ritual cannibalism simply did not exist, that it consisted of rumors with no factual basis, that it lacked first-hand, eye-witness evidence.[67] According to Arens, hardly ever do anthropologists claim to have witnessed the act of cannibalism themselves; their accounts are based largely on hearsay.[68] He even asserts that there are instances of anthropologists badgering tribes for stories about cannibalism even when the poor villagers deny it.[69] Many anthropologists have understand-ably felt under attack by Arens,[70] and, in turn, have criticized his motives and methods. Petrinovich, for example, calls him "more of a sensation-hungry journalist than an exact historian"[71] and Hodgkinson notes that most of the anthropological community regard him as a "sensationalist revisionist."[72]

But Arens's charges had a broader, more political purpose. He finds it significant that cannibalism tends to be attributed to primitive people, usually at a time before the white man has come to civilize them. The cannibals are regarded as distant versions of ourselves, "reflections of us as we once were" before we became civilized.[73] And so we have reason to feel superior to these people, a feeling that can lead, among extremists, to xeno-phobia.[74] Pickering also points out how well cannibalism feeds into Western-ers' conviction of the superiority of our culture. We believe that every society has a path of development, and some are more advanced than others. Canni-balism is assumed to be integral to a society at a primitive stage; therefore, any society that is aboriginal also had to be cannibalistic. Such views also justified colonialism: colonists could take over whole blocks of territory and subsume whole societies, convinced that "the dispossessed would benefit from the technological, political, social, religious, and moral superiority of the invader."[75] Tannahill points out that the tendency to demonize these tribes increased as Western Europe sought to colonize remote parts of the

Figure 2. A woodcut from Hans Staden's *The True History and Description of a Country of Savages, a Naked and Terrible People, Eaters of Men's Flesh, Who Dwell in the New World Called America.* Staden depicted himself as the bearded, praying figure on the right. Reprinted in William Arens, *The Man-Eating Myth* (New York: Oxford UP; 1979; print; figure 4).

world and as government officials, traders, and missionaries competed for who could publish the most exotic and horrifying stories of these strange cultures for the pleasure of the reading public.[76] That political agenda is illustrated by classic attributions of cannibalism to pre-Columbian Carib Indians and Aztecs, as in Figure 2.

When Columbus landed on Hispaniola, he saw no signs of cannibalism among the Caribs, but that did not stop him from telling everyone, when he returned to Europe, that the natives of the New World were cannibals. By his third journey to the Americas, he "had become so experienced in these matters that he was able to identify man-eaters by their looks."[77] In Arens's view, Columbus presented this savage picture to justify the slave trade, which was to be the outgrowth of his explorations. He wasn't able to bring back much in the way of spices and gold, but he was able to bring back an equally valuable commodity: slaves. Such barbarians deserved nothing better than slavery, so slavers could believe, in good conscience, that they were helping to save the souls of unspeakable people. In fact, although royal and papal policy at first banned any enslavement of the Caribbean islanders, an exception was made for any tribe thought to be cannibals. Thus, all sorts of tribes were labeled cannibals, whether they were or they weren't, whether they were warlike or whether they were peaceful,[78] and, ultimately, "the indigenous cultures of the Caribbean were all but destroyed."[79]

The demonization of the Aztecs took a different form because, as almost everyone acknowledges, they did engage in violent, cruel sacrifices to the gods, with bodies bound and tortured and hearts dripping with blood. The issue is whether they then ate their victims and, if so, whether it was ritual cannibalism (and thus a barbaric act) or survival cannibalism resulting from food shortages (and so marginally more acceptable). The more melodramatic of the anthropologists have no doubt that it was the former:

> To keep the mystical forces of the universe in balance and to uphold social equilibrium, the Aztec fed their gods human flesh. By the act of consecration the sacrificial victims were incarnated as gods. Through eating the victims' flesh, men entered into communion with their gods, and divine power was imparted to men.[80]

Harris is similarly certain that the Aztecs were cannibals and provides endless bloody details of torture and killing. But he believes that the motive was survival, that food, especially protein and fat, was in short supply, and that the sacrifices to the gods were a necessary part of the Aztec economy, with each dead prisoner given to a member of the community for consumption: "The Aztec priests can legitimately be described as ritual slaughterers in a state-sponsored system geared to the production and redistribution of substantial amounts of animal protein in the form of human

Myers 14

flesh."[81] Thus, Harris suggests with irony, the introduction of domestic animals to the Aztecs was just as much a reason for the decline of cannibalism as the arrival of Christian missionaries.[82] He believes that Europeans could afford to be highly moral about cannibalism because their agricultural economy didn't require them to engage in it. Still, they had just as many bloody wars with just as high a proportion of the population killed—only they weren't eaten.[83]

Arens, as one might expect, doubts very much whether cannibalism ever took place in Mexico at all. He speculates that the rumors of the Aztecs' eating the enemy were a form of military propaganda on both sides,[84] and even questions whether ceremonial sacrifices—a "colorful barbaric scenario" —actually occurred, noting that even in the worst sieges by the conquistadors, the defenders starved rather than eat each other. Resentful of the existence of "such an advanced civilization in the New World,"[85] the Europeans were forced to demonize the Aztecs in order to justify the conquistadors' campaign of exploitation and expropriation.[86] But like the conquistadors and the missionaries, Arens, too, seems to be imposing his own political agenda. He is determined to uphold "'primitive' cultures as ecologically and morally exemplary,"[87] even if it requires the demonization of his anthropologist colleagues.[88] To suggest otherwise would be politically incorrect.[89]

Throughout all these theories and countertheories, the emphasis is on the evils of ritual cannibalism (if it existed at all), but rarely on the bloodshed and killing that must have accompanied it. Western society continues to tolerate violence, bloodshed, and even murder; but is horrified at the possibility that flesh could be consumed as an accepted rite of a culture:

> It is interesting that some anthropologists are willing to concede that human sacrifice of the most brutal sort took place, but are unwilling to accept the fact that ritual cannibalism took place. They can accept the proposition that these people horribly tortured and mutilated living captives, but not that they took a bite afterward. For some, the act of cannibalism appears to be justifiable if it was necessary for people to survive, but not if it was part of the theatre of life.[90]

What's really significant is not whether the reports of cannibalism are or aren't true, but why they have always fascinated so broad an audience, retained their status as a shocking taboo, and so evolved into a cultural myth for the West. Surely, our attitudes toward cannibalism say more about us, our desires, and our fears than they do about the man-eaters. In Petrinovich's paraphrase of Pogo, "we have found the cannibals, and they are us."[91]

Notes

[1]*The Reluctant Cannibal.*

[2]Typical motivational charts are found in Askenasy 224; Goldman 14; and Petrinovich 6. Few anthropologists include sociopathic cannibalism (e.g., Jeffrey Dahmer or Hannibal Lecter) in their charts.

[3]Petrinovich 6.

[4]Petrinovich 15–16.

[5]Garn and Block 106. MacClancy states that, for forty to have a decent meal each day for a month, they'd have to eat eight fat adults (170).

[6]Askenasy 64–65, quoting Tannahill.

[7]Askenasy 69; Cunningham 115.

[8]Dr. John Baker, commenting in Alexander Marengo's *Cannibal.*

[9]Qtd. in Askenasy 80. During recent Russian and Ukrainian famines, parents were known to eat their own children as an "act of Christian kindness" to put them out of their misery, and it has been traditional in China, as early as the famines of 594 BC, for families to swap children so that parents would not have to eat their own (Marengo).

[10]"You begin to crave meat of any sort—you act different to the way you act when there's a supermarket around the corner" (Dr. Timothy Taylor, commenting in Marengo).

[11]Read 59.

[12]Read 84–85.

[13]Cunningham 87.

[14]One of the survivors said that they had specifically emulated the Last Supper and that the "intimate communion among us [was] what helped us to subsist" ("Survivors" A9). See also Tannahill 176.

[15]Cunningham 199. Several of those commenting on the experience of the Andes survivors observe that the subsequent reactions from those in Uruguay, even the relatives of those eaten, were sympathetic. Askenasy asks whether this amnesty from reproach, public and private, would have occurred had the survivors not been members of Uruguay's elite (105). Tannahill also wonders "whether they would have met with quite such general warmth and understanding if they had come from New York's Harlem . . ." (175).

[16]Petrinovich cites another survival experience characterized by a sense of community that led to survival. After a week, three survivors of an air crash in Idaho determined to eat the father of one of them, justifying their decision by attributing to him the desire to help them survive. (He had covered his daughter with his coat just before he died.) They, too, gained the strength needed to walk down to civilization, and they, too, did not deny what they had done, citing the model of communion and their common religious belief. Subsequently, there was no criticism from relatives, clergy, or the law (76).

[17]Much of the material in this paragraph comes from Petrinovich 69–71. Petrinovich also notes that the first person the Andes survivors contemplated eating was the dead pilot, the one person who had no ties to the group (73).

[18]The material in this and subsequent paragraphs about the Donner Party comes from Stewart and from Petrinovich 22–28.

[19]Stewart 130–33.

[20]Petrinovich 24. It's unclear what actually happened. Did they fail to agree on a lottery, or did they have one but disregarded it since the person who lost was particularly well liked? There was also a suggestion that two of the men would shoot it out and the loser would be eaten.

[21]Like the Andes survivors, they showed some delicacy: "They observed only one last sad propriety; no member of a family touched his own dead" (Stewart 133). This did not last, however; later, when a man died, a woman began to butcher his body in the presence of his widow.

[22]A recent documentary about the fate of the Donner Party noted that, under these extreme conditions, the corpses no longer looked like dead bodies; they looked like food (*Snowbound: Curse of the Sierras*).

[23]Stewart 145. Stewart's melodramatic language and high moral tone are typical of writings on cannibalism.

[24]Petrinovich 73. See also Askenasy 170.

[25]Hodgkinson 27.

[26]Askenasy provides a dramatic account of maritime cannibalism in 1899: one of five men on a raft was about to die, but before he did, "the

knife was plunged into his heart, and the blood trickled out to be drunk by the half-famished, half-thirsty mortals by his side. While the fearful feast was in progress, [another man died]. Like birds after fresh prey the man-eaters rushed to the second victim, stabbed him, and sucked the milk-warm blood as it oozed from the great slash about his heart" (87).

[27]Those who died and then were eaten or who lost the lottery were "almost invariably the weakest, most vulnerable, disliked or isolated individuals. Slaves were eaten first, black men before white, women before men, passengers before crew, unpopular members before the rest" (Petrinovich 49). Among the crew, cabin boys were first to go (Hanson 132).

[28]Petrinovich 50.

[29]Petrinovich 51–53.

[30]Petrinovich 60. Apparently, the first two lotteries were disputed, but after the third the boy was killed.

[31]Askenasy 2–10. One woman on the boat was very tough about claiming rights to the blood of her fiance as he died; she fended off all the others, saying later that she did it from pure hunger.

[32]The description of the Mignonette is taken from Simpson and from Hanson.

[33]They didn't want to wait until he died, even though that was imminent, because blood was very life-sustaining, and it "would congeal in his veins" and be undrinkable once he was dead (Hanson 116).

[34]The two mates said that they should all die together, but Captain Dudley was more pragmatic: "It be hard for four to die, when perhaps one might save the rest" (Simpson 61).

[35]Hanson, figure 5, 42.

[36]Simpson 84. Petrinovich confirms that the public is rarely determined to punish or censure those who resort to survival cannibalism (10–11).

[37]Hanson 172.

[38]The court was all in favor of hypocrisy: "For humanity's sake, we must regret that such confessions as have fallen from these rescued men ever came to the light of day" (Hanson 200).

[39]"Bay of Pigs Survivor."

[40]Askenasy 90.

[41]Watson 5.

[42]Stewart 295.

[43]Petrinovich 25. Askenasy wonders whether our apparently built-in revulsion to cannibalism is a result of genetic programming because "cannibalism would be counterproductive to our species' survival" (225). On the other hand, Cunningham points out that one bite does not necessarily lead to future craving (102).

[44]While there has been considerable disagreement about whether the potential for cannibalistic behavior is genetic or cultural, recent studies conclude that the tendency is innate (Arens 130).

[45]"Most human beings appear to need a few taboos, and for the time being cannibalism seems to serve that purpose admirably" (Askenasy 231). In 2003, the trial of Armin Meiwes, the German cannibal whose victim was eager to be eaten, was a top story in newspapers all over the world (see, for instance, Harding 3 and Landler A3).

[46]There are references to cannibalism in Homer, Ovid, Herodotus, and Caesar (e.g., eat the old and women since they're useless for battle) (Cunningham 99). Fairy tales like Hansel and Gretel and Jack and the Beanstalk contain references that would lead outsiders to assume that Western Europe had a history of cannibalism (Arens 148 and Cunningham 100).

[47]*Sweeney Todd* and *Candide* are very successful musicals with prominent references to cannibalism. In "Cannibalism in the Cars," Mark Twain makes a tongue-in-cheek point about the exotic and forbidden nature of cannibalism by having twenty-four respectable businessmen, stuck in a blizzard on a train, choose a selection of victims for dinner by using impeccable parliamentary procedure, debate (youth vs. size), and editorial comment about the succulence of the main dish: "I like Harris. He might have been better done, perhaps, but . . . no man ever agreed with me better than Harris . . ." (14).

[48]Harris 104. Cunningham calls Count Dracula "a cannibal with sadistic tendencies" (101).

[49]Arens 147.

[50]This popular fascination with cannibalism can be found in many of the home pages on the Internet. See, for example, Schechner. Another approach to this solemn taboo is spoof: Trey Parker's film *Cannibal! The Musical* parodies a man accused of cannibalizing members of a group that is traveling West in 1873.

[51]Gardner notes the temptation of people writing about cannibalism to insert juicy details (35).

[52]Diamond calls this "customary cannibalism": "the consumption of human flesh . . . as a non-emergency custom" (25).

[53]Lewis cites the Tupinamba of the Amazon, who treated their prisoners like heros, wined and dined them, and then ritually killed and ate them (75). MacClancy describes the Big Nambas of northern Vanuatu, who ate only their enemies (170), and the Hurons of southern Canada, for whom ritual cannibalism was "a socially approved means of invigorating themselves, of securing peace, of demonstrating tribal strength, and of venting otherwise dangerous feelings" (171–72). During the Crusades, one source, William of Tyre, describes acts of ritual cannibalism among the crusaders, and there are contemporary accounts that attribute both survival and ritual motives, but historian Paul Crawford downplays the issue, stating that the "significance [of cannibalism] to the First Crusade is probably not great." As recently as the Cultural Revolution in China in the 1960s, followers of Mao engaged in cannibalism for the purpose of terrorism, killing teachers thought to be "class enemies," forcing other teachers to cut out the dead man's heart and liver, and then eating them: "The yard was full of the smell of students cooking their teachers." More than thirty years later, in interviews, these cannibals still express great pride in their actions (Marengo).

[54]Tribal cannibalism is an act of revenge, in which the captured enemy is "tortured and reduced to food in the ultimate act of domination" (Sanday 6). According to Daniel Bergner, ritual cannibalism for terror and revenge has occurred as recently as 2003—during civil wars in the Congo (49).

[55]Harris 104.

[56]Qtd. in Askenasy 11–12.

[57]MacClancy 169–70.

[58]Cunningham 104. MacClancy cites the Hua, who ate their parents to replenish their vital essence (170).

[59]Askenasy 11.

[60]Malinowski observed some Trobriand Islanders eating the body of a deceased man as an act of "filial piety"; the sons were clearly revolted by what they had to do, but had no way of escaping it (qtd. in Lewis 71). In her study of the Warí tribe, Beth A. Conklin observed that, in instances as late as the 1950s, "compassionate cannibalism" allowed family members to refrain from consumption since that would be like "self-cannibalism" (qtd. in Miller A15).

[61]For example, the old person could be bound up in a tree, surrounded by a ritual dance; on a signal, he or she would be shaken out of the tree and disposed of in a mass killing (Cunningham 106).

[62]See "Cannibalism."

[63]Diamond.

[64]Cunningham 97–98.

[65]The evidence of six skeletons recently found in a cave site is regarded as "controversial" since the possible reasons for these incisions—including cannibalism—have yet to be convincingly determined. See Bower.

[66]White 348.

[67]Arens 21. Arens refers to the anecdotal evidence and sensational tone found in many accounts of cannibalism and the dramatic reconstructions—"probably happened" or "one would imagine"—that lead the reader to believe that the vilest things occurred.

[68]Arens 36. This view is supported by MacClancy: "There are relatively few authoritative accounts by trustworthy eyewitnesses of anthropophagites in action. The vast majority of accounts depend not on observed events but on stories told to Westerners" (168). See also Goldman 14.

[69]Arens 142–45.

[70]"What Arens essentially did was lay down a challenge: he required other anthropologists to produce proof of ritual anthropophagy," evoking an "emotional response" from the anthropological community (Hodgkinson 27).

(They may also have resented Arens's popular success.) Anthropologists who discover instances of cannibalism attract considerable attention, which can enhance their scholarly reputations. In effect, Arens was accusing anthropologists like White of "fortune-hunting" (Goldman 15).

[71]Petrinovich 13.

[72]Hodgkinson 28. In discussing Arens's theories, Askenasy suggests that what Arens is doing is equivalent to Holocaust denial (49–50).

[73]Arens 19.

[74]Arens 145. According to Arens, we feel free to attribute the vilest behavior to remote tribesmen; if we said similar things about minority groups within our own cultures, we would be heavily censured. Some of the more extreme writings on cannibalism bear out Arens's views. Maerth, for example, spins theories about humans being a mongrel race who originally gained their strength and aggressiveness from eating the superior specimens of hominoid ape.

[75]Pickering 63. Gardner, too, acknowledges that we "attribut[e] cannibalism to alien others [as] an effective instrument of demonization" (28). This is all part of the colonial degradation (and also scapegoating) of subject peoples.

[76]Tannahill 150. MacClancy points out that cannibalism was good for business: "As astute missionaries knew, putting 'cannibal' in the title of their books widened their market and increased sales or donations from fervent Christians" (168).

[77]Arens 44.

[78]Arens 47–51. See also Petrinovich 5. Askenasy alludes to the use of cannibalism by the church as a rationale for colonizing: "Since Christians, of course, did not devour one another, it became their duty to civilize the mindless savages" (231).

[79]Arens 54.

[80]Sanday 7. For a similar discussion of the Aztecs, see Tannahill 86.

[81]Harris 109. Harris calculates executioners would work for four days and nights, continuously, killing approximately 14,000 prisoners; this is an estimate based on two minutes per killing (106).

[82]Harris 110.

[83]Harris 122–23. Harris cites another crucial distinction between Europe and the Americas: Europe tended toward a pattern of imperial expansion, and a successful empire doesn't kill and eat those it conquers; rather, it incorporates them into the empire, with safety exchanged for obedience. If you go in for cannibalism, you'll never be able to negotiate peace because no enemy will ever want to get into your clutches.

[84]In contemporary records, there is a report that the Aztecs ate roasted babies: "Cortes does not confirm or elaborate on this statement, but as a military man, it is likely that he realized the impact this would have on the home front" (Arens 60).

[85]Arens 77.

[86]Hodgkinson 27.

[87]Hodgkinson 28.

[88]Petrinovich 150.

[89]Petrinovich 149.

[90]Petrinovich 101.

[91]Petrinovich 216.

Works Cited

Arens, William. *The Man-Eating Myth*. New York: Oxford UP, 1979. Print.

Askenasy, Hans. *Cannibalism: From Sacrifice to Survival*. Amherst: Prometheus, 1994. Print.

"Bay of Pigs Survivor Says He Turned to Cannibalism." *Seattle Times*. Seattle Times Company, 16 Apr. 1998. Web. 14 Oct. 2004.

Bergner, Daniel. "The Most Unconventional Weapon." *New York Times Magazine* 26 Oct. 2003: 48–53. Print.

Bower, B. "Cave Finds Revive Neandertal [*sic*] Cannibalism." *Science News*. Society for Science & the Public, 2 Oct. 1999. Web. 5 Nov. 2004.

"Cannibalism." *Encarta Online Encyclopedia*. Microsoft Corp., 2004. Web. 5 Oct. 2004.

Crawford, Paul. "The Crusades." *Online Reference Book for Medieval Studies*. Catholic Education Resource Center, 1997. Web. 4 May 2004.

Cunningham, Richard. *The Place Where the World Ends*. New York: Sheed, 1973. Print.

Diamond, Jared. "Archaeology: Talk of Cannibalism." *Nature* 407.6800 7 Sept. 2000: 25–26. Print.

Gardner, Don. "Anthropophagy: Myth and the Subtle Ways of Ethnocentrism." *The Psychology of Cannibalism*. Ed. Laurence R. Goldman. Westport: Bergin, 1999. Print.

Garn, Stanley M., and Walter D. Block. "The Limited Nutritional Value of Cannibalism." *American Anthropologist* 72.1 (1970): 106. Print.

Goldman, Laurence R. "From Pot to Polemic: Uses and Abuses of Cannibalism." *The Psychology of Cannibalism*. Ed. Laurence R. Goldman. Westport: Bergin, 1999. Print.

Hannibal. Dir. Ridley Scott. MGM and Universal Studios, 2001. Film.

Hanson, Neil. *The Custom of the Sea*. New York: Wiley, 1999. Print.

Harding, Luke. "Victim of Cannibal Agreed to Be Eaten." *The Guardian* [London] 4 Dec. 2003: 3. Print.

Harris, Marvin. *Cannibals and Kings: The Origins of Culture*. New York: Random, 1977. Print.

Hodgkinson, Thomas. "Cannibalism: A Potted History." *The Independent* [London] 17 Mar. 2001: 27–29. Print.

Landler, Mark. "Eating People Is Wrong! But Is It Homicide? Court to Rule." *New York Times* 26 Dec. 2003: A3. Print.

Lewis, I. M. *Religion in Context: Cults and Charisma.* Cambridge: Cambridge UP, 1986. Print.

MacClancy, Jeremy. *Consuming Culture.* New York: Holt, 1993. Print.

Maerth, Oscar. *The Beginning Was the End.* Trans. Judith Hayward. London: Michael Joseph, 1973. Print.

Marengo, Alexander, dir. *Cannibal: The Real Hannibal Lecters.* 3BM TV Productions. HBO. 9 Feb. 2003. Television.

Miller, D. W. "Love Me, Miss Me, Eat Me." *Chronicle of Higher Education* 10 Aug. 2001: A15. Print.

Night of the Living Dead. Dir. George A. Romero. 1968. Starz/Anchor Bay, 1999. DVD.

Parker, Trey, dir. *Cannibal! The Musical.* 1996. Troma Team Video. DVD.

Petrinovich, Lewis. *The Cannibal Within.* New York: Aldine de Gruyter, 2000. Print.

Pickering, Michael. "Consuming Doubts: What Some People Ate? or What Some People Swallowed?" *The Psychology of Cannibalism.* Ed. Laurence R. Goldman. Westport: Bergin, 1999. Print.

Read, Piers Paul. *Alive: The Story of the Andean Survivors.* Philadelphia and New York: Lippincott, 1974. Print.

"The Reluctant Cannibal." Comp. Michael Flanders. Perf. Michael Flanders and Donald Swann. *The Complete Flanders and Swann.* Emd International, 1997. CD.

Sanday, Peggy Reeves. *Divine Hunger: Cannibalism as a Cultural System.* Cambridge: Cambridge UP, 1986. Print.

Schechner, Sam. "The New Cannibalism." *College Hill Independent.* Brown Univ., 17 Apr. 1997. Web. 29 Sept. 2004.

Simpson, A. W. Brian. *Cannibalism and the Common Law.* Chicago: U of Chicago P, 1984. Print.

"Snowbound: Curse of the Sierras." *Wrath of God*. History Channel. 2000.
    Television.

Stewart, George R., Jr., *Ordeal by Hunger: The Story of the Donner Party*. New
    York: Holt, 1936. Print.

"Survivors of Andes Air Crash Admit Dead Saved Their Lives." *New York
    Times* 26 Dec. 1972: A9. Print.

Tannahill, Reay. *Flesh and Blood: A History of the Cannibal Complex*.
    Briarcliff Manor: Stein, 1975. Print.

Twain, Mark. "Cannibalism in the Cars." *The Complete Short Stories of Mark
    Twain*. Ed. Charles Neider. New York: Bantam, 1983. Print.

Watson, Molly. "Refugees Ate Bodies as Boat Drifted at Sea." *Evening
    Standard* [London] 21 Mar. 2001: 5. Print.

White, Tim D. *Prehistoric Cannibalism at Mancos*. Princeton: Princeton UP,
    1992. Print.

Explaining the Tunguskan Phenomenon

The Tunguska River Valley in Siberia has always been an area of swamps and bogs, forests and frozen tundra, sparsely populated, and remote and inaccessible to most travelers. It was at dawn on June 30, 1908, that witnesses in the Tungus observed a light glaring more brightly than anything they had ever seen. This cosmic phenomenon, they said, was bluish-white in color and gradually became cigarlike in shape. Just as terrifying to the few people inhabiting that part of Siberia was the tremendous noise that accompanied the light, a noise that was reported to have been heard 1,000 kilometers from the site (Parry, 1961). Some who were in the vicinity were deafened, while others farther away apparently became speechless and displayed other symptoms of severe trauma. The Tungus community refused to go near the site or speak of the occurrence, and some even denied that it had ever happened (Crowther, 1931). The event was so frightening to these simple peasants that many believed it had been an act of divine retribution, a punishment by a god demanding vengeance (Baxter & Atkins, 1976).

Since 1921, when the first perilous expedition to the Tungus region confirmed that a remarkable event had indeed taken place, scientists have attempted to explain what it was and why it happened. One hundred years later, the various theories developed to explain the explosion in the Tunguska Valley have become almost as interesting a phenomenon as the original occurrence. Like doctors trying to diagnose a disease by examining the symptoms, scientists have analyzed the fragmentary evidence and published theories that supposedly account for it. However, no theory has been entirely convincing. The purpose of this essay is to provide a brief description of some of the major interpretations of the Tunguska occurrence and to suggest that, in their efforts to substantiate their theories, scientists can be fallible.

---

[1]Note that APA requires a separate cover page with the student's name, course title, instructor, and date centered at the bottom of the page, and the paper's title centered in the middle (for example, Explaining the Tunguskan Phenomenon). All pages have a short version of the essay's title and the page number at the top. This includes the cover page.

Tunguskan Phenomenon   Morgan 3

At dawn on that day in June 1908, a huge object evidently came from space into the earth's atmosphere, breaking the sound barrier, and, at 7:17 a.m., slammed into the ground in the central Siberian plateau. Moments before the collision, a thrust of energy caused people and animals to be strewn about, structures destroyed, and trees toppled. Immediately afterward, a pillar or "tongue" of fire could be seen in the sky several hundred miles away; others called it a cylindrical pipe. A thermal air current of extremely high temperature caused forest fires to ignite and spread across 40 miles, melting metal objects scattered throughout the area. Several shock waves were felt for hundreds of miles around, breaking windows and tossing people, animals, and objects in the air. Finally, black rain fell from a menacing-looking cloud over a radius of 100 miles. It is no wonder that the peasants of the Tunguska River Valley thought that this was the end of the world (Krinov, 1966; Baxter & Atkins, 1976).

Figure 1. A map of the Tunguska region, showing the extent of the blast's impact and the region's remote location in Siberia. From "What Lies Beneath," by M. Chown, 2001, *New Scientist 171*(2301), p. 17.

Tunguskan Phenomenon   Morgan 4

      For a variety of reasons, this devastating occurrence remained almost unknown outside Russia—and even outside central Siberia—for many years. The Tungus (see Figure 1) is extremely remote, even for Russia, which is such a vast country that transportation and communication between places can be slow and difficult. The few people living in the area who actually witnessed what happened were mostly peasants and nomadic tribesmen, and did not have much opportunity or inclination to talk about what they had seen. There was little publicity, and what there was was limited to local Siberian newspapers (Krinov, 1966). During that summer, there was a lot of discussion in the newspapers of the European capitals about peculiar lights and colors seen in the northern skies, unusually radiant sunsets, some magnetic disturbances, and strange dust clouds (Cowan, Atluri, & Libby, 1965). But, since news of the events at the Tungus River had hardly yet been heard even in Moscow, there was no way for scientists in other countries to see a connection between these happenings.

      It was only in 1921, when Russia was relatively stable after years of war, revolution, and economic problems, that the first expedition to investigate the event at Tunguska actually took place (Crowther, 1931). That it occurred then at all was largely because an energetic Russian scientist, Leonid Kulik, had become fascinated by meteorites. He read in an old Siberian newspaper that, in 1908, a railway train had been forced to stop because a meteorite fell in its path—a story that was quite untrue. Kulik thought that he might become the discoverer of the greatest meteorite ever found on earth and determined to search for evidence that such a meteorite existed. Authorized by the Soviet Academy, Kulik led a series of expeditions to the Tungus River. In 1921, he did not even reach the site, for the route was almost impassable. In 1927, and annually for the next few years, Kulik did, indeed, explore the devastated area and was able to study the evidence of what had happened and listen to the oral accounts of the event provided by those inhabitants who were still alive and who were willing to talk to him. Finally, in 1938–39, Kulik traveled to the Tungus for the last time, for the purpose of taking aerial photographs that might confirm his meteorite theory (Baxter & Atkins, 1976).

Kulik and his fellow investigators believed that whatever had happened at the Tungus River had been caused by a meteorite. So, what they expected to find was a single, vast crater to mark the place where the meteorite had landed. Such a crater, however, was simply not there (Cowan, Atluri, & Libby, 1965). Instead, Kulik found a vast devastated and burned area, a forest of giant trees with their tops cut off and scattered around (Crowther, 1931). In 1928, without the benefit of an aerial view of the region, Kulik concluded from his various vantage points on the ground that, around the circumference of the area where the meteorite had landed, there was a belt of upright dead trees, which he named the "telegraph pole forest." Scattered around the perimeter of the frozen swamp, which he called the "cauldron," were groups of fallen trees, with their tops all pointing away from the direction of where the blast had occurred (Cowan, Atluri, & Libby, 1965). None of this was consistent with Kulik's meteorite theory, and he could only attribute the odd pattern of upright and fallen trees to a shock wave or "hot compressed-air pockets," which had missed some trees and affected others (Baxter & Atkins, 1976). The account of his discovery in the *Literary Digest* of 1929 states that "each of the falling meteoric fragments must have worked, the Russian scientists imagine, like a gigantic piston," with compressed air knocking trees down like toothpicks ("What a Meteor," 1929, p. 34). Kulik continued to insist that the fire and the resultant effect on the trees was the result of a meteorite explosion. But the Russian scientist V. G. Fesenkov estimated that such destruction could only have been caused by an object of at least several hundred meters, and that, if anything of this size or force had hit the ground, it would have left a crater (Baxter & Atkins, 1976).

Kulik found other evidence that could not easily be explained by the meteorite theory. Although there was no trace of a single large crater (Cowan, Atluri, & Libby, 1965), there were numerous shallow cavities scattered around the frozen bog (Olivier, 1928). For several years, Kulik attempted to bore into the ground, seeking evidence that these pits and ridges were formed by lateral pressure caused by gases exploding from the meteorite's impact. Kulik described the scene as "not unlike a giant duplicate of what happens when a brick from a tall chimney-top falls into a puddle of mud. Solid ground actually must have splashed outward in every direction." In this account, the supposed meteorite became "the great swarm of meteors" that "must have traversed" the atmosphere for several hundred miles, pushing ahead of it a "giant bubble of superheated atmosphere" that was "probably responsible" for the burned countryside ("What a Meteor," 1929, p. 33). All the "must have's" and "probably's" make a good narrative, but are not scientifically convincing.

Similarly, Kulik endeavored to explain eyewitness accounts of the huge fireball in the sky that burned one observer's shirt off his back and threw him off his porch (Cowan, Atluri, & Libby, 1965). Such extreme heat waves had never before been known to have accompanied the fall of a meteorite, but Kulik decided that this meteorite was much larger than those previously recorded and that therefore it would have released much more energy upon impact and that would account for such radiant heat (Baxter & Atkins, 1976). So obsessed was Kulik with the idea that somewhere buried in the Tungus swamp was a phenomenal meteorite that he focused the efforts of all the expeditions to the area during his lifetime on digging beneath the frozen tundra and to some extent neglected the examination of other evidence that might have further threatened the theory that he was de-termined to prove (Parry, 1961). Initially, he was successful in convincing the scientific community that his theory was correct. It is most interesting to read excerpts from *The American Weekly* of 1929 flatly asserting that a mete-orite had fallen in Siberia and that Professor Kulik had brought back photo-graphs of the giant crater that he found, as well as small samples of meteoric materials. The article is accompanied by a photograph of Professor Kulik measuring "the main crater, where the largest mass of this celestial visitor buried itself in the earth" (as cited in "What a Meteor," p. 34).

While Kulik's expeditions were still searching for evidence of a mete-orite, other scientists were hypothesizing that the Tunguska explosion might have been caused by a small comet, which would account for the absence of a crater. Comets are composed of ice, frozen gases, and dust, and as they travel around the sun, they develop a long tail. Upon impact, a comet might give off a trail of gases and dust, which would create a bright and colorful night sky similar to that observed after the explosion. This would not be true of a meteorite, which has no gaseous trail and thus leaves no trace in the atmosphere. It has also been suggested that the observed direction of the object's travel was more typical of a comet than a meteorite (Florensky, 1963). If the comet had blown up approximately two miles above the site, that would explain why some trees survived while others did not (Parry, 1961). On the other hand, there is no evidence that a comet had ever crashed on earth before, or caused a comparable change in magnetic and atmospheric phenomena, or even come so close without being sighted (Baxter & Atkins, 1976). Those scientists supporting the comet theory have suggested that, although it is unusual for any comet to come that close to earth without anyone sighting it, the one landing at Tunguska might have been small enough to go by unnoticed. But that idea is contradicted by Fesenkov's estimate that, to cause such destruction, the nucleus of the Tunguskan comet—if there was one—would have been only slightly smaller than those of well-documented comets that were visible at great distances (Cowan, Atluri, & Libby, 1965).

The next major explanation for the cosmic phenomenon at Tunguska could only have been formulated after World War II, when the scientific community had learned how to make atomic explosions and had become familiar with their aftermath. Aleksander Kazantsev, a Russian scientist and (equally important) science-fiction writer, had visited Hiroshima after the atom bomb explosion and had studied the data describing its impact and aftermath. Because of certain similarities in the blast effects—the burnt yet upright trees, the mushroom cloud, the black rain—Kazantsev and other scientists concluded that the blast of 1908 was an atomic explosion estimated at a minimum of ten times the strength of the one at Hiroshima (Parry, 1961). Witnesses had described the blinding flash and withering heat at Hiroshima in much the same way that the Siberian peasants described the frightening blast at Tunguska. The melting heat that Kulik found so inconsistent with his meteorite theory was more consistent with an atomic explosion (Baxter & Atkins, 1976). It is worth pointing out that scientists went on to develop the hypothesis that a nuclear explosion had occurred at Tunguska even though their theorizing was largely based on stories told by ignorant peasants, believers in devils and wrathful gods, who could quite easily have exaggerated what had actually happened to improve their stories. Even though these eyewitness accounts were gathered twenty or more years after the actual event, and had quite possibly entered the folklore of the countryside (Krinov, 1966), they were still regarded as the purest evidence.

To test whether a nuclear explosion might have occurred, scientists examined the trees for radioactivity and for any unusual increase in normal growth patterns, shown by greater spacing between the age lines, that might have been the result of radioactivity. What they found was that some trees at the site grew to be four times greater than what would normally have been expected. Similarly, scabs that appeared on the hides of local reindeer were explained as being the result of radioactive contamination (Baxter & Atkins, 1976). This evidence, by no means conclusive (Florensky, 1963), was cited as proof that such an atomic explosion had taken place, just as Kulik had cited the existence of shallow pits in the terrain as proof that a meteorite had exploded.

Assuming that what happened at Tunguska was the result of an atomic blast, and faced with the fact that nuclear fission was not within man's grasp before the 1940s, Kazantsev and his colleagues concluded that the phenomenon must have involved extraterrestrial beings and that the explosion was caused by a UFO, propelled by atomic energy, that crashed (Parry, 1961). The pattern of devastation on the ground, as seen from the air, suggested that the object took a zigzag path, changing its direction as it came closer and closer to earth. Advocates of the UFO theory argue such a change in direction would not have been possible with a natural object like a meteorite or comet, and that the object—a spacecraft—was driven by intelligent beings who were trying to land without hitting a more densely populated area. They hypothesize that the craft had some mechanical problem that made it necessary to land but that the initial angle of its trajectory was too shallow for landing and would only have bounced the craft back into space. So the navigators tried to maneuver and correct the angle, but swerved, came down too sharply, and exploded (Baxter & Atkins, 1976). On the other hand, it seems just as possible that a natural object swerved or that debris from a nonatomic explosion was thrown in zigzag directions than that navigators from outer space ran into mechanical troubles and crash-landed. If probability is going to be disregarded in order to support one theory, then the same suspension of the natural order of things can be used to confirm an equally unlikely theory.

In the late 1950s, an exploratory team examined the Tunguska site with an advanced magnetic detector and, in 1962, scientists magnified the soil and found an array of tiny, colored, magnetic, ball-shaped particles, made of cobalt, nickel, copper, and germanium (Baxter & Atkins, 1976). According to extraterrestrial-intelligence specialists, these could have been the elements used for electrical and technical instruments, with the copper used for communication services and the germanium used in semiconductors (Parry, 1961). However, controlled experiments would be necessary to make this atomic-extraterrestrial argument convincing.

Scientists who find the UFO and extraterrestrial explanations less than credible have turned to the most recent theories of physics and astronomy to explain what might have happened in the Tungus. Some (including Kazantsev) argue that such an explosion might have been caused by debris from space colliding with the earth (Morrison & Chapman, 1990), or by antimatter, which exploded as it came in contact with the atmosphere (Parry, 1961). Alternatively, the explosion might have been caused by a "black hole" hitting the earth in Siberia and passing through to emerge on the other side. Those opposing these theories point, again, to the absence of a crater and to the numerous eyewitness accounts that describe the shape of the object and the sound of the blast, all of which would be inconsistent with antimatter or black-hole theories (Baxter & Atkins, 1976). However, a 1973 article in *Nature* asserts that a black hole would not, in fact, leave a crater, but would simply enter the earth at a great velocity and that a shock wave and blast might possibly accompany its entrance (Jackson & Ryan, 1973). Comparisons have also been made with a similar but smaller incident that happened in 1930, in a stretch of Brazilian jungle as remote as Tunguska. Eyewitnesses reported the appearance of three fireballs, resulting in a one-megaton explosion and massive destruction of the forest. Coincidentally or not, the explosion occurred at the same time as the yearly Perseids meteor shower. The investigation into this phenomenon has been hampered by the

unavailability of the eyewitness accounts, contained in diaries that are held
by the Vatican (Stacy, 1996).

Even with the trail getting colder, scientists have not given up on
finding out what occurred on June 30,1908. In recent years, conferences
have taken place almost annually, in Moscow and in Krasnoyarsk, Siberia,
to exchange theories and examine on-site evidence. Andrei Ol'khovatov, an
independent scientist with a website devoted to Tunguska, believes that the
explosion was "a manifestation of tectonic energy" related to the release of
atmospheric energy in several notable earthquakes that have demonstrated
some of the same electrical and fiery phenomena (Ol'khovatov, 2001). In
1999, an expedition from the University of Bologna, headed by Dr. Luigi
Foschini and focused on Lake Ceko, not far from Lake Tunguska, used sonar
and underwater cameras before drilling for samples from the lake bed
(Whitehouse, 1999; Foschini, 1999). (Figure 2, a photograph taken by the
Bologna researchers, shows the vast impact of the blast even ninety-one
years later.) Most recently, Dr. Robert Foot of the University of Melbourne
has claimed that the cause of the Tunguska explosion must have been "mirror matter": matter that exists in the universe to spin in the opposite direction from the normal spinning of subatomic material and so "maintain
left-right symmetry in the Universe." Foot says that mirror matter is "very
hard to detect," but "interaction between atoms in the air and mirror atoms"
could happen and might have caused an explosion of Tunguskan dimensions
(Chown, 2001).

What is most fascinating about the Tunguska Valley phenomenon is
that, despite all the advances in science over the past 100 years, investigators cannot now be any more certain of the cause of the blast than they were
in 1921, when Kulik first came near the site. None of the theories presented
is wholly convincing, for all of them rely to some extent on human observers,
whose accounts of events are notoriously unreliable, or hypotheses based
on ambiguous evidence, without the support of controlled tests and experiments. Even the introduction of modern, high-tech equipment has not established a convincing explanation.

Examining these hypotheses about what did or did not land and explode in Siberia does teach us that scientific theories are sometimes based

Figure 2. An aerial photograph of the blast site in 1999, showing some of the 2,200 square kilometers (800 square miles) in which 60 million trees were destroyed. From "Return to Tunguska," by D. Whitehouse, 1999, *BBC News*, retrieved from http://news.bbc.co.uk/2/hi/science/nature/380060.stm

on the selective interpretation of evidence and that scientists, like everyone else, tend to believe their own theories and find the evidence that they want to find. Although the language that they use is very different, the accounts of what happened at Tunguska according to Kulik, Kazantsev, and their other scientific colleagues are not so very different from what the local peasants say that they saw. Both have a closer resemblance to science fiction than science fact.

References

Baxter, J., & Atkins, T. (1976). *The fire came by: The riddle of the great Siberian explosion.* Garden City, NY: Doubleday.

Cowan, C., Atluri, C. R., & Libby, W. F. (1965, May 29). Possible antimatter content of the Tunguska meteor of 1908. *Nature, 235,* 861–865.

Chown, M. (2001, July 28). What lies beneath. *New Scientist 171*(2301), 17.

Crowther, J. G. (1931). More about the great Siberian meteorite. *Scientific American, 144*(5), 314–317.

Florensky, K. P. (1963, November). Did a comet collide with the earth in 1908? *Sky & Telescope, 26,* 268–269.

Foschini, L. (1999, July 28). *Last operations in Tunguska.* Retrieved from the University of Bologna Department of Physics website: http://www.th.bo.infn.it/tunguska/press2807_en.htm

Jackson, A. A., & Ryan, M. P. (1973, September 14). Was the Tungus event due to a black hole? *Nature, 245,* 88–89.

Krinov, E. L. (1966). *Giant meteorites.* London, England: Pergamon.

Morrison, D., & Chapman, C. R. (1990, March). Target earth: It *will* happen. *Sky & Telescope, 79,* 261–265.

Olivier, C. P. (1928). The great Siberian meteorite. *Scientific American, 139*(1), 42–44.

Ol'khovatov, A. (2001, June 28). [Home page]. Retrieved August 19, 2005, from http://www.geocities.com/capecanaveral/cockpit/3240/tunguska.htm

Parry, A. (1961). The Tungus mystery: Was it a spaceship? In A. Parry (Ed.), *Russia's Rockets and Missiles* (pp. 248–267). London, England: Macmillan.

Stacy, D. (1996). Another Tunguska? *The Anomalist.* Retrieved from http://www.anomalist.com/reports/tunguska.html

What a meteor did to Siberia. (1929, March 16). *Literary Digest,* 33–34.

Whitehouse, D. (1999, June 28). Return to Tunguska. *BBC News.* Retrieved from http://news.bbc.co.uk/2/hi/science/nature/380060.stm

·12·
Some Basic Forms for Documentation: MLA, APA, and Endnotes

MLA STYLE

The following is a list of model bibliographical and parenthetical entries for MLA style. The proper bibliographical form that will appear in alphabetical order on your "Works Cited" page is followed by a sample parenthetical documentation that might appear in the text. The sample documentation in this list will usually contain the author's name; but remember that in your essay you will often mention the author's name in your text, thus making necessary only the parenthetical documentation of the page(s) of your source. You can find guidelines for preparing MLA documentation in Chapter 10, on pages 464–474. See also the list of "Works Cited" in the student essay "Looking at Horror Films" in Chapter 11. For more details and examples, as well as guidelines for kinds of sources not listed below, see the seventh edition of the *MLA Handbook for Writers of Research Papers* (2009).

PRINT SOURCES

Book by a Single Author

> Silver, Lee M. *Remaking Eden.* New York: Avon, 1997. Print.
>
> (Silver 84)

Book by Two Authors

> Franklin, John Hope, and Loren Schweninger. *In Search of the Promised Land:*
> > *A Slave Family in the Old South.* New York: Oxford UP, 2005. Print.
>
> (Franklin and Schweninger 94)

Book by More Than Three Authors

> Spiller, Robert E., et al. *Literary History of the United States.* London: Macmillan,
> > 1946. Print.
>
> (Spiller et al. 67)

Edited Collection Written by Different Authors

> Nussbaum, Martha C., and Cass R. Sunstein, eds. *Clones and Cloning.* New
> > York: Norton, 1998. Print.
>
> (Nussbaum and Sunstein 11)

Essay from a Collection Written by Different Authors

> Harris, John. "Clones, Genes, and Human Rights." *The Genetic Revolution and*
> > *Human Rights.* Ed. Justine Burley and Richard Dawkins. New York:
> > Oxford UP, 1999. 201–23. Print.
>
> (Harris 209)

Book Published in a Reprinted Edition

> Orwell, George. *Animal Farm.* 1946. New York: Signet, 1959. Print.
>
> (Orwell 100)

Book Published in a New Edition

Lechner, Frank J., and John Boli, eds. *Globalization Reader*. 2nd ed. Malden:
Blackwell, 2003. Print.

(Lechner and Boli 58)

Work in Translation

Lorenz, Konrad. *On Aggression*. 1966. Trans. Marjorie Kerr Wilson. New York:
Bantam, 1969. Print.

(Lorenz 45)

Book Published in Several Volumes

Tocqueville, Alexis de. *Democracy in America*. Ed. Phillips Bradley. 2 vols. New
York: Knopf, 1945. Print.

(Tocqueville 2: 78)

One Volume in a Set or Series

Spurling, Hilary. *Matisse the Master: The Conquest of Colour, 1909–1954*. New
York: Knopf, 2005. Print. Vol. 2 of *A Life of Henri Matisse*. 2 vols.

(Spurling 288)

Book in an Edited Edition

Kirstein, Lincoln. *By With To & From*. Ed. Nicholas Jenkins. New York: Farrar,
1991. Print.

Jenkins, Nicholas, ed. *By With To & From*. By Lincoln Kirstein. New York: Farrar,
1991. Print.

(Kirstein 190)

(Jenkins xiii)

The second entry indicates that you are citing the work of the editor (not the author); therefore, you place the editor's name first.

Introduction, Preface, Foreword, or Afterword

> Spacks, Patricia Meyer. Afterword. *Sense and Sensibility.* By Jane Austen. New
> York: Bantam, 1983. 332–43. Print.
>
> (Spacks 338)

Article in an Encyclopedia

> "American Architecture." *Columbia Encyclopedia.* 6th ed. 2005. Print.
>
> ("American Architecture")

Notice that no page numbers are needed for either the bibliographical entry or the parenthetical reference. If the article has an author, list the author's name first in the bibliographical entry and use the author's name in the parentheses. If you are citing a little-known or specialized encyclopedia, provide full publication information, including the place of publication and the publisher.

Publication of a Corporation, Foundation, or Government Agency

> United States. Dept. of Justice. *The Federal Death Penalty System: A Statistical
> Survey (1998–2000).* Washington: GPO, 2000. Print.
>
> United States. Bureau of the Census. *Abstract of the Census of Manufactures.*
> Washington: GPO, 1919. Print.
>
> Carnegie Foundation for the Advancement of Teaching. *Strengthening
> Pre-collegiate Education in Community Colleges.* Stanford: Carnegie
> Foundation for the Advancement of Teaching, 2008. Print.
>
> (*Federal Death Penalty* 28)
>
> (Bureau of the Census 56)
>
> (Carnegie Foundation 16)

Pamphlet or Brochure

The entry should resemble the entry for a book. If the author's name is missing, begin the entry with the title; if the date is missing, use the abbreviation *n.d.*

> More, Howard V. *Costa de la Luz.* Turespana: Secretaria General de Turismo, n.d.
> Print.
>
> (More 6)

Classic Work

> *The Jerusalem Bible.* Reader's Edition. Ed. Alexander Jones. Garden City:
>
> > Doubleday, 1968. Print.
>
> Homer. *The Odyssey.* Trans. Robert Fitzgerald. Garden City: Doubleday, 1963.
>
> > Print.
>
> (*Jerusalem Bible,* Job 3:7)
>
> (*Odyssey* 7.1–16)

If you are citing a particular edition of a classic work, identify it in the bibliographical entry and in the parenthetical citation. Subsequent citations need only the book, chapter, and verse "(Job 3:20)."

Article in a Scholarly Journal

Include the issue number, if there is one, both for journals that are paginated continuously throughout a volume and for those that begin each issue on page 1.

> Krcmar, Marina, and Stephen Curtis. "Mental Models: Understanding the
>
> > Impact of Fantasy Violence on Children's Moral Reasoning." *Journal of*
> >
> > *Communication* 53.3 (2003): 460–78. Print.
>
> (Krcmar and Curtis 466)

Article in a Monthly Magazine

> Murray, Charles. "The Inequality Taboo." *Commentary* Sept. 2005: 13–22. Print.
>
> (Murray 18)

Article in a Weekly Magazine

> Rosenbaum, Ron. "Shakespeare in Rewrite: The Battle over How to Read
>
> > Hamlet." *New Yorker* 13 May 2002: 68–77. Print.
>
> (Rosenbaum 68)

Article in a Newspaper

> Goldin, Davidson. "In a Change of Policy, and Heart, Colleges Join Fight against
>
> > Inflated Grades." *New York Times* 4 July 1995, late ed.: 8. Print.
>
> (Goldin)

No page number is required in a parenthetical citation of a one-page article. If a page number is required and the newspaper is divided into separately numbered sections, include the section designation before the page number in both the bibliographical entry and the citation, e.g., *B6*.

Article without an Author

"Embryos and Ethics." *The Economist* 27 Aug. 2005: 64. Print.

("Embryos and Ethics" 64)

Letter to the Editor

Kropp, Arthur J. Letter. *Village Voice* 12 Oct. 1993: 5. Print.

(Kropp)

Editorial

"The Way Out." Editorial. *New York Times* 4 May 2010: A30. Print.

("Way Out")

Review

Borowitz, Andy. "The Scotsman." Rev. of *American on Purpose,* by Craig

Ferguson. *New York Times Book Review* 4 Oct. 2009: 9. Print.

(Borowitz)

Interview

Berger, John. Interview with Nikos Papastergiadis. *American Poetry Review.*

July–Aug. 1993: 9–12. Print.

(Berger 10)

Letters

Hans, James S. Letter to the author. 18 Aug. 1991. TS.

Keats, John. "To Benjamin Bailey." 22 Nov. 1817. *John Keats: Selected Poetry*

and Letters. Ed. Richard Harter Fogle. New York: Rinehart, 1952.

300–303. Print.

(Hans)

(Keats 302)

For unpublished letters, indicate the medium as "TS" (for "typescript") or "MS" (for "manuscript," or handwritten). Published letters are cited like a work in a collection.

Unpublished Dissertation

> Eastman, Elizabeth. "'Lectures on Jurisprudence': A Key to Understanding Adam
> Smith's Thought." Diss. Claremont Grad. School, 1993. Print.
>
> (Eastman 34)

Map or Chart

> *Spain, Portugal, and North Africa.* Map. American Automobile Association,
> 1993–94. Print.
>
> (*Spain*)

Cartoon

> Trudeau, Garry. "Doonesbury." Cartoon. *Charlotte Observer* 23 Dec. 1988: B12.
> Print.
>
> (Trudeau)

ELECTRONIC SOURCES

Using the sample below as a guide, attempt to ascertain as many of the elements of citation as are appropriate to your source. In general, cite the author, title of the work, title of the Web site, sponsor or publisher of the Web site, the date of publication or last update, the medium ("Web"), and your date of access. MLA no longer requires the use of URLs; instead you should provide enough information so that readers can locate your sources easily through standard search engines. If you cannot find some of the information, cite what is available.

> Author's last name, First name, Middle initial. "Title of the Article or Other Document." *Title of Book, Periodical, or Web Site.* Editor or translator of the document or Web site. Print publication information (if any). Name of the sponsor or publisher of the Web site, date of electronic publication or most recent update. Medium. Date of access.

Scholarly Project

> *The Camelot Project.* Ed. Alan Lupack and Barbara Tepa Lupack. U of Rochester,
> 15 Apr. 2010. Web. 4 June 2010.
>
> (*Camelot*)

Book within a Scholarly Project

Skene, Felicia. *Penitentiaries and Reformatories*. Edinburgh: Edmonston, 1865. *Victorian Women Writers Project*. Ed. Perry Willett. Indiana U, 24 Apr. 2003. Web. 28 Feb. 2010.

(Skene)

Information Database

Art History Research Centre. Ed. Leif Harmsen. Dept. of Art Hist., Concordia U. May 2007. Web. 19 Nov. 2009.

(*Art History*)

Article in an Information Database

Jarvis, Edward. "The Increase of Human Life: Part 1." *Atlantic Monthly* Oct. 1869: 495–506. *American Memory*. Web. 12 Feb. 2010.

(Jarvis)

Professional Web Site

UC Berkeley Ancient History and Mediterranean Archaeology. UC Regents, 2009. Web. 15 Feb. 2010.

(*UC Berkeley*)

Personal Web Site

Stallman, Richard. Home page. Richard Stallman, 1996–2010. Web. 3 Mar. 2010.

(Stallman)

Article in a Scholarly Journal

Osborne, Lawrence. "A Pirate's Progress: How the Maritime Rogue Became a Multicultural Hero." *Lingua Franca* 8.2 (Mar. 1998): n. pag. Web. 17 Mar. 2010.

(Osborne)

Cite a scholarly journal found online as you would a print publication, then finish the entry with the medium and date of access. If the journal does not include page numbers, use "n. pag." in the bibliographical entry and only the author's name in the parenthetical reference.

Article in a Newspaper

> Kelly, Michael. "Non-Judgment Day at Yale." *Washington Post*. Washington Post
> Company, 18 Dec. 2001. Web. 20 Jan. 2010.
>
> (Kelly)

Article in a Magazine

> Blumenthal, Sidney. "Cheney's Coup." *Salon.com*. Salon Media Group, 23 Feb.
> 2006. Web. 25 May 2010.
>
> (Blumenthal)

Newsgroup Posting

> Watson, Hunter. "Soviet Collapse." *Google Groups: soc.history.moderated*. Google,
> 31 Dec. 2001. Web. 5 Jan. 2009.
>
> (Watson)

Article from a Database on CD-ROM

> Burke, Marc. "Homosexuality as Deviance: The Case of the Gay Police Officer."
> *British Journal of Criminology* 34.2 (1994): 192–203. CD-ROM. *PsycLit*.
> SilverPlatter. Nov. 1994.
>
> (Burke 195)

After the print publication information, add the medium ("CD-ROM"), the database name (in italics), the vendor, and the date the CD-ROM was produced.

Article from an Online Database Service

> Chase, Bob. "New Respect, Not Reproach." *NEA Today* Feb. 2002. *ProQuest*
> *Direct*. Web. 12 Feb. 2010.
>
> (Chase)

This format is used for an online database that you access through a library subscription or through a service that you subscribe to personally. (Note that you no longer include the name of the library.) After the publication information, add the name of the database (in italics), the medium ("Web"), and your date of access.

Online Book

After the publication information for the book, list the title of the Web site, the date of online publication, the medium, and your date of access.

> Platt, Suzy. *Respectfully Quoted*. Washington: Library of Congress, 1989.
> *Bartleby.com: Great Books Online*. 2003. Web. 12 Feb. 2010.
> (Platt)

E-mail

> Wittreich, Joseph. Message to the author. 12 Dec. 2002. E-mail.
> (Wittreich)

Review

> Cox, Ana Marie. "Easy Targets." Rev. of *Women Who Make the World Worse*, by
> Kate O'Beirne. *New York Times*. New York Times Company, 15 Jan. 2006.
> Web. 20 Oct. 2010.
> (Cox)

OTHER KINDS OF SOURCES

Personal or Telephone Interview

> Nussbaumer, Doris D. Personal interview. 30 July 1988.
> Albert, John J. Telephone interview. 22 Dec. 1989.
> (Nussbaumer)
> (Albert)

Broadcast Interview

> Kennedy, Joseph. Interview by Harry Smith. *This Morning*. CBS. WCBS, New
> York. 14 Oct. 1993. Television.
> (Kennedy)

Include the medium at the end of the entry ("Television" or "Radio").

Lecture

Auchincloss, Louis, Erica Jong, and Gloria Steinem. "The 18th Century Woman."
Symposium: Metropolitan Museum of Art, New York. 29 Apr. 1982. Lecture.
(Auchincloss, Jong, and Steinem)

Live Performance

Tommy. By Pete Townshend. Dir. Des McAnuff. St. James Theater, New York.
3 May 1993. Performance.
(*Tommy*)

Film

Dr. Strangelove. Dir. Stanley Kubrick. Columbia Pictures, 1963. Film.
Kubrick, Stanley, dir. *Dr. Strangelove.* Columbia Pictures, 1963. Film.

Put the film first if you wish to emphasize material from the film; however, if
you are emphasizing the work of the director, list that name first.

(*Dr. Strangelove*)
(Kubrick)

Television or Radio Program

Serge Pavlovitch Diaghilev 1872–1929: A Portrait. Prod. Peter Adam. BBC. WNET,
New York, 12 July 1982. Television.
(*Diaghilev*)

Audio Recording

Tchaikovsky, Piotr. *The Tchaikovsky Collection.* CBS Special Products, 1989.
Audiocassette.
(Tchaikovsky)

Videocassette or DVD

Wuthering Heights. Dir. William Wyler. 1939. Embassy, 1987. Videocassette.
(*Wuthering*)

Work of Art

Brueghel, Pieter. *The Beggars*. 1568. Oil on wood. Louvre, Paris.

(Brueghel)

APA STYLE

The format for documentation recommended by the American Psychological Association is used primarily in the social and behavioral sciences, especially sociology and psychology. It is also often employed in subjects like anthropology, astronomy, business, education, linguistics, and political science.

Like MLA style, APA documentation is based on parenthetical references to author and page. The chief difference is that, in the APA system, you include the work's *date of publication* after the author's name, both within parentheses.

MLA

Primitive religious rituals may have been a means for deterring collective violence (Girard 1).

Brain Theory suggests two extremes of writing style, the appositional and the propositional (Winterowd and Williams 4).

APA

Primitive religious rituals may have been a means for deterring collective violence (Girard, 1972, p. 1).

Brain Theory suggests two extremes of writing style, the appositional and the propositional (Winterowd & Williams, 1990, p. 4).

As with MLA style, if you cite the author's name or the date of publication in your sentence, it is not necessary to repeat it in the parentheses.

In 1972, Girard suggested that primitive religious rituals may have been a means for deterring collective violence (p. 1).

According to Winterowd and Williams (1990), Brain Theory suggests two extremes of writing style, the appositional and the propositional (p. 4).

Here is what the bibliography for these two entries would look like in MLA style and in the style recommended by APA for student papers.

MLA

WORKS CITED

Girard, René. *Violence and the Sacred.* Baltimore: Johns Hopkins UP, 1972.
   Print.

Meric, Havva J., and Margaret M. Capen. "Cognitive Style and Sex: A Study of
   Stereotypical Thinking." *Psychological Reports* 102.3 (2008): 739–44. Print.

APA

REFERENCES

Girard, R. (1972). *Violence and the sacred.* Baltimore, MD: Johns Hopkins
   University Press.

Meric, H. J., & Capen, M. M. (2008). Cognitive style and sex: A study of stereotypical thinking. *Psychological Reports, 102*(3), 739–744.

These are some of the ways that APA bibliographical style for student papers
differs from MLA style:

- Authors' first and middle names are designated by initials. When there are
  multiple authors, all are listed last name first, and an ampersand (&) is
  used instead of *and.*

- Two or more works by the same author are listed chronologically. Instead
  of using a dash for repeated names (as in MLA style), you start each entry
  with the author's full name.

- The date of publication (in parentheses) is placed immediately after the
  author's name.

- In the title of a book or article, only the first word, the first word of the sub-
  title, and proper nouns and adjectives are capitalized.

- The title of a section of a volume (e.g., an article in a periodical or a chapter of a book) is neither italicized nor surrounded by quotation marks.

- The volume number of a journal is italicized; the issue number follows in
  parentheses (not italicized).

- The bibliography is titled *References* rather than *Works Cited.*

Since the identification of sources greatly depends on the dates that you cite, you
must be careful to clarify the dating, especially when a single author has published two or more works in the same year. Here, for example, is an excerpt from
a bibliography that distinguishes among three sources by the same author published in 1972:

Carnegie Commission on Higher Education. (1972a). *The campus and the city:*
   Maximizing assets and reducing liabilities. New York, NY: McGraw-Hill.

Carnegie Commission on Higher Education. (1972b). *The fourth revolution: Instructional technology in higher education.* New York, NY: McGraw-Hill.

Carnegie Commission on Higher Education. (1972c). *The more effective use of resources: An imperative for higher education.* New York, NY: McGraw-Hill.

And here is how one of these sources would be documented in the essay:

In its report *The More Effective Use of Resources*, the Carnegie Commission on Higher Education recommended that "colleges and universities develop a 'self-renewal' fund of 1 to 3 percent each year taken from existing allocations" (1972c, p. 105).

The following is a brief list of model entries for APA style. Each bibliographical form that will appear in alphabetical order on the "References" page is followed by a sample parenthetical reference as it might appear in your text. Whenever there is an author, the sample parenthetical references in this list will contain the author's name; remember that in your essay, you will often mention the author's name (and the date) in your text, with only the page of the source needed in the parenthetical reference. For additional examples of the use of APA style, look at "Explaining the Tunguskan Phenomenon," the third research essay in Chapter 11.

PRINT AND AUDIOVISUAL SOURCES

Book by a Single Author

Silver, L. M. (1997). *Remaking eden.* New York, NY: Avon.

(Silver, 1997, p. 84)

Book by More Than One Author

Franklin, J. H., & Schweninger, L. (2005). *In search of the promised land: A slave family in the Old South.* New York, NY: Oxford University Press.

(Franklin & Schweninger, 2005, p. 94)

When a source has three to five authors, name them all in the first text reference or parenthetical note; then, in all subsequent references or notes, list only the first author's name followed by "et al." For sources with six or more authors, use "et al." in the first reference or note as well. In bibliographical entries, list all authors up to seven. For eight or more authors, list the first six, then an ellipsis mark, then the last author.

Edited Collection Written by Different Authors

Nussbaum, M. C., and Sunstein, C. R. (Eds.). (1998). *Clones and cloning.* New
   York, NY: Norton.

(Nussbaum & Sunstein, 1998, p. 11)

Essay from a Collection Written by Different Authors

Harris, J. (1999). Clones, genes, and human rights. In J. Burley & R. Dawkins
   (Eds.), *The genetic revolution and human rights* (pp. 201–223). New York,
   NY: Oxford University Press.

(Harris, 1999, pp. 209–212)

Work in Translation/Work Published in a Reprinted Edition

Lorenz, K. (1969). *On aggression* (M. K. Wilson, Trans.). New York, NY: Bantam.
   (Original work published 1966)

(Lorenz, 1966/1969, p. 75)

Book Published in a New Edition

Lechner, F. J., & Boli, J. (Eds.). (2003). *Globalization reader* (2nd ed.). Malden,
   MA: Blackwell.

(Lechner & Boli, 2003, p. 58)

Book with No Author

World atlas. (1984). New York, NY: Simon and Schuster.

(World Atlas, 1984)

Article in an Encyclopedia

American architecture. (2005). In *Columbia encyclopedia* (6th ed.). New York, NY:
   Columbia University Press.

("American Architecture," 2005)

Publication of a Corporation, Foundation, or Government Agency

Carnegie Foundation for the Advancement of Teaching. (2008). *Strengthening pre-collegiate education in community colleges.* Stanford, CA: Author.

(Carnegie Foundation, 2008, p. 16)

Article in a Periodical Numbered Only by Volume

Krcmar, M., & Curtis, S. (2003). Mental models: Understanding the impact of fantasy violence on children's moral reasoning. *Journal of Communication, 53,* 460–478.

(Krcmar & Curtis, 2003, p. 466)

Article in a Monthly Periodical

Murray, C. (2005, September). The inequality taboo. *Commentary, 120*(2), 13–22.

(Murray, 2005, p. 18)

Article in a Weekly Periodical

Rosenbaum, R. (2002, May 13). Shakespeare in rewrite: The battle over how to read *Hamlet. New Yorker,* 68–77.

(Rosenbaum, 2002, p. 68)

Article without an Author

Embryos and ethics. (2005, August 27). *The Economist (US), 376*(8441), 64.

("Embryos and Ethics," 2005)

Article in a Newspaper

Goldin, D. (1995, July 4). In a change of policy, and heart, colleges join fight against inflated grades. *The New York Times,* late ed., p. 8.

(Goldin, 1995)

Unpublished Dissertation

Eastman, E. (1993). *"Lectures on jurisprudence": A key to understanding Adam Smith's thought* (Unpublished doctoral dissertation). Claremont Graduate School, Claremont, CA.

(Eastman, 1993)

Film

Kubrick, S. (Director). (1963). *Dr. Strangelove* [Motion picture]. United States: Columbia Pictures.

(Kubrick, 1963)

ELECTRONIC SOURCES

The sixth edition of the APA *Publication Manual* (2010) recommends that you provide the same information for an electronic source as you would for a print source (author, date, title, publication information), and then add information on retrieval. Some journal articles are assigned a DOI (digital object identifier) to make locating a source easier. If an article has a DOI, list it after the publication information. If there is no DOI assigned, then list the URL of the home page of the publication. Include a retrieval date only if the information is likely to change.

For parenthetical references to a document with no page numbers, cite paragraph numbers if they are visible onscreen, using the abbreviation "para." (Smith, 2008, para. 12). If paragraphs are not numbered onscreen and the document has headings, list the heading and the number of the paragraph following the heading to cite the source of a quotation.

Internet Article Based on a Print Source

DiFranza, J. R. (2008). Hooked from the first cigarette. *Scientific American, 298*(5), 82–85. Retrieved from http://www.sciam.com

(DiFranza, 2008, p. 84)

Journal Article with a DOI

Sonibare, M. A., Moody, J. O., & Adesanya, E. O. (2009). Use of medicinal plants for the treatment of measles in Nigeria. *Journal of Ethnopharmacology, 122,* 268–272. doi:10.1016/j.jep.2009.01.004

(Sonibare, Moody, & Adesanya, 2009, p. 270)

(Sonibare et al., 2009, p. 270)

Journal Article without a DOI

Pruett, J. M., Nishimura, N. J., & Priest, R. (2007). The role of meditation in addiction recovery. *Counseling and Values, 52,* 71–84. Retrieved from http://www.counseling.org

(Pruett, Nishimura, & Priest, 2007, "Implications for Counselors," para. 2)

Journal Article Retrieved from a Database

Swingley, D., & Fernald, A. (2002). Recognition of words referring to present and absent objects by 24-month-olds. *Journal of Memory and Language, 46,* 39–56. Retrieved from http://www.elsevier.com/wps/find/journaldescription.cws_home/622888/description#description

(Swingley & Fernald, 2002, p. 46)

If the article has a DOI, list it after the page numbers. If it doesn't have a DOI, list the URL of the journal's home page in the retrieval statement.

Article in an Internet-Only Magazine

Blumenthal, S. (2006, February 23). Cheney's coup. *Salon.com.* Retrieved from http://www.salon.com

(Blumenthal, 2006)

Document from a University Web Site

Stimson, S. C., & Milgate, M. (2001). *Mill, liberty and the facts of life.* Retrieved from University of California at Berkeley, Institute of Governmental Studies website: http://www.igs.berkeley.edu

(Stimson & Milgate, 2001, p. 12)

Document from a Private Organization's Web Site

American Civil Liberties Union. (1999). *Worker's rights.* Retrieved March 4, 2000, from http://www.aclu.org/issues/immigrant/workerrights.html

(American Civil Liberties Union, 1999)

Paper Presented at a Conference or Symposium

> Patrick, W. C., III. (2001, February 13). *The threat of biological warfare.* Paper presented at the Marshall Institute's Washington Roundtable on Science and Public Policy. Retrieved from http://www.marshall.org/PatrickRT.htm
>
> (Patrick, 2001)

Newsgroup Posting

> Watson, H. (2001, December 31). Soviet collapse [Electronic mailing list message]. Retrieved from http://groups.google.com/group/ soc.history.moderated
>
> (Watson, 2001)

If the newsgroup does not archive postings, do not include the posting in the "References" list, but cite it in the text as follows:

> (B. Spatt, personal communication, April 25, 2002)

NUMBERED BIBLIOGRAPHY

In this method, used primarily in the abstract and engineering sciences, you number each entry in your bibliography. Then, each citation in your essay consists of only the number of the work that you are referring to, placed in parentheses. Remember to include the page number if you quote from your source.

> Theorem 2 of Joel, Shier, and Stein (2) is strengthened in the following theorem:
>
> The following would be a consequence of the conjecture of McMullen and Shepher (3, p. 133):

Depending on your subject, you arrange your bibliography in alphabetical order (biology or mathematics) or in the order in which you cite the sources in your essay (chemistry, engineering, or physics). Consult your instructor or a style sheet that contains the specific rules for your discipline.

ENDNOTE/FOOTNOTE DOCUMENTATION

Documentation for many academic books is provided by *footnotes* or *endnotes.* In this system, a sequence of numbers in your essay is keyed to a series of separate notes containing publication information, which appear either at the bottom of the pages where the numbers appear (footnotes) or on a separate page at the end of the essay (endnotes). It also often includes a bibliography at the end of the essay.

This brief excerpt from a biographical essay about Ernest Hemingway shows you what the endnote/footnote system looks like.

> Hemingway's zest for life extended to women also. His wandering heart seemed only to be exceeded by an even more appreciative eye.[6] Hadley was aware of her husband's flirtations and of his facility with women.[7] Yet, she had no idea that something was going on between Hemingway and Pauline Pfeiffer, a fashion editor for *Vogue* magazine.[8] She was also unaware that Hemingway delayed his return to Schruns from a business trip to New York, in February 1926, so that he might spend some more time with this "new and strange girl."[9]
>
> [6]Hemingway 102.
>
> [7]Sokoloff 84.
>
> [8]Baker 159.
>
> [9]Hemingway 210 and Baker 165.

If your instructor asks you to use endnotes or footnotes, do not put parenthetical source references, as in MLA or APA style, anywhere within the text of the essay. Instead, at each place where you would insert a parenthetical reference, put a number to indicate to your reader that there is a corresponding footnote or endnote.

When inserting the numbers, follow these rules:

- The note number is raised slightly above the line of your essay. Many word processing programs have provision for various styles of documentation, including inserting footnotes/endnotes.

- The notes are numbered consecutively: if you have twenty-six notes in your essay, the number of the last one should be 26. There is no such thing as "12a." If "12a" appears at the last moment, then it becomes "13," and the remainder of the notes should be renumbered.

- Every note should contain at least one separate piece of information. Never write a note that states only, "See footnote 3." The reader should be told enough to make it unnecessary to consult footnote 3.

- While a note may contain more than one piece of information (for example, the source reference as well as some additional explanation of the point that is being documented), the note should have only one number. Under no circumstances should two note numbers be placed together, like this: [6,7].

Unless your instructor specifies otherwise, use endnotes rather than footnotes and include a bibliography.

The *format of the bibliography* is the same as the "Works Cited" format for parenthetical documentation that was described in Chapter 7 and Chapter 10: the sources are alphabetized by last name, with the second and subsequent lines of each entry indented. The entries themselves are the same as the forms for MLA bibliographical entries listed at the beginning of this chapter. The bibliography starts on a new page following the list of endnotes, or following the essay if you are using footnotes.

The *format of the notes* resembles the bibliography entries in reverse: the first line of the note is indented five spaces, with the second and subsequent lines flush with the left margin. The note begins with a raised number, corresponding to the number in the text of the essay; the author's name is in first name/last name order; author and title are separated by commas, not periods; publication information is placed in parentheses; and the note ends with the page reference and a period.

Start the list of endnotes on a new page after the text of the essay, numbering it (and any subsequent pages) in sequence with the rest of the pages. Center the title *Notes* one inch from the top of the page, double space, and begin the first entry. Double space both within entries and between entries.

Here is a list of seven notes, illustrating some of the most common forms, followed by a bibliography consisting of the same seven sources:

NOTES

[1]Lewis 43.

[2]Himmelfarb 85.

[3]Cox 196.

[4]Martines 113.

[5]See C2.

[6]Heinze.

[7]Crawford.

WORKS CITED

Cox, Harvey G. "Moral Reasoning and the Humanities." *Liberal Education* 71.3 (1985): 195–204. Print.

Crawford, Paul. "The Crusades." *Online Reference Book for Medieval Studies.* Catholic Education Resource Center, 1997. Web. 4 May 2001.

Heinze, Andrew R. "Jews and American Popular Psychology: Reconsidering the Protestant Paradigm of Popular Thought." *Journal of American History* 88.3 (2001): 950–78. *Expanded Academic ASAP.* Web. 14 Feb. 2002.

Himmelfarb, Gertrude. "Observations on Humanism and History." *The Philosophy of the Curriculum.* Ed. Sidney Hook. Buffalo: Prometheus, 1975. 81–88. Print.

Lewis, Helen Block. *Psychic War in Men and Women.* New York: New York UP,
1976. Print.

Martines, Lauro. "Mastering the Matriarch." *Times Literary Supplement* 1 Feb.
1985: 113. Print.

See, Carolyn. "Collaboration with a Daughter: The Rewards and Cost." *New York
Times* 19 June 1986, late ed.: C2. Print.

Another kind of endnote or footnote, known as the *short form*, should be used
when you are citing the same source more than once in your essay. The first
time you cite a new source, you use the long form, as illustrated above, which
contains detailed information about publication history. The second time you
cite the same source, and all subsequent times, you write a separate note, with
a new number, but now you use a shorter form, consisting of the author's name
and a page number:

8Lewis 74.

The short form can be used here because there is already a long-form entry for
Lewis on record in a previous note. If your bibliography contained two works
by Lewis, then you would have to include an abbreviated title in the short form
of the note:

8Lewis, *Psychic War* 74.

The short form makes it unnecessary to use any Latin abbreviations, like *ibid.*
or *op. cit.*, in your notes.

For an example of the use of endnote documentation in a full-length essay,
see "Is Eating People Really Wrong?" in Chapter 11. For advice about using
footnotes rather than endnotes, and for more examples and guidelines for
kinds of sources not illustrated above, see the seventh edition of the *MLA Handbook for Writers of Research Papers* (2009).

NOTES PLUS PAGE NUMBERS IN THE TEXT

If you are using only one or two sources in your essay, it is a good idea to include one footnote at the first reference and, thereafter, cite the page number of
the source in the text of your essay.

For example, if your essay is exclusively about Sigmund Freud's *Civilization
and Its Discontents*, document your first reference to the work with a complete
note, citing the edition that you are using:

*Sigmund Freud. *Civilization and Its Discontents.* Garden City:
Doubleday, 1958: 72. All further citations refer to this edition.

This single note explains to your reader that you are intending to use the same edition whenever you cite this source. All subsequent references to this book will be followed by the page reference, in parentheses, usually at the end of your sentence.

> Freud has asserted that "the greatest obstacle to civilization [is] the constitutional tendency in men to aggression against one another . . . " (101).

This method is most useful in essays on literary topics when you are focusing on a single author, without citing secondary sources.

Appendix A

Writing Essay Examinations

Instructors give essay examinations for three reasons:

- To make sure that you have read and understood the assigned reading;
- To test your analytical skills;
- To find out if you can integrate what you have read with the ideas and information that you have learned in lectures and class discussion.

Since your instructor is usually not trying to test your memory, essay examinations are often open-book, allowing you to refer freely to the source. But in any exam, even a take-home assignment, there is likely to be some time pressure. To prepare, you should have read all the material carefully in advance and outlined, underlined, or annotated the text.

READING THE QUESTION

You determine your strategy by carefully examining the wording of the question before you begin to plan and write your essay. First, you must accept that someone else is providing the topic for your essay. The person who wrote the question wants to pinpoint a single area to be explored, and so you may have very little scope. However restrictive it may seem, you must stay within the boundaries of the question. If you are instructed to focus on only a small section of the text, summarizing the entire work from beginning to end is inappropriate. If you are asked to discuss an issue that is raised frequently throughout the work, paraphrasing a single paragraph or page is pointless. Do not include extraneous information just to demonstrate how much you know. Most instructors are more impressed with aptness and conciseness than with length.

The controlling verb of the question will usually provide you with a key. Different verbs will require different approaches. You are already familiar with the most common terms:

summarize; state; list; outline; condense; cite reasons

What is sometimes forgotten under pressure is that you are expected to carry out the instructions literally. *Summarize* means condense: the reader expects a short but complete account of the specified subject. On the other hand, *list* should result in a sequence of short entries, somewhat disconnected, but not a fully developed series of paragraphs.

Other directions may be far broader:

describe; discuss; review; explain; show; explore; determine

Verbs like these give you a wide scope. Since they do not demand a specific strategy, be careful to stay within the set topic, so that you do not explain or review more than the readers want to know about.

Still other verbs indicate a more exact method of development, perhaps one of the strategies that you have already worked with in Assignment 4 in Chapter 5:

compare and contrast; illustrate; define; show the reasons; trace the causes; trace the effects; suggest solutions; analyze

Notice that none of the verbs so far has provided an opportunity for personal comment. You have been asked to examine the text, to demonstrate your understanding of its meaning and its implications, but you have not been asked for your opinion. However, several verbs do request commentary:

evaluate; interpret; criticize; justify; prove; disagree

Although these verbs invite a personal response, they do not give you freedom to write about whatever you choose. You are still confined to the boundaries of the set subject, and you should devote as much of your essay as possible to demonstrating your understanding of what you have read. *A brilliant essay that ignores the topic rarely earns the highest grade.* If you have worked hard to prepare for the essay, you would be foolish to ignore the question. Don't reinterpret the directions in order to write about what is easiest or what would display your abilities to best advantage or what you figured out earlier would be asked. Just answer the question.

PLANNING AND DEVELOPING THE ESSAY

Even when you have worked out what you are expected to write about, you are still not ready to start writing. Your reader will also judge the way in which your essay is constructed, so organize your thoughts before you begin to write. No elaborate outline is necessary.

Guidelines for Planning and Developing Your Essay

1. *List some of the main points that come into your head, reduce the list to a manageable number, and renumber the sequence.* This process does not take very long and it can prevent unnecessary repetition, unintentional omissions, mixed-up sequences, and overemphasis.
2. *Develop each point separately.* Don't try to say everything at the same time. Consult your list, say what is necessary about each item, and then move on to the next.
3. *Develop each point adequately.* Each reason or cause or criticism deserves convincing presentation. Unless you are asked for a list, don't just write down one sentence and rush away to the next item. You will write a more effective essay by including some support for each of your points. Do not make brief, incomplete references to ideas because you assume that the reader will know all about them. It is your responsibility to explain each one so that it makes sense by itself.
4. *Refer back to the text.* Whenever possible, demonstrate that you can cite evidence or information from the assigned reading. If you think of two possible examples or facts, one from the source and one from your own experience or knowledge, and if you haven't enough time to include both, the safe choice will come from the source. However, you must always mark the transition between your own presentation of ideas and your reference to the source by citing its title, or the name of its author, or both.

ANALYZING AN ESSAY AND AN ESSAY QUESTION

Carefully read through George Stade's "Football—The Game of Aggression." Assume that you have previously read this essay and that you have between forty-five minutes and an hour to answer the following question:

Although he acknowledges that it can be violent, George Stade suggests that football may serve a constructive social function. Considering some of his descriptive comments about the sport, explain why football may not be as healthy for society as Stade implies.

FOOTBALL—THE GAME OF AGGRESSION
George Stade

There are many ways in which professional football is unique among sports, and as many others in which it is the fullest expression of what is at the heart of all sports. There is no other major sport so dependent upon raw force, nor any so dependent on a complex and delicate strategy; none so wide in the range of specialized functions demanded from its players; none so dependent upon the undifferentiated athletic *sine qua non,* a quickwitted body; none so primitive; none so futuristic; none so American.

Football is first of all a form of play, something one engages in instinctively and only for the sake of performing the activity in question. Among forms of play, football is a game, which means that it is built on communal needs, rather than on private evasions, like mountain climbing. Among games it is a sport; it requires athletic ability, unlike croquet. And among sports, it is one whose mode is violence and whose violence is its special glory.

In some sports—basketball, baseball, soccer—violence is occasional (and usually illegal); in others, like hockey, it is incidental; in others still, car racing, for example, it is accidental. Definitive violence football shares alone with boxing and bullfighting, among major sports. But in bullfighting a man is pitted not against another man, but against an animal, and boxing is a competition between individuals, not teams, and that makes a great difference. If shame is the proper and usual penalty for failures in sporting competitions between individuals, guilt is the consequence of failing not only oneself and one's fans, but also one's teammates. Failure in football, moreover, seems more related to a failure of courage, seems more unmanning than in any other sport outside of bullfighting. In other sports one loses a knack, is outsmarted, or is merely inferior in ability, but in football, on top of these, a player fails because he "lacks desire," or "can't take it anymore," or "hears footsteps," as his teammates will put it.

Many sports, especially those in which there is a goal to be defended, seem enactments of the games animals play under the stimulus of what ethologists, students of animal behavior, call *territory*—"the drive to gain, maintain, and defend the exclusive right to a piece of property," as Robert Ardrey puts it. The most striking symptom of this drive is aggressiveness, but among social animals, such as primates, it leads to "amity for the social partner, hostility for the territorial neighbor." The territorial instinct is closely related to whatever makes animals establish pecking orders; the tangible sign of one's status within the orders is the size and value of the territory one is able to command. Individuals fight over status, groups over *lebensraum*[1] and a bit more. These instincts, some ethologists have claimed, are behind patriotism and private property, and also, I would add, codes of honor, as among

[1] Literally, living space. The word is often most associated with the territory thought by the Nazis to be essential to Germany's political and economic security.

ancient Greeks, modern Sicilians, primitive hunters, teen-age gangs, soldiers, aristo-
crats, and athletes, especially football players.

The territorial basis of certain kinds of sports is closest to the surface in foot-   5
ball, whose plays are all attempts to gain and defend property through aggression.
Does this not make football *par excellence* the game of instinctual satisfactions, especially among Americans, who are notorious as violent patriots and instinctive
defenders of private property? . . . Even the unusual amity, if that is the word, that
exists among football players has been remarked upon. . . . And what is it that corresponds in football to the various feathers, furs, fins, gorgeous colors by means of
which animals puff themselves into exaggerated gestures of masculine potency?
The football player's equipment, of course. His cleats raise him an inch off the
ground. Knee and thigh pads thrust the force lines of his legs forward. His pants
are tight against his rump and the back of his thighs, portions of the body which
the requirements of the game stuff with muscle. . . . Even the tubby guard looks slim
by comparison with his shoulders, extended half a foot on each side by padding.
Finally, the helmet, which from the esthetic point of view most clearly expresses
the genius of the sport. Not only does the helmet make the player inches taller
and give his head a size proportionate to the rest of him; it makes him anonymous,
inscrutable, more serviceable as a symbol. The football player in uniform strikes
the eye in a succession of gestalt[2] shifts; first a hooded phantom out of the pale-
olithic past of the species; then a premonition of a future of spacemen.

In sum, and I am almost serious about this, football players are to America what   6
tragic actors were to ancient Athens and gladiators to Rome: models of perenni-
ally heroic, aggressive, violent humanity, but adapted to the social realities of the
times and places that formed them.

[2]I.e., perceptual.

ANSWERING THE QUESTION

At first, you may have some difficulty determining the focus of your essay
since the question includes more than one key word to help you work out your
strategy. The main verb in this question is *explain*. You are being asked to account for something, to help your reader understand what may not be entirely
clear. *Explain* also implies persuasion: your reader must be convinced that your
explanation is valid.

- If the question asked you to explain *something that is confusing* in Stade's
  essay, your task would be to provide an interpretive summary of some
  part of the text. For example, you might have been asked to explain the
  differences, with illustrations, between violence that is occasional, incidental, and accidental, discussing the implications of these distinctions for
  sports in general.

- If the question asked you to explain *some related point that Stade omits* from his discussion, your task would be to extend his reasoning, perhaps to discuss causes or effects, or to contrast and compare. For example, you might have to explain why football lends itself to a greater degree of violence than other sports, or explain the parallel between the way football players and animals defend their territory.

- If the question asked you—as it does—to *evaluate the author's reasoning* in forming his conclusions, you would then examine Stade's "almost serious" conclusions and demonstrate—explain—the limitations of his arguments and examples; in other words, argue against his position.

The essay question raises the point that Stade may have underestimated the harmful effects of football, a sport so violent that it could undermine the social benefits that it otherwise provides. To answer the question, then, you must accept the assumption that Stade may be overenthusiastic about football, *whether or not you agree,* and proceed to point out the implications and the shortcomings of his analysis. In a sense, writing a good essay depends on your willingness to allow your views to be shaped by the examiner's, at least for the duration of the exam.

The question defines the *limits* as well as the strategy of your essay. It does not permit you to dispute Stade on grounds that are entirely of your choosing. You are firmly instructed to focus your attention on the conflict between violence and social benefit. It would be foolish to ignore these instructions and write only about the glories of football or to condemn the sport for reasons unrelated to the violence of its play.

What should you be evaluating in your essay, and how many comments are "some"? Stade makes the following points in support of his view that football can be a useful social ritual:

- It fosters individual strength and determination.

- It develops cooperation and teamwork.

- It teaches players how to acquire and defend territory and thus encourages nationalism and the patriotic defense of one's country.

- It provides players and spectators with the opportunity to act out their aggressions in a controlled and relatively harmless way.

These points should certainly be on the list of paragraph topics that you jot down as you plan your essay. Since these ideas are embedded within the paragraphs of Stade's essay, you should use your own ordering principle—least violent to most (potentially) violent might be a good choice. Each of your paragraphs should begin with a description of one characteristic of the sport as Stade presents it, followed by your own explanation of the social disadvantages or benefits that might result.

Resist the temptation to devote too much space to a single aspect of the sport. For example, if you spend too much time discussing Stade's comments about uniforms and the extent to which the football player is magnified and dehumanized by his padding and his helmet, you may not be able to develop your discussion of whether football encourages patriotism or a more divisive and dangerous nationalism. Stade's essay is based on his belief that people participate in sports as a way of expressing passions and impulses that have no place in our normal daily occupations. He implies that, if this outlet is eliminated, our instincts for violence may spill over into activities where they would be far more dangerous. This argument has often been used to justify violence as depicted on television and in the movies. While you are not expected to analyze the issue with the expertise of a trained psychologist or sociologist, your essay should reflect your awareness of and your views on Stade's conception of football as a way of controlling our aggressive instincts.

INTRODUCING YOUR TOPIC

Examination essays, like all essays, require an introduction. Before beginning to explore some of the issues inherent in George Stade's analysis, you should provide a short introduction that defines the author's topic and your own. Your later references to his ideas will need a well-established context; therefore, try to define Stade's conception of football (which might differ from someone else's) right at the outset of your essay. Although the introduction need not be longer than two or three sentences, *cite your source*—the name of the author and the name of the essay, both properly spelled—and state exactly what it is that you and your author are concerned about. To demonstrate the frustration of reading an introduction that is shrouded in mystery, look at the first paragraph from a student essay answering the question that has just been analyzed:

> The attitude of the author of this essay is highly supportive of a sport that may be the most violent in the world. It is true that players acquire a lot of skills and learn about teamwork, as well as receiving huge sums of money and becoming public idols. However, there are also risks and dangers that result, for spectators and those watching on television, as well as for those on the field wearing team uniforms, which he fails to point out in this brief essay.

"He," of course, is George Stade, and the sport under discussion is football. The student had read and understood the source essay, but is so eager to begin commenting on Stade's ideas that she fails to establish a context for her arguments. Here is a more informative introduction:

> In "Football—The Game of Aggression," George Stade presents the game of football as a necessary evil and a useful social ritual. He does not deny that the game, more than most sports, is based on a potentially lethal kind of aggression. But, contrasting football with other sports, he finds that it also encourages a sense of teamwork and an instinct for patriotism, which can be valuable both to

the individual and to society. Left unclear is whether ritualizing violence through sports does, in fact, result in a less violent society, or whether watching football players maul each other in weekly combat only encourages spectators to imitate their heroes.

PRESENTING YOUR ESSAY TO THE READER

Students often choose to divide their time into three parts. For example, if you have forty minutes during which to write an essay, try the following timetable:

- ten minutes to analyze the question and plan a strategy
- twenty minutes to write the essay
- ten minutes to proofread and correct it

During in-class examinations, students often waste vital minutes by painstakingly transcribing a new copy from their rough drafts. While *your handwriting must be legible*, it is not necessary to hand in a clean copy. Instructors expect an exam essay to have sentences crossed out and words inserted. They are used to seeing arrows used to reverse sentences and numbers used to change the sequence of paragraphs. It makes no sense to write the last word of your first draft and then, without checking what you have written, immediately take a clean sheet of paper and start transcribing a copy to hand in. Because transcription is such a mechanical task, the mind tends to wander and the pen makes errors that were not in the original draft. Take time to proofread your essay, to locate grammatical errors, and to fill in gaps in continuity. As long as your corrections and changes are fairly neat and clear, your instructor will not mind reading the first draft and will probably be pleased by your efforts to improve your writing.

Readings for a Research Essay

The essays in this appendix are sources for you to work with if your instructor asks you to write a research essay based on Assignment 12 (p. 454). These readings form two groups: periodicals and academic books. Your instructor may ask you to use either group or both as the basis for your essay. Or (with your instructor's permission) you may wish to supplement these essays with additional sources of your own choosing.

GROUP A: PERIODICALS

The Nation 15 July 1991: 79–120.

Note: This special issue of *The Nation* consisted of many short essays on patriotism. The following authors are included here:

Burnham, Walter Dean

Cuomo, Mario M.

Glasser, Ira

Ivins, Molly

Jackson, Jesse L.

Postman, Neil

Shannon, William H.

"Debating How Best to Love Your Country." *The New York Times* 1 July 2000: B7.

Lukacs, John. "When Democracy Goes Wrong." *Harper's* Apr. 2005: 13–18.

GROUP B: ACADEMIC BOOKS (ORDERED BY DATE)

Tocqueville, Alexis de. *Democracy in America*. Vol. 1. 1835. Trans. Arthur Goldhammer. New York: Penguin, 2004.

Tolstoy, Leo. "Patriotism, or Peace?" *Essays, Letters, Miscellanies*. Vol. 2. New York: Scribner's, 1913.

Walzer, Michael. "Civility and Civic Virtue in Contemporary America." *What It Means to Be an American*. 1974. New York: Marsilio, 1992.

Kristol, Irving. "Urban Civilizations and Its Discontents." *Reflections of a Neoconservative*. New York: Basic Books, 1983.

Axinn, Sidney. "Honor, Patriotism, and Ultimate Loyalty." *Nuclear Weapons and the Future of Humanity*. Ed. Steven Lee and Avner Cohen. Totowa: Rowman, 1986.

Nathanson, Stephen. "Military Service and Unjust Wars." *Patriotism, Morality, and Peace*. Totowa: Rowman, 1993.

Viroli, Maurizio. "Patriotism without Nationalism." *For Love of Country: An Essay on Patriotism and Nationalism*. New York: Oxford UP, 1995.

McLean, Scott L. "The War on Terrorism and the New Patriotism." *The Politics of Terror: The U.S. Response to 9/11*. Ed. William Crotty. Boston: Northeastern UP, 2004.

Group A: Periodicals

WALTER DEAN BURNHAM
Professor of government, University of Texas

The Nation (7/15/91)

Patriotism at its best is the affirmation of certain essential human values that bond one individual to another, in what one might call a country-specific way. Patriotism at its worst is fetishistic idolatry, the worship of the tribe and hence of oneself. It is one of three great emotive expressions that mark modern history, the other two of course being religion and socialist internationalism. As has been the historic case with religion and socialism, patriotism readily lends itself to manipulation of mass publics by politicians and other elites seeking "hot buttons" to push.

It is this sort of patriotism (or perhaps better, patrioteering) that prompted John Quincy Adams to comment that whenever he saw a politician start to wave the flag, he felt an "involuntary apprehension of mischief."

Patriotism is thus an inescapably, deeply ambiguous phenomenon. What does it mean to "love one's country"? Rallying around the flag can be a fundamentally valuable human response to challenge. Who can view the history of the Civil War or World War II and think otherwise? Still, there tends to be a left-right split in defining the meaning of loving one's country that parallels the two sides of this force. A relatively little rallying around the flag, viewed in historic time, goes a long way; World War II does not happen very often. But efforts to promote it are continuous, with or without anything in the environment that looks like a rational threat. The other approach, no less motivated by love of country, is more critical. The reason this is so is that important elements of our national value system promise things that the social, economic and political systems are not delivering. This gap between promise and performance in the United States centers on the structural deficiencies of a capitalist civilization and of its associated political system in the realization of those values. A patriot committed to the elevation of the human condition in the United States has ample ground within its structure of values and traditions for sustaining a critical stance. However, the tribal-worship side of the force can infinitely appeal to many or most of us. Doing the other kind of patriotism will thus always be uphill, not to mention steady, work.

What America means to me is, ultimately, the ideal of a society where no arbitrary limits are placed on anyone's ability to reach and enjoy the plenitude of his or her potential as an adult human being. The historic American accomplishment in this regard has of course often been desperately flawed along lines of race, gender and class. But it has nevertheless been mighty. We too often tend to forget this. In some important respects, this ideal is not that far removed from Marx's primordial vision; there were good reasons for his ardent support of the Union cause during the American Civil War. And it is somewhere in this plane that the best ideals of the historic left and of the American value system come very close together. Needless to say, these are all great generalities; and God, as always, is in the details. But the vision endures, and it is no mean vision either.

Perhaps I can lend a certain autobiographical concreteness to the discussion. My forebears arrived on these shores across a span of time extending from 1620 to 1878. I have been very happily married for a generation to a woman whose parents arrived here in 1929 from Ireland, where they and their forebears had endured seven centuries of imperialist and racist oppression. None of these people were rich and famous, but they generally prospered, and they did their part to build the country. Various members of this family tree served in colonial wars, the American Revolution, the War of 1812, the Civil War and World War II. I myself served in the armed forces during the Korean conflict, with distinct pride if without much pleasure. (A half-generation later I was one of many who became unalterably opposed to the Vietnam War, but I saw and still see nothing inconsistent in this.) The tree includes Protestant, Catholic and Jewish elements, and I take pride in each of these traditions.

This is after all a very American story. The United States is a palimpsest; it is always being "written over," as it becomes something else over time from what it was. Being an aggregation of every race and people under heaven, it lacks the assured cultural definition of national identity that one finds in European nation-states. That creates the space for political entrepreneurs to play a politics of divide-and-rule, a chief feature of the current regime under which we live. It also has contributed to such exercises in pathology in the name of patriotism as the House Un-American Activities Committee, Senator Joseph McCarthy and their latter-day successors. These too are American stories. They underscore why it is necessary that those with a different concept of patriotism resist all efforts by the patrioteers, those specialists in invoking the Idols of the Tribe, to control the meaning of this rich and ambiguous power in the land.

MARIO M. CUOMO
Governor of New York

The Nation (7/15/91)

Like most of us, my family and I owe this nation a great debt for most of the many good things that have happened to us. So my patriotism rests on profound gratitude. But it goes beyond that. It is a love of country that calls not only for active support but also for candor and, occasionally, even tough love.

Patriotism, for me, is rooted in the belief that my country will behave in a decent and civilized manner toward those who live in it and those who live outside it. To me, that means the guarantee of a strong constitutional system that upholds the principles of freedom and protects its people; a political leadership that is chosen in open elections; a philosophy of government that reflects a commitment to helping those who can't help themselves; and a manner of relating to other sovereign nations that is governed by international legal precepts.

The term "patriotism" seems to be raised most often in the context of military action and at times has been used as a test of support for our country's military activities. But I understand it to include a respect for contrasting viewpoints, an acceptance of dissent, a tolerance—and even a welcoming—of the clashing diversity of voices that is uniquely American. In our democracy, patriotism ought not be the blind endorsement of a particular government administration, nor should it require rigid conformity to whatever the majority dictates. A proper patriotism would recognize that there are no absolutes when it comes to solving our social or international problems, except the standard by which we must judge all goals— our willingness to help one another, and to help others.

IRA GLASSER
Executive director, American Civil Liberties Union
The Nation (7/15/91)

As Samuel Johnson noted, patriotism is often used by grasping politicians as a cloak for self-interest. Sometimes the American flag itself has been used as a cloak for self-interest by those who wrap themselves in it even as they act to undermine what the flag represents.

But there is another kind of patriotism, reflected not so much by devotion to the flag as by a commitment to the founding principles that the flag represents. "Patriotism" is a strong word and generates strong emotions; we ought not abandon it to those whose purpose is to undermine the founding principles, such as those codified in the Bill of Rights. Supporting those principles is what ought to characterize American patriotism, and we should contest our adversaries both for the definition of the term and its proprietary use.

Liberty means that even in a democracy the majority cannot be allowed to rule everything. Rights require the establishment of legal boundaries for democracy itself, forbidden zones of freedom where individuals reign supreme and where the government, and majoritarian preference as well, may not prevail.

The Bill of Rights, flawed as it was by slavery and lesser imperfections, was adopted because the original citizens of the United States insisted upon it. Those are *our* traditional American values. Our brand of patriotism consists of fighting for those values and insisting that they are the essence of what it means to be an American. It is up to us to make patriotism a synonym for freedom of conscience and expression, fundamental fairness and equality.

MOLLY IVINS
Columnist, *Dallas Times Herald*
The Nation (7/15/91)

The times I feel a great rush of affection for this country are almost always touched off by either the land or the people. I love the land and I usually think of it in terms of the West, because that's where I've spent most of my life. I love the Texas Hill Country, the Big Bend and the endless space around Lubbock (truly an acquired taste). I believe the east rim of the Grand Canyon is sublime, the Grand Tetons almost heartbreakingly beautiful and, another acquired taste, the Red Rock country of southern Utah has grown on me over the years. Southern Louisiana and northern New Mexico are other favorites.

It's silly to generalize about 250 million people, but I dearly love the spunk, irreverence and let's-get-her-done practicality of so many Americans. Ted Morgan, a writer who had the misfortune to be born French, not one of life's lighter crosses, and the good sense to become an American, once observed that the charm of

Americans is that whenever we are confronted with any given problem, we immediately mount horse and charge off in 360 different directions. I have a great relish for the ensuing stampede. As Marianne Moore once said, "It is an honor to witness so much confusion." I am fond of the terminal common sense of Midwesterners, the dotty charm of Southerners and the relish with which Texans approach damn near everything.

I tend to be suspicious of patriotic spectacle because I dislike being emotionally manipulated. "Reely big shews," like the '84 Olympics in Los Angeles, remind me of Hitler's Nuremberg rallies. And, God knows, we have had enough sleazy politicians wrap themselves in the flag and use patriotism to cover up their sins to make the entire nation cynical. Carl Jung said that sentimentality and brutality are "sisters," never very far apart. I must confess, however, to a weakness for Fourth of July fireworks and John Philip Sousa marches. I find the Lincoln Memorial by moonlight almost unbearably moving, and I was thrilled when the tall ships came into New York Harbor on the Bicentennial Fourth of July.

I believe patriotism is best expressed in our works, not our parades. We are the heirs of the most magnificent political legacy any people has ever been given. "We hold these truths to be self-evident. . . ." It is the constant struggle to protect and enlarge that legacy, to make sure that it applies to all citizens, that patriotism lies. When some creepy little shit like Richard Nixon (whose understanding of the right of the people peaceably to assemble and to petition the government for redress of grievances is so profound that he proposed to send teamsters, thugs, and murderers out to "break the noses" of antiwar protesters) becomes President, our heritage is diminished and soiled in such an ugly fashion.

Vote, write, speak, work, march, sue, organize, fight, struggle—whatever it takes to secure the blessings of liberty to ourselves and our posterity. Ran across one of our good guys right at the end of the last session of the Texas Lege, just a few weeks ago. He said he felt like a country dog in the city. "If I run they bite my ass, if I hold still, they fuck me." Calling all country dogs: It's a helluva fight.

JESSE L. JACKSON
President, National Rainbow Coalition
The Nation (7/15/91)

One afternoon in Greenville, South Carolina, when I was 9 years old, my father was raking leaves. The man came outside to offer us a drink of water, and when he left I asked, Why does that man speak differently from us? "He's German," said my father, and he stopped and leaned on his rake. "He's German. I fought in Europe so they could have freedom. I'm proud to be a veteran of that war." His eyes clouded over. "But now he's here, and he can vote, and I cannot. I helped free his people, now I'm raking his leaves."

It is a paradox of the human spirit that even after such brutal oppression and disregard for human rights, we are still so patriotic and love our country so much. It is our land; we cultivated it and helped to build it. But it is not our government. Indeed, fighting for a better government is the patriotic thing to do.

America at its best guarantees opportunity, and so fighting to expand the horizons of oppressed people is an act of patriotism. Yet too often, those who dare expand our nation's democracy and make it true to its principles are victims of naked aggression, aggression led not by street fighters but by the White House, Congress and the courts. The founding writers of the Constitution envisioned a nation in which people of African descent were three-fifths human, in which their own mothers and daughters and sisters had no right to vote, in which Native Americans had no right to live. Thomas Jefferson expressed the American dilemma when he wrote:

> For in a warm climate, no man will labour for himself who can make another labour for him. This is so true, that of the proprietors of slaves a very small proportion indeed are ever seen to labour. And can the liberties of a nation be thought secure when we have removed their only firm basis, a conviction in the minds of the people that these liberties are of the gift of God? That they are not to be violated but with his wrath? Indeed I tremble for my country when I reflect that God is just. . . .

Through patriotism we have made America better. We have gained the right to vote. Women and African-Americans have changed the course and character of the nation. And my father's faith in his country has been sustained in the lifetime commitment of his family to make America better. Yet those who have fought for the highest and best principles of our country, the true patriots, have been vilified and crucified. The true patriots invariably disturb the comfortable and comfort the disturbed, and are persecuted in their lifetimes even as their accomplishments are applauded after their deaths.

Today, politicians are proud to pronounce that we have abolished slavery. But in its time, slavery was the political center, and abolitionists were punished for their moral strength. Today, politicians hold up the gains of women. Yet in its time, denial of the vote to women was the political center; the women's suffrage movement sought the moral center, and was punished for its patriotism. Those who fight for civil rights, open housing, environmental laws, peace and international cooperation, and veterans of domestic wars—the real patriots—receive no parades.

We must never relinquish our sense of justice for a false sense of national pride. "My country right or wrong" is neither moral nor intelligent. Patriotism is support for the highest ideals of the nation, not for whoever happens to be in the White House. As citizens we must continue to fight for justice and equality so that we might make a better nation and a better world. We must give credence to our invitation: "Give me your tired, your poor, your huddled masses yearning to breathe free," for the character of our nation is rooted in the affirmation of these ideals for all of our people.

NEIL POSTMAN
Professor, New York University School of Education
The Nation (7/15/91)

As I see it, a patriot is someone who organizes his or her political and social val-   1
ues around a set of national ideals. Patriotism does not imply love of government
and certainly does not require that one ignore the gap between a nation's ideals
and its practices in actual social life. In fact, one of the important principles of the
American Creed is that citizens have an obligation to criticize government and other
actors in society when the disparity between ideal and reality becomes too great.

I consider myself a devoted American patriot because the American Creed, which   2
developed out of the epoch of the Enlightenment, is humanistic and liberal and has
a universalist dimension. It expresses the essential dignity of human beings and
confidence in the value of decisions arrived at by common counsel rather than by violence. It explicitly states enlightened conditions of political association in the First
Amendment to the Constitution. These ideals have formed my own consciousness, and I have found no reason to reject them.

It sometimes happens that people who were born and raised in America are so   3
insulted by the imperfections of government and social life that the nation's ideals
become invisible to them. When this happens, it is well to remember that Chinese
students expressed their impulse to freedom and democracy by making their papier-
mâché version of the Statue of Liberty; or that students in Prague in protest over
government oppression read aloud from the works of Thomas Jefferson. It also
helps to remember the American Creed by talking to immigrants who have come to
America, recently and in the past, and who know well why they left their own native land and why they have come here.

WILLIAM H. SHANNON,
Monsignor, professor emeritus, Nazareth College
The Nation (7/15/91)

In recent weeks we have experienced a good deal of an unprincipled (or per-   1
haps I should say "unthinking") type of patriotism. There are people who, before the
gulf war began, seemed to think it unjust and therefore unjustifiable. But once we
were in it, their attitude became one of unquestioning support for the war effort.
These are the people who felt and still feel that, if you didn't support the war, you
were letting our servicemen and -women down. The attitude seems to be: As long
as we're in it, let's win it. Questions such as, Is our cause just? Are we observing
the kind of restraint that the principle of proportionality requires? seem to have disappeared into the question, How soon can we win?

There may well be people who supported the war for moral reasons, but it is   2
difficult to avoid thinking that what is being called patriotism today is, on the part
of many people, a combination of "group narcissism" (which turns us in on ourselves

and enables us to see military victory for our side as the highest good of the moment) and a "neurotic obedience" (which leaves decisions in the hands of authority figures and thus relieves us of the anxiety of making our own decisions and accepting the consequences of our own initiatives). This kind of immature patriotism can take on hysterical dimensions. Soon after the end of the war, I saw on the television news pictures of a town where there were villages and yellow ribbons everywhere. One woman interviewed said she was almost afraid not to follow suit, even though she was opposed to the war. Her fear was that if she did not conform her home would be vandalized.

Does this mean, then, that patriotism is a quality of questionable morality? Is patriotism an evil? At this point I would like to bring in an old friend who tends to be forgotten today: St. Thomas Aquinas. Aquinas lists patriotism under the virtues. And he sees it as a potential part of the virtue of justice. In fact, the name he uses for it may sound strange to us. He uses the name "piety." Piety for him is the virtue that moves us to offer honor and respect to those to whom we are indebted. He says we are indebted first of all to God; hence we owe piety to God. We are indebted to our parents; hence we owe piety to them. We are also indebted to our homeland; hence we owe piety to our homeland and to our fellow citizens. The piety we owe to homeland and all its people is what Aquinas means by patriotism.

3

I want to stress the point that he considers patriotism as a potential part of the virtue of justice. This surely means that patriotism must look to justice as its primary mentor. This means that anything that is against justice is surely against the virtue of patriotism. Hence to support and defend our country on any occasion where we are convinced its actions may be unjust is not patriotism at all. As a part of justice, patriotism demands that we make moral judgments on the course of actions that our country may take. A patriotism that refuses ever to call one's country to account for the morality of its action is no true patriotism at all. It is a bogus patriotism.

4

I say all this because I think that patriotism has become a bad word for people who, because they see it so widely abused to cover actions that are not patriotic at all, want to banish the word entirely from their own vocabulary. Like the man on the way from Jerusalem to Jericho, the word "patriotism" has fallen among robbers who have stripped it of its true meaning. I want to be like the Good Samaritan and rescue it from the damages it has suffered and restore it to its own good, healthy meaning.

5

DEBATING HOW BEST TO LOVE YOUR COUNTRY:
Do You Fight Off Assaults on the System or Fight to Make the System Better?

New York Times (7/1/2000)

Norman Podhoretz is the editor at large of Commentary *magazine, a senior fellow of the Hudson Institute and the author of* My Love Affair with America. . . . *Victor Navasky is the publisher and editorial director of* The Nation, *the Delacorte professor of maga-*

zine journalism at Columbia University and the author of Naming Names, *a study of the Hollywood blacklist. For many years they have disagreed, often vehemently, about the issues that shape American life. For this Fourth of July weekend,* The New York Times *asked them to discuss patriotism. The moderator of the discussion was Barry Gewen, the editor of Arts & Ideas and an editor in the Book Review of* The Times.

Q. Norman, you begin your new book, *My Love Affair with America,* with the quotation from Samuel Johnson: "Patriotism is the last refuge of a scoundrel." This is probably the single most famous quote about patriotism, and it prompts the question: Has patriotism gone out of style? | 1

Podhoretz. Well, I think Johnson was wrong and this was a most uncharacteristic remark for him, a fervent Tory, to have made, since conservatives, generally in Europe anyway, had been associated with patriotic sentiment and the nationalist sentiment. | 2

Has patriotism gone out of style in America? The answer is certainly yes, as of very recently. But my own feeling is that it's slowly coming back. We see signs of this resurgence of patriotic sentiment in various sectors of the culture. The most salient, I suppose, would be the enormous success of Tom Brokaw's two books on the World War II generation. I think the success of a movie like *Saving Private Ryan* is another sign, a sign of a new respect for the kind of virtues that were traditionally associated with patriotism or love of country. | 3

Navasky. Well, about Samuel Johnson: Ambrose Bierce had an amendment to Johnson. I think he said, "I beg to submit, sir, it is the first." In other words, patriotism is not the last refuge of scoundrels, it's the first. | 4

I don't agree with that. But I think it depends what your definition of patriotism is. I would suggest that in the Vietnam era the people who were protesting the war included a large number of patriots. My definition of patriotism would involve fighting to make sure your country lives up to its highest ideals. And from that perspective even those who burn the flag—not all of them but some of them—may have been as patriotic as those who wrapped themselves in the flag. | 5

So the word may be coming back in some way, but the struggles to make America the best it can be have been going on, it seems to me, since the Revolutionary War. | 6

Podhoretz. I would like to take issue with the definition that Victor is offering. To define American patriotism as struggling to make the country live up to its best ideals has in practice generally meant denigrating the country for not doing so. The ideal is very often the enemy of the real. | 7

The conditions under which Americans have actually lived in one generation or another is the country that one either loves or does not love. One can be critical of the country while loving it, just as one can be critical of one's wife or husband or lover in personal life. But I would submit that the people who burned the flag during the Vietnam War or people who spelled the name of the country with a K to suggest an association with Nazi Germany or people who saw no difference | 8

An act of patriotism. Norman Podhoretz, whose new book is *My Love Affair with America*, says he thinks patriotism is slowly coming back into style.

An act of patriotism? Victor Navasky says he thinks that even extreme forms of protest have sometimes been necessary in the struggle for the American dream.

between America and the Soviet Union during the cold war, morally or politically, were not patriots.

Navasky. I guess I don't pretend to know the motives of the folks who chose the   9
burning of the flag as their way of protesting the Vietnam War, but I do know that going back to the beginning of our history, and right up through the abolitionist movement and the movement for labor rights in the 1920's and 30's and the movement for civil rights in the 60's, those people who fought to achieve the American dream of equal rights for all were scorned at the time as, in effect, unpatriotic and later on as Communists.

Q. Let me ask Victor a question about patriotism and liberals and the left. In   10
the period around World War II, there was no embarrassment on the left about engaging in traditional patriotic activities—flag waving, Fourth of July celebrations—but these symbols of patriotism seem to have disappeared from the left. Do those symbols now totally belong to conservatives and the right, or does the left have some call to them also?

Navasky. Sure, there was a shared symbology that went across the ideological   11
board. Irving Kristol has written an essay, which Norman cites in his book, where he said that there is a holy trinity associated with American patriotism and it includes the Constitution, the Declaration of Independence and the flag. I would say two out of three isn't bad. To me, the authentic symbols of our country start with the covenants, the Declaration of Independence and the Constitution. The flag is important only for the principles that it represents.

Q. Next question: is there a good patriotism and a bad patriotism?   12

Podhoretz. Yes, though my own view is that patriotism has been so ridiculed   13
and has been so out of fashion that spiritual and moral balance require an emphasis on patriotism as a good thing. I mean, most people would say that when patriotism becomes chauvinistic or jingoistic or even simply nationalistic, it becomes aggressive and dangerous. But the heritage that we fight for is not merely one of rectifying wrongs of the past, such as slavery or discrimination, and trying to create conditions that are more in consonance with what is promulgated, both in the Declaration and the Constitution; it's also to fight off assaults on the system of government that was designed by the Founding Fathers.

Q. Victor, is there a good patriotism and a bad patriotism?   14

Navasky. Stephen Decatur, who said, "Our country right or wrong," said first,   15
"May she always be in the right." And that's a good part of patriotism—to fight to have your country be in the right. A destructive part of patriotism is when it slips into a kind of nationalism which makes you hate other countries, put your country's interests first when you think it's behaving in an immoral and unjust way. So that confusing patriotism with unconditional support for a government policy, it seems to me, does damage, and core damage, to the meaning of citizenship in our democracy.

Podhoretz. But to denigrate the country, to call it foul names, to desecrate its   16
symbols, should not be given the name of patriotism. People who want to do that

are free to do that in this country. But I don't think they ought to then wrap themselves in the flag that they've just burned.

Navasky. When Frederick Douglass made his famous speech where he said that freedom requires rain and thunder and lightning, what he was talking about was that you have to do a lot of nasty and uncomfortable things to bring the plight of folks who don't have freedom to the national attention. And that is a part of a patriotic America-loving act. It's not an America-hating act to try to bring the African-American community to its entitlement.

17

Podhoretz. In the civil rights movement, the early civil rights movement in the late 50's and early 60's, the most effective means blacks employed happened to be not nasty, whatever, but nonviolent resistance. Which was perceived by everybody in this country as noble and admirable and which made the sheriffs who were attacking them with water hoses look ignoble and evil. So I don't agree that nasty things necessarily have to be done.

18

Q. A great deal of the historical scholarship of the last few decades has examined and brought to light the negative aspects of American history—slavery, the treatment of American Indians, the detention of Japanese Americans during World War II. How do we fit these negative aspects of American history into education programs for our children?

19

Podhoretz. Well, I think they have to be faced up to honestly. Children have to be taught that these things happened. They also have to be taught that many— in fact, I think all of the ones you mentioned—were acted upon, were corrected. And that they were corrected through the resources of the American constitutional and institutional structure.

20

It's very important to teach children that the history of this country is on the whole a glorious one, not an inglorious one. That this is a country to be proud of, including for the way it has dealt with what I would say are the inevitable blemishes and warts. I think that we as a socio-political-economic system rank with such great civilizations of the past as fifth-century Athens and Elizabethan England. Not, as I say in my book, in the production of artistic monuments, though we haven't done so badly in that department either, but in the provision of more liberty and more prosperity to more people than has existed anywhere else on earth, whether present or past. And this, too, has to be taught to our children and should be emphasized.

21

Navasky. I think the way you teach the abolitionists, for instance, is that you make clear that, in terms of your own values, the abolitionists were greater patriots than the plantation owners against whom they were fighting. That the folks who were organizing the workers, in my judgment, were greater patriots than the mine and mill owners who were exploiting them. That the real patriots during the Vietnam War were the folks who resisted it. And the patriots during the civil rights movement were indeed, as Norman said, the folks who adopted passive resistance. And it worked to a degree there.

22

Podhoretz. I have nothing against the abolitionists, but I would say that my hero in the Civil War is not John Brown but Abraham Lincoln. They were very

23

different and they were not on the same side. And it makes a big difference whether you think it's Abraham Lincoln who should be celebrated or John Brown.

Navasky. I think they both should be celebrated, as should Frederick Douglass.   24

Podhoretz. Well, I agree with you about him.   25

Q. What impact, if any, has multiculturalism had on our idea of patriotism?   26

Navasky. I think it requires a revision to this classic notion of my country right   27
or wrong, first of all, depending on when your own group became part of the tradition and entitled to the rights that other folks got.

Secondly, I think the real contribution of multiculturalism to our culture to-   28
day is the right of people to establish their own identities and define their own identities.

And thirdly, multiculturalism suggests that we have a series of competing alle-   29
giances. One of them is love of family. A second is love of tribe or culture or whatever it is. A third is love of country. And a fourth is one's relationship to the international community. And it seems to me the most valuable kind of patriotism is one which honors the other relationships rather than competes against them.

Podhoretz. Well, here we go again. I think multiculturalism is a perversion   30
of the traditional American idea of pluralism. The ideal was that in the public sphere—in the public schools—the rule of assimilation prevailed. That is, if an immigrant came to this country, he was expected—and, indeed, wished—to learn English and to absorb the traditions of his new country, to become an American, to be Americanized. Nothing prevented that individual from remaining loyal, within the private sphere, to the tribe and the family. You were free as an individual to live in both worlds if you chose. But what you were not free to do was to refuse to assimilate to the culture of this country. Nobody was going to arrest you or anything of that sort, but you would certainly limit your opportunities for employment, for advancement and for participation, including civic participation.

I think that multiculturalism doesn't so much help to give people the power to de-   31
fine their own identities as it keeps them apart from the rest of the community. So I think it's a bad thing and I think it is not—does not—contribute to a healthy patriotism.

Q. Now each of you, if you want, can take a minute or two to say something in   32
summary. Norman?

Podhoretz. Yeah, why not. I'll take a crack at it.   33

I think intellectual honesty requires us to recognize that we have emerged from   34
a period during which America-bashing, as some call it, or denigration of America, has prevailed, particularly among intellectuals, not so much among most people, but among the elites. I believe this has begun to change. I hope it has begun to change.

Navasky. I guess patriotism is best expressed in the struggle to make this a   35
better place. And it is not best expressed in saluting the flag or in parades down Fifth Avenue but in writing, in marching, in suing, in voting, in going to court, whatever it takes to fulfill the promise of the Bill of Rights.

from WHEN DEMOCRACY GOES WRONG
John Lukacs
Harper's, April 2005

Adapted from Democracy and Populism, *by John Lukacs, published in February by Yale University Press. Lukacs is the author of* A New Republic, *among many other books.*

Much has happened since Alexis de Tocqueville published the first volume of *Democracy in America* in 1835. America is not what it was then; the American people are not what they were; and America is no longer the only prototype of democracy in the world. Perhaps now, when all around us seethes the still-spreading tide of the democratization of the world, it is time for Tocqueville's theme to be reversed. For a book remains to be written with the title *American Democracy* that examines how American political and social conditions differ from French or British or Japanese or Russian or Ruritanian democracy. Tocqueville invites such a line of inquiry when he writes of his book:

> My aim has been to show, by the example of America, that laws, and especially customs, may allow a democratic people to remain free. But I am very far from thinking that we ought to . . . copy the means that it has employed to attain this end; for I am well aware of the influence which the nature of a country and its political antecedents exercise upon its political constitution; and I should regard it as a great misfortune for mankind if liberty were to exist all over the world under the same features.

And yet: the evolving history of the democratization of the world is well-nigh inseparable from the Americanization of the world. "The world must be made safe for democracy": this hapless idea of an American president, Woodrow Wilson, has endured well beyond the revolutionary ideas of his goateed contemporary, the demagogue Lenin. Wilson's extreme ideas have since been espoused by Democratic and Republican presidents alike, among them Richard Nixon, Herbert Hoover, Franklin Roosevelt, and now George W. Bush. Perhaps Wilson's mindless phrase ought to be reversed as well, for "how to make democracy safe for the world" is a big question that Tocqueville would have instantly understood.

Many of Tocqueville's questions are more relevant than ever. Is democracy the rule of the people or, more precisely, rule by the people? No, it is rule in the name of the people, which is far more complicated. In its predominant sense democracy is the rule of the majority, but here liberalism must enter. (It did not and does not always.) Majority rule must be tempered by legal assurances of the rights of minorities, and of individual men and women. And when this temperance is weak, or unenforced, or unpopular, then democracy is nothing more than populism. More precisely, it is nationalist populism.

Neither "nationalism" nor "populism" was a term used by Tocqueville. He understood such phenomena, but these words did not exist in the French language

during his lifetime. They do exist now, however, and our question is how traditional democracy can survive when traditional liberalism has decayed. Tocqueville
did not have to face this, but we do. . . .

For much of the nineteenth century, democracy was feared by both liberals and   5
conservatives. Serious thinkers from both camps spoke against the principle of popular sovereignty, and against what Tocqueville called "the tyranny of the majority."
Those who did not reject democracy entirely tried their best to circumscribe it.
They were aware that liberty and equality are not identical, that their aspirations are
not necessarily parallel and indeed often antithetical, and that to insist on one at
the expense of the other could be disastrous.

But after 1870 the practice (or at least the evocation) of democracy was, willy-   6
nilly, adopted by almost all liberals, as well as by many conservatives, and, as a result, some of the principal differences between the two camps began to fade. The
time of their great dialogue, especially in Europe, came to an end. It gave way to
two enormous new movements, nationalism and socialism, which ultimately dominated most of the twentieth century. And of these two, nationalism proved to be the
more powerful and enduring.

The terms "nationalist" and "nationalism" appeared only in the late nineteenth   7
century, because "patriot" and "patriotism" already existed, and, at least for a while,
it seemed that these were sufficient. When, a century earlier, Samuel Johnson
uttered his famous dictum that "patriotism is the last refuge of a scoundrel," he
meant nationalism, but that word did not yet exist. These two inclinations, patriotism and nationalism, divergent as they are, still often overlap in people's minds.
(When, for example, Americans criticize a "superpatriot," what they really mean is
an extreme nationalist.)

Patriotism is defensive; nationalism is aggressive. Patriotism is the love of a par-   8
ticular land with its particular traditions; nationalism is the love of something less
tangible, of the myth of a "people," and is often a political and ideological substitute for religion. Patriotism is old-fashioned (and, at times and in some places, aristocratic); nationalism is modern and populist. A patriot is not necessarily a
conservative; he may even be a liberal of sorts. In the twentieth century, a nationalist could hardly be a liberal. Hitler well understood the difference, declaring in
Mein Kampf, "I was a nationalist, and not a patriot."

Obscured though they are by political terminology, nationalism and socialism have   9
indeed dominated American politics too throughout the twentieth century. Except for a few details, America's welfare institutions do not essentially differ from
those of other democratic nations, and, political rhetoric notwithstanding, such
measures are accepted by the great majority of Americans and by both of their
political parties. Meanwhile, the United States has not been immune to the appeal of
nationalism, which is always stronger than that of socialism. While the Republicans
tend to be more nationalist than socialist, the Democrats tend to be more socialist than nationalist. This has been so for at least eighty years. Some time in the future it may change, but not yet. . . .

Group B: Academic Books

from DEMOCRACY IN AMERICA (1835)
Alexis de Tocqueville

In 1831 at the age of 26, Alexis de Tocqueville traveled from France to the United States to survey the American prison system for the French government. The two volumes of Democracy in America *were published in France after his return.*

There exists a love of country that stems primarily from the immediate, disin-   1
terested, and indefinable sentiment that ties a man's heart to the place where he was born. This instinctive love is intimately connected to a liking for ancient customs, respect for elders, and memory of the past. Those who feel it cherish their country as a man might love his ancestral home. They love the tranquillity they enjoy and value the peaceful habits they acquired there. Attached to the memories that the place evokes, they find it pleasant to live there even in obedience. It is not uncommon for such love of country to be further exalted by religious zeal, in which case it can work miracles. It is itself a kind of religion: it does not reason, it believes, it feels, it acts. Some nations in a way personify the fatherland and glimpse its image in the prince. They transfer to his person some of the sentiments that constitute patriotism. They boast of his triumphs and take pride in his power. There was a time under the old monarchy when Frenchmen felt a kind of joy at surrendering utterly to the arbitrary rule of their monarch and were proud to proclaim that "we live under the world's most powerful king."

Like all unreflective passions, such love of country inspires great but transitory ef-   2
forts rather than persistent ones. It is apt to save the state in time of crisis only to allow it to wither in time of peace.

When a people is still simple in its mores and firm in its belief, and society rests   3
tranquilly on an ancient order whose legitimacy is not contested, such instinctive love of country can flourish.

Another, more rational form of patriotism also exists: it is less generous, less ar-   4
dent perhaps, but more fruitful and durable. This second form of patriotism is born of enlightenment. It develops with the aid of laws, grows with the exercise of rights, and eventually comes to be bound up in a way with personal interest. People understand how their country's well-being influences their own. They know that the law allows them to contribute to that well-being, and they take an interest in their country's prosperity, initially as something useful to them but later as their own handiwork.

In the life of a nation, however, there may come a time when ancient customs are   5
transformed, mores decay, faiths are shaken, memories lose their prestige, but enlightenment has yet to complete its work and political rights remain insecure or limited. At such times the only light in which men can see their country is a feeble and dubious one. Patriotic feeling no longer attaches to the soil, which to the people who live on it has become mere inanimate earth; or to ancestral customs, which they have learned to see as confining; or to religion, of which they are skeptical; or

to the laws, which they do not make; or to the lawmaker, whom they fear and despise. Hence they cannot see their country anywhere, in either its proper guise or any other, and they withdraw into narrow, unenlightened selfishness. They have escaped prejudice but not yet embraced the empire of reason. Lacking both the instinctive patriotism of monarchy and the considered patriotism of a republic, they find themselves stuck somewhere between the two, surrounded by confusion and misery.

What to do in such a situation? Retreat. But nations no more revert to the sentiments of their youth than do men to the innocent desires of childhood. Though they may long to feel such feelings again, nothing can revive them. So there is no choice but to proceed forthrightly and with all deliberate speed to make the case that the interests of individuals and of the nation are inextricably intertwined, because disinterested love of country has vanished forever. 6

Far be it from me to suggest that in order to achieve this end, full political rights must immediately be granted to all men. Nevertheless, the most powerful way of persuading men that they have a stake in their country's fate, and perhaps the only way still available to us, is to see to it that they participate in its government. The civic spirit today seems to me intimately intertwined with the exercise of political rights, and I think that from now on the number of citizens in Europe will rise and fall in proportion to the extension of such rights. 7

How is it that in the United States, whose residents, leaving customs and memories behind, came only recently to the land they now inhabit, where they met as strangers for the first time and where, to put it bluntly, it is scarcely possible for a patriotic instinct to exist—how is it that everyone in the United States takes an interest in the affairs of his town, county, and state as though they were his own? The answer is that, within his own sphere, each person takes an active part in the government of society. 8

In the United States, the common man has understood how the general prosperity affects his own happiness—a very simple idea, yet one of which the people in most countries have only a very limited grasp. What is more, he has become accustomed to looking upon that prosperity as his own handiwork. He therefore identifies the public fortune with his own, and he works for the good of the state not only out of duty or pride but, I would almost venture to say, out of greed. 9

There is no need to study American institutions and history to understand the truth of what has just been said; American mores will instruct you sufficiently. Because the American takes part in everything that is done in his country, he believes that he has an interest in defending everything about it that is criticized, for it is not only his country that is attacked but himself. Thus one finds his national pride resorting to every artifice and stooping to every puerile expression of individual vanity. 10

Nothing inhibits ordinary social intercourse more than the irritable patriotism of the American. A foreigner may be prepared to praise a great deal in the United States, but some things he would like to criticize, and this the American absolutely refuses to allow. 11

America is therefore a land of liberty where, in order not to offend anyone, a foreigner must not speak freely about individuals or the state, the people or the government, public or private enterprises, indeed about anything he finds there, except perhaps the climate and soil. In fact, one encounters Americans prepared to defend even the latter two things as though they had had a hand in making them. 12

In these times we must make up our minds and dare to choose between the patriotism of all and the government of a few, for we cannot have both the social strength and vitality that come from the former and the guarantees of tranquillity that the latter occasionally provides. 13

from PATRIOTISM, OR PEACE? (1913)
Leo Tolstoy

Count Leo Tolstoy was a philosopher and social reformer as well as Russia's most distinguished novelist—the author of War and Peace *and* Anna Karenina. *In 1896, Tolstoy wrote "Patriotism, or Peace?" as part of a letter commenting on a clash between the United States and Great Britain over boundaries in Venezuela.*

Often, when one asks children which they choose of two incompatible but eagerly desired things, they will answer, "Both." "Which do you wish—to go for a drive, or to play at home?" "To go for a drive and to play at home." 1

Exactly so with the Christian nations, when life itself puts the question to them, "Which do you choose—patriotism or peace?" They answer, "Patriotism and peace." And yet to combine patriotism and peace is just as impossible as to go for a drive and to stay at home at one and the same time. 2

The other day a conflict arose between the United States and England over the frontier of Venezuela. Salisbury did not agree to something; Cleveland wrote a message to the Senate; patriotic, warlike cries were raised on both sides; a panic occurred on 'Change; people lost millions of pounds and dollars; Edison said he was devising machines to kill more men in an hour than were killed by Attila in all his wars; and both nations began to make energetic preparations for war. 3

But, together with these preparations for war, alike in England and America, various writers, princes, and statesmen began to counsel the governments of both nations to keep from war, insisting that the matter in dispute was not sufficiently serious for war, especially as between two Anglo-Saxon nations, peoples of one language, who ought not to go to war with each other, but ought rather in amity together to domineer over others. Whether because of this, or because all kinds of bishops, clergymen, and ministers prayed and preached over the matter in their churches, or because both sides considered they were not yet ready; for one cause or another, it has turned out there is to be no war this time. And people have calmed down. 4

But one would have too little penetration not to see that the causes which have thus led to dispute between England and the States still remain the same; that if 5 the present difficulty is settled without war, yet, inevitably, to-morrow or next day, disputes must arise between England and the States, between England and Germany, England and Russia, England and Turkey, disputes in all possible combinations. Such arise daily; and one or other of them will surely bring war.

For, if there live side by side two armed men, who have from childhood been   6 taught that power, riches, and glory are the highest goods, and that to obtain these by arms, to the loss of one's neighbors, is a most praiseworthy thing; and if, further, there is for these men no moral, religious, or political bond,—then is it not clear that they will always seek war, that their normal relations will be warlike, and that having once caught each other by the throat, they separate again only, as the French proverb has it, *pour mieux sauter,*—they draw back to take a better spring, to rush upon each other with more ferocity?

The egoism of the individual is terrible. But the egoists of private life are not   7 armed; they do not count it good to prepare, or to use, arms against their competitors; their egoism is controlled by the powers of the state and of public opinion. A private person who should, arm in hand, deprive his neighbor of a cow or an acre of field would be at once seized by the police and imprisoned. Moreover, he would be condemned by public opinion, called a thief and a robber. Quite otherwise with states. All are armed. Influence over them there is none; more than those absurd attempts to catch a bird by sprinkling salt on its tail, such as are the efforts to establish international congresses, which armed states (armed, forsooth, that they may be above taking advice) will clearly never accept. And above all, the public opinion which punishes every violent act of the private individual, praises, exalts as the virtue of patriotism, every appropriation of other people's property made with a view of increasing the power of one's own country.

Open the newspapers on any day you like, and you will always see, every moment,   8 some black spot, a possible cause for war. Now it is Korea; again the Pamirs, Africa, Abyssinia, Armenia, Turkey, Venezuela, or the Transvaal. The work of robbery ceases not for an instant; now here, now there, some small war is going on incessantly, like the exchange of shots in the first line; and a great real war may, must, begin at some moment.

If the American desires the greatness and prosperity of the States before all nations, and the Englishman desires the same for his nation, and the Russian, Turk, Dutchman, Abyssinian, Venezuelan, Boer, Armenian, Pole, Czech, each have a similar desire; if all are convinced that these desires ought not to be concealed and suppressed, but, on the contrary, are something to be proud of, and to be encouraged in oneself and in others; and if one's country's greatness and prosperity can be obtained only at the expense of another, or at times of many other countries and nations,—then how can war not be?

Obviously, to avoid war, it is necessary, not to preach sermons and pray God for   10 peace, not to adjure the English-speaking nations to live in peace together in order to domineer over other nations, not to make double and triple counter-alliances, not to intermarry princes and princesses, but to destroy the root of war. And that is, the exclusive desire for the well-being of one's own people; it is patriotism. Therefore, to destroy war, destroy patriotism. But to destroy patriotism, it is first necessary to produce conviction that it is an evil; and that is difficult to do. Tell people that war is an evil, and they will laugh; for who does not know it? Tell them that patriotism is an evil, and most of them will agree, but with a reservation. "Yes," they will say, "wrong patriotism is an evil; but there is another kind, the kind we hold." But just what this good patriotism is, no one explains. If good patriotism consists in inaggressiveness, as many say, still all patriotism, even if not aggressive, is necessarily retentive; that is, people wish to keep what they have previously conquered. The nation does not exist which was founded without conquest; and conquest can only be retained by the means which achieved it—namely, violence, murder. But if patriotism be not even retentive, it is then the restoring patriotism of conquered and oppressed nations, of Armenians, Poles, Czechs, Irish, and so on. And this patriotism is about the very worst; for it is the most embittered and the most provocative of violence.

Patriotism cannot be good. Why do not people say that egoism may be good? For this might more easily be maintained as to egoism, which is a natural and inborn feeling, than as to patriotism, which is an unnatural feeling, artificially grafted on man. **11**

It will be said, "Patriotism has welded mankind into states, and maintains the unity of states." But men are now united in states; that work is done; why now maintain exclusive devotion to one's own state, when this produces terrible evils for all states and nations? For this same patriotism which welded mankind into states is now destroying those same states. If there were but one patriotism—say of the English only—then it were possible to regard that as conciliatory, or beneficent. But when, as now, there is American patriotism, English, German, French, Russian, all opposed to one another, in this event, patriotism no longer unites, but disunites. To say that patriotism was beneficent, unifying the states, when it flourished in Greece and Rome, and that it is also similarly and equally beneficent now, after eighteen centuries of life under Christianity, is as much as to say that, because plowing was useful and good for the field before the sowing, it is equally so now, when the crop has come up. **12**

It might, indeed, be well to let patriotism survive, in memory of the benefits it once brought, in the way we have preserved ancient monuments, like temples, tombs, and so on. But temples and tombs endure without causing any harm; while patriotism ceases not to inflict incalculable woes. **13**

Why are Armenians and Turks now agitated, being massacred, becoming like wild beasts? Why are England and Russia, each anxious for its own share of the inheritance from Turkey, waiting upon, and not ending, these butcheries of Armenians? Why are Abyssinians and Italians being massacred? Why was a terrible war within an ace of outbreak over Venezuela; and since, another over the Transvaal? And the Chino-Japanese war, the Russo-Turkish, the Franco-German? And the bitterness of conquered nations: Armenians, Poles, Irish? And the preparations for a war of all **14** nations? All this is the fruit of patriotism. Seas of blood have been shed over this passion; and will yet be shed for it, unless people free themselves of this obsolete relic of antiquity.

Several times now I have had occasion to write about patriotism; about its entire incompatibility, not only with the truly understood teaching of Christ, but with the very lowest demands of morality in a Christian society. Each time my arguments have been met either with silence, or with a lofty suggestion that my ideas, as expressed, are Utopian utterances of mysticism, anarchism, and cosmopolitanism. Often my ideas are summed up, and then, instead of counter-arguments, the remark only is added, that "this is nothing less than cosmopolitanism!" As if this word, cosmopolitanism, had indisputably refuted all my arguments.

Men who are serious, mature, clever, kind, and who—this is the most important matter—stand like a city on a mountain top; men who by their example involuntarily lead the masses; such men assume that the legitimacy and beneficence of patriotism are so far evident and certain, that it is not worth while answering the frivolous and foolish attacks on the sacred feeling. And the majority of people, misled from childhood, and infected with patriotism, accept this lofty silence as the most convincing argument; and they continue to walk in the darkness of ignorance.

Those who, from their position, can help to free the masses from their sufferings, and do not do so, commit a vast sin.

The most fearful evil in the world is hypocrisy. Not in vain did Christ, once only, show anger; and that against the hypocrisy of the Pharisees.

But what was the Pharisaic hypocrisy compared with the hypocrisy of our own time? In comparison with our hypocrites, those among the Pharisees were the justest of men; and their art of hypocrisy was child's play, beside ours. It cannot be otherwise. All our lives, with their profession of Christianity, of the doctrine of humility and love, lived in an armed robber camp, cannot be other than one unbroken, frightful hypocrisy. It is very convenient to profess a doctrine which has, at one end, Christian holiness and consequent infallibility, and at the other end, the heathen sword and gallows; so that, when it is possible to deceive and impose by holiness, holiness is brought in play, while, when the deceit fails, the sword and gallows are set to work. Such a doctrine is very convenient. But a time comes when the cobweb of lies gives way, and it is no longer possible to keep up both ends; one or other has to go. This is about to happen with the doctrine of patriotism.

Whether people wish it or do not wish it, the question stands clear to mankind, *How can this patriotism, whence come human sufferings incalculable, sufferings both physical and moral, be necessary, and be a virtue?* This question, of compulsion, must be answered.

It is needful, either to show that patriotism is so beneficent that it redeems all those terrible sufferings which it causes to mankind; or else, to acknowledge that patriotism is an evil, which, instead of being grafted upon and suggested to people, should be struggled against with all one's might, to escape from it.

C'est à prendre ou à laisser, as the French say. If patriotism be good, then Chris-   22
tianity, as giving peace, is an idle dream, and the sooner we root it out, the better. But
if Christianity really gives peace, and if we really want peace, then patriotism is a survival of barbarism, and it is not only wrong to excite and develop it, as we do now,
but it ought to be rooted out by every means, by preaching, persuasion, contempt,
ridicule. If Christianity be truth, and we wish to live in peace, then must we more
than cease to take pleasure in the power of our country; we must rejoice in the
weakening of that power, and help thereto.

A Russian should rejoice if Poland, the Baltic Provinces, Finland, Armenia, should   23
be separated, freed, from Russia; so with an Englishman in regard to Ireland, India, and
other possessions; and each should help to this, because, the greater the state, the
more wrong and cruel is its patriotism, and the greater is the sum of suffering upon
which its power is founded. Therefore, if we really wish to be what we profess to be,
we must not only cease our present desire for the growth of our state, but we
must desire its decrease, its weakening, and help this forward with all our might. And
in this way we must train the rising generation; we must educate them so that, just
as now a young man is ashamed to show his rude egoism by eating everything and
leaving nothing for others, by pushing the weak out of the way that he may pass himself, by forcibly taking that which another needs: so he may then be equally ashamed
of desiring increased power for his own country; and so that, just as it is now considered stupid, foolish, to praise oneself, it shall then be seen to be equally foolish
to praise one's own nation, as it is now done in divers of the best national histories, pictures, monuments, text-books, articles, verses, sermons, and silly national
hymns. It must be understood that, as long as we praise patriotism, and cultivate it
in the young, so long will there be armaments to destroy the physical and spiritual
life of nations; and wars, vast, awful wars, such as we are preparing for, and into the
circle of which we are drawing, debauching them in our patriotism, the new and to
be dreaded combatants of the far East. . . .

CIVILITY AND CIVIC VIRTUE IN CONTEMPORARY AMERICA
from *What It Means to Be an American* (1974)
Michael Walzer

Michael Walzer, a philosopher at the Institute for Advanced Study at Princeton University,
writes about politics and ethics and is particularly well known for his work on just and
unjust wars.

"We have physicists, geometers, chemists, astronomers, poets, musicians,   1
painters," wrote Rousseau in 1750, "we no longer have citizens. . . ."[1] Here in the

[1] Jean-Jacques Rousseau, "Discourse on the Sciences and Arts," In *The First and*
Second Discourses, edited by Roger D. Masters (New York: St. Martin's Press, 1964),
p. 59.

United States we still do have citizens, but it is frequently said of them that their commitment to the political community is less profound than it once was, that there has been a decline of civic virtue and even of ordinary civility, an erosion of the moral and political qualities that make a good citizen. It is hard to know how to judge statements of this kind. They suggest comparisons without specifying any historical reference point. They seem to be prompted by a variety of tendencies and events which are by no means uniform in character or necessarily connected: the extent of draft resistance during the Vietnam War, the domestic violence of the middle and late 1960s, the recent challenges to academic freedom, the new acceptance of pornography, the decline in the fervor with which national holidays are celebrated, and so on.

Perhaps one way of judging these (and other) phenomena is to ask what it is we   2
expect of citizens—of citizens in general but also of American citizens in particular, members of a liberal democracy, each of whom represents, as Rousseau would have said, only 1/200,000,000th of the general will. What do we expect of one another? I am going to suggest a list of common expectations; I shall try to make it an exhaustive list. Working our way through it, we shall see that we are the citizens we ought to be, given the social and political order in which we live. And if critics of our citizenship remain dissatisfied, then it will be time to ask how that order might be changed.

Loyalty, Service, Civility

1. We expect some degree of commitment or loyalty—but to what? Not to   3
la patrie, the fatherland; that concept has never captured the American imagination, probably because so many of us were fathered in other lands. Not to the nation; the appearance of an American nationality was for a long time the goal of our various immigrant absorption systems, but this goal has stood in some tension with the practical (and now with the ideological) pluralism of our society. Most of those who mourn our lost civility would not, I think, be happy with an American nationalism. Not to the state, conceived abstractly, but only to a particular kind of state: our allegiance is to the republic. Now that is a very special kind of commitment, stripped of the mystical connotations of loyalty in Old World countries. We stand, partly by necessity, partly by choice, on narrower ground. Ours is a political allegiance, and our politics is Judaic or puritan in character; it does not lend itself to ritualistic elaboration. Our holidays are occasions for speeches, not for ceremonial communions; our inaugurations are without sacramental significance. We are rightly unwilling to make spectacles of our celebrations, and for that reason it has been virtually impossible to adapt them to the needs of a mass society. There is a certain cynicism today about the symbolic expressions of American loyalty—perhaps because no one can imagine 200,000,000 people celebrating the Fourth of July, simultaneously and together, in some way that isn't repellent to liberal sensi-

bilities. Surely it is a commendable feature of our public life that we do not press the occasion upon our citizens.

Our passivity in this regard probably has something to do with the triumph of sec-   4
ularism in the republic. The content of many American celebrations—Memorial Day and Thanksgiving, for example—is or was markedly religious in character and must lose much of its resonance as religion loses its hold. On the other hand, we have always denied that any particular religious belief or even religious belief in general was necessary in an American citizen. Now that denial is being tested, not as to its justice, but as to its practicality. Understandably, people are worried; for it is often said that loyalty has to be collectively symbolized and acted out if it is to be sustained. The appropriate symbols and actions, however, must grow naturally out of our common life; they cannot be invented, conjured up, pulled out of a politician's hat. If we have not tried to substitute the goddess Reason for the Christian God, as Robespierre tried to do in France, surely that too is to our credit. But the symbols and actions don't grow naturally, and liberal loyalty seems to be sustained in some other way—not through communal celebrations but through private enjoyments, as writers like John Locke undoubtedly intended. One gets a different kind, and perhaps a different degree, of loyalty then, but there is no reason to think that one doesn't get the kind and degree a liberal republic requires.

2. We expect citizens to defend their country, even to risk their lives in its de-   5
fense. In American lore, the minuteman, who rushes to arms when his country is in danger, long ago came to represent the citizen at his best. But it has to be said that this colonial hero and his successors, the militiamen of the nineteenth century, were essentially volunteers who did not always agree with the politicians in the capital or even with their local commanders as to when the country was in danger. They claimed a kind of local option which was for years the despair of American military planners.[2] Nor is it, after all, any sign of civic virtue merely to rush to arms. In August 1914, Austrians and Germans, Frenchmen and Englishmen, flooded the enlistment offices, but we would not want to explain their military enthusiasm by reference to the quality of their citizenship. Indeed, in an earlier America, the readiness of the inhabitants of the Old World to die at the behest of their states and sovereigns would more likely have been understood as a sign of the poverty of their lives and their lack of moral independence. The same attitude explains the old American hatred of conscription. It was thought an infringement of individual liberty and a sure sign of tyrannical government when family and home were invaded and young men dragged off to war. When James Monroe, then Secretary of War, first proposed a draft in 1814, Daniel Webster assured him that the country would not stand for it:

[2] See Marcus Cunliffe, *Soldiers and Civilians: The Martial Spirit in America, 1775–1865* (Boston: Little, Brown, 1968), especially chaps. 6 and 7.

In my opinion, Sir, the sentiments of the free population of this country are greatly mistaken here. The nation is not yet in a temper to submit to conscription. The people have too fresh and strong a feeling of the blessings of civil liberty to be willing thus to surrender to it. . . . Laws, Sir, of this nature can create nothing but opposition. A military force cannot be raised, in this manner, but by the means of a military force. If the administration has found that it cannot form an army without conscription, it will find, if it ventures on these experiments, that it cannot enforce conscription without an army.[3]

We have come a long way since those days, a way marked as much by changes   6 in the external world as in our domestic society. The domestic changes have been made only gradually and, as Webster predicted, in the face of constant opposition. It is worth remembering how recent a creation the docile draftee is before we mourn his disappearance (has he disappeared?) as a loss of American virtue. In 1863, the first conscription law was fiercely resisted—over one thousand people died in the New York draft riot of that year—and it was massively evaded during the remainder of the Civil War. The draft was still being evaded on a large scale in World War I, particularly in rural areas where it was easy to hide. And who can say that the young men who took to the woods in 1917 were not reaffirming the values of an earlier America? They would have grabbed their rifles readily enough had the Boche marched into Kentucky. Perhaps that is the only true test of their citizenship.

The citizen-soldier defends his hearth and home, and he also defends the politi-   7 cal community within which the enjoyment of hearth and home is made possible. His fervor is heightened when that community is in danger. Armies of citizens, like those of Rome or the first French Republic or Israel today, are born in moments of extreme peril. Once the peril abates, the fervor declines. The armies of great powers must be sustained on a different basis, and the long-term considerations that lead them to fight here or there, in other people's countries, when there is no immediate or visible threat to their own, can hardly be expected to evoke among their citizens a passionate sense of duty. Perhaps these dozens have an obligation to fight, in obedience, say, to laws democratically enacted, but this is not the same obligation that American publicists meant to stress when they made the minuteman a mythic figure. It has more to do with law-abidance than with civic courage or dedication.

3. We expect citizens to obey the law and to maintain a certain decorum of be-   8 havior—a decorum that is commonly called civility. That word once had to do more directly with the political virtues of citizenship: one of its obsolescent meanings is "civil righteousness." But it has come increasingly to denote only social virtues; orderliness, politeness, seemliness are the synonyms the dictionary suggests, and these terms, though it is no doubt desirable that they describe our public life,

[3] Speech in the House of Representatives, December 9, 1814, reprinted in Lillian Schlissel, ed., *Conscience in America* (New York: E. P. Dutton, 1968), pp. 70–71.

orient us quite decisively toward the private realm. Perhaps this shift in meaning is a sign of our declining dedication to republican values, but it actually occurred some time ago and does not reflect on ourselves and our contemporaries. For some time, we have thought that *good behavior* is what we could rightly expect from a citizen, and the crucial form of good behavior is everyday law-abidance. Has this expectation been disappointed? Certainly many people write as if it has been. I am inclined to think them wrong, though not for reasons that have much to do with republican citizenship.

If we could measure the rate and intensity of obedience to law—not merely the nonviolation of the penal code, but the interest, the concern, the anxiety with which citizens *aim* at obedience—I am certain we would chart a fairly steady upward movement in every modernizing country, at least after the initial crisis of modernization is past. Contemporary societies require and sustain a very intense form of social discipline, and this discipline is probably more pervasive and more successfully internalized than was that of peasant societies or of small towns and villages. We have only to think about our own lives to realize the extent of our submission to what Max Weber called "rational-legal authority." It is reflected in our time sense, our ability to work hard and methodically, our acceptance of bureaucratic hierarchies, our habitual orientation to rules and regulations. Consider, for example, the simple but surprising fact that each of us will, before April 15, carefully fill out a government form detailing our incomes and calculating the tax we owe the United States—which we will then promptly pay. The medieval tithe, if it was ever a realistic tax, was socially enforced; our own tax is individually enforced. We ourselves are the calculators and the collectors; the tax system could not succeed without our conscientiousness. Surely the American income tax is a triumph of civilization. There are very few political orders within which one can imagine such a system working; I doubt that it would have worked, for example, in Tocqueville's America.

But I want to turn to two other examples of our relative civility which speak more directly to the concerns of our recent past, which have to do, that is, with violence. In 1901, David Brewer, an associate justice of the U.S. Supreme Court, delivered a series of lectures on American citizenship at Yale University, in the course of which he worried at some length about the prevalence of vigilante justice and lynch law.[4] This was the peculiarly American way of "not tarrying for the magistrate." "It may almost be regarded," Brewer said, "as a habit of the American people." Clearly, our habits have changed; in this respect, at least, we have grown more law-abiding since the turn of the century. The police sometimes take the law into their own hands, but they are our only vigilantes; ordinary citizens rarely act in the old American way. This is not the result of a more highly developed civic

9

10

---

[4]David Brewer, *American Citizenship* (New York: C. Scribner's Sons, 1902), pp. 102 ff. From the same period, see also James E. Cutler, *Lynch-Law: An Investigation into the History of Lynching in the United States* (New York: Longmans, Green, 1905).

consciousness, but it is a matter of improved social discipline, and it also suggests that, despite our popular culture, we are less ready for violence, less accustomed to violence, than were earlier generations of American citizens.

We are also less given to riot; if nineteenth-century statistics are at all reliable, our   11
mobs are less dangerous to human life. The most striking thing about the urban riots of the 1960s, apart from the surprise that greeted them, for which our history offers no justification, is the relatively small number of people who were actually killed in their course. By all accounts, riots were once much bloodier: I have already mentioned New York's "bloody week" of 1863. They also seem to have been more exuberantly tumultuous, and the tumult more accepted in the life of the time. Here, for example, are a set of newspaper headlines from New York in 1834:[5]

A Bloody Fight
Mayor and Officers Wounded
Mob Triumphant
The Streets Blocked by Fifteen Thousand Enraged Whigs
Military Called Out

These lines describe an election riot, not uncommon in an age when party loyalties were considerably more intense than they are now and a far higher proportion of the eligible voters were likely to turn out on election day. The accompanying news story does not suggest that the rioters or their leaders were extremists or revolutionaries. They apparently were ordinary citizens. Our own riots are also the work of ordinary citizens, but not of the contemporary equivalents of Whigs, Orangemen, or even Know-Nothings. Riots today seem to be peculiarly disorganized, each of them less a communal event than a series of simultaneous acts of individual desperation. They are more frightening than the earlier riots and also less dangerous. Perhaps this change is appropriate to a liberal society: if civility is privatized, then so must incivility be. Crime in contemporary America is something like a diffused, disintegrated riot.

This last example suggests a certain tension between civility and republican citi-   12
zenship. Indeed, in the early modern period, one of the chief arguments against republicanism was that it made for disorder and tumult. Faction fights, party intrigue, street wars; instability and sedition: these were the natural forms of political life in what Thomas Hobbes called "the Greek and Roman anarchies," and so it would be, he argued, in any similar regime.[6] He may have been right, in some limited sense at least. The improvement in social discipline seems to have been accompanied by a decline in political passion, in that lively sense of public involvement that presumably characterized the enraged Whigs of 1834 and other early Americans. I shall

[5] Quoted in Cunliffe, *Soldiers and Civilians*, p. 93.
[6] *De Cive*, XII 3.

have more to say about this when I turn to the general issue of political participation. But first it is necessary to take up another aspect of our new civility.

Tolerance, Participation

4. We expect citizens to be tolerant of one another. This is probably as close as we can come to that "friendship" which Aristotle thought should characterize relations among members of the same political community. For friendship is only possible within a relatively small and homogeneous city, but toleration reaches out infinitely. Once certain barriers of feeling and belief have been broken down, it is as easy to tolerate five million people as to tolerate five. Hence toleration is a crucial form of civility in all modern societies and especially in our own. But it is not easily achieved. Much of the violence of American history has been the work of men and women resisting its advance in the name of one or another form of local and particularized friendship or in the name of those systems of hierarchy and segregation that served in the past to make pluralism possible. It's probably fair to say that resistance has grown weaker in recent years; the United States is a more tolerant society today than at any earlier period of its history. Of course, we need to be more tolerant; it's as if, once we commit ourselves to toleration, the demand for it escalates; it is no longer a question of a recognized range of religious and political dissidence, but of the margins beyond the range. Even the margins are safer today; more people live there and with less fear of public harassment and social pressure. It is precisely these people, however, who seem to pose a problem for us, who lead us to worry about the future of civic virtue. A curious and revealing fact, for their very existence is a sign of our civility.

The problem is that many Americans who find it easy (more or less) to tolerate racial and religious and even political differences find it very hard to tolerate sexual deviance and countercultural lifestyles. One day, perhaps, this difficulty will be remembered only as a passing moment in the painful development of an open society. But it doesn't feel that way now; it feels much more drastic, so that intelligent people talk of the end of civilization, all coherence gone, the fulfillment of this or that modernist nightmare. For surely (they say) political society requires and rests upon *some* shared values, a certain spiritual cohesion, however limited in character. And a commitment to moral laissez-faire does not provide any cohesion at all. It undermines the very basis of a common life, because the ethic of toleration leads us to make our peace with every refusal of commonality. So we drift apart, losing through our very acceptance of one another's differences all sense of kinship and solidarity.

This is undoubtedly overstated, for the fact is that we do coexist, not only Protestants, Catholics, and Jews; blacks and whites; but also Seventh Day Adventists, Buddhists, and Black Muslims; Birchers and Trotskyites; sexual sectarians of every sort, homo and hetero. Nor is it a small thing that we have made our peace with all these, for the only alternative, if history has any lessons at all, is cruelty and

13

14

15

repression. Liberalism may widen our differences as it widens the range of permissible difference, but it also generates a pattern of accommodation that we ought to value. It would be foolish to value it, however, without noticing that, like other forms of civility, this pattern of accommodation is antithetical to political activism. It tends to insulate politics from group conflict, to promote among citizens a general indifference toward the opinions of their fellows, to freeze the intolerant out of public life (they are disproportionately represented, for example, among nonvoters). It stands in the way of the personal transformations and new commitments that might grow out of a more open pattern of strife and contention. It makes for political peace; it makes politics less dangerous and less interesting. And yet our notions about citizenship lead us to demand precisely that citizens *be interested* in politics.

5. We expect citizens to participate actively in political life. Republicanism is a 16 form of collective self-government, and its success requires, at the very least, that large numbers of citizens vote and that smaller numbers join in parties and movements, in meetings and demonstrations. No doubt, such activity is in part self-regarding, but any stable commitment probably has to be based and is in fact usually based on some notion of the public good. It is, then, virtuous activity; interest in public issues and devotion to public causes are the key signs of civic virtue.

Voting is the minimal form of virtuous conduct, but it is also the easiest to mea- 17 sure, and if we take it as a useful index, we can be quite precise in talking about the character of our citizenship. Participation in elections, as Walter Dean Burnham has shown, was very high in the nineteenth century, not only in presidential contests, but also in off-year congressional and even in local elections.[7] Something like four-fifths of the eligible voters commonly went to the polls. "The nineteenth century American political system," writes Burnham, ". . . was incomparably the most thoroughly democratized of any in the world." A sharp decline began around 1896 and continued through the 1920s, when the number of eligible voters actually voting fell to around two-fifths. Rates of participation rose in the 1930s, leveled off, rose again in the 1950s, leveled off again—without coming close to the earlier figures. Today, the percentage of American citizens who are consistent nonparticipants is about twice what it was in the 1890s. By this measure, then, we are less virtuous than were nineteenth-century Americans, less committed to the public business.

The reasons for this decline are not easy to sort out. Burnham suggests that it 18 may have something to do with the final consolidation of power by the new industrial elites. The triumph of corporate bureaucracy was hardly conducive to a participatory politics among members of the new working class or among those farmers who had been the backbone of the Populist movement. Some workers turned to socialism (Debs got a million votes in 1912), but far more dropped out of the political system altogether. They became habitual nonvoters, at least until

[7] Walter Dean Burnham, "The Changing Shape of the American Political Universe," *The American Political Science Review*, LIX (March 1965), 7–28.

the CIO brought many of the men and women it organized back into electoral politics in the 1930s. If this account is right—and other accounts are possible—then nonvoting can be seen as a rational response to certain sorts of social change. No doubt it was also functional to the social system as a whole. The decline in participation during a period of increasing heterogeneity and rapid urbanization probably helped stabilize the emerging patterns of law-abidance and toleration. Certainly American society would have been far more turbulent than it was had new immigrants, urban dwellers, and industrial workers been actively involved in politics. That is not to argue that they shouldn't have been involved, only that people who set a high value on civility shouldn't complain about their lack of civic virtue.

A recent study of political acts more "difficult" than voting—giving money, attending meetings, joining organizations—suggests that there was a considerable increase in participation in the course of the 1960s.[8] Not surprisingly, this increase coincided with a period of turmoil and dissension of which it was probably both cause and effect. One might impartially have watched the events of that time and worried about the loss of civility and rejoiced in the resurgence of civic virtue. The connection between the two is clear enough: people are mobilized for political action, led to commit themselves and to make the sacrifices and take the risks commitment requires, only when significant public issues are seized upon by the agitators and organizers of movements and parties and made the occasion for exciting confrontations. These need not be violent confrontations; violence draws spectators more readily than participants. But if the issues are significant, if the conflict is serious, violence always remains a possibility. The only way to avoid the possibility is to avoid significant issues or to make it clear that the democratic political struggle is a charade whose outcome won't affect the resolution of the issues—and then rates of participation will quickly drop off. 19

The civil rights and antiwar agitations of the 1960s demonstrate that there are still dedicated citizens in the United States. But the activity generated by those movements turned out to be evanescent, leaving behind no organizational residue, no basis for an ongoing participatory politics. Perhaps that is because not enough people committed themselves. The national mood, if one focuses on the silence of the silent majority, is tolerant and passive—in much the same way as it was tolerant and passive in the face of prohibitionists or suffragettes or even socialists and communists in the 1930s: that is, there is no demand for massive repression and there is no major upsurge in political involvement. It is also important, I think, that the two movements of the sixties did not link up in any stable way with either of the established parties. Instead of strengthening party loyalty, they may well have contributed to a further erosion. If that is so, even rates of electoral participation will probably fall in the coming years, for parties are the crucial media of political 20

[8] Sidney Verba and Norman H. Nie, *Participation in America: Political Democracy and Social Equality* (New York: Harper & Row, 1972), especially chap. 14.

activism. These two failures—to mobilize mass support, to connect with the established parties—may well suggest the general pattern of political life in America today. For most of our citizens, politics is no vocation. They think it a duty to vote, but they have no deep commitment to a creed or party, and only about half of them bother to vote. Beyond that, they are wrapped up in their private affairs and committed to the orderliness and proprieties of the private realm. Though they are tolerant, up to a point, of political activists, they regard politics as an intrusion and they easily resist the temptations of the arena. This makes life hard for the smaller number of citizens who are intermittently moved by some public issue and who seek to move their fellows. It may help explain the frenetic quality of their zeal and the way some of them drift, in extreme cases, into depression and madness. The institutional structures and the mass commitment necessary to sustain civic virtue simply don't exist in contemporary America.

URBAN CIVILIZATION AND ITS DISCONTENTS
from *Reflections of a Neoconservative* (1983)
Irving Kristol

An elder statesman of neoconservatism in America, Irving Kristol was the founding editor of the Public Interest, *a journal of social and cultural comment, and is presently a senior fellow of the American Enterprise Institute.*

The founding fathers saw democracy in America as resting upon two major   1
pillars. The first, whose principles and rationale are so superbly set forth in *The Federalist Papers*, was the "new science of government" which made popular government possible in a large and heterogeneous republic. This new science designed a machinery of self-government that has to be considered as one of the most remarkable political inventions of Western man. The machinery is by now familiar to us; representative and limited government, separation of powers; majority rule but refined so that it had to express the will of various majorities elected in various ways; a diffusion of political and economic power which would thwart the intentions of any single-minded faction no matter how large and influential, and so on and so forth. The basic idea behind all these arrangements was that the pursuit of self-interest was the most reliable of human motivations on which to build a political system—but this pursuit had to be, to use one of their favorite phrases, the pursuit of self-interest "rightly understood," and such right understanding needed the benevolent, corrective checks and balances of the new political machinery to achieve decent self-definition—that is, to converge at a point of commonweal.

The second pillar envisaged by the founding fathers was of a spiritual order—   2
and the fact that most of us today prefer to call it "psychological" rather than spir-

itual would have been taken by them as itself a clear sign of urban decadence. To designate this pillar they used such phrases as "republican morality" or "civic virtue," but what they had constantly in mind was the willingness of the good democratic citizen, on critical occasions, to transcend the habitual pursuit of self-interest and devote himself directly and disinterestedly to the common good. In times of war, of course, republican morality took the form of patriotism—no one, after all, has ever been able to demonstrate that it is to a man's self-interest to die for his country. In times of peace, republican morality might take the form of agreeing to hold public office; since the founding fathers assumed that the holders of such office would be men of property, to whom the pleasures of private life were readily available, and since they further thought of political ambition as a form of human distemper, they could candidly look upon public service as a burden as well as an honor. But whatever the occasion, such a capacity for disinterested action seemed to them—as even today, it still seems to some—a necessary complement to the pursuit of self-interest rightly understood.

from HONOR, PATRIOTISM, AND ULTIMATE LOYALTY (1986)

Sidney Axinn

Sidney Axinn, an emeritus faculty member at Temple University, is a social and political philosopher who has written extensively about the philosopher Kant and whose current interest is military ethics.

This passage is excerpted from a longer essay. At this point, Axinn is asking whether military honor and loyalty to one's country justify the use of nuclear weapons in war. He has concluded that it is wrong for civilized nations to use nuclear weapons even when they have been attacked because civilians as well as combatants would be destroyed and because the devastation might deter rather than encourage an early surrender: "The heroes at Hiroshima were not Americans."

Patriotism and Morality

The issues involved in nuclear war can be put in terms of a moral antinomy. An antinomy is a pair of statements that assert *opposite* positions, but positions such that *each* is attractive or impressive. By clearly distinguishing between a particular thesis and its opposite (or antithesis), and considering the advantages and disadvantages of each, it is sometimes possible to gain considerable clarity about a problem. In our case, we shall examine the antinomy between those who take patriotism to be the ultimate loyalty, and those for whom morality is more important.

The four terms "honor," "morality," "loyalty," and "patriotism" need to be reviewed before we look at the antinomy. Following the Kantian tradition, I have taken *morality* to mean treating everyone by the same set of rules. (I ignore, in this context, serious distinctions such as between intention and consequence, individual and group, etc.) *Honor* refers to the faithfulness with which one keeps promises and carries out duties, regardless of personal cost. For *military honor*, the promise and the duty are to act without violating the laws of warfare. Since the laws of warfare require that the *same set of rules* holds for all sides in a conflict, military honor is a special case of morality—the moral demand is that the same set of rules bind everyone. In sum, obedience to military honor is always moral, but all cases of moral behavior need not be military.

By *loyalty* one refers to a relationship between an individual and a beneficiary, such that the individual is willing to sacrifice at least something for the sake of the beneficiary. Varieties and degrees of loyalty may be distinguished in terms of the extent of the sacrifices and the goals of the beneficiary for whom they are made. For present purposes, we can specify fanatical loyalty as the case in which an individual is willing to sacrifice *anything* for any goal of the beneficiary. By "ultimate loyalty," we shall mean loyalty to the one most important beneficiary in someone's life. Patriotism, of course, means loyalty to one's nation. The variety and strength of the loyalty can vary.[12]

> THESIS: The moral response requires the sacrifice of anything needed to defend the interests of one's ultimate loyalty, one's nation.
>
> ANTITHESIS: The moral response requires that some things never be sacrificed, regardless of the goal at stake.

Observations on the Thesis

To be without loyalty is apparently to be without honor. Since honor involves holding to one's commitments, there must be commitments or there is nothing to honor. In this sense, "loyalty" and "commitment" are synonyms. The ordinary image of loyalty is the case in which two friends are walking together. If one is attacked by bullies, the other is expected to come to his or her aid. To run off rather than sacrifice one's safety is to show that friendship, or that particular friendship, is not a serious loyalty. Most of the world's friendships are probably based on something less than the principle of "I would die for you." Loyalty can be measured by the degree of sacrifice that it is worth. There is an obvious difference between a casual acquaintance and someone who is willing to get his hands dirty to help a friend.

Two questions arise on the relationship between loyalty and patriotism. Are there limits to the sacrifice that is morally required to protect one's basic loyalties? And, second, is the nation a morally proper object of loyalty? The position of the thesis, above, is that moral value requires an absolutely basic and supreme loyalty. With no such absolute in one's life, all is reduced to the petty play of selfishness. We can understand selfishness, but we give it no honor. On this view morality means the willingness to sacrifice, and serious morality means the willingness to sacrifice

3

4

5

anything for the sake of one's ultimate loyalty. We might call this position *moral monism*, from my viewpoint an unfortunate vestige of monotheism.[13]

Even if one accepted moral monism, the thesis forces consideration of a second question: what can stand as an ultimate attachment, an absolute loyalty? Historically, people have taken their basic loyalties to be their families, lovers, religious leaders, god or gods, king or fatherland and, recently, their political form of government. The term "nation" sometimes includes both the sense of one's countryland and also its political structure. (When a choice must be made between the land and the form of government, loyalties become sharpened, e.g., when a country is invaded but escape is possible.) (I have not included the ultimate attachment, to oneself, because it is considered to be opportunism, and usually [?] denied the moral vocabulary.) The debate over nuclear warfare can ignore most of the list of possible and actual loyalties and come down to the choice between one's nation and mankind.

6

The question becomes whether any single nation is worth the sacrifice of not merely one's own life, but of a significant part of mankind. To place such ultimate value on a nation is to hold the position that must be called the religion of nationalism, which is a variety of religious fanaticism. Let us consider the historical situation in which atomic bombs were used to protect our nation. Suppose that we had not used atomic bombs on Hiroshima and Nagasaki, and instead had negotiated a surrender of our country to the Japanese. First, a great many human beings would not have been killed in those two cities. And now, almost 40 years later, what would be the difference? Perhaps we would be selling our cars, cameras, and TV sets to the Japanese! If, instead of their surrender to us, we had surrendered to the Japanese emperor, we might have negotiated for many of the same changes in the Japanese government. Perhaps their renunciation of war might not have been made part of their constitution, and we would now not be embarrassed by the effort to persuade them to add their own military efforts to ours in the Pacific area (pacific?).

7

If one looks at a nation 20 or 30 years after a war, it is not always easy to understand whether it won or lost that war. The point is that whatever the characteristics of a nation, perhaps characteristics so morally sublime that they are worth making the nation an ultimate loyalty, time and the war itself will make changes in that nation. These changes may be so large as to alter the basis for bestowing one's highest loyalty. Of course, these observations are based on the history of essentially pre-nuclear wars. With atomic and nuclear bombs, the changes in any nation that remains after such a war must be enormous. Whatever the original foundation of loyalty, and however profound the basis for patriotism before a nuclear war, the entity that remains after such a war might be so dramatically different that one's prewar love for his country might change to post-war hate.

8

Suppose that one contemplates a sacrifice of many human lives, but a sacrifice that results in preserving the patterns of government, the political, economic, and social structures that now exist. Would a sacrifice for that goal, maintaining exactly

9

what we now have, be morally defensible? The very question seems empty and frivolous, because as soon as we frame it we realize that all of our structures undergo change. The serious question therefore becomes whether we are willing to sacrifice for one prospect of future change or another such prospect. Suppose we have a fantastic loyalty toward the U.S. Constitution. We understand that it has been and will be subject to amendments, but we would rather die than live under a different constitution. How different? Ours changes through different interpretations of the courts and administrative bodies, plus the differences made by repealing amendments and adding new ones. While it takes an expert constitutional lawyer to understand and predict the present and future applications of the constitution, we hope that all citizens understand certain broad features of our basic document. Our military, on induction, swear to uphold the constitution, and we hope that they have some understanding of what this means (we are either too confident or too worried to test that assumption). We avoid certain problems by ignoring the constitution in the further developments of military life after that moment during induction, at least in the military life of enlisted men.

My point in these considerations is that the nation is not a clear and acceptable   10
moral absolute. *We can't accept the thesis*, the assertion that the nation is to be an absolute loyalty for us. That position is a romantic hangover from the image of a good slave or servant; it is undignified for a mature stage of mankind's history.

Observations on the Antithesis

According to the antithesis, morality must never be sacrificed. Morality means   11
treating everyone by the same set of rules. (While the conception of morality has had many other interpretations, I shall assume that Kant was right about his analysis of the common and essential core of the idea.)

Since our antinomy is concerned with "the moral response," the choice between   12
thesis and antithesis is a decision on what is to be taken as morality. For the thesis, morality may require that the same set of rules apply to all members of one's own nation, but not to citizens of other or "enemy" nations. For the antithesis, morality requires that at least some of the rules apply to all humans, regardless of citizenship. Further, the thesis may countenance different rules within the citizenship of the nation if that is needed for national defense (for example, lying to fellow citizens, unequal sacrifices by them, etc.). In order to hold to the thesis without embarrassment, nations at war regularly describe the enemy as less than human. If only "we" are fully human, then the antithesis may be empty and ignored. After a war nations rediscover the fact that the enemy is also human. I take this pattern to be consistent with the viewpoint above, the view that the thesis is not a morally acceptable choice.

The War Conventions are taken to express the boundaries of military honor,   13
and they do so because they are a set of rules that apply equally to all parties. Military honor requires, on paper, an impressive level of honesty toward the enemy. I

offer two examples from our FM 27-10, the specifications of "Good Faith," and of "Parole." After the Hague article 24 on permissible ruses of war, our Field Manual adds, "Absolute good faith with the enemy must be observed as a rule of conduct." This is followed by a long list of legitimate ways of

> mystifying or misleading the enemy against which the enemy ought to take measures to protect himself. It would [however] be an improper practice to secure an advantage of the enemy by deliberate lying or misleading conduct which involves a breach of faith, or when there is a moral obligation to speak the truth. For example, it is improper to feign surrender so as to secure an advantage . . . to broadcast to the enemy that an armistice had been agreed upon when such is not the case would be treacherous [p. 22].

The matter of parole is similar. U.S. military personnel are forbidden to give parole (their word that they will not escape), except for temporary purposes. If they do so, they are bound by the Geneva POW Convention "on their personal honour scrupulously to fulfill, both towards the Power on which they depend and towards the Power which has captured them, the engagements of their paroles or promises (p. 72). Conclusion: the accepted demands of military honor require that we choose the antithesis. Morality insists that some rules apply to everyone, enemy or not.

Consequences of the Antinomy

Given the above viewpoint on morality, can conventional warfare be waged morally? If it is fought under the restrictions of the Geneva and Hague Conventions, conventions that apply equally to everyone, it can be carried on with honor. Honor, again, is the consistent commitment to agreed upon rules that hold for all. The urgent question since Hiroshima is the status of atomic and nuclear warfare. Such warfare violates the essentials of the "laws of warfare."   14

Four of the elements of war with honor are each at risk or obviously violated by nuclear weapons. First, the distinction between combatant and noncombatant is eliminated. Second, the distinction between belligerent and nonbelligerent nation is eliminated, since fall-out cannot be controlled. Third, the restriction on unnecessary suffering is eliminated. Fourth, the restriction on hostages is ignored, since cities become hostages. Conclusion: nuclear warfare violates the minimum demands of military honor.   15

[12] These varieties of loyalty are developed further in Axinn, "Loyalty and Ultimate Commitments," a paper delivered at the May 1983 A.P.A. meeting in Chicago.

[13] I argue that such monism is a variety of fanaticism, in "Ambivalence: Kant's View of Human Nature," *Kantstudien*, No. 2 (1981), pp. 169–74.

MILITARY SERVICE AND UNJUST WARS
from *Patriotism, Morality, and Peace* (1993)
Stephen Nathanson

Stephen Nathanson, who teaches philosophy at Northeastern University, has specialized in the ethical aspects of legal and political issues.

Throughout Patriotism, Morality, and Peace, *Nathanson attempts to describe "a moderate form of patriotism that allows some citizens to defend their country and some to choose not to." In this chapter, Nathanson is extending his earlier point that "willingness to fight in a war must be conditional on a judgment that the war itself is morally justified."*

There are four types of views about the morality of war. One view, sometimes called "realism" or "realpolitik," is the idea that war is an amoral activity, something that nations do but that is beyond the scope of moral evaluation. Wars happen just as earthquakes and tidal waves happen, but, like these natural disasters, war cannot be judged from a moral perspective. Despite its apparent callousness, this approach often strikes people as sophisticated and realistic. It makes the moral judgment of war appear to be naive and inappropriate.

Whatever its initial appeal, this is not a plausible view. First, it ignores the crucial element of human decision, which is central to war but absent from natural disasters. Second, it is not a view that national leaders could express publicly. They work hard to cloak their activities in moral terms. Even if this is done cynically, it is evidence of the force of moral reasons in generating public support for war. Moral reasons have political force. Third, "realpolitik" makes no sense for citizens who are called to risk their lives for their country. They must have reason to believe that what they are doing is morally worthy. Classifying war as amoral would, in effect, deprive it of the justifications it needs to mobilize people's support. The attempt of the "realist" to denigrate the role of moral evaluation in this area is itself naive and unrealistic. It overlooks the fact that if enough people think a war is not worthwhile, then leaders will have a difficult time actually engaging in war.[8]

Among views that actually evaluate war morally, there are three possible approaches. The extreme militarist view is that war is always morally good. The extreme pacifist view is that war is always immoral. Neither of these views is widely held. Most people believe that war is sometimes justified, but they see it as a regrettable activity that is only justified by some form of necessity. Since absolute pacifism and extreme militarism are very much minority opinions, I shall not deal with them here and will focus on what I take to be the dominant view about the morality of war.[9]

The dominant moral view is that war should be neither totally approved nor totally condemned. According to this view, while war is a terrible activity, it may be morally permissible and even morally obligatory under very restricted conditions. This view is elaborated in the so-called "just war theory," which is an attempt to articulate the criteria by which wars may be evaluated.

There are two parts of just war theory, the *jus ad bellum* and the *jus in bello*. The jus ad bellum criteria set the standards that must be met to justify entry into a war, while the *jus in bello* criteria set the standards that govern the actual means of fighting of a war. A fully just war is one that is entered into under the right conditions and fought in the right way.

The following summary oversimplifies these requirements, but it will be sufficient for this discussion. According to the *jus ad bellum* criteria, one may engage in war if, first, one has a just cause, a serious enough, morally acceptable reason for doing so. Wars of aggression do not satisfy this requirement, while wars of self-defense do. Second, the war must be declared by a legitimate authority. Third, one must have the right intentions; that is, one must actually be motivated by such things as the desire to defend oneself or resist aggression. One cannot merely use these reasons as a cover for actions that have other aims. Fourth, entry into war must be a last resort. If there are other, peaceful ways of resolving a conflict, they must be tried first. War is justifiable only if all other options have been exhausted. Fifth, one must have a good chance of success. Finally, war must be a proportionate response. It would not be appropriate to go to war if the evil that the war will cause will be much greater than the evil that is being resisted.

These are the conditions that must be met to justify entry into a war. They are not the only conditions that need to be met, however. A country that has good grounds to enter a war may nonetheless act wrongly if it conducts the war in immoral ways. Even if one's cause is just, one's fighting may be immoral if it violates *jus in bello* (justice *in* war) constraints. In particular, while fighting a war, one must be discriminate, seeking only to kill and injure enemy soldiers and avoiding the intentional killing of civilians who are uninvolved in the fighting. Likewise, disabled soldiers and those that surrender must be well treated. Finally, the damage that one does in individual battles must be proportionate to the military value of winning that particular battle.[10]

This is not the place to elaborate or defend these requirements, but it is worth noting that they are widely accepted and are grounded in both ethical and religious beliefs, in military codes and traditions, and in international law. Even when political and military leaders feel free to violate them, they nonetheless pay "lip service" to these criteria and actively misrepresent facts to make it appear that they are adhering to them.[11]

Just War and Individual Responsibility

The just war criteria appear to have the form of necessary and sufficient conditions for engaging in war morally. That is, in order to fight a just war, one must satisfy both the *ad bellum* conditions for justified entry into a war and the *in bello* conditions for justified means of fighting. Failure to meet either test renders the war unjust.

What does this view imply for individual citizens who might be called to fight   10
for their country? The most natural application of just war theory to individuals
implies that individuals may only fight in a just war, a war that satisfies both the *ad
bellum* and the *in bello* criteria. If a person's country enters a war unjustly or if, in
the course of the war, immoral forms of fighting will be required, then morality
does not permit participation in that war. Moreover, given the seriousness of the
moral violations involved in immoral killing and injuring, it would be a person's moral
duty to refuse military service. From this perspective, unconditional willingness to
fight on one's country's behalf violates the moral duty individuals have to refrain
from morally unjustified acts of killing and injuring.

While I find this the most natural way to understand the implications of the just   11
war tradition for individual citizens, my interpretation differs from that of Michael
Walzer, whose book *Just and Unjust Wars* contains an influential contemporary statement of just war thinking. Walzer appears to hold that the morality of a person's
participation in a war is independent of the morality of the war itself. Moreover,
he bases this view on his own interpretation of the just war criteria. If he is correct, unconditional willingness to fight for one's country is morally permissible and
is sanctioned by just war theory itself. His argument, then, represents a serious challenge to my view that such participation is wrong and that willingness to serve in
war should be conditional on the war's being just.

Walzer's view is that individuals are responsible only for the morality of their own   12
actions in a war and not for the overall morality of the war itself. He writes:

> We draw a line between the war itself, for which soldiers are not responsible,
> and the conduct of the war, for which they are responsible, at least within their
> own sphere of activity. . . . [B]y and large we don't blame a soldier . . . who fights
> for his own government. . . . We allow him to say what an English soldier says
> in Shakespeare's *Henry V*: "We know enough if we know we are the king's men.
> Our obedience to the king wipes the crime out of us.". . . Not that his obedi-
> ence can never be criminal; for when he violates the rules of war [i.e., the *in bello*
> criteria], superior orders is no defense. The atrocities that he commits are his
> own; the war is not.[12]

In this and other passages, Walzer suggests that it is morally right for individual
citizens to fight for their country even if it is engaged in an unjust war. In order to
act morally, they need only avoid violations of the rules of war, the *in bello* criteria.
They are not responsible for whether the war satisfies the *ad bellum* criteria.

I believe that this view is too permissive. By sanctioning participation in unjust   13
wars, it frees individuals from the duty to consider the morality of a war before
supporting it by acts of killing and injuring. It is, in fact, a version of the view expressed
by the slogan "My country, right or wrong," since it implies that whether one's country's cause is just or unjust is irrelevant to whether one ought to fight for it.

To anyone familiar with Walzer's writings, it will seem odd to attribute any version 14 of this hyper-patriotic slogan to him. It is especially odd because later in his book Walzer explicitly says that citizens "cannot avoid" the pressing questions "should we support this war? should we fight in it?" (64).[13] Nonetheless, in the passage I have quoted, Walzer emphasizes the distinction between the two sets of just war criteria and claims that individual soldiers are responsible only for their own compliance with *jus in bello* rules and not for the war as a whole. For him, the *ad bellum* and *in bello* criteria represent a moral division of labor. The responsibility for judging the war as a whole belongs to political leaders and ordinary citizens but not with actual and potential soldiers. They need only worry about their own personal acts of war.

Given the moral seriousness of killing and injuring and the immorality of unjust 15 wars themselves, there is a strong presumption in favor of the view that people have no right to fight in unjust wars and are morally blameworthy for the harms they inflict in the course of such wars, even if these harms are limited to the killing and injuring of enemy soldiers. Why does Walzer reject this? Why does he insist that soldiers on both sides of a war have an equal right to kill one another, even when those on one side are fighting a war of aggression, while those on the other are defending against attack?

One of Walzer's main arguments comes in the form of a reply to those who claim 16 (as I have) that people ought not to serve "if they know the war to be unjust." Walzer answers that this knowledge is "hard to come by." Modern states, he says, give reasons for their wars and it

> takes courage to doubt these reasons. . . . [M]ost men will be persuaded to fight. Their routine habits of law-abidingness, their fear, their patriotism, their moral investment in the state, all favor that course. Or, alternatively they are so terribly young . . . that they can hardly be said to make a moral decision at all. (39–40)

In other passages, Walzer stresses the lack of individual volition involved in mod- 17 ern wars, contrasting modern soldiers, who do not choose to go to war, with the knights of old who did. Of the thousands who died in the battles of World War I, Walzer says that they died

> simply because they were available, their lives nationalized, as it were, by the modern state. They didn't choose to throw themselves at barbed wire and machine guns in fits of patriotic enthusiasm. (35)

He refers several times to participation in war as a form of "servitude" and stresses the idea that individuals are usually unable to resist military service.

There is certainly some truth in the points Walzer makes. Nonetheless, they do 18 not undermine the view that people ought not to serve in unjust wars. A person may believe that service in unjust wars is morally wrong and still agree with Walzer that people who serve are not morally blameworthy if they have no way of knowing the war is unjust, if they are so habituated to obeying the law that they cannot violate it, or if they are so young that they cannot make an independent moral judgment. Facts like these may provide *excuses* for people who have fought wrongly, but they do not provide a *justification* for having done so. They do not show that citizens ought to fight for their country in an unjust war.

Throughout his discussion, Walzer overlooks both the distinction between justifications and excuses and the distinction between rights and duties. As a result, he does not differentiate between three different views. These are:

1. The "duty to fight" thesis: Citizens have a *duty* to fight for their country, even if it is engaged in an unjust war; i.e., it is morally wrong *not* to fight.
2. The "right to fight" thesis: Citizens have a *right* to fight for their country, even if it is engaged in an unjust war; i.e., it is morally *permissible* for them to fight.
3. The "no blame" thesis: Citizens who fight for their country are *not* morally *blameworthy*, even if it is engaged in an unjust war.

Since many of Walzer's statements are ambiguous, it is often hard to tell which thesis he is defending. He might be defending a duty to fight, a right to fight, or an excuse for those who fight on the wrong side. Or, he could be defending all of these views.

Walzer appears to reject the "duty to fight" thesis in a footnote late in his book. Speaking of people who refuse to serve in an unjust war, he says,

> They act very well if they refuse to fight, and we should honor those . . . who have the self-certainty and courage to stand against their fellows. (299n)

If those who refuse to fight are to be honored, then Walzer must not think that their refusal violates a duty to fight.

The same note provides evidence that Walzer holds both views 2 and 3, the "right to fight" thesis and the "no blame" thesis. After writing that we should honor people who refuse to fight in unjust wars, he adds: "That doesn't mean . . . the others [i.e., those who do fight] can be called criminals." As thesis 3 says, those who fight are not to be blamed for doing so. Finally, speaking of people who oppose a war because it is unjust, he says, "we should expect opponents of the war to refuse to become officers or officials, even if they feel bound to share combat risks with their countrymen" (300n). This final comment suggests that a sense of solidarity might lead one to fight in a war one disapproves. Walzer's apparent approval of this choice indicates that he holds view 2, the thesis that people have a right to fight for their country, even if it is on the wrong side of a war.

While Walzer wants to defend a right to fight in an unjust war, his argument fails to establish this conclusion. At most, Walzer's argument supports the third and most limited of the three views, "Citizens are not morally blameworthy for fighting for their country, even if it is engaged in an unjust war." It does nothing to justify thesis 2, "Citizens have a right to fight for their country, even if it is fighting an unjust war."

In fact, the argument fails even as a defense of thesis 3, the "no blame" thesis, since 23 it provides a blanket denial of blameworthiness. Even if one accepts Walzer's view that people are not blameworthy for immoral actions if they have no way of knowing that the actions are immoral or cannot avoid them, one might still insist that people are blameworthy for participating in war if they can know that the war is immoral and have the capacity not to serve. Walzer's argument provides no excuse for people in this position and hence no basis even for thesis 3, the most limited of his claims.

One part of Walzer's argument is especially odd, for he treats the fact that it 24 "takes courage" to doubt the government's reasons for the war as a valid excuse. Later in his book, Walzer argues that the *in bello* rules require soldiers to accept increased risks to their own lives in order to avoid killing noncombatants (see 151–156). Surely, satisfying this rule requires considerable courage.[14] It is odd for Walzer to expect people to have the courage to risk their lives to uphold *jus in bello* rules, while he thinks it is too much to expect them to risk social disapproval in order to uphold the *jus ad bellum* criteria.

At best, then, Walzer's argument establishes that certain factors may excuse some 25 people for participating in unjust wars. It does not show that such participation is a duty or a right. Nor does it show that fighting is always excusable. In saying this, I do not mean that all who fight should be considered war criminals. That kind of legal blame is different from the moral blame that I am discussing. My key point is that Walzer's argument fails to provide either a justification for serving in an unjust war or a blanket excuse for doing so. It does nothing to justify unconditional willingness to serve or to relieve people of the duty to consider the nature of the war they are being called on to fight. . . .

Summing Up

Many people believe that patriotism requires unconditional willingness to fight for 26 one's country in its wars. I have tried to show that this view is false. A patriot may be a pacifist, rejecting war altogether. Likewise, patriots who care about their country and are willing to make sacrifices on its behalf may nonetheless draw the line at supporting it in an unjust war. Countries ought not to fight unjust wars, and individuals ought not to fight in them. Patriotic people have both a right and a duty to judge their country's cause before supporting it in a war.

[8] For more sustained critiques of realism see Michael Walzer, *Just and Unjust Wars* (New York: Basic Books, 1977); Robert Holmes, *War and Morality* (Princeton: Princeton University Press, 1989), ch. 2; and Marshall Cohen, "Moral Skepticism

and International Relations," in Charles Beitz et al., eds., *International Ethics* (Princeton: Princeton University Press, 1985).

[9] For a survey of various views, see Martin Ceadel, *Thinking about Peace and War* (Oxford: Oxford University Press, 1987).

[10] For fuller accounts of the just war criteria, see William O'Brien, "Just-War Theory," in J. Sterba, ed., *The Ethics of War and Nuclear Deterrence* (Belmont, Calif.: Wadsworth, 1985), 30–44; and James Childress, "Just-War Theories: The Bases, Interrelations, Priorities, and Functions of Their Criteria," in M. Wakin, ed., *War, Morality, and the Military Profession*, 2nd ed. (Boulder, Colo.: Westview, 1986), 256–76.

[11] Cf. Walzer on hypocrisy, *Just and Unjust Wars*, xv, 19–20.

[12] Michael Walzer, *Just and Unjust Wars*, 38–39. Subsequent page references are in the text.

[13] Likewise, his earlier book *Obligations* (New York: Simon and Schuster, 1971) presents and defends the views of anti-war dissenters.

[14] In Tim O'Brien's novel about the Vietnam war, *Going after Cacciato* (New York: Dell Publishing, 1980), the soldiers are deeply resentful of an officer who forces them to search tunnels for civilians before destroying the tunnels. The burdens of complying with the *in bello* criteria are substantial.

PATRIOTISM WITHOUT NATIONALISM
from *For Love of Country* (1995)
Maurizio Viroli

Maurizio Viroli teaches in the department of politics at Princeton University. He has a particular interest in Machiavelli and in republicanism.

In the epilogue of For Love of Country, *Viroli has been considering the idea that we should be willing to make major sacrifices for our country, but that we should be able to choose the ideals and circumstances that require those sacrifices: "We are still committed to our own country, even though we are committed to what constitutes the best of it." At this point, he begins to discuss Tocqueville's conception of American patriotism.*

In this tradition [of Tocqueville], patriotism means democratic citizenship. It describes a love for a republic that citizens feel as their own business and their own creation; a love coupled with self-interest and pride, but still an essentially political love which translates not into desires for purification, but into the practices of participatory democracy.   1

The patriotism that flourished on the soil of American democracy, remarked   2
Tocqueville, was a rational patriotism which 'grows by the aid of laws and the exercise of rights, and in the end becomes, in a sense, mingled with personal interest'. This patriotism is perhaps less ardent and less generous than the patriotism

that springs from the attachment to the place where one was born,[44] but it is more creative and lasting:

> A man understands the influence which his country's well-being has on his own; he knows the law allows him to contribute to the production of this well-being and he takes an interest in his country's prosperity, first as a thing useful to him and then as something he has created.[45]

Direct participation in the public life of the community, remarks Tocqueville, is the 'only remaining way' to make the citizen feel part of the republic. Civic spirit is the outcome of the 'exercise of political rights'.[46] American citizens have no common culture, no common memories, no common traditions; none the less they are interested in the affairs of their township, of their canton, of their state, because each of them 'takes an active part in the government of society' and is accustomed to regarding the general prosperity and the common good as his own.[47]

In Tocqueville's analysis, American patriotism is love of country that comes from duty, pride, and even greed; it has little in common with the generous, embracing, encompassing, charitable love of country theorized by republican thinkers. And yet, though sober and full of self-interest, it still is a love based on the identification with the republic obtained through political means; that is, through good laws and political participation. The republican prescription for civic virtue seems to have worked in nineteenth-century America: if the *patria* treats the citizens justly, if it allows them to participate in public life, they are likely to consider her as their own common good and love her with passion and reason.

Republican patriotism, at least on American soil, is a lively intellectual tradition. It was republican patriotism, writes Charles Taylor, that fuelled 'the sense of outrage' that motivated Americans to react against Nixon's violations. It was a sense of outrage, he specifies, that was based neither on calculation of long-term interests, nor on general commitment to the principle of liberal democracy, but on a particularistic attachment, that is, a widespread identification with 'the American way of

3

4

---

[44] *Democracy in America*, ed. J. P. Mayer (New York, 1969), 235. Tocqueville contrasts rational patriotism with the patriotism which 'mainly springs from the disinterested, undefinable, and unpondered feeling that ties man's heart to the place where he was born. This instinctive love is mingled with a taste for old habits, respect for ancestors, and memories of the past; those who feel it love their country as one loves one's father's house'. This patriotism however often goes together with devotion to the monarch as the personification of the nation.

[45] Ibid. 235–6.

[46] Ibid. 236.

[47] Ibid. 236–7.

life' defined 'by a commitment to certain ideals, articulated famously in the Declaration of Independence and Lincoln's Gettysburg address'.[48] Republican patriotism has not only been an important ideological support for freedom in the past, Taylor remarks, but 'will remain unsubstitutably so for the future'.[49] As the example of Watergate shows, a 'patriotism of the right' on the part of the citizens is essential to preserve the rule of law; that is, the very foundation of a liberal democracy. However, Taylor argues, a 'patriotic liberal regime' leaves out another equally fundamental requirement of republican patriotism and of the good republic, namely participatory self rule. Though it recognizes it, it regards self-rule as 'purely instrumental to the rule of law and equality'. In a procedural liberal society patriotism is therefore unlikely to reach its full potential.[50]

Republican patriotism, remarks Taylor, places the main emphasis on political participation. It was not primarily concerned with freedom in the modern sense of negative liberty and equal protection of individual rights, but with 'participatory self-rule'. Political participation reinforces bonds of civic friendship, a sense of common history, and the feeling of belonging to a common political entity which constitutes the essence of patriotism. Though differently argued, and based upon a different evaluation of the theoretical and cultural relevance of republicanism, Taylor's prescription is close to that of Walzer and Schaar: patriotism grows in a republic that allows for and encourages democratic self-government.   5

All the theorists that have argued in favour of a patriotism based on the idea that to love one's country means to love the republic as a political community based on the principle of common liberty, with its own culture and way of life, are in fact indicating the possibility of a patriotism without nationalism. It is a patriotism that stresses that the citizens' love can and must be obtained primarily by political means; that is, through the practice of good government and through justice. And by justice they mean the protection of civil rights and the political rights of the citizens. To be loved by its citizens, the republic must not tolerate discrimination and privileges and must allow the citizens to participate in public life. To love the republic they must feel close to it; they must feel it as theirs, which means to feel their fellow-citizens dear, worthy of respect and compassion. The emphasis on citizenship is not only motivated by the argument that popular sovereignty guarantees that laws aim at the common good, but also that direct political participation reinforces attachment to the republic.   6

This sort of patriotism makes possible the civic virtue that a good republic needs. Properly understood, civic virtue is a love of the republic or the fatherland expressed as a moral vigour that permits the citizens to act for the common good and to resist the enemies of common liberty. Like all virtues, civic virtue also de-   7

[48] 'Cross-Purposes: The Liberal-Communitarian Debate', 174.

[49] Ibid. 175.

[50] Ibid. 175–8.

mands an effort; it asks to enrich private life, not to dissolve it into public commitment. The deeds that civic virtue requires the citizens to accomplish are greater than the achievements of private life; but only in the sense that they sustain the liberty of each and every citizen. Although civic virtue expresses itself in the public realm, it deeply affects the customs and private life of a people. Understood as love of common liberty, it cannot be a threat to civility, orderliness, and decorum. In fact, civic virtue is a weapon against the powerful or the licentious who do not want to accept the self-restraint and moderation that civil life requires.

As I have argued, patriotism of liberty does not need social, or cultural, or religious, or ethnic homogeneity. If the fatherland is less than a republic in the classical sense, citizens cannot be virtuous: they cannot love a state that treats them unjustly (though in fact they sometimes do). If the fatherland is more than a good republic—if it is a good republic and a religious or cultural or social community— civic virtue will probably reach its maximum. It may also, however, degenerate into the zealot's love of oneness, not the citizen's political love. This implies that to see the right sort of patriotism grow, we need not strengthen homogeneity and oneness but work to strengthen the practice and the culture of citizenship. **8**

The cultural, religious, or social unity of ancient republics (whether or not these ancients[sic] republics were really as virtuous as political writers believed is a question unimportant for our purposes) cannot be reproduced in the modern world. But this does not mean that civic virtue is unattainable. Modern citizens too can love their republic, if the republic loves them, if it protects their liberty, encourages political participation, and helps them to cope with the inevitable hardships of the human condition. Though less ardent, the political love of modern citizens might be sufficient to sustain the republic and common liberty. **9**

Understood as love of common liberty, political virtue is not a dangerous virtue. The observation that patriotism is inevitably bound to produce bigotry, intolerance, and militarism, is correct for other types of patriotism, but does not apply to the patriotism of liberty that I have been advocating in this book. A charitable love of liberty produces only liberty. Bigotry, intolerance, and war are the products of another love; that is, love or longing for oneness or uniqueness. There seem to be two distinct, though partially overlapping, pathways to civic virtue: the path of homogeneity and that of liberty. Our way should be that of liberty; that is, a political way. We do not need more citizens attending national festivals with great fervour; nor do we need more citizens willing to offer their lives to protect their country's religious or ethnic or cultural unity. We need, instead, more citizens willing and capable of mobilizing when one or more citizens are victims of injustice or discrimination, when unfair laws are passed or constitutional principles are violated. **10**

Patriotism is different from heroic self-abnegation. The former requires us to do something more than attending to our private business; the second demands the sacrifice of our personal concerns and even our life for the common good. The virtuous citizen goes to the public square or the meeting room when he or **11** she has to, but then he or she goes back home, or to his shop, or to join his friends. The hero sacrifices all to the republic. His love of the republic is more than a political love; it is a love enhanced by religious identification or passion for glory. But republics, except for extraordinary circumstances, need less than that; they need citizens who can practise civic virtue as a completion of private life and private interest.

What Rousseau said to the citizens of Geneva applies also to us: we are neither Spartans, Athenians, nor Romans. And yet we are, or should be, concerned with liberty. We need civic virtue to prevent and to rebut the challenges to liberty that occur in our societies. The conception of patriotism and political virtue that I advocate in this book seems to me to be within our reach. However, it may not be: maybe modern citizens are no longer capable of committing themselves to 'more generous objects' and 'nobler interests', to use John Stuart Mill's words;[51] maybe we are too culturally, socially, and religiously divided and too inclined to identify with our own tribe to be able to commit ourselves to the common liberty.

In many cases, we can in fact protect our individual liberty and our welfare and the welfare of our family by not fighting for the common liberty, or otherwise sacrificing for the common good. We can surely protect our liberty without helping to protect the liberty of all members of society. By virtue of class, race, and gender, we are often insulated from violations of liberty committed against others belonging to a different class, race, or gender. We neither see nor feel the connection between our liberty and the liberty of others. We are no longer capable of compassion.

One can reply that to believe that we can protect our individual liberty without being concerned with common liberty is imprudent because it allows ambitious and arrogant men to impose their power over the laws and corrupt public institutions, thereby putting us at their mercy. Though perfectly rational, this argument is not sufficient to mobilize a passion like the love of liberty nor, more importantly, to defeat passions like avarice and cowardice which are the most powerful obstacles to civic virtue.

A more powerful drive to civic virtue is, perhaps, necessity: when corruption and oppression become unbearable, citizens sometimes retrieve a sense of public commitment. In times of extreme decay of public life, a sense of national or patriotic dignity or honour may also come to sustain virtue. We have, however, many examples of endless endurance of and adaptation to corruption and oppression: there are no sure roads that lead to a renaissance of civic virtue.

The best way to help the rebirth of civic virtue—the best way for political philosophers—is to outline a conception of patriotism that is acceptable and within our reach. The conception of patriotism as love of common liberty is, I believe, both morally sustainable and a reflection of current practices in our own times. In our

12

13

14

15

16

---

[51] *De Tocqueville on Democracy in America*, ii, in *Collected Works*, ed. J. M. Robson (Toronto, 1977), xvii. 168–9.

own societies there are citizens defending other citizens who have been victims of injustice; citizens mobilizing against corruption and crime; citizens of different tribes invoking justice for all. They indicate for us the shape of a possible virtue and of patriotism at its best. What makes it possible is its political nature. We need more of them, and a better theory may do some good: to change our understanding of patriotism may help us to reinforce the sort of virtue that democracy needs and, more importantly, not to waste political and intellectual energies searching for an impossible or dangerous virtue.

THE WAR ON TERRORISM AND THE NEW PATRIOTISM
from *The Politics of Terror: The U.S. Response to 9/11* (2004)
Scott L. McLean

Scott L. McLean chairs the political science department at Quinnipiac University and is an analyst for the Quinnipiac Polling Institute. His specialties are American political thought and public opinion.

In his overview of patriotism in American history, McLean begins with a discussion of Thomas Paine, who coined the phrase "sunshine patriot" for those who choose not to make sacrifices for their country. McLean points out that "shocking events" like 9/11 have the power to reinvigorate a nation's sense of patriotism, but that it is also possible to manipulate patriotic feelings for political purposes.

The American founders in the eighteenth century faced a dilemma not encoun-   1
tered by European states, which built allegiance by identifying themselves with their particular national cultures. The constitutional framers instead had to construct a national identity to fit a newly established regime of vast continental scale based on an individualistic philosophy (Hayes 1928). They began their philosophy of patriotism with the idea that humans are naturally free and isolated individuals who construct government and agree to obey it in order to better serve their private purposes, mainly the security of their persons and property. They realized that state governments and local culture held a more powerful sway on the affections and loyalties of citizens than the new federal government. The prevailing conception of patriotism, held mainly by their opponents, was based on the belief that active citizenship is the expression of one's identification with local community (Dietz 1986, 270; Viroli 1995, 63). A government of the scale envisioned by the framers would inevitably be more impersonal and require more compromises than smaller and more intimate communities are accustomed to make. Their solution to this dilemma lay not in constructing a federal government with the ability to force states to comply with national policies. Instead, the framers argued that loyalty to large-scale organizations depends on their ability to act effectively in the lives of individuals. As Alexander Hamilton defended his idea of national government in the 27th *Federalist Paper* (1787), stable and "energetic" administration against "internal and

external danger" over time will "touch the most sensible cords and put into motion the active springs of the human heart" and "conciliate the respect and attachment of the community" (Hamilton, Madison, and Jay 1982, 133).

Hamilton and the other founders were by no means confident that the federal government would become the supreme object of national loyalty. Rather, they hoped that as citizens became accustomed to consistent and energetic federal administration over the parts of their lives in which they took the most interest, the government would in time be able to make a claim on their loyalties at least as strong as their attachments to civic groups, locality, or family. They envisioned that people would come to see their self-interest coincide with the stability and strength of the federal government and its ability to defend the nation's security.

This variation on the social contract theory had its limits. The framers doubted that enlightened self-interest was sufficient to motivate citizens to risk or sacrifice their lives for the nation-state. They hoped instead that citizens would learn the ability to see themselves as *more than* self-interested individuals, to feel obligations beyond the self and immediate family. For the most part, though, leaders in that system would be required to appeal to private interests in their calls for public sacrifices.

Alexis de Tocqueville, a young French aristocrat touring America in 1830, recognized this dilemma when he said that the "instinctive patriotism" of the old monarchy, based on "a reverence for traditions of the past," incited "great transient exertions, but no continuity of effort" (Tocqueville 1990, 1: 242). In modernity, instinctive patriotism is gone, and "the country assumes a dim and dubious shape in the eyes of citizens" (Tocqueville 1990, 1: 241). The risk was that instinctive patriotism would be replaced by a chauvinistic nationalist pride that "resorts to a thousand artifices and descends to all the petty tricks of personal vanity" (Tocqueville 1990, 1: 244). In its sentimental guise, patriotism becomes more an expression of veneration for the state, scarcely able to steer a course toward a life of civic involvement and service.

He thought that the only alternative was for the United States to develop a "more rational" patriotism based on active participation in civic life. It was a patriotism "less generous and perhaps less ardent," but "more creative and more lasting" than instinctive patriotism. "It is nurtured by the laws; it grows by the exercise of civil rights; and in the end, it is confounded with the personal interests of the citizen" (Tocqueville 1990, 1: 242). Civic attachment would have to be forged in the small sacrifices of time and energy citizens make in their active involvement in churches, town meetings, social clubs, and political parties. Patriotism in a modern democracy, at its best, would be something more than unenlightened egoism and something less than unreflective identification with the nation. Tocqueville saw that there were some advantages of this union of patriotism and self-interest, but he worried that Americans would mistakenly see even their noblest, most generous, and self-sacrificing instincts as merely a product of self-interest: "They are more anxious to do honor to their philosophy than to themselves" (Tocqueville 1990, 2: 122). He believed it was true that participation would likely begin in calculations of self-interest, but over time "men attend to the interests of the public, first by necessity, afterwards by choice; what was intentional becomes an instinct, and by dint of working for the good of one's fellow citizens, the habit and the taste for serving them are at length acquired" (Tocqueville 1990, 2: 105).

The links between local civic activity and national patriotic sentiment grew increasingly difficult to sustain as America entered its industrial phase, and government became ever more bureaucratic and distant from citizen control in the twentieth century. The older U.S. patriotism has been visible at times. In a national crisis, one's identity as a "patriotic citizen" may temporarily trump other identities, and public interest might trump private concerns. But in the long run, willingness to make even small sacrifices must be reinforced by popular culture and sustained by governmental institutions that will channel people's energies into public life. Even then, the content of that identity and the ways in which the burdens of patriotism are to be distributed depend on what historian Mark Leff calls "the politics of sacrifice" (Leff 1991). In a national crisis, the mystique of home front sacrifice can permeate the political landscape. But, Leff argues, these changes in the vocabulary of political obligation and membership do not imply open-ended commitments to civic life or erasure of private life and personal interests. Even though sacrifice is based on underlying conceptions of patriotism, it is nevertheless malleable to the interplay of prevailing interests (Leff 1991, 1318). Particular circumstances can "tip the scales" toward certain conceptions of patriotism and distributions of "sacrifice," and the post-9/11 political environment is no exception.

6

Acknowledgments

Norm R. Allen Jr. "True Patriotism." Originally published in *Free Inquiry* Magazine, June/July 2004. Copyright © 2004, the Council for Secular Humanism. Reprinted by permission of the publisher.

Americans for Medical Progress Web site home page. www.ampef.org. Courtesy of Americans for Medical Progress.

Warren S. Apel. "The Flag Burning Page." www.esquilax.com. Reprinted by permission of Warren S. Apel.

Sidney Axinn. "Honor, Patriotism and Ultimate Loyalty." From *Nuclear Weapons and the Future of Humanity*, edited by Avner Cohen and Steven Lee. Copyright © Sidney Axinn. Reprinted with the permission of Rowmann & Littlefield Publishers, Inc.

David P. Barash. Excerpted text from "Evolution, Males, and Violence" by David P. Barash. Originally published in the *Chronicle of Higher Education*, May 24, 2002. Reprinted by permission of the author.

Walter Berns. Excerpt from *Making Patriots* by Walter Berns. Copyright © 2001. Reprinted by permission of the University of Chicago Press and the author.

Jane Bernstein. "Victim of Circumstance." Appeared in *The New York Times*, Magazine Section, April 2, 2000. Copyright © 2000 by Jane Bernstein. Reprinted with permission of Brandt & Hochman Literary Agents, Inc.

Blanche D. Blank. "A Question of Degree." Excerpt from "Degrees: Who Needs Them?" Originally published in *AAUP Bulletin*, Autumn 1972. Reprinted by permission of Joseph Blank.

Celestine Bohlen. "O Say Can You See What That Flag Means?" From *The New York Times*, December 16, 2000. Copyright © 2000 by The New York Times Company. Reprinted with permission.

Leon Botstein. "Let Teenagers Try Adulthood." From *The New York Times*, Op-ed page, May 17, 1999. Copyright © 1999 by The New York Times Company. Reprinted by permission.

Walter Dean Burnham. Excerpts from *The Nation*, July 15/21, 1991. Copyright © 1991. Reprinted by permission of Walter Dean Burnham, Professor Emeritus, Erwin Chair in Government, the University of Texas at Austin. He is the author of many books and articles on American government and politics, and is particularly noted for his work on critical realignments in U.S. political history. Courtesy of Walter Dean Burnham.

Christopher Clausen. "An Army of One." From *The American Scholar*, Volume 72, No. 4, Autumn 2003. Copyright © 2003 by Christopher Clausen. Reprinted by permission of The American Scholar.

Lizabeth Cohen. "Feminizing Public Space." From *A Consumer's Republic* by Lizabeth Cohen. Copyright © 2003 by Lizabeth Cohen. Used by permission of Alfred A. Knopf, a division of Random House, Inc.

Gail Collins. "Too Sparing in Their Use of Water." Excerpt from *America's Women* by Gail Collins. Copyright © 2003 by Gail Collins. Reprinted by permission of HarperCollins Publishers.

Stephanie Coontz. "The Curious History of Mother's Day." From *The Way We Never Were: America's Families and the Nostalgia Trap* by Stephanie Coontz. Copyright © 1997 by Basic Books, a division of HarperCollins Publishers, Inc. Reprinted by permission of Basic Books, a member of Perseus Books, LLC.

Bill Coplin. "Lost in the Life of the Mind." Originally published in *The Chronicle Review*, September 3, 2004, Volume 51, Issue 2, page B5. Reprinted with the permission of the author.

Bernard DeVoto. "The Easy Chair." Copyright © 1943 by *Harper's* Magazine. All rights reserved. Reproduced from the February issue by special permission.

Billie Wright Dziech. "Forcing Greek Organizations to Go Coeducational Won't Lead to Greater Diversity." Originally published in the *Chronicle of Higher Education*, April 2, 1999. Reprinted with the permission of the author.

Fendrich, Lippit, and Malamud. "In This Year's Fashion Jungle, Beastly Patterns Are the Sincerest Form of Fakery." Originally published in the *Chronicle of Higher Education*, December 1, 2000.

Shannon E. French. "When Teaching the Ethics of War Is Not Academic." Originally published in the *Chronicle of Higher Education*, March 21, 2003. Reprinted with permission of the author. Dr. Shannon E. French is an Associate Professor of Philosophy in the Department of Leadership, Ethics, and Law at the United States Naval Academy and author of the book *The Code of the Warrior: Exploring Warrior Values, Past and Present*. Published by Rowman and Littlefield Publishers, 2003.

Neal Gabler. "Our Celebrities, Ourselves." Originally published in the *Chronicle of Higher Education*, March 14, 2003. Reprinted with permission of the author.

John Taylor Gatto. "Against School: How Public Education Cripples Our Kids and Why." Copyright © 2003 by *Harper's* Magazine. All rights reserved. Reproduced from the September issue by special permission.

Todd Gitlin. "Disappearing Ink." Reprinted with the permission of Todd Gitlin.

Ira Glasser. Excerpts from *The Nation*, July 15/21, 1991. Copyright © 1991 by Ira Glasser. Ira Glasser was the Executive Director of the American Civil Liberties Union from 1978 until his retirement in 2001. Reprinted with permission.

Robert Goldstein. Excerpt from *Burning the Flag: The Great 1989–1990 American Flag Desecration* by Robert Goldstein. Copyright © 1996 by Robert Goldstein. Reprinted by permission of Kent State University Press.

Marshall Gregory. "A Liberal Education Is Not a Luxury." Originally published in the *Chronicle of Higher Education*, September 12, 2003. Reprinted with permission of the author.

Pat Hagan. "Falling on Deaf Ears." From *New Scientist*, August 28, 2004. Reprinted with permission of New Scientist.

Anne Hollander. Excerpted text from *Sex and Suits* by Anne Hollander. Copyright © 1994 by Anne Hollander. Reprinted by permission of the author..

Eric Hoover. "Crying Foul Over Fans' Boorish Behavior." Originally titled, "Colleges Want Students to Make Noise, Politely." From the *Chronicle of Higher Education*, April 9, 2004, Volume 50, Issue 31, page A1. Copyright © 2004, The Chronicle of Higher Education. Reprinted with permission.

In Defense of Animals home page. Reprinted with permission of Elliot M. Katz, DVM, President & Founder. www.idausa.org.

Molly Ivins. Excerpts from *The Nation*, July 15/22, 1991. Copyright © 1991 Molly Ivins. Reprinted by permission of the author.

Sandeep Jauhar. "When Doctors Slam the Door." From *The New York Times*, Magazine Section, March 16, 2003. Copyright © 2003 by The New York Times Company. Reprinted with permission.

Leon Kass. "The End of Courtship." From *The Public Interest*, Winter 1997. Copyright ©1997 Leon R. Kass, M.D. Reprinted by permission of the author.

Irving Kristol. Excerpts from *Reflections of a Neoconservative* by Irving Kristol. Copyright © 1983 by Irving Kristol. Courtesy of the author.

Jeffrey Rosen. Excerpt from *The Naked Crowd* by Jeffrey Rosen. Copyright © 2004 by Jeffrey Rosen. Used by permission of Random House, Inc.

Bertrand Russell. Excerpt (pp. 228–231) from *The Social Responsibility of Scientists* by Bertrand Russell. Copyright © 1994 by The Bertrand Russell Peace Foundation. Reproduced by permission of Taylor & Francis Books (UK) and the Bertrand Russell Foundation.

Diana Schaub. "The Pillars of the Temple of Liberty." From *The Survival of Culture: Permanent Values in a Virtual Age*, edited by Hilton Kramer and Roger Kimball. Copyright © 2002 by Hilton Kramer and Roger Kimball. Reprinted with permission of Ivan R. Dee, Publisher.

William H. Shannon. Excerpts from article originally published in *The Nation*, July 15/22, 1991. Reprinted with permission of the author.

Carl Singleton. "What Our Education System Needs is More F's." Originally published in the *Chronicle of Higher Education* (1954). Reprinted by permission of the author.

Roger Sipher. "So That Nobody Has to Go to School If They Don't Want To." From *The New York Times*, Op-ed page, September 21, 1967. Copyright © 1967 by The New York Times Company. Reprinted with permission. All rights reserved.

George Stade. "Football—The Game of Aggression." Reprinted by permission of the author.

Edward Tenner. Excerpt from *Our Own Devices: The Past and Future of Body Technology* by Edward Tenner. Copyright © 2003 by Edward Tenner. Used by permission of Alfred A. Knopf, a division of Random House, Inc.

The New York Times. "Comparing Notes." Originally titled: "Pandora Compares Passages Plagiarism Graphic." From *The New York Times*, May 31, 2003. Copyright © 2003 The New York Times Company. Reprinted by permission. All rights reserved.

The New York Times. "Debating How Best to Love Your Country." From *The New York Times*, July 1, 2000. Copyright © 2000 by The New York Times Company. Reprinted with permission.

The New York Times. "300 Killed by Fire, Smoke and Panic in Boston Resort." From *The New York Times*, November 30, 1942. Copyright © 1942 by The New York Times Company. Reprinted with permission.

Time. "Catastrophe: Boston's Worse." From *Time* Magazine, December 7, 1942. Copyright © 1942 Time, Inc. Reprinted by permission.

Alexis de Tocqueville. Excerpts from *Democracy in America* by Alexis de Tocqueville. Copyright © 2000. Reprinted by permission of the University of Chicago Press.

Maurizio Viroli. Excerpted text from pp. 181–187 in *For Love of Country* by Maurizio Viroli. © 1995. Reprinted by permission of Oxford University Press.

Michael Walzer. "Civility and Civic Virtue in Contemporary America." From *Social Research Journal*, Winter 1974, 41:4, pp. 593–611. Copyright © 1974. Reprinted with the permission of Social Research.

Michael Welch. Excerpt from *Flag Burning: Moral Panic and the Criminalization of Protest.* Copyright © 2000 by Aldine Publishers. Reprinted by permission of Transition Publishers.

Alan Wolfe. Excerpt from *Moral Freedom: The Search for Virtue in a World of Choice* by Alan Wolfe. Copyright © 2001 by Alan Wolfe. Used by permission of W. W. Norton & Company, Inc.

Fareed Zakaria. Excerpt from *The Future of Freedom: Illiberal Democracy at Home and Abroad* by Fareed Zakaria. Copyright © 2003 by Fareed Zakaria. Used by permission of W. W. Norton & Company, Inc.

Wilbur Zelinsky. "Flag and Eagle." Excerpt from *Nation into State: The Shifting Symbolic Foundations of American Nationalism* by Wilbur Zelinsky. Copyright © 1988 by the University of North Carolina Press. Used by permission of the publisher.

Art Credits

Figure 1-1. By permission of the *Atlantic Monthly*.

Figure 1-2. Photofest.

Figure 2-1. Jon Gardiner/Duke University/Icon Sports Media.

Figure 3-1. Reproduced from: R. H. Macy & Co., Inc. 1957 Annual Report, courtesy of the Robert F. Wagner Labor Archives, New York University, from its Department Store Workers—Local 1-S Collection. By permission of Macy's and Federated Department Stores, Inc.

Figure 4-1. Gordon M. Grant.

Figure 4-2. Culver Pictures.

Figure 5-1. From "Falling on Deaf Ears" by Pat Hagan, *New Scientist*, Vol. 183, Issue 2462, August 28, 2004, p. 36. Reprinted by permission of *New Scientist*.

Figure 7-7. Illustration of the online catalog of the Columbia University Libraries. Reprinted with permission.

Figure 7-8. By permission of Ingenta.

Figure 7-9. By permission of Google.

Figure 7-10. By permission of Google.

Figure 7-11. © NTPL.

Figure 8-1. Reproduced by permission of In Defense of Animals.

Figure 8-2. Americans for Medical Progress (www.amprogress.org).

Figure 10-1. New York Times Graphics.

Figure 12-1. John Kobal Foundation/Getty Images.

Figure 12-2. Photofest.

Figure 12-3. © John Springer Collection/CORBIS.

Figure 12-4. By permission of the British Library.

Figure 12-5. From Hans Staden, *The True History of His Captivity*, 1557, by Malcolm Letts, NY: Routledge, 2004.

Figure 12-6. From "What Lies Beneath," *New Scientist*, July 28, 2001, p. 17. Reprinted by permission of New Scientist.

Figure 12-7. University of Bologna (Giusepe Longo), www.th.bo.infn.it/tunguska/.

Figure 12-8. Chris Maynard for the *New York Times*.

Figure 12-9. AP Images.

Index